J. W

To Live for You!
To Die for You!

Portrait of Mahler by John Searight.

To Live for You!
To Die for You!

THE LIFE OF
GUSTAV MAHLER

by

John Searight

Published in Association
with
The Gustav Mahler Society of the United Kingdom
2009

Published by John Searight in Association with
The Gustav Mahler Society of the United Kingdom 2009

First Impression – 2009

ISBN 978 0 95616 950 1

© John Searight

John Searight has asserted his right under the
Copyright, Designs and Patents Act, 1988,
to be identified as Author of this Work.

Printed in Wales at
Gomer Press, Llandysul, Ceredigion SA44 4JL

In memory
of
Pamela Załuski

Contents

Acknowledgements

I am indebted to the numerous Mahler authors whose books have surrounded me during this literary journey, especially Henry-Louis de la Grange whose massive and definitive four-volume biography has been an invaluable source of information. I would also like to express my gratitude to the many friends, musicians and experts who have been so generous with their time and assistance, especially

Prof. Henry-Louis de la Grange
Marie-Joe Blavette and Sonia Popoff (Bibliothèque Gustav Mahler, Paris)
Christl Lieben (Vienna)
Dr. Robert Mahler (London)
Sir Brian McMaster CBE
Dr. James Pritchard (Chairman, Gustav Mahler Society, U.K.)
Katharina Ulbrich (Bad Hall)
Pierre Velik (Klagenfurt)
Muzeum Vysočiny, Jihlava

to

Lorna Hepple and Anne Smith MBE, for their patience in reading my manuscript

and to

Iwo Załuski, composer, concert pianist and fellow author, for driving me around Europe and for his constant advice and constructive criticism over nearly a decade.

PROF. HENRY-LOUIS DE LA GRANGE
BIBLIOTHÈQUE MUSICALE GUSTAV MAHLER
11 BIS, RUE DE VÉZELAY
75008 PARIS

For John Searight,
One of those Mahler admirers for whom
I am happy to have worked all my life!
With cordial greetings
Henry-Louis de La Grange

Foreword

Gustav Mahler once famously remarked to Jean Sibelius that 'the symphony must be like the world, embracing everything'. Mahler was a revolutionary composer who portrayed the sounds of nature in his symphonies, such as birdsong, alongside peasant dances, military bands and bugle calls remembered from his childhood spent in the garrison town of Iglau. He had an unhappy childhood, and even as an adult he frequently felt thwarted in his ambitions due to his background, considering himself to be 'thrice homeless – as a native of Bohemia in Austria, as an Austrian among Germans and as a Jew throughout the world; everywhere an intruder, never welcomed'. An exaggeration of course, but his remark reflected his constant struggle against anti-Semitism.

Most of his lieder were generally well received during his lifetime, but his semi-autobiographical symphonies, into which he poured out his soul, had a very stormy ride. They are not only a kaleidoscopic reflection of the music of his time, but a nostalgic glance at the passing of romanticism and an almost prophetic glimpse into the future. His influence was immense. The young composers of the Second Viennese School, in particular Schoenberg, Berg and Webern, were inspired by him, and his influence on those who would follow is without question, Shostakovich and Britten being two prime examples.

With two very important Mahler years approaching, 2010 being the one hundred and fiftieth anniversary of his birth and 2011 the centenary of his death, we can expect many performances of his works and the appearance of numerous publications. John Searight's biography is a valuable addition to Mahler literature. It is accessible, informative and at the same time entertaining. Over nearly a decade his researches have taken him to many European countries. He challenges the myth that Mahler was a dark, brooding character who was preoccupied with death, an obsession, John Searight believes, of which there is little evidence in either his music or his ambitious career as a superlative conductor. It is hoped that those who read this biography will adopt a more balanced view of a remarkable man, one who had a profound and lasting influence on the course that music would follow right up to the present day.

Brian McMaster

Chapter 1

Childhood and Student Years
Kalischt . . . Iglau . . . Prague . . . Vienna

THE CZECH-MORAVIAN Highlands is an area of gently rolling hills, of forests and rivers, dotted with little villages, sleepy and quiet. It was in one such village in Bohemia, close to the border with Moravia that, on the 7th of July 1860, Gustav Mahler was born. That village was Kalischt.

Kaliště, as the village is called today, has not changed a great deal. The old distillery buildings remain, overlooking the village pond, which Mahler referred to as the 'smelly' pond, and the nearby church on the village green. Just behind the church was the house where Gustav was born – not exactly luxurious, for there was no glass in the windows. Unfortunately the house was destroyed by fire in 1937, but, with the walls more or less intact, a new building was erected using the same ground plan. On the side there is a rather splendid plaque commemorating the centenary of his birth.

During the first half of the nineteenth century, the inhabitants of Kalischt numbered around five hundred. They were almost entirely ethnic Czechs, an exception being the family of a German-speaking, Jewish door-to-door salesman, Šimon Mahler, who had settled in Kalischt with his wife Marie in 1827. Marie, a very determined lady who was not afraid of hard work, peddled drapery around the local villages, and she continued to do this throughout her life. On one occasion at the age of eighty she was arrested for selling 'unlicensed goods'! Furious she demanded an audience with the Emperor, who was so impressed by the gritty determination of this indefatigable old lady that he granted her an immediate pardon. One can see where Mahler's own characteristic traits of hard work and determination came from. Marie's father, Abraham Bondy, owned the local distillery, and in 1838 Šimon Mahler took over the lease and later became its owner. Most of the liquors on sale were potato or barley based, using large amounts of caraway seeds and aniseed.

The Emperor Franz Joseph's reign over the Austro-Hungarian Empire, made up of many different nationalities and minority groups, lasted for no less than sixty-eight years. It was therefore no wonder that there was a constant threat of strife and even revolution. Under Franz Joseph the pendulum constantly swung between constraint and freedom. He was by and large a good Emperor, devoted to his people, yet often influenced by the turbulence of the times and by stifling Austrian bureaucracy.

It was during the time of Maria Theresa that the Jewish minority had been allowed to settle in an area of low population and of little importance, the area of the Czech-Moravian highlands in South-eastern Bohemia. But anti-Semitism still remained. In 1848 the Jewish taxes were abolished and religious freedom was granted, but it was not until 1867 that the Jews finally gained full civil and political rights.

Inevitably anti-Semitism did not vanish overnight and Jewish families, despite their new rights, continued to struggle. They were often disadvantaged in their efforts to improve their status, not so much in relation to their village neighbours, but in their dealings with officialdom and the bourgeoisie in the towns and cities, especially Vienna. In fact, between 1909 and 1911, a certain Adolf Hitler, having just turned twenty, was living in Vienna and was already showing an interest in anti-Semitism.

One of the anti-Semitic laws in force at the time of Šimon Mahler's wedding stated that only the eldest son of a Jewish family was allowed to marry. Šimon was not the eldest son and consequently all of his children were registered as illegitimate. The few in Šimon's position who were permitted to marry (a strictly limited number) were usually only given permission after making a sizeable payment.

Bernhard Mahler, Gustav's father, was born on August 2nd 1827, and inherited his parents' determination to succeed, both financially and intellectually. He was an avid reader, even when driving his cart. He turned his hand to working in small factories and shops, and even became a tutor for a while before taking over his father's distillery business. By the age of thirty he was well on the way to gaining financial independence.

In 1848, with the relaxation of the anti-Jewish laws, the Mahlers managed to expand their business and Bernhard was soon in a position to take his trade to nearby towns. It was on one of these trips that he met Marie, one of six daughters of Terezie and Abraham Hermann, a wealthy soap manufacturer from Ledetsch. They married in 1857 and the dowry that Bernhard received enabled him to buy a home in Kalischt. It was, however, very much a marriage of convenience both for Bernhard and for his father-in-law, Marie having been forcibly separated from the love of her life. As Mahler later commented, his parents were as ill suited as fire and water. He was hard, selfish and unbending; she, by nature, gentleness itself and sensitive, but physically weak. She suffered from a heart problem, made worse over the years by the endless succession of births and deaths of her children, not to mention her husband's abrasive and often cruel behaviour.

Their first son, Isidor, was born in 1858, but died the following year. And then, on the 7th of July 1860, Gustav was born. It was at this time that Bernhard made plans to move to the town of Iglau (Jihlava) where he would be able to expand his business considerably. The move took place on the 22nd of October 1860. Their home was the first floor apartment of number 265 Pirnitzergasse (now number 4 Znojemská).

In the second half of the nineteenth century, Iglau was one of the more thriving Moravian towns. The population in 1860 numbered around 18,000. On the 1st of January 1860 a railway license had been granted to build the Austrian north-south line. The service began on the 25th of January 1871, connecting Iglau with neighbouring towns, the line terminating in Vienna. Anticipating the new railway service, many factories were built in the 1860s and 1870s. Industries included glass, tobacco, cloth and shoes, as well as a new brewery, which began producing beer on April 4th 1861.

Iglau had several schools, including a secondary grammar school. The hub of the town's life was based around the very large central square. In the upper part promenade concerts and Sunday processions were held, as well as regular military parades, and in the lower part there was a bustling weekly market. It was in this square that Gustav, at the age of five, began wandering around entertaining the public on his little accordion, and he took every opportunity to march behind the military bands!

The town had a well-established musical tradition. Records show that a choir school existed as early as 1571. In 1819 a *Musikverein* was established and symphonies by composers such as Haydn, Pleyel, Mozart and Winter were regularly performed, as well as choral works. The town theatre, which had been built in 1850, became the centre for music, with concerts, operas and operettas being performed there, as well as plays. The building still exists, although a new theatre has been opened alongside it. Another important venue for music lovers was the dance hall in the new Hotel Czap.

Ever since the mid eighteenth century, Iglau had been an army town with several military barracks, including one in a former Dominican convent on Křižová Street. During Mahler's childhood, a number of units, some of them Hungarian and Croatian, were stationed in and around the town, but the regiment that the young Gustav liked best was the 49th Infantry because of their colourful uniforms and band. The army bands performed regularly in public as their contribution to the town's cultural life, and their size and the variety of instruments used began to expand to include such instruments as horns and trombones.

Bernhard Mahler's liquor trade continued to flourish. He was an enterprising and shrewd businessman, at times quite ruthless. He was frequently fined by the local court for such offences as arguments, fights, taking advantage of prostitutes, illicit business dealings and on one occasion for insulting a district policeman. With trade booming, by the end of 1872 he was able to buy the house next door, number 264. This house had a courtyard and gave him the space he needed to increase his production considerably.

The previous owner was the mother of Heinrich Fischer, the music director of the town's choral society as well as the choir of the Jacobskirche, the large and impressive church just off the central square. It was through him that Gustav was introduced to the wider world of music, and he became a very close friend of his son Theodor. The two boys spent a great deal of time playing together, exploring and swimming. Gustav began to love and absorb stories, and many was the time when they would listen attentively to Nanni, Theodor's nursemaid. One of the stories she told them was *Das klagende Lied*, the strange and rather dark tale that would be the basis for the first of Gustav's major works.

Their new home, today owned by the local council, the building having been renovated and with plans to turn the upper floor into a Mahler museum, consisted of a large kitchen, entrance hall, two bedrooms and a gentleman's living room where Bernhard had his desk and a small library. On the wall Gustav's father later hung a framed certificate stating that he, Bernhard Mahler, was a middle class citizen of Iglau!

The tavern was on the ground floor and the distillery and shop overlooked a courtyard at the rear. On the first floor lived the servants, wet-nurse and bartenders. These employees came mostly from the Iglau and Ledetsch areas. Mahler heard and learnt many of the folk songs sung by these servants and the customers in his father's bar, and there were frequent occasions when he would have listened to the music of folk dances; in Iglau the most frequently performed was the ländler *Hat Schó*. Gustav would absorb all the different types of music he heard, no matter how banal. On one occasion, during a particularly awful quarrel between his parents, he had run out of the house only to be confronted by a man with a barrel organ churning out the popular song, '*Ach, du lieber Augustin.*' The conflict between his emotional state and the song stayed with him throughout his life, a conflict that was reflected in many of his major works.

As we have seen Gustav had shown musical ability from a very early age. In fact it was said that he could learn tunes almost before he could speak. At the age of six, when visiting his grandparents in Ledetsch, he had discovered a piano in their attic. He recalled how the keys were above his head, but that he had still managed to 'plonk out' the odd tune that he had heard, much to the astonishment of all those present. So impressed was his grandfather that, to the delight of Gustav, he gave him the piano which arrived in Iglau by ox cart the following day. When he was seven he composed his first composition, much influenced by the deaths of his brothers Karl and Rudolf: 'Polka with a Funeral March Introduction', almost a contradiction, but reflecting the conflicting emotions of the deaths in his family and the merrymaking in his father's tavern. Only a year later he began to give music lessons.

The Mahlers attended the new synagogue, which had opened in 1863. Bernhard, however, was not a strict conformer to the Jewish religion. He had named his first child in accordance with his Jewish ancestry, all the others being linked with the German speaking society that he favoured. This was further underlined when, having become aware of Gustav's musical talent, he managed to get him enlisted in the Jacobskirche choir. Whilst a chorister there Gustav was introduced to many great choral works such as Mozart's Requiem and Rossini's Stabat Mater. Not only did singing in the choir help with his musical development, it was also good for Bernhard's own standing with the town's mainly Christian community and thereby good for business! Bernhard saw in his son's ability the chance of some reflected glory, and so he set out to promote Gustav as a young virtuoso and was prepared to make some financial sacrifices to this end.

Apart from tuition with Fischer, he had piano lessons from a violinist, Johannes Brosch, Kapellmeister Viktorin of the Iglau Theatre and from Wenzel Pressburg, a former pupil of Anton Bruckner. Bernhard Mahler made a point of being present during these lessons to make sure that his son was attentive and that he was getting his money's worth! This, of course, was completely unnecessary as Gustav was always very eager to learn.

Gustav Mahler's childhood was far from being a happy one. His mother Marie was loving but weak with a heart defect, bearing child after child, most of whom did not survive – she gave birth to fourteen, eight of whom died in infancy or early childhood. Gustav could hardly have known his mother not either pregnant or recovering from childbirth, and the dreadful contrast of constant merrymaking by his father's inebriated customers and the succession of deaths of his brothers and sisters left an indelible mark. In total contrast to his mother, his father was ruthless, often abrasive, even cruel at times, and certainly out for his own ends. He was also unfaithful to his wife, often seducing the servant girls. It was not only Gustav who suffered, of course. In this atmosphere of tension and morbidity, his sister Justine even played at death by lying on the bedroom floor surrounded by candles. It was a conflicting existence, almost bizarre, with the children's bodies being carried out and Bernhard's clients coming in to satisfy their liquid needs.

Gustav's love of nature started in his early childhood. He would escape from the traumas of home and school by running down to the beautiful valley of the River Jihlávka, which lies behind the town walls below the Jacobskirche. It was there that he felt freedom, where he could drift into a dream world, where he could commune with nature – as his future wife Alma put it, he dreamed his way through childhood. On one occasion, so the story goes, his father took him down there for a walk in the forest and, his mind on business no doubt, forgot him. The sun set and night approached, and he sat for hours listening to the nocturnal sounds, almost as though he were listening to what the forest was saying. Already the seeds were being sown for some of his great works of the future, such as his *Third* and *Seventh Symphonies*.

Bernhard also took Gustav on frequent trips across the Highlands to visit relatives. As he sat next to his father, he saw and was captivated by the hills and the forests. One of his regular trips was to Ledetsch to visit his grandparents, and they often stopped in Kalischt to buy shoes from the local cobbler. These journeys through the Highlands and the blue haze of the distant horizons would, many years later, provide nostalgic memories for Mahler, such as when he was writing the *Abschied* in *Das Lied von der Erde*. His love of nature was not a romantic one, but an all-embracing wonder of creation, its harshness as well as its beauty.

It is almost certain that the first school that Gustav attended was the public school on Brünnergasse, but little is known about this stage in his education as no official documents or even registers have been traced. In 1869 he transferred to the German Secondary Grammar School (Gymnasium) situated behind the church of St. Ignaz at the upper end of the town square. The building is now a district archive.

Gustav was not a very successful pupil, in fact he ended his first year at the Secondary Grammar nineteenth out of thirty-one. In his report, dated February 4th 1870, the only subjects for which he received praise were gymnastics and religion; both areas would continue to interest him in the future. As for the rest, he was a dreamer, inattentive and at times impatient, and the results showed. He and Theodor Fischer would frequently go swimming and boating together. Many years later, Theodor recalled how Gustav always showed kindness and that he had a real sense of justice. In fact he was quite intolerant of injustice, something that would remain with him all his life.

Gustav's insatiable appetite for reading became a concern for his parents, especially his father who tried to restrain him. Considering Bernhard's own interest in reading and study this is surprising, although perhaps he was concerned that reading too much would hinder Gustav's musical progress. This was important for Bernhard as well as for his son, for he clearly desired to be able to bask in any future reflected glory to help satisfy his Jewish pride. Gustav, frustrated by his father's restraints, had to hide in order to satisfy his literary desires. One refuge was on the roof of the house, which he managed to reach through a loft window. On one occasion he was spotted by a neighbour and given a good hiding by his father, who then had the window bricked up to prevent any repetition.

Realizing his exceptional gift for music, Bernhard supported him in every way he could and it was no surprise that he became the focal point of the family. An example of this was the way his brother Ernst slaved after him, tidying his belongings and cleaning his shoes, Gustav repaying him by playing the piano. This 'slaving' by his brother was particularly helpful, for Gustav had frequently suffered beatings from his father for his untidiness.

As well as the experience and musical knowledge he gained as a chorister at the Jacobskirche, he attended many performances of operas and operettas at the town theatre. These included works by Offenbach, Donizetti, Flotow, Lortzing and Schubert. All these experiences, together with his rapid progress as a pianist, brought about his first major public appearance at the Iglau Theatre on the 13th of October 1870. It was a great success, although regrettably there is no record of the works that he performed. The local press described him as a virtuoso in the making. Bernhard was delighted, and his standing in the local community leapt up another notch or two. Despite this success, he showed admirable restraint and did not try to push Gustav too hard which might have caused a backlash. However, he was concerned over his son's lack of progress at school, and so decided to send him to Prague to further his studies.

It must have been with a mixture of fear of the unknown, relief to be away from his father, yet missing the rest of his family, that the eleven-year-old Gustav left Iglau for Prague. Bernhard had arranged for his son to lodge in the home of Moritz Grünfeld and his large family – he had eleven children – in Celetná Street. They owned a music shop, and they were indeed a very musical family. Gustav was to receive music lessons in their home, and was to attend the prestigious Nové Město Gymnasium for his general education. The whole plan looked ideal on paper, but it turned out to be disastrous.

The Grünfeld family treated him cruelly, even taking away his clothes and shoes for their own children to wear, sometimes leaving Gustav to walk around barefoot. The food he was given was so basic and meagre that it was barely enough to keep him going. On the other hand, the Grünfeld children were well fed, healthy and boisterous in complete contrast to the pale, thin Gustav with his painful shyness, who became an easy target for their mischievous pranks. He was homesick and desperately unhappy. He tried to lose himself in his dream world, but he was close to breaking point. One day a teacher asked him what he wanted to be when he grew up, and he replied, probably through a mixture of anger and frustration, 'A martyr.' It was hardly surprising that his school results were even worse than before, coming sixty-fourth out of sixty-four at the end of the winter semester.

One incident would remain in his memory for the rest of his life. Possibly lost in a daydream, he had sauntered into one of the rooms in the Grünfeld home only to be confronted by the nineteen-year-old Alfred Grünfeld vigorously making love to a maidservant. At first he was shocked rigid, and then ran to the assistance of the girl whom he thought was being violently attacked. The couple were understandably furious with the boy and swore him to silence, but the incident had left its mark.

Bernhard, hearing that all was not well, set off for Prague to investigate. On seeing his poor, miserable, undernourished son, he immediately took him to a restaurant, then collected his belongings and, furious with the Grünfelds, made post haste back to Iglau.

Nothing had changed. The unhappiness, the rows and bitterness in the Mahler home continued just as before, but Gustav, having survived the Purgatory of Prague, was mentally a little stronger, more mature and glad to be back amongst people he knew and familiar surroundings. He returned to the Gymnasium to continue his education, and renewed his music studies with increased vigour – his safety valve and door to the future.

Later that year, in November 1872, Gustav took part in a special concert at the theatre to mark the anniversary of Schiller's birth. After an orchestral first half of the program, he mesmerized the audience of eight hundred by playing Liszt's *Variations on the Wedding March from Mendelssohn's Midsummer Night's Dream*, receiving wildly enthusiastic applause.

Not long after his latest success, on the 20th of April 1873, he took part in another concert, this time to mark the marriage of the Archduchess Gisela to Prince Leopold of Bavaria. He played Thalberg's *Fantasie on Themes from Norma*. With each performance his reputation as a pianist increased and such words as 'Wunderkind' began to be uttered. By popular demand he encored the Thalberg in the Czap Hotel a month later in yet another gala concert, a mostly choral programme to mark the foundation of the new Iglau male voice choir. But alongside his musical successes and the adulation he was now receiving, the unhappiness of his home life remained. Deaths of his siblings continued. Arnold and Frederick had both died in 1871, and in May 1873 Alfred too passed away. The abuse of his frail mother, whom he loved so dearly, continued from his rough, thoughtless father for whom he never showed any real affection at any stage during his life. But Gustav was growing up and more able to cope with all this. However, on April 13th, 1874, an event occurred that was the most shattering the young man had yet experienced.

Ernst, his thirteen-year-old brother, just a year younger than he was, and to whom he was especially close, died after a long illness from a heart complaint. It was he who had helped Gustav with mundane day-to-day tasks and who had loved to hear him play the piano, discuss music and play games together, and they had comforted each other during times of family stress. Throughout his long illness, as Mahler later recounted, he had sat by his bedside for hours on end, reading him stories, trying to keep his spirits up. And now that he was gone, Gustav felt very lonely. The memory of those painful months would remain with him always. This event, in a way, marked the end of his childhood, and his determination to succeed in music really took flight.

He began to compose an opera, probably based on the play *Herzog Ernst von Schnaben* by Johann Uhland, written in 1818. The libretto was by Josef Steiner, a friend of Gustav. With its altered title, *Herzog* having been dropped, it was probably an *in memoriam* to his deceased brother. Regrettably, when he returned to Steiner's home the following year to resume work on the opera, he discovered that his friend's aunt had had a clear out and, not realizing the importance of the papers, had consigned them to a bonfire.

It was at this point that Gustav Schwarz came onto the scene. He was an elderly manager of a large country estate not far from Iglau. Whilst clearing an attic, he had discovered some manuscripts by Sigismund Thalberg and was seeking someone with musical knowledge to have a look at them. Mahler was recommended by a friend of his, and, apart from playing through the Thalberg manuscripts, he played extracts from the opera he had been working on. Schwarz was astounded at the ability of the young man, and realized that something had to be done to enable him to go to Vienna, to the famous Conservatory, so that his musical career might be well and truly launched.

Gustav had inherited one particular aspect of Bernhard's character – his ambition and determination to succeed. Yet at the same time he was learning to be diplomatic, to use other people's influence to further his cause. Realizing that Schwarz might well be the key to his future at the Vienna Conservatory, he wrote to his elderly admirer thanking him for his hospitality and encouragement, but pointing out that his 'dear father' might be a stumbling block as he would almost certainly consider such a move to be detrimental to his studies in Iglau. Following the Prague *débâcle*, Bernhard was understandably anxious, not only over the effect such a move might have on his son's ordinary studies, but also over a youth of his age mixing with undesirable company in the big city, as well as the cost involved.

On Saturday the 4th of September 1875, Gustav Schwarz visited Bernhard and Marie, and thankfully his persuasive powers succeeded. The decision was taken to at least get the opinion of the Conservatory's eminent professor of piano studies, Julius Epstein. It is presumed that Schwarz took Gustav to the professor's home in Baden, to the south of Vienna. Not only was Epstein a renowned pianist and teacher, but also a close friend of Brahms, and therefore had considerable influence. The visit was a success, Epstein being duly impressed by the fifteen-year-old. Arrangements were made for Bernhard to meet the professor. He still had reservations, but Epstein managed to convince him that Gustav had an exceptional talent that had to be given a chance to blossom. To Bernhard's credit, he accepted the professor's advice, despite his worries and the very high financial costs that he would have to bear. Epstein took immediate steps to have Mahler enrolled, and this took place on the 10th of September 1875 – as student number 326. He would be a student at the Conservatory for three years, at the same time completing his studies at the Gymnasium in Iglau as an external student.

Vienna! What a thrill it must have been for the fifteen-year-old – a dream come true. Vienna, the Mecca of music and art, the city of Mozart with its magnificent new Ringstrasse, begun in 1857, to replace the forbidding fortifications which had surrounded the inner part of the city. It was a splendid tree-lined boulevard connecting most of the public buildings of importance such as the Rathaus, the Parliament, major museums and parts of the Hofburg Palace. 1867-1873 had been years of economic boom. 1869 had seen the opening of the splendid Court Opera House, designed by Eduard van der Nüll and August von Sicardsburg, and a year later, not far from the Hofoper and close to the Karlsplatz, the Musikverein building, housing a superb new concert hall and the *Gesellschaft der Musikfreunde* – the Conservatory where Mahler would study. All this exciting new development had been the inspiration of the Emperor himself, Franz Josef.

Unlike his departure for Prague as a timid ten-year-old setting off into the unknown, he arrived in Vienna positive, excited and ambitious, and he would later be joined by his close friend Theodor Fischer, as well as Emil Freund (from his class at the Gymnasium in Iglau) and Gustav Frank, a cousin of his.

Julius Epstein, a kind and generous man and highly regarded, took Gustav under his wing. The respect, affection and gratitude that he held for Epstein would remain with him always. As his piano tutor Epstein realized the young man's potential and managed to have him installed as an advanced student, thus bypassing the initial, more mundane areas of study. For harmony he studied with Robert Fuchs and composition with Franz Krenn.

Two of the first friends Gustav made at the Conservatory were Rudolf Krzyżanowski and Hugo Wolf. Wolf's later claim to fame lay mainly with his fine Lieder, notably the *Italienisches Liederbuch*, the *Spanisches Liederbuch* and the *Mörike Lieder*, and he was regarded by many as the natural successor to Schubert. On the other hand Wolf was something of a wild card, rebellious and showing little respect for his teachers, especially Hellmesberger. As a result he was thrown out of the Conservatory in 1877. The three students shared a passion for Wagner's music, and what a thrill it must have been when the great man himself came to Vienna in November 1875 to oversee productions of *Lohengrin* and *Tannhäuser*, both conducted by Hans Richter. One day Mahler made a point of being in the foyer of the Hofoper as Wagner was leaving, but through shyness he missed the chance to help him on with his coat, a lost opportunity that he would regret for the rest of his life. Wolf, on the other hand, over-the-top as usual, one day took it upon himself to open the carriage door for Wagner outside the Imperial Hotel where he was staying, then ran hell-for-leather to the Hofoper in time to open the door once more for him to get out! Wagner was the idol of most of the students at that time, and on one particularly wild evening, Mahler, Wolf and Krzyżanowski decided to sing highlights from *Götterdämerung* with great gusto, and consequently were thrown out of their digs by a very irate landlady!

Another brilliant student joined the Mahler circle. This was Hans Rott, a composer Gustav later referred to as 'the founder of the new symphony'. Among other students he would meet, and one who would become an important figure in his life, was Arnold Rosenblum who would later change his name to Rosé. He became leader of the Court Opera Orchestra, which also performed as the Vienna Philharmonic Orchestra for orchestral concerts. He would marry Gustav's sister Justine, and his brother Eduard would later marry Gustav's sister Emma, born that October. Another important figure was Franz Schalk who as a conductor would become one of Mahler's assistants.

Gustav worked hard at his studies and gave piano lessons to make ends meet as Bernhard was unable to afford the high fees demanded by the Conservatory. Most of his pupils were sent to him by Julius Epstein, one being his own son Richard. Epstein had to approach the committee to have Mahler's fees halved, presumably by the awarding of a scholarship. There was little argument, for it was generally recognized that Gustav was one of their prize students (in fact Epstein himself may well have subsidized his fees). As Fuchs recalled years afterwards, he was a regular truant from his harmony lessons, but that there was nothing he wasn't able to do. As a consequence the technical side was to cause him struggles later on, and he may have come to regret his truancy.

During the holidays, Gustav always went home to his parents in Iglau, now as a confident young man and a successful student. He remained very close to his mother and brothers Alois and Otto, sisters Leopoldine and Justine, as well as little Emma. He even felt a degree of gratitude to his father, despite all his failings, for his eventual support and financial sacrifice that was enabling him to study at the Conservatory. During his first summer break Krzyżanowski stayed at the Mahler home and together they organized a charity concert at the Czap Hotel in Iglau, the proceeds to help his old school. The programme included works by the two young men as well as by Vieuxtemps, Schubert and Chopin. It was a great success, not only with the audience, but the press too, who praised both Mahler's pianistic prowess as well as his compositions.

Back in Vienna, Mahler and his two close friends Hugo Wolf and Rudolf Krzyżanowski shared a room. Poor, often hungry, but with mutual interests, they gave each other support in their musical activities, as on the occasion when Mahler was desperately trying to finish a concert piece and his friends gave him space by sleeping rough on benches on the Ringstrasse! They shared their food and even clothes, such as the time when Mahler had been sent an overcoat that was far too big for him. Having walked around for a few days resembling a cartoon character with the coat trailing on the ground behind him and looking thoroughly absurd, he gave it willingly to Krzyżanowski as it fitted him perfectly!

Most of Gustav's student works have been lost or were destroyed by him personally, one exception being the movement for his *Piano Quartet in A minor*. It appears that he had intended destroying this as well, but he could not find it. In fact it was not until 1973 that it was first made public by the composer Peter Ruzicka from Hamburg after he had come across it in the U.S.A. Probably composed in 1876, the movement shows the influence of Brahms with no clues as to Mahler's later music. Nevertheless, as a student work, it was successful.

Thanks to the help given him by Julius Epstein, Mahler became an exceptional pianist and at the end of his first year at the Conservatory he was awarded the top prize for his performance of the first movement of Schubert's *Sonata in A minor*. He won again the following year, this time by playing the *Humoresque* by Robert Schumann, but despite his undoubted gift, any thoughts of making a career as a pianist were soon dispelled when he heard the Beethoven sonatas played by Anton Rubinstein. Although initially he intended never to perform again, he did intermittently, especially during the early part of his career. It was not just the fact that he felt he could not compete with Rubinstein, he had begun to realize that composition was his true métier.

Mahler's feelings towards his professors were very mixed. For Julius

Epstein he had nothing but respect and fondness, for Hellmesberger only coldness because of his anti-Semitic views. One of Mahler's disappointments during his years at the Conservatory was over a symphony he had written. Hellmesberger had agreed to conduct it, but while rehearsing the work he discovered a few errors in the orchestral parts. He threw the conductor's score onto the floor, stormed off virtually accusing Mahler of being incompetent and refused to have anything more to do with it. The young man must have been devastated, not to mention humiliated.

Another professor he really admired was Anton Bruckner, then fifty-two. Mahler was not one of his students, but he and Krzyżanowski frequently attended his lectures. As a composer, Bruckner did not have many supporters, but as a man he had great appeal. He was open, friendly and, as Mahler later recalled, had 'an almost childlike nature.' A strong friendship developed which was to last for many years and, as a man of sincerity he exerted a considerable influence on Mahler, for which he was eternally grateful. The two students, as well as Hans Rott (who may well have introduced them to him), used to attend concerts with Bruckner, who always delighted in their company. Bruckner also happened to be a great admirer of Wagner, having attended the very first performance of *Der Ring des Niebelungen* at Bayreuth in 1876.

The strength of affection shown by Mahler and Krzyżanowski for Bruckner was underlined on December 16th 1877 when a revised version of his *Third Symphony* was performed by the Vienna Philharmonic Orchestra. This was his '*Wagner*' symphony, dedicated to the great composer, and therefore very important to him. The event was a calamity due to a combination of Bruckner's poor conducting and a thoroughly unsympathetic orchestra. The majority of the audience left the concert hall before the end, with only a handful, mostly students, remaining. These included Mahler and Krzyżanowski. Bruckner was distraught, but his publisher Theodor Rättig remained interested in the work and asked for a piano duet transcription. Because of their unflinching support, Bruckner gave the task to Mahler and Krzyżanowski. It was a great success and, as well as being published, the two students were able to perform the transcription at the Conservatory. The elderly composer gave Mahler the manuscript of his *Third Symphony* with heartfelt thanks.

Many of his critics accused Bruckner of writing symphonies that were little more than 'pseudo-Bach through Wagner'. Such an attitude was totally unfair. They are great cathedrals of sound. He was an important composer with a very individual voice. Many regard his *Eighth Symphony* to be his finest, but his unfinished *Ninth*, with its great *Adagio*, is almost 'Mahlerian' in its intensity.

However, Mahler's friendship and admiration for Bruckner led to a considerable problem. The eminent Johannes Brahms was hostile to students, modern ideas and especially to Bruckner and, consequently, Mahler, Krzyżanowski, Rott and Wolf were on his black list. This would cause a profound upset for Mahler in the future although his respect for Brahms would last until the latter's death in 1897.

In 1878, Mahler received his diploma. He was now at the point where he would have to decide which direction to go, how to forge his career. Little is known about the years 1878-1880, but it is clear that Mahler went through the typical traumas of a young man. He, like a number of other young musicians in Vienna, became a vegetarian. This was as a result of an article in the October 1880 issue of the *Bayreuthe Blätter*, in which there was a piece by Wagner, 'Religion and Art', putting forward his strong views in support of vegetarianism . . . a bloodless diet to save mankind! Mahler also became a socialist. It was during this period that he composed his first important work, *Die Argenauten*, an overture now lost, which he entered unsuccessfully for the 'Beethoven Prize' in 1878. He then began work on a cantata, *Das Klagende Lied*, inspired by the story that Theodor's nursemaid had read to him years before. This was to be his first major and surviving work, not influenced by composers such as Bruckner, but in his own voice.

In the same year Hans Rott, who had studied organ music with Bruckner and who was a soul mate of Mahler's, left the Conservatory. Mahler later referred to their relationship as 'like two fruits from the same tree'. Rott had submitted the first movement of his symphony in a composition competition, but despite Bruckner's support, it had ended up being the only entry not to receive a prize. He completed the symphony in 1880, but after such incidents as threatening passengers in a train with a gun, convinced that Brahms had filled the carriages with dynamite, he was pronounced insane and sent to an asylum. He died of tuberculosis on the 25th of June 1884 aged just twenty-five. Mahler was shattered by the news, the man who had opened the door to the new era of the symphony, now dead. The influence of Rott's Symphony on him was immense, with its Ländler movement, and the adagio, which was, in a way, a forerunner of the great adagio of his own *Third Symphony*. So much of Mahler's music reflects memories of times past, and he deliberately let himself be influenced by Rott's Symphony in his own *Second*, *Fifth* and *Seventh Symphonies* as well.

Returning to 1878, Mahler, having received his diploma, returned to Iglau. He spent some time with his friend Emil Freund in Seelau, about twenty-eight miles from his childhood town. He began to experience typical youthful notions about God, life and the universe, laced with angst and a feeling of inability to move forward. Yet his romantic side, his love of nature and his dreams of a perfect world came to the fore. Life was an irony; whither should he go?

He continued to eke out a living by giving piano lessons and was given the task of teaching the children of Moritz Baumgarten. The Baumgartens lived near Budapest, and he soon grew more than a little tired of this task, longing to return to his friends. He wrote to Steiner saying that he couldn't cope with his present way of life for much longer. He felt frustrated, almost suicidal. His letter was a young man's *cri du coeur* and as in the past he sought refuge in nature and would escape to the fields. He spent time with Fárkas, a local shepherd, listening to the mournful tunes he played on his shawm accompanied by the sounds of nature and cowbells. Just as he had absorbed the folk songs, dances and military band music of his early years, so he continued to commit to memory the whole world of sound into which he would constantly dip later on when composing.

At last, in August 1879, the year in which Alma Schindler, his future wife, was born, he was able to return to Emil Freund's home in Seelau and then back to Iglau where he soon fell madly in love with Josephine Poisl, the postmaster's daughter. She was one of his piano pupils and he dedicated three songs to her: 'Spring', 'A winter's Song' and 'A May Dance', as well as the poems 'The Sun has Risen' and 'Forgotten Love'. These works in many ways anticipate his first major song cycle, *Lieder eines fahrenden Gesellen* of 1884. However, Josephine did not reciprocate his feelings and the would-be romance ended in March 1880 when she married Julius Wallner, a professor at the Gymnasium in Iglau.

In April 1880, Mahler returned to Vienna to study art, archeology and philosophy at the university, as well as attending a music course given by the well-known critic Eduard Hanslick, a friend of Brahms and therefore inevitably very anti-Wagner. Gustav continued work on *Das Klagende Lied* as well as his *Nordic Symphony* which was never completed and is now lost without trace. He, along with Wolf and Kzryżanowski, having become left-wing vegetarians, met others of the same inclination such as Victor Adler, a young physician and politician who later on became the instigator of social democracy in Austria, the writer Hermann Bahr, and Friedrich (Fritz) Löhr, who struck up a close friendship with Mahler. It was also during this period that he renewed acquaintance with a former student of the Conservatory, the viola-player Natalie Bauer-Lechner.

Born in 1858, she was the daughter of a bookseller in Vienna. Although graduating before Mahler's arrival at the Conservatory, she had been given permission to continue to use its facilities while her younger sister Ellen was studying there. Discovered by Brahms when she was just fifteen, for a long time she was the only woman to play his *Violin Concerto*. She became the viola-player of the Soldat-Röger String Quartet. Founded by Marie Soldat-Röger in 1895, it was an exclusive women's quartet based in Vienna. Natalie would later become a constant companion of Mahler's

over a period of several years. She kept a record of their time together and
Mahler's life in general and is probably the most reliable insight into his
character that we have.

It was at about this time that the *Rübezahl* affair took place. Hugo Wolf
had come up with an idea for an opera based on the *Rübezahl* tale. Mahler
was enthusiastic, saying that he was convinced that the story could well be
turned into a comic opera and he set to work immediately, producing a
libretto in little over a week. Wolf, meanwhile, was still 'researching', and
when Mahler showed him his completed libretto, he was furious that he
had jumped the gun and decided to scrap the whole project. Mahler,
however, argued that he thought the idea had great possibilities and
continued to work on it on and off for the next few years, although he
never completed the opera, blaming his conducting commitments. But the
disagreement with Wolf, even though unintended, was the first crack in
their friendship and was the bad seed that was to germinate later on.

It was at this point that Rättig, the publisher for whom he and
Kzryżanowski had produced the piano duet version of Bruckner's *Third
Symphony*, suggested that he ought to have an agent, so he introduced him
to Gustav Löwy with whom Mahler signed a five-year contract. It was not
long before a possible first appointment was being offered – to be the music
director for a summer season at the tiny festival theatre at the little spa
town of Hall in Upper Austria.

At exactly what point Mahler decided to take up conducting seriously as
a career is uncertain, although it was probably more likely that he drifted
into it through necessity rather than desire. At this early stage he must
have been pinning his hopes on *Das klagende Lied* which was nearing
completion. He probably thought that his new work would be the
launching pad for his career as a composer. The offer on the table must
have caused him doubts. A job in a small, musically insignificant backwater
hardly had much appeal. Why should he bother? How would it look on his
C.V.? However, he accepted the offer, partly due to pressure from his
mother to find a worthwhile job as she was becoming anxious over her
son's drifting into a rather dubious, post student existence. Friends and
acquaintances in the music world also advised him to accept the post,
purely for experience and to give him something definite to get his teeth
into. The final push probably came from Julius Epstein who had supported
him so steadfastly during his time at the Conservatory. He wanted to see
his star pupil and young friend begin a career that he was convinced would
lead to great things. Mahler, as always, bowed to his advice. So, it was off
to Upper Austria, his first appointment, and although he continued to have
doubts about the idea, it would, after all, only be for a few weeks.

Chapter 2

First Appointments
Bad Hall . . . Laibach . . . Olmütz . . . Kassel

Das klagende Lied . . .
Lieder eines fahrenden Gesellen

I
N MAY 1880, Mahler arrived in the little spa town of Hall in Upper
Austria, today known as Bad Hall. It is situated approximately twenty
kilometres to the west of Steyr and forty kilometres south of Linz, and at
the time had around eight hundred inhabitants. It was a sleepy little town where
the well heeled came to take the iodine-impregnated waters for all manner of
ailments. Today there is a delightful town museum, the Forum Hall, which has a
room specifically set aside for Mahler memorabilia. It is just beside the gates
that lead to the impressive Kurhaus and other spa buildings and the well laid-
out park with fountains and a bandstand, behind which is the spot where the
Festival Theatre stood.

The theatre had been constructed by Josef Hillischer, the manager of the
spa, who had also had built a villa for his family close by. The 'theatre' was
little more than a wooden barn, not very well disguised by various external
decorations. It could seat around one hundred and ninety, had a small
gallery and an orchestra pit just big enough for the fifteen musicians
Mahler would have at his disposal. The theatre is no longer there, a stone
and brick replacement having been built in 1883 with a seating capacity of
five hundred, so the old wooden structure was abandoned to the elements.
In 1921 the balcony, being in a dangerous state, was removed. Having been
used for various agricultural and storage purposes, it fell into terminal
disrepair before finally being burnt down in 1969. On the 17th of
September, 2003, a simple monument with a commemorative plaque was
erected on the site where the old wooden theatre had once stood, with an
inscription saying, '*An dieser Stelle stand das alte Bad Haller Theater, in
dem der Komponist Gustav Mahler im Sommer 1880 dirigierte*' ('On this
spot stood the old Theatre of Bad Hall where the composer Gustav Mahler
worked as a conductor during the summer of 1880').

From boredom in Hungary, heartbreak in Iglau, time-killing back in Vienna and now this! For the ambitious young man this must have been depressing in the extreme. At first all those thoughts of giving-up must have come flooding back. Bad Hall – had he been familiar with English at that time, surely he would have agreed! This was a test by Löwy to find out more about Mahler's character and his determination to be a success: succeed in a place like Hall and he could go far. But for the eager young conductor, already showing signs of being a perfectionist and intolerant of low standards, having to deal with an indifferent group of jobbing musicians who spent the day providing background music for the benefit of those who were taking the waters, equally indifferent singers and being paid a pittance for his efforts – what was the point?

On arrival he had found digs in the nearby village of Pfarrkirchen, well within walking distance of the spa. The rooms he had were in the large Unteres Gasthaus, later known as Baderhaus due to the therapeutic baths that had been installed as part of the service. The building now has a plaque commemorating Mahler's brief stay in the village.

Mahler was in for a few surprises. As Alma later wrote, he soon discovered that there were other duties that Hillischer expected of him. He had to make musical arrangements for his tiny ensemble, sing parts himself if necessary and he was even expected to perform on stage (this he refused to do). In addition he was expected to do cleaning, sort out music stands and chairs, put ready the orchestral parts and clear everything away after each performance. He even had to wheel the director Zwerenz's baby around the park during the intervals! Frau Zwerenz, incidentally, just happened to be the star of the cast!

And the works that had to be performed? A full list for the summer of 1880 is not known, but they were mostly operettas. We do know that *Drei Paar Schuhe* (Three Pairs of Shoes), libretto by Görlik and Berla with music by Millöcker, and a one act operetta by Offenbach, *Die hochzeit bei Laternenichein (Le Mariage aux Lanternes)*, were performed in June. The winter season in nearby Steyr had included *Die Fledermaus* as well as other works by Offenbach and Suppé, all, of course, 'watered down'.

Depressed as he must have been, Mahler refused to give up. Writing to his friend Albert Spiegler, he referred to the Hall brigade as 'dung flies', and that they were not going to get the better of him. He asked Spiegler to contact Lipiner to whom he had entrusted *Rübezahl*, the opera he had been working on. He asked for the manuscript to be sent to him as he wanted to continue composing the music – he needed something to satisfy his artistic needs. However, it was not long before he was dismissed by Zwerenz for failing to turn up for a performance. He had been socialising with a group of cultured young men, including a well-known portrait painter Heinrich von Angeli, anything to get away from the tedium of the Festival Theatre. And so his first appointment ended in unfortunate circumstances, but he had been well and truly bitten by the conducting bug.

On his return to Vienna he immediately contacted Löwy, asking if he could find him a winter job as a conductor. As it so happened, Zwerenz, of all people, had been appointed to take charge of the theatre in Iglau for the winter season and, forgiving him for his misdemeanour at Hall, he offered Mahler the conducting job in his home town for the winter season of 1880-1881. At first glance this must have been tempting, but Mahler decided that he had to aim higher and so turned down the offer. That autumn became a mixture of good and sad news. Mahler was still very upset by Rott's spiral into insanity and the suicide of one of Emil Freund's friends, a girl Mahler had met and liked very much. However, on the first of November, he had at last finished *Das klagende Lied*, which he nicknamed his 'child of sorrow'.

Das klagende Lied . . .

It had indeed been as a child of sorrow that he had first listened to Nanni, Theodor Fischer's nursemaid, reading them the fairy-tale *Das klagende Lied*. Mahler's cantata is a work of great importance; the first composition in which his unique style came into being. It has many of the ingredients we expect from Mahler: contrasting emotions, the use of military and folk ideas, and an off-stage orchestra. This had to be far enough away to be able to play fortissimo, yet sounding pianissimo – a device he used later with particularly good results in his *Second Symphony*. The effects, the drama, the rhythms – it almost begs to be an opera rather than a concert piece. It has the unmistakable stamp of the composer who regarded it as the first of his works worth preserving, naming it his Opus 1. It is a cantata on the grand scale for chorus, soloists and large orchestra, so much so that the critic Max Kalbeck remarked in 1901, somewhat sarcastically, that in comparison the collapse of Valhalla at the end of Wagner's *Götterdämerung* was a purely local matter! Perhaps this was rather over-doing it, but in so saying he nevertheless acknowledged the scale of the piece. (Kalbeck, along with other critics, took delight in tearing Mahler's works to pieces). The fact remains it was a great, youthful celebratory launch to his composing career. It may be flawed but it is a precursor filled with the seeds of the great works to come. Michael Tilson Thomas describes it as 'a great torso of a piece containing many beautiful things and other moments that are so clumsy'.

It is in three parts and lasts some sixty-five minutes.

Part One: A stately queen of great beauty is seeking a husband. She makes a promise to wed the man who finds a particularly lovely flower, which only grows in a forest. Tempted by the challenge, two brothers set out to find it. The younger of the two discovers it, but his jealous brother then kills him.

Part Two: A wandering minstrel happens to be walking through the forest when he sees a bone belonging to the dead man. He picks it up and carves it, making a flute. When the minstrel starts to play the instrument, it relates the tale of the fratricide that had taken place.

Part Three: The day of the marriage arrives, and the minstrel enters the palace and plays his flute, which again tells its mournful tale. The elder brother, now the King, is furious, leaps up from his throne and barges his way through the crowded hall. He grabs the flute and plays it himself, and the 'Singing Bone' publicly accuses him of the dreadful deed. The Queen collapses, the wedding guests flee in horror and the palace falls in ruins.

Mahler later removed the first part, *Waldmärchen*, feeling that the work benefited without the nearly half-hour introduction. He also reduced the number of soloists from four to three by omitting the bass part. (He gave the score of the *Waldmärchen* to his sister, Justine, and her husband's nephew, Alfred Rosé, instigated its first performances on Radio Brno in 1934 and on Vienna Radio in 1935). But despite its grandiose scale, it is just a fairy tale based on an old German story in the anthology put together by Ludwig Bechstein (1801-1860), together with ideas from the Brothers Grimm story of fratricide, *The Singing Bone*.

Mahler wrote to Emil Freund saying that his 'child of sorrow', as he called it, had to be performed, and he would bring about its performance by any means he could think of. It was a creation of which he was rightly proud, and he banked on it as his ticket to greater things.

As it happened, he had to wait for twenty years, but in 1881 he decided to enter it for the Beethoven Prize, the competition run by the *Gesellschaft der Musikfreunde* for the benefit of past and present students of the Conservatory. This, of course, was the same competition for which Rott had entered the first movement of his *Symphony*, only to be unceremoniously dumped by the jury. Mahler must have been concerned about this, as it was well known that he and Rott had been close and the jury tended to be rather conservative.

They met in December and awarded the prize to Robert Fuchs, Mahler's former harmony teacher. His brother Johann Fuchs had been on the panel, and he had had a low opinion of Mahler while he was a student. Among others on the jury were the anti-Semite Hellmesberger, which of course had not helped, Mahler's composition teacher Franz Krenn from whose lectures he had often played truant, the famous and abrasive critic Eduard

Hanslick, the conductor Hans Richter and composers Karl Goldmark and Brahms, who, of course, was fully aware of Mahler's feelings towards Bruckner! So, even though it was an innovative work, ahead of its time, which may not have helped, its failure to win was no great surprise.

Disappointed as he inevitably was, he never lost faith in his Opus 1 and did not destroy it along with his other early works. Two years later in 1883 he was to send *Das klagende Lied* to Franz Liszt, obviously feeling that with his support a performance would be virtually guaranteed, but he returned it insinuating that the music was interesting, but the text awful. Mahler shelved *Das klagende Lied*, convinced that its time would come, and indeed continued to revise it right up to its first performance in Vienna on the 17th of February 1901. Nevertheless, he later blamed its failure to win the Beethoven Prize as being responsible for his stressful life as an opera conductor, although looking back it is hard to see how his character would have allowed him to live as a reclusive composer.

Mahler was in the process of discovering just how obstinate Vienna could be. Haydn, Mozart and Schubert had all struggled to be accepted in the Austrian capital, and as for poor Bruckner . . . On the other hand Beethoven and Wagner had breached the bastions of narrow-mindedness through their solid determination; Mahler would try to emulate them.

There is not a lot known about his life during the months following the disappointment over the failure of *Das klagende Lied* in the Beethoven Competition. We know that he spent Christmas and the following summer holidays in Iglau with his family as well as some time in Seelau with Emil Freund. At last good news came when Löwy contacted him informing him that Alexander Mondheim-Schreiner, the director of the theatre in Laibach, wanted him to be his conductor for the following season.

Laibach, now Ljubljana in Slovenia, was definitely an improvement on Bad Hall. For a start it was a large town with a population of around one hundred thousand, as opposed to the eight hundred or so in his previous post. It was a university town and had a cultural tradition, but the theatre, the Landestheater, was only marginally better than the Festival Theatre at Hall. It was at least a proper and reasonably stylish building, not a wooden structure, but it still only boasted an orchestra of eighteen or so players, a mixed chorus of about fourteen, albeit more professional. Nevertheless, musical ambitions were greater despite his being forced to work on a shoestring budget with employees having to double-up singing, acting and even carrying out more mundane duties such as work in the box office. In fact Mahler's first task was to conduct a performance of Gounod's *Faust* with only one man in the chorus!

However amateur this set-up may have seemed, it was an invaluable experience for Mahler who was to include operas by Mozart, Verdi, Weber and Rossini during his employment there. It was at this time that he decided to grow a moustache and beard to make himself look older, and he managed to entice singers of a higher calibre to appear as guest artists.

The local newspapers were reasonably impressed with the first opera under his full control, *Il Trovatore*, and they praised the work he had put into the subsequent performance of *Die Zauberflöte* at the end of October. His reputation grew production by production, and when the time came for his benefit concert he had become something of a celebrity. This took place on March 23rd, 1882 with a performance of *Alessandro Stradella* by Flotow. When he entered the pit, the orchestra played a fanfare and the audience went wild, and afterwards he was presented with a laurel wreath. Everyone knew the effort he had made to raise the standards at the Laibach Theatre – despite the 'performances' of one or two prima donnas, one of whom made her protestations on the top of his piano by slapping her thighs! The season ended at the beginning of April and, travelling via Trieste, thereby catching his first ever glance of the sea, he returned to Vienna.

Bad Hall had, on the whole, been a bad experience, but his months as conductor at the Laibach Theatre had been a valuable education and had boosted his confidence as a conductor. It had also widened his knowledge of the repertoire, his ability to interpret and how to adapt under difficult circumstances. Most important of all, he had learnt how to deal with fellow artistes, the press and the public, most of whom had nothing but praise for his work at the Landestheater. It is strange that there appears to be no evidence that efforts were made to renew his contract. Probably Mahler himself had decided that, valuable as the experience had been, enough was enough and it was time to move on to higher things.

On returning to Vienna he resumed the waiting game, but now with greater confidence after the knowledge and experience he had gained at Laibach. He knew that it would only be a matter of a short time before the next opportunity came his way. With the onset of summer, he decided to return to Iglau via the Baumgartens, and it was during this visit to his hometown that, on 19th of September 1882, he was given the task of conducting the opera, *Boccaccio* by Franz von Suppé. This guest appearance caused considerable excitement in the town. The reviews were superlative as might have been expected with the return of its increasingly famous son, but after the adulation had died down, Mahler was to make scathing comments about the lead singer, a certain Fraulein Hassmann, insinuating that she was the least talented female singer he had met for a long time!

During the following months, Mahler continued giving piano lessons in Vienna, and resumed work on *Rübezahl*. The boredom and impatience began to return. In December he wrote to Salzburg, enquiring about a conducting post there, but after only being offered the possibility of an assistant's post, he decided not to pursue the matter. Since his return to Vienna, Mahler had been particularly frustrated by his inability to find suitably peaceful lodgings. Wherever he went he seemed to come up against the noise of screaming babies or amateur musicians in neighbouring apartments, but despite this he did manage to make some progress with both the libretto and score of *Rübezahl*, the opera he was destined never to finish. Just as he was becoming desperate to find somewhere where he could work in peace, the possibility of another short-term conducting job was offered.

Olmütz (Olomouc) is situated on the River Morava, northeast of Brno. At that time it had a population of around twenty thousand, and was, in many ways, very similar to Iglau in that it had a reasonable cultural tradition. The Municipal Theatre, dating from 1830, was able to seat a thousand and stood in the main square. The orchestra was usually made up of around twenty-four musicians and there was a chorus of about thirty, with seventeen soloists able to be called upon. Although hardly the type of position Mahler had been hoping for, at least it appeared to be an improvement on his previous posts, would give him added experience and was certainly better than continuing to languish in frustration and boredom. Poor Mahler had no idea what he was letting himself in for.

Still only twenty-two, he took up his new job on the 10th of January 1883. The Municipal Theatre was in a badly run-down state, short of money, sets, artistes and enthusiasm. Before Mahler's arrival, the director, Emanuel Raul, had managed to alienate the public by putting on new and not particularly good works, which had inevitably led to a slump in attendances and revenue. Mahler, in a letter to Friedrich Löhr, compared the situation he found himself in to being like a thoroughbred horse asked to pull a cart whilst harnessed to oxen! He told his friend that from the moment he arrived, he felt as though he were about to face the Day of Judgement. Of course these dire circumstances that he found himself in would not deter him from doing his level best to shake the apathy out of the place. As a musician he knew it was his duty, as well as knowing that to bring about some success in such a situation would do his future prospects no harm.

After his very first rehearsal members of the company left in a fury complaining of sore throats, and swearing that they would never work for him again. It would seem that initially he had made a point of not introducing himself, let alone holding conversations with them. He even went into the theatre bar and, having been greeted by asides and glances from the imbibing cast, asked for water. He was still a staunch vegetarian and this also caused raised eyebrows, such as on the occasion when he ordered a meal of spinach and apples in a restaurant and then began a rather public lecture on the benefits of abstaining from meat and of not wearing wool next to the skin. This caused something of a disturbance amongst the other patrons and he was persuaded to leave. Inevitably great curiosity arose about the new, rather eccentric young man who had taken charge of the performances at the Municipal Theatre. He was not popular, far from it, but a certain respect began to emerge when improvements began to become evident.

One of the early decisions he made was that he would not entertain conducting works by Wagner and Mozart. To him, it would be almost sacrilegious to subject such masterpieces to the inadequacies of Olmütz. However, after a great deal of cajoling considerable progress was made. His first real success, both with the public and the press, most of whom had been anti-Mahler up until then, was the Olmütz première of *Un Ballo in Maschera* by Giuseppe Verdi – at least successful when compared to the disastrous productions prior to his arrival in the town. Compliments abounded and Mahler must have given a great sigh of relief, knowing that he was winning the uphill struggle.

On 13th of February, an event occurred that really upset him, causing him to lose control of himself in public. This was the death of Richard Wagner whom he considered to be a musical 'god' and one of the greatest composers of all time. It was known that the young conductor's father, Bernhard, was a sick man, and the story goes that the critic Manheit saw Mahler running down the street crying into his handkerchief. Thinking that he had received bad news about his father, he was about to console him when he cried out, 'The Master is dead!' Such was the esteem in which he had held the great German composer.

Despite the success of *Ballo*, Mahler continued to find his work at the artistically inadequate theatre in Olmütz almost as painful as Bad Hall and Laibach. He was unhappy, had no friends and was beginning to suffer from his strict vegetarian diet for which no one had the least sympathy in an area where meat was almost the staple food.

Having acted as accompanist at a lieder recital given on the 25th of February, he turned his attention to the next project, the first production of Bizet's *Carmen* to be staged in Olmütz. This took place on the 10th of March. Again, both press and public acclaimed Mahler's work, and there were further performances that were equally successful. The last of these was on the 17th of March, another success despite the fact that the lead soprano and five members of the chorus had left just before the first night, having to be replaced at the last moment, as well as the children's chorus being prevented from taking part!

Mahler was rightly regarded as the saviour of the Municipal Theatre. His time there was drawing to a close, and his benefit concert was almost a repeat of that at Laibach with wild applause and a large laurel wreath. Yes, the Olmütz theatre had been rescued from its downward spiral, but there, was no way that Mahler could have made a silk purse out of a sow's ear, and, indeed, when he did leave on the 18th of March, a large proportion of the company departed as well.

The young perfectionist had continued to be frustrated by sub-standard artistes and an incompetent management, but he had been as determined as ever to achieve the highest standards he could under the circumstances. To him conducting was not a routine job, but a vocation, a privilege and a duty to be the representative of the composer in any performance, no matter where and regardless of any difficulties. After all, he himself was an ambitious composer about to burst into bloom, and he knew how he would feel if some laissez-faire conductor should take the reins of one of his works. He firmly believed that laziness and incompetence were personal insults to composers.

An important visitor to the Municipal Theatre for one of the performances of *Carmen* happened to be the producer, Karl Überhorst from the theatre in Dresden, which, of course, was in a different league from Olmütz. He was mightily impressed by the young conductor's achievements against all odds and told Mahler that he would be glad to use his influence for any posts he might apply for in the future.

Next stop, a quiet interlude back in Vienna at the privately owned Carl-Theater near the Prater, where he would be the chorus director for a season of Italian opera. Not a great deal is known about this stage in the early part of his career, but it must have been a great relief to be able to work in Vienna and not to have full responsibility for the performances.

Following this short engagement, Mahler spent some time with his friend Fritz Löhr at his home in Perchtoldsdorf, not far from Vienna. Löhr later recalled how they went for many long walks together in the countryside, discussing music and literature, 'abandoning themselves to nature . . . two hearts in harmony.' They wandered through old, untouched Austrian villages and trod in the footsteps of Beethoven in the Heiligenstadt area. This holiday was a much-needed breath of fresh air for Mahler, and he managed to shake off the dust from the three trials he had endured at Hall, Laibach and Olmütz. Löhr became one of his closest friends and, after the deaths of Bernhard and Marie, he willingly kept a fatherly eye on Mahler's surviving brothers and sisters and their education.

Meanwhile, behind the scenes moves were being made to find Mahler another post. Löwy had heard that a kapellmeister's position at the Royal and Imperial Theatre in Kassel was vacant. Kassel was a vibrant industrial city about midway between Cologne and Leipzig, and the theatre came under the auspices of Berlin. Löwy immediately wrote to the intendant, Baron von Gilsa, a retired Prussian officer who had been awarded the Iron Cross among many other medals, and at the same time contacted Karl Überhorst asking him to provide a suitable reference. This the latter did willingly as he had promised Mahler he would at the end of his time at Olmütz. Mahler travelled to Kassel for a week's trial which he completed successfully. He signed a very detailed contract on the 31st of March, 1883, one interesting clause being that Löwy's five per cent should be deducted at source, probably a reaction to the muddled nature of Mahler's finances. The contract was for three years at a salary of two thousand marks a year, and in addition he would receive extra money towards his day-to-day expenses. It was by far the furthest that the twenty-three year old had yet travelled, both geographically as well as from a career point of view. It was his first appointment at an important opera house, and from the 1st of October he would have the rather grandiose title of Royal Musical and Choral Director bestowed upon him. At last! One can almost imagine him punching the air with delight and shouting out a resounding 'Ja!'

But . . .

First, it was back to Vienna, doubtless bubbling over with excitement and eager to tell all his friends the good news, including Bruckner who must have been delighted that, at last, his young supporter had got his foot firmly on the ladder to success. He was then, of course, very keen to visit Iglau to see his family and friends, not knowing when the next opportunity might arise, for he had to begin work at the Kassel theatre on the 21st of August.

No sooner had he arrived in Iglau than the arm-twisting began. A concert had been arranged by the Red Cross to raise money for a relief fund set up to help those who had been made homeless in a recent earthquake on Ischia. It was to be an important event with the Archduke Eugen as the guest of honour. It had been decided to have a mixed programme of recitals, drama and a short operetta, *Das Kaffeekränzchen,* by Karl Kuntze, which Mahler had been asked to conduct and accompany on the piano. Hans Bruckmüller, a local musician, was asked to turn the pages for him. Doubtless Mahler had his mind on greater things, and he found this task and the operetta itself an affront to his status. He began to make snide comments to the cast, made little effort to rehearse them properly, and on the evening itself he became so wound-up that he suddenly leapt to his feet, slammed the piano lid, and much to the astonishment of all present, shouted at Bruckmüller to take his place as he did not want anything more to do with it. Having calmed down, he reappeared to join the violinist Mila von Ottenfeld for a recital including the *Kreutzer* sonata. Bruckmüller had resumed his position as page-turner, and to make sure that he kept up, Mahler set about kicking him each time he wanted a page turned. Bruckmüller quite understandably soon got fed up with this and returned the compliment, Mahler calling him a . . . something-or-other. The audience became quite mesmerized by all this. The violinist was embarrassed beyond words being under the mistaken impression that the insult might have been aimed at her! Eventually the whole scene dissolved into applause and laughter. This was to be Mahler's final concert in Iglau.

The differences Mahler encountered in Kassel, compared to his previous posts, were considerable. He was mightily relieved to be working with professionals in a theatre which could seat as many as 1,600 and with an orchestra of around fifty, but the very professionalism of the outfit in the much sterner Prussian part of Europe, combined with the fact that his contract placed him under the control of the Berlin administration rather than the theatre management, soon began to cause problems. The Baron, Adolph Freiherr von und zu Gilsa, continued to wield his officer's stick, and Mahler soon had a rude awakening, being given an endless list of petty tasks and paperwork.

No less than three times in September he found himself in trouble with the authorities. He was fined for making too much noise with his feet during rehearsals and performances and for refusing to leave the podium to conduct an off-stage chorus. He was also sanctioned for causing some of the women to burst into hysterical laughter during a dress rehearsal. As a result of this, he was ordered to have a chaperone present whenever he was in the company of one of the female members of the company!

He soon discovered that, despite his magnificent title, he was in fact second to Wilhelm Treiber, who insisted on reserving for himself all the most prestigious productions and landed Mahler with the lesser works in which he had no interest. Nevertheless he was given the opportunity to première operas by Delibes, Adam and Meyerbeer, as well as the chance to create a new production of *Un Ballo in Maschera*, with which, of course, he was very well acquainted. But the restrictions placed upon him, the lack of artistic freedom that he had been used to in the past and the constant boarding school attitude of the management, noting every slightest misdemeanour, soon began to eat away at Mahler's enthusiasm, and it was not long before he began to question the wisdom of remaining in Kassel.

Having recovered from the initial shocks of his new job, he pulled himself together and, as was always the case, his dedication to the music came to the fore. He must have enjoyed the higher standards of performance he was now able to achieve. Yet he was not happy and kept a look out for work in a less draconian establishment. There was something of an irony here, in that Mahler, in his zeal for the achievement of high standards, was himself difficult to work for, especially for any musicians who dared to give less than one hundred per cent. There were in fact clauses in his contract which made him responsible for the punctuality, quality of performance and the general discipline of the orchestra and chorus. He later recalled how on one occasion the musicians had got so aggrieved with his excessive demands that certain individuals turned up for one rehearsal armed with cudgels with rather unfriendly intentions! Probably exaggerated, but indicative of his determination to achieve the reputation of a perfectionist, and his ultimate goal to be recognised as one of the top conductors in his profession.

Another learning curve for Mahler was how to cope with nit-picking critics. Early reviews criticised his tempi and his physical exertions on the podium. By January 1884, he was beginning to react to the unhappy atmosphere of the house and began to make determined efforts to seek out pastures new.

An opportunity came in the same month with the visit of Hans von Bülow and the Meiningen orchestra. Bülow was one of the most eminent figures in the music world. He had been a staunch supporter of Wagner, conducting the premières of both *Tristan und Isolde* and *Die Meistersinger*, but after the composer had successfully enticed his wife Cosima, daughter of Franz Liszt, to join him, Bülow changed camps and become an equally staunch Brahms supporter! Nevertheless, despite the complications of his private life, he was revered as a musician, and was famous for his attention to detail and the immaculate performances given under his direction. On some occasions he even insisted that his players should perform standing up and play from memory. It was hardly surprising that he became something of a role model for Mahler, who took the bull by the horns and wrote a long letter to him in a somewhat gushing and grovelling style. Mahler told him that he was a musician wandering in darkness and confusion and, having attended Bülow's concert, he knew that he could be his saviour. He begged him to take him on as a pupil and even offered to pay for the privilege.

Mahler, of course, was bound to Kassel by his contract, and there was no way that Bülow would become involved in disputes with the Kassel authorities. Even so, receiving such an over-the-top letter from the young conductor would not have helped. In his letter Mahler had criticised his present employers, said how unsatisfied he was in his present post, and begged Bülow for a reply. Bülow sent him a blunt, dismissive note pointing out that he was an inexperienced young man and had much to learn, including how to approach his elders and betters. He sent Mahler's letter to Treiber who was delighted to hand it on to Baron von Gilsa, and Mahler found himself in an even worse predicament than he had been before. The saving factor, which prevented his instant dismissal, was the high standard of his work.

Thoroughly miserable, Mahler had no alternative but to carry on, only now his every move was being watched and criticised. Maybe partly because of his dejected state, he entered into a new love affair, this time with Johanna Richter, a very attractive although rather second-rate singer in the company. She was a welcome distraction, as was a sudden request to compose incidental music for an entertainment based on *Der Trompeter von Säkkingen*, a poem by Victor von Scheffel. Mahler wrote to Fritz Löhr telling him that he had composed the music in just two days and that he was very satisfied with the results, although he had little time for 'Scheffel's affectation' and considered his own work to be far superior to that of the poet. The entertainment took place on the 23rd of June as the last item of a concert programme. Much to his delight, everyone, including the critics, went over-board in their praise for his work. Unfortunately, as with most of Mahler's early compositions, the score was either lost or destroyed, although the later discarded *'Blumine'* movement of his *First Symphony*, was a by-product.

The day after the concert Mahler left for his summer break. Having visited his parents in Iglau he went to stay with Fritz Löhr at his home in Perchtoldsdorf to spend a few days relaxing and putting his troubles to the back of his mind. Löhr then travelled with him back to Iglau, and he later recalled how they had spent many hours walking in the beautiful countryside close to the town, listening to Bohemian musicians and watching youngsters dancing in the open air, profound, sad and yet joyous. He had found the experience so moving, and later reflected the 'earthy charms' of this world in his music.

Before returning to Kassel, Mahler visited Dresden, no doubt to tell his tales of woe to Karl Überhorst. Whilst there he went to performances of *Così fan tutte* and *Tristan und Isolde*, and was introduced to the conductor Ernst von Schuch, who would later become a friend and supporter.

At the end of August he was back in Kassel, and his words in a letter to Löhr, 'God help me!' rather summed up his feelings. He had seen Johanna again but found her distant and unresponsive, despite having written two love poems, which he had dedicated to her. These two poems were the starting point that later resulted in his song cycle, *Lieder eines fahrenden Gesellen* (Songs of a Wayfarer), which he would dedicate to the singer. Mahler also told Löhr that as a result of his recent visit it could still be a possibility that he might be offered work in Dresden.

Lieder eines fahrenden Gesellen
(Songs of a Wayfarer)

Mahler wrote the poems, with piano accompaniment, in December, but he later revised the score as an orchestral version. This set of songs marked a leap forward in the quality of his creativity. They can be placed in the same bracket as Schubert's *Winterreise* and Berlioz's *Les Nuits d'Été*, and they provided seeds from which many ideas would emerge while he was composing his *First Symphony*. They are heartfelt gems and, as Mahler was to do in succeeding works, he placed himself at their centre – the Wayfarer is clearly the composer himself.

Wenn mein Schatz Hochzeit macht. (When my love becomes a bride)
The first song proclaims that when the love of his life becomes another's bride, that day will be a day of bitterness, and he will go to his room and will weep the tears of loss. He compares her voice to the singing of a sweet little bird and her beauty to the beauty of nature in spring, but spring is over and so is her singing, and he will spend the night in sorrow.

Ging' heut' morgen übers Feld. (As I walked this morning through the field)
The second song is a lively acclamation of the beauties of nature and is full of *joie de vivre*. Everything is wonderful, but doubt returns at the end when the Wayfarer questions whether his happiness would ever flower, and he is resigned that it won't.

Ich hab'ein glühend' Messer. (I have a burning knife)
The third song plunges to the depths of despair with the repeated words, 'O weh! O weh!' (Woe is me! Woe is me!), occurring no less than five times. The Wayfarer sings of a knife in his breast, which destroys all pleasures and peace, and whenever he looks up at the heavens or wanders through golden fields, he sees his lost love, even in his dreams. So distraught is he that he would welcome death.

Die zwei blauen Augen von meinem Schatz. (My love's two blue eyes)
The fourth and final song deals with acceptance and recovery. The Wayfarer reluctantly accepts his rejection, and is ready to say farewell to his love and to go out into the wide world. He sets off into the night across a dark and forbidding heath with no one to bid him farewell, his only companions being love and sorrow. Eventually he comes across a linden-tree where, at last, he can relax and sleep. When he awakes he finds that the tree has showered him with blossom and he feels refreshed. The song ends with the words, '*Lieb' und Leid! Und Welt und Traum!*' (Love and sorrow! And world and dream!).

Apart from being moving little masterpieces, these songs, in their orchestrated versions, established the orchestral song cycle. This was an idea first used by Berlioz in his *Nuits d'Été* and later by Wagner in the *Wesendonk Lieder*, but Mahler's song cycle, and those that he wrote subsequently, have an entity and are like miniature song-symphonies, telling their story on a journey through the conflicts of nature and human existence. Here are two personal reactions to them, written years later. First, Harvey Grace in *The Musical Times* (1927): 'If this is typical Mahler let us have a lot more of him', and Benjamin Britten in his diary (1931): 'Lovely little pieces, exquisitely scored – a lesson to all the Strausses and Elgars in the world'.

With the continuing and ever-worsening difficulties Mahler was facing in his work, combined with his emotional turmoil over Johanna, he was becoming desperate to leave Kassel. Some interesting news reached him that Angelo Neumann had recently been appointed director of the German Theatre in Prague. Neumann, a former singer, had a first class reputation in both the artistic and administrative spheres. Mahler felt that he was a man he would very much like to work for, so he wrote to him inquiring if there was any possibility, saying that he was young, enthusiastic and eager to progress, and suggesting that he contact Überhorst in Dresden for a reference. Mahler had learnt his lesson about how not to write letters, no gushing prose or grovelling here, his style precise and to the point. As a result Neumann replied, suggesting that he contact him again when his appointment had appeared in the newspapers. Mahler also wrote to Bernhard Pollini in Hamburg and Max Staegemann in Leipzig offering his services.

The end of the year arrived, and on New Year's Eve Mahler joined Johanna. In a letter to Fritz Löhr he tells his story of sorrow. They were alone, but talked little. When the bell chimed midnight she burst into tears, but would not let him comfort her. Instead she went into another room where she just stood staring out of the window. She returned, still weeping, and Mahler knew that their affair, which had always been rather one-sided, was definitely at an end. He pressed her hand and went out into the cold, bell-tolled night, alone and despairing.

The end of January brought what he had been hoping for. He had been accepted as a conductor at the Leipzig Stadttheater on a six-year contract, starting in July 1886 working alongside Arthur Nikisch. He immediately wrote to Löhr telling him the good news, but also stating that in the long term Vienna was his target, for there was nowhere else that he could really feel at home.

Meanwhile he still had some work to do at Kassel. For a few months, on Mondays, when his presence was not required at the theatre, he had been working with a choir in Münden, and his labours bore fruit in a performance of *The Seasons* by Josef Haydn. Both the public and the critics had nothing but praise for his efforts and the general high standard attained. One of the soloists happened to be Johanna Richter.

Later in the year, from the 29th of June until the 1st of July, a music festival was to take place in Münden, the works to be performed being the *St. Paul* oratorio by Felix Mendelssohn and Beethoven's *Ninth Symphony*. It had been planned for the Kassel orchestra to take part but, with Hofkapellmeister Wilhelm Treiber not invited and the consequent ballyhoo in the press, they withdrew. Baron von Gilsa tried to persuade Mahler to hand over the reins to Treiber, but with his confidence growing by the day and with Leipzig on the horizon, he delighted in telling Baron Adolph Freiherr von und zu Gilsa that he had no intention of doing so. The days of bowing and scraping and living in fear of the Prussian ex-officer were well and truly over.

He told Fritz Löhr in a letter dated 12th of May that factions were battling it out with 'Up Mahler' and 'Up Treiber', and that he had bluntly informed the intendant that they did not share each other's artistic values. However, a compromise was reached with Treiber to be responsible for the rehearsals and Mahler to be the conductor at the performances. This compromise itself brought about the first blast of anti-Semitism that Mahler would suffer from throughout his career. Word spread that Mahler, the Jew, would be taking all the plaudits, while the Germans would be doing all the hard work.

Any remaining chance of the Kassel orchestra taking part was now dashed, and Mahler was forced to create an orchestra by rounding up musicians from nearby towns, including a military band. Far from giving up, and as a matter of principle, he was determined that the festival would be a great success. He rehearsed and rehearsed his makeshift orchestra and choruses, who at first grumbled at his unrelenting demands, but soon realized that they were beginning to attain standards of which they had not thought they were capable. One of the soloists was Rosa Papier, criticized by the press, but who would re-emerge later in his career. He had become so wrapped up in his work for the festival, that, on one occasion, having boarded a train for Münden, he sat for ages going through a score. Suddenly he looked up, wondering why the train's departure had been delayed so long, and peering out of the window he saw to his astonishment that his carriage had been shunted into a siding – it had not been part of the train for Münden which had left on time.

When the festival came the results were astonishing, given the circumstances. Mahler had won and Kassel had lost. Baron von Gilsa and the Berlin administration knew that they had little choice but to let him go, and with the intendant's recommendation, the latter having to all intents and purposes lost his 'disciplinary control' over Mahler. The date of the termination of his contract was brought forward from the 1st of September to the 1st of July, in other words he would not be welcomed back in Kassel after the Münden Festival.

Mahler had a year to fill in and somehow to earn a living. He was not relishing the thought of returning to his earlier rather 'Bohemian' existence in Vienna. He had virtually given up hearing any more from Neumann in Prague, when, out of the blue, the good news came – he was to be the head Kapellmeister and he had to take up his post by the 12th of July, the 15th being the day of the first rehearsal for a new production of *Lohengrin* which he was to conduct. He was thrilled – Wagner, at last, and plans for *Der Ring des Nibelungen, Tristan und Isolde* and *Die Meistersinger* to follow.

In a letter to Löhr at the end of June, Mahler told him his feelings about the future, regretting that his Prague appointment could not last for more than a year because Max Staegemann had made it quite clear that he had better forget any idea of being released from his Leipzig contract. Neumann and Staegemann were archrivals, and Mahler quipped that it was not a bad thing to have *Herren Direktoren* squabbling over him!

Before his departure from Kassel, he had been presented with a large diamond ring, a gold watch and other presents besides by the Münden Choral Society. He told Löhr that unfortunately he had had to dispose of the gold watch to pay off debts, and that he'd probably have to do the same with the other gifts to make ends meet in the near future, including his train fares to Iglau, where he would spend three days, and then on to Prague.

So Kassel was in the past, as was his love affair with Johanna Richter. His stay there had been such a mixture of pain, happiness and eventual success, but above all it had been an incalculably invaluable experience. He had learnt the importance of discipline in a large theatre organization, albeit not in the manner dished out by von Gilsa and the Berlin administrators. He had learnt the necessity of restraint in his future work, and he was also beginning to see the value of using 'politics' in his dealing with people connected with his profession. A few months after his departure, Mahler wrote to Baron von Gilsa saying that he had learnt a most valuable lesson: one must be prepared to obey in order to know how to command, as well as acknowledging that he had been a thorn in his side. He had defused a situation that could have gone on festering. His confidence had grown apace and he had met and impressed many in the music world with his success at Münden, including Felix Weingartner and, more importantly and despite his earlier rebuff, Hans von Bülow.

Chapter 3

Prague . . . Leipzig

_____

Die drei Pintos
First Symphony

MAHLER ARRIVED IN Prague on the 13th of July 1885, a date he had been anticipating eagerly. It is strange in a way that he had embraced the idea of Prague so wholeheartedly. He must have had memories of his previous painful and cruel existence as a youngster while staying with Moritz Grünfeld and his family, but Prague, the capital city of Bohemia, was a beautiful city, historic and cultured. His work would be at the German Theatre. This had become very run down until the arrival of Angelo Neumann who had begun the onerous task of pulling it up by its bootstraps. Who better to aid him in this task than the highly ambitious young conductor he had managed to acquire, even if only for one a year. Neumann, a Wagner disciple and much respected by the great composer, even succeeded in persuading the managers of the theatre to buy the Bayreuth sets and costumes he had previously used on his international Wagner tours.

The chief conductor at the Deutsches Landestheater was Anton Seidl, but there was also Ludwig Slansky, a Czech conductor and former first violinist at the theatre who was of the old school and consequently anti-Neumann. Neumann had no hesitation in giving preference to Mahler, for he wanted new blood and vitality in his re-vamping of the Deutsches Landestheater which was in direct competition with the recently built Czech National Theatre.

Mahler's first task was to rehearse *Lohengrin* for Seidl, and both he and Neumann acknowledged the young conductor's skill and enthusiasm by giving him the honour of conducting a special performance of Cherubini's *Der Wasserträger* on the 18th of August to celebrate the Kaiser's birthday. On such an auspicious occasion it was inevitable that Mahler should become a household name in the city. The success of the performance prompted Neumann to give Mahler charge of a production of *Don Giovanni*, Slansky having declined saying that the people of Prague would not be interested; extraordinary really as Mozart had composed the opera for the people of Prague. Mahler's fresh approach aroused great interest, even though some critics did question his tempi. He was beginning to get used to this criticism and indeed his tempi would continue to cause raised eyebrows throughout his career. It could be argued that this was often due to the inability of some critics to find anything else to make adverse comments about! However, the majority were impressed with his efforts and the high standard of the performance.

With new productions of *Die Meistersinger, Das Rheingold* and *Die Walküre,* Mahler was thrilled and really felt that his career as a top flight conductor had at last taken off. The production *of Die Meistersinger* on the 25th of October was the first uncut performance, lasting four and a half hours. Kulhanek's review in the *Prager Tagblatt* sang the praises of both the production and Mahler himself. Slansky inevitably felt bitter, as it was clear that Neumann considered Mahler to be his number one conductor, despite his over-energetic antics on the podium, which reminded Neumann of Hans von Bülow's conducting. 'Hot-head' and 'firebrand' were two descriptions he used.

Meanwhile, as was becoming his wont, once again he fell in love with one of the singers. Her name was Betty Frank. News of this latest affair spread fast, even as far as Iglau. Emil Freund wrote to him advising him to tread very carefully, especially as his parents were by now very frail and might be upset by this latest affair. Mahler obviously felt deeply about Betty Frank as she became the first artiste to sing three of his songs, including *Hans und Grethe,* which was encored at a charity concert held in the winter garden of the Grand Hotel on the 20th of April, 1886.

Whenever time permitted, he would visit the Czech National Theatre to hear works by his fellow compatriots such as Dvořák and Smetana, thus showing his feelings towards the Czech majority in the city with whom he felt a special kinship, rather than the German minority. This was a good tactical move on his part, but undoubtedly he loved to hear the music of his homeland and childhood.

In his letters to his parents, Mahler repeatedly invited them to travel to Prague so that they could see him conducting. His mother desperately wanted to make the trip, but Bernhard had a kidney infection and was suffering from swollen ankles. With his ill health he had become even more cantankerous than usual, and Justine, who was shouldering the responsibility of looking after their parents, was finding it increasingly difficult to cope. Mahler wrote a comforting letter to her, praising her for her unstinting dedication. He tried to calm her and begged her to show patience and understanding towards Bernhard, for his behaviour could surely be put down to his illness. But tension began to increase in the home and Marie began to suffer from severe asthma attacks. There was no way now that she could travel to Prague, but the family was greatly looking forward to Gustav's visit that summer.

Following the Wagner productions, Fritz Löhr spent three weeks in Prague. This was a particular delight for Mahler, who had warned him in advance that his beard had gone and he now sported a dashing moustache. No longer did he feel the need to make himself look older – his confidence had soared. He also informed Löhr that he was sharing rooms with a colleague, the Swedish baritone Johannes Elmblad, at Langegasse 18. The house belonged to a printer by the name of Schulz, whose children had regular singing lessons, one of the songs being *Bruder Martin* (to the same tune as *Frère Jacques*), which was later to appear in Mahler's *First Symphony*.

Löhr was concerned about his friend. It appeared that Mahler had no social life at all, this despite being something of a celebrity in the city, with people readily recognising him. Löhr was impressed by Mahler's conducting and he had noticed that his podium style had become more stable, yet still suffused with youthful passion. But with this youthful passion came the same problem he had suffered from in Kassel, although obviously under totally different circumstances – his failure to accept authority. Mahler never had been, nor ever would be, a ballet enthusiast, and he managed a head-on clash with the ballet coach Bertha Milde in connection with a production of Gounod's *Faust*. They did not see eye to eye and neither would give ground. Neumann became involved and supported Milde, almost as a matter of principle. Neumann's blood boiled when masterpieces such as Wagner's operas were tampered with, and he had always loathed having to serve up 'bleeding chunks' for the benefit of the evening dress brigade. Now here was his ballet mistress messing about with *Faust*. Of course Mahler was right, and he agreed with him, but he had to learn obedience or go. Mahler was furious and became quite abusive, but Neumann stood his ground. His young conductor had to learn a lesson about accepting decisions from above, even if he was correct in his assessment of the over-weight and uninspiring Milde. Things became rather tense between the two men, but Neumann managed to defuse the situation by publishing a particularly flattering letter about Mahler, at the same time wishing him a great future!

As a result of this conflict, Mahler's feelings about Prague had changed, for the time being at least. No longer was he desperate to stay, although of course he had no choice in the matter. His pride had been dented, but Neumann, feeling that a lesson had been learnt, softened the blow by asking him to conduct his first performance of Beethoven's *Ninth Symphony*. This was a last minute assignment, with just two days and a single rehearsal with a small string section, before the performance. Despite this, it was a great success. Among those to congratulate him was Guido

Adler, then a professor at the German University in Prague. This was the same concert, held in the Grand Hotel, when Betty Frank sang three of his songs. Relations between Neumann and Mahler, however, never really recovered and he continued to refuse to give way on any artistic dispute. He himself was fully aware of the problem and was inevitably concerned about facing the far more formidable Arthur Nikisch in Leipzig. However much he had begun to have second thoughts about the forthcoming move, there was no way he could get out of his contract, especially now that he was regarded as a rising, if controversial, star.

During his last few weeks at the Deutsches Landestheater Mahler conducted a number of operas, notably Meyerbeer's *Le Prophète*, Gluck's *Iphigénie en Aulide*, which was to be one of his greatest successes in Vienna in 1907, and Beethoven's *Fidelio*.

In a way, despite the difficulties, he must have had regrets about leaving Prague where he was at least in the Austrian Empire, whereas in Leipzig he would be a foreigner. Not only that, he would no longer have the degree of control he had been enjoying. In Leipzig he would inevitably have to play 'second fiddle' to Nikisch. His immediate reaction to these concerns was to write to Staegermann giving him a list of recommendations and requests, thereby hoping to put himself into a positive frame of mind. Among his recommendations were operas by Dvořàk and Smetana, which doubtless would have made him feel more at home.

So Mahler left Prague and a tearful Betty Frank, his contract having come to an end on the 15th of July. It had been a great leap forward in his career and for the first time he had enjoyed the experience of a degree of artistic freedom. He had gained immense confidence with his virtual control over the performances at the Deutsches Landestheater (Neumann permitting), and he had experienced the immense satisfaction of being able to conduct many of the great operas of the likes of Mozart and Wagner. His talent was now recognized by most, despite the inevitable small band of critics who would always be waiting to do him down.

Between leaving Prague and taking up the reins of his new job in Leipzig, he managed to spend a few days in Iglau visiting his ailing parents and his younger sister Justine, on whom they were becoming increasingly dependent. Of all his surviving brothers and sisters, Justi was the one of whom he was particularly fond and grateful for all the personal sacrifices she was making. He must have been very saddened by the state of his parents, no doubt tinged with a sense of guilt that circumstances had inevitably prevented him from seeing more of them. Yet pride in their rising star of a son must have allayed this to a certain extent.

The Leipzig Neues Stadttheater was in the premier league of European opera houses, and although Mahler faced the prospect of being a mere assistant to Arthur Nikisch, whose career, ironically, had been launched by Neumann while the latter was at Leipzig, it was undoubtedly another leap forward. The theatre seated 1,900 and was modern, luxurious and boasted an orchestra of seventy-six. Leipzig, with a population of three hundred thousand, had an impressive musical pedigree: the home of J. S. Bach, Wagner's birthplace and the Gewandhaus Orchestra, brought to prominence by Mendelssohn.

Mahler wrote to Justi telling her that he had settled in well, that the air was good and suited his health. He informed her that he had a very amiable landlord, whose congeniality was helped by a regular supply of opera tickets, and that the members of the orchestra were showing him great respect.

Nikisch had incredible charisma, and musicians under him were spellbound. He was only five years older than Mahler, had studied at the Vienna Conservatory and had already been at the Leipzig theatre for eight years. He was a cult figure with musicians and public alike. Tchaikovsky was mightily impressed with his conducting, describing him as calm with no excess movements, yet extremely powerful and full of self-control. Mahler knew full well that he would have his work cut out to compete or even establish himself, hence the recommendations he made well before his arrival, which were obviously intended to indicate that he meant business. He launched himself into his new post with vigour. Musicologist and critic Max Steinitzer recalled that he did not exactly make himself popular with soloists, choir or the orchestra, and referred to him as 'the glowering Austrian'. He was intolerant of stupidity in words or actions, and it was easy to read his thoughts from his rather too obvious facial expressions! Mahler had asked to conduct *Tannhäuser* and this he was able to do, as well as *Der Freischütz*, *La Juive* and *Rienzi*, but despite his burning desire to conduct *Der Ring des Nibelungen*, Staegemann made it clear that this was Nikisch's domain. The conflict had begun.

Mahler wrote to Director Staegemann on the 6th of November, reminding him of an agreement they had made that whenever the *Ring* was staged he would share the conducting with Nikisch. On the 27th of November he went a step further, asking to be released from his contract! Actually he and Staegemann had quite a good relationship away from the theatre. Mahler was frequently invited to his home, tactfully praising the singing ability of the director's daughters. Despite Mahler's protests and hints about leaving, Staegemann managed to calm him down. Inside Mahler seethed, and he managed to upset singers and musicians alike with his excess of zeal – he was now determined to out-do Nikisch! But Staegemann knew his worth, was patient, diplomatic with his employees, and waited for the young firebrand to recover his equilibrium.

Mahler had put out feelers for alternative employment and had even written to Baron von Gilsa asking for his support. By the end of the year he had received no less than three invitations: from Bernhard Pollini in Hamburg, Karlsruhe and from Neumann who, probably thinking that Mahler had found himself in a quicksand situation, invited him to return to Prague with a very tempting offer. However, it was not in Mahler's nature to take a step backward, and anyway matters were beginning to settle down.

On moving to Leipzig he had once more become lonely and very homesick. This came to a head at Christmas, and in a way mirrored the sad New Year's Eve he had spent with Johanna Richter in Kassel. He wrote to Fritz Löhr, telling him how he had spent Christmas Eve all alone, just staring out of the window at the happy windows opposite, filled with lights, Christmas trees and merry-making. His mind was with his sick parents 'waiting sadly in the dark' and the rest of his family and friends, and he admitted that he had wept.

In January 1887 a new development took place. Nikisch had been offered a post at the Royal Opera House in Budapest, and the prospect of his rival leaving obviously pleased Mahler, although he did tell Löhr that they had moved from a state of daggers drawn to a more civilized peaceful coexistence. He had made up his mind that if Nikisch stayed he would move to Hamburg where he had been offered an extremely good contract with a salary of 6,000 marks per annum, three months holiday and the pick of the operas to be performed, including *Tristan und Isolde, Fidelio* and *Don Giovanni*. There is no doubt that he wanted the job, but he knew that if Nikisch left, there was no way that Staegemann would release him. He also mentioned that Neumann was still trying to persuade him to return to Prague, but Nikisch decided to stay, so that was that.

No sooner had Mahler resigned himself to remaining in Leipzig than fate intervened on his behalf. In February 1887 Nikisch became seriously ill with a lung infection, as a result of which Mahler was asked to take control of *Der Ring des Nibelungen.*

Working under pressure was something that Mahler was always good at. At the last moment he had to take responsibility for *Il Barbiere di Siviglia* and the new production of *Die Walküre*. For the latter he managed to persuade the administrators of the desirability of lowering the orchestra pit, as it had been in Bayreuth, as well as the introduction of Wagner tubas. Apart from a few criticisms concerning the balance of sound with the new arrangements, success and praise were the order of the day. Word spread fast, and Mahler even received an invitation to take up a post in New York, but, with his new found power in Leipzig, he was reluctant to move anywhere for the time being. He had well and truly established himself with both the press and the public and, although Nikisch was recovering, he knew that it would be a long time before he would have the strength to regain his former position of authority.

With Nikisch's illness and subsequent convalescence in Italy, Mahler's life became a whirlwind of productions, the success of which brought astonishment even to some of his critics, most notably with performances of *Fidelio* and the Leipzig première of Offenbach's *Les Contes d'Hoffmann* in March and April. To give some idea of his hectic schedule, in March he conducted no less than seventeen operas, and all this activity helped to distract him from the problems of his family in Iglau. He even tried to make arrangements for his mother and father to move to Leipzig so that he could be near them, although nothing came of this. Success built upon success and in May *Siegfried* brought out superlatives almost unheard of, and even the die-hard critics such as the pro-Nikisch Krause capitulated.

Through all this, Mahler had almost become an adopted member of the Staegemann family, but in the background lurked another problem, already hinted at in a letter to Löhr. In August 1886 he had told his friend that he had received a letter from Betty Frank, who obviously still missed him greatly, asking him to clarify his feelings towards her, which he did 'with sincerity'. As far as he was concerned the affair was over, and two months later he told Löhr that he had met someone rather special in Leipzig – the 'type of person who tempts one to act foolishly'. He said he would be careful, lest he land himself in difficulties again. This lady was Marion Mathilde von Weber, whose husband, Captain Karl von Weber, was the grandson of Carl Maria von Weber of *Der Freischütz* fame. She was four years older than Mahler and had three children. Löhr must have had that feeling of, 'Here we go again!'

By now Staegemann clearly held Mahler in higher esteem than Nikisch, but his sense of loyalty and sympathy towards Nikisch, who had recovered sufficiently to resume work, resulted in *Götterdämmerung* being given to him rather than to Mahler. Mahler was unhappy, but he realized only too well that in the long term he would gain the upper hand, and so he agreed to stay for a further year, the carrot being to conduct six Wagner operas, including *Die Meistersinger*. One opera Mahler conducted in November 1887 was *Tannhäuser*, attended in person by Cosima Wagner who had come to visit her late husband's birthplace. What she thought of Mahler's conducting we do not know, but she never invited him to conduct at Bayreuth. Whether this was due to his conducting or the fact that he was Jewish is open to question. The previous month he had made another important acquaintance. The young Richard Strauss, his opposite number in Munich, had arrived in Leipzig to conduct his own *Symphony in F minor*, and an arm's length friendship began, based mainly on mutual respect.

Mahler's visits to the von Weber household became frequent, not just because of his feelings towards Marion, but also because her husband had approached him over the possibility of completing an unfinished comic opera by Carl Maria von Weber, *Die drei Pintos*. At first he refused, but then changed his mind, probably because it gave him the opportunity to see Marion regularly. Carl Maria had only made initial forays into the work with less than half sketched out and practically no orchestration. The libretto was in dire need of revision and Captain von Weber, a part time playwright, undertook this task with Mahler's guidance. It is quite clear, even from the sketches, that this is not vintage Weber, or as the critic Eduard Hanslick put it, 'weak Weber'.

On one of his visits to the Weber household Mahler came across an important source of inspiration, an anthology of poetry entitled *Des Knaben Wunderhorn*. These poems, filled with all the emotions, animals and gentle humour, captivated him. They were to become central to his compositions up to and including the *Fourth Symphony*.

With Nikisch now physically weakened by his recent illness, Mahler launched into the 1887-1888 season with increased vigour, determined to establish himself as the number one conductor at the Stadttheater. However, it must be remembered that he had always had the greatest respect for Nikisch as a conductor, considering his interpretations to be very akin to his own. This he made quite clear, despite the obvious rivalry, a rivalry that had spread to critics and public alike. Leipzig had become split in their loyalties between the old order and the new.

The première of *Die drei Pintos* took place on the 20th of February, 1888 at the Leipzig Stadttheater, and its success pricked up ears in other opera houses, notably Hamburg, Dresden and Vienna, as well as interest being shown as far afield as London, Paris and even in America. Mahler's old adversary Baron von Gilsa attended as well as Bernhard Pollini, the intendant of Hamburg, a number of well-respected conductors and the inevitable phalanx of critics, including the redoubtable Eduard Hanslick, who complemented Mahler on his efforts to complete the unfinished opera, saying that the music had good taste and a good sense of theatre. It was to be a considerable success and the nearest Mahler ever came to composing an opera of his own.

Three months before the première Richard Strauss had made his feelings quite clear in a letter to Hans von Bülow, referring to Mahler's work on the sketches as a masterpiece, but he had only heard the first act. Bülow's opinion of the opera as a whole was 'antiquated trash'. Strauss, probably fearful of differing from Bülow, then criticized the second and third acts as being indifferent and Mahler's orchestration as something of a disaster. There were traces in the orchestration of his own *First* Symphony, which he was working on at the time. On the other hand, Bernhard Vogel, writing in the *Neue Zeitschrift für Musik*, praised the completed *Die Drei Pintos* as enriching the repertoire of German comic opera. Controversy abounded, but the success of the opera was undeniable. It was performed no less than sixteen times in Leipzig that season. It was also a financial success for Mahler, who had received ten thousand marks in advance from the publishers, with more to come for each performance wherever it was staged. His debts were cleared and he was able to send a thousand marks to his parents, making it clear that he did not want the money to be invested in his father's liquor business, but to be spent on themselves. He told them that fame had come at last and that he had been introduced to the guests of honour at the première, the King and Queen of Saxony.

Despite the conflicting views of the critics, one thing that greatly amused Mahler was that two parts of the opera that had been singled out for praise, the first Chorus of Students and the Ballad of the Cat Mansor, were in fact entirely his own work. He told his former teacher, Heinrich Fischer that they had 'fallen into the trap and praised MY pieces', thinking that they were Weber inspirations. He would say nothing for the time being, but he was itching to see their reaction when they found out their mistake!

For Mahler it had been a labour of love, in more than one sense! The Gustav-Marion affair began to get dangerously serious and, according to his future wife Alma, writing in her memoirs, they even made plans to elope. He had arranged for Marion to meet him on a train, but alas she failed to turn up. In a way he must have been relieved, probably aware that he was in serious danger of putting his career on the line as well as upsetting his sick parents and family who were becoming increasingly dependent on him. The details and the degree of passion between the two rely on Alma's sometimes rather creative memoirs, so reliability is open to question. The English composer Ethel Smythe recounts, probably with a degree of exaggeration, an incident that apparently took place while Karl von Weber was travelling by train to Dresden. Having known about the clandestine affair for some time, yet at the same time trying to pretend that it did not exist, he had got to the point when he was unable to tolerate it any longer. He suddenly went berserk, laughed hysterically, drew a revolver and began blasting away at the headrests in his carriage. He was arrested and taken to an asylum where he remained until he had recovered sufficiently to be able to return home so that Marion could look after him.

Ethel Smythe, a forceful and courageous woman who was also a conductor and suffragette, met Mahler during these whirlwind months: 'I saw little of him, and we didn't get on; I was too young and raw then to appreciate this grim personality, intercourse with whom was like handling a bomb cased in razor-edges'. Her words are an indication of the single-mindedness and zeal of Mahler the conductor and now Mahler the composer.

One thing is certain, Mahler's affair with Marion had triggered off a creative surge that not only brought about the performing version of *Die drei Pintos*, but, more importantly, the *First Symphony*. Indeed, the *Blumine* movement, later to be discarded, had been written for and dedicated to Marion, a fact discovered by the conductor Wilhelm Mengelberg when he visited her years later.

A month before the première of *Die drei Pintos*, Mahler had written to Fritz Löhr hinting that he had been hard at work composing. He was overwhelmed with inspiration – 'the sluice-gates' had opened. He was referring to a symphonic poem, which later developed into his *First Symphony* and, as he later told Max Marschalk, it had been inspired by love, where his love affair had ended. Not just Marion, but memories of Johanna Richter and Josephine Poisl emerging in themes drawn from the *Lieder eines fahrenden Gesellen* and one of his early songs, *Maitanz im Grünen*, composed in 1880 for the daughter of the Iglau postmaster, and his love of that time.

In parallel with work on his 'symphonic poem', Mahler had also been composing a symphonic *trauermarsch*, which he called *Totenfeier*, subsequently adapted and used as the first movement of his *Second Symphony*. He later told Natalie Bauer-Lechner that he had imagined himself lying dead, surrounded by wreaths – perhaps a link with his sister Justi's death act as a child.

With this potent mixture of activities, the composing as well as other distractions, his conducting had begun to flag, and Nikisch, now recovering, began to re-establish himself. Inevitably Staegemann began to show concern regarding Mahler's dedication to the Stadttheater.

On the 9th of March 1888, Emperor Wilhelm I, King of Prussia, died. To show respect, the Stadttheater closed for ten days, ten days that Mahler devoted to composing. The *First Symphony* was taking shape fast, and by the end of May it was finished. Initially he called the work 'Symphonic Poem' – it was not until 1896, when he also discarded the *Blumine* movement, that he changed the title to Symphony. He wrote to his parents and to Fritz Löhr telling them the good news. He said that the music had flowed out of him 'like a torrent'. He also told Löhr that he had been stuck at his desk for six weeks to complete the task.

He played the work, not only to the Webers, but to the Staegemanns as well, and the director of the Stadttheater fully appreciated the reason why Mahler had become preoccupied during the preceding months. But even with the symphony completed, Mahler's mind was still with his new creation and he found it hard to regain his footing as a conductor at the level he had previously attained. Staegemann had to have a disciplined conductor at the Leipzig Stadttheater to support Nikisch, and Mahler in his present frame of mind certainly did not fit the bill. To complicate matters further, news from Iglau was not good. His father was terminally ill, his mother very sick, Justi exhausted looking after them, his brother Alois wanted to launch himself into a business career, fifteen-year-old Otto needed support in his desire to follow in Gustav's footsteps to become a musician, and there was also thirteen-year-old Emma to be thought of. As Löhr later recalled, he kept all this emotional turmoil to himself. It was therefore no wonder that Mahler, torn in so many different directions, was giving the impression that his attitude to his work was not as it should have been.

Mahler was very grateful to Staegemann for his understanding and patience, and so in April he made a big effort to mend his ways, becoming involved in eleven productions that month including *Die drei Pintos* and three Wagner operas. But his good intentions were to no avail. The momentum to end his time at the Stadttheater was gathering speed. His Leipzig days were drawing to a close, whether due to Nikisch or Staegemann or both, or just a feeling that it was time for a change. One factor that undoubtedly added fuel to the fire, was that Angelo Neumann had contacted Mahler with the view of his conducting *Die drei Pintos* in Prague. This leaked out when, on the 20th of April, the *Prager Abendblatt* published an article with the news of Mahler's imminent return. This of course would have been strictly against his Leipzig contract. Certainly Mahler's situation was exacerbated as a consequence of a clash he had had with stage manager Albert Goldberg, whom he had never particularly liked and who had considerable influence at the Stadttheater, especially over Staegemann. Goldberg had made his opinion clear that Mahler was no longer capable of carrying out his responsibilities. It is possible that he actually wanted to leave Leipzig. He may have thought that, with his new found fame and his 'revelatory' *First Symphony*, it was time to take the next step forward, but it would have been a rash move with no job to go to. He must have been aware of the rumours that were spreading fast that, despite his abilities, he was gaining a reputation for being difficult to work with, not to mention the scandals of his private life. One thing is certain: Mahler would no longer tolerate a subordinate role.

On the 16th of May he wrote a long letter to Staegemann asking to be released from his contract, citing Goldberg's attitude towards him, combined with the former's support for his stage manager, to be the reason. The following day, he wrote to Staegemann again formally requesting that his contract be terminated. His wish was granted. He left a few days later into an uncertain future, clutching the score of his new creation. Shortly after his departure, Nikisch conducted a *Ring* cycle, just to prove that he was, and always had been, Leipzig's first choice conductor!

First Symphony, in D

Mahler's *First Symphony*, born out of a potent mix of love and childhood memories, was a truly remarkable achievement, ground-breaking and inevitably controversial.

In its first version it consisted of five movements, later reduced to four when he discarded the *Blumine* movement (dedicated to Marion von Weber on her birthday). His starting point had been his earlier *Lieder eines fahrenden Gesellen*, the cycle of four songs dealing with disappointment in love and love of nature, using material from these songs in the symphony. Originally he gave the 'symphonic poem', as he at first called the work, the title 'Titan' after the novel by the German author Jean Paul. Mahler provided this title and an accompanying programme to help concertgoers through his new world of music. He admitted that his guiding notes were put together afterwards, but as with all titles and programmes, he later scrapped these ideas as people were beginning to rely upon them too literally, and he wanted his music to speak for itself. But behind it all there remained his own personal, autobiographical plan: the hero, himself of course, travels on a journey from childhood memories, of merrymaking, of death and despair, to early loves, and then, in the great final movement, victory of good over evil. As with most of his works, he continued to work on the score, and ten years later he completed the revised edition.

Mahler himself declared that his new symphony would be a type of music the world had never before experienced, and he regarded the score to be the greatest he had so far produced and quite indescribable. He later wrote to Strauss in 1894, saying that his intention had been to depict the struggle for victory, a victory which is furthest away when the hero thinks it is at its closest – a spiritual struggle reflecting the difficulty of becoming a hero. According to Natalie, he regarded it as the most spontaneous and daring of all his compositions. Neville Cardus considered it to be 'the most original symphony of the 19th century'. It was the first part of a journey, Mahler's own spiritual journey reflected in music.

First Movement: Langsam, Schleppend. Wie ein Naturlaut – Im Anfang sehr gemächlich
(Slow, drawn out with sounds of nature. At first, very soft)

It is a misty dawn and nature awakes. The atmosphere is fresh and clear. As Michael Tilson Thomas so aptly describes it, 'it is like walking on eggshells', so fragile, with the full body of the strings playing harmonics on the note A. (In his first version the strings played a straight A. It was not until the symphony's second performance that Mahler, not satisfied with the original effect, had the idea of using harmonics). It is mysterious, beautiful, calm, but fraught with danger as far as the musicians are concerned. It is like a giant curtain opening onto a scene of tranquility, with little birdcalls – a cuckoo played by a clarinet – and distant fanfares by the brass heralding the spring morning in anticipation of the drama to come. It is, in a way, his version of 'From Bohemia's Woods and Fields.' What a revolution, what a challenge for the performers! One can detect the influence of Wagner, but taken a stage further into Mahler's own music world, one that is almost childlike, innocent, delightful and full of astonishment. This is the world of his childhood memories, of the forests and lakes of his homeland, inevitably leading the listener into the unhappiness and tragedies of his family. The movement's main theme emerges, an Allegro based on the second of the *Lieder eines fahrenden Gesellen*, '*Ging' heut' Morgen über Feld*' – 'Wandering through the field this morning, the dew still on the grass, a merry finch spoke to me, 'Hey, you. Good morning indeed, isn't it?' The sun vanishes, but only temporarily, and then this remarkable first movement draws to a conclusion, filled with the exuberance of youth.

Second movement: *Kräftig bewegt, doch nicht zu schnell*
(Moving powerfully, but not too quickly)

The second movement is a typical Mahler *ländler*, the type of Bohemian-Moravian folk dance that he had often watched as a child in Iglau. It is in complete contrast to the first movement, rhythmical, somewhat brash, possibly laced with the bucolic atmosphere of his father's tavern and with a brief waltz section at its centre. It is full of orchestral stamping and galumphing, turning its back on the beauties of nature in the first movement. It acts as an intermission in the greater scheme of things. (The original second movement was the later discarded *Blumine*, using ideas drawn from his score for *Der Trompeter von Säkkingen* and, as mentioned before, dedicated to Marion von Weber. The *Blumine* movement was not performed again until 1967).

Third movement: *Feierlich und gemessen, ohne zu schleppen.*
(Solemn and deliberate, without dragging)

After this necessary breathing space, we are plunged into a movement of gloom. Mahler originally described his third movement as 'Funeral march after Jacques Callot'. The idea came to him from a well-known picture entitled The Huntsman's Burial, which he must have seen in a book of children's stories. It depicts the huntsman's coffin on its way to the grave, carried by stags and a fox sitting on top of it. It is accompanied by a cortège of animals and birds and a band comprised of cats, frogs and crows, and the gravedigger, a boar. The movement opens with a brooding rendition of *Bruder Martin (Frère Jacques)*, which he had heard frequently performed by the children of Schultz, his landlord in Prague. This develops into a quicker section to help the cortège on its way, before dissolving into a lovely, dreamlike sequence inspired by the fourth of the *Gesellen* songs, in which the wanderer sings of the Linden Tree beneath which he often slept, showered with blossom, forgetting life's pains. But this peace does not last, and the grotesque funeral march returns. Of course, Mahler never intended for all these details of animals and so on to be taken literally. The picture was his own starting point, a satirical burlesque with the music very much his own story, clearly showing his bitter-sweet sense of humour. Nevertheless, one must not take this movement too lightly; after all, it is his 'hero's' funeral march.

Fourth movement: Stürmisch bewegt; energisch
(Tempestuous movement; energetic)

The Fourth Movement bursts upon us without a pause with a barnstorming explosion. Mahler described it as 'an outburst of a deeply wounded heart', and his own description was *'Dall' inferno al paradiso'*. It is a titanic fight between good and evil, between darkness and light. It is Mahler shaking off the shackles of his past. After the bombast has died down, there emerges one of the most delectable passages he would ever compose, and out of it comes the conclusion. It is Mahler rising like the Phoenix from the ashes of despair and into a bright future, jubilant, with the magnificent victory chorale, with echoes of the *Alleluia* chorus from Handel's *Messiah*: 'And he shall reign for ever and ever.' This is his ultimate ambition, to achieve immortality through his creations.

And what did the world think of his *First Symphony*? Mahler would have to wait until the 20th of November 1889 to find out.

Having left Leipzig, Mahler made haste to Iglau. He was depressed at the sight of his parents and he must have felt deep remorse that he had not been able to help them and his sister Justi more than he had, and indeed that he had not visited them more often. But they had always been in his mind and he had done his best to help both financially and morally.

So Mahler in Iglau, filled with concerns for his parents, Justi and the rest of his family, once more faced an uncertain future, apart from his forthcoming trip to Prague to conduct *Die drei Pintos*. At least his Weber completion had brought him a degree of financial stability for the first time in his career, which enabled him to ease the burdens of his family. However, he now felt he was on the right path. Despite his extra-musical reputation, he had become a well-known and respected conductor, and his *First*

Symphony was waiting to be performed. It was a work he was certain would bring about fame for him as a composer overnight, if only he could get it played, but whichever direction he turned, the consensus was that it was too modern, too risky. He even tried to persuade Richard Strauss in Munich. He would have to be patient. During his stay in Iglau, he continued work on the *Totenfeier* (Funeral Rites), based on part of the epic poem by Adam Mickiewicz, a Polish writer, and translated by Mahler's friend Siegfried Lipiner.

Mahler was welcomed back in Prague like the Prodigal Son, although everyone knew that it would only be a short stay. He conducted *Die drei Pintos* five times in August to great acclaim and then began rehearsing Cornelius's *Der Barbier von Bagdad,* an opera he was particularly fond of, managing another confrontation with Angelo Neumann.

Already the wheels were turning behind the scenes, helped by some of his friends, especially Guido Adler. Budapest wanted Mahler. After a further brief stay in Iglau, he set off for Vienna. His brother Otto was about to launch into music studies at the Conservatory, the fees to be paid by Gustav, but the main purpose of his visit to Vienna was to meet a representative of Baron Franz von Beniczky, the intendant of the Budapest Opera. As a result he received an almost immediate invitation to travel to the Hungarian capital. He found the Budapest Opera to be in a badly run-down state, but he nevertheless realized the important status of the position he was being offered. It would mean hard and probably ruthless work, which of course was no problem for him! But if he could drag the Opera up from its state of stagnation, even if it meant an interruption to his composing, he knew full well that his status in the music world would be second to none.

Chapter 4

Budapest

Des Knaben Wunderhorn

IN AUGUST 1879, having completed his task of giving piano lessons to Moritz Baumgarten's children, Mahler had left the Budapest region a poor, struggling young man, filled with angst and depressed about his future prospects. If anyone had told him that a mere nine years in the future he would return to Budapest as Director of the Royal Hungarian Opera, he would rightly have thought him out of his mind!

The terms of his contract were fantastic. He would have complete control over the Opera, answerable only to Beniczky, who was very happy to leave all artistic matters in Mahler's hands. He would have a basic salary of ten thousand gulden plus expenses, he would get four months leave and he would have substantial funds at his disposal from the treasury. Mahler was becoming something of a specialist in landing jobs with opera companies in dire need of help. Budapest was no exception. Despite a magnificent new opera house, complete with the latest hydraulic stage equipment and seating 1,200, and generous subsidies from the treasury and even from the Emperor himself, it was in a state of stagnation and suffering from inept management. Attendances had fallen badly and there was a general laissez-faire attitude. The place needed a good shake-up. But even before he arrived questions were being asked in the press about the appointment of this young Jew whose previous experience hardly justified such a lofty position.

The journalist, Ludwig Karpath, whom Mahler was to get to know very well over the years, recalled how one day returning from a walk he passed by the Opera House. Always on the look-out for a story, he saw a little man he had not seen before disappearing rapidly up the stairs leading to the office of the Director. On enquiring who he was, he was told that the little man was the new director and that his name was Gustav Mahler. Karpath, like most people in the city, had never heard of him – his appointment had been kept top secret. This was news! He dashed to his newspaper office with the scoop; no one there had heard of him either.

On the 10th of October 1888, in an address to the members of the Opera, Mahler laid his cards on the table. He made it clear that dedication, utter devotion and to work with the utmost vigour would be expected from all employees of the Budapest Royal Opera at all times. In this he included himself as well.

One approach that he hoped would help to cure the prevailing lackadaisical attitudes was to insist that in future all productions would be sung in Hungarian, to use Hungarian artistes whenever possible, and if outsiders had to be brought in, that they too would have to sing in Hungarian. In the past it had not been uncommon for several languages to be used in the same production, which of course was a nonsensical practice.

This promotion of nationalist culture was in fact a courageous principle to adopt. For someone who spoke only a few words of Hungarian, this was quite a sacrifice and an added burden to the many he already faced having to shoulder. It was not long before he began to regret his decision, finding it painful, and he longed to hear German being sung again. This nationalist approach raised some eyebrows, coming from a young, Jewish non-Hungarian whom many considered to be grossly overpaid, and many suspected his motives. Two newspapers that did give him support were the *Pester Lloyd* and the *Neues Pester Journal*, both German, and their critics August Beer and Viktor von Herzfeld respectively. However, Mahler played his cards carefully and diplomatically, and he decided to take a back seat until the new year, assess the situation and then come in a with a bang with *Das Rheingold* in January 1889, the beginning of a new Hungarian Ring cycle. He began planning, auditioning and supervising work on the libretti of *Das Rheingold* and *Die Walküre* in the early autumn.

Meanwhile he left the conducting to Sándor Erkel, although remaining closely involved. A short Donizetti season, Bizet's *Pearl Fishers* and *Lohengrin* were all staged successfully. Behind the scenes much progress was being made – a general tightening-up. But Mahler, the workaholic, continued to insist that his staff put in as much effort as he made, an unrealistic demand, especially when compared to the level of dedication to which they had become accustomed. The orchestra was inevitably the hardest hit and rebellious murmurings began to be heard. Mahler immediately countered this by threatening instant dismissal should anyone fall out of line, saying that he would rather use a military band until he was able to hire an orchestra from Berlin! So once again he had clashed swords with his musicians over what he considered to be the prevailing unacceptable standards that had regrettably become accepted as the norm. His search for suitable soloist singers continued to go well, although rumours began to circulate, doubtless due to his previous reputation, regarding his 'Brünnhilde', Arabella Szilágyi, to whom he was giving a great deal of attention preparing her for the part!

His whirlwind preparations for the new 'Hungarian' productions of *Das Rheingold* and *Die Walküre* filled his life during the last few weeks of 1888. But his utter dedication to the Opera, not helped by his own personal nature, resulted in loneliness. He had not had the time, nor wanted the distraction, of an active social life. He wrote to Max Staegemann on the 20th of December saying that he expected to have a very lonely Christmas, the theatre being closed and with no close friends. However, he had much to look forward to in the New Year.

Mahler became increasingly worried by the letters he was receiving from Justi. His sister wrote of the steady decline in their father's health, together with a worsening of his bad temper. He was becoming more and more difficult for Gustav's long-suffering sister to cope with, and he detected a note of despair, wondering whether she would be capable of continuing to shoulder the burden. He wrote to her consoling, encouraging, sympathising, but pointed out that his responsibilities in Budapest were such that it would be extremely difficult for him to visit Iglau at that time, although of course he would if a real crisis should take place. He sent a food parcel to his parents just before Christmas that included Hungarian apples and pears, and he offered to send them money should they fall short.

The New Year came and with it a performance of *Die drei Pintos* in Vienna. Although not an unqualified success, at least it kept his name before the Viennese music circles, especially as the revered and feared critic Eduard Hanslick wrote a positive review. And then, eight days later, on the 26th of January 1889, Mahler launched the Budapest Opera into his new Hungarian *Ring* cycle. He had thrown himself into every aspect of the production, and had even had the orchestra pit lowered as at the Bayreuth Festspielhaus. Being the perfectionist he was, he had focussed on all aspects of the production, not just the music, and his enthusiasm frequently caused him to go into a spin, dashing in all directions at once. Inevitably there were some who delighted in mocking him behind his back, but few failed to recognise his dedication and held a secret admiration for what he was trying to achieve.

This new *Ring*, opening with the performance of *Das Rheingold* on the 26th, had been eagerly awaited by the press and public alike. The house was packed. Mahler entered, lifted his baton and the great drama began. The first deep stirrings of the *Genesis* motif, so low that the double basses are tuned down a semitone to play the sustained E-flat, emerged from the depths of the waters of the Rhine. One of the most magical preludes had begun, the audience held its breath. Suddenly smoke and flames appeared. No, it was not part of the spectacular production; it was the prompter's box on fire! Mahler tried to continue, but was forced to interrupt proceedings when faced with the grand entrance of firemen in place of the Rhinemaidens! After an unscheduled thirty-minute interval, the performance began again. In a way this mishap played into Mahler's hands, for now the audience was fully behind him, willing success. And success it was. There were roars of approval, and the critics August Beer and Viktor von Herzfeld joined in the acclamation.

If the performance of *Das Rheingold* had been a success, *Die Walküre*, performed the following evening, caused an uproar of adulation. The audience shouted time and again for Mahler to appear on the stage, even after the first act as well as at the end. He was presented with a laurel wreath, Beniczky enthused, and the critics, even those who had frequently questioned Mahler's appointment, applauded as one. Mahler the 'hero' was now loved, admired and sought after socially. From being lonely over Christmas, he was now in great demand and probably began to treasure any time he was allowed to spend on his own!

His life was a succession of highs and lows. It seemed that every time he reached a pinnacle of success, a hammer blow would fall. Following his recent successes in Budapest, he almost certainly paid his last visit to his father, who died shortly after on the 18th of February aged sixty-one. Although he had never really loved his father, he must have felt gratitude that he had paved the way for his career in music. He returned to Iglau for the funeral.

Marie, already in very poor health, began to go downhill fast, and Justi, having nursed her father through increasingly difficult times and now having to do the same for her mother, was nearing the end of her tether, despite help from her sister Leopoldine. Mahler, obviously very concerned for his sisters, especially Justi, wrote regular letters of support, sending food parcels and offering to pay doctors' fees and other bills. He told his sisters that under no circumstances should they deprive themselves of anything and that they should indulge themselves in some little luxuries. But he warned them not to be frivolous for difficult times might lie ahead and he had to watch his own financial position, especially as he would have to pay for his musically gifted brother Otto's education. He would have loved to have been able to help more in person, to be with them in Iglau, but his work prevented him from doing so other than for the occasional short visit. During his brief stay Mahler sorted out family affairs as best he could, sending Otto to Vienna to study at the Conservatory and arranging for the winding-up of his father's business. His other brother, the somewhat irresponsible Alois, was due to begin his military service.

Mahler had left Budapest for his father's funeral as the 'conquering hero', but when he returned he came face to face with cynicism in some quarters. There were those who accused him of turning the Budapest Opera into a lesser Bayreuth, with much of the traditionally beloved repertoire side-lined, an unfair criticism for operas such as *The Marriage of Figaro, The Barber of Seville* and *Die Freischütz* were all performed, although it was true that at this point the repertoire was weighted in favour of Wagner. This was hardly surprising for the creation of the new Hungarian *Ring* would inevitably take centre stage, as well as performances of *The Flying Dutchman* and *Lohengrin,* but the seeds of future difficulties were being sown.

A little bit of relief came in April with a visit from Fritz Löhr, who later recalled how they had spent a great deal of time walking around the city and the surrounding countryside. He also mentioned that Mahler played him music he had been composing, sketches for his *Second Symphony.* Another visitor was the Austrian composer Wilhelm Kienzl. They had met previously in Kassel, and Mahler was pleased to see him again, inviting him to a rehearsal of *Le Nozze di Figaro.* Afterwards they had dinner together, and Mahler told him how he longed to hear German being sung again, a longing that became more acute day by day. Kienzl described Mahler as a man living on his nerves, continually stamping his right foot and chewing the ends of his moustache!

The end of the season came, and the consensus of opinion was that it had been very successful, both administratively and artistically, and the voices of the cynics and even the anti-Semitic mumblings of some were slapped down, for the present at any rate. No one could argue about Mahler's achievements, resurrecting the Hungarian National Opera from a state of near collapse to one of spectacular revival in just nine months. But once more the clouds began to gather.

He was exhausted after his first hectic season in Budapest, worried by the on-going problems facing his family, anxious about Justi and the rapidly deteriorating health of his mother, and, as if all this was not enough, he himself was afflicted with haemorrhoids. Nevertheless, as soon as he was able to, he spent a few days in Iglau. Apart from his concern for his mother and Justi, he was becoming worried about his oldest sister Leopoldine who was suffering from persistent headaches. To make matters worse, thirteen-year-old Emma was going through a teenage rebellious stage. It was thought prudent under the increasingly difficult circumstances to send her away for a while. But the adrenalin continued to flow, and after his visit to Iglau at the end of May he went to Vienna. From there he travelled to Prague and then to Munich where in July he had an operation for his painful ailment.

Instead of giving himself time to recuperate he went straight to Salzburg, then to Bayreuth and finally to Marienbad as the guest of Beniczky, who must have been very concerned about his state of health, insisting that he should take a few days complete rest. But even as he tried to relax and take the waters, a new problem loomed. Sándor Erkel, his right hand man at the Opera, was trying his utmost to get away, having become increasingly frustrated with having to exist in Mahler's shadow. Mahler himself had suffered likewise during his Leipzig days and he fully sympathised. He returned to Budapest via Iglau, realising that his mother did not have long to live.

The new season began with Mahler suffering both mentally and physically, relying on morphine to see him through the opening production of *Lohengrin*. As far as the audience was concerned it was a great success, although August Beer did have reservations, resurrecting the murmurings of the previous season that there was too great a German content in the planning. This persuaded Mahler to postpone the new productions of *Siegfried* and *Götterdämerung*. Quite frankly he probably welcomed the opportunity to do so under the circumstances.

On the 21st of September he dashed to Iglau, having heard that his mother's condition had worsened. He found Justi in a state of near collapse, so bad in fact that, having found a nurse to look after his mother, he rushed her to Vienna to see a specialist. To his dismay, on their arrival in Vienna, he found that Poldi (Leopoldine), his twenty-six-year-old sister, who had been suffering from neuralgia, was also in a bad way. He must have felt like screaming. His mother dying in Iglau, both Justi and Poldi dangerously ill in Vienna, constantly in the back of his mind the irresponsible, debt-ridden Alois, at present doing his military service, and he knew that he had to be back in Budapest as soon as possible. Yet he was now head of the family, feeling a responsibility that he knew he would be unable to fulfil as he would have liked, no matter how hard he tried. Having heard that his mother had rallied to a degree, and receiving reassurance from the specialist in Vienna, he allowed Justi to return to Iglau to continue nursing Marie. He had to go back to Budapest, especially as Erkel had his mind firmly on leaving. But no sooner had he arrived than he heard that Poldi had died on the 27th of September, and a fortnight later he received news that his mother had passed away as well. Marie was buried in the Jewish cemetery in Iglau next to her husband, Bernhard. Later Mahler had a sombre black monument erected in their memory. Fritz Löhr recalled Marie as being a model of warmth, tenderness and kindness.

Mahler was devastated and must have felt a degree of guilt that he had not been with her at the end, but his responsibilities had torn him hither and yon. It appears that he did not attend the funeral either. The ever-faithful Fritz Löhr, now married and working as an archaeologist in Vienna, realising the state Mahler was in, took Otto and fourteen year old

Emma under his wing, while Justi travelled to Budapest to live with her brother.

For the time being, his family responsibilities could take a back seat. Having taken a few deep breaths, he embarked on his next project, and a very personal one at that – the première of his *First Symphony*, then entitled 'Symphonic Poem in Five Movements', which was to take place on Wednesday the 20th of November in Budapest.

Once again the gossipmongers became active. Mahler, the most eligible bachelor in Budapest, was apparently all set to marry Bianca Bianchi, a singer he had been working with in preparation for a chamber concert to be held on the 13th of November. At this concert she sang the first performances of three of Mahler's songs: *Frühlingsmorgen, Erinnerung* and *Scheiden und Meiden* to great acclaim, and both she and Mahler were given a great ovation. In his review, August Beer used words such as 'subtle', 'talented' and 'noble'. But the rumours concerning Mahler's likely marriage to Bianchi were just gossip. It later emerged, according to someone who had known Arabella Szilágyi personally, that Mahler had had his eyes on his Brünnhilde, although nothing actually came of the relationship other than a mutual deep affection and gratitude.

A week after the chamber concert on the 13th of November came the night that he hoped would really launch his career as a composer. *Die drei Pintos* and his songs had brought his name before the public, the former having been performed in a number of cities, but he felt confident that his *'Symphonic Poem'* would be a huge success and profitable at that. Fritz Löhr and Otto arrived in Budapest and were present at the final rehearsal on the morning of the 19th and were both very moved by the occasion. Mahler was obviously delighted with the efforts the orchestra had made and told them so by letter – a tactful move to ensure every effort the following day!

The concert was held in the City Hall, and Sándor Erkel was to conduct works by Cherubini before and Mozart and Bach after Mahler's work. Erkel was still very much a popular figure and continued to have a large, sympathetic following in Budapest, so the audience was inevitably divided into two factions even before the start. Supporters of Erkel also numbered those who were critical of Mahler as Director of the Royal Opera and had arrived for the performance determined to voice their disapproval. The shock effect of the music itself only fuelled their intentions.

With the on-going conflict between the pro-Mahler and pro-Erkel factions, it was almost inevitable that the *'Symphonic Poem'* would prove to be controversial. Mahler's supporters applauded after each movement in competition with a cacophony of boos from the opposition. This increased in the second part, both after the funeral march using the *Brüder Martin (Frère Jacques)* theme and after the final movement. Most of the critics were none too complimentary, such as Viktor von Herzfeld, normally a staunch supporter of Mahler the conductor, who used such words as 'bizarre', 'mediocre' and 'painful dissonances'. The only critic who was truly supportive was August Beer who, although saying that it was obviously a youthful work and that he was none too keen on the finale, stated that the composer showed talent, that he was a gifted orchestrator and could go on to greater things. Beer considered that Mahler, who had waited five years before having his work performed, should be respected. He complimented him on the supreme efforts that he had made to recreate the stream of ideas that had come to his mind in a musical form. The Hungarian press was virtually unanimous in condemning the work, their feelings summed up by von Herzfeld who commented that Mahler would always be welcomed onto the podium, so long as he did not conduct one of his own works!

One amusing incident that apparently occurred came with the almighty 'crash' at the beginning of the finale, when a fashionable lady, who had been sitting demurely close to Fritz Löhr, shot up into the air scattering all her belongings onto the floor. Löhr commenting on the effect the music had had on the audience in general said that the music had 'startled them out of their mindless routine'.

Mahler later recalled how after the performance most of his friends were frightened to be associated with him, and he felt as if he had some contagious ailment, and that any mention of either the work or the performance was strictly taboo. One exception was Ödön von Mihalovich whom he contacted later, remembering 'with deep emotion' how he had not deserted him following the 'unhappy performance'. He must have been bitterly disappointed with the reactions. He had not taken the public and press by storm as he had dreamt he would, but he must have half expected this. Attitudes towards music in Europe at the time were conservative to say the least, and no more so than in Hungary. Many concertgoers wanted nothing more than polite, gentle evenings, and did not wish to be disturbed or challenged in any way by 'modern music', let alone by a foreigner, a Jew and someone who had been thrusting more and more Wagner into the repertoire of the Royal Opera. Controversy was something that he would have to learn to live with; it would be his shadow throughout his life. Nevertheless his new work hit the headlines, set tongues wagging, and even if misunderstood, it triggered off an undoubted eagerness and curiosity to see what he would come up with next.

The cartoonists had a field day. One, which appeared in the *Bolond Istók* on the 24th of November, showed Mahler, hair on end and cheeks puffed out, blowing into an enormous brass instrument. Out of it are being propelled at great velocity dogs, foxes, rabbits, a cockerel and other creatures, while members of the audience take cover, protecting their ears in horror, and Hans Koessler, a friend of Mahler's and a professor at the music academy, thumps a huge publicity drum.

It is quite clear that Mahler himself was dissatisfied with his Symphonic Poem as performed on the 20th of November 1889. Over the following years he would repeatedly revise the score, changing the orchestration and even dropping the *Blumine* movement, which he had based on music he had composed for the play, *Der Trompeter von Säkkingen*. The conductor Bruno Walter remembered how Mahler would throw away reams of manuscript, some sheets of which Walter managed to rescue. On one occasion Mahler, aware of this, handed him the abandoned *Blumine* movement. It was only by actually hearing the music played by an orchestra that he realised that further work on the score was definitely needed, such as the opening which came across as far too thick and heavy, a rather 'sultry' dawn, and not the crisp Alpine-like one portrayed by the fragile harmonics that we know today. His revision of the score continued for ten years, always seeking to recreate the sounds in his head with greater clarity. More than any other composer he would write copious notes and instructions for conductors, musicians and singers to follow in order to create his sound, and he later made it quite clear that if others after him discovered ways of improving his scores, it was their duty to do so! (He himself became well known for doing just this to scores by such musical 'gods' as Beethoven, Bach and Schumann, among others).

After the dust had settled, and Mahler had turned his concentration once more towards matters at the Royal Opera, the niggling started again. Despite all his considerable achievements at the Opera, both financial and artistic, the Hungarian press renewed their criticising – too much German opera, not enough Hungarian music and too few foreign guest stars. Mahler, who had made every effort to promote local talent, must have felt that he could not win. A new conflict had begun to gather momentum between those who considered that he had pushed 'Magyarisation' too far, and those who wanted more, and when he cut the last act of Meyerbeer's *Les Huguenots*, all hell broke out in the press, including strong words from August Beer. Mahler retorted that it improved the work. The arguments raged; Mahler stood his ground. He and Erkel continued to share the conducting, Mahler including further performances of *Das Rheingold, Die Walküre* and *Lohengrin* on his list.

On the 16th of December, Gustav and Justi travelled by train to Vienna for Christmas as guest of the Löhrs, and of course met up with Otto and Emma who were living with them at the time. This was the first family get-together since the deaths of their parents, and gave Mahler a welcome and much needed break from the stresses of recent months, although he did have to dash up to Iglau briefly to tie up the loose ends after the sale of his late father's business. He arrived back at the Löhrs just as they were lighting the candles on the Christmas tree.

In the New Year Mahler conducted further performances of *Das Rheingold* and *Die Walküre* and suffered further variations on a not too original theme from the press, but the most interesting event was a performance of Beethoven's *5th Symphony*, which he conducted for the first time, and from memory. He had made alterations to the orchestration to suit a modern orchestra in a large concert hall, such as an increase in the size of the wind and string sections. He also made other changes, including the use of an E flat clarinet in the Finale. Controversial of course, but something Mahler would continue to do, as indeed he encouraged others to do concerning his own works. Not change for changes sake, but change to adapt to new, modern situations.

His position at the Royal Opera began to take a downward turn. He became increasingly frustrated by the belt-tightening, which in turn inevitably contributed to a watering down of the quality of the performances and also prevented him from launching new productions. He was never able to complete the 'Hungarian' *Ring*, and he was unable to find sufficient local talent of the quality he sought. He became irritable, unpopular with the artistes and was fully aware that the success of his first year, when he had resurrected the Royal Opera from a state of near disaster, was under threat. There is no doubt that some of the blame directed towards him was justified. One article at the end of January noted that no Hungarian opera had been sung for a over a year, yet *Die Walküre* had been performed no less than eleven times during the same period; even Beer was becoming critical.

Mahler had felt relatively secure so long as Beniczky was in control of affairs, and indeed between them they had managed to stabilize the financial side of the Opera, but questions were being raised over the choice of repertoire and the quality of some of the artistes being employed. Another criticism was that Mahler had been concentrating on conducting the new productions, whereas the core repertoire had been left in the hands of Erkel. But the emotional turmoil that Mahler had been subjected to must be taken into account, together with his painful physical ailment! Aware of the mounting problems, he was determined to win his way back.

A welcome break came in May, following a suggestion from Beniczky that he and Justi should go on a tour of Northern Italian cities to hear new works and to recruit a new tenor and soprano. Some changes in personnel were needed for the coming season in order to fend off the early signs of public apathy. In addition Beniczky thought that such a trip would broaden Mahler's horizons for he felt that his conductor was in need of a 'musical transfusion'. One of the operas he heard was *Cavalleria Rusticana*, which he immediately fell for and made sure was included in the programme for the following season. He wrote to Fritz Löhr's wife, Uda, from Florence, saying that they'd been having a 'glorious time' and that Justi was 'positively flourishing!'

Meanwhile, Fritz Löhr had rented a large house in Hinterbrühl, not far from Vienna, and Gustav joined the Löhrs for the summer, relaxing in the peaceful surroundings of the Wiener Wald. Justi, having spent a short time with a Dr. Fellner at Franzensbad, a small spa in Bohemia, joined Gustav, Fritz and Uda. It had been a long time since Mahler had been able to relax, exercise, reflect on his past, the future and to compose, and it was during this holiday that he completed the first set of nine *Wunderhorn Lieder.*

Des Knaben Wunderhorn

Between them, Achim von Arnim (1781-1831), a Prussian aristocrat, and Clemens Brentano (1778-1842), a wandering minstrel, gathered together a huge number of German poems and songs, which were published as two volumes in 1806 and 1808. They gave their collection the title, *Des Knaben Wunderhorn* ('The Youth's Magic Horn'), the title of one of the poems, which was actually of French origin. They sent the first volume to Goethe, dedicating it to him, and he was delighted and endorsed their efforts. This dedication, and Goethe's enthusiasm for the anthology, probably attracted Mahler's attention, for he himself had for many years been a disciple of the great German writer and philosopher.

It was during his Leipzig days that Mahler had first discovered *Des Knaben Wunderhorn* in the von Weber household. He was attracted by many of the poems. Full of magic, myths and tales of German folklore, some humorous, some sinister and others lyrical, he found the collection fascinating. Realising that they had hardly been touched by other composers, he decided that this goldmine of material would become his. Over a period of twelve years he was to write twenty-four songs. The well-known cycle, *Des Knaben Wunderhorn,* were not the first songs he wrote using these texts. Before these came a collection of nine entitled *Lieder und Gesänge aus der Jugendzeit,* the first of which was composed for the von Weber children while he was in Leipzig. The last of this group he completed during his summer holiday with the Löhrs in Hinterbrühl in 1890.

The titles of this first collection of *Wunderhorn* settings are as follows:

> *Um schlimme Kinder artig zu machen.* (To make badly behaved children polite)
> *Ich ging mit Lust einen grünen Wald.* (I walked with delight in a green wood)

Aus! Aus! (Over! Finished!)
Starke Einbildungskraft. (By virtue of a strong imagination)
Zu Strassburg auf der Schanz. (In Strasbourg on the ramparts)
Ablösung im Sommer. (Summer relief)
Scheiden und Meiden. (Separating and fleeing)
Nicht Wiedersehen! (Never to meet again!)
Selbstgefühl. (Self-sentiment)

Just as Arnim and Brentano had adapted the original material for their publications, so Mahler did likewise, even adding extra stanzas to *Ich ging mit Lust einen Grünen Wald, Aus! Aus!* and *Ablösung im Sommer.*

The main and most well known collection, which Mahler called *Des Knaben Wunderhorn,* he composed between 1892 and 1898, and these he orchestrated, unlike the first nine songs which were for piano only. Apart from being outstanding lieder, they provided him with a great deal of music material that he would use in his *Second, Third* and *Fourth Symphonies,* which have become known as the *Wunderhorn* symphonies. These songs have great depth and are a personal statement on man, his place in creation and his destiny. Several of the songs are quite substantial in length, brilliant and subtle in their orchestration, yet never problematical for the soloist. There is never the feeling of them being overpowering, too big for their subject matter, nor do they outstay their welcome.

Der Schildwache Nachtlied (1892) (The Night Song of the Sentinel)
This is a dialogue between a sentinel and his girl friend. It is midnight, and the soldier is being sent away. Military in character, Mahler uses drum rolls, trumpet calls and march rhythms, doubtless remembered sounds from his childhood, and an area he would return to time and again.

Verlor'ne Müh (1892) (Wasted Effort)
Contrasting with the first song, this one is in the style of a Ländler, the local folk dance regularly performed in the Iglau area. It is a short, charming dialogue between a young man and his girl friend.

Trost im Unglück (1892) (Consolation in Misfortune)
Another song with a military flavour, as a hussar and his girl prepare to part.

Wer hat dies Liedlein erdacht? (1892) (Who Thought up this Little Song?)
A simple love song, again using the ländler rhythm.

Das Irdische Leben (1893) (The Earthly Life)

This is in complete contrast to the previous songs. It is a dialogue between a mother and her child; the starving child pleading for food, the mother doing her best to console him saying that the harvest will soon be reaped, the corn threshed, and then she will be able to bake bread. But all this is to no avail for the child dies. Mahler summed up this miniature tale of horror as depicting Destiny, which does not always provide what man seeks, for Fate is seldom in a hurry to deliver what we need.

Des Antonius von Padua Fischpredigt (1893) (St Anthony of Padua's Sermon to the Fish)

A song of mocking humour based on the tale of St. Anthony of Padua, who, finding his church empty, goes down to the river and preaches to the fish. They swim up in their shoals: eels, carp, pike and a whole variety of other species, all looking up at him. Mahler told Natalie Bauer-Lechner that the thought of the scene, with the fish sticking their stiff necks above the surface looking up at the saint, made him laugh out loud. Having heard the sermon, they swim away none the wiser, forgetting St. Anthony's words, the carp still gaping, the pike thieving, the cod remaining fat, the eels intent on love and the crabs walking backwards: a satire on mankind. Mahler mentioned that there was a strong influence of the Bohemian music of his childhood in these songs, especially *Fischpredigt*.

Rheinlegendchen (1893) (Rhine Legend)

After the cynicism of *Fischpredigt*, Mahler returned to a more childlike charm. As he told Natalie, this song differs from the earlier ones he had written for the von Weber children in that it is more direct and tender, and he described the orchestration as 'butterfly colours'. It tells of the love of a lad in the fields for a princess, but the only way he can contact her is by throwing his ring into the Rhine where it will be swallowed by a fish. Eventually it will be caught and served up on the king's table, whereupon the princess will claim the ring and bring it back to him – a simple folk tale of charm.

Lied des Verfolgten im Turm (1895) (Song of the Persecuted in the Tower)

A return to a darker theme, one of despair, but behind the loneliness of the prisoner there is a message of freedom of thought, remembering happier times and the girl he loves.

Lob des hohen Verstandes (1896) (In Praise of High Intellect)

Humour returns in a song competition between a nightingale and a cuckoo. The judge they choose is an ass, who surely would be able to hear clearly with his long ears! As Mahler remarked, the words are a dig at the critics.

Es sungen drei Engel (1895) (Three Angels Sang)
A song about the forgiveness of sin. At the Last Supper, St. Peter asks Jesus for forgiveness, and the latter tells him to fall on his knees and pray to God. The song ends with four lines on the theme of heavenly joy.

Urlicht (1892?) (Primal Light)
A moving song, almost hymn-like, that plots the bitter path to heaven and the efforts of the soul to see God, the inevitable asking of questions, the temptations to turn back, and yet the hope of everlasting bliss.

Das himmlische Leben (1892) (Heavenly Life)
This in many ways is the greatest of the *Wunderhorn* songs and would have a profound influence on his symphonic writing during the following years. An angel sings of heavenly pleasures, peace and innocence, far from the clamour of the world. It is heaven as seen through the eyes of a child.

Wo die schönen Trompeten blasen (1895) (Where the Fine Trumpets Blow)
This is one of the longer songs and is another dialogue between a young soldier and his sweetheart. He arrives at her home at dawn, preparing to go to war. She weeps and he promises to return within a year. Meanwhile his house will be the green turf. Mahler made many alterations and additions to the original poem. It is almost a mini tone poem, punctuated by trumpet calls, and there is the feeling that maybe the soldier is in fact a ghost returning to visit his girl.

Each of these *Wunderhorn Lieder* is a miniature masterpiece, and in each song, Mahler used an ensemble tailor-made for the text, never over-powering, the orchestration almost chamber-like in its clarity.

Back to the summer of 1890, and his holiday with the Löhrs in Hinterbrühl. With relaxation, a self-imposed regular routine and diet, as well as exercise, his health improved. The peace and quiet he experienced there being, in a way, a foretaste of future summer retreats, broken only by two brief trips to Vienna and one final visit to Iglau to tie up some loose ends. The Löhrs had made plans to go to Italy, so Mahler rented an apartment in Vienna for Justi, Otto and Emma before he returned to Budapest in late August to prepare for the forthcoming season.

As he set to work on a new production of *Don Giovanni*, which was to launch the new season on the 16th of September, rumours became rife that Beniczky, always a supporter of his, was about to leave. This must have been a source of anxiety for him. Despite various diva antics, *Don Giovanni* was a success. Beer questioned certain tempi and the quality of some of the solo singing; Herzfeld was full of praise for Mahler's approach. But Mahler's relations with his singers and musicians did not improve. Indeed, the situation became so bad that it had become almost impossible to advertise performances in advance, for singers had taken it upon themselves to 'go sick' at the last moment.

Confusion reigned, and Mahler was becoming more and more furious and understandably intolerant of such an amateur and childish approach to their chosen profession. One incident involved two male singers who had decided to disrupt a rehearsal by larking around, changing their lines in a somewhat dubious fashion. Mahler lost his temper and they in turn challenged him to a duel, even going so far as providing seconds. Beniczky asked the two singers to apologise, but they refused. Beniczky then backed down, although he told them that he would not permit a duel to take place. So it was clear that Beniczky no longer had much control over affairs. Although the incident blew over, gossip became widespread in the city about 'Mahler, the despot'! In a letter to Justi, written towards the end of September, he mentioned that he was already negotiating with Bernhard Pollini, the Director of the Hamburg Opera, over a possible contract to take effect before the 1891-1892 season. He told Justi not to mention this to anybody.

It was at around this time that he renewed his acquaintance with Natalie Bauer-Lechner, whom he had first met during his student days in Vienna. 'A friend in need is a friend indeed'! The unsavoury situation that Mahler found himself in, and Natalie's recently broken marriage, contributed to a close relationship developing between the two of them. They had similar outlooks on music and life, and Natalie, who was obviously very attracted to Mahler, was more than willing to be not only sympathetic to his plight, but eager to form a close relationship that would last for over ten years. She became his close friend, confidant and diarist, for which we have a great deal to be thankful for.

The Hungarian versus Jewish 'foreigner' battle took on new life with the forthcoming appointment of the one-armed ex concert pianist, Count Geza Zichy, known to be a rampant nationalist and anti-Semite, who would replace the tired Beniczky in January 1891. Zichy had made it clear that he intended taking charge of artistic matters, and Mahler instinctively knew that, despite having a further eight years on his contract to run, it was time to seek employment elsewhere. He rightly decided to milk the situation knowing that Zichy would be only too delighted to replace him.

Because of the difficulties of finding enough good as well as willing local
talent, Mahler decided to employ non-Hungarian stars. One of these was
Lilli Lehmann, who sang in Italian and French, thus going completely
contrary to Mahler's earlier announcement that he would do away with
operas sung in a mixture of languages. But under the circumstances he was
prepared to take the risk. She had performed with the Royal Opera before,
in 1887 in *Fidelio*. Mahler had originally contacted her with the hope that
she would agree to sing in a Wagner opera, but she had refused. Lilli
Lehmann had a deep respect for Mahler and for what he was striving to
achieve – excellence with sacrifice! They became friends, a friendship and
collaboration that would last for twenty years. She later wrote that she
respected Mahler's undoubted talent, hard work and artistic integrity. She
said that she had always stood by his side when trouble arose, and that he
was more often than not misunderstood. In short, she had a great
admiration for the man.

The highlight of Lilli Lehmann's visit to Budapest was without doubt
her performance as Donna Anna in *Don Giovanni*. As luck would have it,
Brahms just happened to be in Budapest at the time to conduct two of his
own works in an orchestral concert. It was suggested to him that the
production of *Don Giovanni* at the Royal Opera was worth going to.
Having at first mumbled that he'd never heard a satisfactory performance
of *Don Giovanni*, he was persuaded to accept the invitation, albeit
reluctantly and rather rudely, declaring that he would far rather go for a
drink. Thankfully his friends prevailed and he grudgingly agreed to attend,
saying that it might provide a suitable stimulus for a sleep before going to a
tavern.

Not a lot of sleep was had, for Brahms, having hardly closed his eyes at
the beginning of the overture, grunted and then began to enthuse. At the
interval he insisted on meeting Mahler, embracing him and telling him that
he had never heard such a good performance of *Don Giovanni*. Mahler
spent some time with Brahms after the performance, and he later informed
Justi that the old man had said that he had never heard Mozart played so
stylishly, and he told Löhr that Brahms had praised him in an astonishing
way; this from a man who was renowned for being far from easy to please.
Of course Mahler was delighted, not only by the compliment from the old
die-hard composer, but because it gave a boost to his desire to go on to
greater things, to get away from Budapest with its petty-nationalism and
anti-Semitism. Brahms, who had rejected Mahler's own *Das klagende Lied*
nine years before when he was a student at the Conservatory, would now
be counted as a supporter, even a friend.

If *Don Giovanni* had been a tremendous success, Boxing Day would
exceed it. He introduced Budapest to Mascagni's new opera, *Cavalleria*

Rusticana, which he had discovered on his Italian trip the previous summer. He had predicted that it would be an outstanding success, and he was right. There was ecstatic applause after every scene, and the performance was acclaimed unanimously, everybody agreeing that Arabella Szilágyi had been outstanding as Santuzza. Mascagni wrote to Mahler a few days later sending his heartfelt thanks.

Not long after this latest triumph, Beniczky's retirement took effect. He wrote of the achievements that he and Mahler had brought about, both artistic and financial, and he was loyal and grateful to Mahler to the end. But of course such sentiments carried no water for Zichy. By agreement Mahler's contract was shortened to a further two years, which did not bother him in the slightest, nor even the censure that was imposed on him, preventing him from airing any grievances. He was determined to leave; Hamburg was his next goal. Talk of his imminent departure soon spread throughout the city, and, as was so often the case, a large section of the public wanted him to stay. With the atmosphere becoming increasingly hostile, he told Justi that he had had to take on the dual role of soldier and diplomat. But Mahler was still not going to leave except on his terms, and his patience paid off. Zichy became impatient and offered him compensation of 25,000 gulden, which he accepted without more ado. He wrote to Justi exclaiming, 'Hooray! I'm free!'

Mahler's final act at the Royal Hungarian Opera was a performance of *Lohengrin* on the 16th of March 1891. The audience went so wild in his support and against Zichy that it took some time for order to be restored. Because of these demonstrations, Zichy decided that it would not be a good idea for Mahler to have an official farewell benefit evening. The public regarded him as a martyr and Zichy as the devil who had driven him out. Mahler's supporters, however, presented him with a gold baton as a token of appreciation for all his hard work and achievements during his time in Budapest. Count Albert Apponyi, a member of the Hungarian Parliament, was another supporter who sang his praises. He afterwards commented that he had never met anyone so gifted, not just as a musician, but also as a stage manager and director as well. He would later write recommending him to the Vienna authorities stating that he had been utterly dedicated and had outstanding ability, not just from a musical point of view, but with every aspect of running a successful opera company.

Mahler wrote a tactful letter of farewell, thanking the public and those who had worked for the Royal Opera for their support and wished them well for the future. August Beer wrote applauding Mahler for everything he had achieved, virtually from scratch, and for elevating the Hungarian Opera to a position unimaginable when he had arrived. Others were not so charitable, feeling it was high time he went. Zichy, in his memoirs, while not doubting his musical gifts, cited Mahler as being the root of most of the discipline troubles at the Opera when he took over as intendant. There may have been an element of truth in this, for Mahler was never very tolerant of fools and slovenliness. Those who were aware of the real situation knew that these were very one-sided and totally unjust comments, but then he and Mahler were like oil and water. Mahler's Budapest days were in some ways the final part of his education as a conductor and opera director.

Chapter 5

Hamburg . . . Part One

Second Symphony

IN SOME RESPECTS Mahler's position at the Hamburg Municipal Theatre was a step backwards. Apart from the tail end of his Budapest days after Zichy had taken control, Mahler had been virtually in charge of all artistic and administrative affairs directly linked to the Opera with Beniczky rubber-stamping his decisions. In Hamburg he was to return to the position as first Kapellmeister and would have to swallow his pride, accepting decisions made by those in authority, particularly the self-made impresario and former singer, Bernhard Pollini (alias Baruch Pohl). But Pollini <u>was</u> a former musician and forward looking, unlike most of the old-school intendants Mahler had worked for in the past. Pollini was a shrewd businessman and talent scout, and he was known to be very demanding of his personnel.

As a former singer himself, Pollini's main concern was a high standard of performance from his star vocalists. Contrary to the prevailing policy at Budapest, he constantly sought guest appearances from foreign artists of renown such as the soprano Katharina Klafsky, who also happened to be the husband of second conductor Otto Lohse, and the Czech contralto Ernestine Schumann-Heink. The latter later recalled how Mahler was an idealist who found it difficult to accept that the musicians in front of him, with their shortcomings, were not geniuses like himself. She wrote that as a result he became something of a musical tyrant, which was sad because when he was not on the podium he was kind and lovable. On the other hand, Pollini was quite happy with his musicians so long as the public came – that was all that mattered. His attitude was rather strange for an ex-performer, his only concerns being the quality of his singers and the financial health of the theatre. He regarded Mahler's insistence on good, expressive acting as somewhat eccentric, but being fully aware of his new conductor's ability, allowed him to do more or less as he pleased provided that his budget was not affected! Such an attitude obviously flew right in the face of Mahler's approach, for he had always shown the utmost concern with every aspect of a production, musical and otherwise. Pollini had built up the Hamburg Municipal Theatre, raised huge funds, and he had seen it attain the status of a top rank European theatre, complete with the latest electric lighting. Mahler inevitably held him in deep respect for in many ways he was a man after his own heart, and not forgetting that it was he who had clamoured to obtain his services in the first place.

The city was an eye-opener for him. Shortly after his arrival on the 26th of March 1891 he wrote to Justi telling her how beautiful and vibrant it was with its magnificent harbour, electric tramway and what he considered to be a very healthy climate. Hamburg, formerly a free Hanseatic city state, independent of the Hapsburg and Prussian Empires, considered itself to be superior to both Berlin and Vienna, so it was quite an honour for Mahler for his services to have been sought after by Pollini. Another very famous conductor, highly active in the city and responsible for most of the symphony concerts, was none other than Hans von Bülow, whom Mahler had met whilst he was learning his trade in Kassel. (He had paid a visit to Kassel with his Meiningen Orchestra, when Mahler, desperate to leave, had begged him to be his saviour and von Bülow had waved him away. Shortly afterwards Mahler had impressed him at the Münden Festival).

Hans von Bülow was a very determined, forthright and widely revered conductor who was most insistent on hard work, quality and obedience from his musicians, as well as good behaviour from audiences – very like Mahler in fact. Many stories were told of his 'Beechamesque' quips. The composer J.B. Foerster recalled how, on one occasion, he had glanced up at the gallery stating that he would only begin when a certain gentleman had stopped picking his teeth! On another, following sustained applause after a performance of Beethoven's *Ninth Symphony,* he thanked the audience on Beethoven's behalf expressing his regret that the composer was unable to be present. He then set about an encore of the Finale, but only after informing the audience that it would be pointless rushing to the exits because he had had all the doors closed!

Mahler was thrown in at the deep end, for on Easter Day, the 29th of March 1891, having hardly unpacked his bags, he introduced himself to the Hamburg audience by conducting Wagner's *Tannhäuser* to great critical acclaim. Josef Sittard used words such as 'a motivating force . . . superb achievement . . . electrifying . . . a genius', and praised Mahler's influence on the musicians who had sounded like a totally different orchestra. More praise came from another critic, Carl Armbrust, who even compared him to Bülow. He pointed out the fine balance of freedom of interpretation given to his singers, yet the whole performance remained completely under his strict control, a quality the like of which Hamburg had not experienced up until that time.

Following the brilliant success of *Tannhäuser*, Mahler's contract was rewritten. He was to receive 14,000 Reichsmarks instead of 12,000 and would become director of the Opera at the beginning of the following season. Pollini's gratitude extended to allowing him to use his villa as his home instead of the Streit's Hotel until he managed to find a suitable apartment. The staff would remain to attend to his every need.

Tannhäuser was followed by *Siegfried*, and present was Hans von Bülow who afterwards wrote to his daughter Daniela saying that Mahler was equal to the greatest. Referring to the musicians, he quipped how he had made them 'dance to his tune'. So in one fell swoop he had conquered the public, the press and Hans von Bülow, and all this had been achieved even without an orchestral rehearsal. No greater ally could he have had at that time and he made a point of attending as many of Bülow's concerts as he was able to. Mahler always sat in the first row at rehearsals and, as he told Löhr, Bülow would look down at him during particularly beautiful passages, pass scores to him of works with which he was not familiar, bow and even talk to him from the podium. All this may seem rather strange, but their relationship was becoming one of great mutual respect and, in a way, Bülow came to regard Mahler as his protégé.

Friend of Pollini's (still), friend of Bülow's, who was of course greatly admired by press and public, Mahler soon found himself fêted and dined all over the city. As he told Justi, he was rapidly becoming 'a famous star'. The only major problem he had was finding suitable accommodation that he could afford. Eventually he found an upper apartment in a large house overlooking gardens and fields, ideally peaceful and conveniently close to Pollini's villa.

Pollini lost no time in exploiting his star conductor. During April and May, bearing in mind that Mahler had only taken up his post at the end of March, he conducted no less than thirty-five performances, including a Wagner season, which culminated on the 18th of May in a performance of *Tristan und Isolde,* a work he had been longing to conduct and with which he would always be closely associated.

So ended the season on a high, and Mahler left for his summer break, first with his brothers and sisters in Perchtoldsdorf near Vienna before going on to Bad Gastein in the Tyrol for a brief visit to Pollini. Whilst there he also happened to meet up with Natalie Bauer-Lechner, with whom he spent many happy hours walking in the magnificent surroundings. Having taken the waters at Marienbad, which he told Justi had not agreed with him, he set off for Bayreuth to attend performances of *Tannhäuser* and *Parsifal.* Finally he embarked on a hectic tour of Scandinavia, during which he came face to face with a Salvation Army band on board a ferry, which Mahler found to be 'an interesting encounter'. Up on deck, with the vessel heaving up and down in the heavy swell, he was much amused by their performance. After almost an hour of tuning up, the ensemble, consisting of three guitars, violin and trumpet, was joined by some rather painful singing. This in turn was accompanied by groans and retching of a number of passengers leaning over the side of the ship!

It had hardly been a very restful holiday, but then the adrenalin must have been flowing freely after his wildly busy and successful introduction to the Hamburg Stadttheater. It had not been entirely enjoyable either, for he mentioned in a letter to Emil Freund how lonely he had been.

At the end of August he was back in harness, bracing himself for his first full season. It soon became clear that his honeymoon period with Pollini was at an end. He knew that the orchestra and chorus respected him, although the solo singers were divided. It was now clear beyond doubt that Pollini's main interests were a good press and how much profit he could make, regardless of artistic integrity. Mahler told Natalie that fate appeared to be dictating that his life should be blighted by struggles and confrontations, yet his heart remained true. He would continue to make every effort, sticking to his principles.

Apart from a cooling of his relations with Pollini, he was also having further accommodation problems. With his apartment just two doors away from Pollini's villa, he had thought it prudent to seek alternative arrangements and was forced to spend two months in the rather noisy Hotel Royal. He told Justi that he could not see his position in Hamburg to be anything other than a stopgap and that he longed for Vienna.

The season opened with *Fidelio,* followed by *Die Meistersinger* and *Tristan und Isolde.* In the middle of September his mind turned once more towards his own works, and he wrote to Bülow asking him if he could pay him a visit. He arrived clutching his *Totenfeier* and duly played it to Bülow, who walked over to the window, his hands over his ears. Mahler wrote to Löhr telling him that the renowned conductor had been horrified and became quite agitated. Mahler was distraught, his newfound supporter giving him a blunt rebuff, and as a result denting his confidence, fortunately only temporarily. However, his respect for Bülow remained intact, for he was without doubt the greatest Beethoven conductor of his time, a very respected critic who had done more than any other to further the cause of composers such as Wagner and Bruckner. Despite his incomprehension of Mahler's music, he remained a loyal supporter of Mahler the conductor, whose confidence was strengthening all the while. He was now famous, listened to, regarded as one of Europe's finest conductors, and all this did much to compensate for his disappointment over Bülow's derisory comments about *Totenfeier*. He wrote to Emil Freund, telling him that he had been reading Friedrich Nietzsche, and that his words might well have an overwhelming influence on his life. He received a letter from Heinrich Krzyżanowski, Rudolf's brother, who offered to write a libretto for him. Mahler was delighted, although he had to decline the offer, for the present at any rate.

Apart from a performance of *Don Giovanni* to mark the centenary of Mozart's death, the final month of 1891 was relatively quiet. Mahler's main preoccupation centred on preparations for the German première of *Eugene Onegin*, an opera that he had definite reservations about, referring to it as 'mediocre'. Tchaikovsky himself had planned to conduct. The date fixed was the 19th of January. Tchaikovsky, however, found rehearsing in German difficult. Impressed with Mahler's meticulous preparation and knowing that Mahler himself was very keen on conducting the première, he handed over the baton to him. Tchaikovsky was delighted with the performance, describing Mahler as a genius. The press praised him as well, yet at the same time pointing out the opera's weaknesses stemming from a lack-lustre and rather action-less libretto. Nevertheless, it was another red-letter day for Mahler's reputation.

After a considerable gap in his composing, he launched himself into the *Wunderhorn* songs with increased vigour. A torrent of inspiration resulted in no less than five orchestrated songs being completed by the 22nd of February, including one of the most important, *Das himmlische Leben,* which would later become the final movement of his *Fourth Symphony.* He instinctively knew the worth of these songs and was already planning to use them in his symphonies. This creative burst resulted in his adopting a far more positive outlook, and made such matters as Pollini's increasing jealousy appear less important and threatening. This had been exacerbated by a performance of *Fidelio,* when Mahler was showered with gifts, bouquets and no less than twenty-seven laurel wreaths! But he was finding it increasingly difficult to restrain himself from doing something he might afterwards regret, and he wrote to Justi saying again how he yearned for Vienna.

Meanwhile he had been in contact with Sir Augustus Harris, manager of the Covent Garden Opera, who was determined to stage a Wagner season in London. Harris had already signed contracts for singers from Budapest as well as Hamburg, and Mahler, while enthusiastic over the prospect of a new challenge, was also keen on the idea of a temporary reprieve from the Pollini problems at home.

It was a tradition for the Hamburg Opera to give a concert of sacred music on Good Friday. In addition to Mozart's *Requiem,* it gave Mahler particular pleasure to be able to include Bruckner's *Te Deum* in the programme. It was greeted with enthusiasm by the critics, much to Mahler's delight. He wrote to Bruckner about the concert, praising his *Te Deum* and telling him how the audience had been very moved and had remained motionless at the end. He received a reply from the venerable composer thanking him and saying how frustrated he had been over all those years of not being recognised. Mahler wondered whether he too might suffer the same fate. Once again Justi was having financial as well as emotional difficulties and Mahler, whose main concern was that she should have some enjoyment in her life after her traumas in Iglau, wrote a consoling letter to her. One concern they shared was Otto. Mahler was sure that he had the potential of becoming a superb musician, perhaps even better than himself, but Otto's attitude at the Conservatory had been wayward to say the least. He left that April diploma-less, although this news was kept from Gustav for the time being. As for Alois, there really was no hope, having recently escaped imprisonment by a hair's breadth for his ever-increasing debts.

The only encouraging news from Justi was that a very strong friendship had grown between her and Natalie. Gustav instructed his sister to find a place where they could stay for the summer, somewhere secluded and healthy where he could relax and recharge his batteries. He suggested that she should take Natalie with her on this quest. Unable to stand the noisy environs of the Hotel Royal any longer, he returned to the Streit Hotel, even though it was more expensive.

The main event at the end of the 1891-1892 season was a Wagner festival, Mahler having been entrusted with all the major operas. With the Hamburg season drawing to a close, he became preoccupied with his next task – preparations for the visit to London. He began a crash course in English with his friend Arnold Berliner, not surprisingly finding it very difficult to become fluent in such a short space of time! As far as he was concerned he regarded the forthcoming London engagement to be a good investment for the future, even though it would mean curtailing his summer holiday.

Covent Garden, like Hamburg, had recently been refurbished with electric lighting having been installed. Augustus Harris, who had previously organised a German season at Drury Lane in 1882, was a dedicated man of the theatre and decided that it was high time that London be introduced to *The Ring*. Mahler found Harris to be a man not entirely of his own persuasion, for his tastes veered towards popularism, rating huge crowd scenes and historical pageant higher than the quality of a score. Ironically he had labelled *Das Rheingold* 'a damned pantomime!' but like most impresarios, public acclaim and good receipts were his great delight. Several of the singers he had hired were names known to Mahler, such as Katharina Klafsky and Ernestine Schumann-Heink. In addition to *The Ring* there would be performances of *Fidelio*, *Tannhäuser* and *Tristan und Isolde*. The season would run from the 8th of June until the 23rd of July.

Mahler boarded a steamer at Cuxhaven on the 26th of May, not alone, but with a complete opera company consisting of twenty-four solo singers, a full orchestra and chorus, two additional conductors as well as stagehands. Little did he know what a barnstorming success his venture would turn out to be. The press reports said it all:

Andrew Nicholson in *The Times*: 'If the rest of the Wagnerian trilogy is to receive the same justice that was accorded to *Siegfried* . . . the present year will be indeed remarkable in operatic history . . . From beginning to end scarcely a single detail, either in the orchestra or on the stage, fell short of perfection . . . Herr Mahler, the admirable conductor, sits, or rather stands, not close to the stage, but in the middle of the players. The effect of the beautiful scenery was immensely enhanced by the absence of all light in the auditorium during the acts.'

Hermann Klein of *The Sunday Times* described Mahler as 'rather short, of thin, spare build, with a dark complexion and small piercing eyes that stared at you with a not unkindly expression . . .' He also found him very modest and his use of English amusing. This is born out in some of his letters. Even though he had been making a big effort to learn the language, he came out with some classic expressions, such as 'Yours truly was tops again!' and 'I am quite done up!'

Bernard Shaw, having been present at the performance of *Siegfried*, wrote, 'I have to chronicle several curtain calls for the energetic conductor, Herr Mahler. He knows the score thoroughly, and sets the tempi with excellent judgement . . . We all breathed that vast orchestral atmosphere of fire, air, earth and water with unbounded relief and invigoration.' Shaw did also say, however, that without doubt the Covent Garden Orchestra could perform the score better, given the chance.

The report in *The Athenaeum* on the 11th of June: 'It would be impossible to over-praise the efforts of the orchestra under Herr Mahler . . . It would be well for conductors to attend these performances if only for the purpose of watching the methods by which Herr Mahler gains the desired effects.'

The Illustrated London News on the 18th of June: 'Herr Mahler is a Wagnerian conductor of the first order. He proved this, not only by a perfect acquaintance with every detail of the wonderful score, but by the rare unity of spirit with which he inspired his mixed orchestra of ninety-six German and English executants . . .'

The Musical Times on the 1st of July: (on a performance of *Tristan*) '. . . It is worthy of note, as a characteristic indication of the tone and temper of the audience who frequent Wagner opera, that when a cat appeared and remained on the stage for some little time in the last act, there was not the faintest ghost of a giggle throughout the vast auditorium.'

More feelings of awe came from another young composer to be, Ralph Vaughan Williams, who considered that Mahler's conducting was simply outstanding. He remarked how he had wandered home completely dazed and had suffered several sleepless nights. Another man of music who heard and was overwhelmed by *Tristan* was Henry Wood, then only twenty-two.

Mahler was dumb-struck by his reception, and he wrote to Arnold Berliner after the performance of *Fidelio* saying that, despite some barracking from certain critics, the audience had gone wild and he had been forced to take a bow after every act, to repeated chants of 'Mahler!' Also present was Paul Dukas, who wrote of one of the most incredible performances he had ever witnessed and that he had had the feeling of being present at the première of this most sublime work. The fact that it was sung in German caused some raised eyebrows as Londoners had been used to hearing it in Italian. Mahler had also included the *Leonore 3 Overture*, placing it between Acts One and Two, which was criticised in some of the reviews. (Later, in Vienna, he would use the overture as a bridge into the last scene).

Despite the undoubted success of his six weeks in London, which included ten extra performances, Mahler was now more than ever eager to concentrate on composing, and regretted missing most of his summer break from the Stadttheater.

Weary after the Hamburg season and now almost on his knees, he finally left London on the 23rd of July and headed for Berchtesgaden to join Justi, Emma and his brothers Otto and Alois for his summer break. In the beautiful surroundings he took particular delight in going for long mountain walks. During this short holiday he found time to visit Fritz Löhr in Sankt Gilgen, as well as Amalie Joachim in Salzburg, who was planning to sing two of his songs in Berlin. By the end of August it was time to return to Hamburg, and he decided to break his journey by calling in on his old friend Heinrich Krzyżanowski in Munich. Whilst in London he had received the news that cholera had been spreading from South-east Europe and Russia, and it was while he was at the Krzyżanowskis' that he heard that it had reached Hamburg. The city had been hard hit with over nine thousand deaths.

Understandably Mahler was unwilling to return. He wrote to Arnold Berliner thanking him for inviting him to stay at his home on the outskirts of the city, but told him that he had had a severe infection of the intestine and considered it to be very unwise for him to return for the time being. There was no point in rushing back anyway because inevitably the Stadttheater would not be opening until the epidemic had subsided. So he continued his holiday at Berchtesgaden, although obviously concerned about the situation and when it would be safe for him to travel. In fact the theatre opened on the 16th of September, but Mahler did not arrive until a week later. Pollini was furious and held him in breach of contract, despite the fact that Mahler was still unwell, and initially fined him a whole year's salary – 12,000 marks! There was no way that he could have paid such a sum, but luckily a mutual friend managed to defuse the situation. Any remaining respect that he had had for Pollini dissolved and a deep and festering antagonism began to develop between the two men.

Mahler returned to the podium of the Stadttheater at the beginning of October, but it was not long before it became clear that Bülow's health was deteriorating. There had been an occasion the previous season when Mahler had been put on stand-by to take over one of his subscription concerts, but he had recovered. Now the situation was different and he had to deputize for him at the December 12th concert. Unfortunately this prevented Mahler from attending the première of his songs 'Der Schildwache Nachtlied' and 'Verlor'ne Müh', sung by Amalie Joachim in Berlin. Mahler, the 'God' of the Stadttheater, was now a target for the press as Bülow's replacement in the concert hall. They accused him of trying to imitate Bülow, of putting his own interpretation onto the classics and daring to tinker with the size of various sections of the orchestra, just like Bülow in fact, although they did not dare criticise him! These adverse comments may well have had the effect of diminishing Mahler's previously high social status in Hamburg.

Mahler spent Christmas at the home of Frau Lazarus, a friend and admirer of Bülow's. It is probable that it was there that he met an Austrian by the name of Hermann Behn. Born into a well to do family in 1859, he was himself a composer and former pupil of Bruckner's. His compositions included no less than nine volumes of lieder. Behn was also an admirer of Wagner's music, making arrangements of some of his scores for two pianos, as well as Bruckner's *Seventh Symphony*. With so much in common, they struck up an immediate friendship.

The New Year brought renewed problems for Mahler regarding his brothers. Alois, debt-ridden and as irresponsible as ever, developed tuberculosis, and poor Justi was once more thrust into full time nursing. Otto, his music career neglected having left the Conservatory, was about to do his military service, which would probably put a full stop to Mahler's hopes for his naturally gifted but lazy brother. He was far from pleased, especially by Otto's selfishness and ingratitude after all the help, financial and otherwise, that he and others had given him. He still hoped Otto's gift as a musician could be saved and decided to take a harder line, encouraging him to fight his own battles. As far as Alois was concerned, Mahler's sympathy was wearing very thin. Not only had he become a financial burden but an emotional one as well, especially for Justi. Mahler began to contemplate the possibility of finding him work in some far-flung country, Argentina being a possibility!

During the early part of 1893 Mahler turned his mind to revising his *First Symphony* as well as writing sketches for his *Second* and orchestrating the *Lieder eines fahrenden Gesellen*. Not a great deal of note took place at the Stadttheater, although on Good Friday he conducted the first performance of Bruckner's *Mass No. 1 in D minor*. The old man wrote a letter of deep gratitude, calling him 'a hero', for he felt himself surrounded by rejection, even hostility. Mahler, with his affection and a deep respect for him, must have been very saddened by the crass ignorance of the critics and the public, who were gullible enough to believe what they read. This frustration and annoyance on Bruckner's behalf was countered by the reaction to his own benefit concert. A full house heard Beethoven's *Fifth Symphony* and *Fidelio*, and Mahler was gratified and indeed very moved by a tribute written by Hans von Bülow that accompanied the inevitable laurel wreath, referring to him as 'The Pygmalion of the Hamburg Opera' – a tribute Mahler treasured for the rest of his life. The operatic year ended with *Die Meistersinger* and *Der Ring des Nibelungen*, which Justi attended.

With the 1892-1893 season over, he returned to Austria with Justi, not to any of his usual places, but to a new venue discovered by her and Natalie – Steinbach in the Salzkammergut on the beautiful Attersee. It appeared to be an ideal place to spend the summer for there were also friends in the neighbourhood, including Victor Adler, the physician, socialist leader and admirer of Wagner, and the newspaper editor Engelbert Pernerstorfer and their families, both men friends from Mahler's student days. This was to be the first of Mahler's summer retreats, a place where he could unwind and turn his mind to the greatest love of his life, composition.

The haven that they had discovered was an inn named the *Gasthof zum Höllengebirge*, (The Inn of the Mountains of Hell, now named *F. Föttinger Gasthof*). The name hardly does justice to the fabulous and very peaceful surroundings. It was named after the Höllengebirge, mountains that rise dramatically behind the village of Steinbach that provide an inspiring contrast to the placid Attersee, across which the inn faced. A large building complete with sun terraces, it looked out over a meadow that gently sloped down to the water's edge. It was surrounded by natural beauty, peaceful in front, dramatic behind, and would be perfect for Mahler's essential rambles, which he not only loved for the exercise and fresh air, but were also an essential source of inspiration. Indeed, he would always carry a notebook to jot down ideas lest they be forgotten. All this was thanks to Justi and especially the devoted Natalie, who had manoeuvred her way into becoming an accepted part of the family, although she harboured a deeper hope that one day Mahler might propose to her. They rented five rooms on the first floor, which Gustav and Justi were to share with Otto, Emma and Natalie. The rooms were sparsely furnished, the only items of luxury being a leather sofa that had to be wheeled from room to room and a Bösendorfer baby grand piano on loan from the manufacturers. Tired out after months of hard labour in Hamburg, he now gave his full concentration to composition. With Mahler unable to relax and with the adrenalin continuing to flow, Natalie voiced concern over his health, suggesting that he should ease up. He was furious at her fussing, saying that creation was all-important and no sacrifice too great. For him this was a holiday with a purpose and he instigated a strict routine: up at six-thirty, spending the morning composing, not to be disturbed, and lunch to be served when he was ready. His companions always knew when he had had a productive morning, for after lunch he would celebrate by smoking a cigar.

During this summer, apart from further work on the *Wunderhorn Lieder*, he concentrated on his *Second Symphony*. Already he had virtually completed the first movement, which he had based on the *Totenfeier*, as well as additional sketches. He had told Natalie that his aim was to complete the *Andante* and the *Scherzo*. He also mentioned the importance of having extended periods for composition so that his music could stream out unhindered; not for him odd moments and picking at ideas. In many ways his attitude to composition was very similar to that of the impressionist artists – bold sweeps and explosions of colour, capturing unique moments of inspiration.

At the time of its composition, Mahler had regarded his *First Symphony* as a musical revolution, which in many ways it was, and that it would take the world by storm, which it didn't. However, despite his disappointment, he soon began to realise that it did have shortcomings and so began his decade of revision. He had the same feeling of innovation about the *Second*, despite Bülow's comments about *Totenfeier*, which he had written some five years before. Since then he had learnt a great deal, and his enthusiasm for the new work soon came to the boil. Having finished the *Scherzo*, the full sketch of the *Andante* was completed in a week and he was thrilled with the result, but he held his feelings in check, telling Natalie that what seemed superb while the ink was still drying, might not have the same appeal a few months thence.

The conversations he had with Natalie on the subject of music, and his compositions in particular, are most enlightening. At this time there were the first suggestions that he was beginning to doubt the wisdom of using titles and programmes, wanting the music to speak for itself. Nevertheless he did write programmes for both the *Second* and *Third Symphonies*, obviously with the intention of making them more accessible, but he would later drop these. He told her that his music was a reflection of his own life and the world about him, and that if his existence became one of perfect peace, he didn't think he would be able to create anything of value! He informed her of his struggles with composition, such as with the *Scherzo* of the *Second* and how he had doubted its quality. While writing it he had had the feeling of being guided by an external force, almost uncomprehending what he was creating. He compared it to a blind hen managing to find a grain of corn. Even though at the time of writing the *Scherzo* he had felt reservations about it; upon reflection he found it 'awesome'.

When Mahler's mind was in full compositional flight, all else would take second place. He became blinkered, almost hypnotised by the act of creation. He told Natalie that very often it was far from easy, frequently painful, and he compared it to a woman giving birth – the pain followed by an overwhelming joy – or like a pearl, an object of beauty brought into being through the agony of the oyster. This act of creation, the birth of a new work, to him was an almost sacred and very personal act and one that had to be respected, and should under no circumstances be overheard or interrupted. Unwelcome noises were particularly infuriating to him, and he predicted that in the future noise pollution would be outlawed in the same way that smells were – how right he was!

But the Steinbach vacation was not all work. He went on regular walks, a particularly enjoyable one being on the 7th of July, his birthday, when they all set off for a lengthy hike, taking with them a picnic complete with birthday cake. A few days later, Fritz Löhr came to stay for a fortnight, and the two friends, as well as Otto and Natalie, spent many hours discussing the works and merits of various composers, and naturally Mahler played him the three new *Wunderhorn* songs. Wagner of course was beyond criticism, and Mahler said that whenever he felt down, he only had to think of Wagner for his spirits to rise – he was unique, a genius, a revolutionary and a worthy successor to Beethoven. What else could be achieved? Wagner's genius had shaken the world of music and he was precisely right for the people of his time, an essential ingredient for such a gift to be recognised. Mahler mused that 'the harvest is over, with only scattered ears of corn left to be gathered in'. Brahms, yes, but as far as Bruckner was concerned, despite the undeniable sincerity of his old friend from the Conservatory, he had reservations. Nevertheless he made it clear that he would always do his level best to get Bruckner's works performed, for they had a magnificence and depth, even if he questioned their form. He had always revered him as a man, and was saddened that his works had not been fairly judged during his lifetime. As for Liszt, he regarded his music to be very second rate. Mahler was a man ahead of his time and it would take several decades for his music to achieve the impact he had hoped for. For him both content and form had to be in perfect balance to withstand the test of time.

The summer at Steinbach drew to a close. Mahler was disappointed that he had been unable to complete his *Second Symphony*. He wanted the last movement to be choral, following the example of Beethoven's *Ninth*, but despite all his efforts he had failed to find a suitable text that would fire his imagination. Otherwise his break had been a great success. In addition to continuing work on his *Second Symphony*, he had also written the three *Wunderhorn* songs: *Das irdische Leben, Des Antonius von Padua Fischpredigt* and *Rheinlegendchen*. Justi and Natalie had indeed found just the right retreat for him. Before leaving he made arrangements for a small building to be constructed in the meadow behind the inn and at the water's edge, for he needed somewhere where he could work undisturbed with an uninterrupted view over the Attersee to give him inspiration.

Justi and Natalie took this matter in hand, buying the land from the leaseholder Anna Scheicher, and seeking the services of a local architect, Franz Lösch from nearby Schörfling. Lösch later recalled how Mahler had said that he needed to be close to the lake's edge so that he could hear the lapping water, for it had a special language of its own which helped him to compose. The hut was to be a simple structure with just one room, with windows on three sides, a stove, a table, chairs and the loaned Bösendorfer baby grand. This was to be the first of Mahler's famous *Häuschen*, or composing huts.

On the 23rd of August, two days before leaving Steinbach, he wrote to Alois. His patience with him exhausted, he made it clear that from now on he was on his own. He would not be sending him any more money. He told him to find employment and hoped that he would become 'a useful member of society'.

Mahler's return to Hamburg was not nearly as painful as he had feared, apart from having to find new lodgings, for his previous abode, which overlooked a zoo where the public were frequently entertained by a military band, had become unbearable. Having visited a number of addresses, he decided on a two-roomed flat overlooking open ground, which would do as a stopgap. The season began and performances of *Der Freischütz* and *Die Meistersinger* were applauded, and, with Tchaikovsky himself present, Mahler also conducted a special performance of *Iolanta*.

Hardly had he settled into his new flat when sickness struck the household. Justi had just arrived for a visit and he was naturally concerned for her health, especially as cholera was still widespread in parts of the city. The day after her arrival Mahler fell ill with stomach pains, diarrhoea and a high fever. Justi presumed the worst and determined to look after him despite the obvious risks to her own health. When his condition worsened, she became so upset that she decided to die with him and even shared the same spoon with which she was feeding him. Fortunately it turned out that he had not contracted cholera but some other virus and, being otherwise robust, he recovered from his ailment in a remarkably short space of time.

After only a fortnight's absence he was back at work facing a busy autumn schedule. The highlight, as far as Mahler was concerned, was a concert to be held on the 27th of October. In addition to other works, the first part of the programme would include his *Wunderhorn* songs *Das himmlische Leben, Verlor'ne Müh, Wer hat dies Liedlein erdacht, Der Schildwache Nachtlied, Trost im Unglück* and *Rheinlegendchen*. After the interval, and hoping for a better reception than it had received in Budapest, the newly revised version of his *First Symphony*, still referred to as a symphonic poem entitled '*Titan*', would be performed. He was not to be disappointed. The Lieder were given a very enthusiastic applause, but '*Titan*' was a sensation. Yes, there was a minority who let fly with boos, probably pre-planned, but they were completely drowned out by the thunderous applause of the majority, which included the musicians themselves. Such a reception did much to defuse the 'anti' section of the critics, although Joseph Sittard, complimentary to Mahler as a conductor, regarded the Lieder as 'monotonous', had 'distorted harmonies' and 'meandered on crude musical stilts'. As far as the *Symphony* was concerned, he regarded having to sit through it as 'a penance for a great many sins'. To him it was too long, undisciplined and lacked poetic and musical content of quality. But by now Mahler was used to the sour grapes of some of the critics. Far more important to him was the general reaction of the public and his musicians. On the other hand, Ferdinand Pfohl, writing in the *Hamburger Nachrichten*, considered the *Symphony* to be outstanding, especially the *Marche Funèbre*. As always the critics were divided, probably between the narrow-minded and the forward-looking, and with the inevitable touch of anti-Semitism lurking in the background in some cases. A repeat performance of the *Wunderhorn Lieder* by the same singer, Paul Bulss, in Wiesbaden generated only a lukewarm reception, which was very disappointing for Mahler following the Hamburg success.

Boosted by the Hamburg reception of his *Wunderhorn Lieder* and the '*Titan*' *Symphony*, and having come across his original manuscript of *Das klagende Lied*, he decided that it was a work well worth resurrecting, and so he set about making a clear and more presentable copy of the score. He instinctively felt that it was an important work and should be performed and, on rediscovering the cantata, he was astounded by how mature and original it was.

Christmas came and the New Year and, with his fair copy of *Das klagende Lied* complete, on the 2nd of January he conducted Verdi's *Falstaff*. It was an overwhelming success and hailed as a masterpiece. The other New Year production was Smetana's The *Bartered Bride,* which Mahler was delighted to be able to conduct, for he had always held his fellow countryman in the highest esteem. Starring in the production was Berta Lauterer, Josef Foerster's wife, and their collaboration cemented the friendship between the two composers. Foerster would often visit Mahler in his apartment, which had the air of a music workshop with scores scattered everywhere and the famous laurel wreath presented to him by the then ailing Hans von Bülow, dedicated to *'Dem Pygmalion der Hamburger Oper'*. Von Bülow, once the arch critic and now the fervent supporter, would soon be indirectly the source of inspiration.

It was during this period that the mutual respect and cooperation between Mahler and Richard Strauss really began to flourish. Strauss had played Mahler his opera *Guntram* on the piano and he had been very impressed. On the 2nd of February he wrote to Strauss asking him to bring the score with him on his next visit so that he could follow it 'as a conductor'. Strauss on his part offered to include the *'Titan' Symphony* in one of his programmes at the Weimar Festival. In his letters to Strauss Mahler also mentioned his own uncertain position at the Hamburg Opera. Pollini, according to Mahler, was playing his usual game of chess, having actually approached Strauss with the idea of his joining the Hamburg staff. At one moment he was trying to demote Mahler so that he himself could enjoy more of the reflected glory and the next he was summoning him to his office to sign a new contract, to which suggestion Mahler replied that he had already prepared himself for his departure. He had indeed applied to Munich and Berlin, both to no avail. He wrote to Fritz Löhr making his feelings quite clear. He was Jewish, and Jews would not be acceptable, and he was certain that the same would apply to Vienna, his ultimate goal. Mahler, with his own personal ideas and interpretations of the great works of the masters, would result in a 'repulsive dog-fight'. These places were not interested in a fresh approach, especially coming from a Jew. He stressed that it was only through the out and out support of Brahms and Bülow that his standing in Hamburg remained so high. At this point he felt stuck. He could no longer take a gamble for he had the continuous financial drain of his brothers and sisters to think of. It must have been a great relief to him that his brother Otto was about to begin a musical career as a choir director and second conductor at the Leipzig Opera. Pollini caved in, and a new five year contract was presented to Mahler with all his demands agreed to. One of the interesting clauses of his new contract was an agreement permitting him to conduct further London performances. Checkmate to Mahler!

As already mentioned, Bülow's health had been in rapid decline, and Mahler was asked to take over his conducting commitments. He would be released from his opera work when necessary to fulfil the engagements. Upon Richard Strauss's recommendation, Bülow, accompanied by three of his friends, Fraulein Peterson, Frau Schiff and Frau Lazarus, went to Egypt for some sun and warmth, but hardly had they arrived in Cairo when, on the 12th of February, Mahler's friend and supporter died from a brain tumour. Despite being prepared for the inevitable, Hamburg was shocked and saddened at losing the much revered musician. Mahler was asked to conduct Beethoven's *'Eroica' Symphony* at a memorial concert, although he had only been a second choice. Strauss had been the first choice, but he had declined. He conducted the work concealed behind a bust of Bülow, which was surrounded by plants. By all accounts the performance was very special and emotional and, in a small way, added to Mahler's stature.

Bülow's funeral took place on the 29th of March 1894 in the Michaeliskirche. Such had been his standing in the city that the occasion was on the scale of a state funeral. During the ceremony the choir sang music from Bach's *St. Matthew* and *St. John Passions* and Brahms's *Requiem*, and a rousing performance of Friedrich Klopstock's *'Aufersteh'n'* (to be resurrected). This was what Mahler had been waiting for. The pure sound of the children's singing overwhelmed him. He compared it to being struck by lightning. His feelings towards Bülow, the great emotional occasion and the *'Aufersteh'n'* – everything became clear: it was 'sacred inspiration'! He now had the basis for the finale of the *Second Symphony*. Later that same day, Foerster paid Mahler a visit and found him hard at work. As soon as he entered, Mahler shouted excitedly words to the effect of 'I've got it!' It was not just to be a setting of Klopstock's ode, but a starting point, the text an inspiration that Mahler would work on and extend to meet his own needs. His search was over, a search which had taken him through much of the world's greatest literature including the Bible, and he was now well on his way towards completing what would turn out to be one of his greatest and most popular works, and indeed one for which he would continue to harbour a special affection.

The three ladies who had accompanied Bülow to Cairo had taken on the roles of 'professional mourners', weeping and wailing at every opportunity, which infuriated Mahler, and he quipped sarcastically that he feared they might establish a museum to display Bülow's chamber pots and other personal items! At his annual benefit concert he conducted Beethoven's *Seventh Symphony* with his usual controversial tempi. This sparked off the critics, but the audience loved the performance. Afterwards he was presented with gifts which included a particularly magnificent laurel wreath interlaced with gold, no doubt in appreciation for his hard work during Bülow's illness and at his funeral. Mahler (deliberately?) forced the cancellation of the proposed London trip by demanding too high a salary. He had other things on his mind, his *Second Symphony* and trying to persuade Pollini to stage *Guntram*, but despite his efforts Pollini showed no interest. The première took place in Weimar in May, the same month that Strauss had arranged for the '*Titan*' to be performed. Also, on the 11ᵗʰ of May, the wedding took place between Richard Strauss and a singer by the name of Pauline de Ahna, a formidable lady for whom Mahler was to have little time.

Strauss was entrusted with the preliminary rehearsals of the '*Titan*', and Mahler, accompanied by Otto, arrived to conduct the final rehearsal and the performance, which took place on the 29ᵗʰ of May. It was almost back to the bad old Budapest days with a most unfavourable reaction from a large section of the audience, although as always there were those who applauded him. He felt that controversy was more important than polite applause, and the orchestra, after he had sweetened them with a barrel of beer, had declared their approval. He told Arnold Berliner that when dogs started to bark, he knew he was moving in the right direction. Nevertheless he must have been upset. The critics, having sharpened their nibs beforehand, had their usual field day. So ended the season, and Mahler was only too relieved to return to the peace and quiet of Steinbach so that he could complete his *Second Symphony*.

He was very eager to see the *Häuschen*, which had been constructed for him the previous autumn, and he was not disappointed. The instructions he had left with Justi and Natalie for the builder before his departure the previous year had been carried out to the letter. There it stood by the water's edge, surrounded by an abundance of June flowers in the meadow behind the inn. Inside the furnishings were as he had asked, with the baby grand taking up much of the floor space. It was, and is, a very special place. It is no wonder that he was inspired to write such wonderful music with the fabulous views across the mirrored waters of the Attersee to the blue, misty hills beyond. It is still there today, even though it had to be reconstructed after years of neglect and having been used for a variety of purposes including a slaughterhouse, a laundry and even as a public toilet! The rebuilt *Häuschen* stands in the middle of a camp and caravan site, but it nevertheless retains a certain magic, having been restored to much as it was in Mahler's time. Inside is a baby grand, a few basic items of furniture and a collection of framed photographs and memorabilia.

With the top priority for this summer break the completion of the *Second Symphony*, Gustav had asked Justi to try to persuade Natalie not to join him at Steinbach, for he felt that her fussing, something which had begun to irritate him the previous summer, would distract him from the important task at hand. It was not that he had come to dislike her, far from it, for at least she was an ally and kindred spirit, but her desire to marry him had made her over-possessive. As a result she did not visit Steinbach during the summer of 1894, and her absence resulted in a gap in her invaluable recollections.

Mahler resumed his summer routine: 6.30 to the *Häuschen* where breakfast would await him, his sisters keeping out of his way during the morning and fending off any source of noise, natural or otherwise, which might disturb his train of thought. Under no circumstances should he be interrupted. They had to wait for lunch. Times varied and quite often he would not emerge until three o'clock. In the afternoons he would swim, row across the lake or hike in the fields and mountains or along the forest tracks, perhaps to a local village such as Weissenbach at the southern end of the Attersee. Apparently while he was working on the Finale of the *Second Symphony* he became so uptight that Justi and Emma began to fear for his health, but after three weeks of blinkered existence, both text and score in sketch form were finished.

On the 29th of June he wrote to Fritz Löhr informing him of the safe delivery of the Finale, and that both father and offspring were as well as they could be under the circumstances. The 'child' had been baptised '*Lux lucet in tenebris*' (Light shines in the darkness). In a letter to Berliner a few days later, he described his new work as 'majestic' and 'colossal', and in another letter that it was the most important work he had yet created. He told Strauss that he had shed his old skin and that the new skin was a better fit. His new work, compared to his previous symphony, was like a man to an infant.

Second Symphony, in C minor
(In five movements, for soprano, contralto, chorus and orchestra.)

The *Second Symphony* is a notable advance on the *First*, yet it is a continuation of the same story. The hero of the *First* (Mahler himself) is borne in a solemn funeral procession, and at the end is resurrected in a blaze of glory. In a letter dated the 26th of March 1896 to the critic Max Marschalk, one of the few who understood and supported him, Mahler posed such questions as, What is the purpose of life? Why must people suffer? Is it nothing but a cruel joke? . . . These are questions that must be answered. It could have been that after all the adverse reactions to the *First Symphony*, however remarkable and ground-breaking it might have been, he was burying the disappointments of that work and resurrecting himself as a composer. It is the first of the so-called *Wunderhorn* symphonies in which he was to use material from already composed songs based on the *Wunderhorn* poems, either sung or instrumental, although in the *Second* and *Third Symphonies* they are but interludes in altogether grander canvases. The *Second* is a journey through death, despair, memories, the search for God, purification and at last spiritual ecstasy. Mahler wrote several sets of programme notes explaining what lay behind each movement, having been asked to clarify his scheme by the likes of Natalie, Bruno Walter and later his wife Alma, but as with all programmes he subsequently rejected them, wanting the music to speak for itself. In 1901 he told Alma that he regarded explanatory notes as being the equivalent of a crutch for a cripple, and made no more sense than asking God to write a programme for creation! He likened them to doctrines of religion, which would only mislead and distort, and so were undesirable, although at this stage in his career he did need a programme for his own purposes to act as a skeleton upon which he could flesh out his ideas, to be discarded once the work was completed. After all, by this time he was seeking to be recognised as a composer of absolute symphonic music, not a writer of symphonic poems. It was through music that he sought the answers to the meaning of existence. Some seek through the written word, some through art or through organised religion. Mahler never had, nor would ever have, any desire to abandon himself to organised religious doctrine. He was a believer in God as a universal force, the great inexplicable creator, and his music, so personal and yet with such a universal message, was his spiritual path into the great unknown.

First movement: Allegro maestoso (mit durchaus ernstem und feierlichem Ausdruck.
(With serious and solemn expression throughout)

This first movement is not a funeral march, not in the pictorial sense as in the March to the Scaffold in the *Symphonie Fantastique* by Berlioz, but funeral rites; perhaps closer to being a successor to the *Marcia funèbre* of Beethoven's *Eroica*. The listener is thrown into the deep end with a great thrust from the strings, leading into the sombre theme of mourning, but it is not a 'weepy', it has more of the feeling of *Siegfried's Funeral March* in *Götterdämmerung*. The movement has a true symphonic structure, and there are quieter, more lyrical passages. There is the great *Dies Irae*, the trumpets playing a suggestion of the *Resurrection* theme. The movement progresses like a tidal wave, building up to an enormous and terrifying climax, only to pass and leave the emptiness of mourning, and then the final two octave collapse into nothingness. After such a sapping experience, both for musicians and audience alike, Mahler insisted that there should be a five minutes pause before the beginning of the second movement.

Second movement: Andante moderato: sehr gemächlich.
(Very leisurely)

The second movement is one of light relief, of happy memories, yet tinged with sadness at the loss of innocence. It is a ländler, and Mahler himself called it almost 'Schubertian'. It is delightful and was an immediate success when played in concerts on its own, even before the symphony itself took wing. It is like a gentle smile after the grim-faced first movement.

Third movement: In ruhig fliessender Bewegung
(In a tranquil, flowing movement)

There is real irony here of man's disillusionment and reluctance to accept his failings. It is a distorted image of the world. Mahler's explanation to Natalie was that it depicted the hero having lost all notion of genuine happiness and even identity in a world gone crazy. He uses ideas from his *Wunderhorn* song about St. Anthony's fruitless sermon to the fish, but in this context it takes on the form of an ironic *scherzo*, the humour of the original being replaced by a more sinister mood. The *Fischpredigt* music weaves in and out of the score, sometimes interrupted, and then the *Glaube* faith motif (later to come to the fore in the Finale) makes its first appearance in a beautiful central passage. This in turn is interrupted by the return of the restless *Fischpredigt* music, punctuated by threatening fanfares, timpani and 'screams' from the orchestra, or as Mahler put it, 'the shriek of a tortured soul'. There is a further brief appearance of the faith motif, before the perpetuum mobile nature of the movement finally grinds to a halt. On its completion, Mahler was particularly pleased and indeed was astonished by his creation, and he told Natalie that he had not been aware of its quality while he had been composing it.

Fourth movement: 'Urlicht': Sehr feierlich, aber Schlicht (Choralmässig)
(Very solemn, yet simple – like a hymn)

Out of the pain of the last somewhat bizarre movement flows the peace of the 'Urlicht' (Primal Light), another of the *Wunderhorn* songs. It tells of the path to God, often painful and beset by temptations, and the eventual goal of eternal happiness. '*Ich bin von Gott und will wieder zu Gott!*' (I am of God and will return to God). It is a very spiritual movement, perhaps a homage to Bruckner, and acts as a quiet prelude which leads into the mighty Finale.

Fifth movement: Im Tempo des Scherzo: Wild herausfahrend
Maestoso, sehr zurückhaltend – sehr langsam und gedehnt
Aufersteh'n, ja aufersteh'n, wirst du mein Staub'
(In the tempo of the *scherzo*: wildly bursting forth. Dignified, held back –
very slow:
'You shall rise up, yes rise up my dust')

In total contrast to the quiet simplicity of the *Urlicht*, the last movement is colossal and totally overwhelming. What a marvellous foil the *Urlicht* is coming between the bitter sarcasm of the Scherzo and the succeeding torrent of emotion that is the Finale. It deals with the death of all living things, the Day of Judgement and finally resurrection.

Once the initial outburst has subsided, we hear the distant sound of horns, reminiscent of shofroth, the ram's horn trumpets used by the Jews of old during religious ceremonies as a summons to prayer. The movement's emotional journey moves from fear to unmitigated terror and finally to ecstasy. The confidence with which Mahler fashioned this gigantic finale at this early stage in his symphonic career is astonishing. It calls for gigantic forces including ten horns, eight trumpets, off stage brass, soloists, chorus and organ. It was in fact the largest concert work to be composed since the Berlioz *Messe des Morts* and yet, throughout the symphony, there are passages of great delicacy, almost chamber in quality, which make the climaxes that much more overwhelming. The Finale also shows Mahler's use of effects: bird calls, distant fanfares from the off stage brass, the chorus remaining seated when they first enter. The latter direction is so essential for they emerge from a passage of expectant calm and their hushed entry, singing the opening of the *Aufersteh'n*, is truly magical. For the huge chorus to stand up, accompanied by inevitable rustling, would completely destroy the atmosphere. Of course they do stand when it comes to the great climax. The music is almost operatic, yet deeply spiritual, it is both personal and at the same time a message for all mankind.

Mahler told Bruno Walter that in this vast work the listener is clubbed to the ground and is then raised up on the wings of angels. He told Natalie that to call the work a symphony in the traditional sense would be inaccurate. For him the symphony must develop into an all-embracing symphonic world, using all the latest musical innovations, for like life itself he saw music as an evolving art.

He put the final touches to the score of the *Second Symphony* after two trips. First he paid a brief visit to Brahms who was staying in nearby Ischl, the spa made famous for having Emperor Franz Joseph's summer residence. He was pleased to see the old composer who received him warmly, even though he made sarcastic remarks about the *Häuschen*, calling it '*Wasserhäuschen*' because of its proximity to the Attersee, and he nicknamed Mahler's new work '*Wassersymphonie*'! Having seen the score, Brahms remarked that up until then he had considered Richard Strauss to have been the foremost iconoclast, but Mahler had taken over the mantle as the king of the revolutionaries! The other journey was to Bayreuth at the invitation of Cosima Wagner, which both surprised and delighted Mahler for until then she had been renowned for her anti-Semitism. While he was there he attended performances of *Parsifal, Lohengrin* and *Tannhäuser* from the comfort of the Wagner family's box.

On arrival back in Steinbach, having seen Otto at the Krzyżanowskis' en route, and having heard that his brother had been well liked at the Leipzig Opera and was now about to move to Bremen, Mahler spent the last days of his summer break completing the *Second Symphony.*

So ended a hectic but very productive summer, and he returned to Hamburg knowing that he had created something rather special.

Chapter 6

Hamburg . . . Part Two

Third Symphony

WITH HIS POSITION in Hamburg considerably strengthened after the successes of the previous season, and with a more subdued Pollini, Mahler faced a very busy year at the Opera. Following the death of the much-respected Bülow, he had to shoulder the responsibility for the subscription concerts in addition to his duties as Opera Director. Nevertheless, his confidence was higher than ever, boosted by the completion of the *Second Symphony*. This he played to his friend Josef Foerster, who was staggered by the new work. Mahler had also found a new and much larger apartment, more befitting a man in his position, where his sisters would soon join him.

During the summer, Pollini had made a new appointment, a young man of eighteen by the name of Bruno Schlesinger. He was an enthusiastic young musician who had become fascinated by the controversies arising from Mahler's 'Titan' Symphony following the Weimar performance, especially the 'Funeral march after Jacques Callot'. Having made up his mind that he was going to meet the composer, he had approached Pollini, who offered him a job as co-répétiteur, or assistant coach.

Bruno Schlesinger would later change his name to Bruno Walter, and he would become not only a great supporter and friend of Mahler's, but also one of the greatest conductors of his symphonies. Indeed, Mahler was to dedicate his *Ninth Symphony* to him, and Walter was to conduct the posthumous premières of both the *Ninth* and *Das Lied von der Erde*. He first caught sight of Mahler outside Pollini's office, and later described him as being short, pale and thin, with a long face and raven black hair. He wore glasses, but they could not hide his remarkable eyes. The lines on his face betrayed sadness as well as humour. When Pollini introduced him to Mahler, Bruno Walter put on an air of exaggerated confidence, which caused considerable amusement, and Mahler immediately took to the young man.

He did not have to wait long for an opportunity to establish himself.

Mahler was in the process of preparing for a performance of a new opera by Engelbert Humperdinck, *Hänsel und Gretel*, a work that Mahler came to admire greatly – no wonder, as such fairy tale material fell into the same bracket as the poems from *Des Knaben Wunderhorn*. An added attraction was that Humperdinck was a Wagner disciple like himself. The pianist who had been employed for the rehearsal was having difficulties coping with the music, so Mahler turned to Walter and asked him if he felt he would be capable of playing the score, which of course was completely new to him. This he did without any problem. Mahler was impressed and gave him further tasks, including rehearsing the chorus for a production of *Lohengrin*, which he also carried out very successfully, despite being his first experience with a chorus.

Bruno Walter's reminiscences of Mahler the conductor are fascinating. He painted a picture of a person of extremes, a man who was a genius, and yet at times almost demonic. His personality was electric, his instructions clarity itself, and he compelled those around him to act with almost blind obedience. He was intolerant of incompetence, yet at the same time he warmed to those who had talent and showed enthusiasm. His sudden changes of facial expression matched his mood swings, at one moment pained, the next humorous, at another angry, and then kindness itself. These constant variations of mood were reflected in his movements. He had an irregular gait: stamping his feet, rushing ahead, suddenly standing still, and so on, his pace constantly erratic. Relax he could not, and he must have been a difficult person to be close to, but Bruno's devotion knew no bounds. He later regarded that his close relationship with Mahler had been a great blessing on his whole life, and this despite the fact that Mahler by nature was a man self-absorbed in his music and his inner turmoil. According to Bruno he was no educator, but for those who had talent and were able to accept his personality, the dedication and inspiration that flowed from him was education enough. In the years to follow those who had neither talent nor the will to submit themselves to his stringent demands inevitably fell by the wayside. He was a hard taskmaster, no more so than with himself.

Another vivid portrait of Mahler's character at this time came from the soprano Ernestine Schumann-Heink, a Czech singer who sang at the Hamburg Opera between the years 1883 and 1898. Her advances having been rejected by him, she set about spreading rumours that he was a homosexual. Later on, though, she remembered him as one of the greatest conductors of his time, though his constant quest for unobtainable perfection resulted in him being hated. She described him as being a nervous, thin man who, once he had a baton in his hand, became a tyrant, and yet away from the podium he was kindness itself, sensitive with an overwhelming love of nature down to the smallest flower. He was a complex character, almost schizophrenic, and he was consequently misunderstood and condemned by many. Despite the fact that he was not particularly enamoured by her, she admitted that he had given her a great deal of help, and for that she was grateful.

Pollini's attitude to the Stadttheater, always with the balance sheet at the back of his mind, was to stage as many different operas as possible. So long as the singing was of a reasonable standard, the productions themselves did not concern him. This clashed head on with Mahler's insistence on meticulous preparation and stage performance. Consequently Mahler was never satisfied with the finished results at the Hamburg Opera, despite the fact that he dragged it up to be one of the foremost companies in Europe. He rightly considered that all aspects of a production, whether musical or visual, were equally important in the realisation of a composer's vision.

Despite the lack-lustre productions and the incompetence of Franz Bittong, the stage manager, Mahler never compromised himself with his allotted task as music director, and on this front at least he always demanded the highest possible standards, bearing in mind the rather mixed bag of musicians that he had at his disposal. Even though some were exceptional, the orchestra, under-paid and frequently demoralised, did not show anything like the dedication of their conductor. He later told Natalie that their attitude to their art had been nothing more than as 'a cow to be milked'. Nevertheless most did show some respect for him, both as a musician and also because they were fully aware that he too had little time for Pollini. Mahler did his best to bring about a pay increase for the musicians, although at the same time making it quite clear to them that their financial plight was no excuse for a drop in standards. His podium gymnastics of previous years had now subsided, for with greater experience and maturity he found he was able to instil discipline and even fear by simple movements and facial expressions. The quality of performance he managed to achieve, despite all the aforementioned problems, was remarkable.

Just as he would not tolerate lack of effort from his musicians, so he was equally intolerant of 'ignorant' or noisy audiences. Bülow's approach had been one of sarcastic remarks; Mahler's was altogether much harsher, even venomous. Noise, whispering, applause at the wrong moments he would not stand for, and his effect on the audiences became similar to that on the musicians – discipline and fear of stepping out of line! Bruno Walter wrote of Mahler's abundance of vitality that produced an electric atmosphere and performances that reflected the fire from the man within. None but the faint hearted could resist his passion and dedication to music. According to Walter the atmosphere was magical, and that neither during the two years he worked with him at the Hamburg Opera, nor during the six when he was with him in Vienna, did he ever see the spell, created through 'edge of the seat' tension, broken.

At the end of September the new production of *Hänsel und Gretel* was launched. The public loved it, and there were over thirty performances during the 1894-5 season.

Otto was continuing to exasperate Mahler, his lack of commitment at times driving him to distraction. Already he was contemplating leaving his post in Bremen. Justi wrote a stinging letter to Otto, rebuking him for his insolence and ingratitude for all the help he had received. This letter was much amended by Mahler himself and is the last known letter to Otto.

The end of October saw the beginning of a series of eight subscription concerts, which Mahler had taken over from the late Hans von Bülow. Foerster had become a regular visitor to Mahler's apartment, and he marvelled at the meticulous way he prepared each piece of music prior to performance, stamping his own interpretation on each work. The scores were ablaze with his markings. The series began successfully. The first concert consisted of Mozart's *Symphony in G minor, K550, Volkslieder* by Brahms, sung by Amalie Joachim with Mahler at the piano, and Beethoven's *Seventh Symphony*. Present at the concert was the pianist-composer Ferruccio Busoni, whom Mahler invited to a lunch along with Hermann Behn. Mahler told Behn that he thought his lieder were splendid, and that he would do his best to get them performed, a wise move by Mahler, for Behn had considerable influence in Hamburg.

Many of the critics, especially Sittard, set about picking holes in the first subscription concert in every way possible, the result being that attendances at the subsequent concerts dwindled. Sittard continued to attack Mahler during the rest of the series. He particularly disliked his string orchestra version of Schubert's *Tod und das Mädchen*, and even the final concert, dedicated to the recently deceased Anton Rubinstein when his *Ocean Symphony* was performed, was duly panned and poorly attended. Sittard summed up his feelings towards Mahler by commenting that he thanked God that he was unique! And yet there were those such as Foerster who realised the brilliance of his interpretative approach and his desire to constantly re-think each piece he conducted. Nowadays of course it is common practice for a conductor to stamp his own thoughts on a work, but at that time most played safe by simply going through the motions.

As well as the subscription concerts and his work at the Opera, Mahler also managed to find the time to put the finishing touches to the score of his *Second Symphony*, which he completed before Christmas.

The New Year triggered off hectic activity as Richard Strauss had agreed to conduct the first performance of the first three movements of Mahler's

Second Symphony in Berlin. Although having completed the score a few weeks earlier, Mahler wanted to try out the three movements himself so that he could make any necessary corrections before sending the score to Strauss. Hermann Behn was in the small audience present, and he was so impressed that he promised him that he would make a four-hand arrangement, which Mahler later praised, the two men playing it in the presence of Frau Lazarus, the Viennese widow who had been a close friend of the late Hans von Bülow.

Mahler wrote several letters to Strauss at the end of January and the beginning of February. He told him that the three movements were ready, proclaiming them faultless and, surprisingly, considerably easier than the *First Symphony*. He also told Strauss that he had arranged for the two preludes from the latter's opera *Guntram* to be performed, a work that Strauss was having the greatest difficulty persuading any German opera company to stage. He told Strauss that he wished to be present at the first rehearsal of the *Second Symphony*, or even conduct it himself. He required extra musicians and he himself would be prepared to bear the cost, and an extra rehearsal which he would pay for as well if necessary.

Meanwhile, Pollini was insisting that Mahler conduct virtually every evening at the Hamburg Opera, so when rehearsals began for the *Second*, he found himself having to commute to Berlin by night train for the morning rehearsals, then dashing back to Hamburg in time to conduct the evening opera. The strain on him must have been intense, especially as just before this gruelling schedule began, he had received tragic news. On the 6th of February, Otto, his gifted musician brother, not yet twenty-two, had shot himself. In his pocket was found a lock of his mother's hair. At the time he was staying in Vienna with a friend of Friedrich Löhr's, Nina Hoffmann, wife of the artist Josef Hoffmann, whom Wagner had given the task of designing the sets for the first *Ring*, staged at the first Bayreuth Festival in 1876. She herself became well known as the biographer of Dostoyevsky, the Russian writer, whose poetry Mahler came to love. The reasons behind Otto's suicide are not known for certain. Perhaps the public ridiculing of parts of his two symphonies (his third remained unfinished) had sent him into deep depression. He did not have the strength of character his elder brother possessed. Press reports, while praising Otto as a gifted and dedicated musician, suggested that he was a dreamer, negative in outlook, given to bouts of depression and that he had found life's struggle a particularly heavy burden. Mahler, of course, was devastated by his death, having regarded him as potentially a more gifted musician than himself; a brother whom he and Justi had done their best to nurture and groom for a great career in music. The strength of Mahler's feelings can be discerned by the fact that later he could not bear the thought of opening a trunk containing Otto's possessions. Inside were his brother's manuscripts as well as the manuscript of the first three movements of Bruckner's *Third Symphony*, which the old composer had given Mahler in gratitude for his support, and that he had passed on to Otto. This was discovered after Mahler's death when Alma sent for the trunk. But she found that it had already been looted, although the Bruckner manuscript was still there and became one of her most prized possessions. Mahler, unable to leave Hamburg because of all his commitments there, as well as the hectic preparations for the performance of the first three movements of his *Second Symphony* in Berlin, asked his old friend Emil Freund to deal with legal matters arising from Otto's suicide.

The Berlin performance of the first three movements of the *Second Symphony* took place on the 4th of March 1895. The audience was small and largely made up of two factions, those sympathetic to Mahler (including many invited friends) and a pack of hostile critics licking their lips in anticipation! The Austrian composer Wilhelm Kienzl sat between Richard Strauss and the conductor Karl Muck, and in 1926 he remembered how impressed he had been with the first movement. Turning towards Kienzl, Strauss had declared wide-eyed that there appeared to be no limits to musical expression, while Muck, horrified, had growled that it was atrocious. Strauss at this time appeared to have had his doubts about the work, and was certainly not prepared to appear too enthusiastic. As a result the relationship between Mahler and Strauss cooled temporarily. Strauss, ever the populist, presumably felt that too close a public friendship with his controversial counterpart might damage his own blossoming standing in the music world. The friendly section of the audience was naturally very appreciative, demanding curtain calls and giving Mahler a great ovation; the critics predictably acerbic, using words such as 'tasteless . . . monstrous . . . bizarre . . . tortuous'. One critic who did give Mahler his due was Oskar Eichberg, the music critic of the *Berliner Börsen Courier*, who wrote that it was unfair to judge a work when heard only in part. He declared that Mahler was a composer whose new music was important and should be listened to. It was rich and the orchestration colourful, and he looked forward to hearing the complete symphony. He also praised Mahler's conducting. Mahler was so grateful to Eichberg that he wrote to him on the 30th of March thanking him for his kind remarks, which had meant so much to him. He told him that he felt that his lot as a composer at that time was like being on Calvary, and how every new work that he presented was repulsed and so had to be shut away in a drawer. However he felt confident that, with sympathetic encouragement from people like Oskar Eichberg, the time would come when his music would win through.

Another writer who had shown appreciation for the first three movements of the *Second* was Oskar Bie, writing in the March edition of the magazine *Neue deutsche Rundschair*. As with Eichberg, Mahler wrote him a letter of thanks, saying how important it was to him to read such an encouraging article after all the narrow-minded attacks he had suffered. He told Bie that his music was 'lived', so how could those who were not 'alive' understand it, people who were oblivious to the monumental changes that were taking place at that time. He added that he felt he was constantly tilting at windmills, and suggested that they should meet some time in the future so that they could become better acquainted. At least with the encouraging articles by these men Mahler could look forward to his summer's composing with the knowledge that he did have some supporters in the press.

The grand finale of the season of subscription concerts was a performance of Beethoven's *Ninth Symphony*. For some time Mahler had been researching documents written at the time or shortly after the first performance, and he came to the conclusion that Beethoven, by then completely deaf and therefore unable to try out and hear the music he had written, would probably have been dissatisfied with the orchestration, especially when taking into account the changes that had taken place in the modern symphony orchestra of the 1890s. He decided to increase the brass and woodwind sections, and even arranged for some of the brass to play off-stage prior to the entry of the tenor in the Finale. Of course, Mahler had been attacked by the critics and the purists before. On this occasion, even though the changes had been carried out for genuine reasons and after a considerable amount of research, he appeared to be 'cocking a snook' at his detractors. Much to his delight the reaction on the whole was very positive. The audience applauded ecstatically and the critics held their fire, although some inevitably complained about his alterations. An added surprise came from his old adversary Sittard who called him a genius as a conductor!

Unfortunately the subscription concerts had not turned out to be the usual financial success. The much respected Bülow was still missed by the public, and Mahler, who had tried to provide a more varied programme by including a greater number of recent works by composers such as Bruckner, Richard Strauss, Rubinstein and Brahms, had become a controversial director of this series of concerts. This combined with a continuing bombast from the critics had resulted in attendances dwindling. As a consequence the season ended with the almost inevitable, another tiff with Pollini, and the usual conflict between standards and artistic values on the one hand and profits on the other. Pollini had also reneged on his agreement with Mahler that he would allow him to conduct two pieces from Strauss's opera *Guntram* at a matinée concert. Mahler, not a man to break promises, was furious. He had told Strauss of his plan to conduct the prelude to the last act as well as a tenor solo. Mahler's immediate reaction was to send his resignation to Pollini, although it was neither accepted nor was there even a reply. On the 8th of June Mahler wrote to Strauss telling him that whatever the future might hold, he would continue to do his level best to get *Guntram* staged. He also congratulated him on his latest symphonic poem, *Till Eulenspiegels lustige Streiche*, which Strauss had completed on the 6th of May.

Mahler left Hamburg for his summer break a tired and frustrated man. Increasingly he had had the urge to resign, and so, having returned to Berlin to lay plans for the future performance of the complete *Second Symphony*, he made his way to Vienna, his ultimate goal. Having heard that the director Wilhelm Jahn's health had become a cause for concern, Mahler wished to pay his respects to the intendant of the Hofoper, Josef von Bezecny in order to pave the way for the future.

At last, with a sigh of relief, he was back in Steinbach – and composition. The Attersee, the mountains, the forests, the meadows of wild flowers and his *Häuschen* beside the lapping waters of the lake provided almost immediate inspiration. During the summer of '95, Natalie again joined Mahler and his sisters. On her arrival she found that he had already started work on his *Third Symphony*. The blaze of wild flowers around the *Häuschen* had aroused the muse, and it was not long before he had composed a minuet entitled '*Was mir die Blumen auf der Wieser erzählen*' (What the flowers in the meadow tell me). From this seed grew his largest work to date, the huge *Third Symphony*, his 'Creation Symphony', a great hymn of love to nature and the supreme power of God, the creator. It depicted the gamut of man's emotions and his place in the scheme of things. Mahler told Natalie that this new work would at last earn him applause and money! It would be a work laced with humour and laughter at the world, but he said this with his tongue in his cheek, for he was fully aware that yet again people would struggle to understand. It would be a work born out of the struggle and sorrow of his first two symphonies, and only through knowledge of these would his *Third* be fully appreciated. So he set about this new epic composition, which he would not complete until a year later.

A new form of exercise, which he took to with great enthusiasm, was cycling, and Natalie enjoyed accompanying him on his rides. They loved the independence that this means of transport provided, although Natalie voiced her dislike of the poor roads and bad weather. She called the bicycles 'little iron horses', and on fine days what could be better than a ride followed by the soothing bliss of a dip in the lake. On one occasion Mahler persuaded her to accompany him swimming from shore to shore of the Attersee! As before, Mahler, intoxicated by the wonders of nature and inspired by the magnificent scenery, strode out on his mountain walks, notebook in hand, jotting down ideas as they came into his head. The mountains, forests and meadows were like a magnet, drawing him into the overwhelming Alpine vistas and creation in all its guises, beauty, cruelty *et al.*

Work on the new symphony went on apace, and Natalie and Justi had their work cut out ensuring that Mahler was not disturbed by any noise while he was in the *Häuschen*. Farmers were bribed with beer, buskers paid handsomely to keep away, cowbells muffled, and noisy animals in the vicinity removed or eaten! Crows were a problem, and a dead one was suspended outside the *Häuschen*. They also erected a scarecrow dressed in one of Justi's swimming costumes, a coat belonging to Emma and one of Natalie's hats. For Mahler to pour forth his mind and soul into his music, he had to work in splendid isolation, removed from those he loved with only the natural surroundings as his companions, for nature was the catalyst that composed in him.

The plans for the symphony were becoming grander by the day. Mahler's conception of the term 'symphony' was taking on a new form. He told Natalie that to him the word 'symphony' referred to a musical world constructed with the aid of all the technical means available, with the eternally new and evolving content influencing the form of the work. He told her that it was essential that he must continuously learn how to express himself in new ways – his music must evolve. Apart from '*Was mir die Blumen auf her Wieser erzählen'*, Mahler also managed to compose four more movements: '*Was mir die Tiere im Walde erzählen*' (What the animals in the forest tell me), the idea coming from one of the Wunderhorn songs, '*Ablösung im sommer*', '*Was mir die Nacht erzählt*' (What the night tells me), inspired by a poem from Nietzsche's '*Also Sprach Zarathustra*', and another Wunderhorn based movement entitled '*Was mir die Morgenglocken erzählen*' (What the morning bells tell me). Mahler's use of a text by Nietzsche was in keeping with the current fashion, for Nietzsche was very popular, Richard Strauss also using his philosophy as the basis for his symphonic poem based on '*Also sprach Zarathustra*' (1895-1896). The fourth movement Mahler composed that summer was a huge *Adagio*, '*Was mir die Liebe erzählt*' (What love tells me). All these movements were sketched out and their preliminary scores completed. He told Natalie that the provisional titles of the symphony's movements would be:

> Summer marches in.
> What the flowers in the meadow tell me.
> What the animals in the forest tell me.
> What night tells me.
> What the morning bells tell me.
> What love tells me.
> What the child tells me.

He toyed with two possible titles for the symphony: 'The Happy Life' and 'A Summer Night's Dream', both of which he would later drop. In addition to this creative torrent, he also found the time to compose two more of his *Wunderhorn Lieder*: '*Lied des Verfolgten im Turm*' and '*Wo die schönen Trompeten blasen*'. His excitement over the new symphony can be gleaned not only from his conversations with Natalie, but also from letters he wrote to Fritz Löhr towards the end of August, in which he referred to the new work as the most individual piece he had written to date. He told Fritz that it was in a grand symphonic form and would last for about one and a half hours. It was very personal and by far his best work to date.

So ended his summer break of 1895, and what a productive one it had been. He again visited Berlin on his way back to Hamburg to check on the arrangements for the forthcoming première of the complete *Second Symphony*. Despite the relief at being able to move into a house of their own on the outskirts of Hamburg, which the ever-faithful Justi, aided by Emma, had organised, Mahler felt unwell and exhausted. The previous season at the Hamburg Opera, the preliminary performance of the first three movements of the *Second Symphony* and having to make arrangements for its official première in Berlin, due to take place at the end of 1895, had begun to take its toll. In addition his hectic summer of composing, which must have left him emotionally drained, moving house once more, and now having to face the 1895-1896 season at the Hamburg Opera culminated in a return of haemorrhoids. He was in considerable pain and was even suffering haemorrhages.

The bitter relationship between Mahler and Pollini continued as before. The much-acclaimed soprano Katharina Klafsky had decided to leave for America, together with her conductor husband Otto Lohse. Mahler wrote to Arnold Berliner telling him that the intendant had made no attempt to replace Lohse, thus leaving him as sole conductor and having to take to the podium every day, the only positive note in this letter being that he described his new home as 'magnificent'. To ease the almost impossible burden on Mahler, Felix Weingartner was appointed to take over the 'Bülow' concerts for the 1895-1896 season. Klafsky's departure for America forced Pollini to find a replacement for her. A young, inexperienced soprano was recommended to Pollini by a Viennese music teacher, a retired singer by the name of Rosa Papier. The young twenty-three year old Austrian was to play a significant part in Mahler's life over the following six years. Her name was Anna von Mildenburg.

Frightened by the high-voltage atmosphere of the Hamburg Opera and feeling very lonely in a foreign land, the young singer had a spectacular first meeting with Mahler. In her *Erinnerungen*, published in 1921, she remembered her first piano rehearsal at the theatre. She was singing the

part of Brünnhilde in *Die Walküre* with her répétiteur, both quite happy
with the way she was performing, when suddenly the door burst open to
reveal a short, tanned man in a grey summer suit, hat in hand and umbrella
under his arm. He slammed the door and told the répétiteur to continue. So
this was Director Gustav Mahler! Anna, with eyes closed and scared stiff,
turned to continue, but Mahler suddenly stamped his foot, threw his hat
and umbrella onto the piano and dismissed the unfortunate accompanist
forthwith, and took over the rehearsal himself. She continued to sing, no
reaction coming from the maestro, until she finally broke down and burst
into tears. At first he was silent, then he shouted at her, and the terrified
expression on her face caused him to break into fits of laughter. When
Anna had calmed down, he made encouraging remarks, but told her that
she would have to continue crying until the time came when she would sink
into mediocrity, at which point nobody cried. Her initial fear of him soon
gave way to respect and her confidence began to gather strength. As all
artists found, so long as they showed dedication he would be a great
support for them, inspire them and enable them to reach standards they
had hitherto not dreamt of. Mahler knew that he now had at his disposal a
star in the making, and Anna, having recovered from the shock of her first
meeting with the Director, was more than happy to place herself in his
hands. His demands were considerable. She accepted his search for
perfection and in return Mahler showed her great kindness.

Many years later, Mildenburg recalled Mahler's character, a picture built
up over the years she had known him. She described him as unique,
combining many facets. At times people regarded him as almost demonic,
yet at others humorous. On occasions he had the simplicity of a child,
especially in his astonishment at the wonders of nature, at others he was
deep and contemplative. He could be filled with happiness, serenity, even
humility. Yet these positive sides to his character were often unseen by
those who worked under him, hidden like the far side of the moon. To
some he appeared insensitive, unapproachable, an ominous man who
frequently caused upsets through his sarcasm, and yet he rarely hurt people
intentionally.

Pollini objected to the amount of time Mahler and Mildenburg spent
together and rumours soon took wing that they were having an affair. She
made her debut as Brünnhilde in *Die Walküre*, a performance that
staggered everyone who was fortunate enough to be present, not least
Pollini, who could see box office receipts soaring! The critics, though
mentioning the obvious that her voice was not yet at its peak and that she
lacked experience, were otherwise full of praise. Mahler had at last found
his ideal dramatic soprano and went out of his way to help and cosset her
during these early days. His attitude to the other singers remained much as

before: praise when they performed well and carried out his wishes, fury when they didn't. At such times he would transfix them with his eyes and frighten them into submission! It was a common occurrence for him to leap up onto the stage and harangue them in public. Yet as always he helped those whom he considered were making an effort, both as a sympathetic conductor and with words of encouragement. The adulation that soloists such as Anna received from the public, constantly surrounded by their fans, contrasted with the post-performance loneliness that Mahler felt. Often he would leave the theatre alone to seek some light refreshment in a café, although he managed to counteract these feelings to a certain extent with the knowledge that each success might help to sow seeds for the future. During these months Weingartner became a regular visitor, and they spent a good deal of time discussing Mahler's compositions, including the as yet unfinished *Third Symphony*. Another frequent visitor was, of course, Anna, whom Weingartner considered to be a lovely girl with a voice to match!

Mahler spent hours with her nurturing her undoubted talent, whenever possible on a daily basis, not only coaching her as a singer but also working on her acting ability. He made her practise gestures and facial expressions in front of a mirror. The inevitable happened. Mildenburg became besotted with Mahler and as a result a stormy love affair began. Mahler sent notes to her dressing room, one being after her performance as *Aida* on the 21st of November conducted by Bruno Walter, when he praised her saying that she had sung beautifully, and that a certain lapse was not her fault but a consequence of Walter's conducting. He told her that he had breathed every breath with her, that he was very satisfied with her performance – it had been a great success. It was hardly surprising that it was not long before the relationship between the two began to cause problems. Mildenburg, by nature a passionate and potentially fiery character, a star thrust into the spotlight at such a young age, found it impossible to keep her relationship with Mahler under wraps. Inevitably the gossipmongers began to have a field day, much to his embarrassment. Not only did her loose tongue cause him more difficulties at the Opera, but also he was afraid that his sisters, especially the devoted Justi, would become upset. Consequently he deliberately began to give Anna the 'cold shoulder' in public, which upset her, and when she became upset, so did Mahler! As fond as he was of Anna, he began to become concerned that this affair would begin to affect his standing at the Opera as well as his dedication to the cause of music, which at this time, and in the years to come, would always remain his top priority. And yet, having found someone whom he loved so much, she fuelled the desire in him to succeed as a composer.

The most important event of the year as far as Mahler was concerned was almost upon him – the first complete performance of his *Second*

Symphony in Berlin, which was to take place on the 13th of December 1895. The Berlin impresario Hermann Wolff had had doubts concerning the financial viability of the symphony being performed, especially after the total lack of public interest when the first three movements had been played. Consequently Mahler had been forced to seek financial backing. Most of this came from his friend Hermann Behn and from Wilhelm Berkhan, also from Hamburg. Behn was particularly enthusiastic, and even paid for the engraving of his own piano transcription of the symphony.

Mahler set off for Berlin to supervise the final preparations for the concert. On the 8th of December he wrote a lengthy letter to Anna. His infatuation with her was typical of a man under extreme stress. He pleaded with her not to use cosmetics, either internal or external! To him she was perfection as she was. He told her how he and Behn had visited a foundry near Grunewald to acquire some bells for the end of the symphony, no orchestral ones being able to produce the sound he wanted. This brief excursion, only half an hour by train, had obviously lifted his spirits, for he described the beautiful snowy landscape sparkling in the sunshine and the kindly old white haired man at the foundry. The trip had been a welcome but only too brief escape from the selfishness and turmoil of city life. His letter becomes nothing less than a love letter, full of kisses, darlings and the like, and ends with 'Your Gustav'.

Mahler threw himself into the rehearsals with all his customary vigour, his enthusiasm typified by a member of the Berlin Philharmonic demolishing a drum after repeated requests from the conductor that it must be hit harder! This incident apart, the rehearsals went well and he was more than pleased with the musicians and the overall sound. He wrote to Anna on the 10th of December saying that the performers had been 'carried away' in their enthusiasm. They had supported him to the hilt, and through sheer effort and determination they had overcome all the difficulties of learning the new work.

Justi and Emma arrived to attend the concert, but Natalie was unable to as she was committed to perform in a concert in Vienna, much to Mahler's disappointment. Justi, having suffered the embarrassment of the acrimonious reception of the previous concerts of his music, was understandably anxious. Despite the success of the rehearsals, and proving Wolff's predictions to be correct, public interest in the première was negligible. Mahler, concerned that the concert hall might be half empty, set about arranging for complimentary tickets to be distributed to musicians and students studying at the Conservatory, as well as inviting all the friends and fellow composers he could think of. By doing so at least there would be an opposition to the traditionally hostile press. He had taken a huge gamble financially, but then his future as a composer was at stake.

The day of the concert arrived and Mahler was not a well man. He had arrived in Berlin with a persistent headache, and on this day of all days he was virtually struck down with a migraine, such was the stress he was under. Ashen and clearly ill, he managed to overcome the pain and threw himself wholeheartedly into the performance. His physical state must have sent waves of sympathy throughout the concert hall. Natalie recalled Justi's account of the reception of the new work. The enthusiasm and applause increased in volume with each movement, and Justi's overall reaction was that this enthusiastic response was for a 'once in a lifetime' event. Apparently grown men were seen in tears and young people emotionally threw their arms around each other, and yet the audience remained gripped by the drama and in anticipation until the moment came when the chorus entered, at which point there was an audible gasp of relief and wonder. Not surprisingly, after the gigantic and very moving ending of the symphony, the audience cheered and cheered, surrounding the shattered figure of Mahler who was near to collapse on the podium. Most who were present, including such eminent figures as Engelbert Humperdinck, Arthur Nikisch and Felix Weingartner, had to accept that Mahler was now a force to be reckoned with. Mahler, the composer, had made the breakthrough. Humperdinck afterwards wrote a letter offering his congratulations, which pleased him greatly. Bruno Walter later remembered the performance as being superb and quite overwhelming and despite the malice of some, the general impression was one of a great and very original composition. In his view, this performance marked the emergence of Mahler, the composer, and the sight of him on the podium, sick yet at the same time inspired, made Walter certain that his calling was to devote his career to the cause of Mahler's music. Walter referred to the *Second Symphony* as a 'tragic symphonic dream of man's fate and confident faith'.

However, most of the critics continued to attack Mahler, considering the new symphony to be bombastic, overblown 'Wagner', too long and banal, but there were some, such as Max Marschalk, who were more sympathetic. He wrote to Mahler saying that he supported the direction in which he was taking music. For this Mahler was deeply grateful, and he wrote to Marschalk on the 17th and 20th of December thanking him for his support, yet regretting the 'brick wall' of the critics in general. He told Marschalk that he had asked his publishers to send him a copy of the piano version of the symphony. So 1895 ended on an encouraging note and Mahler must have had great hopes for the future.

The Christmas period was very hectic with performances of *Oberon* and *Le Nozze di Figaro*, both featuring Anna von Mildenburg, Mahler managing to capture scattered moments of respite with his sisters. On the 30th of December he wrote to Friedrich Gernsheim, the Berlin chorus director who had supported him so steadfastly during the preparations for the première of the *Second Symphony*. He thanked him profusely for his support, and told him how glad he was to have such an ally. He also asked him to pass on his gratitude to the Stern Choral Society for their dedicated efforts. He obviously had plans to have Gernsheim's *Third Symphony* performed sometime in 1896, as he told him that it was on his desk in front of him as he wrote the letter. Mahler was very impressed with the work, calling it a masterpiece, but he mentioned that Pollini was seriously ill, and consequently it would be difficult to make any definite future plans. With Pollini not so involved in matters, life became somewhat easier for Mahler, although this did not change his desire to seek employment elsewhere, which of course included his long-term ambition – Vienna.

The stormy love-work relationship between Mahler and Anna continued apace, and rumours became rife after it was discovered that a rehearsal room they had been using had been left in a state of complete disarray, with scores and furniture scattered everywhere!

In the middle of January, Natalie, whose quartet had been booked for a concert in Hamburg, visited Mahler and his sisters. She was impressed by their home and the peaceful surroundings with views of meadows and orchards. It was during this stay in Hamburg that she heard Mahler and Bruno Walter playing Behn's piano duet version of the *Second Symphony* at Behn's home. The impact on her, even in this watered-down version, was tremendous, doubtless aided by a very over-the-top commentary by the composer.

Anna, launching herself into her new roll as *Norma* in the opera by Bellini, showed signs of jealousy with Natalie's repeat visit to Hamburg in February. Mahler must have welcomed Natalie's steady friendship to counteract the volatile Anna, and he begged her to try to be with him in Berlin the following month when the revised version of the *First Symphony*, as well as his *Lieder eines fahrenden Gesellen,* would be performed.

Mahler's love for Anna was becoming an obsession. His letters became more and more extraordinary; to him she was a 'girl to die for'! She was more important than anything else in his life (not true, of course). The purple prose flowed, but to a certain extent he exaggerated in his letters, partly due to an apparent cooling of the relationship on Anna's part. She knew what she was doing. Mahler had been the launch pad for her success, and now she was playing with him like a fish on a line.

Preparations for the forthcoming Berlin concert of Mahler's music were in the hands of Wolff once more, who, although not expecting financial rewards, must have felt that after the full performance of the *Second Symphony* Mahler might just turn out to be an important composer of the future. Nevertheless he showed little desire to be of practical help, and

Mahler himself was forced to carry out most of the background work. He and his sisters stayed at the Palace Hotel, and a number of friends arrived, including Natalie, the Behns and Foerster, personal support that was much needed.

Mahler worked himself to the bone, for he was determined that this concert should be a success, yet advance ticket sales were deplorable. Once again he had invested his own money to the tune of several thousand marks, yet advance takings were a paltry forty-eight! Complimentary tickets were again handed out to any who could attend, yet the hall remained half empty. Those who were present on the 16th of March gave him a reasonably warm reception, apart from the inevitable few, who had infiltrated with the one intention of booing and hissing.

The concert began with the first movement of the *Second Symphony*, followed by the *Lieder eines fahrenden Gesellen* and finally the revised version of the *First Symphony*, now without its *Titan* title and the *Blumine* movement. The performances went well, but Mahler was hurt by the poor public response, and he was fully aware that he still had not made the breakthrough that he longed for. One person who was present and deeply moved, was his former co-conductor from Leipzig, Arthur Nikisch, who had come to Berlin with the sole purpose of hearing Mahler's works. Mahler must have been both surprised and delighted, and Nikisch was so impressed that he promised that he would arrange for the first three movements of the *Second Symphony* to be played under his baton during the following winter season. Yet this was but one small crumb of comfort. In a reply to a letter from Annie Mincieux, a writer and portrait painter in Berlin who was a fervent supporter of his, Mahler said that if he were not such a stubborn person, determined to hold his head up despite all the problems and criticisms which constantly rained down upon him, he would rather lead the simple life of a farmer, close to nature. But he thanked her for her words of encouragement. He told her how pleased he was that another person was able to understand his 'experience', for the only experience he had grown used to was the pain from the thorns in his crown, the main ones being the majority of the critics who continued to pour scorn on him with comments such as 'pointless . . . vulgar . . . an endurance test'.

He told Natalie that people still had not tuned in to his way of thinking and consequently they were unable to understand his music. He was becoming convinced that he would not live to witness success. Natalie did her level best to console him, even bashfully kissing him good night after the inevitable post concert reception. But, upset as he was by the public's failure to accept his works, other problems were looming. Anna, through her loose tongue, had ensured that virtually everyone in Hamburg knew all about their relationship. Added to this embarrassment, Pollini had become very ill with heart problems, and Mahler began to feel increasingly insecure. It was time to take action. Contact was made with the Court Theatre in Schwerin and also with Vienna. The replies were much the same; they would not consider employing a Jew.

Depressed as he was, he nevertheless managed to lose himself in his *Third Symphony*. When Natalie arrived in April he was hard at work orchestrating the second movement, 'What the flowers in the meadow tell me'. Working on this movement in particular must have been a tonic for him, and he told Natalie that it was the most carefree music he had written. It was fresh, light and full of grace, yet it is overtaken by a storm with the flowers' very existence in peril. Typical Mahler, yet this movement brought back happy memories of Steinbach and his *Häuschen* in the flower-filled meadow by the Attersee. It must have acted like a tranquillizer, yet, as Natalie wrote in her recollections, Mahler always suffered agonies when he was writing music, agonies as well as great joy. Mahler referred to this as nervous excitement and it was always accompanied by unpredictable and often extreme changes of mood. He asked himself, why did he have to suffer in this way? Why did he have to subject himself to such a martyrdom? Yet there were lighter moments too, and with good weather they went for long walks together, Natalie doing her level best to act as a counsellor!

Pollini had managed to upset Bruno Walter on a number of occasions, and, despite the intendant's failing health, Walter had decided he wanted to move on from Hamburg. He realized that there were no real opportunities for promotion. Reluctantly, Mahler agreed with his decision and recommended the young conductor to Dr. Löwe of the Breslau Opera. Mahler looked upon Walter as a kindred spirit and one of the few who understood and genuinely supported him, and with Bruno Walter's adulation of him and his music, the two men were determined to remain in touch.

The 1895-1896 season drifted towards its close. It had been exhausting emotionally with the Berlin concerts of his works, his affair with Anna von Mildenburg and his ever-increasing desire to leave Hamburg. The personal insults he had received from Schwerin and Vienna over his being a Jew had hurt him deeply, but he would not be put off by such mindless comments. He contacted Rosa Papier, Anna's teacher in Vienna, and asked her to work behind the scenes on his behalf, naturally in the strictest confidence. The season ended with a sparkling performance of *La Traviata* and a Wagner festival, and Mahler was only too delighted to leave Hamburg on the 3rd of May for his summer break.

On his way to Steinbach he met up with critic and composer Max Marschalk in Berlin. He had been in regular contact with him over the previous weeks, determined to cultivate his support, likewise Marschalk with Mahler, for the former hoped that his own works would see the light of day under Mahler's baton. Mahler then visited Leipzig and Dresden to promote his *Second Symphony,* before arriving in Vienna on the 5th of June to meet Rosa Papier, as well as calling on Fritz Löhr and other friends.

He arrived in Steinbach in the pouring rain, and it rained and rained, but he had only one task on his mind: the completion of the *Third Symphony.* Calamity! He had forgotten to pack the drafts of the first movement, the very movement that he had to work on the most, and to make matters worse the rented piano had failed to arrive on time. Natalie, once more spending the summer with Mahler and his sisters, under the circumstances found him very difficult to live with. She described him as being like a grounded eagle with pinioned wings. Mahler wrote to Anna in a terrible state – would his summer be wasted? Having recovered his equilibrium, he contacted Hermann Behn who was on holiday, begging him to return to Hamburg to find the score. Behn replied, promising to have the manuscript sent on post haste.

Mahler did not waste these early days at Steinbach, for he set about writing music to another of the *Wunderhorn* poems, entitled 'Lob des hohen Verstandes' ('In praise of great understanding'), which to all intents and purposes was a tongue in cheek dig at his 'friends' the critics. Much to his relief the manuscript arrived safely on the 19th of June, the piano having been installed in the *Häuschen* by then. He wrote to Behn thanking him profusely, referring to the missing pages as the first movement's 'entire embryo'. In this letter he mentioned that Justi, Emma and Natalie were all very depressed, saying that they would not spend another summer in Steinbach. Their feelings were doubtless exacerbated by a combination of Mahler's frustration at having forgotten to pack the manuscript and the atrocious weather. But once the initial problems of the score and piano had been resolved, he became much more tolerant and easier to live with.

According to Natalie, keen as he was to complete the *Third Symphony,* he did not show his usual obsession with composing to the exclusion of everything else. Whereas previously his composing had been a whirlwind of creation, he was finding the *Third Symphony* more problematical. It was altogether more complex, more groundbreaking, so large that he told Natalie that he could have called it 'What the mountains tell me'. She wrote how he worked with incredible intensity from eight to twelve, followed by an hour to recover and wind down before being able to meet the others for lunch. The tension and Mahler's excitement began to affect Justi, Emma and Natalie who all had to escape at times to preserve their sanity, Natalie frequently to practise her viola.

In a letter to Anna, Mahler described his new symphony as a journey from inanimate nature all the way to God's love! He told Natalie that it was so much larger than life, such a gigantic work, that it made anything human belong to a pygmy world by comparison. It frightened him the way he was taking music and what the future for music might hold. It was almost as if he were being swept along, unable to escape, and he found it difficult to believe that he himself had written the score.

Mahler, naturally elated, completed the sketch of the first movement on the 28th of June. The struggle was over, although he told Natalie that he still had to work on it, for really it was still only a skeleton. He told her that it was the maddest thing he had ever written and had decided on the titles of 'Pan's Awakening', to be followed by 'Summer Marches in'. It was overwhelming, gigantic and surely no one would have the courage to perform it during his lifetime, and anyway he would be the only person able to conduct it. How wrong he was! Once more his creativity had come to the boil, the new symphony sweeping him along like a tidal wave. He became totally preoccupied and was easily irritated by the smallest of distractions. Natalie recalled living with him at such times was extremely wearing, a bit like being in a little boat tossed about by the waves. They continued to walk, cycle and discuss his work, but when they were out he would frequently lose himself in his thoughts, always with a notebook at hand to scribble down ideas no matter where he was. Indeed he considered that these notes made on the move included some of his best ideas.

He remarked to Natalie that he hoped to goodness that he would know when his compositions began to weaken – his greatest nightmare – for one bad one would destroy the rest. He sincerely hoped that he would end his days at the height of his powers. No matter what the state of a composition, clarity was of the essence. Every instrument must be heard so must be used in a manner that would promote its own special qualities. He had learnt his lesson from his earlier compositions, such as the *First Symphony*, which he had had to re-score, and indeed he would have to do the same with future works, including the *Fifth Symphony*. A great deal of extra work was needed to achieve this clarity, but if a composition was worth creating, then it was also worth the extra effort. According to Natalie, his rule was; 'Whatever you do, do it as well as you can!'

On the 2nd of July, he had written to Bruno Walter inviting him to stay in Steinbach in the middle of the same month, by which time he must have hoped that work on the symphony would be nearly finished. With the orchestration nearing completion, and the weather improved, he decided to pay his annual visit to Ischl to visit Brahms. He set off on his bicycle and found the old man sad and ill. He had recently attended the funeral of his much loved friend Clara Schumann, and he himself was terminally ill with liver cancer. Nevertheless, he managed to lift himself from the gloom that had enveloped him and welcomed his guest. He showed considerable interest in the way his career was developing and in his music. They went for a short walk, deeply discussing the future of music. They came to a bridge over a stream and paused to look at the foaming water. Brahms, the traditionalist, ever more so in his old age, voiced displeasure at the way music was going. Mahler pointed at the eddies in the water as they passed beneath them, turned to Brahms and asked him, smiling, 'Which is the final one?' Mahler must have been aware of the fact that this was to be their last meeting.

Following a brief visit to Salzburg, where he met the influential journalist Siegmund Singer, he headed for Aussee to meet a former Budapest colleague, the Hungarian composer Ödön Mihalovich. The main reason for these meetings was to seek their support in his quest for a move to the Vienna Hofoper. He wrote to Anna, telling her about these visits and that he had been suffering from severe migraines.

Mahler returned to Steinbach on the 16th of July, the day before Bruno Walter's visit. The weather was superb, and Walter remembered how he arrived by steamer to be met by Mahler at the landing stage, his host insisting on carrying his bag. When Walter stopped to look up in awe at the Höllengebirge mountains towering above him Mahler told him not to bother to look for he had already composed them in his symphony!

Bruno Walter found Mahler to be very relaxed, at one with his surroundings and enjoying good food, especially tasty sweets. He took his young visitor to the *Häuschen*, and Walter recollected how when the door was opened, his head was showered with beetles!

One of Mahler's literary joys at that time was Cervantes' *Don Quixote*. He found it very moving, yet at the same time he thought the goings on between the Don and his servant hilariously funny. Mahler had befriended two kittens and he delighted in watching them at play. When he went for short walks he would take them with him in his pockets, stopping every now and then to watch them play, but his fascination ceased quite suddenly when he discovered them consuming a bird.

On the 25th of July Natalie found Mahler to be particularly cheerful as he emerged from the *Häuschen* – the end of his travails was nigh. He compared the feeling to that experienced by a swimmer swimming to a distant shore. At first nothing but water, half way across and still no sight of the end, but quite suddenly there was the shore and the lapping waves. (Natalie must have known the feeling well after their swim across the Attersee the previous year). Then on the 28th she reported that the *Third Symphony* was finished. On her return from a cycle ride she met Mahler who told her that he was very happy with his work, although there would inevitably have to be some tidying up. She was particularly moved when she discovered that he had placed the sketches for the first movement on her table with a note addressed to 'my dear friend Natalie'. He described the work as a seed grown into a tree, healthy and fully developed and bearing fruit.

Third Symphony, in D minor
(In six movements, for alto, children's and women's choirs and orchestra)

The final choice of titles for the six movements were as follows:

> Part One
> Pan awakens: Summer marches in
> Part Two
> What the flowers in the meadow tell me.
> What the creatures of the forest tell me.
> What man tells me.
> What the angels tell me.
> What love tells me.

However, on publication these titles were dropped.

At first Mahler had intended a seventh movement, the *Wunderhorn* song, *'Das himmlische Leben'* (The Heavenly Life). This song had been the original 'seed which grew into the tree', and it is easy to see why he wanted to use it to end the symphony, but after such a massive work and a very long and moving sixth movement, it would have been an anti-climax. (He later used it as the Finale of his *Fourth Symphony*).

First Movement: Kräftig, entschieden
(vigorous, resolute)

This first movement is quite extraordinary, especially considering the time when it was written. At around forty minutes, it is by itself longer than many symphonies and indeed the longest orchestral movement Mahler would compose. Although he had referred to it as 'the maddest thing' he had written, but for maddest perhaps we should read most courageous. It was the last movement of the symphony to be composed. Following the emotion filled *Second Symphony*, his original plan had been that it should be filled with humorous ideas, but on its completion little humour remained. The proportions had grown to such an extent that he had almost lost control of the movement.

In a manner similar to the opening of the *Second Symphony*, the listener is thrown straight into the drama with an opening march theme for eight horns, not dissimilar to the finales of Brahms's *First* and Beethoven's *Ninth* (in homage to Beethoven and the ailing Brahms?). The movement depicts the great battle between Pan, the Greek God of the forests, fields and fertility, who represents summer, for Mahler the season of creation, and winter. His first thoughts had been centred around Dionysus, whose labels were similar to Pan's, being the God of fruitfulness and vegetation, especially of the vine, his other name being Bacchus. However Mahler decided that he preferred the more down to earth nature of Pan, finding what he represented to be closer to his own nature. Musically the movement is also a battle between major and minor, with brass and percussion to the fore, and as his title suggested, summer is victorious with Pan marching in. The movement culminates in a brief almost Bacchanalian celebration of new life over the frozen gloom of winter. Mahler threw caution to the wind in a way that brought the comment from the composer Ernst Křenek that it was almost surrealist. It was experimental, wild and very daring for its time. It grabs the listener by the lapels and will not let go until the conflict has been resolved. It is therefore no wonder that Mahler had indeed considered it to be the maddest thing he had written.

Second movement: Tempo di Menuetto. Sehr mässig.
(very moderately)

After the massive first movement, what could follow? Typically for Mahler the answer was something completely different! The title, 'What the flowers in the meadow tell me', exactly sums up the mood of this short movement, about a quarter the length of the first. Inspired by the flower-filled meadow in which his *Häuschen* stood, it is romantic, nostalgic, a gentle ländler. There is an icy blast in the middle when the peaceful scene becomes transformed by dark, heavy skies and the flowers bend in the storm, but the storm is short lived and the opening spirit of the movement is restored. Like the second movement of the *Second Symphony*, it immediately won favour and was performed out of context on a number of occasions, including under Weingartner and Nikisch. Mahler did not approve of this practice, but he did not fight against it either for at least his music was being heard.

Third movement: Comodo, Scherzando, ohne Hast.
(without haste)

For this beautifully descriptive music of the animals of the forest, he used material from one of his early songs, *Ablösung im Sommer*, one of the *Lieder und Gesänge*, which tells the tale of the death of the spring cuckoo and how the summer nightingale will take his place. Out of the 'forest murmurs' comes the distant sound (off stage) of a post-horn, the introduction of man into the animal world. The effect is magical; doubtless a nostalgic memory from his childhood and the bugle calls from the barracks. At first it is like a distant dream with no threat to the natural world, but the peace of the forest is then shattered – man has arrived. Mahler, as always, gives clear directions in the score in order to achieve his desired, almost theatrical effect of the stagecoach emerging from the distance, rushing forwards and then receding.

Fourth movement: Sehr langsam, misterioso.
(very slow, mysterious)

This is the pivotal movement. It was Mahler's intention for the last three movements (4,5 and 6) to be played without any pauses, and whereas the first three deal with the natural order of things, humanity has now arrived and with it the spiritual quest. In a similar fashion to the fourth movement ('Urlicht') of the Second Symphony, so this one introduces the human voice. The words are by Nietzsche from his poem Also sprach Zarathustra, 'O Mensch! Gib Acht!'. The alto sings of the night, warning man to take heed. She sings of heartache and suffering and how they must be overcome, joy alone being preserved for eternity. After the wildness of the first movement, the lightness of the second, the descriptive writing of the third, we now encounter an altogether more sombre mood that hangs like a heavy cloud until, at the very end, a ray of sunshine penetrates the gloom with the words, 'All joys search for eternity!'

Fifth movement: Lustig im Tempo und keck im Ausdruck.
(cheerful in tempo and bold in expression)

For this movement, Mahler turned to one of his Wunderhorn songs, Es sungen drei Engel (Three Angels sang). It is a short, light movement, flowing straight out of the fourth, and is for alto solo and a double chorus of women and children. It lasts for approximately four minutes and has frequently caused problems for impresarios, the choruses having to sit patiently through at least an hour and a quarter before being asked to sing a mere four minutes in total! It tells of the disciples at the Last Supper, of forgiveness and heavenly joy. It comes as a breath of fresh air, with the children imitating the sound of chiming bells.

Sixth movement: Langsam, ruhevoll, empfunden.
(slow, tranquil, with feeling)

One of the unusual characteristics of the final movement is that Mahler wrote a purely orchestral slow movement to end his mammoth symphony.

He told Natalie that his decision to do this, despite not being normal practice, was that to him the *Adagio* was a 'higher form'. Tchaikovsky's *Pathétique Symphony* was another case in point, composed three years before Mahler's *Third*, although totally different in concept. To achieve the aura he was seeking, one of awe, wonder and reverence, spectacle would have been completely wrong. After all, Mahler himself said that the title 'What love tells me' could almost be 'What God tells me', for God and love are indivisible.

A forerunner of the final movement of the *Ninth*, this great *Adagio* is one of the most beautiful and heartfelt of all Mahler's creations. The mood is reminiscent of Wagner's *Parsifal*, totally free of schmaltz, just great and moving nobility as Mahler pays homage to the wonders of the natural world. It is a call to prayer, a benediction, it is 'What love tells me'. The listener is gently carried forward, caressed and drawn into this sublime aura of love. Eventually the movement builds to an almost orgasmic climax at 24 in the score, out of which serenity returns. This section looks forward to the final part of the last movement of the unfinished *Tenth*. The symphony ends in a mood of complete optimism, and a long, sustained chord, punctuated by the timpani, declares 'Love is victorious! Doubt is banished'.

Mahler's music had developed into music of contrasts on two particular levels. The lower one, the earth-bound, had become a blend of the wild, frequently jarring, and the music of every day that included ländler and bugle calls. The transcendent or 'higher music' embraces the searching soul: a synthesis of 'being'. It was no wonder that his detractors accused him of eclecticism. His symphonic worlds are built from these building blocks, and together with his experimentation with instruments both traditional and new, he created the 'Mahler sound'.

Before Bruno Walter's departure from Steinbach, Mahler played him the completed *Third Symphony*. Even hearing it being played on the baby grand in the *Häuschen*, Walter was staggered. To him it was a shattering musical experience, and he was awestruck by its grandeur and the gamut of the many facets of nature. Yet it was not merely nature, *Naturlaut*, as Mahler called it, depicted in the music, but deeply spiritual and a window into its creator's soul. It had been a summer to remember for the young conductor. He felt greatly privileged and his friendship with him had become even stronger. He had also developed a special affection for Mahler's younger sister, Emma!

And so summer was near its end, and Mahler, overwhelmed by his own creation and feeling a certain emptiness now that his *Third* was finished, was filled with gloom at the prospect of yet another season at the Hamburg Opera. Following visits to Siegfried Lipiner in Berchtesgaden and Bayreuth for a performance of Wagner's *Ring*, it was time to say good-bye to Steinbach. The inn had been sold. The new owners had increased the price for their rooms to such an extent that he felt unable to book for the summer of 1897. Despite its drawbacks of accommodation, climate and extraneous noises, he had grown fond of Steinbach and his *Häuschen* – the place of such inspiration. The knowledge that he would not be able to return added to his despondency. Before leaving he went for one final walk, and looking down at the *Häuschen* and the Attersee, the tears began to flow.

En route to Hamburg, he visited Rosa Papier in Vienna to further his case for a post at the Hofoper. Apparently they were still not well disposed to the idea of appointing a Jew, but this was not only due to anti-Semitism. The authorities were simply unaccustomed to appointing anyone who was not a member of the State religion, namely Roman Catholicism. He turned to Munich, but the reaction there was the same. Would there be no escape? Pollini was still in harness, and relations between the two men could only worsen. On his return, Mahler discovered that Pollini had appointed Rudolf Krzyżanowski as an assistant conductor, Mahler's friend from his student days. This was good in one respect, for every friend was more than welcome, but his arrival was liable to cause upsets in the prevailing poisonous atmosphere. Pollini's plan was to give Krzyżanowski many of the operas particularly dear to Mahler, such as *Tristan und Isolde* and *Die Meistersinger*. Not only that, Pollini also intended foisting onto Mahler works that he knew full well he had little time for. If their friendship became too obvious, Krzyżanowski might well be tarred with the same brush as Mahler. Katharina Klafsky and her husband, the conductor Otto Lohse, had returned from America in time for the new season.

Despite his worsening situation at the Hamburg Opera, Mahler, more mature and shrewd in his dealings with Pollini and his shenanigans, was not going to give in. He was not prepared to leave Hamburg until a suitable alternative came his way, preferably Vienna, which, regardless of the negative reactions up until then, remained his goal. Standards at the Vienna Opera had been in decline for some time, and following the departure of director Franz Jauner in 1880, the post being temporarily filled by Dingelstedt, the authorities were urgently seeking a man of quality to take over the reins. During these troubled times, one man provided some continuity, Hans Richter, a much respected conductor. Jauner's successor was Wilhelm Jahn, well known as both a musician and conductor of quality. Friction between Richter and Jahn was eagerly anticipated by the Vienna coffee house gossips, fanned by the press. The two men, however, walked more or less in tandem, Jahn giving Richter the Philharmonic concerts, while he himself concentrated on the Opera.

Mahler's season began with *Tannhäuser*, with Katharina Klafsky and Anna von Mildenburg in the cast. Krzyżanowski's season started with *Tristan und Isolde*, starring his wife, Ida Doxat. Mahler continued with *Figaro*, followed by *Fidelio*, again with Klafsky in the role of Leonore. A few days later, on the 29th of September, Klafsky suffered a fatal heart attack in her sleep. Her popularity was underlined by the mass grief that followed her demise, her funeral taking on the proportions of a state occasion.

News reached Mahler that Bruno Walter was having a difficult time in his job in Breslau. Apparently he had the feeling that he was in danger of being elbowed out by the conductor Leopold Weintraub, the instigator of much ill feeling. On the 12th of September Mahler wrote to Walter telling him to take courage and not to give in, but to remain pleasant to everyone. However, if things became impossibly difficult, not to hesitate to write and he would do his best to exercise his influence behind the scenes. Mahler did write a letter to Theodor Löwe telling the Direktor of Breslau that Weintraub was worth less than one of his young conductor friend's nail clippings! This letter was not actually posted, so presumably the situation had eased. Also in September, Mahler wrote to Max Marschalk, informing him that the score of the latter's opera, *Lobentanz*, had arrived safely, that he liked it and looked forward to it being produced.

Natalie, who stayed with Mahler in Hamburg during September and October, wrote of his daily routine: up at 7 a.m., cold shower and then breakfast on his own – a time of quiet and no distractions that he valued greatly. He would read poetry and literature by authors such as Goethe and Nietzsche, and then concentrate on his own work. It was during Natalie's stay that Mahler completed the fair copy of the first movement of the *Third Symphony* (the manuscript bears the date 7th of October 1896). Following his work session, it was off to the Opera, a brisk walk of about forty-five minutes. Her account of Mahler at rehearsals is quite amusing. He remained a hard taskmaster. He compared himself to an animal tamer, whipping his musicians to ever-higher standards and greater concentration, treating them harshly whenever 'the beast of impotence and laziness lifts its ugly head!' Despite his feelings about the Hamburg Opera, he was nevertheless determined to keep up and if possible improve standards, and thereby his reputation, for he knew that any slacking on his part might jeopardize his plans for the future. He continued to wait for '*die Berufung zum Gott der südlichen Zonen*' ('the call of the god of the southern regions'). Then it was home for a late lunch, a siesta, a visit to his copyist Otto Weidig, and a walk before returning to the Opera for the evening performance. Walking for Mahler was so important, not only for the exercise, but to clear his mind, to focus on the creative activities of the day.

She described him as being very untidy, both of his person and belongings, and his room was usually a disaster area. This made a surprising contrast to his meticulous approach to music and the Opera, but then he was completely focused on music, almost possessing tunnel vision. When criticized over this, his reply was that it was his nature and that if his nature had been different he would not have been capable of writing his symphonies! Natalie commented on his swings of mood from an extrovert, bubbling excitement to introverted silence, from happiness to gloom. Despite these mood changes, he would always remain loyal to his friends, who knew that they could trust him in every way.

One of the operas that Natalie went to see was *Carmen*, which she had already been to twice before and loved. However, she told Mahler that it was a work she did not want to hear too often, lest she became tired of it. Mahler, who also loved the opera, told her that this would be highly unlikely because the orchestration was so superb, everything written with clarity in mind – Mahler's own principle. Every time he conducted it he discovered something new in Bizet's superb scoring with its delicacy and clarity and his experimentation creating new sounds. He foretold that this was the path music would take, rather than the impressionism of composers such as Claude Debussy. He regarded *Carmen* as one of the great operas, although perhaps not quite in the same league as those by Wagner, Mozart and Beethoven's *Fidelio*. While walking and talking with Foerster, the latter suggested that Beethoven's opera was greater than those of Wagner. Mahler agreed with him, saying that two great minds think alike, although this was probably said with his tongue in his cheek.

One evening, before Natalie left Hamburg, he played her the completed first movement of the *Third Symphony*. She had been longing to hear it and she was suitably astonished, Mahler quite beside himself with excitement as he played.

The first public performance of part of the *Third Symphony* took place on the 9th of November when Arthur Nikisch conducted the second movement, the *Blumenstück*, or 'What the Flowers of the Meadow tell me', in Berlin. It was greeted with great enthusiasm and even such die-hards as the critic Sittard could do nothing but praise Mahler. Despite his dislike of individual movements from his symphonies being performed in isolation, he was obviously delighted – for once he had managed to get the critics ('curs' as he had called them in a letter to Bruno Walter) onto his side. Suddenly Mahler the composer had become hot news and he was asked to provide a biographical outline by several writers for articles to be written about him. Following this success, Nikisch arranged for a further performance of the *Blumenstück* in Leipzig, with Mahler being invited to conduct the first three movements of his *Second Symphony*. He found the orchestra to be very sub-standard and their attitude pitiful. The acclamations following the Berlin concert were not to be repeated. Quite to the contrary – Leipzig did not want to know. Mahler, depressed, wrote to Marschalk saying that his work at the opera gave him less time to compose than one of the 'matadors' of the concert hall. He could only write music on 'red letter' days, when all emotional experiences would stream out in concentrated form into the new work he was composing.

Meanwhile, his friends Rosa Papier, Siegfried Lipiner and Ödön Mihalovich, the Hungarian composer, had been busy supporting his cause for appointment to the Hofoper. Lipiner, who held the important position of Librarian of the Austrian Parliament, had both visited and written to the management of the Court Theatre praising Mahler and discounting rumours concerning his suitability. Word had spread that his temperament was a problem. Lipiner pointed out in no uncertain terms that he was dedicated, passionate about music and had great self-control. Another ally of Mahler's was Count Albert Apponyi, ever grateful for his sterling work at the Budapest Opera. In the New Year, Apponyi, aware that the Vienna Opera was facing a crisis over the health of the incumbent conductor and director, Wilhelm Jahn, wrote to Vienna highly recommending Mahler. Jahn was suffering from an eye complaint, which made conducting increasingly difficult. In his letter Count Apponyi stated that Mahler's work at the Budapest Opera had been quite exceptional. He made it clear that it was due to the incompetence of Count Géza von Zichy, that Budapest had lost a director who had managed to pick up the Budapest Opera, lifting it to new heights both artistically and financially. He praised Mahler's excellence in all fields of opera production, and suggested that an approach should be made to Brahms, asking the old man about the performance of *Don Giovanni* that he had attended, conducted by Mahler on the 16th of December 1890. He concluded that the Vienna Court Opera would be very fortunate if it managed to gain the services of such a man. Bezecny was very impressed, and presumably both Prince Rudolf Liechtenstein, the Lord Chamberlain, and Prince Alfred Montenuovo, the chief administrator of the Opera, were also shown the letter. On the other hand, Cosima Wagner, ever the anti-Semite, did her level best to put a spoke in the wheel – a Jew at the Vienna Opera? Never! Her intolerant attitude to his candidature was in complete contrast to her views of him as a conductor of Wagner's music, for as such she held him in the highest regard, but her anti-Semitism prevented her from ever inviting him to conduct at Bayreuth. She, as did Princess Metternich, backed Felix Mottl, and even Ernst von Schuch of Dresden would have been preferable. Hans Richter was also against Mahler being appointed.

Despite all the controversy, Bezecny was determined to acquire Mahler's services, for he knew of no other who would be better suited to the unenviable task of revitalizing the Vienna Court Opera. The odds were beginning to swing in Mahler's favour. One more person had to be won over, the man he hoped to replace – Jahn. The opportunity arose when three movements of Mahler's *Second Symphony* were performed in Dresden under Ernst von Schuch. Jahn attended the concert, and the audience, which included King Albert of Saxony, and nearly all of the critics were very enthusiastic. Mahler met Jahn, who promised to consider supporting his application, should he have to resign because of his eyesight, which of course was inevitable. Even so, at this juncture, Jahn was under the impression that, should Mahler be appointed, he would become an assistant conductor on a temporary basis until his eyesight improved. Another, and very influential supporter to arise, was the renowned critic Eduard Hanslick.

On his return from Leipzig, Mahler discovered that the stage manager, Franz Bittong, Pollini's puppet, had caused complete chaos with the rehearsal schedules, with singers being required to attend rehearsals of different operas at the same time. Mahler took immediate steps to overrule Bittong, who moaned that he had only been carrying out orders, and wrote a very blunt letter to Pollini pointing out the inadequacies of his stage manager. It was time for Mahler to make a more formal approach to Vienna. He contacted the Intendant, Bezecny, formally applying for the post of conductor at the Vienna Court Opera, at the same time saying that he had become a Catholic before leaving Budapest – not true, although he had set the wheels in motion. He was in fact baptized on the 23rd of February 1897.

To all intents and purposes, Mahler had been engineering a *coup d'état*, manipulating his contacts, whether politicians, journalists, artists, aristocrats or former employers and colleagues. Aside from his ambitions, he did harbour concern over taking up a conductor's post in Vienna. In a letter to Arthur Seidl on the 12th of February he wrote that he had heard that the appointment lay between Felix Mottl, then in Munich, and himself. His main worry was that having shouldered the immense responsibility and workload at the Hofoper, his main aim in life, that of composing, might be forced to one side. Nevertheless, he had made up his mind to leave Hamburg no matter what, and he asked to be released from his contract before a planned tour in March that would include a visit to Russia. Pollini had made his feelings towards Mahler quite clear to Julius Steinberg, a critic from Prague. He had asked him to help engineer his departure, for he was no longer sure who was in charge. His resignation was therefore accepted, although initially it would not be effective until May. Upon Mahler's recommendation, Anna had gone to Bayreuth to study the role of Kundry in Wagner's *Parsifal* with Cosima Wagner for the forthcoming Bayreuth Festival. Mahler wrote to her, telling her that she would soon be standing on the stage of Bayreuth, home of one of the greatest spirits in man's history.

Mahler, presumably feeling guilty that he had been out of touch with Richard Strauss for quite a while, sent him a copy of the full vocal score of the *Second* Symphony, together with Hermann Behn's piano arrangement. On the 22nd of February, Strauss replied thanking him, addressing him as '*Mein lieber Freund*', saying that he would love to perform the work and praising the piano version. He ended his 'thank you' by saying that he had thought Mahler had forgotten all about him, calling himself the 'first Mahlerian'. Before the March tour Mahler had planned to attend a performance of the second, third and sixth movements of his *Third Symphony*, to be played by the Königliche Kapelle Orchester in Berlin under their conductor, Felix Weingartner, who had been persuaded by Hermann Behn to conduct the movements. Excited by the prospect, Mahler wrote to influential friends such as Max Marschalk, Arnold Berliner and Arthur Seidl telling them the news and obviously hoping that they would attend. Seidl, however, replied that regretfully he would not be able to. In a long letter to him, Mahler declared his happiness at having a critic of his standing as an ally, and how sad he was that he would not be present at the première of the three movements of the *Third*.

The concert took place on the 9th of March. After the success of the première of his *Second Symphony* in the same city, he expected a similar warm reception for the *Third*, but the première of the *Second* nearly two years previously had been with the Berlin Philharmonic and before a largely invited audience. The *Blumenstück* was given good applause, not surprisingly since it had already received virtually unanimous praise. But then the audience split into the usual two factions, the rowdiness becoming almost a mêlée. Mahler must have been reminded of the première of his *First Symphony*. This, too, was a disaster, and he was only too glad to leave Berlin for Moscow.

In the train, he wrote to Anna telling her about the uproar in the audience, which had reached its climax when Weingartner had insisted on him taking a bow! He told her that the 'enemy' had won, Justi was distraught and he fully expected the press to have a field day. He wrote to Max Marschalk, begging him to reply saying that he at least understood his music. He added that he found Moscow quite beautiful – perhaps, he thought, life had become a dream and he would wake up on Mars! Mahler was unwell, and he told Anna that he had not eaten for two days, for every time he tried to eat his stomach rejected the food. This illness, accompanied by the inevitable migraine, was probably post-traumatic stress brought on by the recent Berlin *débâcle*, and he recovered to appreciate the beauty of snow-clad Moscow, the sleighs in the streets where every other building appeared to be a church, with passers-by beating their breasts and crossing themselves as they passed each one. Nikisch arrived in the city to prepare for a forthcoming concert, and although Mahler was delighted to see him, his arrival proved to be a problem. The Moscow public had grown to like Nikisch and it was his concert that they were looking forward to. Mahler's concert, which included Beethoven's *Fifth Symphony,* as well as works by Wagner, Gounod and Chopin, was not a great success either with the audience or with the critics, who questioned his tempi and called his conducting theatrical. He was glad to leave, and set off for Munich where he was due to conduct two concerts with the Kaim Orchestra.

Munich was a possible alternative to Vienna, should his application there fall through. He found the orchestra to be very receptive to his demands and he took great pleasure in working with them. However, his interpretation of Beethoven's *Fifth Symphony* again caused controversy. He was accused of being anti-traditionalist, especially with his unusual tempi and his tinkering with the instrumentation in the last movement.

The final engagement of his tour was Budapest, where he was greeted as a returning hero! The concert on the 31st of March again included Beethoven's *Fifth*, but Budapest's audience and critics voiced their approval, as they did for the *Blumenstück*. Mahler was lauded, presented with laurel wreaths and was guest of honour at a banquet after the concert. The city knew what it had lost when Mahler had been virtually forced to leave.

In Vienna there had been a flurry of activity with Jahn's inevitable departure looming over the horizon. Mahler had been summoned to meet Bezecny on the 3rd of April – his dream was about to come true. Ferdinand Pfohl, the music critic of the *Hamburger Nachrichten*, remembered meeting Mahler shortly after he had heard that Bezecny wanted to see him in Vienna. Ludwig Karpath met Mahler outside the Hamburg Opera, congratulated him warmly, and, not knowing that Mahler had already been received into the Roman Catholic Church, expressed his surprise that he had been accepted for the post. Mahler replied that by converting to the Catholic faith he had merely changed his coat. In other words, it was simply a conversion of convenience and he remained the same person inside.

The following day, he signed a contract accepting the post of conductor at the Vienna Court Opera, at first for one year, at a salary of 5,000 florins. He wrote to Karpath thanking him for his help behind the scenes, at the same time voicing his concern over the news that Bezecny had decided to resign – would the anti-Semitic press focus on his appointment? The critics did indeed sharpen their knives, spreading rumours that Mahler would instigate a thorough shake-up of staff at the Hofoper. He described the situation in another letter to Karpath as 'a wasps' nest'. Life in Vienna would be an almighty struggle, at least to begin with, but he was prepared to take the bull by the horns and win! He told Fritz Löhr that he fully expected to be led a dance in Vienna, but stated that he intended to call the tune. Mahler's return to his spiritual home, for him spiritual both as a man and as a musician, was about to take place.

At his farewell concert in Hamburg on the 24th of April, he conducted *Fidelio*, with Anna as Leonore, and Beethoven's *Third Symphony*. The audience went wild. A succession of presentations of laurel wreaths followed, and he thanked all those who had stood by him during his time in Hamburg. It was an emotional farewell, not least from Anna von Mildenburg, though they would meet again.

Chapter 7

Vienna . . . Part One

MAHLER HAD ALMOST achieved his goal. Vienna had beckoned, but initially he would be employed solely as an assistant conductor. Ever since his student days he had wanted to return to the cultural capital of Europe, but he was under no illusions as to the stony path that lay ahead. He would have to combat the anti-Semitic element of the press, typified by an article in the *Reichpost* on the 14th of April 1897. Although saying that he would have to be given the opportunity to succeed, it referred to him as the Jew-boy, and that the Jewish press now had a champion. The article went on to question whether his podium antics could justify the high claims made by the Semitic press. And yet Vienna was not entirely an anti-Semitic city. Emperor Franz Joseph and most of the royal family were tolerant of all communities in the very cosmopolitan capital of the Austrian Empire. The Emperor himself left the running of the Hofoper in the hands of Prince Rudolf Liechtenstein, the Lord Chamberlain, who in turn passed on the responsibility for the administration of the Vienna Opera to Prince Alfred Montenuovo, a no-nonsense and efficient organiser whom Mahler grew to respect, and who in turn became a staunch supporter of his.

The battle lines were drawn up, and Mahler, in a letter to Arnold Berliner on the 22nd of April, foresaw the conflicts that lay ahead, expecting many months of hostility from those who would not or could not co-operate. He pointed a finger at Hans Richter whom he suspected of stirring up trouble.

An important occasion in the world of art had taken place on the 3rd of April when the Society of Austrian Artists (*Vereinigung Bildender Künstler Österreichs*, which became known as the Vienna 'Secession') met and appointed Gustav Klimt as its president. Among those elected onto the executive committee were the artists Carl Moll and Koloman Moser (well known as the designer of many of Austria's postage stamps during the early part of the twentieth century). Another important member of the Secession was Alfred Roller, who became famous as an innovative stage designer. There was also the writer Hermann Bahr, an acquaintance from Mahler's time as a student, although they had never become close friends, and who later married Anna von Mildenburg. All these men were to become involved in the Mahler story. The Secessionist movement aimed at revitalising the visual arts with fresh ideas – almost parallel to Mahler's attitude to music – and to shake off the dust of the previous decades. Their motto was, 'For each Age its Art, to Art its Freedom'. The cultural revolution of Vienna was about to take wing.

Fin de Siècle Vienna was a city of contradictions. Although devoted to the arts, it was a city of intrigues, of gossips in the coffee houses, light-hearted yet deep-down full of spite. The Empire had an aging Emperor, and, at the same time, a young revolutionary spirit. Politics was in a state of turmoil. The two main political parties were the right wing Christian Democrats, led enthusiastically by Karl Lueger, the city's mayor and an anti-Semite who would later impress a young man by the name of Adolf Hitler. The left wing Social Democrats were led by Victor Adler, Mahler's friend from his student days. The Social Democrats were the people's party, organising May Day parades through the city that usually culminated in massed gatherings in the city's main park, the Prater. It was only thanks to Montenuovo that Mahler survived. In the past, the emperor and the nobility in general had taken pride in supporting and furthering the ambitions of great composers such as Haydn and Beethoven – what greater kudos than to stage a première of work by such eminent artists in one's palace! Those days had gone. Even Wagner, having landed himself in financial difficulties, had been forced to flee Vienna dressed as a woman in order to escape imprisonment. As a result the city lost the opportunity to stage the première of *Tristan und Isolde*.

Largely taking the place of the nobility's influence in the arts were the Jews, always eager to promote their patriotic fervour in the capital. The proportion of Jews in the city was around ten per cent, yet twenty-five per cent of university students were Jewish. Some prominent critics and musicians were too, including Eduard Hanslick (by birth, although brought up a Catholic) and Julius Korngold, his successor as chief music critic of the *Neue Freie Presse*. There was Max Graf, the music historian, Guido Adler, a musicologist of renown, the young composers Arnold Schoenberg, Alexander von Zemlinsky and Karl Goldmark, the great author and librettist Hugo von Hofmannstal, who would write the libretti of several of Richard Strauss's operas, including *Elektra, Der Rosenkavalier, Ariadne auf Naxos* and *Die Frau ohne Schatten,* and the concertmaster of the Vienna Philharmonic, Arnold Rosé, later to marry Justi and whose daughter was to die in a concentration camp during the Second World War.

Arnold Rosé (né Rosenblum) was born in Jassy in what is now Romania. He was one of four brothers who had all shown an aptitude for music at an early age, which resulted in the family moving to Vienna so that they could receive a music education of the highest order. In 1881, at just eighteen years of age, he was appointed concertmaster of the Vienna Philharmonic, a position he was to hold for fifty-five years. In 1882 he founded what was to become the renowned Rosé Quartet. So Mahler, the Jew turned Catholic, was to be in good company. The problems were his position and the machinations of the anti-Semitic section of the press. But for the first time in his career, he found himself moving to a new post in a city where he already had many friends and acquaintances. He could count on their support and was guaranteed a social life with as many invitations as he would care to accept.

For some years, Vienna had had to cope with mass immigration, mostly from the over-populated areas of Moravia and Southern Bohemia, Mahler's own region. Since he had arrived in Vienna as a student in 1875, the population had almost doubled to over 1,718,000. Housing, unemployment and poverty had become serious problems, and Vienna had become a city of haves and have-nots. The years of traditional, comfortable, staid living were rapidly coming to an end – revolution was in the air, both political and artistic, the latter typified by the founding of the Secession.

Mahler arrived in Vienna on the 27th of April 1897, and booked into the Hotel Bristol, his temporary abode until he could find a suitable place of his own. He paid courtesy visits to Bezecny, the intendant of the Opera, as well as Eduard Wlassack, a close friend of Rosa Papier's and a very influential person behind the scenes at the Hofoper. On the evening of his arrival he was the chief guest at a dinner party organised by Rosa Papier, his loyal supporter and teacher of Anna von Mildenburg. Rosa had taken part in a performance of Mendelssohn's *St. Paul* under the composer's baton during his time at Kassel.

Having survived the initial onslaught of inquisitive reporters, and after visiting as many people of influence as time would permit, Mahler, the new assistant conductor at the Court Opera, set to work. Hans Richter had buried his hatchet and was amiable towards the thirty-seven year old newcomer. Mahler wrote to Ludwig Karpath, telling him that at his meeting with Jahn on the 2nd of May, he had been treated kindly and offered *Don Giovanni* for his debut on the 11th. He told Karpath that this had not been his choice – he had suggested *Tannhäuser* – but in the circumstances he had had to accept gracefully. Mahler was fully aware that patience and tact were paramount, for Jahn's days at the Opera were numbered.

Between the 2nd and the 4th of May, Pollini was in Vienna, and just happened to be staying at the Hotel Bristol. Hermann Bahr, who had business with the Hamburg Opera Intendant, recalled how, while they were deep in discussion, Mahler had burst into the room like 'an element of nature'. Bahr had thought that his face was familiar, but at first did not recognise Mahler, who was apparently irritated by his presence, wanting to speak with Pollini. Bahr remembered how Mahler had stormed around the room, stamped his feet and then shot out through the door as quickly as he had arrived! The two men looked at each other and burst out laughing. Mahler, giving a good impression of 'a cat on hot bricks', was without doubt suffering from nervous tension. However, he need not have worried. Hans Richter, as well as the ailing Jahn, received him into their fold with kindness and, knowing his passion for Wagner's operas, gave him *Lohengrin* instead of *Don Giovanni* for his debut. Meanwhile he made a whistle-stop visit to Venice to attend the première of Leoncavallo's *La Bohème*, where he met up with Pollini for the occasion. Mahler reported back that it was not in the same league as Puccini's opera of the same name and could not recommend staging it in Vienna.

Rumours that he was about to take over the Directorship from the almost blind Jahn were at this point unfounded, but it was not difficult to read between the lines. Added to this, Mahler's reputation as a ruthless perfectionist had sent shudders down the spines of many members of the Vienna Philharmonic. However, Jahn himself had introduced him to the orchestra and, although frosty to begin with, Mahler, with tact and patience to the fore, soon brought about a thaw.

On the 11th of May, Mahler conducted *Lohengrin* after only one rehearsal. It was an outstanding success. He had won over the musicians, banishing all doubts about his ability, dedication and attitude to them – beforehand there had even been rumours of a walk out. They were impressed with Mahler, and he in turn was flattering in his comments about their musicianship, as well as the marvellous acoustics of the Opera House. Natalie wrote that he had 'breathed something of the Holy Spirit into *Lohengrin*'. He received wild applause from the audience, and afterwards, as he left by the stage door, he was congratulated by a large crowd of young musicians, many of who were students at the Conservatory. Among them was Josef Reitler who summed up his feelings by declaring that the operatic experiences of the past seemed to be petty and banal by comparison. Mahler was very touched by this, for acceptance by young people meant a great deal to him. He could breathe a deep sigh of relief, for he had conquered Vienna in one fell swoop. The critics too were enthusiastic. Ludwig Speidel, writing in the *Fremden-Blatt*, stated that no greater consideration could have been shown to Jahn, the ailing Director, than to have a man of such ability at his side, and that, given the opportunity, Mahler's artistic influence would be beneficial to the Opera. Richard Heuberger (*Neue Freie Presse*) declared Mahler to be confident, spirited and an excellent dramatic conductor whose influence went a lot further than the footlights.

After just one performance, people were aware that a new era was about to begin. Robert Hirschfeld, of the *Wiener Abendpost*, described Mahler's conducting by saying that every slightest movement had meaning, his intentions made clear. His eyes were everywhere, for he was totally involved in every aspect of the production, whether concerning musicians, singers or chorus – everywhere, in fact, except for the score, which he knew by heart. Finally, Karl Kraus (*Breslauer Zeitung*) declared that Mahler was a 'Siegfried' who would do away with old bad habits. What a beginning! The press unanimous in their praise, the musicians and singers behind him, the public bowing before him – he was on Cloud Nine!

On the 17th of May, he wrote to Anna saying that his troubles were behind him, that all Vienna hailed him enthusiastically, and that the entire staff of the Opera was very taken by him. Indeed, everything was just splendid. He told her that he had been assigned *Die Walküre, Siegfried, Figaro* and *Zauberflöte* in the days to come.

Natalie remembered accompanying him to a performance of *Die Meistersinger* under Hans Richter's baton. Afterwards, Mahler declared that Richter had conducted the first act like a master, the second act like a schoolmaster and the third act like a master cobbler! Such was his attitude towards one of the great conductors of the day and a protégé of Wagner. He told Natalie that he had every intention of shaking up the Court Opera once he had become Director – casting, scenery, costumes, everything. Rumours abounded in Vienna concerning what he might do, but he gave no indication in public as to his plans; he was wisely biding his time.

Before Justi and Emma arrived in Vienna, Ludwig Karpath spent a good deal of time with him, walking through the streets, discussing what the future might hold. Mahler had also befriended Arnold Rosé, the leader of the orchestra. He had met him before, but now that they were working together, the two men became much closer. Another name from the past was Hugo Wolf, who had been a contemporary of his at the Conservatory. Wolf was clearly delighted that Mahler had been appointed conductor at the Hofoper, especially as he was now confident that his friend would see to it that his opera, *Der Corregidor*, would be performed there.

Jahn, facing the reality of his failing sight and delighted with the universal acclamation of Mahler's *Lohengrin*, was grooming him to be his successor. And then ill health struck. At first Mahler was suffering from no more than a cold, but it worsened, fever took hold and his throat became infected. Justi was still in Hamburg tying up domestic loose ends, so Natalie nursed him. Somehow he managed to struggle from his sick bed to rehearsals, even though he had virtually lost his voice. Fortunately, under the circumstances, *Die Walküre* had to be cancelled due to Luise von Ehrenstein (Sieglinde) falling ill, so he was able to concentrate his efforts on

The Magic Flute. One change he made was to halve the string section, telling the musicians that his action was not intended to please them, but rather that Mozart's music needed the extra delicacy of a smaller number of musicians to recreate the magic of the score. Whereas he had had only one rehearsal for *Lohengrin*, for *The Magic Flute* he had ten, and the performance was an outstanding success. Despite his poor health, Mahler had made an important point: he was not just a conductor of 'modern' music such as Wagner, he was equally adept at the classics. He had proved himself before a discerning Vienna, conducting outstanding performances of works by his two favourite opera composers – Mozart and Wagner, the former while he was a very sick man. This must have earned him a great deal of respect and sympathy.

Mahler's health continued to deteriorate and his throat infection resulted in an abscess that had to be lanced. There was no way he could continue with his hectic schedule so, under advice from doctors, he left Vienna with Justi, Emma and Natalie for Kitzbühel to rest and recuperate. Having been forced to give up Steinbach and his beloved *Häuschen*, his thoughts returned to finding a replacement where he could continue composing during his summer breaks. Unfortunately, hardly had they arrived in Kitzbühel, when scarlet fever struck the area, so they were forced to move on. In a letter to his friend Adele Marcus in Hamburg, he mentioned that he had only 'three enemies in Vienna: Jahn, Richter and Fuchs'. Although Robert Fuchs had never warmed to Mahler, it is strange that he should say this about Jahn and Richter who had behaved very civilly towards him after his arrival. Perhaps he meant that they were the only obstacles in his way preventing him from taking full charge of the Vienna Opera, his words probably tainted by his physical state and the dreadful weather. On the 12th of June he wrote to Anna telling her about his state of health and how he would almost certainly have to undergo a further operation on his throat in August. Nevertheless he still hoped to be able to attend her debut at Bayreuth on the 19th of July, when she would be performing the role of Kundry in *Parsifal*. In fact he did not, for he thought that his presence there might provide the gossipmongers with ammunition.

He received news that, on the 13th of July, he had been made Deputy Director of the Court Opera, his task to take over Jahn's responsibilities during his illness. There was only one more step to go, although all might have been in vain for on one occasion, just before Mahler and his companions arrived in Vahrn in the South Tyrol, he had nearly come to an unfortunate end. Whilst out cycling in the Ridnaun Valley near Sterzing, he had lost control of his bicycle, swerved off the road and had only managed to save himself from falling into a ravine by clinging onto a conveniently positioned bush!

He loved Vahrn and decided that it would be ideal as his new summer retreat, although not for 1897, for this year would be a barren one as far as composing was concerned. His health had begun to improve and he was able to enjoy the relaxation, fresh air and exercise. Natalie remembered a conversation she had had with him when he spoke to her about the important influence of the sounds of nature on man. In recent days he had almost been driven mad courtesy of a particularly enthusiastic cockerel. He told her that all basic rhythms and themes were based on nature's own, whether harmonious or discordant, sublime, tragic or humorous.

Suddenly rumours concerning the former relationship between Anna von Mildenburg and Mahler reached the Tyrol. Almost inevitably she had set her mind on following him to Vienna, setting the wheels in motion through her former teacher, Rosa Papier. On hearing this Justi was furious, and Natalie, still secretly in love with him, even more so. She wrote to Rosa Papier pointing out that such a move would be disastrous for Mahler. Aware of Natalie's feelings, he wrote a much calmer letter to Rosa Papier saying that he would welcome such a talented singer in Vienna, but time was on their side and it would be better not to rush things. Although still clearly very fond of Anna, he had learnt his lesson about not becoming too involved with his leading ladies, let alone one who, through her indiscretions in Hamburg, had caused considerable embarrassment. Yet he would not stand in her way, and he knew that apart from her undoubted ability as an artist, such a move would please his friend and ally Rosa Papier. However, if she did arrive, she would be treated in the same way as any other soloist. He made this abundantly clear to Anna.

His sisters stayed on in Vahrn, while he and Natalie went cycling in the Toblach area for a few days, a particularly beautiful and dramatic part of Austria just north of the Dolomites. Mahler was greatly impressed, and he would return to Toblach during the last years of his life.

With courtesy visits to Eduard Wlassack, Hanslick and then Jahn at his villa in Styria, events were moving apace. He stayed with Jahn for two days, and found the Director a sad old man, yet very kindly disposed towards him. Mahler knew that it would not be long before he would be invited to step into his shoes.

He returned to Vienna to face a deluge of problems, literally in one sense for the city and the surrounding countryside had suffered torrential rain and floods, causing widespread disruption. Despite the resulting difficulties, especially the inability of many of the Opera staff, including Hans Richter, from being able to get to work, the season opened on the 1st of August with another well-received performance of *Lohengrin*, Mahler himself being singled out for praise. Having to shoulder full responsibility with the absence of both Jahn and Richter, he had been given an excellent opportunity to prove his administrative skills, but he must have been very relieved when Richter arrived four days after the opening performance. Doubtless very grateful for Mahler's handling of affairs in his absence, Richter graciously gave him the forthcoming productions of *Das Rheingold* and *Die Walküre*.

Meanwhile, another acclaimed performance, this time of *Le nozze di Figaro*, once more underlined the fact that Mahler's skill lay not just with more recent German repertoire. The public, the Opera personnel and the critics were full of praise, yet Mahler himself was still not a well man. Bruno Walter wrote to him concerned about his forthcoming military service, fearing that it might lessen his chances of becoming an accomplished conductor. Mahler wrote back advising him to get his military service out of the way as soon as possible, saying that when he became Director of the Hofoper, he would do his level best to have him engaged as his assistant.

Mahler had done much to establish himself, and although perhaps he did not now have a mountain to climb, he still had to negotiate a tricky summit – Hans Richter. Hungarian by birth, he had been an essential part of the Viennese music scene for two decades. A close friend of Wagner, who had admired his conducting ability and had entrusted him with the first *Ring* cycle at Bayreuth, his name had become synonymous with quality. He had been an outstanding and very versatile member of the Vienna Philharmonic, and as their conductor they had come to regard him as their own. He would be a difficult act to follow, and yet many thought that a new act, a new breath of life, was needed. Cautiously they thought that Mahler might just be the man to carry out this delicate task. Mahler believed that dedication and discipline were the prerequisites for artistic success, and these foundations had become weakened at the Hofoper and must be restored. There was to be no sudden revolution, for Richter would be re-elected conductor and chairman of the orchestra in May 1898; the change had to be one of transition. But Mahler was acting director, and when Richter approached him with a request for six weeks leave, he granted his request willingly.

Hugo Wolf, determined to have his opera *Der Corregidor* performed in Vienna, went out of his way to offer renewed friendship to Mahler, who, on the look out for new material for the Hofoper, was encouraging with his response, but with no promises for the foreseeable future. Wolf was very disappointed, for he thought that Mahler would have dropped everything to get *Der Corregidor* staged. Top priority for Mahler, though, was the *Ring* cycle only days away; it would be a true test of his authority over the personnel of the Court Opera. He was determined not to be a mere shadow of Richter – this would be <u>his</u> *Ring*.

On the 10th of August Mahler moved into an apartment at Bartensteinstrasse 3 where he, Justi and Emma would live until the following August. Natalie arrived in Vienna on the 24th of August, the day before *Das Rheingold,* and she found him working almost around the clock, not just on musical matters, but with the burdensome administrative ones as well. She wrote that on the 25th of August, the day of the performance of *Das Rheingold,* his excitement was like that of a child at Christmas. He had only been able to have one rehearsal, and this he spent going over the passages that it had become the custom to cut and that he had restored. He had decided to carry out Wagner's wish that the work should be performed without a break. Natalie's account of this *Ring* cycle provides a real insight into Mahler's approach. She compared him to a sculptor, whose chiselling had brought the 'stone' *Das Rheingold* to life, imbuing it with his own vision. The impact was unforgettable, and maybe only Wagner himself could have released the elemental, nature-inspired force of the work in such an impressive way. Despite such ecstatic thoughts from Natalie, Mahler himself was not entirely satisfied with the quality of the performance. Arnold Rosé blamed this on the fact that the musicians were none too familiar with the work! The orchestra's leader promised an improvement with *Die Walküre.*

As it turned out, *Die Walküre* was even less satisfactory, capped by an astonishing incident, which rather summed up the prevailing attitudes at the Hofoper at that time. In the last act there is an important timpani roll, and when Mahler cued nothing happened. The timpanist had gone, replaced by another musician who had missed his entry! Apparently the timpanist had left to catch the last train to his home in the suburb of Brunn, and this was not the first time he had done this. Mahler almost hit the roof. Despite the fact that it was midnight, he sent the unfortunate man a telegram, hoping that it would give him a sleepless night, ordering him to report to his office first thing in the morning. The meeting took place and, although carpeting the man, he learnt that the player's basic salary was just 63 guilders a month, nowhere near enough to support himself, let alone a family, in Vienna. The incident, although unfortunate to say the least, did have a positive after effect. Mahler put at the top of his list of priorities an improvement in musicians' salaries, even if it meant economising in other areas. This did his standing with the orchestra no harm at all.

Nevertheless, the general opinion was that *Die Walküre* had been a success, despite Mahler's remark that 'the dust of sloppiness and inaccuracy lies an inch-thick'. Afterwards Sophie Sedlmair, who had sung Brünnhilde, rushed up to him to kiss his hands. *Siegfried* was the most successful part of the cycle, the Forest Murmurs magical, the awakening of Brünnhilde full of splendour. Like *Das Rheingold* and *Die Walküre* all cuts had been restored, the love scene between Brünnhilde and Siegfried performed intact. Mahler had regarded the cut in this scene to be particularly unforgivable, for it gave the impression that Brünnhilde was a harlot by leaving out the essential build-up when she makes Siegfried aware of the enormous sacrifice she is making. In *Götterdämmerung*, he restored the Brünnhilde-Waltraute scene in the first act, but he was unable to include the normally excised Norns scene due to a lack of suitable performers, much to his regret. Apart from this, the only cut remaining in the whole cycle, *Götterdämmerung* was a triumph. At the end his name was chanted repeatedly and he was given overwhelming applause, encored by a huge crowd of young musicians and students at the stage door. Hugo Wolf was so impressed with the clarity of detail in Mahler's *Ring* that he said he had heard things he had thought he would never hear except in his thoughts when reading the score.

In the eyes of Vienna, the anti-Semitic section of the press apart, who, as expected, nit-picked and compared him unfavourably with Richter, the little man had become a giant of the podium. Yet Mahler was not satisfied, remarking how regrettable it was that great composers had to compose works for 'that pigsty, the theatre . . .'. Would he ever be satisfied? The answer: emphatically no.

The writing was on the wall for Jahn who, on his return to Vienna on the 1st of September, was asked to resign. At first he resisted, but aware of the public support for Mahler and having been bribed with a title from the Emperor and the prospect of an increased pension, he agreed reluctantly. Mahler had achieved his goal – almost. Richter was still there but he was now supporting him, for he had no option, and it would only be a matter of time before he too left. Mahler's appointment took effect as from the 8th of October with a starting total salary of 12,000 florins.

Having achieved a position of almost unlimited power, Mahler rolled up his sleeves and set to work reorganizing and reforming the Court Opera; out with the old, in with the new – the great shake-up was about to begin, regardless of his popularity. He wrote to the music critic Max Marschalk saying that his life was totally taken up with theatrical business, with all his senses and emotions turned inside out. He felt almost a stranger to himself, and he wondered how it would all end. And there was one great frustration, which bit into his soul: he had neither the energy nor the time to compose. The honeymoon period was well and truly over.

Top priority was to get rid of the claques, those raucous, frequently bribed fan clubs, whose members were hell-bent on interrupting proceedings by cheering their chosen stars. Claque members were even encouraged by some of the musicians, as well as other employees of the Court Opera, by being given complimentary tickets. Mahler abolished the practice of issuing free tickets. He insisted that the stars of both opera and ballet should make no contact whatsoever with claque members, and not to acknowledge any out of place applause. He even arranged for detectives to be in the fourth gallery of the auditorium. This was successful to start with, but bad habits did creep back, although to a lesser extent. Latecomers, except those privileged with seats in boxes, would not be allowed in until a suitable break in the music, no matter what their social standing. Auditorium lights would be dimmed during performances. Soloists who had outgrown their usefulness would be removed and new singers brought in. These would include Vienna-born Anna von Mildenburg, Erik Schmedes, Theodore Reichmann, Leopold Demuth, Selma Kurz, Marie Gutheil-Schoder, Friedrich Weidemann and Leo Slezak. Any musicians whose ability or attitude fell below Mahler's demanding standards would be replaced. Traditionally the conductor's rostrum had been placed just in front of the stage. Mahler had it moved back to the balustrade so that he could communicate properly with the orchestra, and he had a telephone installed to facilitate contact with back-stage. He wanted complete control, especially after two unfortunate incidents when the curtain rose to reveal a stagehand still at work, and on another occasion when a tenor and a chorus girl were following amorous pursuits! Mahler would accept nothing less than one hundred per cent dedication. To him music was a sacred art, and anyone who showed less than total respect for the great works was not welcome. His perfectionist approach affected all departments of the Court Opera, not just music but also staging, scenery, costumes and even the administration. The laissez-faire times were over; the days of muddles, of unimaginative choice of repertoire, cancellations and stale productions. To avoid cancellations, Mahler insisted on all main parts having understudies.

Prince Montenuovo, although taking care not to become too personally involved, supported Mahler in his reforms. It was not long before the fears of many began to become a reality, and his initial popularity inevitably began to suffer. Yet, as had always been the case with Mahler, those who did show real dedication would always have his support, gratitude and admiration. Vienna, the laid back city of socialising, an attitude which pervaded every sphere of Viennese life including music, had been forcibly awakened by a little dictator! Mahler was summoned for an audience with the Emperor, who told him that it had not taken him long to establish himself as master of the Court Opera.

In order to liven up the repertoire, Mahler sought out new works. In so doing it was not surprising that several contemporary composers proffered their operas, but he was only after works of real quality. He even turned down Josef Foerster's new opera, *Eva*. And then there was Hugo Wolf. Mahler had made a rash promise that he would make sure that *Der*

Corregidor would be staged once he held the reins in Vienna. Wolf had been banking on this to launch his career in the top league of opera composers. He had already made his name as an excellent writer of Lieder, so, on the 18th of September and brimful with confidence, he headed for Mahler's office at the Opera. His aim was to secure a definite date for its production. Very tired and under considerable strain with all the new responsibilities on his shoulders, Mahler was in no mood to be pushed around by Wolf, even though they had been friends since student days. The meeting became acrimonious. Mahler left Wolf under the pretext of having been summoned by the Intendant. For Hugo Wolf the result of the meeting was a nervous breakdown. In his mentally disturbed state, he paid a visit to one of the singers of the Court Opera, Hermann Winkelmann, telling him that he, Wolf, was the new Director of the Court Opera. When Winkelmann tried to tell him that Mahler was in charge, he replied that he had already got rid of him. Wolf became increasingly aggressive, going around telling everyone that Mahler had been dismissed. He had even written a speech that he planned to read to the employees of the Opera. He became so abusive and violent that he had to be restrained, and he was taken to a private secure establishment. He did recover sufficiently to be able to attend a concert of some of his Lieder, but believing that Mahler might still stage *Der Corregidor* he withdrew the performance rights from the Court Opera!

Wolf's condition worsened and, having tried to commit suicide, he realised that he was a danger to himself, and voluntarily returned to the asylum where he died six years later.

A visitor to the Mahler apartment in the Bartensteingasse that autumn was Bruno Walter. Vienna and the splendour of the Court Opera in particular took his breath away, and he remembered having a thoroughly enjoyable lunch with Gustav, Justi and Emma. During his visit to the city, he also met many of Mahler's friends whom he had heard so much about, many becoming his friends too during the decades to come.

New productions for the autumn of 1897 included two of Mahler's favourites: *Zar und Zimmermann* by Albert Lortzing, and *Dalibor* by Bedřich Smetana. At first glance these were courageous choices, but it was a typical Mahler move to test his newly acquired authority, especially *Dalibor*, for Smetana, who hailed from his own Bohemia-Moravia homeland, was regarded as a 'provincial' composer. Would he be criticized for imposing such music on the Viennese? For him this staging of *Dalibor* was a labour of love. He had taken it upon himself to be responsible for every aspect of the production, and everyone worked hard for him. Both productions were a great success. The music critic Max Kalbeck, writing in the *Neues Wiener Tagblatt* on the 5th of October, referred to Mahler as the

'Hofoper's new miracle worker', and how, with such performances, a new era had begun for the Vienna Court Opera. Every performer had achieved a praiseworthy standard. He had managed to save the Court Opera, which was 'sick to the core', from potential ruin. Kalbeck did, however, wonder if Mahler's choice of a Smetana opera had political motives, for there were a great number of Czechs in the audience, including a number of Czech politicians – a guarantee of an ovation for their fellow countryman! Natalie stated that she had never been witness to a production so perfect in every detail. She wrote how new life had been breathed into the singers, the previously 'stiff' chorus now becoming totally involved with the performance and that the musicians had surpassed themselves.

After a further performance of *Zar und Zimmermann* on the 9th of October, Mahler rushed up to Natalie and told her that his appointment as artistic director had officially gone through; the last piece of the jig-saw was in place. Most of the press greeted the news enthusiastically, the anti-Semitic faction being forced to bite their tongues. Josef Scheu, writing in the *Arbeiter-Zeitung* on the 16th of October, declared that Mahler's appointment could only be welcomed with a great deal of happiness and expectation, while Karl Kraus, in the *Breslauer Zeitung*, stated that there was now a 'new hope in Vienna'. The terms given to him were very generous. The appointment was for life, only to end by mutual consent between the Emperor and himself. His salary was to be 12,000 gulden, with a further 1,000 in bonuses, and on retirement he would receive an annual pension of 3,000 gulden – a guaranteed income for when he decided to compose full time.

Already he was feeling the strain. He wrote to Max Marschalk saying that he was swamped with work in his new all-consuming job, so much so that all his senses and emotions felt as if they had been turned inside out. When Natalie suggested that his new position enabled him to rule as 'Lord and Master', as Mahler himself had declared, perhaps now he would be able to have his symphonies performed. He replied that at that moment he was not particularly bothered whether his own works were accepted earlier or later. He told her that he had begun to feel like a stranger to himself, almost a different person. Of course he would have loved to have his symphonies played, but the pressures of work together with the inevitable controversies that would arise from their performance, had put the idea right out of his head. Anyway, he did not wish to give ammunition to anti-Semitic journalists.

One of the foremost of Vienna's music critics was Max Graf. He described Mahler the conductor as almost 'demonic', out of whom streams of nervous energy flowed. He described his conducting in his early years at the Hofoper as particularly energetic, with his baton darting forward like the tongue of a snake. He would stare, shoot stinging glances when necessary, give cues in one direction while waving his baton in another, and sometimes jump up from his conductor's chair as if he had suffered a sting. He was all movement and fire – just as his whole life was at that time. Later, with age and experience, he no longer had to prove himself in this way. With the onslaught of ill health he mellowed, outwardly at any rate.

The next Mahler 'renovation' was *Die Zauberflöte*. The revitalized production, with cuts restored, brought out the opera's fairy tale quality, its simplicity and naïveté. Mahler's Queen of the Night was no mere mortal, but a divine mother figure with billowing black cloak and flowing hair, 'sheltering all in her nocturnal lap'.

Eugene Onegin, *Tristan und Isolde*, *Tannhäuser* and *Der fliegende Holländer* followed, all with cuts restored and with Mahler's vision permeating every aspect of the productions.

The performance of *The Flying Dutchman* was a revelation. Mahler had not intended to create a new production, but he found so many inadequacies in the existing effort that he found himself bit by bit creating an entirely new one. The staging, the singing and the orchestral playing were all outstanding. The only fly in the ointment was the tenor Winkelmann's 'unofficial' claque that included his son, who interrupted proceedings at a crucial moment. Mahler was livid and he gave the singer a piece of his mind – his feelings were so strong that he admitted that he had felt like beating him up! After the performance, the culprits lay in wait for Mahler outside the stage door. They must have been very taken aback when he gave them a severe dressing down and a lecture on when and when not to applaud! They then clapped him and in response he told them that that was most acceptable as he was now making an exit!

Musicians and singers were forced to adapt to his very individual way of conducting. They had been used to time beaters; Mahler had no truck with this method. For him the melodic and rhythmic content, the moulding of the music, interpreted by him and his musicians in a unique reading was his credo. Consequently each of those under him had to think, interpret and create, not just rely on a mechanical baton-waver. Concentration was of the essence, especially as he would frequently change his tempi from performance to performance. He was fully aware of this, but he considered it good for the singers and musicians; laziness was out, they had to be totally focused, paying very close attention to the conductor. This novel approach resulted in every performance being a unique, fresh occasion, and completely banished the staleness that had pervaded the Court Opera over the previous years.

The Court Opera, probably aided and abetted by Rosa Papier, persuaded the Hamburg Opera to allow Anna von Mildenburg to make guest appearances in December. She appeared in *Die Walküre, Lohengrin* and *Fidelio*, all conducted by Hans Richter, which removed the ammunition of favouritism from those critics who had been waiting with pens at the ready. She was little short of a sensation. Mahler had played his cards carefully, and Anna, as well as Leopold Demuth, also from Hamburg, was given a contract. His poaching of singers from Europe's top opera houses was well under way.

Mahler's most treasured Christmas present in 1897 was the news that his *First* and *Third Symphonies,* their piano reductions and the orchestral parts of the *Second Symphony* were to be published by Eberle in Vienna, who had also published Bruckner's symphonies. This was thanks to the musicologist Guido Adler, also brought up in Iglau and who had studied with the same piano teacher, Brosch, and whom Mahler had befriended as a student when they were both members of the Wagner Society in Vienna. Adler had managed to procure a grant of 3,000 gulden towards the total cost of 12,000 gulden from the *Gesellschaft zur Förderung deutscher Wissenschaft, Kunst und Literatur in Böhmen*, a society founded to promote the arts, literature and science. The whole idea was Adler's, and it was a mighty relief for Mahler, for it meant that his scores would at last be readily available throughout Europe. Adler, who had worked hard behind the scenes on his behalf with his application to the Hofoper, was now instrumental in spreading the word far and wide about Mahler the composer.

In the New Year, a famous star of the opera world arrived in Vienna for guest performances in *Fidelio, Norma* and as Donna Anna in *Don Giovanni.* This was Lilli Lehmann, who would become a regular visitor to the Hofoper. The performance of *Don Giovanni*, under Hans Richter, very nearly had to be cancelled due to the sudden illness of Fanny Mora who was due to sing the part of Donna Elvira. Mahler, having managed to find a replacement at the eleventh hour, sitting in the director's box with Justi and his close friend Nina Spiegler, apparently spent much of the evening shouting down the speaking-tube, lambasting all concerned over ridiculous costumes, make up, props, lighting and the general incompetence of the stage management. Much still needed to be done.

At the end of January Bezecny resigned, to be replaced by the new Intendant, August Plappart, the post now with considerably reduced powers. In the future, most decisions would be made by the two directors, Mahler and Richter, later just Mahler, and would be finalized by the Lord Chamberlain, Prince Liechtenstein. Bezecny, on his departure, had patted himself on the back for his wisdom in appointing Mahler; Plappart curiously congratulated the Court Opera for having a director they could follow 'with their eyes shut' – hardly the case during performances!

February came, and with it the beginning of Anna's contract with the Court Opera. When she visited Mahler in his office, he apparently kept her at arm's length, making it abundantly clear that she would be treated just like any other member of the company. Although he had already mentioned this in a letter to her some months before, it must still have come as a shock to her, but he was adamant that their relationship should be strictly professional. In his letter the previous July, he had pointed out that her arrival in Vienna would be controversial enough, that any unfortunate gossip would result in his position becoming untenable and he would be forced to resign. Nevertheless, he assured her that he would do everything possible to further her career as a singer. Inevitably their relationship cooled, Anna managing to control her emotions. She took her amorous pursuits elsewhere, becoming involved with Mahler's friends Siegfried Lipiner and Ludwig Karpath. Eventually, in 1909, she married Hermann Bahr.

Following *The Ring* cycle, with Mahler conducting *Das Rhinegold* and *Siegfried* and Richter taking charge of *Die Walküre* and *Götterdämmerung*, very reluctantly he felt obliged to stage Leoncavallo's *La Bohème*. His view of this opera had not changed since he had attended the première in Venice. Despite Mahler's condemnation of the work, Jahn had promised the composer that it would be staged at the Hofoper. A promise had been made, and Mahler had to fulfill it. Originally it had been planned for November 1897, but a dispute concerning Ernst van Dyck, one of the lead singers, caused a postponement. Rescheduled for February, van Dyck again caused problems pretending to be sick. Mahler immediately installed his understudy. Leoncavallo, having arrived in Vienna, was furious. He threatened Mahler with legal action, interrupted a rehearsal, involved the press and even the Italian ambassador. Mahler would not be dictated to by singers or visiting composers, and in this he was backed by Prince Liechtenstein. The newspapers had delighted in serializing the conflict, and by doing so had aroused public interest in the affair. When the evening came, the house was packed, and by far the greatest applause before, during and after the performance, was for Mahler himself. As for the opera itself the critics were not impressed, all agreeing that it paled into insignificance alongside Puccini's *La Bohème*, but Hanslick and his colleagues nevertheless praised Mahler's efforts. He had stood his ground and won, and in so doing had made his message quite clear that he would not tolerate tantrums and interference. He won himself the nickname of *Korporal vom Tag*!

The composer and cellist Franz Schmidt had joined the Vienna Court Opera Orchestra in October 1896, and he later remembered how Mahler's arrival had been 'like a catastrophe of the elements', shaking the edifice to its foundations; everything weak had to give way. As a result many singers were to pack their bags over the following months. These included Ernst van Dyck, Theodor Reichmann and Hermann Winkelmann, as well as two-thirds of the orchestra who were either dismissed or pensioned off. Schmidt remarked that by 1900 he was the senior cellist after just four years!

Richard Dehmel, the poet, sent Mahler some of his work hoping that the composer would be suitably impressed and would set some of his poems to music. Mahler thanked him but pointed out that with his onerous job as Director of the Hofoper, he would be unable to even consider composing anything for the foreseeable future. He would have neither the time nor the strength to write music for at least two years. Mahler told Natalie how bored he was with his job, now that the Court Opera was 'dancing on my finger-tip'. He was finding little satisfaction with his work and he disliked being constantly in the limelight with people grovelling before him. His inability to even contemplate composing was eating into his soul.

Yet, as so often happened in his life, an unexpected joy lay just around the corner. Partly due to the fast spreading news of Guido Adler's efforts and generosity in arranging for the forthcoming publication of Mahler's first three symphonies, there arose renewed interest in having his music performed. The Kaim Orchestra of Munich included the *Andante* from the *Second Symphony* in a concert in Vienna, while in Frankfurt the second movement of the *Third Symphony* was performed. Both were praised, but playing 'bleeding chunks of Mahler' out of context, especially these short, gentle movements, was far from ideal.

In the same month, March 1898, an even more important event took place. Angelo Neumann, whom Mahler had worked for at the German Theatre in Prague, had contacted him with a proposal to have his *First Symphony* performed on the 3rd of March. A former fellow-student of Mahler's at the Vienna Conservatory and first kapellmeister at the German Opera, Franz Schalk, would take charge of the rehearsals. Before setting off for Prague, he penned Schalk a list of suggestions. Among these were: a fifth trumpet in the last movement, a second harp, and the largest body of strings possible, but only musicians of quality. The first movement, the opening of which, he wrote, was not music, but the sounds of nature, should be played very delicately except for the big climax. The ending of the last movement would benefit from a large horn section. He also pleaded with Schalk to take special care with the score as it was his only copy!

When Mahler arrived and entered the German Theatre for the final rehearsal, the very large orchestra greeted him with great warmth. He was obviously very touched by this, for he overlooked a number of mistakes and weaknesses, and at the end he diplomatically told them how pleased he had been with their playing. The performance itself was a tremendous success. Fond memories of his short spell in Prague and admiration for the rocketing success of their fellow countryman fuelled the adulation of the audience and resulted in encouraging reviews from the press. Laurel wreathes and other presentations followed the concert, and afterwards he was guest of honour at the inevitable lavish banquet attended by many whom he had known in his Prague days, including Neumann, as well as Guido Adler and Siegfried Lipiner who had travelled from Vienna for the occasion. He left Prague on a high and spent a few days of deserved rest during Easter week in Abbazia on the Adriatic coast. He was completely exhausted and was once more being troubled by a painful recurrence of his problem with the nether regions. The success of the Prague concert must have increased his longing to be able to put pen to staves once more. He ruminated with Natalie about the past and how things might have turned out differently, how if Brahms, Goldmark, Hanslick and Richter had awarded him the Beethoven prize for *Das klagende Lied*, he would not have been condemned to a life of hell in the theatre.

On the 6th of March, the *Second Symphony* was performed in Liège under Sylvain Dupuis. It was an outstanding success, and Mahler wrote to Dupuis thanking him for his dedication and for achieving such a wonderful result, captivating audience and press alike. Dupuis hoped that a further performance would take place the following year.

On his return from his Easter break, Mahler had to face the last lap of the 1897-1898 season. There was a new and much praised production of *Aida*. There were also performances of *Norma, Fidelio, Tristan und Isolde* and *Götterdämmerung*, all with Lilli Lehmann making guest appearances. Out of the blue came an approach from New York – would the grass be greener over there? Certainly the work load would be lighter, he would earn more and, most important of all, his employment would be for just seven months of the year, thus giving him valuable time in which he could return to his first love, composing. Nothing came of this overture at this stage in his career, but the seeds were sown for the future.

The season ended and there was general satisfaction with Mahler's first at the Court Opera. Much to the surprise of some, he and Richter had managed to work in relative harmony, the strain of the latter's previously very heavy conducting schedule having been reduced considerably. Inevitably rumblings of discontent continued in some quarters, and Mahler's anti-Semitic foes were still out there waiting to pounce at every opportunity, but so long as he had the majority on his side, especially the all important Princes Liechtenstein and Montenuovo, their influence was limited.

Mahler's health had continued to deteriorate, and he was forced to

abandon his post on the 5ᵗʰ of June for a haemorrhoid operation. For
recuperation he returned to Vahrn, but unlike previous summer holidays it
was to prove neither particularly pleasant nor productive, for he was in
constant pain following the surgery. Nevertheless, he did go on walks and
one in particular gave him great enjoyment. Natalie had suggested it as she
remembered it as being one of her favourites as a child. Mahler too was
impressed by the magnificent views of the snow-capped mountains and the
Dolomites in the distance, although he would have enjoyed the outing more
under different circumstances. As a matter of principle, for a summer
without any composing would have depressed him severely, he did manage
to orchestrate two more of the *Wunderhorn Lieder*. These were *Lied des
Verfolgten im Turm* (Song of the Persecuted Prisoner in the Tower) and *Wo
die schönen Trompeter blasen* (Where the Fine Trumpets Blow).

On the 30ᵗʰ of July he wrote to Hermann Behn telling him that he was
still in constant pain, that he had at least done a little composing and that
his sister Emma had become engaged to Arnold Rosé's brother, Eduard, a
cellist in the Boston Symphony Orchestra. He was pleased that she had
found a suitable future husband and that his responsibility for her would
soon be at an end, but sad that she would be crossing the Atlantic. He
would miss her.

Back in harness after his summer break convalescing in Vahrn, and with
his very successful first year behind him, Mahler was all set to launch into
the 1898-1899 season. On the 10ᵗʰ of May Richter had been re-elected as
conductor of the Vienna Philharmonic and chairman of the committee in
charge of orchestral matters, and should therefore have chaired the
planning meeting for the forthcoming season. With Richter not in the best
of health Mahler chaired this meeting in his place, and he made it
abundantly clear that he had every intention of including a number of
works new to Vienna. Eyebrows were raised and Richter, not wishing to
cross swords with his younger counter-part, decided to step down. His
excuse was that he was suffering pains in his right arm which would hinder
his ability to conduct. On the 2ⁿᵈ of September Richter officially resigned.
Deep regret was voiced by the orchestral committee, and Mahler was duly
appointed conductor for the Philharmonic concerts of the 1898-1899
season. He was now in control in both the opera house and the concert
hall, and it was the same orchestra who performed at the two venues.
Richter, who had lifted the reputation of the Vienna Philharmonic to a
position unsurpassed in Europe, was respected and loved by the concert-
going public. The tall, bearded figure was to be replaced by the short,
nervous dynamic re-thinker who never held tradition sacred just for its own
sake. 'Honest Hans', as Mahler called him, recovered well enough to
continue his conducting career in England.

The first operas that Mahler conducted that season were a further two performances of *Lohengrin* and one of *Die Meistersinger*, Mahler replacing Richter for the latter. Two new singers at the Hofoper were Erik Schmedes, a Danish tenor who was to become one of Mahler's favourites despite the fact that on occasions he had to be coaxed out of taverns to attend rehearsals, and Anna von Mildenburg who had been given a permanent contract. These two singers performed together in many productions and proved to be an excellent combination.

Initially Mahler's attitude to the orchestra had by and large been one of pleasantness and cooperation and the musicians had responded to his professional approach, but now that he held the reins things would be different. Even though the members of the Vienna Philharmonic were the same that he faced daily at the Opera, as a concert orchestra they were an independent body, and so it had been the musicians themselves who had approached Mahler, asking him to succeed Richter. Mahler was the man of the moment and the orchestra decided that it would be worth giving him a trial year, knowing that his increasing fame would certainly result in full houses. Indeed, when it was announced that he would be taking over the Philharmonic concerts from Richter, the whole series was quickly sold out. He was fully aware of the orchestra's faults and weaknesses as well as their strengths and his aim was, as always, 'perfection'. At the Opera, when Prince Liechtenstein suggested that it was not required of Mahler to bang his head against the wall, the latter replied that it would be the wall that would be holed! This was his attitude; he would win. At the same time he was more than ready to praise and reward those who proved their worth, and not just the musicians and singers. One example was when he paid the stagehands one gulden each as a meal allowance so that they would not have to go home to eat during the lengthy *Ring* rehearsals. Wlassack and Plappart, Beniczky's successor as Intendant, objected strongly before reluctantly agreeing. On the next occasion they would not pay, so Mahler, to fulfill his promise and to retain their good will, paid the stagehands out of his own pocket. He would always champion the causes of any whom he thought were being hard done by, and he continued to battle on behalf of the technicians, eventually bringing about a pay increase for them in 1900. As for any children involved in productions, he would always give them treats.

Rehearsals, rehearsals, rehearsals . . . as Schoenberg said later, an inadequate conductor would be bereft of ideas after three, but a great one would still seek improvements after nine. Mahler would criticize, praise, but rarely gave the impression that he was totally satisfied. He let musicians and singers alike know that their jobs were only secure so long as they continued to carry out his exacting demands. After the easy-going

Richter-Jahn era it was no wonder that malcontents began to rise to the surface,

The September 1898 *Ring* cycle was widely praised. Among those singled out were Sophie Sedlmair, Erik Schmedes, Josef Ritter and Leopold Demuth, and as for Anna von Mildenburg, she was quite outstanding as Brünnhilde. *The Ring* was given uncut, including the first Vienna performance of the Norn scene. Mahler, as ever, was not wholly satisfied, but he knew that he was on the right path. This *Ring* cycle had become the talk of the city.

The 'catastrophe of the elements' referred to by Franz Schmidt had struck. The comfortable and popular atmosphere of the Richter years had changed to one of uneasiness, of not knowing what to expect next. Mahler re-thought every work, not just once but for every performance. He often appeared to be oblivious to the feelings of the musicians. He was prepared to be controversial, even to shock. He would delve into the very heart of each score and interpret it in the way that he considered the composer would have wished. It was therefore no wonder that some musicians rebelled, criticizing his attitudes, methods and even his style of conducting. They vented their feelings in an article published anonymously in the *Deutsche Zeitung*, describing his conducting as being like a dervish or someone with St. Vitus's dance, his left hand 'lost in delirium tremens'. His aim was to entertain the public rather than providing clear indications for the orchestra (it was true that audiences were frequently mesmerized by him!). The article also slated Mahler for tinkering with scores, such as the inclusion of an E flat clarinet in Beethoven's *Coriolan Overture*. The whole tone of the writing was decidedly anti-Semitic, even the title bore the words 'Jewish Régime', and there were suggestions that he personally had been responsible for Richter's departure. It complained of his harsh, insensitive treatment of the musicians, and warned that he might well end up with no orchestra. The timing of the article was designed to hurt. As the rehearsals had not been open to the public, it must be presumed that certain members of the orchestra were to blame. Mahler had been forewarned by the editor, the item having been included without the latter's approval. It was published on the 4th of November, just two days before the first Philharmonic concert, but Mahler did not rise to the bait; there was no need, for his position and standing appeared to be invincible.

On the 28th of October, Mahler had written to Bruno Walter, who was at that time a conductor in Riga, offering him a post at the Hofoper. Concerned over the consequences of terminating his contract as well as the reception he might receive in Vienna, especially from the anti-Semites, he insisted that should he accept the offer he must be announced as the official successor to Richter. He also wondered whether he was experienced enough for such a position. Mahler wrote back saying that conductors were always learning and not to worry about whose successor he would be, but to grab the opportunity. Walter declined the offer, much to Mahler's regret.

For his first Philharmonic concert on the 6th of November, Mahler had decided that the programme should consist of the *Coriolan Overture*, Mozart's *Symphony No. 40 in G minor* and Beethoven's *Third Symphony*, the *'Eroica'* – a wise choice, for not only were Mozart and Beethoven two of his favourite composers, but of the Viennese as well. Furthermore, the *'Eroica'* had also been performed at Richter's farewell concert. Its inclusion provided an indication of continuity as well as an opportunity for a comparison between Richter's traditional approach and the fresh interpretation of Mahler. The audience in the Musikvereinsaal, and most of the critics, were enthusiastic, although some inevitably questioned his interpretations. Even Hanslick was complimentary, remarking in the *Neue freie Presse*, 'All's well that begins well'. He wrote that, despite these being works that the musicians could play in their sleep, Mahler, through his extensive rehearsing, had brought about a renewed spirit and dedication. Hanslick used words such as 'delicate textures . . . clarity . . . grandeur . . . power . . .'. Max Kalbeck wrote that the audience, cool to begin with, grew warmer as the concert progressed, and that at the end of the *Eroica* there was enthusiastic applause. He also mentioned that Mahler had conducted everything from memory, and that his conducting was calm, his gestures economical. So much for the critics of his over-energetic style of conducting often witnessed at the Opera, and such descriptions of him as being like a galvanized frog! Volatile at times he might be in rehearsal, but it was during rehearsals that the energetic work was done. Without doubt the balance of opinion was in Mahler's favour, and the rebels in the orchestra were silenced, fearing that otherwise their careers might be in jeopardy.

On the 19th of November, Gustav and Justi moved into an apartment in a magnificent new building designed by the Secessionist Otto Wagner. It is on the corner of Auenbruggergasse and the Rennweg, the entrance being at Auenbruggergasse 2. Close to the Schwarzenbergplatz, it was in an ideal situation for him, being only a short walk from the Musikverein concert hall of the *Gesellschaft der Musikfreunde* and the Opera. Almost opposite, on the other side of the Rennweg, is the Belvedere Palace, now one of Vienna's premier art galleries and famous for its large collection of paintings by Gustav Klimt. The delightful palace grounds provided a quiet place where Mahler frequently took exercise. The listed apartment block remains very much as it was in Mahler's day with the entrance hall, the spiral staircase and the apartments themselves little changed, even with the original kitchen stoves! Mahler had a telephone installed so that he could communicate with the Opera at any time, and the management of the Opera provided him with a car, although he would often prefer to walk.

The second Philharmonic concert took place the following day. The programme consisted of Weber's *Oberon Overture*, Schubert's *Eighth ('Unfinished') Symphony* and the *Symphonie Fantastique* by Berlioz. The overture was very well received, Mahler's conducting of the Schubert less so, and the *Symphonie Fantastique* was greeted with a degree of hostility from the audience and the critics, many leaving the Musikvereinsaal before the end. This was not so much a reaction to his conducting as a failure to appreciate the music. Mahler was upset for, although fully aware that it was not a work of the very highest caliber, it had been innovative for its day and was in many ways a forerunner of his own symphonic thinking. One fact became clear from the first two Philharmonic concerts, he was his own master and, as Kalbeck noted, even when he 'made mistakes' they were made with conviction. Two further Philharmonic concerts were held in 1898. On the 4th of December the main works were Brahms's *Second Symphony* and a new work by Dvořák, his symphonic poem *Heldenlied*, played in the presence of the composer. The last concert of the year was held on the 18th of December and included Bizet's *Roma*, Wagner's *Siegfried Idyll* and Beethoven's *Eighth Symphony*. Mahler's standing as a conductor continued to improve. Most of the critics were on his side, many wondering at the depth of his interpretations.

Meanwhile work at the Opera had continued to forge ahead with performances of Boieldieu's *La Dame Blanche, Der Freischütz* and the first complete Viennese performance of *Tristan und Isolde*. All inevitably had the Mahler touch, not just in terms of the music, but the productions as well. Out went the traditional, rather staid sets; in came simplicity and the greater use of lighting to achieve effects. Electricity had been introduced into opera houses between 1885 and 1890, and 1898 had seen the installation of an electrical control board at the Hofoper. Controversy inevitably continued to reign, but so too did curiosity and surprise with every performance. It was no wonder that in his attempts to lure Bruno Walter to Vienna, Mahler told him that he had better agree to come before 1900 otherwise, with his ridiculously heavy schedule, he might well be dead!

1899 opened with another bout of anti-Semitism, this time stirred up by Karl Lueger who had been elected mayor of Vienna in 1895 and was to remain in that office until the outbreak of the First World War. A charity concert for the poor had been planned, and Lueger made it very clear that he would not countenance the 'Jew Mahler' conducting it. Members of the orchestra however had other ideas. They had appointed him as their conductor, and they would not be pushed around by the likes of Lueger.

Mahler stood well back from this tasteless controversy, but the whole affair inevitably rekindled the anti-Semitic articles in the press.

On the 15th of January, only days after the abandoned charity concert, the fifth Philharmonic concert was to take place. Mahler, far from taking cover, was at his most controversial. Before the concert he told Eduard Hanslick that he was ready for battle. Why? Because he was to conduct his own arrangement for string orchestra of Beethoven's *Quartet in F minor, Op 95*. He warned Natalie that 'all the Philistines, to a man, will rise up' in protest, and would not even consider just listening and probably enjoying a new way of performing the *Quartet*. The main point of the exercise was his usual one of adapting works to suit a particular location. The score remained Beethoven's, but with a fuller sound more suited to a concert hall, rather than being played by 'four paltry fiddlers'. Following the charity concert *débâcle*, the opposition was spoiling for a fight, and so was Mahler! When booing broke out, he sent a message threatening to have that part of the hall cleared should it continue. His threat worked, but the reception was icy. The other works were Schumann's *First Symphony* and the Vienna première of Tchaikovsky's *1812 Overture*. Members of the press were predictably critical of Mahler's tinkering with the Beethoven *Quartet*, the general opinion being that a quartet was designed to be a dialogue between four musicians, so how dare he . . . The Schumann was praised, but some considered the *1812 Overture* to be rather vulgar. Mahler had a soft spot for Schumann's symphonies, and he told Natalie that their lack of popularity had been largely brought about by the very unfair antagonism shown towards them by Wagner which had done their reputation great harm. This is why he had included Schumann's *First* in the 15th of January concert, hoping that the performance might rekindle interest.

Four days later, on the 19th of January, Mahler arrived in Liège to conduct the encore performance of his own *Second Symphony*, promised the previous year by Sylvain Dupuis. Grateful as he was for the latter's sterling work on his behalf, Mahler was disappointed by the quality of the orchestra and general organization, but having become used to Vienna this was almost inevitable. Diplomatically he kept his feelings to himself and was tactful and appreciative. The performance on the afternoon of the 22nd of January was a tremendous success. The public repeated their adulation of ten months before, and almost all the critics sang the work's praises, even though the *Journal de Liège* printed a caricature of Mahler the conductor, depicting him as 'a gnome leaping out of a magic box'! Despite the fact that he had not particularly liked Liège as a town, he returned to Vienna touched by the genuine warmth of the people.

The seeds of Guido Adler's generosity in having Mahler's works published were beginning to bear fruit. On the 8th of March he was invited to conduct his *First Symphony* in Frankfurt. The orchestra applauded, the audience were polite, the press critical. Whereas the *Second* was an almost overwhelming emotional experience, the *First* continued to be more problematical.

The last two Philharmonic concerts of the season included Bruckner's *Sixth Symphony*, revised by Mahler, which received mixed reviews, and an all-Beethoven programme. This last concert, held on the 19th of March, included the *Seventh Symphony* and the *Piano Concerto No. 5 in E flat*, the *'Emperor'*, in which the soloist was his friend from his Leipzig days, Ferruccio Busoni. It was an outstanding success, and the critics heaped praise on all concerned. Mahler had wanted the season to end on a high, and it had. However the Beethoven concert was not his last, for on the 9th of April he conducted the Vienna première of his own *Second Symphony*.

A few friends were allowed to attend the rehearsals so long as they kept out of sight. At first the orchestra was mystified by the score, even doubting its worth, but the more they rehearsed the clearer the vision became. Most of the musicians rose to the challenge with increasing willingness, although the small die-hard anti-Mahler faction took the opportunity to launch another campaign against him with a similar article to the one they had penned just before the first Philharmonic concert. But this group of troublemakers was on a losing wicket, swamped by the increasing enthusiasm of the majority. The concert was in aid of the Nicolai Society for the Sick, Mahler having waived any suggestion of a fee. This annual affair was named after the composer and founder of the Philharmonic concerts, Otto Nicolai, the first having taken place in 1860. Conductors of these charity events were chosen by the members of the orchestra, and it was considered to be an honour to be asked. Mahler's demands on the musicians can be summed up by two incidents reported by Natalie. In the first, a timpanist was admonished for not beating his drums loudly enough during the passage depicting the bursting open of the graves. The timpanist warned that the skin would split to which Mahler replied, so be it. The skin survived (just), but a drumstick did not! The second incident involved a cymbal clash, again not loud enough. Mahler insisted that the unfortunate player clash the cymbals louder and louder. Giving up any thought of refinement, the musician let rip with all his might, to which Mahler shouted, 'Bravo . . . now louder still!'

The Musikverein was packed, the audience expectant facing the huge orchestra, chorus and soloists arrayed on the platform. The first movement was applauded, the second, already heard and liked by the Viennese, received enthusiastic clapping. The *Scherzo* baffled some of the audience, but the *'Urlicht'* they took to their hearts, Mahler having to repeat it in order that it should flow straight into the fourth movement, for the third, fourth and fifth movements were designed to be played without a break. Following the hushed entrance of the chorus in the *Aufersteh'n*, the music building to the great sounds of the closing bars of the symphony, the audience went wild, and following numerous recalls to the platform, he was applauded all the way out of the building and into the street. An added bonus was that the expected booing and hissing of his foes had been completely swamped. He appeared to be winning his battle against them.

The euphoria of the concert was to a certain extent countered by the scepticism of some of the critics, and this depressed Mahler for he must have hoped that his *Second Symphony* would win them over. He was accused of self-interest in having his symphony performed, guaranteeing applause by ensuring a large 'Jewish' audience, that the music was cacophonous, anti-art, banal and so on. As usual he had his allies, among them Ludwig Karpath of the *Neues Wiener Tagblatt,* who answered the question some had asked as to whether it was really a symphony at all by giving a resounding 'Yes', but pointed out that it was not a symphony in the traditionally accepted form. The correspondent of the *Wiener Abend post*, on the other hand, although regarding the work as highly serious, thoughtful and noble, could not accept it as a symphony, but merely a collection of five separate, unrelated pieces. The *Neue Freie Presse* made the cryptic comment that it was just a piece of 'imaginary theatre'. Certainly the most hurtful review came from Hans Liebstöckl writing in *Die Reichswehr*, the gist of whose article assumed that, having suffered Mahler's *Second*, the symphony itself was sick, probably terminally.

Upset as he was, his determination to further his cause as a composer was not weakened, and he set to work revising parts of his *Third Symphony* and *Das klagende Lied*, polishing them up ready for their imminent publication. The critics would not leave him alone. Once the public excitement over the *Second Symphony* had died down they set about criticizing him for his selection of operas and his casting, and this, combined with interference from the Opera's administration, especially from Wlassack and the new intendant Plappart, irritated Mahler considerably. He even had thoughts of leaving. He countered their negative attitude by issuing a forty-three page memorandum on the 24th of April, making his case for his handling and influence in every aspect of opera production from scenery to musical matters, from finance to costumes. The inefficiencies and artistic shortcomings of the past had to be rectified, and he made it quite clear that, as Director, he should have overall responsibility. He must have felt a deep sense of ingratitude, but at least Liechtenstein and Montenuovo remained on his side.

During his first season in charge of the Philharmonic concerts, Mahler's

Meanwhile, he faced increasing problems with his conducting schedules. Richter was still absent, presumably permanently, and the assistant conductor Johann Fuchs was ill. Ferdinand Löwe, formerly director of the Kaim Orchestra of Munich, had failed to adapt to the operatic needs and standards of Vienna, and the guest conductors who had been engaged were no better. On the 4th of October Fuchs died and Mahler decided that urgent action had to be taken. He opened negotiations with Franz Schalk, a Viennese who was proving to be a success in Prague.

One of the new productions planned for the early part of the season was *The Demon* by Anton Rubinstein. Completed in 1875, it had been the first opera to be sung in Russian in London where it was staged in 1888. In the cast was Anna von Mildenburg, and in a letter to Emma, Justi wrote that Anna was in excellent voice, as good as she had been in her Hamburg days. Justi told Emma that they were seeing less of her, maybe just once or twice a week, since she had begun an affair with Mahler's old friend Hermann Behn. Another leading singer in the production was an established favourite of the Viennese, Theodor Reichmann, and he and Mahler began a duel of wills. Reichmann objected to Mahler's staging ideas, but however much he tried to placate the singer and justify his plans, Reichmann's vitriol became more extreme by the day. He compared working for Mahler to being harnessed to a 'tyrannical yolk'. He criticised his conducting and his dictatorial attitude. Matters grew even worse when Mahler gave the part of Hans Sachs in *Die Meistersinger* to another rising star, Leopold Demuth. He had already sung the role in Bayreuth, but Reichmann considered the part to be his. Mahler, doing his level best to dampen down the flames, continued to work with Reichmann on the Hans Sachs role, and when later he did sing the part his performance was given great acclamation. His attitude changed; Mahler was great, he himself had been wrong!

Natalie wrote that the performance of *Die Meistersinger* on the 27th of November 1899 was the first to be staged uncut. Mahler had a profound love for this opera, and he told her that should all German art vanish it could be resurrected and put together again from this one work. To him it made all else seem virtually worthless and superfluous. An exaggeration of course, but it clearly showed his high regard for Wagner's masterpiece. All the seats were sold, nobody arrived late and no one left before the final curtain. The performance was astonishing, marred only by whistling and catcalling from an anti-Mahler group in the gallery. The rest of the audience did their level best to drown them out, but their persistence rather spoiled an otherwise fantastic evening. He must have been particularly pleased with the success of Selma Kurz as Eva. The press were virtually unanimous in their praise, despite the inevitable jibes by a few anti-Semites. Apparently, as Mahler left the Opera house, a young admirer took him unawares and kissed his hand.

Mahler's position as conductor of the Vienna Philharmonic had been in doubt throughout the summer and early autumn. The small group of die-hard malcontents had recruited more musicians to support their cause for his removal. They tried to persuade Richter to return, but he declined the offer. Mahler was decidedly annoyed by their attitude, especially as these were the very same musicians who played for him at the Hofoper, and whose salaries and working conditions he had done his best to improve. So upset was he that he threatened to resign from his post as conductor of the Philharmonic Concerts unless he could rely upon their united support. Realising the turmoil that would ensue from his resignation, almost all the musicians gave him a vote of confidence, yet underneath the surface the seeds of discontent were beginning to germinate

The first Philharmonic Concert of the season was to take place on the 5th of November. Mahler was still seething and the rehearsals produced fireworks. Following Weber's *Euryanthe Overture* and Mozart's *Symphony No. 41 in C*, the concert was to end with Beethoven's *Fifth Symphony*. Mahler made his feelings quite clear over the decidedly lackadaisical attitude of most of the orchestra while rehearsing the latter. He particularly criticised the way they played the opening of the symphony. The atmosphere became very strained, tempers began to fray, and he retorted by suggesting that the musicians keep their rage for the performance so that at least the opening of the symphony might be played correctly! Natalie recorded Mahler's views. The opening should be like a wild assault; the subsequent pauses like the efforts of a giant to fend it off with his fist. Beethoven was supposed to have remarked, 'Fate hammers on the door'. Mahler considered he might have said simply, *'Das bin Ich!'* Mahler regarded himself as being the only conductor of his time capable of realising Beethoven's vision, and he could only achieve this by 'terrorizing' the musicians, compelling them to transcend their own personal egotistical abilities. He was convinced that the way Beethoven's symphonies had been performed in the past must be brought up to date. The size of the normal symphony orchestra had increased to such an extent that the strings would normally outnumber an entire orchestra of Beethoven's time, let alone the new developments that had taken place in the instruments themselves. A new balance had to be worked out. For Mahler, Wagner was his model, and he too had suffered criticism in his efforts to adapt Beethoven's symphonies to the modern orchestra. When Mahler was convinced over a musical matter he would not be deflected from his aim, regardless of the consequences.

Following the fiery rehearsals, the performance was eagerly awaited. It was a complete sell-out, and both the audience and the press waited in anticipation of Mahler's tinkering with the orchestration, particularly in the last movement. Controversy reigned, although the changes were barely noticeable, so skilfully had Mahler adapted the score. Some critics stuck by their preconceived venomous comments, others were surprised and more positive and a few actually praised his vision and conducting. As for the *Jupiter Symphony*, the praise was virtually unanimous and some reviews even ecstatic. Thus, despite the attitude of certain members of the orchestra, the Philharmonic season had begun on a successful note, yet tinged with controversy; a combination that would guarantee good attendances at subsequent concerts.

On the 3rd of December, the Philharmonic concert programme consisted of Brahms's *Third Symphony* Dvořák's *Die Waldtraube* (The Wood Dove) and Beethoven's overture, *The Consecration of the House*. According to Natalie, Mahler had had secret desires to make cuts in the Brahms, but restrained himself fearing the furore this might cause, which many would consider to be disrespectful to the recently deceased composer. As much as he admired his chamber music, he felt that Brahms's symphonies were earth-bound with no vision of the greater scheme of things. However profound and true to his beliefs he had been as a composer, to Mahler Brahms had been a prisoner of earthly existence; he had never glimpsed the view from the summit. Consequently, his symphonies would never be of the greatest influence on the future of the art. Nevertheless, he had a deep respect for the man and his music and the performance showed this. It was a great success and for once the critics were united in their praise.

Two weeks later to the day, came the last concert of the year. Brahms was again included, this time his *Violin Concerto in D*, performed by Marie Soldat-Röger (Natalie was a member of her string quartet), but the main work was to be Beethoven's *Sixth Symphony ('The Pastoral')*, and it was this that was the focus of attention. The question that was on everyone's lips was, what would Mahler do this time? He had a special fondness for the work, especially at this time with his own symphony of nature so recently completed. Mahler considered that a successful performance of 'The Pastoral' would only take place if the conductor had a special affinity with nature, and in his opinion few of his contemporaries would qualify on this count. Natalie wrote that his interpretation was something completely new. The second movement, *Andante molto moto* (Scene at the brook), was played so slowly that there was complete astonishment in the hall. He stated firmly that the music had to flow gently, indeed like a little brook. The expected abuse that he had braced himself for did not materialise. Praise was the order of the day. Having recovered from the shock, the critics decided that they loved the babbling brook and were impressed by the mighty thunderstorm. Even his adversaries in the press such as

Theodor Helm praised the performance, and Robert Hirschfeld wrote that he was so overwhelmed by its beauty that it had brought tears to his eyes!

After a short break with Justi and Natalie in the village of Rodaun to the southwest of Vienna, Mahler braced himself for whatever the New Year, the first of the new century, would throw at him. It was not long before the anti-Semitic journalists had once more rolled up their sleeves. Anti-Mahler articles appeared in the *Deutsches Volksblatt* and *Deutsche Zeitung*, both publications really going to town in a blatantly libellous fashion. They accused him of all manner of misdemeanours during his time in Hamburg, from the personal to financial 'irregularities', and warned that he would be the ruin of the Hofoper. Mahler, who normally did not respond to such articles, felt that they had gone too far, and he feared that if they continued in this vein his standing in the world of music might well be thrown into jeopardy. He went to see Prince Montenuovo to put the record straight. He need not have worried, for the Lord Chamberlain was not to be fooled that easily by the press.

At the first Philharmonic concert of the year on the 14th of January, Selma Kurz performed five of Mahler's songs taken from *Des Knaben Wunderhorn* and *Lieder eines fahrenden Gesellen* with orchestral accompaniment. Entrusting the singing of his own lieder to Selma, he showed not only his love for her as a singer, but a deepening, more personal feeling as well. Eduard Hanslick considered these orchestral songs to be worthy successors to the songs of Berlioz, such as *Les Nuits d'Été*, and he was impressed by Mahler's orchestration, stressing that he had handled the task 'with masterly skill'. He felt that works by members of the 'musical Secession', other composers including Richard Strauss and Hugo Wolf, might prove to be the music of the future. He also added that Selma Kurz, singing the songs from memory, had done so in a most expressive manner. This concert took place only a month after Anna von Mildenburg had sung a rather grand, if none too warm, performance as Isolde (according to the critics).

Rumours of a relationship of an intimate nature between Mahler and Selma Kurz began to circulate, and with some justification. He had been spending a disproportionate amount of time with her, and his long letters to her are filled with words such as 'love . . . darling . . . embrace . . .'. At one point they even contemplated marriage, but their relationship cooled. Mahler, doubtless remembering the problems caused by Anna during his Hamburg years, must have come to his senses. Anyway, it was written that the Director should not be married to another employee of the Court Opera.

On the 19th of January there was a guest appearance by the Australian soprano, Nellie Melba at a concert conducted by Richter. Melba had endeared herself to the orchestra by donating her fee to their pension fund, so they gave her generous backing! Mahler and the press were in agreement that her singing was somewhat soulless despite her undisputed talent, Mahler deciding that he preferred listening to a clarinet. On the 22nd he conducted the première of a new fanstasy opera by Alexander von Zemlinsky, *Es war einmal* (Once upon a Time). Zemlinsky was a young and very talented composer, still in his late twenties, who had impressed Viennese music circles, including Brahms. *Es war einmal* was very popular and given numerous performances, although Mahler had mixed feelings about the quality of the work. Still, Zemlinsky was clearly a gifted composer, perhaps one to watch for the future.

The following month saw the anniversary of the performance of Mahler's *Second Symphony* at the 1899 Nicolai Concert in aid of the Opera pension fund. The 1900 event was to be held on the 18th of February, and Mahler had chosen Beethoven's *Ninth* for the occasion, on the face of it a choice that would almost guarantee success and general approval, but, as always, he insisted on his own interpretation of the work that included retouching the score. Following the storm that had greeted his similar treatment of Beethoven's *Fifth* the previous November, he anticipated the inevitable controversy by writing an explanatory leaflet to be handed out to patrons. He defended his actions by stating that in no way would he ever contemplate altering Beethoven's masterpiece, but that he had taken into consideration the development of instruments since Beethoven's time, especially the brass. This, together with the composer's total loss of hearing and his innovative use of the orchestra to create new sounds, necessitated some changes in the orchestration. Mahler considered that to do so was his duty, and wrote that he was following in the tradition of Richard Wagner who had spent his life doing his utmost to 'rescue' Beethoven's symphonies from 'decadence and neglect'.

The concert was a tremendous success, and Mahler was given one of the greatest ovations he had yet received. It had been a sell-out, so it was repeated four days later. But some of the critics, hardened men as they were, were not swept up in the tide of emotion. Richard Heuberger, writing in the *Neue Freie Presse* on the 19th of February, regarded his retouching as irresponsible; it was an act of barbarism, which flew in the face of Beethoven's vision. While stating, perhaps sarcastically, that he and his fellow critics were full of admiration for the Director of the Hofoper, he emphasised that it was time to stop such practices. Other reviewers accused him of 'disfiguring' Beethoven's music, saying that Wagner's interpretations should not have been applauded, and that Mahler had been self-indulgent. Only Max Kalbeck provided a more balanced review, justifying Mahler's approach. Needless to say, he would not be deflected from his deeply held beliefs on retouching, just as he himself declared that others should do the same to his works should the need arise.

One amusing retort from Mahler came following a comment from Prince Liechtenstein after the concert. Having congratulated him on the performance, he remarked that he had heard other tempos. Mahler's reply came in the form of a rhetorical question, when he asked if his highness had ever heard the work before! How attitudes have changed today, with performances played on period instruments living happily alongside others by a modern orchestra. This is as it should be, for both are correct in their own ways.

At the end of February Richter finally resigned, having given twenty-eight years of service to Vienna. It is interesting that in a letter to Mahler he considered that even he had been the victim of thoroughly brutish criticism, although without the Jewish label. Mahler and Richter parted on amicable terms, Mahler to face the oncoming battles at the Hofoper, Richter to England and the Hallé Orchestra. At least a line had been drawn under the old regime, although inevitably some put the blame for Richter's departure squarely on Mahler, his 'Jewishness' and his 'tampering' with well-loved repertoire. The finger was also pointed at him for the loss of other established stars, such as Marie Renard and Ferdinand Löwe, replacing them with his own favourites. There was clearly an element of truth in this in that he was happy to let well-established singers go if they felt they could not fall in with his methods and the rigorous standards that he expected of them.

The highlights of the remaining concerts of the second half of the season included Bruckner's *Fourth Symphony*, a performance for which Mahler was criticised for making cuts! Also played were the *Variations on a Theme of Haydn* by Brahms, a work Mahler was particularly fond of, and Schubert's *'Great' C major Symphony*, for which Mahler was praised for not making any cuts! The concert season had been a success financially, and despite the on-going campaign of criticism he continued to receive from some of the newspapers and journals, he was invited to continue as conductor of the Philharmonic Concerts for the following year. All but three members of the orchestra voted in his favour.

On the 22nd of April Richard Strauss wrote to Mahler under the pretext of asking him if he had an orchestrated version of the Austrian National Anthem. He told him that he was in the process of writing a ballet entitled *Kometentanz*, an 'astral' pantomime, and he wondered whether Vienna would consider staging it. Strauss told him that a performance in Berlin on the 9th of April of three of Mahler's orchestrated songs, sung by Emilie Herzog, had been given a positive reception by the audience. He enquired if the *Third Symphony* had been published, for he was eager to conduct 'What the flowers tell me' in Paris the following winter. In a postscript he stated that he had only included Mahler's songs to ensure the latter's acceptance of *Kometentanz*, admitting that that was the way he was!

Mahler replied saying that his ballet was accepted in advance, subject to his seeing the scenario regarding the cost of staging it. He asked Strauss not to perform 'What the flowers tell me' out of the context of the *Third Symphony*, lest it be misunderstood performed in isolation. He told Strauss that he would gladly send him a copy of the *Third Symphony*, although he did not expect him to conduct it due to its duration of nearly two hours and the difficulties of assembling the necessary forces.

With Selma Kurz well established and becoming very popular, Mahler's attention now focussed on a singer from Weimar – Marie Gutheil-Schoder. Coached by Richard Strauss, Mahler placed her in the same category as Anna von Mildenburg. Her voice may not have been as good as Anna's, but from a dramatic point of view she was at least her equal. She had already made guest appearances at the Hofoper. A strong-willed character, fully prepared to stand her ground against Mahler on dramatic matters, she had already caught the attention of the critics. They had shown considerable enthusiasm for her very personal, striking interpretations of the parts she had so far sung. Even if her voice was not the finest, she had undoubted star quality, and Mahler was praised for his success in signing her in the face of considerable competition from several other opera houses. He had chosen one of his favourite works for her to make her debut as a star of the Court Opera on the 26th of May: *Carmen*. It was a tremendous success. Richard Heuberger, writing in the *Neue Freie Presse* on the 27th of May, stated that the production was magnificent, and that Marie Gutheil-Schoder was remarkable. Natalie referred to her as an outstanding dramatic artist, and wrote that Mahler had called her 'a musical genius'. From all accounts Natalie was closer to the mark. Mahler had ended the season on a high note, and the almost incessant 'scribbling' against him from some quarters was, for the time being at least, pushed into the background.

The Philharmonic Orchestra had been booked to provide several concerts in Paris at the World Exhibition, and as their permanent conductor they wanted Mahler to travel with them. He was none too keen on the idea of this excursion as it would eat into his holiday and reduce his composing time, but having been invited he had to accept. He suspected that it might turn out to be a financial embarrassment, for June was a holiday month for the Parisians and there would be the inevitable competition from other events at the World Exhibition. He therefore insisted that a contingency fund of twenty thousand kronen be set up.

On arrival he discovered to his dismay that the posters advertising the concerts referred to him as 'Gustav Malheur' or 'disaster'! He was driven to the Austrian embassy where he was to be the guest of the ambassador, so at least he would have a relatively quiet, distraction-free residence during his visit. The concerts were to be held at the Théâtre Municipal du Châtelet and at the huge, acoustically terrible Palais du Trocadéro. With so many distractions at the Exhibition, good attendances necessitated extensive publicity. This had not taken place, which resulted in disappointingly small audiences and the consequent distribution of a considerable number of free tickets. The programmes consisted of works recently performed in Vienna in order to keep rehearsals to a minimum.

Those who did attend the concerts voiced their pleasure and most of the critics were favourably disposed towards Mahler, although there were raised eyebrows over some of his interpretations, especially 'his version' of Beethoven's *Fifth Symphony*! Among the most appreciative was the writer and critic Catulle Mendès, whose praise for Mahler and the Philharmonic was abundant. One thing had really impressed him. He had heard that Mahler had a highly-strung, at times volatile personality, and yet his conducting was simple and dignified. Perhaps fatigue and the extremely hot weather had played their part. Mahler did in fact pass out before one of the concerts and missed the beginning. Pierre Lalo, the composer Edouard Lalo's son, writing in *Le Temps*, praised his fresh approach to the works of the masters and regretted that he had not been able to perform one of his own works, stating that he was one of the most remarkable composers of his time.

Among those who had attended the concerts were composers Camille Saint-Saëns and Gustave Charpentier. Other important figures included the statesman Georges Clemenceau, his younger brother Paul Clemenceau and Colonel Georges Picquart, the latter two becoming close friends of Mahler's. The Paris home of Paul Clemenceau and his wife Sophie had become a venue for artists, and it was there that the art critic Berta Zuckerkandl, Sophie's sister, met August Rodin and other artists of standing. Picquart and Paul Painlevé, a well known mathematician and later Prime minister, and other members of this circle who admired Mahler, made a point of attending his concerts outside Austria whenever possible. Berta Zuckerkandl's salon in Vienna was where the idea of the Secession had first been mooted, and she would become an important player in Mahler's life.

Due to the poor advance publicity and the resulting poor attendances, not helped by the multiplicity of diverse attractions at the World Exhibition, the guarantee fund for the Philharmonic's visit had virtually run out. Mahler held crisis talks with Baron Albert Rothschild asking him to bail them out. He was a regular benefactor, but was at first unwilling to pay more than his annual gift of four thousand kronen. They needed four times that sum to settle debts and return home. They were offered a further five concerts, but piling on the agony was not what either Mahler or the Philharmonic sought. The Paris visit was already taking away ten days of his composing time. Eventually Baron Rothschild agreed, although they did not have to take up his offer in full as attendances at the final two concerts at the Trocadéro were better than had been expected.

In the first of these concerts Mahler had almost brought the house down with his interpretation of the *Symphonie fantastique* by Berlioz. Bruckner's *Fourth Symphony* and Beethoven's *Third Symphony* were played at the final concert, and at the end he and the Philharmonic were cheered. This ovation was followed by a particularly sour piece by the music critic Henry Gauthier-Villars, who declared that the performance of Beethoven's *'Eroica'*, 'chopped up' by Mahler, was definitely not to his liking, and that although there was a large audience, Beethoven was certainly not present!

All in all, Mahler had not enjoyed his visit to Paris. With all its history, beautiful buildings and its size, musically he considered Paris to be like Iglau when compared to Vienna. His opinion was doubtless coloured by the turmoil and, in his mind, distasteful atmosphere pervading the city during the World Exhibition. In a letter to Nanna Spiegler he complained of the uproar all around him, which did not provide the right atmosphere for music making. He had enjoyed the first few days walking in the countryside around Paris and he had visited Versailles. He and Ludwig Karpath had been to the Opéra-Comique to see *Le Juif polonais* by Camille Erlanger on the recommendation of Lilli Lehmann. He had seen parts of the World Exhibition and wondered at the lights, referring to them as like a scene from the Arabian Nights. But he told Nanna Spiegler that *'la gloire'* – as he called the Paris celebrations – would not have suffered at all without the music. Maiernigg and the Wörthersee beckoned and, as he put it, they crept away from Paris with their tails between their legs! However, Mahler knew that through all the trials and tribulations and his handling of numerous difficult situations, including the financial embarrassment towards the end, the members of the Philharmonic were genuinely grateful to their conductor. The relationship between Mahler and his musicians had been strengthened, for the time being at least.

Justi had arrived in Maiernigg while Gustav was still in Paris. She wrote to her sister Emma, telling her that the *Häuschen* in the forest looked like something out of a fairy tale and that the building of the villa was going ahead well. She told Emma that unfortunately the nearby Villa Antonia, which they had booked for that summer, was very cramped, her bedroom doubling up as the dining room.

On the 23rd of June, Mahler, accompanied by Arnold Rosé, arrived at the Wörthersee. Gustav's first priority was to inspect the newly built *Häuschen* in the forest, the *Waldhäuschen* as he called it. The building was much more substantial than the one at Steinbach. It was larger with plenty of room for a grand piano, his scores and books – Kant, Goethe and Bach always at hand. It had thick stone walls, shuttered windows on three sides, the door at the rear and it was surrounded by a terrace. There was a separate toilet cabin nearby that was also used as a nesting box by an owl. Mahler jokingly suggested that a plaque be placed above the door commemorating the fact that the famous composer Mahler sat there regularly! It was perfect; a place where he could compose undisturbed, the only noises coming from the birds and the wind in the trees. The spot still has an idyllic atmosphere today. Although inevitably restored, the *Häuschen* houses a collection of Mahler memorabilia, and only a short distance down a rather overgrown path heading west are the remains of the wrought iron gate and railings he had had erected to keep out intruders. He loved the spot so much that he decided as a matter of course to take breakfast there daily, despite the distance from the Villa Antonia and the steep and often muddy path up which the unfortunate maid would have to struggle whatever the weather. Just as at Steinbach, Mahler planned a strict daily routine, which he considered an essential discipline to aid him in his work and to avoid wasting precious time.

Natalie wrote that he was pale and exhausted after his travails in Vienna and the heat and frustrations of Paris. As a result he found it impossible to settle down to compose. He was both mentally and physically drained, and in his depression he feared that he might never be able to compose again. He found it difficult to pick up the threads of his *Fourth Symphony*, which had lain dormant since the previous summer in Aussee. Natalie and Justi were understandably concerned.

After a few days, they noticed that he was becoming more wrapped up in his thoughts and that he was spending longer up in the *Häuschen*. On the 6th of July he wrote to Richard Strauss, telling him that his *Fourth Symphony* would probably be more practical than its two predecessors and, given a good performance, through it his music might at last be understood. He also told Strauss that he knew of no one whom he would rather have to conduct his 'monster', the *Third*! The 7th of July marked Mahler's fortieth birthday, but he was in no mood to celebrate for the muse had reawakened in him. He began to spend as much as eight to ten hours up in the *Waldhäuschen*.

As well as working on his *Fourth Symphony*, Mahler devoted some time to studying Schubert's chamber music, and he told Natalie that he could fully sympathise with him in his desire to study counterpoint, even in his last days. He admitted that he too had a weakness on that front, proper foundations not having been laid during his student days. As a result he found this aspect of composition particularly wearing. Another score that he had brought with him was Hans Rott's *Symphony*. Studying his former fellow-student's manuscript saddened him. This work, by a man whom he considered to be the founder of 'the new symphony', was close to his heart and thinking. He believed that they were 'two fruits from the same tree', so much had they in common. What a tragedy it had been when his friend had lost his mind and died at such a young age. What might they have achieved together had he lived?

The surroundings of the *Häuschen* were beginning to seem slightly less idyllic. The birds disturbed him. At first he tried scarecrows, and when they took no notice of these he tried firing blanks to discourage their presence, but they kept coming back. News of the strange 'music recluse' had spread, and patrons at a local hotel arranged for musicians to climb up through the forest to entertain him! Sounds of dogs barking, an occasional barrel organ and, when the wind was in an unfavourable direction, he would sometimes hear the distant sounds of a military band from the far side of the Wörthersee.

Work on the *Fourth Symphony* continued to go well, despite the 'barbarity' and 'childish whims' of some in the vicinity. On the 15th of July he set off on his own for a few days walking and cycling in the Ampezzo Valley in the Dolomites, south of Toblach (now Dobbiaco). He wanted to get away from the regular disturbances and to rest mentally, for he had been in no fit state to concentrate on composition after the preceding months of stress in Vienna. On the 19th he returned sunburnt, refreshed and eager to get back to the task that was uppermost in his mind, the completion of his *Fourth Symphony*. He felt more relaxed and with the windows wide open and breathing in the fragrant forest air the music began to flow. He loved the *Häuschen* and its surroundings, and he longed for the day when he would be able to move into his villa at the water's edge.

The new routine that he set himself was to work from seven until midday, and then from four o'clock until seven in the evening. With windows flung wide and at one with nature, Mahler worked feverishly at his task. He felt that his 'second self' (the 'self' that is active during sleep) had incredibly been active throughout the winter months of nightmares in Vienna, and he was fully aware that his composition had reached a higher level. So wrapped up in his work was he that he cared little for his appearance, and on one occasion, while out cycling, unshaven and sloppily dressed, he was stopped by the police who had mistaken him for a vagrant! He informed them that he lived nearby, and hearing his accent accepted his story and let him go. Mahler told Natalie that he had made a personal bet that he would complete the score of the *Fourth* before the Villa was finished.

He was on target. Although the building was ahead of schedule at one stage, it was not expected that the villa would be completed before the end of the summer. On the 5th of August the *Fourth Symphony* was finished.

Fourth Symphony, in G
(In four movements, for orchestra and soprano solo)

Following the enormity of the 'Symphonic Worlds' of the *Second* and *Third Symphonies*, the *Fourth* is, as Max Kalbeck wrote in January 1902, a longing for simplicity. In musical terms, it mirrors Christ's words: 'Unless you become as a little child you will not enter God's kingdom'. On the face of it this new work appeared to be Mahler's reply to those who accused him of being a musical megalomaniac, but pandering to the critics was not in his make-up. Following its two enormous predecessors, it was hardly surprising that he decided to use a smaller canvas. By his standards it is short, lasting about fifty minutes, although today it is usually stretched by anything up to a further fifteen minutes. The orchestra is much reduced in size. There is an emphasis on the strings, with triple woodwind but with no trombones or tuba, only limited percussion, no chorus, just a soloist at the end, and only one passage of genuine fortissimo, an indulgence for which he was rapidly gaining something of a reputation. The *Fourth Symphony* marked a big advance in his technical mastery. It has chamber-like qualities, Mahler himself saying that his new economy of scoring resembled that of a string quartet with its greater clarity and transparency, and he predicted that orchestras would find it difficult to play with each musician having to perform like a soloist. A challenge indeed!

Mahler's hope that his *Fourth* would be more readily understood than his previous symphonies was not to be. This was typified by a report in *The Musical Courier* after a performance in New York in November 1904, which referred to Mahler's 'Drooling and emasculated symphony', 'grotesquerie' and for the listener, 'painful torture'! Another critic described it as a 'black mass', and William Ritter, the Swiss critic and artist who would later become one of Mahler's staunchest supporters, likened the first movement to 'Daniel in the lion's den, like a lady in tights performing acrobatics in a menagerie!' The new symphony was a logical successor to the *Third*, for after all the last movement had originally been intended as the *Third's* finale. It was out of this movement, the *Wunderhorn* song 'Das himmlische Leben' (The Heavenly Life) that the whole work grew. So, the last movement was the first to be composed, and within it are ideas that permeate the preceding movements. As the critic Max Graf commented, the symphony should really be heard from back to front!

First movement: *Bedächtig. Nicht eilen.*
(Deliberate. Not hurried)

Neville Cardus compared this movement to a musical *Alice through the Looking Glass*, with melodies and rhythms growing and shrinking, 'scuttling around like rabbits', and the themes lengthened and shortened like 'Mad Hatters and March Hares'! At around seventeen minutes it is half the length of its counterpart in the *Third*. It is full of Viennese charm, sleigh bells, bird calls from the woodwind and an almost Haydnesque theme played by the strings – compare that with the explosive opening of the *Second!* Mahler described it as a journey under clear blue skies, what could be called 'a celestial sleigh-ride'. Or is it? The philosopher and musicologist Theodor Adorno asked the question, are the jingling bells perhaps a court jester? Was it Mahler poking fun at his critics? Certainly his original idea had been to call the symphony 'Humoresque', a title he had conceived for his 1892 set of orchestrated *Wunderhorn* songs.

The sleigh bells refrain, repeated five times during the course of the movement, anticipates their reappearance in the final movement. But the sleigh bells are not the only surprise on an unsuspecting audience. The Haydnesque or even Schubertian theme goes through all manner of transformations and fragmentation, breaking up into independent motives, combining and recombining in ever-new contrapuntal combinations. He described this process to Natalie as 'kaleidoscopic rearrangement'. None present had ever heard the like of it before, and many thought it a sick joke! It was in fact one of the very first examples of neoclassicism, which would become increasingly popular with composers later in the century. On its journey towards 'The Heavenly Life', the music passes through the gamut of emotions, albeit fleetingly – even the occasional ogre makes a brief appearance – and at one stage is brought to a halt in a *'hiatus in manuscriptus'* (Neville Cardus). The general mood, however, is forward-looking and one of happiness laced with humour.

Second movement: *In gemächlicher Bewegung. Ohne Hast.*
(Easy motion. Without haste)

If the audience had been shocked by the first movement, the second was an even greater surprise. Mahler referred to it as *'Freund Hein spielt auf'*. Hein, a folklore creation representing Death, begins playing – he plays the fiddle. The solo violin is tuned up one tone higher, to be played unmuted, loud and clear to sound rough with out-of-tune dissonances to give the impression of a rustic, unskilled fiddler. This is a *danse macabre* that includes a ländler. Weirdly humorous yet spooky, shadowy and grotesque, Mahler commented that people shouldn't take it too seriously for it was nothing but cobwebs!

Third movement: Ruhevoll
(Calm)

This is undoubtedly the heart of the symphony and is one of his greatest creations. Mahler described the music as 'divinely serene, yet a profoundly sad melody runs through it that can only have you laughing and crying at the same time . . .' The sometimes sinister fun and games of the first two movements are now behind us. In this third movement we have a tension between peace and drama, and weaving through its twenty or so minutes is the thread of love, occasionally interrupted by moments of anguish. It is a reflection, a cleansing, a preparation for 'The Heavenly Life'.

The movement is based on two principal themes, one in the major, the other in the minor. The first is one of serene meditation, the second unrest and yearning. The first goes through a series of variations; the second is restated at various points. There is also a bass *passacaglia* theme, which is also varied. Mahler was particularly fond of this *adagio*, calling it 'my first real variations'.

The movement opens peacefully with the celli playing a heart-rending melody, apparently inspired by a recumbent effigy on a tomb with arms crossed, in eternal sleep. An oboe takes up the tune, a long lament, a cleansing of impurities in readiness for eternity. This is the essence of this movement – a shedding of earthly woes and encumbrances. But there are fleeting moments of hope and humour with the tempo changing gear, yet always returning to serenity. The point comes when the music appears to die, giving us the feeling that this beautiful movement has drawn to a close. But no, Mahler has another card up his sleeve, a real surprise – a huge climax, the only one in the entire symphony. The orchestra explodes with fast arpeggios, glissandi, crashing cymbals, pounding timpani and the brass portraying the opening of the gates to paradise. And then, with tentative steps, we are led forward. In a state of perfect peace, the music flows gently into the final movement, the *Wunderhorn* song, '*Das himmlische Leben*' (The Heavenly Life) – the end yet at the same time the starting point of the whole symphony.

Fourth movement: Sehr behaglich.
(Very comforting)

Following on from the third movement without a break, comes the final destination of the symphony – 'paradise gained' as Neville Cardus called it. The full title that Mahler gave the song was '*Wir geniessen die himmlische Freuden*' ('We enjoy the heavenly pleasures'). Mahler stated that the soprano should sing in a light, childlike fashion. Indeed the very nature of the words suggests a heaven full of simple earthly pleasures, yet free from the cares and aggravations of the world. It is a vision of paradise with food aplenty, music, dancing, singing and generally having fun! In other words a child's view of Heaven, the sleigh bells reappearing between each section. It has lightness and charm and touches of gentle humour. Today regrettably much of Mahler's music is dragged out, thereby changing the whole intention behind it, and this particular movement is very much a case in point. By doing so, greater gravitas and emotion may result, but at the same time Mahler's concept is totally changed. *Das himmlische Leben* is a prime example of this. Mahler's piano roll recording lasts 7:19, the duration of Bruno Walter's 1945 recording (and he should know Mahler's intention better than anyone else) lasts 7:36, yet the norm nowadays is around 9:15. The slower pace results in a loss of the feeling of innocence, of childlike excitement, and instead the movement becomes more adult, more dignified. This is definitely not what Mahler had in mind.

So we have completed the journey as told by 'the child', from the sleigh ride under blue skies, through the Hallowe'en-like *Scherzo*, the love and sadness of the *Adagio*, the opening of the gates to paradise and then Heaven itself. But is it that simple? Adorno's theory of a jester may have some truth, but I wonder whether there might be a much darker side that lies beneath the sunny exterior. Like Adorno, I pose a question: Could this symphony be subtitled 'Memories of an unhappy childhood'? Even though Mahler had rejected the idea of having programs, he did leave various clues.

Might the first movement be not a joyous sleigh ride, but a memory of those trips he made sitting next to his abrasive father on the horse drawn cart through the Bohemian countryside? Do the sleigh bells depict the jingling harness? There are certainly birdcalls, cocks crowing and other sounds of nature, as well as moments of a darker hue. And what of the *Scherzo*? Could this be a memory of the unpalatable combination of drunken revelries on the ground floor of their house in Iglau and the sick and dying children in their apartment above? And one memory that would remain with him always was his discovery of Justi lying on the bedroom floor pretending to be dead, candles by her side casting ghostly, flickering shadows on the walls. There seems to be an interesting link here with his first known piece, composed when he was around seven – *Polka with Introductory Funeral March*; in this case ländler with Freund Hein and his fiddle! He told Natalie that while writing the *Adagio* he had been inspired by the memory of his mother's smiling face as seen through a veil of tears, remembering the cruelty and suffering she had endured. Finally *Das himmlische Leben*. This was one of a pair of *Wunderhorn* songs, the other being *Das irdische Leben* (The Earthly Life), about a small boy who is starving and who repeatedly pleads with his mother for food. She keeps making empty promises, and at the end he dies. Might this be a memory of the gruesome time he spent with the Grünfeld family in Prague when he too was often deprived of food, most of his clothes stolen and his life made a complete misery? I am sure that at this time the eleven year old Gustav must have dreamt of a 'heavenly' existence of food aplenty and fun and games. Incidentally, Mahler's original plan for the symphony was to include both songs; The Earthy Life followed by The Heavenly Life.

As we have seen this was his most disciplined score so far and marked a clear advance in his skill as an orchestrator. For the first time he placed considerable emphasis on counterpoint, and with it the group of symphonies inspired by the *Wunderhorn* poems came to an end, and a new era in his symphonic writing was about to begin.

With the *Fourth Symphony* completed, Mahler felt a certain emptiness. He still had a few days of his holiday left to try to relax and prepare himself for the 1900-1901 season in Vienna. His feelings for Maiernigg and its surrounding countryside continued to grow deeper by the day and he already looked forward to the following summer when at last he would be able to move into his new home. He spent most of the remaining days walking, cycling and swimming.

On one Sunday walk along a woodland path towards Klagenfurt he and his companions, including Justi and Arnold Rosé, heard a cacophony of noise from a forest clearing. It was a summer fête in full swing, complete with barrel organ, shooting galleries, merry-go-rounds and even a military band and a male voice choir adding to what Natalie described as 'a witches Sabbath'. They fully expected him to explode! However, he took them all by surprise by exclaiming, 'That's polyphony!' It reminded him of the remembered sounds of his childhood in Iglau. He told her that nature is polyphony, such as the songs of thousands of birds. The only difference between those sounds and polyphony in music was that the composer ordered and harmonised them logically.

With batteries recharged, both physically and mentally, Mahler returned to Vienna on the 15th of August. Three days later he replied to a letter from his close friend Nanna Spiegler, telling her how wonderful the summer had been and how he now felt ready to face the oncoming winter. He wrote of the importance for him to be alone with nature when all things trivial would vanish. He did not relish the forthcoming struggles in Vienna, especially as he was still half in the world of his *Fourth Symphony*. He told her how different it was from its predecessors; he had to follow new paths, learn new skills, for one always remains a beginner! His fondness for Nanna and her husband Albert was quite clear for he almost begged them to come and spend some time near Maiernigg so that they could see more of each other.

Mahler had plans for launching a season of Mozart operas. This did not come about, probably for financial reasons, but he did put on a new production of *Cosi fan tutte*. This was performed on a specially designed small, revolving stage, similar in size to those used in Mozart's time. It was a triumph. Max Kalbeck stated that he had never before heard such ensemble and even Hanslick was complimentary. Among those taking part were Marie Gutheil-Schoder and Leopold Demuth. The only rumblings of criticism were of the opera itself, particularly the libretto, and the production was taken off after only seven performances. Nevertheless Mahler himself had been universally praised – a good start to the 1900-1901 season.

Following *Cosi* came a new production of *Die Zauberflöte* in which Mahler and Gutheil-Schoder, who sang the part of Pamina, received further critical acclaim. His latest discovery was proving to be a very popular singer, for the time being at least.

Despite the appointment of Franz Schalk to replace Richter, Mahler was still short of an assistant conductor. It had become imperative that the post be filled as soon as possible to alleviate the strain of having to cover for a second assistant. He still wanted Bruno Walter, who was eager to oblige, but the young conductor could not free himself from his Berlin contract. Mahler tried to sign Leo Blech, but he would not be released from the Prague Opera. He wrote to Walter, emphasizing that he was the assistant he wanted and that he would wait however long it might take. As things turned out it would be almost a year before Walter was able to make his Vienna debut.

The newly established Hugo Wolf Society of Munich, founded to promote Wolf's music and whose name was to be changed the following month to The Munich Society for Modern Music, had asked Mahler to conduct his *Second Symphony* at a concert on the 20th of October. Delighted with the prospect of his work being performed there, Mahler, Justi and Natalie travelled to Munich on the 15th. Although hardly expecting the orchestra to be of the same calibre as the Vienna Philharmonic, he was disappointed by the lack of numbers, especially in the string sections. The chorus, particularly the men, proved to be a problem and he had to arrange extra rehearsal time at his own expense, and a totally inadequate soprano had to be replaced before the final rehearsal. Mahler, the perfectionist as always, was anxious to say the least.

The reception that both he and his *Second Symphony* were given surpassed his expectations. A cloud of bewilderment had settled over many in the audience during the first movement, but by the end of the symphony the atmosphere had developed into one of ecstasy. Afterwards Mahler attended a party given in his honour, and it was there that he met a young musicologist by the name of Ludwig Schiedermair who had written in his book 'Gustav Mahler' (1900) of a tirade by the composer on the subject of programme notes. The other guests were astounded when Mahler suddenly leapt from his chair and proclaimed, 'Death to programmes!' He declared that audiences should use their own thoughts and imaginations, for how could they read and listen at the same time? Music should speak for itself for it reveals far more than words. At the back of his mind he obviously had the thought that he did not wish to be bracketed with Richard Strauss and his use of programmes.

In their reviews of the concert the members of the press were reasonably complimentary, although comparisons were made with Richard Strauss; in one case his symphony was compared to *Also Sprach Zarathustra*. This must have infuriated Mahler. However, taken as a whole, he must have been very satisfied. The composer Ludwig Thuille commented that he did not know if he should show admiration or envy that Mahler had brought before the public such a powerful composition.

Following the success in Munich of his *Second Symphony*, Mahler planned a concert in Vienna for the 18th of November that would include his *First Symphony*, the other works to be performed being Beethoven's *Prometheus Overture* and Schumann's *Manfred Overture*. He obviously thought that, with his music being more readily accepted, the time was right for Vienna to hear his previously controversial *First*. He was shocked by its reception. The delicate harmonics and dawn chorus at the beginning were 'given the bird' by sections of the audience, in particular from those whose concert-going was more of a social rather than a musical occasion. The second movement provided some respite, but matters grew worse from then on with the pros and the antis trying to outdo each other. Nothing had changed; memories of the Budapest *débâcle* must have come flooding back when even his friends had avoided him, and afterwards, as he himself put it, he 'went around like a leper'. The latest performance ended with a cacophony of boos, shouts and a few bravos from the more brave of his supporters, and even many members of the orchestra found it hard to suppress their mirth. Of course there were many present who were shocked by the rowdiness of the vociferous minority. The critics were vitriolic to say the least, led by the famous remark by Eduard Hanslick: 'One of us must be mad, and it isn't me!' Mahler was both hurt and furious and he swore that he would never ever under any circumstances compose any music simply to gain popular acclamation.

Mahler, whose authority and respect at the Hofoper had been increasing steadily, now had to face the same musicians, many of whom had shown contempt for his *First Symphony* and whose loyalty to him had been seriously brought into question. He, who had done so much to improve their pay and working conditions, felt badly let down. He confronted the orchestra with a blunt statement reminding them that he was in charge, that he would decide which works were to be performed and that if they did not like it he would resign immediately. His words defused the situation for the musicians knew full well on which side their bread was buttered. The furore over Mahler's *First* subsided, and a Beethoven concert on the 16th of December, to mark the 130th anniversary of his birth, was well received by both the audience and critics. Mahler's work at the Opera had continued unabated at its usual hectic pace, and December saw a complete *Der Ring des Nibelungen*. It too was a great success, with the singer Theodor Reichmann, with whom he had previously had a difference of opinion, eating humble pie in a congratulatory letter complimenting him, expressing his 'heartfelt admiration' and promising to show great improvement himself.

Mahler, utterly exhausted, would normally have taken a holiday over the Christmas period, but he was determined to finish the revision of his *Fourth Symphony* so that it could be published early in the New Year. Natalie wrote that he spent a few hours each morning on this task, including a complete reworking of the *Scherzo*. He told her that he was still finding counterpoint difficult due to that gap in his training.

January saw a new production of Wagner's *Rienzi*, Mahler again shaking off the dust from the tired existing one with his usual enthusiasm. As was to be expected he was concerned with every aspect of the production including the stagecraft. He told Natalie how fed up he was with overacting and unnecessary gesticulation which would often ruin an otherwise good performance. To this end he persuaded August Stoll, the chief stage director, to make students at the Conservatory practice with their arms tied to their sides! He gave Anna von Mildenburg as an example. She had begun as a thoroughly clumsy actress until he had schooled her both on and off the stage, at work and in her daily life. Mahler had insisted that she practise in front of a mirror. In her early days at the Hofoper, when she had had problems walking in long dresses, sometimes even stumbling, Justi advised her to wear similar long garments at home in order to get used to wearing them. As a result of this training Mildenburg had become one of the greatest dramatic actresses in the opera world. This is born out by Justi's remarks after the December *Ring* cycle: Anna had been 'incomparable . . . dominating . . . a genius'; so inspired by Mahler, and he in turn so moved by her.

With the mounting stresses and strains of work, exacerbated by the insulting reception of his *First Symphony,* Mahler fell ill just before the first performance of his new production of *Rienzi*. He was forced to take to his bed with an acute bout of tonsillitis. Nevertheless, despite his ill health, he insisted on conducting the performance itself. To make matters worse, on the morning of the première two of the lead singers scheduled for that evening, Hermann Winkelmann and Anna von Mildenburg, fell ill. Fortunately Anna recovered, but Mahler was forced to track down Erik Schmedes to take Winkelmann's place, eventually finding him taking a Turkish bath! The evening turned out to be a success, the press reserving their adverse comments for the opera itself considering it to be second-rate Wagner and not worth all the expense and effort put into its revival.

For Mahler the 27th of January 1901 proved to be a black day for two reasons. One of the truly great composers, Giuseppe Verdi, whom he greatly revered, died in the Grand Hotel in Milan after suffering a stroke. The same evening Mahler conducted a performance of Beethoven's *Ninth Symphony*. The applause was overwhelming, yet the critics were particularly spiteful, dredging up all the old accusations of his 'scandalous' interference with Beethoven's score and his inability to bring out the true majesty of the work.

Upset by yet more mud being thrown at him by the press, feeling run down and still not fully recovered from tonsillitis, he threw himself into his next task and a very personal one at that. *Das klagende Lied*, his first major work, which he had entered unsuccessfully for the Beethoven Prize back in 1881, had recently been published. It would be performed for the first time in the Grosser Musikvereinsaal on the 17th of February at a special concert of the Vienna Singakademie, supported by singers of the Schubertbund. The orchestra, naturally, would be that of the Hofoper, and the soloists Elise Ellizza, Anna von Mildenburg, Edith Walker and Fritz Schrödter. There was a great deal of talk in the coffee houses prior to this concert, with posters proclaiming the participation of five hundred performers.

Mahler wrote to Fritz Löhr enclosing a ticket. He told Löhr that almost every seat had been booked by season ticket holders and he added as a postscript that he felt tormented and low. He also wrote to Bruno Walter urging him to attend the dress rehearsal on the day of the concert, wanting him to be present to give his advice on any matters that might arise. He also mentioned that should there be further performances outside Vienna, he, Walter, would be the conductor.

Das klagende Lied was an emphatic success with the audience and, predictably, yet another target for the critics, who came out with words such as 'eccentric . . . folly . . . corybantic hubbub . . . bombastic . . .' Although recognising that it was a work of his youth and that he had learnt a great deal since, they begged the question, 'Why bother to perform it?' Some did however appreciate odd moments of quality, praising the orchestration. Despite the broadsides from the press, which he must have anticipated, at least his 'child of sorrow' had been well received by the audience and he immediately considered a further performance.

Three days later, on the 24th of February, he conducted Bruckner's *Fifth Symphony*. He had got his scissors out and made numerous cuts and alterations. Mahler's fond memories of the kind old professor at the Conservatory were not reflected in his music, which he had always felt was second-rate. He considered his cutting of the score to be something of a salvage operation, but his views were not widely shared. There was uproar! How dare he tamper with the work of such a revered man! There were however some who had the courage to sympathise with his actions, including Max Kalbeck, but the controversies that surrounded Mahler were proving to be too much for the Philharmonic and this was to be his final concert with them.

That same evening he stood before the same musicians conducting a performance of *Die Zauberflöte*. Tired out and with failing health, those close to him had become very concerned. Never having fully recovered from tonsillitis, this had been followed by a severe bout of influenza and a recurrence of haemorrhoids, but as always he had been reluctant to rest and give his body a chance to recover. In the audience that evening was a twenty-two year old girl – a great fan of the Director of the Hofoper. She later described his appearance that evening, saying his face was like Lucifer, his cheeks pallid and his eyes glowing red like burning coals. She had turned to those who were with her, stating that nobody could carry on for long in such a state.

Her name was Alma Maria Schindler.

Chapter 9

Vienna . . . Part Three
Alma

Rückert Lieder

ALMA WAS BORN on the 31st of August, 1879. Her father, Jacob Emil Schindler, was one of the best known and most fashionable landscape artists of his generation. He loved music and had a fine tenor voice. As a young man he had shared a studio with a fellow artist, Hans Makart, and according to Alma they gave lavish parties. One regular visitor was Franz Liszt who would sometimes entertain the other guests by playing the piano into the early hours. Her mother, Anna von Bergen, had been a singer with a promising future in light opera and operetta until her marriage when she gave up all thoughts of a singing career.

From 1884 the Schindler home was a fifteenth century manor house situated in parkland beyond the Vienna woods. Plankenberg Manor, part of the estate of Prince Karl Liechtenstein, was said to be haunted, and Alma and her younger half-sister Grete (conceived illegitimately by Anna two years after Alma's birth) spent nights trembling with fear. Despite the grand building that was their home, the family was not wealthy, it was sparsely furnished. But Alma loved their environment and her doting father; her mother less so, for she found her fussy, short-tempered and interfering. The girls spent hours watching their father paint, listening to the stories he would tell them. One of these was Goethe's *Faust*, and so moved were they that he gave them the book to read, but hardly did they have the book in their hands when their mother snatched it from them considering it to be inappropriate. She reprimanded her husband and the quarrel left an indelible mark on Alma's mind. She was more than ever determined to read *Faust*!

Emil loved both his daughters but, inevitably, Alma was his favourite – his 'princess' as he called her – and he went out of his way to open their eyes to the wonders of nature and the beauty of landscapes, both so very close to his own heart. At the same time he loved indulging in luxuries that he could ill afford. He had little time for schools so the girls' education was solely in the home. He was a Catholic, Anna a Protestant and the girls were brought up in their father's faith. Ever the romantic, Emil created a shrine to the Madonna complete with regular supplies of candles and flowers.

Interest in Emil's paintings continued to grow, and in 1889 Crown Prince Rudolf commissioned him to produce a series of pen-and-ink drawings of the towns on the Adriatic coast. Ten-year-old Alma was really excited at the prospect of this adventure. The family, together with Carl Moll, a promising artist and Emil's pupil and assistant, boarded a freighter, which called in at all the chosen ports, including Ragusa and Spizza. After several weeks they reached Corfu where Emil was free to paint purely for his own enjoyment. They had rented a cottage and a piano, and it was during their stay that Alma first began to compose. She spent a good deal of time indoors away from the abuse of some local children aimed at the 'foreigners', and it was during their stay on the island that she began to realise just how important music would be for her in her life.

Crown Prince Rudolf was so delighted with the drawings that he asked Emil to accompany him on a trip to the Orient later that same year. With a sizeable and much needed boost to the family funds, they were on the verge of departing when news reached them that Crown Prince Rudolf had died. On the morning of the 30th of January, he and Baroness Maria Vetsera had been found shot at the imperial hunting lodge at Mayerling, south west of Vienna. At first it was thought that they had committed suicide, but doubts arose and their deaths remain a mystery to this day.

Shocked and disappointed, the Schindlers unpacked; their great adventure to the Orient but an unfulfilled dream. Nevertheless, Emil's income continued to improve and the family financial situation with it, so much so that in 1892 they decided to spend a holiday on Sylt, an island in the North Sea. Again Carl Moll travelled with them, but their first real holiday turned out to be a disaster. Fifty-year-old Emil became unwell and the girls spent much of the time on their own going for walks. One day they asked if they could go to a local restaurant for lunch and it was while they were there that a very upset Carl Moll arrived to fetch them. Alma recalled how instinctively she knew that her father had died and how tearfully they had run across the sand dunes in a howling wind. The girls were locked in their bedroom so that they would not be able to see their father, but a determined Alma found a way to get out for nothing would stop her from seeing Emil. She described him lying in his coffin as being like a 'noble Greek statue', looking so much smaller than he had been in life. They took Emil back to Vienna for burial, his coffin hidden in a piano box for part of the journey as the Hamburg area was under a strict cholera quarantine.

Emil's importance as an artist was later given due recognition when a monument was erected to his memory in the Vienna Stadtpark, taking its place close to other statues of Vienna's greats such as Schubert and Mozart.

Alma lost herself in her music and reading. She had counterpoint lessons from Josef Labor, a blind organist, and when she discovered Wagner she managed to ruin what she described as her beautiful mezzo-soprano voice by spending hours on end 'screaming Wagner'.

Carl Moll had continued to live with Anna and her daughters and his developing interest in her mother disgusted Alma. Emil's former pupil had become the new father figure of the household. After a brief and unsuccessful attempt at schooling, Moll took on the task of educating his reluctant stepdaughters at home. Alma was blossoming into a very beautiful girl and was already turning eyes at parties. She was coming out of her shell and desired to make new friends. One of these was Max Burckhard, the director of the Burgtheater. He had been a friend of Emil's. Despite being twenty-five years her senior, it was to such men of maturity that she turned. Through Burckhard's influence Alma, just seventeen, began to broaden her literary horizon, which in turn inspired her to compose. Apparently she had no desire for him as a man, although he undoubtedly found her very attractive, bouncing back following rebuff after rebuff. He was a fit man who loved outdoor pursuits such as rowing, swimming, cycling and mountain climbing, and loved to spend time alone communing with nature. Although nothing came of the relationship he was good for Alma, helping to fill the gap left in her life following the death of her father. The cultured Burckhard gave her much needed love and education and understood her own artistic desires. He took her to operas and the theatre and to the Mozart Festival in Salzburg. He introduced her to the works of Friedrich Nietzsche and contemporary poets such as Richard Dehmel and Rainer Maria Rilke, whose poems she would set to music.

In 1897, when Alma was eighteen, Anna married Carl Moll. She was shocked. How could her mother marry someone so inferior to her late father? As Alma put it, she had married a pendulum, whereas her father had been a complete clock! Carl had decided to concentrate more on dealing in paintings rather than creating his own. For business reasons he moved the family from their 'childhood castle', with all its memories, to a house close to the commercial and cultural centre of Vienna. Another link with the past had been broken, but it was not long before a new man came into Alma's life, a thirty-five year-old artist with whom she became infatuated – Gustav Klimt. Considered by many as being a member of the artistic lunatic fringe, Klimt was captivated by her. He wore clothes akin to a monk's habit and lived a decidedly Bohemian life style. Rumours abounded about his relationship with Emile Flöge, a dressmaker, as well as his regular flings with his models. Emil had told Alma to reach for the stars; Klimt was her first! He had become a regular visitor to their new home at Theresianumgasse 6, for he and Carl Moll were founder members of the Secession, Klimt becoming its president.

Alma's earlier bitter feelings towards her stepfather had begun to mellow. As a maturing young lady carving out her own life she had come to accept Carl Moll's marriage to Anna. Alma and Carl went for walks together and he introduced her to many famous people in the world of the arts. One of these was the opera singer Lilli Lehmann. She was thrilled to meet her, and on the 9th of February 1898 Alma attended a performance of *Fidelio*, on the same day writing in her diary that Lehmann was unforgettable as Leonore. Alma wanted to become a star, to achieve something great – but how? Perhaps she could write an opera. She criticized herself for being too frivolous to achieve her artistic aims. She ended by pleading with God that some important mission might be bestowed upon her, that she might achieve something great.

Two days later she was invited to an uncut performance of *Siegfried* conducted by Mahler. She was swept away by the music and she could hardly wait for *Götterdämerung* two days later, which was being staged to mark the anniversary of Wagner's death. Regrettably it had to be cancelled due to the singer Hermann Winkelmann falling ill. A week later she heard Lilli Lehmann again, this time in the title roll of *Norma*. Dancing, parties, concerts, art exhibitions and meeting the famous, life had become a whirl of excitement, but she still carried on with her music lessons. Her own music too remained important to her, and on the 17th of March her diary entry states that she had composed a new song with words by Goethe.

At the same time Alma's interest in art remained strong, which was not surprising when remembering the esteem with which her father was held, coupled with her feelings towards Gustav Klimt! She turned her hand to drawings (as seen in her diary), painting and also sculpture, but Anna Moll became very concerned over her daughter's increasing closeness to him and decided that the relationship should be terminated. This was easier said than done. Having secretly read Alma's diary in which she wrote of a kiss, Anna told Klimt to break off the affair, but this simply resulted in their meetings becoming clandestine. Klimt followed them on holiday to Venice and at one stage threatened to kidnap Alma, an idea she positively loved! The whole situation had become particularly embarrassing for Carl Moll, for he had to work closely with Klimt on Secession matters.

Moll told Klimt to stand back and Alma, thinking that his interest in her had waned, was distraught. In her diary entry for the 11th of May 1899, she used words such as cowardly and betrayed. On the 17th she wrote that she could no longer compose, her creativity spent. On the 25th of June she accused Klimt of refusing to share 'the joys of youth' with her, and yet on the 4th of August she declared that the only person she had ever loved and could probably ever love was Gustav Klimt – he was eternally hers.

On the 3rd of April 1900, whilst walking along the Ringstrasse, Alma met Mahler. She wrote in her diary that she was very taken by him. To her the Director of the Court Opera was a musical God! How thrilled she was when, on the 25th of June, she received a postcard from him from Paris with a view of the Champs Elysées bearing his autograph.

Alma turned her mind once more to composing. To assist her in this she started having music tuition from a new teacher, the twenty-nine-year-old Alexander von Zemlinsky. Helped and encouraged by Brahms, he had become noted as an up and coming composer. He was gaining a reputation as a very good young teacher, one of his pupils being Arnold Schoenberg. Alma described Zemlinsky as 'a hideous gnome'. He was ugly, short and usually unwashed, but when it came to music he exuded great magnetism. He recognised her talent and she respected his strictness as a teacher, for as a woman in a man's world she was determined to prove herself as a composer. Mahler conducted the première of Zemlinsky's opera *Es war einmal* (*Once upon a Time*) at the Hofoper – a new chapter in young Alma's fairy tale life was about to begin; she was reaching for her second star!

She led poor Zemlinsky a merry dance. At one moment she would encourage his advances, the next she would become cold. The numerous letters between them make it quite clear that their relationship was stormy to say the least. Alma was self-centred, expecting men not only to succumb to her charms, but to grovel before her, yet in music matters she showed the greatest respect for Zemlinsky. Usually she had her lessons at home, but sometimes she would go to his studio where she met other budding composers including Arnold Schoenberg. She was thus introduced to the beginnings of the music of the New Viennese School. Alma was not impressed, and in her diary entry for the 1st of December 1900 she describes Schoenberg as 'an aberration'! Whereas she showed great interest in the new ideas represented by the Secession, she showed scant interest, even hostility, towards the 'new' music. Under Zemlinsky's guidance Alma composed a great many songs and a number of instrumental pieces.

The seeds for the Secession had been sown in the salon of Berta Zuckerkandl whose sister, Sophie, Mahler had met in Paris. Berta, a journalist's daughter, was well known in the cultural circles of Vienna. She was married to Emil Zuckerkandl, a professor of anatomy, and at one stage she had been very close to the French statesman Georges Clemenceau. The Zuckerkandls' home was very akin to the Molls' with regular meetings and social occasions involving those in the arts. It was therefore not surprising that the two families got to know each other well. According to Alma's diary, Berta remarked that it was bad enough that Alma had good looks, that her gift as a pianist was infuriating, but being a composer as well made her feel sick! Emil was a strong supporter of Klimt, despite his Bohemian lifestyle, and Berta's influence in the world of the arts was considerable. Mahler too became a friend of the Zuckerkandls.

Alma's social life continued unabated and she revelled in the fact that on every occasion eyes were turned towards her. In her diary she boasted that she was the most beautiful, the most alluring, the most desired person at the parties she attended. One man she had fallen in love with was the singer Eric Schmedes. She saw him regularly and, having danced with him at a party, her name was mentioned in the divorce proceedings of his marriage!

It was not surprising that Zemlinsky's eagerness to teach her began to waver and the lessons became less regular, but Alma still received coaching from Labor. She also continued to see Burckhard, he being a family friend. On the 11th of November she wrote that Mahler was sweet and <u>so</u> bright, yet on the following day she wrote ecstatically about Burckhard, concluding with the words 'Burckhard – my Burckhard!' On the 27th of January her thoughts of Burckhard had worked her up into a frenzy of desire. Yet she still saw Zemlinsky, and on the 31st of January she wrote that she was 'endlessly fond of him'. Burckhard, Zemlinsky, Schmedes and Mahler . . . The 24th of February arrived, the evening she went to the Opera to see *The Magic Flute*, the evening she was so shocked by Mahler's appearance.

Mahler's looks were indeed a forewarning of a near fatality, for that very night he was struck down with a haemorrhage. He had had haemorrhages before in the 'nether regions', but this one was far more severe. (In a letter to Strauss he mentioned that he had lost two and a half litres of blood). Justi managed to contact his doctor, who in turn called in a surgeon who remarked that his life had been saved with only half an hour to spare. On the 3rd of March the *Neues Wiener Journal* announced that he would be operated on the following week and that after the operation he would be going away to convalesce, his conducting duties to be taken over by Franz Schalk. This had been a shot across the bows for Mahler. He was flesh and blood like everyone else and he knew that in the future he would have to be more cautious and reduce his workload. Bruno Walter later wrote that it was at this point that Mahler had aged considerably and had become milder and more tolerant. He had told Walter that in the past he had embraced certainty, but that he had lost it. He would regain it the next day and then lose it the following day. Uncertainty had struck and he was filled with a feeling of insecurity. Great concern was voiced, from Emperor Franz Joseph and Prince Montenuovo down to the man in the street.

The operation had been successful, his convalescence at a sanatorium very beneficial, and at the end of March he and Justi left to spend two weeks in Abbazia near Trieste where he could relax, rebuild his strength and brace himself for the final weeks of the 1900-1901 season.

During his absence from Vienna it was reported in *Die Reichswehr* on the 2nd of April that amongst the ranks of the Philharmonic an anti-Mahler movement was gathering momentum. His fiery temperament and excessive zeal were criticised, as was his supposed favouritism towards certain members of the orchestra – inevitably Arnold Rosé was one, though not mentioned by name. Mahler's reappointment was due to take place in September, and thoughts were being turned towards finding a new man for the post. Mahler had had disagreements with the Philharmonic in the past, but he had done everything in his power to further their well-being and reputation, and he would have been very hurt had he known what was going on behind his back. Ludwig Karpath had sent the newspaper articles concerned to Justine, warning her what was going on. She thanked Karpath, telling him that she would not tell her brother for fear of upsetting him and thereby hindering his recovery. Anyway, Mahler would have to give up the Philharmonic concerts for the sake of his health.

Natalie had joined Justi and Gustav in Abbazia, she still clinging onto the dream that one day Gustav would marry her. With regular gentle walks with the aid of two walking sticks, good food and time to carry out further work on the score of the *Fourth Symphony*, Mahler's health improved rapidly. He had had warnings of the consequences of over-work and he would heed them.

Alma's erratic roller-coaster ride with Zemlinsky continued. She had a lesson with him on the 6th of March, and she wrote that she felt uplifted, that she 'lived in him'. She spent that evening at the Zuckerkandls and among the other guests present was the Secession artist Koloman Moser whom she liked. Two days later she attended a concert that included lieder by Zemlinsky, but he had failed to greet her. This shocked and hurt Alma who was so used to men falling at her feet! She decided to greet him coolly when they next met. This upset Zemlinsky, but he retaliated by telling her that there were occasions when her presence could be an embarrassment. A lesson had been learnt; Alma felt devastated, as her diary makes clear. No sacrifice would be too great to win him back. She would fall to her knees and beg; it was all her fault! On the 15th of March she went to the 10th Secessionist exhibition. She waxed lyrical about Klimt's work but despite sending Zemlinsky a ticket, he failed to turn up. She met him on the 18th of March, but he was cool towards her. On the 23rd, a young architect by the name of Felix Muhr proposed to her. She fended him off by saying that she was too young to make such a decision and that she wished to leave such thoughts for at least six months. She wrote that her 'two darlings' (Burckhard and Zemlinsky) were nearby, and now between them was a Muhr (Fr. *mur*: wall)!

Alma began to see Zemlinsky more often. They went out together, and her diary clearly indicates that her love for him had been well and truly rekindled. From the gloom that had descended on her after their tiff, springtime had brought joy to her heart, but she was distraught when he told her of his plans to leave Vienna in the not too distant future. Despite encouragement from Carl and Anna, who were only too keen on seeing their daughter settle down with a stable, reliable man, there was no way that Alma would marry Muhr, and on the 18th of April she wrote that she and Zemlinsky had embraced and kissed.

When Mahler returned to Vienna, he discovered the full extent of the plots against him, emphasised by the lavish praise that the critics had bestowed on Franz Schalk and Josef Hellmesberger who had deputised for him in his absence. He had already decided not to continue as conductor of the Philharmonic concerts. He bit his tongue and wrote to the committee stating that due to his recent poor health, and with much regret, he would no longer be able to continue as their concert conductor. Nevertheless he would do everything possible to encourage them in their work, and would be delighted to conduct the orchestra on occasions, health permitting. Hellmesberger was duly elected. Josef Hellmesberger came from a prominent musical family, among whom his grandfather, also named Josef, had been the concertmaster of the Vienna Philharmonic and director of the Vienna Conservatory. Josef junior was therefore a popular choice, but with his limited conducting experience it soon became apparent that he was out of his depth. The sighs of relief at Mahler's departure, fuelled by the press, were accompanied by a lowering of standards (not properly acknowledged by the critics) and a substantial drop in ticket sales.

The last few weeks of the opera season saw further conflict, this time sparked off by Mahler giving the part of Hans Sachs in Wagner's *Die Meistersinger* to the younger singer Leopold Demuth. A similar situation of jealousy arose when Eric Schmedes became convinced that Mahler favoured Leo Slezak above him, but such opera star tantrums, however irritating, were not unusual and with careful handling they normally blew over.

The anti-Semitic section of the press, having successfully encouraged the musicians to increase the pressure on Mahler not to continue as conductor of the subscription concerts, concentrated once more on finding fault in every way possible with his work at the Opera. But despite all the trials and tribulations of the previous six months, for Mahler the season did end on a good note for the future – Bruno Walter would be joining him as his assistant conductor. Mahler wrote to him early in June on the day he set off for his summer break, telling Walter that he would be sent a contract which would be for two years at a salary of 6,000 florins. He made it clear that the brevity of the contract was deliberate to facilitate a pay increase when the time for renewal came. He told Walter to keep quiet about his appointment, presumably to prevent any anti-Semitic build up during the summer. He gave Walter his holiday address, and hoped that he might pay a visit during August.

Justi and Natalie had travelled to Maiernigg a few days before Mahler to ensure that everything was as ready as possible for his arrival. Much still needed to be done, but Natalie described the house and its location between the Wörthersee and the forest as having a magical charm and quite enchanting. There were two stone terraces overlooking the lake, and Mahler's attic floor with its balcony was like a watchtower.

Mahler arrived on the 5th of June, and when he saw his new holiday home he said it was almost too beautiful. To him it was like heaven on earth. A further delight was the discovery of a spring nearby. The land was promptly purchased and thereafter Villa Mahler had a constant supply of fresh mountain water. Gustav, mellower after his close brush with death, was less upset by birds while he was composing. He now regarded them as his friends and fellow composers. He had fully expected to find it difficult to get back into composing mode following a particularly tiring and frustrating year, but after only three days the muse in him began to awake, and he started to spend long periods up in the *Häuschen*, although he did not tell his companions what he was working on.

He told Natalie of his undying, even increasing admiration for Bach and the wonders of his polyphony. He considered that he was constantly learning from the old master and felt like a child sitting at his feet. And Schumann – one of the greatest of all composers of songs – should be held in the same regard as Schubert. Mahler began to jot down musical thoughts whenever they came to him, and as always he had a notebook in his pocket for this purpose. It was so easy to forget an idea, and by building up a collection he would have a ready source of material to dip into whenever the need arose.

During this summer he kept up a regular correspondence with Richard Strauss, who was very eager to see his opera *Feuersnot* staged in Vienna, and Mahler, eager to oblige, had sent the work to the censor. No reply had yet been received, but Mahler warned Strauss that a few cuts might have to be made. As part of the on-going chain of reciprocal gestures, Strauss told him that he wanted to make the *Third Symphony* the centrepiece of the 1902 Krefeld Festival, which he was in the process of planning. Of course Mahler would conduct. Strauss told him that ideally he would have liked it to be performed in Berlin, but the orchestra was too small and the cost of hiring the additional forces necessary too great. Instead, Strauss proposed conducting the new *Fourth Symphony* in Berlin that winter, but Mahler told him that the parts would not be ready in time, and that Berlin had not been sympathetic to his music in the past. It was a work that was very close to his heart and, anyway, he had already promised Munich the première. Returning to the *Third*, Mahler stressed that any performance must follow his instructions to the letter, but that if he himself were not to conduct it he knew of no one else more suitable than Strauss capable of tackling 'this monster'. Strauss reassured him that at the Krefeld Festival all the resources required would be available and that he would have complete control. Strauss told him that he would very much like to conduct the *Fourth* <u>after</u> the Munich première. Mahler agreed, saying that it was due to be published in October. He also suggested a performance of *Das klagende Lied* and Strauss replied asking him to send him the score.

The main work that Mahler was concentrating his compositional powers on that summer was the *Fifth Symphony*. He told Natalie that he was finding it particularly challenging, especially the *Scherzo*, and that he envisaged musicians who played the music would have to be of accomplished soloist standard. The new work would be entirely orchestral, for in this symphony the human voice would be entirely out of place. He was not able to complete the *Fifth Symphony* during the summer of 1901, but he did compose eight more songs. Seven of these were based on poems by Rückert, the eighth another from the *Des Knaben Wunderhorn* collection:

Der Tamboursg'sell (The Little Drummer Boy)

The boy is being taken to the gallows for an unnamed crime, a harrowing subject probably reflecting the deaths of Mahler's siblings as well as his own recent narrow escape. It is a song of farewell, and to increase the atmosphere of gloom Mahler uses no violins or violas and the military sounds are devoid of the bright sounds of trumpets. This song marked the end of an era for him, for having completed it he lay aside the *Wunderhorn* anthology which had inspired his first four symphonies and twenty-four lieder. With the *Fifth Symphony* under way and with greater confidence, he could see into a future more personal, even experimental.

Friedrich Rückert (1788-1866), a popular poet of the Biedermeier era, had already inspired Schubert and Schumann to compose some of their finest songs. Now Mahler too was struck by the emotional depth of the poet's works. Dark and brooding, sometimes in praise of love and beauty, they are laced with the mysteries of life, death and eternity. It is no wonder that Mahler was attracted to them for these poems so clearly reflected his own profound thoughts. He composed both piano and orchestral versions, his orchestration tailor-made for each song. They are little masterpieces and the complete antithesis of his huge 'world' symphonies.

Ich atmet' einen Linden Duft
(I breathed a gentle fragrance)

A short, lyrical song, the words reflecting Chinese poetry, it compares the fragrance of a twig of lime to a loved one and ends with the words 'love's gentle fragrance'. Short it may be with only eight lines of poetry, but it is a miniature of such delicacy, the voice being used as one of the instruments. Wagner had used voices in this way, and Mahler adapted and used the master's practice to perfection.

Blicke mir nicht in die Lieder
(Do not look at my songs)

Rückert's lines in this poem reflect Mahler's own attitude towards composition, the poet asking not to be disturbed until his task has been completed. While these parallel feelings appealed to Mahler, he nevertheless considered this brief song to be one of his least important and quipped that this would probably ensure that it became the widest acclaimed; a typical sarcastic swipe at the ignorance of many contemporary concert-goers! Such acclamation did not materialise. However, its brevity and comparative lightness act as an important interlude between its heavier, more profound companions in much the same way as the *scherzos* in his symphonies.

Um Mitternacht
(At midnight)

Like the *Second Symphony*, *Um Mitternacht's* journey is from fear and loneliness, through resignation and suffering to a confident embrace of faith in the beyond. It is noble and unsentimental, and is scored for wind, brass, piano, harp and drums. From pessimism to optimism, it ends on a particularly grand note, unique in its conception for its time. It cries out for applause!

Ich bin der Welt abhanden gekommen
(I am lost to the world)

Of this group of four songs based on the poetry of Rückert (a fifth, *Liebst du um Schönheit,* to be added the following year), *Ich bin der Welt abhanden gekommen* is by far the most important and personal. It is Mahler at his most sublime and is clearly the forerunner of the as yet to be composed *Adagietto* of the *Fifth Symphony,* and much later Richard Strauss's *Four Last Songs,* composed between 1946 and 1948. For *Um Mitternacht* Mahler had used no strings, here strings are to the fore and the scoring as delicate as gossamer. As with all his songs, the orchestration was perfectly tailored to suit the poetry. He told Natalie that this song was 'his very self'. It is full of emotion, yet restrained so as not to become sentimental. The lyrics speak of a hermit-like existence, blinkered to the realities of the world, lost in a heavenly dream of tranquillity – hardly reflecting Mahler's life, although Rückert's words must have rung true during Mahler's long hours in his *Häuschen* up in the forest, far away from the stress and hurly-burly of Vienna. Of course he was not able to shut out the Hofoper from his mind. Indeed, his secretary visited him on several occasions to keep him in touch! Arnold Rosé came to stay and conversations inevitably drifted towards Vienna, but Mahler enjoyed Rosé's company and together with Natalie they spent pleasurable evenings playing chamber music. Rosé had another matter on his mind too; he was becoming increasing drawn towards Justine.

The other Rückert poems that had attracted Mahler's attention were from a collection of 425 poems on the subject of the death of children, the *Kindertotenlieder.* On the face of it this was a somewhat morbid selection, but Mahler was clearly moved by Rückert's poetry, written in memory of two of his own children who had died. One of these children was named Ernst, inevitably bringing back memories of the death of his own brother by the same name in 1874. The grief that Mahler suffered at the time came flooding back and he determined to compose a song cycle in remembrance. The summer of 1901 saw work on three of the *Kindertotenlieder.* These will be discussed in a later chapter.

That summer had been a particularly productive one for Mahler. He loved his new home and *Häuschen* and the beauty and peace of the surroundings, just occasionally disturbed by unruly interruptions from inebriated revellers shouting abuse from passing boats. For the last part of the holiday Justi and Arnold Rosé left to spend time together on their own. During these final days Mahler confided in Natalie as never before. He invited her to come up to the *Häuschen* so that he could play and discuss with her his new compositions. He even presented her with the autographs of seven of the eight lieder he had written that summer, *Ich bin der Welt abhanden gekommen* being the sole exception. Rested and more than happy with the fruits of his labours, Mahler, accompanied by Natalie, left Maiernigg on the 26th of August. The weather was cold for the time of year, and they huddled together for warmth. Natalie must have thought that at last Mahler's thoughts might turn towards marrying her, but his mind was on Vienna and having to face the new and what would turn out to be a particularly momentous season there.

The merry-go-round of Alma's flirtations began to wear her down. Her aunt Mie, of whom she was very fond and whose advice she usually heeded, told her that she looked unwell, saying that it was probably caused by all the secret letter writing her niece had been involved in. Mie tried to dissuade her from contemplating marriage to Alexander von Zemlinsky. She told Alma that he was a Bohemian, ugly and stubborn. Grete, Alma's half-sister, also added her concern saying that he was too weak for her, but the more warnings she received the stronger her determination became. Alex was the man for her! Pressure increased for her to marry Muhr. Her mother even threatened to forbid Alex from entering their home. Confrontations between Alma and her mother became very heated, Alma telling her in no uncertain terms not to interfere and that she herself would decide whom she would marry. Burckhard continued to pursue her energetically, Alma allowing him to go only so far and not permitting the ultimate sacrifice, although she wrote in her diary on the 24th of July that she longed to be raped – 'Whoever it might be'!

On the 15th of September Alma wrote that her mother had absolutely forbidden her from visiting Zemlinsky at his home. The pleasures in her heart were accompanied by ever increasing pain. Her frustration is mirrored in her diary entry of the 24th of September, in which she wrote that she had observed two flies copulating, and how envious she was.

The following day the family moved to their new home, a semi-detached house on the Hohe Warte in a fashionable northern suburb of the city. Living in the adjoining house was the artist Koloman Moser. Alma liked the building, but it was further from the centre of Vienna, from Alex and from the cultural circles she adored. She declared that she felt that death was closing in on her.

Mahler's reaction to the first performances of the new season was one of disappointment, even frustration. Standards of both singing and orchestral playing were lack-lustre. The inspiration and fire that he had brought to the Hofoper seemed to have disappeared. He had, however, managed to acquire the services of the tenor Leo Slezak whose contract took effect as of the 15th of September. Ever since his much-acclaimed performance in *Guillaume Tell* the previous January, Mahler had been determined to wean him away from the Berlin Opera. Anna von Mildenburg was having an affair with the writer Siegfried Lipiner, Mahler's socialist friend whom he had first met whilst a student at the Conservatory. Lipiner, aware of Mildenburg's former feelings towards the Director of the Hofoper, was keeping a close eye on her communications with Mahler censoring or even dictating her letters to him. Mahler was both hurt and annoyed by this and told Mildenburg that if she wished to contact him to have the decency to do it in person, not through an intermediary. Maiernigg already began to seem a distant dream.

A ray of sunshine came with a visit from Josef Foerster and his wife Berta Foerster-Lauterer. Mahler was delighted to renew his friendship with his Hamburg friends, but an even greater joy was the arrival of Bruno Walter to take up his post as his assistant.

Bruno Walter made his debut at the Hofoper on the 28th of September. It was no small-scale work that Mahler had given him for the occasion, but Verdi's epic opera *Aida*. He had been determined that Walter's debut would not only be a hit with the audience, but would also hit the headlines! Very often he would feel decidedly uncomfortable while listening to a performance conducted by someone other than himself. Natalie recorded that on this particular occasion Mahler, sitting in his box, was completely satisfied with Bruno Walter's conducting. He could delegate to his young assistant with confidence. Walter himself was very pleased with the way the evening had gone, and his confidence was further boosted by the congratulations he received from his friends. To Walter, Mahler the conductor was something of an idol, an ideal to which he aspired. He wrote to his parents telling them how cordially Mahler had received him.

Almost inevitably many of the critics had pre-planned an assault on the young conductor. Walter, although he had become a Protestant, was Jewish by birth. They used this fact as an excuse to launch a particularly unpleasant campaign against him. How dare Mahler employ such a young, inexperienced conductor! Max Graf in *Die Musik* accused Walter of imitating Mahler's method, which was probably largely true as, after all, he was his mentor! According to Graf he used the same movements, gestures and looks. His mannerisms were simply a plagiarism of Mahler's. Yet Graf did have the honesty to mention that he did show promise and was in full control of both the orchestra and the cast.

Mahler had warned Walter about the largely hostile press, particularly those of an anti-Semite persuasion, so the young conductor was prepared for the onslaught and knew that his reply had to be excellence on the podium. Even so he was understandably upset, especially when Mahler told Walter's wife Elsa that it appeared he was losing the battle with the press. Walter, however, like Mahler, was not one to give in easily and he determined to fight on and win.

Thus the opening of the 1901-1902 season had proved to be stormy with broadsides being aimed at both men. Mahler was criticised for his 'financial and artistic mismanagement'. Some accused him of adopting a policy of 'out with the old, in with the new' and of using the prestigious Hofoper as a testing ground for unproven artists, Walter being the prime example. Mahler's promotion of Marie Gutheil-Schoder above the incumbent stars of the Court Opera angered some, such as Theodor Helm, when she had been cast as Venus in *Tannhäuser*. On the other hand she was praised by others for her performance in Nicolai's *Lustigen Weiber*. The controversies continued and would always continue, for Mahler was never one to take the easy path of automatically accepting the status quo.

Frustrated by the restrictions placed upon her by her mother and the environs of her new home, the October entries of Alma's diary were centred around Alex von Zemlinsky, her desire for him taking on a new intensity. He visited her on the 5th of October, ostensibly to give her a music lesson, but he arrived late having missed his train and they spent the time that remained kissing and cuddling. Burckhard visited on the following day with a similar intention, bearing a bouquet of roses, but Alma's mind remained firmly on Alex. She wrote that she wanted to be a carpet under his feet, a bed that he could lie on. How her body and soul yearned for the short, ugly, yet sweet Alex.

One afternoon, while walking along the Ringstrasse, Alma met Berta and Emil Zuckerkandl. They told her that Sophie, Berta's sister, and her husband Paul Clemenceau were spending a few days with them. They had arranged a dinner party and among the invited was Gustav Mahler. Would she like to come? Her immediate reaction was to decline the invitation. She admired Mahler as a conductor, but he was from a Jewish family, and Alma, like so many in the echelons of Viennese society, preferred not to mix with members of that race. She had also heard rumours, and doubtless read in the press, of his reputation regarding his leading ladies, in particular Anna von Mildenburg, as well as the famed unpredictability of his personality. She had been present at the performance of his *First Symphony* on the 18th of November 1900 and had disliked it. She feared that her presence might prove to be an embarrassment and that Mahler's lack of tact might upset her. True also was the fact that she found such formal gatherings difficult due to the tinnitus from which she suffered.

Plans for the dinner had to be postponed due to Mahler's other commitments, much to Alma's relief, but a new date having been chosen, Berta persisted by telling her that among the other guests invited were Burckhard and Klimt. Alma accepted! Also invited was the artist Alfred Roller, a tall, imposing figure born in Brno in Moravia, and who was to play an important role during Mahler's tenure at the Vienna Court Opera.

Alma arrived with Carl Moll as her mother was not well and unable to attend. The twenty-two year old Alma immediately attracted Mahler's attention and he found it difficult to take his eyes off her. At the dinner table Berta had placed Alma between Burckhard and Klimt, with Mahler sitting opposite next to Sophie Clemenceau. A great deal of giggling and laughter came from Alma and her amorous companions, and Mahler, still finding it hard to take his eyes off her, broke off his quiet, polite conversation with Sophie Clemenceau and asked if they could share the joke. At which point the door opened and another guest arrived – Zemlinsky! He had come hot foot from a recital by the Czech violinist Jan Kubelik. Zemlinsky, apologising for his late arrival, enthused about the brilliance of the violinist until Alma muttered that recitals by virtuosi did not interest her. From across the table Mahler exclaimed, 'Nor me'.

With dinner over, Mahler engaged Alma in a discussion on the subject of beauty. An example he gave was Socrates. Alma cited Zemlinsky who, despite his physical ugliness, was to her beautiful. She must have felt pangs of guilt having contradicted Alex over the recital by Kubelik and then having virtually, although not deliberately, ignored him. Zemlinsky had written a ballet entitled *Das goldene Herz,* which he had sent to the Director of the Hofoper for consideration. Alma asked him why he had not had the decency to reply. When Mahler, embarrassed, promised that he would, but said that he found it difficult to understand Hugo von Hofmannsthal's story and symbolism, Alma said that she would explain it to him. She told him that she had been studying composition with Zemlinsky. Mahler's eyes lit up and he asked her to visit him at the Hofoper so that he could see one of her compositions. He was impressed by the way she had stood up for Zemlinsky. Alma had grown to like Mahler as the evening had progressed, although she wrote that he was extremely restless. He was all oxygen – go too close and you would get burnt!

Mahler and Burckhard together left the Zuckerkandls' and the subject of conversation was Alma. Mahler told him that initially he had found her to be merely a pretty young girl, yet during the course of the evening he had begun to appreciate her intelligence. The fact that she was indulging in a serious activity, especially composition, appealed to him. He began asking a reluctant Burckhard about her. His reply, 'Those who know Fräulein Schindler are aware of what she is. Those who do not should not ask', must have sunk deep into Mahler's mind. It parallels his instruction towards the end of his life regarding the inscription on his gravestone, when he made it clear that just his name would suffice, for 'Those who come to look for me will know who I was; the rest do not need to know'.

The following day Alma, accompanied by Berta and Sophie, set out to visit Mahler at the Opera. When they arrived they saw him standing impatiently outside his office. He welcomed them cordially, took Alma's coat, and led them into his inner sanctum. All the time his eyes were on the twenty-two year old, virtually ignoring Berta and Sophie. The Director of the Hofoper was already coming under her spell. He took his guests through to the auditorium where he was due to conduct the dress rehearsal of Offenbach's *Les Contes d'Hoffmann*.

One reason why he had decided to put on *Les Contes d'Hoffmann* was that he knew it would guarantee packed houses, thereby providing the necessary means to be able to stage new productions of works by Wagner and Mozart. He had revised the libretto and music and had prepared three casts in order to have as many performances as possible during the winter months. The objective was achieved, but with such repetition Mahler reached the point when he could not stand the opera!

Alma was very impressed by his control and his eye for detail with every aspect of the production, even at one point despatching Marie Gutheil-Schoder to her dressing room to have the slits in her costume sewn up for the sake of decency! Twice Mahler came over to speak to them.

The following morning Alma received a poem:

> It happened overnight!
> Never would I have thought
> That counterpoint and the rule of form
> Would once more weigh heavily on my heart.
>
> Thus over one night
> They overwhelmed
> And all the voices joined
> Homophonically in a single tune.
>
> It happened overnight
> – I remained awake –
> So that the instant of a knock
> My eyes would shift towards the door!

> I hear it: Word of Honour!
> In my ears it rings
> In the manner of a canon:
> I gaze at the door – and wait!

The poem was unsigned, yet Alma guessed who had written it. She showed it to her mother, but Anna completely rejected the idea that Mahler had written it. Why should a man of his importance bother to write such a thing for a young girl?

Flattered as she undoubtedly was, Alma's obsession with Zemlinsky continued. On the very day that she received the poem there is no mention of it in her diary, the whole entry devoted to Alex with a mixture of philosophical and carnal thoughts, from her belief that art emanates from love to her desire to kiss his loins!

On the 11th of November Alma attended the première of the new production of *Les Contes d'Hoffmann*, which she thoroughly enjoyed, despite having been suffering from a stomach complaint all day and having had to put up with the persistent Muhr at dinner. The next day she wrote that she felt 'absolutely nothing' for Alex. The roller-coaster ride continued.

On the 19th Alma attended a performance of Gluck's *Orpheus*. Bruno Walter was conducting and Mahler sat in the Director's box. She stared up at him and eventually caught his attention. Afterwards he invited Alma and her mother to take refreshments in his office. He was gracious and kind. Conversation turned to the Hohe Warte, Mahler saying that he knew their home well as he often took walks to Heiligenstadt, passing their house on the way. Anna was impressed and replied that should he be walking in that direction to be sure to pay them a visit, an invitation that he readily accepted. He said that he looked forward to doing so after his return from Munich where he was to conduct the first performance of his *Fourth Symphony* to be given at the fifth Kaim concert on the 25th. Anna had been won over by Mahler, but Carl Moll, on being told of the encounter and the invitation to their home, was not amused. He did not want his stepdaughter to become involved with a man with such a dubious reputation, one largely created by the press of course. Mahler had become engraved on Alma's heart, yet she felt a considerable feeling of guilt that he was beginning to replace Alex. Mahler was like a magnet, and she could not help but be drawn towards him.

On the 20th of November, Mahler, accompanied by Natalie and Justine among others, took the train to Munich for the Kaim performance of the

4th Symphony. Natalie wrote that he was disappointed with the orchestra. Having performed his *Second* the previous year with considerable success, the musicians struggled with the complexities of the new work, and Natalie described how Mahler in order to salvage the situation had to work like a sculptor chipping away at a block of stone, gradually fashioning something akin to his vision.

The audience had prepared themselves for another Mahler extravaganza. The smaller orchestra and the apparent simplicity of themes took them by surprise, and many found his new musical language hard to follow. Natalie reported that applause at the end of the first movement was punctuated by hissing, which became worse after the second movement. Only the last movement received genuine applause. Mahler was upset, particularly so when the musicians failed to attend the post concert reception. Disappointment and antagonism reigned. Many of those who had been so moved by the *Second Symphony*, and had expected more of the same, made it clear that they had little time for the *Fourth*. Theodor Kroyer, writing in *Die Musik*, damned the work, using such descriptions as deceitful, unoriginal and tasteless. He considered that the weeds that had germinated in the *Third* had now grown into a tangled mass of thorny vegetation. Mahler himself had predicted the outcome, that the *Second* would be used as a stick with which to bludgeon the Fourth to death.

William Ritter, the Swiss artist and art critic, had walked out of the last rehearsal considering the work to be a complete scandal. He nevertheless attended the première. He described the first movement as being like 'Daniel in the lions' den, like a lady in tights performing acrobatics in a menagerie!' He was no more impressed by the second movement, saying that the audience had been confronted by teasing goblins. As for the long slow movement, the heart of the symphony, it was too long and without character. And yet, upon reflection, he felt that the music had left an indelible mark on him. He could not get it out of his mind. It affected his sleep. On the one hand he disliked and rejected it, on the other he could not help but admire it.

Three days later Mahler visited Alma. When he arrived she was in the middle of a music lesson with her old teacher Robert Ground. Anna invited him to stay for a meal, an invitation Mahler accepted. He said that he would have to phone home to let Justine know. The Molls did not have a telephone, so he had to walk to the local post office, accompanied by Alma. Walking along the snow-covered streets, he told Alma how much she had been in his thoughts and his concern that his tunnel vision towards the arts had now been broken by thoughts of her. As was typical of Mahler regarding mundane things, his shoelaces kept coming undone, and when they reached the post office he could not remember his telephone number!

It was on this visit that he proposed to Alma, not in the usual romantic way, but hinting that if she were to marry him she would have to accept that he had to remain entirely free from material worries, lest his dedication to music should suffer. Distractions might result in him losing his job at the Opera. Alma must have been very taken aback by this approach, so different from the way her other suitors had grovelled before her.

The following day he sent her his songs that had so far been published, which she and Zemlinsky played through. In her diary she stated that she was disappointed, feeling that a thread of insincerity ran through them. She would let him know her feelings. With Zemlinsky sitting next to her, her love for Alex was once more rekindled. During the following week her emotions seesawed from one to the other. She had several visits from Mahler and together they played through his songs. She was still not impressed, whereas his ardour grew. On several occasions, upon leaving Alma's home on the Hohe Warte after the last bus, he had to walk back to the Auenbruggergasse off the Rennweg to the south of the city centre – quite a distance in the early hours, but nothing to Mahler, the keen walker who now had an extra spring in his irregular step! Alma wrote in her diary that a number of things about him did not appeal to her, such as his smell, his singing voice and his speech – apparently he could not roll his rrr's. She wrote, 'What if Alex becomes famous?' This clearly indicates one of her priorities – to be married to a man of wealth and fame, to be at the centre of Viennese cultural society. If she married a man of great influence in music circles, surely her own compositions would be performed, a dream she did not want to relinquish. She questioned herself, was it the man or the Director of the Court Opera that she loved? It certainly was not as a composer that she loved him, for she had disliked his *First Symphony* as well as his songs.

On Wednesday the 4th of December Mahler conducted a performance of *Les Contes d'Hoffmann*. Alma was in the audience, and he turned and smiled at her on several occasions – 'my Gustav' as she referred to him. The following Saturday he visited her. She wrote how they had kissed repeatedly, of their embraces, although she considered him to be fickle, yet she realised the path that she must surely follow. Despite her reservations concerning certain traits of his personality, the difference in their ages, his Jewish blood, opposition from many including her stepfather, he had displaced Zemlinsky. She felt that Gustav's influence was already changing her, but would it be for the better? What would the future hold? In her diary she refers to him as the purest person she had ever met. She accepted his proposal of marriage, but her mind remained in turmoil. She thought she knew the direction she should go yet she dreaded having to tell Alex.

On the 8th *Das klagende Lied* was delivered to Alma for her appraisal. She liked the text but found the music somewhat weak, although she imagined that some parts would probably sound acceptable. That evening she went to a performance of *Die Zauberflöte,* which she described as heavenly, and again Mahler had turned to her and smiled at appropriate moments.

The following day Muhr visited her and she told him of her love for Mahler. A distraught Muhr threatened to commit suicide, his jealousy prompting him to tell her that some doctor had diagnosed that Mahler had an incurable illness – a rumour rife at the Opera. She felt sorry for Muhr, but his words had upset her greatly, and she still had to tell Alex.

Mahler had to go to Berlin to conduct the *Fourth* as part of a concert organised by Richard Strauss. On the 9th of December he wrote a very warm, informal letter to Anna Moll telling her that his planned trip to Berlin would be longer than expected as he had been asked to go to Dresden to help with the rehearsals of his *Second Symphony,* which was to be performed on the 20th. He would therefore be away for two whole weeks. The thought depressed him, for he would miss them all so much.

He arrived in Berlin on Tuesday 10th of December, having spent the previous evening telling Justine about Alma. Bruno Walter, in a letter to his parents dated the 30th of December, stated that Justi had had no inkling that Mahler and Alma would become engaged. He wrote that Justi would never have left Mahler to fend for himself, and therefore her own engagement to Rosé was a direct consequence of Gustav and Alma's engagement. In fact the news had not particularly surprised Justi, her brother having spent so much of his valuable spare time away from home. Gustav's fear that Justi might be jealous was laid to rest with her promise to show friendship towards Alma. In actual fact Justi was relieved for the way was now clear for her to marry Arnold Rosé. Alma, on her part, was determined to get on well with her future sister-in-law. Indeed, in her diary entry for the 10th, she wrote that Mahler's sister was in her heart. Gustav asked Alma to visit the Zuckerkandls the following day. Justi would be there and this would be an ideal opportunity for Alma to meet her. In her diary Alma stated that she had got on 'quite well' with her, and Justi, writing to Gustav, said that she had been entranced by Alma and that she was 'as pretty as a picture'.

On the 12th Alma took a deep breath and wrote to Alex begging forgiveness for the new direction of her love, at the same time asking him not to desert her as a friend and ending the letter 'Your Alma'. The deed done, her weeks of turmoil were over. She could now focus more clearly on the future. Two days later she visited Justi at Mahler's Auenbruggergasse apartment. Justi found her pleasant enough, but Alma felt uneasy. Justi eyed her suspiciously. She, who had looked after her brother for so long, wanted to be sure that Alma was the right partner for him. She considered the 19-year difference in their ages and Alma's string of affairs to be inevitable risks. Mahler, away from his work, liked to be alone or with only the closest friends and was certainly not one for high society, whereas Alma was quite the reverse. She even feared that Justi might try to sabotage the proposed marriage, but these fears were groundless, Justi having already told her brother how much she liked her. But Mahler too was concerned about the difference in their ages. He told Justi that Alma was little more than a pretty girl, yet he was in the autumn of his life. What would happen when the winter came? Justi tried to put his mind at rest by saying that when Alma became a mother she would settle down and there would be nothing to worry about on that count, and anyway with his exceptional gifts he would remain young longer than she would! But Mahler's concern was fully justified as the future would confirm.

Gustav wrote a number of long letters to Alma pouring out his love for her and using his pet name for her, 'Almschi'. He repeatedly begged her to write to him, and legibly, as her handwriting was not one of her strong points. The most important letter at this time was dated 19th of December and was posted in Dresden. It differed from the others he wrote during this trip in that it was in the form of a long sermon to Alma on her past and what form the future should take. This was the other side of Mahler, the dictatorial. In love he might be, but ground rules had to be laid down. He wanted to make it abundantly clear to her that the likes of Burckhard and Zemlinsky must cease to be of any deep concern, although she should treat them with due respect. These individuals were no longer of great importance, but they had threatened to overwhelm her spirit in the past in an unhealthy way. She had shown signs of becoming vain. She must focus on him and no one else. He criticised her for referring to her music as 'my music' and wanted her forthwith to regard <u>his</u> music as hers as well. She should sacrifice herself to <u>his</u> art at the expense of her own. Mahler's dictate of 'lay down your life and follow me' was a tough one, especially as regards her own music. Alma wrote that Mahler did not think anything of her music and a lot of his, yet she thought nothing of his and a great deal of hers. There was no room for compromise. She wrote in her diary that she could accept neither, for in her opinion Mahler's art, unlike Zemlinsky's, was not very good. To give up everything for that would be a 'lie'. As for his demand that she should cease composing, she considered such a suggestion appalling and deeply hurtful. Mahler wrote that he could not envisage a husband and wife both composing. She should be his wife, to support him and not a fellow composer. Her duty was to make him happy, to give herself entirely to him. He pleaded with her to be honest and open, to discuss everything with her mother. There must be no secrets between them. In short, Mahler wanted a wife who was prepared to take charge of all domestic affairs to leave him free to concentrate on music, in much the same way as Justi had. He demanded a reply to his letter, telling Alma that it would be collected from her the following Saturday.

This was a new experience for Alma, for in the past she had become used to being a puppeteer with her suitors being dangled from her fingers like marionettes. Now she found herself in a situation where the roles were being reversed. Questions flashed across her mind – was she doing the right thing? Did she really want to become subservient to this man so much older than she with his awkward habits, let alone his Jewish background? Would her marriage to him open a minefield of controversies? She was hurt by Mahler's demands, and Anna even tried to persuade her daughter to call off the affair. But these doubts she soon dismissed. She was in love with both the man and his lofty position. She would become the wife of the Director of the Court Opera and thereby be at the hub of Viennese cultural life and, although she would not admit it, she secretly rather enjoyed being dominated by this man of power.

Mahler's reception in Berlin had been warm. As a guest and friend of Richard Strauss, the audience attended the performance of the *Fourth* with open minds. The *Adagio* was especially well received, not least by Strauss who was quite overwhelmed by it. Not so the critics who attacked Mahler mercilessly.

Mahler returned, Alma had swallowed her pride and their affair was back on an even keel, Alma having a clearer understanding of what marriage to Gustav would entail. Her mother and Carl Moll still had reservations, but her mind was made up. The inconsistent Alma no longer felt it purely a matter of marrying a man of fame and power. His health had not been good over the preceding months. He was overworked, underweight and needed someone to care for him. Alma wrote in her diary that she would dedicate herself to this task, the one facet of Mahler that she knew she could dominate.

Alma again visited his apartment to see Justi, and on the 23rd of December Mahler took Justi to Alma's home to meet Anna and Carl and to propose officially to Alma in their presence. That evening Alma wrote in her diary that from then on only Gustav would have 'a place in her heart', and no longer would she lust after other men! On Christmas Day she went to his apartment. Later in the day he had to go to the Opera for a performance of *Tannhäuser*, she remaining behind with Justi. Following their awkward beginning, their relationship had improved considerably, Alma writing that she had become very fond of Justi, helped by the knowledge that she was the same flesh and blood as her Gustav.

While preparing to conduct *Tannhäuser*, Mahler's eyes fell on the
introductory page of the conductor's score which Wagner himself had
signed. Faded and well thumbed over the years, he decided to rescue the
autographed page from obscurity. Not only did he consider Wagner to be
'the master', so too did Alma. He tore out the page and took it back to his
apartment to the delight of Alma. They framed it and hung it on the wall
and there it remained until Arnold Rosé paid them a visit. When he saw the
page, he told Mahler that they had been searching high and low for it and
he insisted on taking it back to the Opera. Mahler was embarrassed that
his indiscretion had been discovered and Alma was far from pleased at
losing the great man's fading autograph.

News of their engagement had been leaked to the press, hitting the
headlines on the 27th, much to the delight of the gossipmongers. Among all
the 'sensation' articles, the one that appeared in the *Fremden-Blatt* was not
only more level-headed, but also provided information of their first
encounter when their paths had crossed whilst on holiday near Hallstätter
See in the Salzkammergut. Mahler had sent a card to Alma postmarked the
5th of July 1899, saying that his signature was genuine and to be aware of
imitations. One can presume that the young Alma had been thrilled at
meeting Mahler and had asked for his autograph, but it is unlikely that she
had fallen in love with him at this time. It was probably more to do with
hero-worshipping the great Director, which she continued to do at a distance
at the Hofoper. The question might be asked, did Berta Zuckerkandl
organise the fateful dinner party to bring them together? Mahler's friends,
including the Lipiners, the Spieglers, and even Bruno Walter were all taken
by surprise and were very concerned about this apparent mismatch.

On Sunday the 29th of December Mahler conducted Nicolai's *Die
lustige Witwe*, and Alma, her mother and Justi attended the performance as
his guests, sitting in the Director's box. When she first entered the box, all
eyes and opera glasses were turned towards a very embarrassed Alma who
withdrew in a state of confusion. Anna von Mildenburg, no less, saw the
poor girl in a state of distress and pacified her before ushering her back to
the box.

The following day Alma recalled how they all but made love, restraining
themselves at the last moment. She criticized the conventions of church
weddings. It was quite ironic that she, a Christian by birth, had no feelings
of responsibility in that direction, while Mahler, a Jew (albeit a 'convert' to
the Catholic Church for political reasons) wished to uphold Christian
moral traditions. She, an avid reader, was a follower of the ideas of
philosophers such as Artur Schopenhauer, a writer whom he despised. His
two favourite authors were Dostoyevsky and Schiller, although they both
admired the works of Goethe. Alma had become a freethinker and

something of a rebel when it suited her. There could, however, have been more to it than this. Whatever their mutual desires, Mahler clearly lacked confidence in sexual matters. This became evident on New Year's Day when passion threw Church conventions aside and they tumbled onto a sofa with Mahler 'stiff and upright', only for him to wilt before the act. Alma was understandably upset and deeply embarrassed, but all was well the next day for she wrote only three words in her diary: '*Wonner über Wonner*' (Rapture upon Rapture!), to be followed by a repeat performance the day after.

Having given up everything for him, Alma's reaction was that he should concentrate entirely on her. She was jealous of his friends and managed, often through verbal indiscretions, to cause upset upon upset appearing to do her utmost to alienate them from him. The first victim had been Ludwig Karpath, the writer and critic. Mahler had known him since 1888 and respected him as being one of the few journalists who did not believe in sensationalism and whose articles were generally fair and unbiased. In Karpath's case, Alma repeated to Mahler a comment he had made at a dinner party, when, having defended him against an onslaught of verbal abuse by the composer Goldschmidt, Karpath had added as an afterthought that he himself had been largely responsible for Mahler's appointment as Director of the Court Opera! True he had helped, although his claim was ludicrously exaggerated, but he had made the remark as part of his defence of Mahler. With this remark taken out of context, Mahler was livid. Consequently a row flared up between the two men, Karpath understandably upset, having done his level best to defend him. They calmed down but Alma's tongue had almost caused a rift between her husband to be and one of his few allies in the press.

More serious was her lack of tact at a dinner party at the Auenbruggergasse apartment on the 5th of January. Alma almost boasts about her bad behaviour in her diary, writing that she had had fun 'stunning' the guests with her bad manners. Siegfried Lipiner, whom she had already met and disliked, was a guest. He arrived with his first wife Nanna and her husband Albert Spiegler, his second wife, Albert's sister Clementine, and his mistress Anna von Mildenburg! Also present were Justine and Arnold Rosé, her mother, Carl Moll and Kolo Moser. Alma set about making a string of deliberately contentious remarks. At one point Mildenburg asked her what she thought of Gustav's music. She replied that she did not know much of it and what she did know she disliked. To break the ensuing awkward silence Mahler burst out laughing, and he took Alma into Justi's room to calm her down. The conversation in their absence can well be imagined. When they eventually rejoined the party, he sat her between himself and her mother where she sulked silently like a spoiled child. Mahler's closest friends having thus been upset, suspicion turned to distrust, and a determination to cause a rift between the couple in order to save him from a potentially disastrous marriage. As Lipiner wrote in a letter to him, marrying Alma would mean living in isolation from his friends. Alma described the evening of the dinner party as her being on parade before Mahler's Jewish friends, people he had dragged around since his youth like 'leg irons', people she had no desire to associate with.

His friends had every reason to be concerned. Apart from their age difference, attitudes to religious belief and literature, and Alma's unreliability socially and morally, Mahler the introvert and Alma the extrovert began to find it more and more difficult to understand the depths of each other's souls. Alma herself wrote that communication between them had become more difficult during their regular walks in the gardens of the Belvedere Palace, across the road from Mahler's apartment. Stripping away the physical side of their relationship revealed a question mark of compatibility, which had been brought to the surface since their engagement had been made public. He himself must have had doubts. What he needed was the stability of a Justi and the musical support and sophistication of a Natalie. What he had was a volatile and frequently unreliable young girl who, albeit unintentionally, could well undermine his name and authority. However, as things turned out, and despite her shortcomings, Alma was to become an asset and an inspiration to him.

Amidst all this turmoil, Mahler still had to keep his mind focussed on the musical events planned for the beginning of 1902, two of the most important being the Vienna premières of Richard Strauss's opera *Feuersnot* and his own *Fourth Symphony*.

The day after the embarrassing dinner, Gustav and Alma played through the score of the *Fourth Symphony*. In her diary she wrote that she liked it and was very moved, thus contradicting her earlier view of the work as well as the remark she had made the previous evening regarding his music. Perhaps she was trying to placate him. She confirmed her conversion to the *Fourth Symphony* by being present at the rehearsals, which were often stormy, Mahler losing his temper with musicians when they failed to carry out his instructions to the letter. The gentlemen concerned took umbrage and a vicious circle ensued. The causes of the situation were twofold: his music did not particularly appeal to them, but more importantly he had replaced a number of musicians with new blood, thus producing an atmosphere of ill feeling.

The performance took place at the Philharmonic concert on the 12th of January. Alma attended the occasion but was not feeling well, her ears ringing so that she found it hard to listen to the music. Natalie wrote that the performance was admirable but that its reception was at least as bad as it had been at the Munich concert. She reported that right from the start hostile comments were clearly audible, laughter and hissing punctuated by retaliatory remarks from those who were trying to appreciate Mahler's work. It was almost as if many in the audience had turned up with the sole intention of disrupting and making fun of the symphony. Some considered the work as being little more than a bad joke on the public, others that it could hardly be considered as proper music. Mahler was quite understandably upset, especially as this performance was on home ground. Munich was bad enough, Berlin too as far as the critics had been concerned, the latter occasion causing Strauss to write to Mahler stating that the *Fourth* had incited the gentlemen of the press to perform a St. Vitus's dance! Natalie recalled how Mahler had commented to Bruno Walter that his adversaries were confused, not knowing which end they should begin 'gobbling it up from!'

Taken aback by its small scale when compared to its predecessors, Max Kalbeck described the symphony as a yearning for simplicity and that it was a composition for children and those who wanted to be childlike. He wrote that the themes were barely adequate for a 'dance pantomime' and that the *Symphony* was a conflict between folk and art songs. But there were those who bowed to the music. Among them was the young composer Anton Webern, to whom Mahler was not only a brilliant conductor, but a composer whom he revered and whose compositions, past and future, he longed to become acquainted with.

Natalie, saddened by the poor reception of the *Fourth Symphony* and resigned to the fact that her long-held hope of marrying Mahler was now a forlorn one, faded from the picture. With her departure came the ending of her memoirs of Mahler. One of the most reliable sources of information ceased, to be replaced by the not so reliable memoirs of Alma. Natalie continued to perform with her quartet, but then became ill and lived in almost slum conditions of poverty. She was taken to a nursing home, and thence to an asylum where she died on the 8th of May 1921.

By this time Mahler always anticipated hostility towards his works and as a result he had become more thick-skinned. Having shaken off the dust, he concentrated on the first Vienna performance of *Feuersnot*, the opera having been performed in Dresden two months previously. He wrote to Strauss telling him that all the plans had been made for the first performance on the 29th of January, with the dress rehearsal the previous day. He had wanted Strauss to conduct the première, but commitments in Berlin would prevent him from arriving in Vienna until the last moment, so Mahler himself would take on the responsibility.

Strauss was present at the penultimate rehearsal and was particularly impressed by the orchestra, describing their playing as magnificent and that without doubt it was the finest orchestra in Europe. He was also delighted with the sets, the costumes and the cast, which included Leopold Demuth. All tickets for the première had been sold, and he wrote that the staff of the Court Opera was united in their effort to achieve a great success. He found that the dress rehearsal was less pleasing due to Mahler's far from relaxed approach – typical of Mahler prior to a première, stretching all concerned towards perfection.

Strauss's wife Pauline joined Alma in the Director's Box for the performance. Sitting next to Alma, she apparently fumed, muttering how could her husband produce such shallow, plagiaristic rubbish! Afterwards, Strauss, having been called onto the stage a number of times by the enthusiastic audience, arrived in the Director's Box beaming, only to suffer a barrage of abuse from his wife who accused him of blatant theft. Mahler, on his way up to join Alma, heard the commotion and shut the two of them in a rehearsal room to cool off. Pauline, however, burst out shouting that she was going back to her hotel alone. Strauss begged her to allow him to walk her back. Her reply was that he could so long as he kept ten paces behind her! It is quite clear that Alma took an instant dislike to Pauline. Richard Strauss later wrote that Alma's description of that evening was far from the truth, and his memories of Alma were not exactly charitable. It could be that Alma's account was both biased and exaggerated, she being well known to be economical with the truth on occasions, but there is little doubt that a scene had occurred between the two. Her remarks that Mahler could not stand the opera and did not conduct the performance underlining the point, as he did conduct, and his correspondence with Strauss both before and after the performance contradicts Alma's comments. Although Mahler did not admire the work greatly, he did write a consoling letter to Strauss concerning the reviews in the Viennese press. Having already conducted the opera three times, he hoped to stage it again in the future. One thing that Alma and Gustav did agree on though, was Strauss's main concern – the royalties. They both found his sense of values distasteful. Strauss, however, oblivious of their feelings, wrote to Mahler an almost ecstatic letter glowing with thanks for all his efforts and to all concerned.

Following the Vienna première of *Feuersnot*, Mahler, advised by his doctor, set off for a brief holiday in the Semmering to the southwest of Vienna. Fresh air, exercise and mental relaxation revived him, although he missed his Almschi terribly, and the hours seemed to drag by. Back in Vienna, his focus was set firmly on one date in particular, the 9th of March – their wedding day. He had been invited to conduct three concerts in St. Petersburg, and he put in a formal request for leave to go to Russia, the Hofoper being closed for Easter, which would be during his absence. This trip to Russia was to be their honeymoon.

The 9th of March dawned wet, and Mahler, wearing galoshes, walked to the huge Karlskirche (the Church of St. Charles Borromeo), which is almost opposite the Opera on the south side of the Ringstrasse. Alma, by now one month pregnant, went by cab accompanied by her mother and Justi. The witnesses were Carl Moll and Arnold Rosé. The ceremony was to take place not in the church itself, but in privacy in the sacristy. Alma recalled how Mahler, when kneeling down, missed the hassock on the prie-dieu and ended up on the stone floor, thus accentuating his small stature and making him look like a dwarf, much to the amusement of all present, including the priest. Thus a private ceremony took place, confounding the expectations of those who had heard rumours of an evening wedding.

Afterwards, the two families had a quiet dinner party, before the newly weds returned to their apartment to pack for their honeymoon in Russia. They set off the same evening by train. The following day Justine and Arnold Rosé were married in the same church. For Mahler a dream had come true; for Alma she had achieved her goal of marrying into greatness. Whatever anguish she had caused her husband and would in the future, and however unsuitable she might have appeared to be to his friends, her presence in his life would be immense, a reason for living and a constant source of inspiration.

Chapter 10

Vienna . . . Part Four

Fifth Symphony

MAHLER'S WORKING honeymoon in St. Petersburg proved to be a mixture of hard work, enjoyment at seeing the sights and meeting the friendly, devout Russian people who welcomed the newly married couple enthusiastically. They were met at the station by Gustav Frank, a cousin of Mahler's, who took them on a sightseeing tour. The city, blanketed with snow, delighted them. They were relieved at having left Vienna and the seemingly endless gossip. A number of social events had been arranged for the Director of the Vienna Court Opera and his young wife, from politicians and the aristocracy to members of the Imperial Family. Most of these engagements Mahler did not enjoy, partly due to his dislike of Russian food, but he was fully aware of the diplomatic importance of such occasions.

He had been engaged for three concerts. On the 17th of March 1902 he conducted Mozart's *Symphony in G minor*, Beethoven's *'Eroica'* and the *Prelude and Liebestod* from *Tristan und Isolde*. Alma, in the early stages of pregnancy, had caught a cold and doubted that she would be able to sit through the whole concert, but she was given permission to stand behind the orchestra. She wrote in her memoirs how moved she had been with this performance of the *Prelude* and *Liebestod*, not just by the music, but also by the expression of beauty and exaltation on Gustav's face. So moved was she in fact that she declared to herself that she knew that her mission in life must be to dedicate herself to him and to clear any obstacles that might lie in his path. Mahler caught Alma's cold and virtually lost his voice, which made rehearsing for the remaining concerts rather a burden.

On the 23rd the main works were Tchaikovsky's *Manfred Symphony* and the *Piano Concerto in E minor* by Liszt's former pupil Emil Sauer, who was the soloist. The final concert on the 29th of March included performances of Bruckner's *Fourth Symphony* and Tchaikovsky's *Violin Concerto*.

The reaction of the Russian audiences was very positive. He was given an enthusiastic welcome and generous applause after each concert. Unlike their counterparts in Vienna, they were open-minded, even fascinated by his dedicated and very personal interpretations of the works performed. The public had been forewarned about his attitude to conducting in an article by Max Graf, the Viennese critic whom Mahler knew only too well. The article, published in the *Russkaya muzykal'naya*, was generous towards him. Graf wrote that Mahler's approach to music was in the modern vein, tradition for its own sake meaning nothing to him. Graf even described him as an heir to Wagner. The same journal's review of the first concert followed Graf's lead. The article stated that the performance of the Mozart symphony had been 'Mozart out of costume', the music taking on a new, deeper character. It was a performance without mannerisms, fresh and full of energy. The article praised Mahler for his intellectual approach to the music, his ability to produce light and shade with great clarity of detail, nowhere more in evidence than in the '*Eroica*'. Mention was also made of Mahler's restrained method of conducting, thus supporting Bruno Walter's opinion that he had aged and become less volatile following the illness he had suffered the previous year.

Despite their colds, the inevitably crowded social calendar and the Russian cuisine, Gustav and Alma had enjoyed most of their three weeks in St. Petersburg. They had liked the Russian people and they had found them to be far more friendly, open-minded and altogether more generous in their appreciation of music than many in Viennese society. Only a widespread disinterest, even disdain for Dostoyevsky (one of Mahler's favourite authors) raised his eyebrows! But three weeks were long enough, and they were glad to return to Vienna and their Auenbruggergasse home.

Justi and her husband Arnold Rosé had moved into an apartment in Salesianergasse, conveniently located just around the corner from Auenbruggergasse. Mahler was pleased that they had found a suitable home so close by, not just because of his love for his sister, but also to have his friend and leader of the orchestra nearby as well.

Alma set about organising their own apartment and bringing some much needed order to the rather chaotic domestic finances, not helped by money still owed for the building of the villa at Maiernigg. According to Alma a considerable amount of money had been squandered by Justi and other members of Mahler's family. The very sizeable debt apparently amounted to around fifty thousand crowns. This huge sum may well have been an exaggeration by her, a disparaging remark aimed at her sister-in-law. Alma wrote that Mahler had told her that Justi had no idea how to organise a domestic budget and that as a result he had been in financial difficulties for several years. He passed on this challenge to Alma to see if she could bring about some financial stability and thus no longer suffer the embarrassment of being permanently in debt. The other immediate problem was a neighbour. Alma recalled how the man who had taken a dislike to Mahler and whose room was on the other side of his bedroom, had instructed his servant to play loud music on the gramophone as soon as Mahler returned from the Opera. The servant was duly bribed to discontinue this practice, except when his master was present. Fortunately it was not long before the occupant decided to move out, and the Mahlers took over their rooms to avoid any further irritations as well as to give themselves more space.

Mahler's honeymoon days came to an end in more than one sense, for on his return to work he found himself at the centre of a particularly hot dispute with the orchestra. This autonomous body objected more strongly than ever to his interference by bringing in new blood. An atmosphere not far short of hostility began to rumble on, accentuated by the gentlemen of the press. Far from backing down, Mahler stood his ground. The musicians had to seek permission from the Director of the Hofoper to perform in the Philharmonic concerts. Hitherto verbal consent had sufficed. Mahler's retaliation was to insist upon an annual written permit, which would only be granted if new players had been accepted into the ranks of the orchestra. This dictate he gave in July, which meant that the musicians had much of the summer break to dwell on it and build up their guile.

A special exhibition had been arranged by the Secession to honour the artist Max Klinger. It was to be held in the main hall of the famous (in the eyes of some infamous!) Secession building, nicknamed 'The Golden Cabbage' because of the decorations to its dome. The centrepiece was Max Klinger's statue of Beethoven, with frescos on the theme of the composer, the most important being that by Gustav Klimt. This huge frieze was only intended to be a temporary backdrop. Like an artistic 'symphony', it portrays man's sufferings, fears, his search for happiness through love and his final goal of redemption. The features of the knight in armour in the section *Sehnsucht nach dem Glück* ('Longing for Happiness') bear a close resemblance to Mahler. Klimt later offered a reproduction of this part of the frieze as his contribution to a book of tributes to Mahler which was published in 1910. Having been stored in a warehouse, it was only saved from terminal decay in 1970 and is now regarded by many as Klimt's greatest work. It was a turning point and the beginning of his 'golden' period, which reached its peak with 'The Kiss' in 1907-8. Another fresco behind Klinger's statue was 'Night Descending' by Alfred Roller.

Mahler was asked by Carl Moll, his father-in-law and president of the Secession, if he would arrange for a musical tribute to Max Klinger. The obvious choice was Beethoven's *Ninth Symphony*, the inspiration behind Klimt's frieze, but the friction between Mahler and the musicians at this time made this impossible. The best he could do was to make an arrangement of part of the choral ending for brass and wind instruments. He raised his baton as Klinger entered the exhibition hall and as the music began Klinger was moved to tears. Thus Mahler reconfirmed his support for the Secession.

Mahler, always a man for strict routine, would get up at seven o'clock, have breakfast at his worktable and then set off for the Opera at eight forty-five. A few minutes before one o'clock there would be a telephone call saying that he was on his way home. Fifteen minutes later he would ring the bell at the main entrance to the apartment block to forewarn the cook that he was on his way up and to serve the soup. All energy and bustle, he would burst into the apartment slamming doors behind him, wash and then join his wife for lunch. This was followed by a brief siesta and then a brisk walk with Alma, either in the grounds of the Belvedere or around the Ringstrasse. Tea was at five, then back to the Opera. Alma would follow later and when his work was finished they would return together, eat, read and retire. For Alma, becoming more noticeably pregnant, this routine was hard to get used to, especially for one whose previous existence had been a social whirl!

Towards the end of May Mahler wrote to Professor Alfred Roller inviting him to lunch. He had already met the Moravian artist at the Zuckerkandls' party and at the fourteenth Secession Exhibition. Roller, as a friend of Carl Moll, often visited Alma's parents, and it is therefore probable that Mahler had met him there. With their shared love of opera, it was not long before Roller and Mahler began discussing set design and productions in general. Roller hated the traditional over-blown productions that had become the norm at the Hofoper, especially the treatment of his favourite opera *Tristan und Isolde*. He was convinced that a fresh, simple approach was needed; visually a production must complement the music and let the music speak for itself. Both Gustav and Alma agreed wholeheartedly with his conviction that there should be a fresh approach to set design at the Hofoper. Mahler hoped that Roller might be the man to fulfil this role some time in the future. A new production of *Tristan und Isolde* was in the offing; what better work for Roller to make his debut if Mahler could arrange for him to be taken on board.

At the end of May Gustav and Alma left Vienna for Cologne, en route for Krefeld and the first complete performance of his *Third Symphony*. His earlier letter to Strauss asking him to smooth his path (for the performance had to be flawless) reflects the importance of the occasion, one that could make or break him as a composer. Following the embarrassing reception of the *Fourth Symphony* in Berlin, it was to Strauss's credit that he did his utmost to carry out all Mahler's requests. He knew it had been a gamble to include Mahler's *Third* in the programme of the Krefeld Festival, a programme for which Strauss himself was responsible.

The work was to be performed by musicians from both the Cologne and

Krefeld orchestras, the rehearsals to take place in the German city. Gustav and Alma lived in the lap of luxury at the Cathedral Hotel, the finest in Cologne. After the first rehearsal Mahler wrote to Justine saying that the first, fourth and fifth movements had been rehearsed and that everything had gone extremely well, with no revisions needed. He told his sister that Alma was not well, sickness probably brought on by the very hot and tiring journey combined with her advancing pregnancy. Nevertheless she had attended the rehearsals, making detailed notes on such matters as balance, and Mahler went straight over to her after each movement had been played to discuss her comments. So well had the rehearsals gone that at one point he exclaimed, 'And behold he heard that it was good!'

After the luxury of the Cathedral Hotel, they had to put up with accommodation of a lesser quality in Krefeld. Their new abode was the home of a wealthy silk merchant. Their hosts mistrusted Mahler and were reluctant to provide lodging. They considered him to be that well known theatre director who was about to unleash a monstrous symphony which would give nothing but pain to those who heard it. Matters were not helped when, coming out of his room, he stopped at the top of the stairs to clean his glasses. Having put them back on, he accidentally kicked a pail of water down the stairs, the lady of the house being the unfortunate recipient! The pleasurable days in Cologne had been replaced by discomfort and irritation. The press were lying in wait and continued to pursue the Mahlers wherever they went.

Alma, her pregnancy very obvious and dressed in what was known as a reform dress designed by Koloman Moser, and Mahler, with ill fitting suit and hat in hand rather than on his head and with his peculiar irregular gait, were the butt of jokes, especially from some of the local children. On one occasion a voice yelled out that Mahler had lost his hat. He had in fact left it in a teashop. Having retrieved it, they made all haste to a small hotel where Justi and Arnold Rosé were waiting for them. The young rabble was eventually dispersed by the four of them dousing them with water from an upstairs window.

A large number of composers, conductors and eminent musicians had made the journey to Krefeld, some as performers, others just to attend the Festival dedicated to contemporary music. The young German composer Hans Pfitzner paid Gustav and Alma a visit clutching his latest work, an opera entitled *Die Rose vom Liebesgaten*, hoping that he could persuade Mahler to have it staged in Vienna. Mahler received him very coolly and was far from encouraging, whereas Alma was all smiles. The work was in fact performed three years later, largely due to her influence. Mahler's mind was clearly on his *Third Symphony*, and having already suffered many irritations in Krefeld, did not want any further distractions.

The evening of the 9th of June arrived and the auditorium was packed. Richard Strauss's organisation throughout the preparations had been meticulous. Alma decided to sit on her own rather than with Justi and Arnold. At the end of the enormous first movement, Mahler received an applause the size of which must have taken him by surprise. Strauss marched up to the podium applauding him, thus underlining the reaction of the audience with his personal public approval. As chief organizer of the Festival, Strauss was a popular figure and his own music widely appreciated. He liked to be associated with success, and he did after all have an ongoing reciprocal arrangement with Mahler for each to promote the other's works. After the traumas of the *Fourth Symphony* in Berlin, he must have been taken aback by this spontaneous outpouring of admiration. The first movement may have been given an ovation but, with the audience becoming increasingly engrossed as the symphony progressed, Strauss became more and more subdued. At the end of the last movement, many of those present, including Alma, were moved to tears. She wrote that it was then that she felt her child stirring in her womb and that she was more than ever convinced of Mahler's greatness, a greatness she knew was her mission in life to dedicate herself to. Before the seemingly endless applause subsided, Strauss had slipped out of the hall jealous of the success and afraid that Mahler would take over the mantle of contemporary greatness that he had hitherto enjoyed. In the audience that evening had been Willem Mengelberg, a young conductor from Amsterdam who was to do more than any other to further Mahler's reputation as a composer in Holland and beyond during the first decades of the twentieth century.

After the concert Gustav and Alma were joined by Justi, Arnold and a few other guests for a celebratory meal at a small inn. Strauss was there too making polite conversation, but when he passed Mahler's table he uttered not a word to the hero of the evening. His attitude upset Mahler and left such an unnecessary sour note following an evening of triumph.

Mahler had even managed to win over most of the critics. Typical was the Swiss writer William Ritter. Following an amusing description of his appearance and conducting in which he described him as looking like a defrocked priest, and that he was like a snake charmer with eyes like vipers' tongues, a hypnotist who could 'unleash dragons' with his baton, he wrote of the fantastic 'kaleidoscope of sound'. He described the first movement as stunning and the *Adagio* as the finest since Beethoven. The *Krefelder Zeitung* reported that the applause had lasted for over fifteen minutes and declared the symphony to be of enduring importance. One criticism levelled at Mahler was his refusal to distribute a programme for the symphony so that the audience would have guidelines to follow, but he had come to disown his earlier plans for programmes, wanting the music to speak for itself. The problem was that by depicting the sounds of nature and his use of a post-horn, ländler and the like, many thought that there must be a story unfolding. After all, Strauss gave clear indications for his tone poems. Mahler did on occasions mention titles for the movements, but it was a practice of which he did not approve. Certainly following the first three symphonies no non-musical labels were applied, save for the two *Nachtmusik* movements of the *Seventh Symphony* – hardly a programme. The only exceptions were, of course, the choral *Eighth Symphony* and *Das Lied von der Erde*.

The overwhelming success of the *Third Symphony* at the Krefeld Festival was to be the turning point for Mahler the composer, and Strauss was worried. Publishers began to change their attitude towards his music from reluctance to keen interest, and in European cities, especially German cities, orchestras became eager to perform his works.

Elated by his success, he returned to Vienna to deal with correspondence and end of season matters at the Opera. He wrote to Roller, saying that he was impatient to see his ideas on sets for *Tristan*. A few days later, having seen his sketches, he wrote to him again saying how delighted he was with them, and how much he looked forward to working with him during the 1902-1903 season, signing the letter 'your sincere admirer'. This new and very important partnership would revolutionize opera production. On the 20th of June Mahler left Vienna for his summer holiday at his villa in Maiernigg on the shores of the Wörthersee.

Mahler, longing for peace and quiet away from the tensions of Vienna, was excited at the prospect of the first holiday that he and Alma were to spend together and, even more important, he looked forward to a few weeks devoted to composing. Alma loved the location of the villa, but had reservations about its design, especially the fussy fretwork decorations on the cornices of the cupboards, the removal of which became one of her first tasks. In a relaxed frame of mind and wearing his old holiday clothes, in which Alma wrote it was hard to recognise him, he let her carry on with the alterations to the décor. If this amused her, fine, so long as he could concentrate on composing.

He established the strict routine he needed for his work, a routine that would remain unaltered during all the summers they would spend at Maiernigg. He would rise at six o'clock and ring for the cook to prepare his breakfast before setting off for the *Häuschen*. The cook, carrying his breakfast on a tray, was not permitted to use the direct route, but had to climb up a longer, steeper and often muddy path through the forest. This led to the rear of the building for Mahler did not wish to see anyone until his morning's composing had been done. Having delivered the coffee, bread, butter and jam, she would bustle away post haste lest she should be seen by Mahler who would be coming up the main path. On a fine morning he would have his breakfast al fresco on the small terrace in front of the *Häuschen* before settling down to compose.

His morning's work over, he would return to the villa, swim or row in one of the two boats he owned, sunbathe, swim again and then dress for lunch. The food had to be simple and light without fat or any form of seasoning. After a brief siesta he and Alma would go for a long walk. On occasions he would suddenly stop to jot down ideas in his notebook, thus giving his wife a welcome break from the strenuous, yet inconsistent pace that he set, especially so in her pregnant state. Whenever she was forced to stop through exhaustion, he would smile and say 'I love you'. Alma struggled to adapt to this rigid pattern of daily life set by Gustav. Most of the day she would spend either on her own or on what she referred to as 'the interminable walks'. Sometimes for a change they would board the local ferry, cross the Wörthersee and walk on the far side of the lake. Occasionally, when Gustav became aware of her need for rest, he would row her on the lake. He needed vigorous exercise in the afternoon. Alma wrote that it was because he could not stand the feeling of a full stomach, although after the usual frugal lunch it is unlikely that it was that full! Probably another reason was the necessity for him to release the pent up energy that had accumulated during a long morning of complete concentration on composing. As he mentioned in a letter to Nanna Spiegler, he was up to his eyebrows in work, completing the *Fifth Symphony* begun the previous summer.

At first Alma would while away the time playing the piano while Gustav was up in his *Häuschen*, but one day she asked her husband if he could hear her and he replied that he could, even though he was two hundred feet above the villa and surrounded by trees. She stopped playing, restricting her musical activity to copying pages of the *Fifth Symphony*. Dedicating her life to him and his music was an ideal she was beginning to find hard to embrace. The young girl, so used in the past to being full of the *joie de vivre*, began to find her new existence lonely and dull. Gustav had no interest in such matters as clothes, travel and socialising. His interests were centred on music and the spiritual; he had no time for material things. Nagging doubts began to creep into Alma's head. Her husband's words words, when he told her that marrying a man like him would not be simple and that her only task would be to make him happy, must have remained firmly at the back of her mind. Yet arguing with these doubts were thoughts of love and dedication. To make matters worse, Anna von Mildenburg (Frau M. as Alma referred to her), whose ardour towards Mahler seemed not to have been diminished by his marriage, moved to Maiernigg so that she could be near him! Her uninvited visits, accompanied by a scruffy dog, which she had decided to rescue from a vagrant, began to become both irritatingly regular and embarrassing. To begin with Mahler would escort her back to her house, which was exactly what Mildenburg had in mind, but her devious behaviour began to annoy him. Frau M. even visited Alma when she was on her own, plying her with gossip regarding Mahler's past, but Alma, fully aware of Mildenburg's scheming nature, mistrusted her and would not be influenced.

One afternoon, upon Alma's suggestion, they persuaded Frau M. to join them in performing the last act of *Siegfried*. Tired of listening to their visitor's embarrassing gossip, they thought that such a plan would make her visit more tolerable. Alma wrote that M. was in superb voice, better than she had ever sung on stage. The sound of their performance could be heard from the lake, and soon a flotilla of small boats had gathered in front of the villa for the free concert. When the act came to an end they were given a spontaneous and very enthusiastic round of applause. That same day Frau M's visits ended promptly when Mahler asked his servant to take her home.

In an undated letter to Justi he said that he had received many invitations to conduct his own works during the coming season. He also mentioned that Alma had come to terms with their solitary existence at the villa and that she was quite cheerful, but in fact he was only too aware of her loneliness during the long hours he spent up in the *Häuschen* and the social sacrifice she was making on his behalf, and as a consequence he wrote the last of the group of five *Rückert Lieder*, which he had begun the previous summer.

Liebst Du um Schönheit
(If you love for beauty)

This is the only love song that Mahler wrote and is the only one of the *Rückert Lieder* that he himself did not orchestrate. It was however orchestrated by Max Puttmann who worked for the Leipzig publishers C. F. Khant, first appearing in print in 1905. It is short, simple and the words so clearly reflect Mahler's own feelings towards Alma and life: to love the sun, the spring, the mermaid adorned with pearls, but 'If you love for beauty, youth or treasure do not love me. However, if you love for love's sake, then love me always as I will always love you'.

He did not hand the finished song to Alma, but placed it in the score of *Siegfried*, which was by the piano in the villa. She had been playing parts of the score and Gustav hoped that she would come across the new song by chance. Much to his disappointment she decided not to play music from *Siegfried* for several days, so Gustav picked up the score and suggested that she might play from it for him. His gift fell to the floor. Alma was moved to tears and they played the new song over and over again. The 'love potion' worked, the doubts fled from Alma's mind and her dedication was strengthened.

Fifth Symphony, in C sharp minor
(In five movements)

The day came when Mahler finally completed the score of the *Fifth Symphony* and he took Alma up to the *Häuschen* to play through it for her. She was very impressed, although she had reservations over some parts, especially the chorale at the end, which she said was too much like a hymn and rather boring. He began to answer her criticism by mentioning Bruckner who had often used brass-dominated chorales. Her reply was that Bruckner may have done, but her Gustav was not Bruckner and ecclesiastical chorales were not suited to his nature. Nevertheless, Mahler was very pleased with his latest work, which heralded the beginning of a new phase in his symphonic writing.

The *Fifth* marked a return to a purely orchestral score, the vocal elements of the *Second, Third* and *Fourth Symphonies* being absent. The *Wunderhorn* period was over. The first movement may have *Wunderhorn* echoes such as the poignant theme similar to that used in the song *Der Tamboursg'sell* about a youth awaiting execution that he had composed the previous summer, but by using it in the context of a funeral march Mahler was burying the past and looking forward to new symphonic worlds. He was growing in confidence with the use of polyphony, and by experimenting with the sonorities of instruments, thereby creating new timbres, he stretched their range into hitherto unheard territories. It was through this symphony that the first seeds of the Second Viennese School were sown. He was deliberately turning his back on the past and the childlike innocence of the *Fourth Symphony*, stepping into an altogether grimmer world that reflected his own recent illness and his increasingly stressful life at the Hofoper.

The symphony is in five movements. It is divided into three parts: Part One, the first and second movements, Part Two, the *Scherzo*, which is the longest movement and the heart of the symphony, and Part Three, the *Rondo-finale*, prefaced by the *Adagietto*.

First movement: Trauermarsch.
Im gemessenem Schritt – Streng – Wie ein Kondukt
(Funeral march: at a deliberate pace, severe, like a cortège)

The opening movement strikes a direct parallel with that of the *Second Symphony*. It is a funeral march, and the hero is being laid to rest. The hero is Mahler the symphonist and he is burying his past music in preparation for the growth and flowering of the new music, the music of the future. His choice of a grim *marche funèbre* to open the symphony may also have been a reflection of his recent brush with death following the intestinal haemorrhage he had suffered. The symphony begins with an unaccompanied trumpet fanfare, a foreboding, solemn motif that recurs several times during the movement, punctuating passages at times grief-stricken, sometimes wildly passionate and at other times more gentle and nostalgic. The movement builds to a shattering climax before the opening fanfare returns, first played on the trumpets and then finally given to the flutes which have the last word, and with them the music of Mahler's past dies symbolically.

Second movement: Stürmisch bewegt
(tempestuous, agitated)

Out of the sombre *trauermarsch* and in defiance of mortality the music focuses on immortality. But where to now? Towards Alma the copyist in a sort of musical foreplay? After the gloom-laden first movement the second opens bursting with energy, shaking off the dust from the past. The new journey has begun, although for the time being shadows of the funeral march persist, but now calmer, more reflective. Half way through the movement there is a change of mood. Out of the turbulence and anguish the music takes on a triumphal character in the form of a chorale. Six horns, four trumpets and timpani proclaim the Messiah-like chorale that bears some similarity to the end of the *First Symphony*: 'And he shall live forever and ever'. Mahler is trying to reaffirm his self-belief in the immortality of his music, but the chorale is rudely interrupted by the return of the turbulence that preceded it. The battle continues. The chorale returns, more determined, building towards a victorious climax, but it is cut off in its prime. Victory has yet to be won, and the movement ends mysteriously and inconclusively.

Third movement: Scherzo: Kräftig, nicht zu schnell
(vigorous, not too fast)

This is both the longest movement and the heart of the symphony. Mahler referred to it as 'the very devil of a movement', and foresaw problems in performance with conductors taking it too fast and thereby making nonsense of it. He wondered what people would make of the 'foaming, roaring, raging sea of sound' with 'new worlds constantly being created, only to fall into ruin the next moment'. Aware that it was music ahead of its time, he wished if only he could conduct its première half a century later. Mahler had told Natalie that the *Scherzo* was neither romantic nor mystical. Bustling with energy, it mirrored a human being in his prime.

After a long pause (as indicated by Mahler) the *Scherzo* bursts onto the scene, dispelling the gloom of the first part of the symphony. With a flourish, an ebullient horn solo launches the movement in much the same way as Richard Strauss had done previously in his symphonic poem, *Till Eulenspiegel*. A bustling interplay of Alpine dances and ländler take on the form of the waltz. Mahler is often accused of doing the ländler to death, but Neville Cardus came to his defence, writing that 'Mahler didn't 'murder' the ländler; he ravished it and got it with child'. There are over eight hundred bars of musical effervescence, free from any of Mahler's usual deeper, psychological significance. The music builds to a climax, to be followed by a sombre horn cadence, which in turn is cheekily imitated by pizzicato strings 'tip-toeing' out of the temporary ghostly gloom. The haunting mood returns, but is soon swept aside by a resumption of the earlier ebullience. Once more the horn calls are heard in a quieter, mysterious passage before the movement draws to an exhilarating conclusion.

Fourth movement: Adagietto: Sehr Langsam
(very slow)

The third part of the symphony begins with what is probably the most well known of all of Mahler's symphonic movements, partly due to its use in films such as Luchino Visconti's *Death in Venice*, and also because it is often played out of context as a separate piece. It can be compared to anything from a Valentine card to one of deepest sympathy! Interpretations of the *Adagietto* vary considerably, with timings from Gilbert Kaplan's 7:57 and Abbado at 8.33 to Karajan's 11:53 and Bernstein's 12.10! The indication *Sehr Langsam* (very slow) is misleading taken in isolation, for Mahler goes on to give further instructions <u>not</u> to drag out the music, and at bar 96 there is the word *Drängend* (urgently). Bruno Walter's timing was close to Kaplan's and the former, as a personal friend of the composer, is surely right. The melancholy and despair of Gustav von Aschenbach in *Death in Venice* is not what the music is about and the use of the Adagietto at state funerals has not helped either. The movement was in fact a gift to Alma, a love poem without words. Willem Mengelberg, another conductor who knew Mahler and championed his works, confirmed this view. He claimed that Gustav and Alma had told him that it had been a token of love before their marriage.

It is in total contrast to the other movements of the *Fifth Symphony*. Scored with the utmost delicacy for strings and harp, it bears similarities in mood and subtlety to *Ich bin der Welt abhanden gekommen*, the Rückert Lied he had composed the previous summer in Maiernigg. The *Adagietto* had probably been written shortly afterwards. In the opening bars, the harp plays a motif similar to the middle of the *Lieder eines fahrenden gesellen* song, *Die zwei blauen Augen von meinem Schatz* (The two blue eyes of my sweetheart). The music is very personal, very spiritual, reflecting not only his feelings for Alma, but also the inner solitude of his own creative soul.

Before Mahler had left for Berlin in December 1901, he wrote to Alma saying that there was one voice that drowned out everything else in his heart, a voice that repeated 'I love you, my Alma!' Indeed, this sentiment is reflected in the *Adagietto*. Coincidentally or not, the words 'Ich liebe Almschi' fit so perfectly with the music, repeated over and over again. Mahler was in love with love, and the *Adagietto* could be called his '*Liebesleben*'. It is like a breath of fresh air, an emotional outpouring of his love. It is almost saying that all the turmoil that surrounds it – and him – doesn't matter; this is what is important. It is his *Siegfried Idyll*, his present to Alma. Out of this bliss, emerges the last movement.

Fifth movement: Rondo-finale (Allegro)

The final movement is launched by the first horn, echoed by the strings. A bassoon answers a second horn call and the music takes flight, rich in fugues and polyphony reflecting Mahler's intense study of Bach. It is joyous, celebratory and surges forward with a swagger. Fleeting moments of reflection, a backward glance to the *Adagietto* and even the song *Lob des hohen Verstandes*, which tells of the song contest between a cuckoo and a nightingale. The symphony ends in a blaze of glory with the return of the chorale, which had struggled for existence in the second movement, now brimful with confidence and affirmative, as if saying, with no hint of doubt, 'my music <u>will</u> live for ever!'

Neville Cardus referred to this magnificent symphony as 'one of the seven wonders of the symphonic world', but that was sixty years after its completion and very close to fifty years after Mahler's death. Reflected in this joyful ending is not only Mahler's optimism for the future of his music, but also his equally positive outlook in his personal life.

Summer's end and Vienna beckoned once more. A rejuvenated Mahler returned with an extra spring in his irregular step with the score of his *Fifth* under his arm. All that needed to be done was to produce a fair copy during the winter months.

Renewed attacks from the press welcomed him back to work. The usual criticisms surfaced. He was accused of being irritable, narrow-minded, of neglecting important works and of upsetting both musicians and singers through his policy of 'hiring and firing'. Questions were even asked as to whether he was mentally and physically strong enough to continue following his serious illness during the latter part of the previous season. To Mahler such a tirade was both expected and very much water off a duck's back. However, some new singers had to be found. Apart from anything else, during the previous season Mildenburg had been unable to tackle all the performances assigned to her, partly due to minor ailments and also because she wanted to preserve her voice. Too much had been asked of her and she dug her heels in. Sophie Sedlmair had been her replacement on several occasions. A new signing was Lucy Weidt, whom Mahler had auditioned earlier in the year. At that time she had been unable to join the Hofoper as she was under contract to Leipzig. Her autumn debut was as Elisabeth in *Tannhäuser*. Another important new signing was twenty-five year old Richard Mayr from Salzburg, who had already sung at Bayreuth to great acclaim. He made his Vienna debut in Verdi's *Ernani*, and his potential was immediately recognised.

To celebrate the Emperor's name day on the 4th of October, Bruno Walter conducted the first performance of Mozart's early, unfinished opera *Zaide*. Mahler had approached Robert Hirschfeld asking him to work on both the libretto and the music to make the opera acceptable for performance. Hirschfeld had already carried out a similar task successfully with Haydn's *Lo Speziale*. Such a move could have worked well for Mahler. Hirschfeld was well known for his attacks on the Director of the Hofoper, and by giving him this task, not to mention the royalties concerned, Mahler must have hoped that relations between them might improve. Unfortunately the whole project back-fired, for despite the care bestowed upon the production and a strong cast that included Leo Slezak, it was taken off after only three performances. Hirschfeld was furious and convinced that he had been snubbed deliberately, and he redoubled his campaign against Mahler.

The end of the same month saw the first performance of a new production of *Les Huguenots* by Giacomo Meyerbeer. Among the very strong cast were Selma Kurz, Richard Mayr and Leo Slezak, all of who surpassed themselves. Slezak wrote of how inspiring the rehearsals had been and how Mahler had managed to bring out the very best from every singer. So inspiring in fact that even when Mahler was rehearsing scenes in which they were not involved, not one of them would dream of leaving the rehearsal room. *Les Huguenots* was a tremendous success, the public's enthusiasm not in the least dampened by adverse criticism from the pro Wagnerites amongst the critics, Hirschfeld among them. The anti-Wagner lobby, including Max Kalbeck, were generally complimentary in their reviews.

But all the ups and downs at the Hofoper took second place to another event that autumn – the birth of Gustav and Alma's first child. Alma had been warned by her doctor that the birth might prove to be difficult because of the baby's awkward position in her womb, but they agreed not to say anything to Gustav. The doctor's concern proved to be well founded, for when Alma went into labour on the 3rd of November she suffered excruciating pain. Gustav paced up and down the streets wringing his hands, crying and suffering in sympathy. Eventually she gave birth to a little girl. It had been a breech birth. When Alma told Gustav about the difficulty and that the baby had been born bottom first, he burst out laughing and retorted, 'That's my child! Immediately she shows the world what she thinks of it!' They decided to name her Maria after his mother, and gave her the nickname Putzi. He immediately fell in love with his little daughter, cradling her in his arms as he walked up and down, talking and singing to her and comforting her when she was sick.

Alma took some time to recover from the difficult birth of her first child. On the 25th of November, three weeks after Putzi's arrival into the world, she wrote that she didn't yet feel any deep love for her, and that her love was entirely focussed on Gustav. No maternal instinct had been aroused in her. A fortnight later she wrote that she felt like a bird that had had its wings clipped, that her child did not need her and even referred to her baby as 'that'. True she had not been feeling well, apparently suffering from gallstones, but her attitude to life had become almost entirely negative.

During these difficult days Mahler had been hard at work preparing for the new production of Tchaikovsky's *Pique Dame*. He took Alma to rehearsals and played her music from the opera at home. *Pique Dame* proved to be very successful. He was congratulated by Kalbeck and even by Hirschfeld, and the Tchaikovsky opera became a firm favourite at the Hofoper. Gradually Alma's post-natal depression began to lift, helped by visits from her parents, the Zuckerkandls, the Rosés and even Klimt and Burckhard! At the same time a deepening hatred of Anna von Mildenburg and Lucy Weidt began to well up in her imagination. She was jealous of the way her husband joked with them and teased them. She even went so far as to write in her diary that she was so upset she wished he would never return home!

Following the success of the *Third Symphony* at Krefeld, a number of orchestras laid plans to have the work performed. These included those in Magdeburg, Elberfeld and Nuremberg, but there was to be no repeat of the Krefeld triumph. This was not surprising, for the Krefeld event had been expertly stage-managed by Strauss, had all the necessary resources at hand and of course Mahler himself was conducting, whereas in the above performances musicians and conductors were far from *au fait* with such a difficult, large scale work. Other projected performances were cancelled. The cost of putting on the massive work with its huge orchestra, soloist and the large chorus of women and children, whose contribution lasts little more than four out of the work's ninety-plus minutes duration, was considered to be an unacceptable financial risk. One German city that got cold feet was Wiesbaden, the *Third* being substituted by the *Fourth Symphony* with Mahler himself being invited to conduct the performance.

With the composer himself at the helm, interest and good receipts would be guaranteed. He must have had mixed feelings about accepting the offer at such a delicate time in his personal life, but with concern over the recent inadequate performances of his music he decided that he had to accept. So on the 20th of January he caught the train from Vienna to Wiesbaden, leaving Alma behind with Putzi.

Mahler, in his letters to Alma, described the train journey; the beauty of the snow-covered countryside and how he had eaten a meal in the restaurant car that had disagreed with him. He spent a night in Frankfurt en route. The heating was on in his bedroom and despite all his efforts he could not cool the room sufficiently and as a consequence had woken up with a splitting headache. He described Frankfurt as having an air of efficiency but in his opinion was boringly uniform. He told Alma that whenever his mind turned towards the *Adagio* of his *Fourth Symphony* he could see her face and her 'dear blue eyes'.

As he prepared to enter the concert hall on the 23rd of January, he must have had a feeling of trepidation as to what kind of reception he would receive after the panning that the *Fourth* had received previously. He was pleasantly surprised. At the end of the performance the audience called him back to the podium several times for bows, which he took almost reluctantly remembering the bitterness aroused by the symphony in the past, but he declined to accept the traditional laurel wreath when it was presented to him. Most of the critics were complimentary in their reviews of the concert, wondering what all the previous fuss had been about. The majority declared the *Fourth Symphony* to be a novel work, far from being boring and with superb instrumentation. In their opinion it was the music of the future, and Mahler's ability as a conductor was beyond question. The sour taste left by the Berlin fiasco had been largely overcome.

By far the most important event of the season at the Hofoper, on the twentieth anniversary of Wagner's death, was the new uncut production of *Tristan und Isolde*. Mahler would readily delegate conducting to his deputies Bruno Walter and Franz Schalk, but *Tristan* he liked to reserve for himself. After all, it was his and Alma's favourite opera. This marked the first collaboration between Mahler and Alfred Roller. The première took place on the 21st of February and it was little short of a sensation. Roller, four years younger than Mahler and a leading light of the Secession, had worked in tandem with him to produce stage settings with a completely new concept. In their opinion naturalistic sets had had their day and should be replaced by more atmospheric, thought-provoking designs with a meaning – the Secessionist ideal. Roller's main aim was to make people use their imaginations. In place of the naturalistic pictures his plan was to utilize space and lighting in a symbolic way. The principle behind this revolutionary approach was that of *Gesamtkunstwerk*, a fusion of all aspects of a production to form an artistic unity. Lighting depicting the mood of a particular scene was of paramount importance. With this in mind Mahler managed to get permission for the orchestra pit to be lowered, as it had been at Bayreuth, so that the orchestra lights would not interfere with the stage lighting. Of course the building work concerned could not be carried out mid-season, but it was completed during the summer of 1903.

Eric Schmedes and Anna von Mildenburg sang the leading roles in this landmark production of *Tristan und Isolde*. Operatic history was being made with all the elements fitting together to perfection. Everyone involved was inspired and showed total dedication. Mildenburg gave the performance of a lifetime, despite initial tantrums over Roller's novel ideas. These she soon came to accept when she fell madly in love with him! She may have been past her peak vocally, especially in the upper register, but her acting and her emotional involvement were beyond criticism. Schmedes, whose heart had been won by Mildenburg some years before, gave his all, and Richard Mayr as King Mark surpassed himself too. Mahler's conducting was outstanding, at times calming and at others going close to the edge emotionally, yet never losing control of the flow of the music drama; this, despite his near collapse from a migraine in the dressing room after the Second Act. According to Alma, it was while he was horizontal and deathly pale that Justi made the cutting remark, 'One thing gives me such pleasure – I had his youth, you now have him when he is old!' Alma wrote that with these words any remaining feelings of love for Justi vanished.

The audience was stunned by Roller's staging of *Tristan*, especially by the lighting. Visually they had never before experienced anything like it. Roller, an artist with strong sympathies with the impressionist movement, almost hypnotised the audience, drawing them into the dream world of the opera. He was not interested in just the positioning and brightness of the lights but also the colours, and he would subtly alter the hues to mirror the mood of a particular scene and the emotions of the characters on the stage. In fact the combination of light and colour was quite intoxicating, typified in Act One when Tristan and Isolde imbibe the magic love potion the set was awash with red and orange. The second act, which opened with the moon and a myriad of golden glittering stars in a dark velvet sky, gradually turned to a cold grey and then to a blood red dawn. It was the original *son et lumière*!

For Roller this was a completely new experience. He had always been keen on the theatre and the opera, but taking control of such an epic as *Tristan* at the Vienna Opera as his debut was both thrilling and daunting.

There were errors of judgement, such as not taking into account the different viewpoints of the audience, but he was keen to learn from any mistakes he had made. By tradition the name of the set designer did not appear on the playbill, but by popular demand, and much to Roller's embarrassment, he had to appear on the stage at the end to acknowledge the ecstatic applause. As Guido Adler later wrote, 'the décor of *Tristan* was truly overpowering in its effect'.

Most of the press were full of praise for Mahler, but some critics had reservations about Roller's contribution, for any completely new concept such as his inevitably courted controversy. Questions were asked as to whether the visual aspects of the production detracted from the impact of the music. For example Hans Liebstöckl, writing in *Reichswehr,* stated that there was little of the spirit of Wagner. He summed up the production by stating that it was strangely impressionistic, that the first act was orange-yellow, the second mauve and the third dough-coloured, and that one of the highlights was Herr Schmedes's new nose! Other critics, such as Puchstein in the *Deutsches Volksblatt*, were very complimentary, regarding the 1903 *Tristan* as being the dawning of a new era in opera production. In the audience on the 21st of February had been the young composer Anton Webern. He wrote in his diary about the marvels of the designs, but that all the merit must fall to Mahler himself.

Mahler and Roller thought alike. They respected each other's God-given talents. They both believed in hard work and complete dedication to the task in hand. Neither sought personal acclamation; it was the fruits of their labours that should be judged. Mahler wrote to Roller thanking him, saying how he hoped that the new *Tristan und Isolde* would be just a beginning of their collaboration and a foretaste of things to come.

On the 22nd of February, at 3 0'clock in the afternoon, the day after the triumphant première of the Mahler-Roller *Tristan*, Hugo Wolf died in the asylum where he had lived for four years. This news must have saddened Mahler, bringing back memories of their student days together and the unfortunate affair over Wolf's opera *Der Corregidor*, which had led to his breakdown. The funeral on the 24th was very well attended. Mahler was present, along with a number of singers from the Hofoper and many musicians who had come to pay their last respects to a composer who had promised so much, only to be cut down by insanity.

The next important work to be staged at the Hofoper was Gustave Charpentier's *Louise*. Alma wrote how one day in January 1903 Mahler had told her about a rather remarkable opera that had been sent to him. He described the full score as being brilliant and very dramatic. It included a part for a recently invented instrument, the celesta. He was immediately taken by the delicate sound it produced, and he was to use it himself in many of his subsequent compositions. The première of *Louise* had been given at the Opéra-Comique in Paris on the 2nd of February 1900. Although controversial at the time, this love story set on the hillside of Montmartre had subsequently been a great hit in the French capital. Mahler, always on the look out for new operas for the Hofoper, had decided that *Louise* would be worth staging. He invited Charpentier to conduct, but he declined, telling Mahler that it would be impossible to equal him. However, he would be delighted to attend the Vienna première.

Rehearsals had been going well, with Gutheil-Schoder, Slezak and Demuth in the lead parts, until Charpentier arrived. He then set about criticising the costumes and sets, saying that they were too realistic, too grand and too similar to those used in the Paris production. Alma referred to him as the first of the Surrealists. Typical of his ideas was in a scene in the Second Act. With the first glimmer of dawn over the streets below Montmartre, the Night Prowler appears. He represents the '*Plaisirs de Paris*', which Louise and other young ladies ardently long for. Charpentier wanted this dubious character to have a red light bulb under his coat so that when he opened it the glow of his heart would appear! Another Felliniesque idea was for a dancer in a very short tutu lit by a pink spotlight to perform pirouettes across the stage during the crowning of the muse scene in Act Three. Alma recalled her first meeting with him when she and Gustav had been walking along the Ringstrasse. She described how she had become aware of a strange figure ahead of them with a large black cape flapping like the wings of a huge bird or the sails of a walking windmill.

Alma regarded Charpentier as a very likeable Bohemian, similar to some of the characters in Louise. He gave her a daily bouquet of flowers, one with the message, '*À Madame Mahler, gracieuse muse de Vienne, la muse de Montmartre reconnaissante*'. He was madly in love with her, although his deep respect for Mahler prevented him from doing or saying anything untoward. According to Alma his table manners were atrocious, and he even invited a young lady, a <u>very</u> casual acquaintance, to join him in the director's box!

Also in town around this time were the Strausses. They dined with Gustav and Alma at their Auenbruggergasse apartment. Pauline's behaviour was as embarrassing as ever, and Mahler took Strauss into the next room so that they could have a civilised conversation. In their absence Pauline set about running down her husband, saying that he never spoke to her and was mean financially and with the time he spent with her. When Pauline burst into tears Alma fetched the two men from the next room. Their continuing discourse on musical matters was punctuated by Pauline's demands for information on which were the best hairdressers and underwear shops in Vienna! Alma also recalled how on one occasion she visited Pauline and found, much to her surprise, that she was still in bed. She was about to leave when Strauss arrived bearing a gift of a very expensive diamond ring with which he bribed Pauline to get up. This was just as well since she was due to sing in a concert conducted by her husband!

The première of *Louise* had been a great success with the audience who insisted on Charpentier taking numerous bows, but the press reaction had been very mixed. Gustav and Alma had enjoyed Charpentier's whirlwind visit, but were nevertheless relieved when life regained a degree of sanity. Sanity of course did not equate with inactivity, for Mahler was once more on his travels, leaving Vienna on the 30th of March. His destination this time was the city of Lemberg in the Eastern Austrian province of Galicia (now Lvov in the Ukraine) where he had been invited to conduct his *First Symphony*.

Mahler's hatred of rail travel is clear from the first of his daily letters to Alma. The thirteen-hour journey had made him feel tense and sick and had brought on a migraine. He described the city as being filthy, as were the local Jews who, much to his amusement, ran about 'like stray dogs'. He exclaimed, 'My God, am I supposed to be related to these people?' But the orchestra he found to be very sympathetically disposed towards him, even though the musicians were not of the highest calibre. When he went before them for the first rehearsal he was greeted by a huge fanfare, much to his embarrassment.

On the 31st of March Mahler attended a performance of *Tosca*. The Puccini of *La Bohème* he liked, but *Tosca* he did not. He found it brash and distasteful, and he made a surreptitious exit before the end. During Mahler's tenure in Vienna *Tosca* was never performed at the Hofoper, and in one of his letters to Alma he referred to it as a masterly piece of trash, saying that it appeared to be the case that today any cobbler's apprentice was a brilliant orchestrator!

The performance of the *First Symphony* on the 2nd of April was a great success, so much so that he was asked to conduct it again two days later. Mahler was touched by the response of the orchestra and audience, but was only too glad to head back for Vienna, his Almscherl and Putzi. His *Second Symphony* had been performed the previous evening in Düsseldorf, conducted by Julius Buths, and he wondered whether the audience there had been as appreciative as those in Lemberg. They had, and the music critics for once were full of praise too.

With the Hofoper closed for Easter, the Mahlers had a brief but very welcome break in Abbazia on the Adriatic coast.

The 1902-1903 opera season was drawing to a close. It ended with a spectacular new production of *Aida*. The cast included Lucy Weidt, Slezak, Demuth and Mayr. The sets and costumes dazzled and in the Triumphal

Scene over a thousand performers were on stage. The King of Saxony attended the first performance and afterwards presented Mahler with a medal. But before the summer holiday and the longed-for return to Maiernigg, an event of major significance for Mahler was to take place. Following his Krefeld triumph, and despite his initial jealousy over the success of the *Third Symphony* there, Richard Strauss had arranged for Mahler's *Second Symphony* to be performed in Basel Cathedral as part of the music festival in the city which was to take place from the 12th to the 15th of June in conjunction with the Thirty-Ninth Composers' Congress of the All-German Musical Society. He was naturally thrilled at the prospect of his *Second* being performed at such a venue as well as being <u>the</u> major work at such a prestigious festival. It was to be played at the final concert at 7 p.m. on the 15th. In a letter to Strauss he thanked him, quipping that he would make a famous composer out of him yet. He asked Strauss to give him details of the building, the forces available and the number and length of rehearsals. The preliminary rehearsals were to be in the charge of Hermann Suter.

When Mahler, accompanied by Alma, arrived in Basel, he was delighted to find that Suter had prepared the ground for him meticulously and that the orchestra and chorus were everything he had hoped for. Alma's mother, stepfather and Koloman Moser arrived in time for the final rehearsal. Other friends made their way to Basel, including Arnold Berliner, the physicist whose friendship Mahler had appreciated during his days at the Hamburg Opera, but he was sad that Justi and Arnold Rosé were unable to come. Justi had given birth to a son, Alfred, on the 11th of December and felt it unwise to make the journey, and of course Arnold could not leave Vienna for work reasons.

Two other composers present at the Basel Festival were Hans Pfitzner and Max von Schillings, both of whom were jealous of Mahler and the fact that his *Second Symphony* had been chosen as the climax of the Festival. Pfitzner snubbed him by leaving Basel on the day of the performance, possibly in retaliation for his rejection of his opera *Die Rose vom Liebesgaten* when he had visited him in Krefeld the previous year. His absence was all the more embarrassing as he was a close friend of both Alma and Bruno Walter. Before he left, Pfitzner asked Alma if he might send her the score of his *First String Quartet*; Alma said she would be delighted to see it. Schillings, a self-confessed anti-Semite and friend of Pauline Strauss, did not hide his bitterness at the indifference that Mahler had shown towards his operas. As far as he was concerned Mahler's music was decadent and marked the beginning of the end for German art. He declared that Valhalla was already burning and that Strauss did not stand a chance against 'this Semite'. Yet under this veneer of anti-Semitism,

Schillings had a certain admiration for his *Second Symphony*. He admitted as much having heard the work in Munich in 1900, and he himself was to conduct it in 1910. He was also to contribute to a book of homage to Mahler to mark his fiftieth birthday. But at the time of the Basel triumph, Schillings' colours were nailed to the pro-Aryan mast, a growing fashion in German art that foreshadowed the dark night of Nazi doctrines.

The performance of the *Second Symphony* was stunning. The candle-lit cathedral was packed and, as the Swiss composer Ernest Bloch wrote the following year, the audience had emerged at the end having lived life itself. They had been touched and strengthened. Outside the cathedral a talented Czech musician and composer by the name of Oskar Nedbal knelt before Mahler and kissed his hand, promising that he would ensure that the symphony would be played in Prague; a promise that he kept. So emotional had been the occasion, with such an outstanding performance in an ideal location and followed by applause the like of which few had ever before experienced, it was not surprising that almost all the music critics were swept up in the tide of euphoria. First Krefeld, now Basel; the world was beginning to listen, and Mahler was at last becoming accepted as a major force in contemporary music. To Strauss he had much to be grateful for.

As a result of this double success, C. F. Peters, the influential Leipzig publishers who had works by such composers such as Grieg, Brahms and Wagner in their catalogue, approached Mahler offering to publish his *Fifth Symphony*. With orchestras clamouring to perform his symphonies, giving the publication rights to Peters was a good move both financially and because of the company's reputation.

Exhausted, yet elated, his mind was now focused on his summer holiday – Maiernigg beckoned. He had entered one of the happiest periods of his life; happy, although there remained difficulties in his relationship with Alma. Now not only married but also a mother, she was finding it very hard to say good-bye to her former self – the famed socializer, flirt and one of the most desired women in Vienna. No longer was she in the position to make men grovel at her feet. She missed being able to attend operas on a regular basis. Anna and Carl Moll continued to do so and she had become jealous of their freedom, she having to remain at home to look after her daughter. She was seldom allowed to play music in the evenings, for when Gustav arrived home all he wanted was peace and quiet. She found it hard to resign herself to family life and to being a mother. Gustav on the other hand felt rejuvenated and adored being with his Putzi, who resembled him in many ways with her dark hair and brown eyes. He would delight in carrying her about and singing to her.

With the more peaceful routine of life beside the Wörthersee renewed it was not long before Mahler began composing once more. The major project for the summer of 1903 was the *Sixth Symphony*. According to Alma, he completed two movements as well as sketching out ideas for the rest of the symphony. One of these movements was the gloriously peaceful pastorale, the *Andante*, which reflects not only the surroundings, but also the new-found peace in his own soul. The other movement he finished was probably the *Scherzo*, which Alma disliked. She described it as a depiction of their children at play – completely inaccurate, as Maria was only eight months old, and her sister yet to be conceived! Mahler also worked hard on the opening *Allegro*, a bitter conflict with fate and the inevitable outcome of death. At the beginning of the *Allegro* he composed a soaring theme depicting the different facets of Alma's character: positive, determined, laced with a degree of petulance. He told Alma that he had portrayed her in the music, saying that he was not sure how successful he had been, but that she would have to put up with it as it was. So he had begun to write the symphony which was to attract the unofficial title of 'Tragic'. Taken as a whole it was to be his most gloom-laden, yet written during two of his most contented years. He completed the work the following summer.

However, far from their characters becoming more unified, the differences became more and more noticeable. Feeling frustrated and trapped, and having to spend so much of her time looking after her little daughter, Alma became moody and suffered from nightmares, some with sexual connotations. Apparently one night she dreamt that a large, green snake-like reptile with legs crawled up inside her. She tugged with all her might trying to remove it, but it clung fast onto her organs, and even with the help of her maid the foul creature could not be extricated. Freud would have had a field day!

As much as he loved Alma, in many ways Gustav regarded her as his servant. He had warned her before they were married that she would have to dedicate herself to making his life trouble free and that nothing was to interfere with his God, music. He found her moodiness difficult to handle. He still insisted on her accompanying him on long walks in the forests or beside the Wörthersee, at other times rowing, but such activities had begun to bore her. In the evenings they played the piano together, but Alma's enforced abstinence from composing was becoming increasingly painful. Doubtless with the principle of 'absence makes the heart grow fonder', as well as the desire for some solitude, Mahler decided to set off on his own for Toblach and the area just north of the Dolomites. As it turned out the trip was not very successful. It rained incessantly and he was constantly pestered by swarms of flies, so it was not long before he returned to Maiernigg.

The summer holiday was nearing its end. With the successes of the previous months, Mahler was for once quite looking forward to returning to Vienna. He wrote to his assistant Franz Schalk saying that he would not be returning until a few days after the beginning of the 1903-1904 season, and that he was writing to Bruno Walter to ask him to take charge of *Lohengrin*. He also wrote to Leo Slezak telling him that his first appearance of the new season would be in *Aida* on the 20th of August and that there would be a number of very interesting opportunities for him in the near future, which he was sure would bring him much acclaim.

On the 27th of August Mahler returned to Vienna on his own, leaving Alma and Putzi behind in Maiernigg. He decided not to go straight to the Auenbruggergasse apartment. Instead, on his mother-in-law's advice, he stayed for a few days at a hotel in Kahlenberg close to the Vienna Woods. Mahler loved the place. He told Alma in his letters that he was surrounded by beautiful countryside and that he was being pampered by the owners, yet the hotel was within commuting distance to the Opera. He decided to stay there until she and Putzi returned on the 6th of September. In one of her letters, Alma voiced her unfounded suspicion that her husband was having assignations with Mildenburg, to which Mahler expressed his feelings of such nonsense by writing,

'Himmelherrgottkreuztausenddonnerundhagelsappermentnocheinmal!'

which summed up his feelings perfectly!

On his return to work he was met with a barrage of controversy over the lowering of the orchestra pit. Such complaints as the new level would be a fire hazard, there would be less room to move around (untrue, as the space for the musicians had actually been increased from 47 to 59 square metres) and that the acoustics would be affected (untrue, as Karpath admitted). Some critics were totally in favour of the alteration, one being Julius Korngold, but others continued to moan. Nevertheless the deed had been done and Mahler was reasonably satisfied. His original intention was to have machinery installed so that the depth of the pit could be varied to a maximum of one metre and a half, depending on the work to be performed. This had to be shelved for the time being for structural reasons, the orchestra pit being lowered by just 50cm. However the two main objectives had been achieved: to prevent the musicians' lights from interfering with the stage lighting and to reduce the volume, thus providing a better balance between the singers and the orchestra.

On the 3rd of September he was due to conduct *Figaro*, a performance in honour of Great Britain's King Edward VII who was on a visit to Vienna, but he delegated the responsibility to Franz Schalk. Mahler had decided to postpone his first appearance of the new season until *Tristan und Isolde* on the 14th. This was part of the now established Wagner season that was also to include *Die Meistersinger* and *Lohengrin*, in which the baritone Friedrich Weidermann made the first of a number of appearances that autumn. The talent of the young singer was immediately recognised, and Mahler's latest recruit to the Hofoper was to prove to be a great success. Autumn 1903 also saw a new production of *La Juive* by Fromental Halévy (1799-1862) with Mahler taking a particularly active and dramatic part on the stage as well as on the podium during rehearsals. On several occasions he leapt onto the stage to demonstrate to the chorus how to act 'terrified'!

The steadily improving standards of every department of the Vienna Court Opera won the plaudits of many, not least Emperor Franz Joseph. Mahler was duly summoned to appear before him. The Emperor thanked him for his services to the Hofoper by bestowing upon him the award of the Order of the Iron Crown, third class. Recognition in high places was important to Mahler, not only because it held his critics at bay, but also because two new controversies began to rear their ugly heads. Firstly, in order to achieve recent successes, the Hofoper was running way beyond its budget and secondly Mahler, with his rising fame as both conductor and composer, was spending more and more time away from Vienna.

Orchestras far and wide were showing increasing interest in performing his symphonies. Julius Buths in Düsseldorf was eager to conduct the *Fourth*. Mahler replied that he was delighted at the prospect of his much misunderstood 'persecuted step-child' being played, but warned him that audiences had so far failed to appreciate the humour behind the work. His *Fourth Symphony* had as yet found little joy in the world of music. Arthur Seidl in Munich was another conductor keen to perform his works. On the 21st of October the British première of the *First* was given under the baton of Henry Wood who stated that the occasion was the first time any of Mahler's music had been heard in England. But by far the most important foreign venue was Amsterdam, where his staunch supporter Willem Mengelberg was at the helm.

Mengelberg, so impressed by Mahler's *Third Symphony* at the Krefeld Festival, was determined that his promise be fulfilled that it should be performed by Amsterdam's Concertgebouw Orchestra. Arrangements were made, and Mahler stayed as guest of the Mengelbergs. This was his first visit to Holland, and he wrote to Alma saying that the journey had been unexpectedly eventful for King Leopold 2nd of Belgium and his entourage had shared his train. He told her how at the very first rehearsal his breath was taken away by the sheer brilliance of the orchestra.

The Mengelbergs were the perfect hosts going out of their way to make his stay a memorable one. He was deeply impressed by the Rembrandt paintings in the Rijksmuseum, in particular 'The Night Watch'. Among the interesting people he met was the composer Alphons Diepenbrock who was a deep admirer of his music, and whose future friendship and support he greatly appreciated. In a letter to one of his pupils, Diepenbrock wrote that Mahler believed in the future and that through his music he had the rare gift of being able to change people. Mahler spent many happy hours walking along the canals and enjoying the Dutch countryside, and he could quite understand the inspiration the landscape gave to artists.

Mengelberg's preparatory work with the Concertgebouw of the *Third Symphony* had been meticulous, and the performances on the 22nd and 23rd were fabulous. Gustav wrote to Alma saying that they had been even better than at the Krefeld Festival. Audience, musicians and singers applauded and cheered him in a way he had never before experienced. Amsterdam had embraced him as no other city had or would do during his lifetime. So successful had the *Third* been that Mengelberg persuaded him to conduct his *First Symphony* two days later. The musicians loved it, but the audience did not give it the ovation that the *Third* had received. Many regarded it merely as an interesting early work and consequently applauded politely. Nevertheless Mengelberg, who was determined to have all of Mahler's works performed in the Dutch capital, conducted the *First Symphony* no less than four times early in 1904. As far as the Dutch were concerned, they now regarded him as the greatest living composer, ousting Richard Strauss from that lofty position. Knowing this must have given him great satisfaction! With the help of Mengelberg's influence, Amsterdam had become the Mahler capital of the musical world, and has remained so to this day, save for the dark years of the Nazi era.

On his return to Vienna, Mahler wrote a letter of thanks to Mengelberg, enclosing a number of scores for his perusal, and saying how much he had appreciated everything that he had done for him. He also asked for his kindest regards to be passed on to Diepenbrock.

After fending off controversy surrounding a protracted dispute concerning the stage hands at the Hofoper, the usual autumnal disputes with some of the singers and having narrowly escaped being drawn in to resume his former stressful post as conductor of the Philharmonic concerts, something he could well do without, Mahler was once more about to go on his travels. Frankfurt had asked him to conduct the *Third*. By this time Alma was two months pregnant, and Gustav was upset at being separated from her again so soon after his trip to Holland. He wrote to her on the 28th of November from the station in Vienna telling her to stay in bed as long as possible. Some eyebrows were beginning to be raised over his travels on behalf of his own music. Was he becoming a mere overpaid administrator, delegating many of his musical responsibilities at the Hofoper to his assistants? It was understandable that he wanted to conduct his symphonies in person for there had been several poor performances under the batons of others. Equally, he was fully aware of the potential damage to his reputation as Director of the Vienna Court Opera, and consequently did turn down a number of very appetizing invitations.

Following the successes in Krefeld and Amsterdam, Frankfurt was a disappointment for him. Initially he found the orchestra to be both second rate and not entirely in sympathy with the music, but both attitude and the quality of playing improved as the rehearsals progressed. However the reception, matching the performance, was nothing like those of his previous triumphs and the press were generally sarcastic with little positive to say. In complete contrast, a performance of the *Second Symphony* in Prague, conducted by Oskar Nedbal on the 18th of December, was a major success. Nedbal, who had been present at the triumphant performance in Basel Cathedral the previous June and who had afterwards kissed Mahler's hand in homage, had thus fulfilled his promise to conduct the work in the Czech capital. The acclamation was such that Nedbal immediately made plans for a repeat performance ten days later. Unfortunately Mahler had been unable to attend due to his commitments at the Hofoper and the negative feelings regarding his increasingly frequent travels. However Alma, accompanied by her mother, represented him, Putzi remaining in Vienna with her father.

So 1903 ended on a very positive note, and even Mahler's detractors had to admit that like it or not his music was indeed becoming a force to be reckoned with.

Following a dreadfully received performance of the *Third Symphony* in Munich in January, which duly confirmed Mahler's fears over performances of his works not conducted by him in person, he was on his travels once again, this time to conduct the *Third* in Heidelberg and Mannheim. In a letter to Alma he stated that Strauss was quite right on insisting that he himself should conduct his own works. He also told her that he had been to a performance of Pfitzner's *Die Rose vom Liebesgarten*, but his feelings towards the score remained unaltered – good atmosphere and orchestral colour, but ill-constructed. He described it as being like jelly, a 'primeval slime' containing seeds of life, whose development beyond the invertebrate was doomed to failure. So despite Alma's attempts to champion Pfizner's music, her husband remained unmoved by *Die Rose vom Liebesgarten*. The performances of the *Third Symphony* in Heidelberg and Mannheim were well received and helped to undo some of the damage caused by the ill-prepared Munich event.

Performances of his symphonies and his travels were gathering momentum: another very well received *Third* in Prague at the end of February, the *Fourth*, as always controversial, in Mainz the following month, followed a few days later by another successful *Third* in Cologne. On the 28th of March he returned to Vienna where concern over his increasingly frequent absences continued to fuel controversy. He then joined Alma and Putzi for a few days much needed rest in Abbazia. Despite knowing the importance of conducting as many performances of his symphonies in person, he was becoming decidedly tired of having to live out of a suitcase and of being separated so frequently from Alma and Putzi.

With his wife and daughter remaining on holiday, he returned to Vienna. To ease the loneliness he felt in his apartment, he paid regular visits to Carl Moll and Arnold Rosé. He also took the opportunity in Alma's absence to visit Fritz Löhr and drove out to see Guido Adler. Alma was as usual a somewhat reluctant letter-writer and Mahler complained of this in one of his daily missives to her. Resuming work at the Hofoper, he was confronted by a considerable backlog that had been piling up during his absence. His assistant conductor Franz Schalk was away on sick leave and another assistant, Hubert Wondra, was in hospital after an unsuccessful assassination attempt. Through his tireless hard work Mahler had elevated the Vienna Opera to a position unrivalled amongst the world's opera houses; keeping it there was to be more problematic. Although still dedicated to his work, the Hofoper was becoming something of a thorn in his side. The constant criticism and ingratitude were becoming hard to stomach, and his mind was focussing more and more on his own music and on his family.

With preparations for a new production of Verdi's *Falstaff*, having to conduct *Tristan und Isolde* (somewhat reluctantly according to his letter to Alma of the 7th of April) and making final corrections to the score of his *Fifth Symphony*, which his publishers were awaiting, he understandably felt very overworked. With Alma's return, domestic life was back to normal, but Mahler was facing new singer problems at the Opera. The latest difficulties concerned two of the most important stars, namely Erik Schmedes and Leo Slezak, both of whom were in financial difficulties, the former due to personal excesses, the latter because of missed performances due to illness. Slezak wanted to ease his situation by making guest appearances at venues other than at the Hofoper. In his memoirs, Slezak stated that he was in his *Sturm und Drang* period, and Mahler himself could of course be fiery at times. Slezak described how having requested leave to perform in Graz, he was greeted by a Mahler broadside. How dare he request time off after his recent absence! So infuriated was Mahler, that he slammed his fists on a bank of communication buttons which linked his office with other important departments at the Hofoper. It was not long before hurrying footsteps could be heard converging on Mahler's sanctum. Doors opened with secretaries, fire officer *et al* appearing, only to be greeted by shouts of '*Raus! Raus!*' This was followed by a deafening silence, and as the huge frame of Slezak emerged, his face flushed, one of the eavesdroppers inquired, 'Is he dead?' Slezak wrote a letter of resignation, but the storm blew over, partly because he knew that Mahler was acting within his rights and had the backing of Prince Montenuovo, the chief administrator of the Hofoper. But it was not long before they were both back on even keels. After all they did respect each other's talents and were so important to each other. The resignation was withdrawn and Slezak was given a considerable increase in pay.

The new Roller-Mahler *Falstaff*, the first Vienna production of the opera in German, was widely acclaimed. Roller's sets were praised along with Mahler's musicianship. Mahler loved Verdi's operas and so did the Viennese. There had been difficulties musically with the language crossover, but his fondness for *Falstaff* and his sympathetic handling of the singers ironed these out.

The 1903-1904 season drew to a close. Mahler had steered the Court Opera successfully and much had been achieved despite the inevitable criticism from some. He had successfully launched an attack on the claques, the groups of fans who brashly supported their chosen singers and whose wild applause tended to destroy the flow of an opera. His retaliation was to have the house lights dimmed and latecomers prevented from entering the auditorium. Any whispers or untoward noises would be greeted by a ferocious glare. Audiences soon learnt that when Mahler conducted the audience had to be on its best behaviour! The budget deficit of the previous year had been substantially reduced, and the *Neue Freie Presse* reported on the 22nd of May that Plappart, the general manager, was very pleased. Attendances and receipts had risen well beyond expectations.

Despite his refusal to take over once more the responsibility of the Philharmonic concerts, a greater harmony now existed between Mahler and the *Gesellschaft der Musikfreunde*, helped partly by his friend, the influential Guido Adler. The latter had drafted plans for a complete reorganisation of the Conservatory, with the possibility of having Mahler as Director. He was flattered by the idea and agreed in principle, so long as the post would not impinge on his work as Director of the Hofoper. The plan however never came into being due to ministerial changes in the government.

Apart from Guido Adler's ambitious plans for the Conservatory, he was in the news for another and far more controversial reason. A group of 'modern' composers under the leadership of Zemlinsky and Arnold Schoenberg had decided to found the musical equivalent of the Secession, an idea enthusiastically supported by Schoenberg's pupils Anton Webern and Alban Berg. Mahler, having paved the way with his own music, the Second Viennese School was now being launched and, much to the surprise of many, both he and Adler declared themselves to be in favour of the plan. They neither understood nor liked the avant-garde music of Schoenberg and his fellows, but were equally aware that just maybe the future lay in their hands.

At their invitation, Zemlinsky and Schoenberg visited Gustav and Alma in their apartment. Alma of course was delighted with the idea! Mahler had a genuine desire to encourage their quest for recognition and was certain that Schoenberg's music in particular was of the greatest importance; he foresaw that the world would one day sit up and take notice. The visit however was not a great success. Controversy and entrenched opinions on music matters led to heated arguments. The visitors left in a huff, Schoenberg swearing that he would never set foot in that apartment again; Mahler telling his wife never to repeat the invitation. Tempers cooled after what was little more than a storm in a teacup, and their admiration for Mahler remained untarnished.

His attention was now focussed on Alma whose second child was due any day. For some weeks brisk walking had been out of the question, so she and Gustav had been taking a daily drive in the Prater. On the 14th of June they did just this. On their return they found the Rosés waiting for them, hoping to persuade Alma and Gustav to join them for an evening at the Burgtheater. The play that evening was *Der arme Heinrich* by Gerhart Hauptmann, with whom they had recently socialised. Despite Gustav's concern Alma was determined to go. On their return Alma, totally exhausted, took her copy of the play to her bed to relive Hauptmann's musical verse. Dawn broke and Alma was in labour. Gustav rushed out to summon the mid-wife. On his return he sat by her reading Kant out loud, trying to distract her from the pain she was suffering. Alma described how the sound of his dreary 'incantations' nearly drove her mad. Eventually she begged him to stop. His intentions may have been right, but the choice of material certainly was not. Their second daughter Anna Justine was born at midday. They nicknamed her Guckerl, or Gucki (*Guckern:* to peep), because of her large, staring blue eyes that she had inherited from Alma.

A few hours later, bubbling with childish excitement, Gustav played a prank on Alma while she was asleep. She suddenly awoke to find a huge stag beetle waving its legs close to her face. Gustav had found it and brought it to her because of her love for animals!

Alma was very weak after Anna's birth and she was told that she would need three weeks to recover, thus delaying the beginning of her summer holiday at their villa in Maiernigg. Mahler wrote to Arnold Berliner giving him the news of the birth of their second daughter. He told him that he was about to leave Vienna for Carinthia on his own, leaving Alma and his children in the tender care of Anna Moll. He stated that he considered it a duty to do so for not a day could be wasted. The completion of the *Sixth Symphony* was uppermost in his mind.

Chapter 11

Vienna . . . Part Five

Die Kindertotenlieder
Sixth Symphony

MAHLER'S INTENTION of not wasting a single day in order to complete the score of the *Sixth Symphony* was foiled by the onset of a particularly severe bout of composer's block. He had travelled on his own to his villa in Maiernigg feeling completely drained after such an eventful season in Vienna and his many travels to conduct his symphonies. Even the birth of Gucki, which had given him such pleasure, had taken its toll. Totally exhausted he just could not settle down to compose, and the enervating climate of Carinthia and the poor weather did not help.

He spent the first days of his holiday planning and supervising the creation of a play area for his children. He wrote to Alma about his plans, but she obviously had a paranoia about snakes, as is evident from the strange nightmare she had suffered the previous summer. Her concern now was that snakes from the lake would invade the sandy play area. She had been brought up in a city environment and felt uneasy with the wild life of Carinthia. Mahler tried to pacify her, saying that there really was no need to worry, and that anyway water snakes were not poisonous. He even wrote to Anna Moll, asking her to have a word with her daughter. He read, played the piano and studied scores by Bach, Beethoven and Bruckner and began to feel very lonely. Depressed at his inability to compose, he longed for the arrival of Alma and the children. Did he feel a certain guilt at leaving them behind in Vienna?

The rain continued unceasingly, occasionally punctuated by spectacular thunderstorms – the only form of bad weather that Mahler rather enjoyed for its drama. He managed to do a little work on two of his *Kindertotenlieder*. Then he received a letter from Alma telling him that her departure from Vienna would have to be postponed by a week for medical reasons. With the weather becoming more and more sultry, Mahler was distraught. He decided to break the monotony by taking a trip to the Tyrol.

He travelled on the 10th of July. His destination was Misurina, high up in the Dolomites where the air would be fresher, and he hoped that the magnificent mountain scenery would give him the necessary inspiration and drive to complete the *Sixth Symphony*.

Whilst there he wrote to Alma urgently asking her to find the manuscripts of the second and third movements which he had forgotten to bring with him, telling her to make sure she brought them with her.

Just two days in the Tyrol had worked its magic. The inspiration he sought to complete the finale of the *Sixth Symphony* filled his mind. On his return he went to Klagenfurt to meet Alma, his daughters and their nurse at the station. The loneliness vanished; the music was bursting to see the light of day. The summer routine was re-established, with Mahler spending many hours up in his *Häuschen*. It is strange that during one of the happiest periods of his life he should compose some of the darkest and at times most terrifying music he would ever compose. Quite frequently a feeling of sheer terror would overwhelm him and, in a state of panic, he would abandon the *Häuschen* for his studio on the top floor of the villa. There, closer to Alma and the children, he would continue to compose. These crises, which he blamed on the cruelty of nature and the great god Pan, caused inevitable problems for his wife who had to ensure that silence reigned both inside and outside the house. Alma could not sing or play the piano, the children had to play in near silence and the cook had to carry out her duties without a sound reaching Mahler. Alma began to feel bored and neglected. She felt that she was becoming little more than a friend, mother and housekeeper.

Die Kindertotenlieder

In 1872, six years after Rückert's death, the first edition of the *Kindertotenlieder* collection was published. It contained 425 poems, but because they were of such a personal nature, the poet had never had the will to have them made available to anyone other than his family and very close friends. Rückert and his wife suffered a double tragedy. In 1833 their youngest child, two year old Luise, died from scarlet fever, and only just over a fortnight later their son also died from the same disease. Rückert was understandably shattered by these events, for a long time remaining inconsolable, and it was during the first six months of 1834 that he wrote his poems, *Die Kindertotenlieder*, in memory of his lost children.

The quality of the poems may not be of the highest standard, hardly surprising when writing two or three a day over a period of six months! But this did not worry Mahler in the slightest, for it was their very personal nature that appealed to him, and anyway, he would adapt the poems when setting them to music. Actually he preferred not to use poetic 'classics', saying that to do so would be like an artist painting over a much-revered sculpture!

Having completed the second and fifth songs of this latest collection to his great satisfaction, Mahler was taken aback by his wife's reaction. Alma reproached her husband for daring to set Rückert's poems about the death of children to music; with two little daughters of their own, he was tempting fate! Of course Mahler had begun the *Kindertotenlieder,* composing the first, third and fourth songs, three years previously in 1901 before he had even met Alma. As mentioned before, he had been very moved by Rückert's poems, which the poet had written after the death of two of his own children, one of whom bore the same name as Mahler's younger brother Ernst, whose death had been one of the most shattering events of Mahler's youth. Not only deaths remembered from his childhood, but also of his married sister Leopoldine and Otto as well, the latter so gifted musically and whom Mahler had done his level best to nurture and protect, but who was overcome by despair and committed suicide. But Alma did not know these people and she was unable to fathom the deep feelings of grief that lay within Mahler's soul. These past tragic events had left an indelible mark and he had begun to contemplate his own mortality, as well as of those whom he loved, and the transitory nature of life itself. The completion of the song cycle had therefore been very important to Mahler, whatever Alma's feelings. The songs were a private *in memoriam* to his beloved younger brother, and formed what is without doubt his greatest song cycle.

The importance of *Die Kindertotenlieder* as a pivotal work cannot be overestimated. It was the key that would unlock the door to the wealth of riches that would follow. In his *4th Symphony* he had experimented with a small orchestra, chamber like qualities and the advanced use of variations in the *Adagio* that he referred to as 'kaleidoscopic rearrangement'. *Die Kindertotenlieder* marks a further advance. Tender and compassionate, yet never sentimental, it is the first work of his musical maturity, a forerunner of that great, late masterpiece, *Das Lied von der Erde.* Exquisitely and sparsely orchestrated (the only brass being horns) they belong to a different world to the romanticism of the *Wunderhorn* years. The musicians are used as soloists, an extension of his aim with the *4th Symphony,* and it is only in the final song that the full forces are used. Donald Mitchell suggests that the 20th century chamber orchestra could well have come into being as a result of this work. Apart from his student piece, the movement of a piano quartet, this is the nearest Mahler came to composing a chamber work. It is also the first song cycle to be written originally for orchestra rather than for piano accompaniment and then orchestrated later.

Nun will die Sonn so hell aufgehn
(Now the sun will rise as brightly)
D minor
Slow and melancholic, do not drag.

Following a brief introduction by the wind section with oboe and horn in counterpoint, accompanied by harp and the glockenspiel depicting a miniature, tolling bell, a feeling of mourning is established. The soloist's first line is 'Now the sun will rise as brightly'. These positive sounding words soon dissolve into sorrow when it becomes clear that the night has been one of personal distress when a little lamp (the child) has been extinguished. But the sunlight at dawn is for everyone, and the words of the final line 'Hail to the joyous light of the world!' sound positive, although there is a stark contrast between the joy of the words and the despair in the music. They are sung through a veil of tears.

Nun seh' ich wohl, warum so dunkle Flammen
(Now I see why such dark flames ... you flashed at me; oh eyes!)
C minor
Do not drag, intense but tender.

In the first song the contrast of night and sunlight is the main thread, and in the second the predominant image is eyes. The words speak of destiny being like an enveloping mist, the pain of separation decreed by Fate, and eyes that will shine in the memory like stars in the night sky. There is a contrast here between the warm, comforting sound of the lower strings and the higher, colder sounds from the woodwind and violins, as well as an alternating between minor and major.

Wenn dein Mütterlein tritt zur Tür herein
(When your mother comes in at the door)
C minor
Heavy, muffled.

This third song is Bach inspired, a composer much revered by Mahler who stated that when he retired he intended to spend as much time as possible studying his scores. It opens with a cor anglais and two bassoons playing in counterpoint, with the lower strings playing pizzicato, before the singer enters in a plaintive legato style. The orchestration of this song is notable for the absence of violins, thereby enhancing the pervading darkness.

A father, devastated by the loss of his daughter, no longer looks at his wife when she enters the room but at an empty space where once his daughter would have stood. He remembers her smiling face; a bitter sweet joy that will soon be extinguished.

Oft denk' ich, sie sind nur ausgegangen
(I often think they've merely gone out)
E flat
Calm.

This is a moment of escapism for the mourning parent. The emptiness of the previous song is replaced with forlorn hope and an unwillingness to face up to reality. This self-deception is mirrored in the orchestration that adopts a far more romantic mood. The music has greater warmth, a quicker more natural pace. Despite this, there is a feeling of tension, of restlessness as portrayed by the syncopated rhythms from the basses.

The singer imagines that the children have merely set out on a walk and that soon they will return home. Despair is countered by imagining them up on the hills in the sunshine. Surely they would be found up there?

In the third stanza the music becomes almost ecstatic, the flute and strings depicting the hills bathed in sunshine, and the singer ends with the words 'It's a lovely day!' Yet this is but a dream, and at the very end the music returns to the more sombre mood of the song's opening.

In diesem Wetter, in diesem Braus
(In this weather, in this tumult)
D minor.
With unremittingly painful expressiveness.

The fifth and final song continues the theme of children lost on an outing. Whereas at the end of the previous one the singer imagines the children playing on a hillside bathed in glorious sunshine, here bleak reality returns, emphasised by the use of muted strings. There are feelings of deep remorse and self-reproach for having failed to prevent the children from being taken out in such stormy weather. This turbulence is related to the parent's state of mind, and with great subtlety, Mahler depicts the storm in the music simply by adding additional instruments without once resorting to a fortissimo. The storm is more in the heart of the grieving parent than in the elements.

Once again the singer tries to banish the despair by imagining that the children are not frightened, but safe in the hands of God, just as they would be in their mother's house. *Die Kindertotenlieder* ends calmly, soothingly with music in the style of a lullaby from which the more positive D major emerges. With a solo horn, joined by the lower strings and celesta, a calm resignation reigns. The children are now at peace. It is a timeless, almost hypnotic ending.

With its almost Chinese watercolour approach of suggestion rather than out and out description and a spirituality almost akin to Buddhism, *Die*

Kindertotenlieder, and this song in particular, is without doubt the precursor of *Das Lied von der Erde.*

Filled with a profound lyricism, these songs of loss are both calm and dignified. The subject matter could so easily have resulted in over-emotionalism, but Mahler's restrained writing is all the better for it. Benjamin Britten referred to them as 'heavenly' and 'glorious', and that 'they restore my faith in life'. He stated that it was music 'I think I love more than any other . . .'

As well as using a considerably reduced orchestra when compared to the symphonies, the transparency of Mahler's music in the *Kindertotenlieder* was groundbreaking. Such sources as marches, dances, fanfares and folk music, so prevalent in his work until this time, no longer played a part. This important work was the forerunner of the early songs of such composers as Webern, Schoenberg and Berg.

Mahler declared that he found writing the *Kindertotenlieder* to be particularly painful, and that he felt sorry that the world would one day have to listen to such sad songs. Sad they may be, but there is a thread of light always present; the sun rising in the first, the stars in the second, the candle light and the light of joy in the third, the sunlit hills in the fourth and the 'bright' image of God's protection at the end of the last song. It was no wonder that Mahler was upset by Alma's retort of 'How dare you!'

Despite Alma's feelings about the *Kindertotenlieder*, she described the summer as being both beautiful and serene. Gustav spent many hours with his daughters, especially Putzi with whom he delighted in playing games and reading her stories, and day-by-day the bond between them was strengthened.

Work on the *Sixth* surged ahead, and he told Alma that he had tried to depict her in the great theme in the first movement (the second subject) – a token of his love, quite possibly to placate her over her admonitions regarding the *Kindertotenlieder*. The initial boredom that Alma had suffered was soon dispelled by visits from family and friends, including the Molls, Roller, Burckhard and Zemlinsky! She wrote that 'Z' worshipped her husband like a god, and that Mahler was beginning to like him more and more.

Another visitor during the summer of 1904 was a friend of Alma's, Erica Conrat, the daughter of a wealthy businessman who had been a friend of Brahms. Erica remembered how one evening she was joined by Mahler to watch a firework display, taking place on the far side of the Wörthersee. As was his wont Mahler began to have philosophical thoughts. He told Erica how Goethe, who had always regarded himself as a mere novice in his writing, was full of praise for those who left this life in the heat of creativity. Maybe the sun's fire would last for billions of years, whereas a rocket, like life itself, was a mere flash in time. Yet in the same way life's short span would have meaning if an individual created something worthwhile for posterity. Erica also left a beautiful description of an occasion when she had joined Alma and Gustav for a row across the lake to Krumpendorf. She and Gustav rowed, while Alma held the tiller. She described Gustav's steady rhythm, and how she was afraid of rowing out of time with him while Alma sat with the setting sun flaming through her hair like a red halo. She depicted her as being like some beautiful creature of prey. Erica considered it to be truly wonderful that Mahler, whose eyes were always focussed on the highest, should be married to Alma who symbolised the beauty of the earth.

Roller, whose visit inevitably centred on plans for the coming season at the Hofoper, also wrote about life at Maiernigg. He described Mahler as a careless dresser, showing no concern for his outward appearance, except that is, for his tails – his 'working clothes' – for when he stood on the podium he fully realised the importance of appearing before the public suitably attired. Footwear was of the utmost importance to him whether for walking or conducting. Roller described Mahler's gait: quick short steps with an involuntary irregular rhythm, straight kneed, leaning forward with chin thrust out in a determined fashion. Others found it difficult to keep up with him, including Alma who would usually accompany, often reluctantly. Walking, climbing, cycling, swimming, rowing – he would stretch himself to the limit. He only relaxed in the evening when he would indulge in conversations of depth, read aloud or play the piano, and sometimes enjoy a cigar and a beer, or wine on special occasions. Moderation, decency and cleanliness were forever important in his daily life. Above all was Mahler's very sincere love of nature, which deeply impressed Carl Moll who accompanied him on some of his walks. And yet, according to Alma, there were occasions that contradicted this, such as when he insisted that four cocks should be killed because their crowing was annoying him while he was sunbathing!

And then the day came when the *Sixth Symphony* was finished – a work that Mahler himself declared would pose conundrums that would only be worked out by a generation who had understood his first five symphonies. Today, thanks to regular performances, recordings and a greater understanding of Mahler and his music, it has become one of his most highly acclaimed works.

Sixth Symphony, in A minor
(In four movements)

Scored for a huge orchestra, including such sundry instruments as cowbells, deep bells, whip, hammer, birch sticks, celesta (his recent discovery) and xylophone, it was no wonder that cartoonists had fun at his expense. One depicted Mahler clutching his head and exclaiming, 'My God, I've forgotten the motor horn!' (*Die Muskete*, January 1907). It is however the most classical of all his symphonies, and in the opinion of musicologist Deryck Cooke in the February 1968 issue of *The Gramophone*, it is Mahler's greatest given the formality of motivic control 'of an almost uncontrollable content over such a large span'. Michael Kennedy agrees with Cooke, 'because it is his most perfect reconciliation of form and matter'. Formality it may have with its four purely orchestral movements, the first of which is in clear sonata form with exposition, repeat, first and second themes, development and recapitulation, but it is far from classical in mood. It is forward-looking, one could almost say prophetic of not only the music of the future but also of catastrophes that lay ahead for both Mahler and mankind. His personal happiness at the time of its composition ran parallel with his fears for the future: the destruction of a great cultural heritage and the devastation of war the like of which the world had never known.

First movement: Allegro energico, ma non troppo. Heftig aber markig.
(Vehement, but concentrated)

The symphony bursts into life with a dark march of extraordinary power; determined, even violent at times. Mahler's 'hero' is thrust into grim conflict. The music builds relentlessly towards a massive climax out of which the 'tragic' theme emerges. Quiet the theme may be when compared to the opening bars of the movement, but the fearsome march continues to hover in the background played pizzicato by the strings. This is followed by the second subject, the 'Alma' theme. With major taking over from minor key, it is a passionate portrayal of his wife, but is swamped by a return of the opening march music, xylophone to the fore. A peaceful Alpine interlude follows, complete with cowbells and tinkling celesta. Mahler said of this section that he had tried to depict the final earthly sounds from the valleys that managed to penetrate the loneliness of the mountain peaks. Once again the march returns, more violent, more urgent than before. At the end of the recapitulation the 'Alma' theme reappears triumphant, joyfully rejoicing in victory over the dark forces, for the time being at least.

Second movement: Andante moderato

Mahler's original plan was for the *Scherzo* to be the second movement. However, it is thought that he later changed his mind, feeling that the Alpinesque *Andante moderato*, reflecting the 'Alpine' interlude in the first movement, was a more suitable sequel to the triumphant rendition of the 'Alma' theme. On the other hand, when the *Andante moderato* is placed next to the Finale the contrast makes the onslaught of the crushing final movement even more devastating.

The *Andante moderato* is an oasis of calm in the turbulent scheme of things that is the *Sixth Symphony*. Serene, meditative, nostalgic and innocent, this is one of his most magical movements. There is an air of solitude and detachment from the cares of the world, the only link being the distant sound of cowbells. The cowbells are in fact the only link with the other movements musically, Mahler avoiding any motivic references. He was determined that this *intermezzo* should be a retreat from the world of tragedy; it is a chance to take a breath of fresh air before the turbulent onslaught that is to come.

Third movement: Scherzo. Wuchtig.
(Heavy)

But first the *Scherzo*, described by the Austrian musicologist Hans Redlich as 'a sinister, Hoffmannesque puppet show', partly due to Mahler's use of a xylophone, but it is not music of frivolity or amusement, rather a movement both eerie and disturbing with the seeds of tragedy being sown.

The peace of the *Andante Moderato* is banished by sinister, pounding dance rhythms, which echo the violent march of the first movement. There is no humour in this *Scherzo*, no light relief after the music that had preceded it, for it is filled with hideous leering demons that stamp on their way relentlessly in a dance of death.

After the initial bombast, the music momentarily takes on a more wistful, almost innocent character, but the demons lurk in the shadows awaiting their chance to reassert themselves, which they do to sinister effect. The movement is a struggle between childhood innocence and the harsh reality of life. Throughout, the demons dominate, but at the end the voice of childhood innocence re-emerges but briefly. Alma wrote that 'ominously the childish voices become more and more tragic, before dying out with a whimper'.

Fourth movement: Allegro Moderato – Allegro Energico

The massive final movement is virtually a symphony within a symphony, the first three movements forming a type of prologue. This is not the tragedy of a certain other sixth by a composer of that time, namely Tchaikovsky. There is no sad, self-pity here. Although Mahler's *Sixth* is very personal and painful, it is more akin to Greek tragedy.

The final movement opens with wild glissandi from the harps. Agonizingly, a violin flings itself into the tragedy theme. The music is relentless. Suggestions of other parts of the symphony abound, including the cowbells, but whenever there is a hint of optimism it is submerged beneath great waves of sound. In this movement, Mahler included what he called 'three hammer blows of fate'. Alma remembered how he had explained to her that the Finale was about himself (or the 'hero') and his destruction. Just as he himself had been the 'hero' in his first two symphonies, so he plays the same part in this darkest of works. He wanted the hammer blows to be short but strong and with a dull, thudding sound, the third felling the 'hero' like a tree. He later deleted the third hammer blow, ostensibly because he felt two to be more dramatic than three, but also probably because he was frightened, even superstitious, of including the fatal blow to his own person. Today it is sometimes reinstated. After a plaintive outcry from the brass, the symphony ends in darkest gloom.

Many, including musicologist Deryck Cooke, feel that the *Sixth* is the greatest of all his symphonies. Its classical construction, its very personal nature, its no-holds-barred conflict between light and dark, with darkness the inevitable victor, holds the attention throughout its mighty span. It is also the first of his symphonies to have both feet firmly planted in the twentieth century.

As Mahler predicted, it took a long time before the *Sixth Symphony* became widely accepted and understood, and even today, when performances abound, there are those who are afraid of the work. Among them is the British composer Colin Matthews, who said in an interview on BBC television that for a long time the *Sixth* was a work that he preferred not hear, finding it so powerful that he would be afraid of having a heart attack! This particularly applied to the Finale, which he found so overwhelming that he had not heard it on record, let alone in the concert hall, for over twenty years. And American conductor Michael Tilson Thomas declared that the *Sixth* 'wrecks my health', finding that when he is preparing for a performance he suffers from disturbed sleep, palpitations, poor appetite and a general failure to function properly!

In much the same way this mighty work obsessed Mahler for some time, and he continued to work on the score for a long while after its original conception. So personal, so autobiographical was it that he never rested content, yet at the same time he listened to what others had to say, grateful for any constructive criticism.

Hand in hand with the tragic aspects of the symphony, and the doom-laden message that all the goals and endeavours of man are meaningless in the long run, there is a positive aspect too: music's healing power. The *Sixth* may be imbued with darkest despair, but through Mahler's creation we can share with him our own private feelings of pessimism.

Alma considered that the *Sixth Symphony* was the most heartfelt of all his works, and she wrote that on the day of its completion they both wept. So great was her feeling about the high quality of the work that she described him as being like 'a tree in full leaf and flower'. Mahler wrote to Bruno Walter, telling him the good news of its completion and saying 'I think I have proved myself!' A few weeks later he sent a letter to Arnold Berliner giving him the news that the *Sixth* was finished, adding 'and so am I!' so much had it taken out of him.

He knew that he had created a masterpiece, and his confidence as a composer had reached a high point. This is reflected in a conversation that Alma later recalled. Apparently when out walking she had told Gustav that all she loved in a man was his achievement and the greater the achievement, the greater her love. Her husband pointed out the risk of basing her love solely on what he achieved, asking her what would happen if she met someone else whose achievements surpassed his. Her reply was that she would have to love that person! He brushed this aside by saying that for the time being at least he could not think of anyone else who could compete with him. Such was his confidence, yet he must have felt a trifle concerned by her words. According to Alma, one day he remarked that if only she were to be disfigured by some disease such as smallpox, thereby losing her beauty in the eyes of others, then he would be able to show her just how much he loved her. This conversation, recorded by Alma many years later in her memoirs, clearly shows her continued selfish and shallow attitude towards love; her main quest in life remained social prominence and to be associated with the famous.

As if completing the *Kindertotenlieder* and the *Sixth Symphony* were not enough, Mahler's burst of creativity during the summer of 1904 was not quite finished. He found the mental energy to write the two *Nachtmusik* movements of his next magnum opus, the *Seventh Symphony*. Shorter, lighter and relatively angst free, they provided what was almost an antidote, an unwinding after the other stressful compositions of that summer.

With August on the wane, it was time to return to Vienna. Two major events were uppermost in his mind: a new ground-breaking production of *Fidelio*, which he and Roller had been planning in meticulous detail, and the première of his *Fifth Symphony*, which was to take place in Cologne, both events in October. In Mahler's mind if the emotionalism and musical innovations of *Tristan und Isolde* made it the greatest music drama of them all, Beethoven's *Fidelio* held a unique place above all other operas. He was determined that this new production, controversial as it was bound to be, would take the operatic world by storm. The *Fidelio* of 1904 was typical of his determination to do away with 'tired' productions and to inject a much needed, new, fresh approach that would make not unreasonable demands on the intellects of those present. According to Roller, he had remarked on one occasion 'What you theatre people call your tradition is nothing but convenience and slovenliness'. This remark has sometimes been abbreviated to 'tradition is slovenliness', which is totally misleading and not what he meant at all.

Today many of the Roller-Mahler ideas would seem to be just common sense. For example, in the scene in the first act when the prisoners are let out of their cells, they emerge into the sunlight singing, '*O welche Lust, in freier heben! Luft den Atem Leicht zu*' (Oh what delight to breathe the fresh air . . .). By tradition, they had marched onto the stage from left and right, forming into a smart semi-circle before singing their chorus. With the poor unfortunates struggling to survive in the darkness of the dungeons, such stage directions seemed to Roller and Mahler to be ludicrous. In the new production the dishevelled prisoners staggered, groping their way up from the darkness of the dungeons singly or in twos and threes, bewildered and dazzled by the light. In short the chorus had to act their parts, not forming a neat semi-circle, but looking dejected, yet temporarily elated. Common sense? There was uproar! This was the chorus's big number, their turn to shine and dominate the proceedings, not crawl around like suffering worms from the depths!

Costumes, lighting, sets – all had the Roller touch. Every aspect of the production had been carefully thought out to produce the greatest possible emotional impact. There were the inevitable criticisms. Alma herself considered that some of the lighting was too dark, feeling that as the audience would not be able to see the actions clearly the dramatic impact would be lessened.

Mahler switched the *Leonore No. 3 Overture*, itself virtually a symphonic poem, from the beginning of the opera to a new position before the final scene, when Florestan, having been released from the dungeon, emerges into the sunlit courtyard of the Bastille. The original reason for this was to give Roller the time necessary to change the sets and to do away with the otherwise inevitable pregnant pause accompanied by chatter and coughs. Alma considered this move to be a stroke of genius on his part, making the emotional impact of the final scene that much greater.

Mahler was totally absorbed in every aspect of the new *Fidelio*. It could well have been at the back of his mind that he wanted this production of what he considered to be the greatest of all operas to be a personal memorial to his years at the Hofoper.

The première had to be delayed by three days until the 7th of October due to Mildenburg catching a cold. Unable to sing the role of Leonore on that day, Lucie Weidt stepped in for the first performance, with Schmedes in the role of Florestan. It was a great success. The audience loved it, as did most of the press, although, as always, there were a few anti-Mahlerites such as Robert Hirschfeld who went out of their way to criticise both his handling of the score and Roller's sets. This was to be expected, but with critics such as Kalbeck and Korngold firmly on his side, he must have been well satisfied. With *Tristan* and now *Fidelio* the Roller-Mahler partnership and their Secessionist approach had not only brought fresh air to the Hofoper in Vienna, but would revolutionise opera production worldwide.

Having hit the headlines with *Fidelio*, it was time for Mahler to concentrate on performances of his own music, in particular the première of his *Fifth Symphony* in Cologne. Largely due to the influence of Arnold Rosé as leader of the Vienna Philharmonic, he managed to secure two reading rehearsals in order to iron out any problems regarding the orchestration of the *Fifth*. Alma was present, and she confirmed certain doubts that he must have already harboured on this front. She complained to her husband that he had written a symphony for percussion! Mahler indeed felt that this section of the orchestra was too prominent and made the necessary alterations. It is probable that Alma had grossly exaggerated in her comment concerning the excessive use of percussion. For all his keenness in using a very large, post-Wagnerian orchestra for his symphonies (the *Fourth* being an exception), for Mahler clarity was of the utmost importance. Despite the huge forces he favoured, many passages are almost of a chamber quality, and it may well have been that the percussion element swamped such moments of delicacy. Among others present at these reading rehearsals were Foerster, Schoenberg, Zemlinsky and the music critic Ludwig Karpath. The latter was totally overwhelmed by the *Adagietto*, which he considered to be one of the most beautiful pieces he had ever heard.

Alma had hoped to travel to Cologne with her husband but was unwell and was forced to postpone her departure. She then developed a feverish cold and had to give up any thoughts of joining him for the première of the *Fifth Symphony*.

As usual when they were apart, Gustav wrote to her almost daily. He told her that the first rehearsal had gone reasonably well, although he feared that the *Scherzo*, 'the very devil of a movement', would cause problems for years to come. He was afraid that conductors would make nonsense of it by performing it too quickly, and that audiences would fail to understand 'this primeval music'; if only he could conduct the premières of his symphonies fifty years after his death. As it happened, despite the sterling work of conductors such as Bruno Walter, Willem Mengelberg, Oskar Fried and Dimitri Mitropoulos to name but four, it was the dedication of Leonard Bernstein in 1960 when he mounted a Mahler centenary season with the New York Philharmonic, together with his Mahler recordings of that time, that began the Mahler phenomenon and the consequent widespread popularity of his music – fifty years after his death! But Mahler's initial fears of misunderstanding over his *Fifth* must have been influenced by the even more complex and potentially controversial *Sixth*, which he had just completed.

The performance was barely adequate, Mahler not entirely happy with the quality of the playing. Many in the audience felt uncomfortable during the first movement, disliked the *Scherzo*, were overwhelmed by the *Adagietto* and applauded generously after the *Finale*. Among those who had travelled to Cologne were Arnold Berliner and Bruno Walter. The latter later wrote that in his opinion the première of the *Fifth* was the sole occasion when Mahler had conducted one of his own works in a manner that he felt was less than satisfactory. The orchestration was still problematic, forcing him to make radical alterations.

Mahler, fully aware of the very mixed feelings over his *Fifth* Symphony, wrote to Alma saying that he was about to go for a walk beside the Rhine. He exaggerated by stating that the river was the only resident who would go quietly on its way without declaring him to be a monster!

Most of the German press were about to launch scathing attacks on him, although a few did write sympathetic reviews. One of these was Rudolf Kastner whose article appeared in the *Münchener Neueste Nachrichten* the following month. Mahler wrote thanking him, telling him that he was one of the few whom he believed understood his music. But he missed the anticipated press barrage, for the following afternoon he left Cologne for Amsterdam where he was to conduct two of his symphonies at the invitation of Willem Mengelberg.

Mahler was met at the station by the Mengelbergs, who insisted that he should stay with them rather than in a hotel. Once again he was impressed by the warmth of the welcome he received from the people of Amsterdam. As on his previous visit he enjoyed the company of fellow composer Alphons Diepenbrock on his all too necessary walks. There was a genuine mutual respect, and Diepenbrock's feelings towards him were clearly illustrated by his fury over an article that had appeared in *Weekblad voor Muziek*, in which the anonymous author referred to the *Fourth* as boring,

Mahler as a charlatan, the music as a mindless din and so on; Diepenbrock tried in vain to find out the identity of the offending scribe.

The original plan had been for Mahler to conduct the second performance of the *Fifth* at the Concertgebouw, but Mengelberg, erring on the side of caution, had programmed the *Second* and *Fourth*, the latter to be played twice in the same programme! This double performance of the *Fourth* took place on the 23rd of October and was very well received by the audience and most of the press. His hitherto controversial symphony was applauded warmly at the Concertgebouw, as was the unusual idea of the work being performed twice in the same programme. He wrote to Alma saying that the occasion had been astounding, the audience warm and attentive with excellent playing from the orchestra and singing from the soloist, Alida Oldenboom-Lutkeman – a fat little lady who reminded him of the Molls' housemaid. His previous friendly feelings towards Amsterdam had been confirmed, and he now felt the city to be his musical home.

Rehearsals for the two performances of the *Second Symphony* on the 26th and 27th of October had been going well. This was to be the first time that the work had been heard in Amsterdam. All those present – audience, choirs and soloists – gave Mahler an ovation that he thought would never end, and in a speech following the first performance Mengelberg praised him as a genius and referred to him as the Beethoven of that time. The only fly in the ointment was an unexpectedly cool reception from some of the critics. Having praised the *Fourth*, so slated by the German and Austrian press, they voiced their disapproval of many aspects of the *Second*, which had been generally well received at home! Nevertheless he left Amsterdam happy in the knowledge that his music was in safe hands at the Concertgebouw.

As he boarded the train for his return to Vienna he must have had mixed feelings. He would miss the warm friendship of the people of Amsterdam, and he braced himself for probable criticism for having been away for two weeks conducting his own music, and so early in the season at that. Yet he longed to be reunited with Alma and his daughters.

On a personal basis his return to the Hofoper was not as problematic as he had feared, partly due to the press being distracted by the first performance in Vienna of Delibes' opera *Lakmé* under the baton of Bruno Walter. The acerbic element set about finding fault with the work and its star Selma Kurz.

Mahler's next excursion on behalf of his own music was to conduct his *Third Symphony* in Leipzig, the city where J.S.Bach and Mendelssohn had worked and died, where Schumann had studied and married, as well as being Wagner's birthplace. Where better for his music to be heard and appreciated? His departure was on the 25th of November, having conducted the Viennese première of Richard Strauss's *Symphonia Domestica* two days previously. Despite the opinion of many that Strauss was <u>the</u> German composer of the day, his new work was very controversial. Some considered that Strauss's portrayal of his private life in this way was exhibitionist and in poor taste, but Mahler's conducting was given due praise, even by Robert Hirschfeld who considered that as a conductor he was something of a magician. Strauss, unable to attend, wrote thanking him, saying that he would not forget what he had done on his behalf.

Mahler's arrival in Leipzig did not bode well for a successful concert. He had developed backache on the journey, a stomach upset brought on by the hotel food, and he had been warned that the Winderstein Orchestra was not in the same league as its more renowned rival, the Gewandhaus, which was due to perform the very same evening! But as things turned out he need not have worried. His ailments left him after a good night's sleep, and in the end he managed to shake up the orchestra to the required standard, the musicians eager to please and tolerant of his nagging. Under a lesser conductor they might have rebelled, but they held a deep respect for Mahler.

Immediately after the concert he sent Alma a telegram saying that the performance had been a great success. Most of the audience had shown their appreciation with a lengthy applause, but the critics had thought otherwise and wrote a collection of damning reviews. A notable exception was Paul Zschulich who, although having reservations about certain aspects of the *Third Symphony*, nevertheless considered it be artistically an important work. He regarded Mahler as being very misunderstood, that he deserved respect and that no clear judgement could be made after only one hearing. Thus controversy reigned in Leipzig, and Mahler must have been very disappointed that the occasion had not proved to be another Krefeld.

Hardly had the dust settled in Leipzig, when he was once again rehearsing the *Third Symphony*, this time for its all important Viennese première on the 14th of December in the Vienna Philharmonic's home, the magnificent golden Musikverneinsaal. Things boded well. The relationship between Mahler and the orchestra was on a high, partly due to his ongoing championing of their cause for higher pay, but also because he had become a widely accepted composer in many countries with orchestras far and wide wanting to perform his works. Controversy there might still be, but no one could deny his importance as a new voice in music, not even his staunchest foes.

The performance was a sensation, so much so that a repeat was immediately organised for the 22nd, just eight days later. Schoenberg and Zemlinsky were astounded by the very personal depth of the music, and considered the occasion to be an important landmark in the development of music. In a letter Schoenberg told Mahler that he had bared his soul. He wrote that he had witnessed a world both terrifying and beautiful, tormented and peaceful. In his opinion, as the drama unfolded, there was complete truthfulness in its depiction of the struggle between the forces of good and evil and the torment of man in his struggle for inner harmony. Zemlinsky was equally impressed, telling Alma that he now appreciated how great a composer Mahler was. Julius Korngold, writing in the *Neue freie Presse* on the 15th of December, declared that this performance of the *Third* marked the first great success that Mahler had enjoyed as a composer in Vienna. He described the tremendous ovation that he had been given, not just by the audience, but by the musicians and singers as well. He wrote that the music was sublime and poetic, and praised his technical ability and imagination. At last Mahler had arrived, accepted by Vienna as a composer, and the critical pain he had hitherto suffered might now be relegated to history. Wishful thinking! A broadside of sarcasm and vitriol was aimed at him after the performances of the *Third*. He was accused of plagiarism, vulgarity and self-indulgence, and one critic even suggested that a jail sentence might be appropriate, but despite such animosity the anti-Mahler faction was becoming increasingly Canute-like in their futile efforts to stem the tide of popular acclaim that he was beginning to enjoy.

Over the Christmas and New Year holiday, Gustav and Alma received the usual collection of invitations to social events. Gustav disliked these intensely; small talk and social climbing, and with him as exhibit number one, they went right against the grain. In the past Alma had always enjoyed such gatherings when her beauty was the undisputed centre of attraction, but as Gustav's wife she had become little more than his shadow. In her memoirs Alma described one such occasion. On entering the dining room of his wealthy hosts, Mahler immediately seized an apple from a dish in the middle of the table, sniffed it all over, and then put it down beside the food that had been served for him. This he ate quickly before leaving the room, wanting to be on his own. Social etiquette was not one of his strong points. With his hatred of such events and Alma's embarrassment at such behaviour, they came to a mutual decision to avoid as many such occasions as possible in the future!

The first major event of 1905 at the Hofoper was a new production of *Das Rheingold*. Ever since the success of the Roller-Mahler *Tristan*, the two men had been determined to create a new production of Wagner's *Ring*. Their aim was to complete the cycle as quickly as possible for the sake of unity from a presentation point of view, but due to interruptions and financial constraints Mahler was not to see his dream fulfilled during his remaining years at the Hofoper.

The rehearsals for *Das Rheingold,* which had begun towards the end of 1904, had been fraught with problems. Roller was every bit as determined and at times as abrasive over production matters as Mahler was with the music, and between them they managed to cause a series of upsets.

One such clash was between Roller and the Rhine maidens who were expected to sing and swim while strapped down on their backs in rather uncomfortable baskets, which could be moved about above the stage using cables. This method replaced the unwieldy, unsightly and unstable trolleys that had hitherto been wheeled about the stage. The effect, combined with Roller's lighting and scenery, was of course stunning. Sets, costumes, lighting – everything had been re-thought, the traditional discarded. Adverse criticism came from some of the cast and critics: the lighting was too dark, the costumes more suited to a pantomime, the sets a travesty of tradition, but Roller would not budge, and Mahler gave him his full backing.

Alma wrote that Roller was beginning to dominate Mahler on production matters. This might have appeared to be so, but their close collaboration during the planning stages meant that Mahler was then able to concentrate on the music, leaving the staging to Roller with full confidence. Occasionally Mahler would intervene, such as the occasion when he stopped a rehearsal. Wagner's own instructions were that the two giants, Fasolt and Fafner, should carry Freia off the stage. The two men declared that this was not possible. At which point Mahler leapt onto the stage, picked up Freia, held her up and marched about the stage with her to the astonishment of all those present! Small in stature he might have been, but his physical fitness at this time was not in doubt!

Despite the grumbles from certain members of the cast and the anti-Mahler traditionalist members of the press, the new *Das Rheingold* was generally considered to be another important landmark in the history of the Vienna opera. Julius Korngold described it as magical, the lighting beautiful, that there was a communion between the music and the production itself. Max Graf and Ludwig Karpath were lavish in their praise, not least for Mahler's meticulous conducting of the score.

But with his incredibly heavy music schedule, Mahler's private life was beginning to suffer. So focussed on his work was he that he was scarcely aware of the depressed state of his wife. Alma felt increasingly neglected and at times little more than a mere appendage. She regularly suffered embarrassment in public caused by her husband's absentmindedness, which was sometimes responsible for his lack of social graces. Only the children kept her sane and acted as a channel for her emotions. She dreamed of the music she was forbidden to write, and Zemlinsky . . .

On the 25th of January, two days after the première of the new production of *Das Rheingold*, Mahler was present at a concert organized by the *Vereinigung schaffender Tonkünstler* (the Association of Creative Musicians) of which he was the honorary president. The main works were two symphonic poems: Zemlinsky's *Die Seejungfrau* (The Mermaid) and Schoenberg's *Pelleas und Melisande*. These were greeted by boos, whistles and the slamming of doors as members of the audience fled!

The same association had also organised another concert to take place four days later on the 29th. This was an important occasion that saw the first performances of *Die Kindertotenlieder*, four of the five *Rückert Lieder* (the exception being *Liebst du um Schönheit*) and four of the earlier *Wunderhorn Lieder*. Two of the songs, *Revelge* and *Der Tamboursg'sell*, were the last orchestral arrangements of *Wunderhorn Lieder* that Mahler would write and were still in manuscript form. The importance of these orchestral songs cannot be overemphasised. Mahler had created a new form – sung chamber music, in much the same way as his later composition *Das Lied von der Erde* can be thought of as a song symphony. The orchestration of the songs is quite remarkable for its clarity and inventiveness. The musicians do not provide mere accompaniment, they are soloists in the own right, and Mahler uses the voice itself as an instrument and part of the ensemble, much as Wagner had done in his music dramas. The soloists were Friedrich Weidermann, Anton Moser and Fritz Schrödter, and they were accompanied by a chamber orchestra drawn from the Vienna Philharmonic. Due to the rather intimate nature of the songs, Mahler had decided not to use the large and glamorous golden concert hall at the Musikverein, but instead the smaller Kleiner Musiksaal, or Brahmsaal as it is now known. Inevitably the tickets were soon sold out, and a repeat concert was hastily arranged for the 3rd of February. On this occasion the soprano Marie Gutheil-Schoder joined the other soloists to sing two additional *Wunderhorn* songs.

After the undoubted success of the *Third Symphony*, Mahler quite understandably expected that his songs would be received with at least due respect. Following the very 'modern' works by such composers as Zemlinsky and Schoenberg at the Vereinigung concerts, they seemed to be steeped in tradition by comparison. One cannot help but wonder if such planning on his part had been deliberate.

The audiences were genuinely moved, especially by *Die Kindertotenlieder*, and the critics, apart from immovable Robert Hirschfeld, were in general enthusiastic. In the audience on the 3rd of February was the young composer Anton Webern. A composition pupil of Schoenberg's and studying musicology under Guido Adler, he was greatly impressed by Mahler's songs. He wrote in his diary how thrilled he had been to spend time with him at the post concert reception, and he referred to him as 'a great man'. The baritone

Friedrich Weidermann, writing in the *Grazer Volksblatt*, said that few eyes had remained dry in the concert hall and that the audience surrounded this strangely small and yet great artist with acclamation, flowers, laurel wreaths, gratitude and genuine love.

Mahler's use of the smaller venue with very limited seating and at the same time using very costly soloists and musicians from the Hofoper, not to mention extensive rehearsals, cost a fortune and sounded the death-knell of the Association of Creative Musicians, but it had suited his purposes well.

Although Mahler did not invent the idea of the orchestral song cycle (Berlioz's *Les Nuits d'été* having been composed over half a century earlier), the success of these two concerts sparked off a fashion in this idiom. Younger contemporaries of Mahler such as Alban Berg seized on the idea, and a chain of composers followed suit, most notably Richard Strauss and Benjamin Britten. The latter dedicated his *Nocturne* (Op. 60, 1958), a cycle of eight songs, to Alma in acknowledgement of his debt to Mahler. Britten had met Alma during his time in the United States, and on one occasion, presumably under the influence of her favourite drink Benedictine, she had apparently proposed to him!

Regarding his own music, Mahler's attention once more focussed on his *Fifth Symphony*. Three performances took place: in Dresden under Ernst von Schuch, in Berlin under Arthur Nikisch and in Prague conducted by Leo Blech. In all three cases the work had very mixed receptions from the audiences and the press. The critic of the Czech publication, *Dalibar*, although having certain reservations especially concerning the *Adagietto*, nevertheless regarded it as one of the most important symphonic works of recent times. Richard Batka, writing in the newspaper *Bohemia*, described the very different effect that the music had had on members of the audience – everything from despair to ecstasy. Richard Strauss wrote to Mahler after attending the final rehearsal in Berlin. He said that the *Fifth Symphony* had given him great pleasure, which was only dimmed by the 'little *Adagietto*', although he appreciated the fact that this movement was clearly an audience pleaser. He also praised Nikisch's zeal.

On the 7th of March Mahler departed for Hamburg. He was to conduct the *Fifth Symphony* twice, on successive days. He looked forward to returning to the city where he had enjoyed a happy and fruitful eight years at the Opera. He hoped that his return would be greeted with similar warmth, and that his *Fifth Symphony* would be given the praise it surely deserved. The first rehearsal went badly, and in a letter to Alma he wrote that the work was accursed and that no one understood it. But matters improved. The musicians pulled themselves together and even showed signs of enthusiasm. Between rehearsals Mahler renewed old friendships, in particular with lawyer and musician Hermann Behn and the poet Richard

Dehmel. Both men were at the first of the two performances, which took place on the 13th and 14th of March. They were very enthusiastic, as was the vast majority in the audience who managed to drown out the whistles from the few who had attended solely with that in mind. And the critics? Almost all praised Mahler <u>and</u> his *Fifth Symphony*.

The young conductor Arturo Toscanini, who had already gained notoriety at La Scala in Milan, was in the process of planning a new concert season at the Teatro Regio in Turin. Interested in including new works, he had been sent a copy of Mahler's *Fifth*. He was not impressed. He declared that Mahler was definitely not a genuine artist and that his music showed no signs of genius. In various letters he made such comments as 'hackwork' and 'whining and wailing of violins and woodwind' and that the symphony made him feel nauseous. Quite clearly he did not understand the work. He wrote that if Mahler the composer was anything like Mahler the conductor, then he had to be a very weak interpreter! It would not be long before their paths would cross in New York. Meanwhile the *Fifth* had received its first performance in the United States of America, and although some had reservations, the overall reaction had been positive.

Following the Krefeld triumph of the *Third Symphony* in June 1902, the unfortunate meeting had taken place between Mahler and Hans Pfitzner, when the latter, convinced that he had created a masterpiece, had shown him the score of his new opera *Die Rose vom Liebesgarten* (The Rose in the Garden of Love). Mahler had declared the libretto to be poor, obscure and too long. The wind taken out of his sails, Pfitzner had left feeling humiliated and demoralized, his opera damned. Alma had been very upset and was furious with her husband's inconsiderate treatment of Pfitzner with whom she struck up a friendship. Pfitzner, unlike Mahler, showed enthusiasm for her songs, and she felt in him a kindred spirit. When later Pfitzner sent Alma his *String Quartet in D*, eager for her views on it, he was surely hoping that she would show it to her husband, which of course she did. Mahler, despite the fact that he had little time for him, must have had a guilty conscience for he announced that it was a very important work. He might well have been influenced by Bruno Walter's enthusiasm as well, for his young assistant had promised Alma to do all he could to change his opinion of Pfitzner's music. He agreed to reconsider *Die Rose vom Liebesgarten*, to please Alma, if nothing else. The first performance of the opera had in fact taken place in Elberfeld on the 9th of November 1901, and Mahler had attended a performance in Mannheim on the 31st of January 1904. He had still not been impressed, but the time had come to bury this particular hatchet.

As always, Mahler would not tolerate slovenliness from anyone, especially with a new production and a Vienna première at that. In this respect he was as hard on those under him as he was on himself. Having decided to stage it at the Hofoper, *Die Rose* had to be success. At rehearsals he requested that Pfitzner should sit directly behind him so that he would be able to give advice on such matters as tempo.

Pfitzner made no secret of the fact that he disliked Mahler's symphonies, and ever since their first meeting at the Krefeld Festival he had had amorous inclinations towards Alma. She did not reciprocate, for to her he was merely a friend who appreciated her own music. However the non-musical aspects of Pfitzner's character, which certainly aroused feelings of jealousy and irritation, did not deflect Mahler from his desire to do everything in his power to ensure that the forthcoming production of *Die Rose* was a great success.

In her memoirs Alma recalls how Mahler often invited Pfitzner to the Auenbruggergasse apartment when he himself would not be present! On the face of it this seems to have been a strange tactic to use to combat his jealousy, but it is quite likely that he felt that Alma would soon tire of Pfitzner's company. True she enjoyed discussing and playing music with him, but he could be difficult, especially when Mahler joined them, when their conversations frequently descended into bitter arguments, much to Alma's embarrassment.

May Day arrived and Pfitzner, having attended a rehearsal of *Die Rose*, made a hasty exit and headed post haste to see Alma before Mahler returned to the apartment. Clutching a rose, he came face to face with a crowd of demonstrating workers who were processing along the Ringstrasse. This both angered and frightened him. He dashed down side streets and greeted Alma in a state of considerable confusion. Meanwhile Mahler, who had also met up with the huge procession and who was always happy to make known his socialist sympathies, joined the workers, whom he considered to be his brothers and the future of their nation. Eventually he arrived home, and the contrasting sympathies and experiences immediately sparked off a particularly heated argument. As with their music, so with their political beliefs – the two men were poles apart. Yet Pfitzner could not help admiring Mahler, and his gratitude to him for the care he was taking over the Vienna première of *Die Rose vom Liebesgarten* knew no bounds. Pfitzner was in fact his own worst enemy. He made a habit of upsetting those very people who could enhance his reputation as a composer, perhaps because he had an inferiority complex. He did eventually produce a masterpiece, *Palestrina,* in 1917.

After twice being postponed due to Mildenburg and Schmedes suffering from colds, the première of *Die Rose* took place on the 6th of April. Its unquestionable success was due mainly, if not entirely, to Mahler's meticulous musical preparation and Roller's stunning sets and lighting, which blinded audiences to the work's intrinsic deficiencies, especially the libretto which the press castigated. Numerous performances followed; Mahler had fulfilled his promise and Alma was satisfied.

Four weeks later, on the 3rd of May, a drama of a different nature took place at the Hofoper during a performance of *Die Zauberflöte*. An electrical fault started a fire above the stage. Blue flashes, smoke and shouts sparked off panic in the audience, who began to surge towards the exits. However, the stage lights soon came on again to reveal the large frame of Leo Slezak who did his best to calm down the patrons. Having carried out a quick safety check, Mahler reappeared to shouts of approval and the performance resumed. According to Slezak, Mahler, having thanked him for his part in calming the audience, congratulated him on his first mistake free performance of the scene that followed the resumption. He quipped to the rest of the cast that it needed a house fire to make Slezak sing in tune!

It had been planned to hold the first *Fête musicales d'Alsace-Lorraine* in Strasbourg in 1905, and the organizers decided to invite Mahler and Richard Strauss for the three-day festival. The city was becoming an increasingly important musical centre, and in 1904 a new 1200 seat concert hall, the Sängerhaussaal, had been opened. Strauss himself had already visited the city in 1899 when he had conducted his symphonic poems *Also sprach Zarathustra* and *Tod und Verklärung*. Since then works of his had been performed regularly in Strasbourg, but not Mahler's music. The latter insisted, as a condition of his presence at the festival, that at least one of his works be included in the programme. He suggested the *Fifth Symphony*. This caused shock waves of concern among the organizers due to its length and the cost of performing it, not forgetting the hostile reception it had often suffered in previous performances. Eventually they agreed.

Gustav and Alma set off for Strasbourg on the 14th of May. They stayed at the Grand Hotel de Paris on the Rue de la Mésange. Both Mahler and Strauss were welcomed with great enthusiasm as the two most important figures in contemporary music. A number of Mahler's friends had travelled to Strasbourg, including Georges Picquart and Paul and Sophie Clemenceau, whom he had first met in Paris in June 1900.

Mahler was to conduct his *Fifth* on the second evening of the festival, the 20th of May. It was to be the first work on the programme – he had insisted on this so that the audience would be fresh. (His insistence was also probably to ensure that the orchestra was too!). It was to be followed by Brahms's *Alto Rhapsody*, to be conducted by Ernest Münch, and then Strauss would come to the podium to conduct Mozart's *Violin Concert in G*, followed by his own *Symphonia Domestica*.

A fanfare welcomed Mahler for the performance of his *Fifth Symphony*, and he was given a wild ovation at the end. For the second half of the concert he and Alma sat at the end of the balcony. Another ovation followed the *Alto Rhapsody*, and as a result the choral coda was given as an encore. Strauss became more and more agitated and worried about what the musicians, who were inevitably becoming very tired, would do to his *Symphonia Domestica*. He was overheard making unfortunate comments, referring to the performers as 'circus artists' and the alto soloist as 'a cow'. The singer's husband overheard this and duly exploded, demanding a written apology. The possible alternative being a duel, Strauss duly obliged. Still seething, he conducted his contribution to the concert. This began with Mozart's *Violin Concerto in G* with Henri Marteau as soloist, which Strauss had to get through before conducting his own *Symphonia Domestica*. Alma recalled that the performance of the latter was not very good, but then Strauss had only had two rehearsals, whereas Mahler had demanded four for his *Fifth*.

Afterwards Strauss stormed about yelling abuse at everyone concerned, and refused to accompany Gustav and Alma to the banquet at the Rothaus to be held in their honour. (The Rothaus on Place Kléber no longer exists, although the modern building on the site retains the name 'Maison Rouge'.) However, having taken Strauss back to their hotel, Gustav and Alma managed to pacify him and he was persuaded to attend. Despite a warm welcome when they arrived, Strauss resumed his tirade against the organizers of the concert. Mahler slipped out quietly and rejoined Alma at the hotel much amused by the evening's events.

Mahler had never been over keen on Strauss's music up until this time, regarding much of it as purely commercial and lacking soul, but he had nevertheless always shown interest in his latest endeavours. He and Strauss did not have a great deal in common, but they were useful to each other. Mahler, as director of the Vienna Opera, had considerable influence in the music world and was an ally worth having for the performance of his works, while Strauss, the popular composer, and he too a conductor held in high esteem throughout Europe, was essential to Mahler for his support and influence in getting his symphonies performed. Their wives also had a certain amount in common. Despite disliking each other, they were both good organizers enabling their husbands to get on with musical matters. The big differences between the two women were that Pauline Strauss was not particularly attractive and by nature abrasive, whereas Alma was one of the most beautiful women in Vienna and had great charm.

Leading up to the Strasbourg festival, Strauss had been working flat out on his latest project – the opera *Salomé*. Based on the original French version of Oscar Wilde's play, originally written for the actress Sarah Bernhardt, it was a work so controversial that it had been banned in London for eleven years. The play had only achieved success after its first performance in Germany and was staged no less than 111 times during the 1903-1904 season. When Strauss had told Mahler of his plan to write the opera, the latter had tried to dissuade him because he feared that it would quite likely be rejected on moral grounds, especially in Catholic countries.

Strauss, undeterred, had virtually finished the score just before setting out for Strasbourg. Hoping that Mahler's influence would result in a Viennese première, he took Gustav and Alma to Wolf's music shop in the Place des Étudiants, just off the Place Kléber and close to their hotel. Strauss sat down at one of the pianos in the showroom and proceeded to play and sing (!) his new opera, except for the Dance of the Seven Veils, which he had not yet composed. Mahler was astonished, overwhelmed – it was a masterpiece. This was not the Strauss he had known; here was something new and daring. A small crowd of passers-by had gathered in the little square outside Wolf's, attracted by this extraordinary music and the equally extraordinary performance!

Despite its anti-Semitic content, Mahler was determined that Vienna should have the privilege of staging the Austrian première. One might speculate as to why he was so eager to have anything to do with the work. Without question the opera is a major masterpiece, but could there have been an ulterior motive behind his desire to champion it, especially in the Austrian capital? There is no doubting the anti-Jewish content of the opera. Apart from the obvious gruesome treatment of John the Baptist and Salomé's blood lust, there are also such lines as,

First Soldier:	*Was für ein Aufruhr!*
	Was sind das für wilde Tiere,
	die da heulen?
	(What a tumult! What is all this howling like wild animals?)
Second Soldier:	*Die Juden, Sie sind immer so.*
	Sie streiten über ihr Religion.
	(The Jews, that's how they always are. They constantly squabble over their religion.)

Could it have been that Mahler had thought that, by pulling out all the stops to get the work staged in Vienna, thereby making it abundantly clear that he was supporting an opera that was clearly anti-Jewish, his anti-Semitic opponents might be slapped down and even be made to eat humble pie? Was this Mahler the politician aiming to defuse the hostility of the anti-Semitic press? Of course this is pure conjecture, but it is an interesting thought and certainly no reflection on his friendship with Strauss or the quality of *Salomé*. One could speculate further that it was very surprising that Mahler should find himself running up against a brick wall of opposition to staging the première in Vienna, the anti-Semitic undercurrent being so strong in the Austrian capital. Could it have been that his opponents 'smelt a rat' over Mahler becoming involved in such a venture? Certainly many doubted the sincerity of his conversion to Christianity. Perhaps they felt it was almost as if he were saying, 'Look, I became a Christian, I am a Christian like you. I am no longer a Jew, and here's to prove it!' Of course it is well known that Mahler became a Christian to suit his own ends ('I've just changed my coat', as he had told Ludwig Karpath at the time of his baptism). He had no time for any particular creed or faction, still less for the politics of religion. His belief was in an all-embracing eternal wonder of creation, a mystical force that he strove all his life to put his finger on.

This was to be one of his hardest and bitterest battles, and one that he would eventually lose. While the music was admired, the censor was adamant that it should not be performed at the Hofoper. Dresden had the honour of the first performance on the 9th of December 1905. The Austrian première took place not in the capital, but in Graz in May 1906 with Gustav and Alma present. The *Salomé* affair was one of the most painful rejections that Mahler suffered during his tenure as Director of the Hofoper, and his championing of the work would prove to be a contributing factor to his departure from Vienna two years later.

The Strasbourg festival ended on the 22nd of May with a performance of Beethoven's *4th Piano Concerto* with Ferrucio Busoni as soloist, followed as a grand finale, by the *Ninth Symphony* conducted by Mahler who used his own modifications of the orchestration. Alma regarded it as the most beautiful performance she had ever heard. She recounted how the audience went wild and converged on the small figure of her husband, their enthusiasm so great that she feared for his safety. She recalled how afterwards she, Piquart and Clemenceau had run into the street and round to the rear of the concert hall in search of him. Suddenly they saw him running, hat in hand, pursued by an ever-increasing crowd of exultant admirers. In the nick of time they managed to bundle him into a cab and escaped to a small tavern where they ended the evening celebrating.

As regards the performance of Beethoven's *Ninth*, most of the critics were ecstatic in their praise, calling Mahler 'the Napoleon of the baton', 'the artistic phenomenon' and 'his name ... will shine in the artistic firmament of the future'. As for Mahler's *Fifth Symphony,* words of praise came from some critics, who described it as powerful and ingeniously orchestrated with moments of emotion and beauty. William d'Gelly writing in the *Journal d'Alsace-Lorraine*, quipped that Mahler's love of the trumpet was like the Italians love of macaroni! Of course, not everyone was enthusiastic. The French writer and philosopher, Romain Rolland, a friend of Strauss, considered that Mahler had been mesmerised by thoughts of power, which had gone to his head as with many other German artists. He described his appearance on the podium as being like a dishevelled schoolmaster or minister, and he slammed his conducting of Beethoven's *Ninth*, saying that he had used incredible tempi, that the musicians were falling over each other, and really it was not Beethoven at all, but Mahler. As for his *Fifth Symphony*, he found it mediocre and banal, 'a lavish and strident bric-a-brac'. Whereas Strauss's *Symphonia Domestica* was full of subtlety and light, Mahler's work was like dough that had not risen. However, upon reflection, Rolland later summed him up as an egoist, but nevertheless sincere, and that his almost unbearable workload at the Hofoper prevented him from having much time to dream. He considered that Mahler, the composer, would only be his true self when the time came for him to leave his administrative work behind, but maybe that would be too late. Nevertheless, despite Romain Rolland's feelings, Mahler's presence at the Strasbourg festival had been a notable triumph.

Chapter 12

Vienna . . . Part Six

Seventh Symphony
Eighth Symphony

T HE LONGED-FOR summer holiday in Maiernigg had almost arrived, but first Mahler had to travel to the Austrian city of Graz where the 1905 *Allgemeiner Deutsche Musikverein* Festival was to be held, once again under the directorship of Richard Strauss. Meanwhile Alma had left Vienna for Carinthia with their daughters.

For Mahler, the Graz Festival's main event would be a performance of thirteen of his lieder with orchestra on the 1st of June. At his request this concert would take place in the more intimate surroundings of the Stephaniensaal rather than in the main concert hall, following the double success in Vienna at a venue of a similar size. The soloists who had travelled from Vienna were Anton Moser, Erik Schmedes and Friedrich Weidermann, the latter to end the programme with a performance of *Die Kindertotenlieder*. The audience reaction was every bit as enthusiastic as at the two Vienna concerts, and at the end he was acclaimed with tears, cheers and laurel wreaths. As far as the public was concerned he was the unquestioned star of the festival, and this inevitably upset other contemporary composers whose works were also performed there.

The day after his Graz triumph Mahler returned to Vienna. With their apartment closed for the summer, he stayed with Anna and Carl Moll. His final and very important conducting date of the season was a performance of Richard Strauss's opera *Feuersnot* that took place on the 5th of June. Two days later Willem Mengelberg and Max von Shillings joined him and the Molls for lunch, an event that gave Gustav much pleasure.

Once more settled in Maiernigg, Alma and her daughters resumed the summer routine. In her diary she wrote that she longed for Gustav, and that she was spending most of her time copying music for her husband. Yet the ambitions of her past, her desire for fame as a composer were forever at the back of her mind. Nevertheless she stated that the only reason for her existence was to serve her husband. This she continued to do in practical matters too. She had managed to sort out the chaotic state of his finances, brought about by his generosity to his brothers and sisters who had squandered much of it irresponsibly, and by Justine's poor financial management. By this time most of the debts had been repaid, one of which was a considerable sum owed to Justine, money she had lent Gustav towards the cost of building the villa in Maiernigg.

His holiday was in danger of being delayed by a special gala concert that Prince Montenuovo had arranged in honour of the Shah of Persia (the '*schwein*' of Persia as Mahler referred to him in a letter to Alma!). Montenuovo understandably wanted him to conduct this event, but he was determined not to lose valuable composing time in Carinthia, for the completion of the *Seventh Symphony* was his top priority. Consequently a medical certificate was acquired which stated that he was exhausted and needed immediate rest!

Despite keeping herself occupied by copying music for her husband, playing the piano and looking after the children, Alma's frustration once more set in. Dedicated to his music as she was, in her diary she admitted that in her heart she had been unfaithful to him. Her bouts of depression were not helped when she accidentally toppled over an oil lamp, the flames quickly taking hold in the sitting room. Having regained her equilibrium after the inevitable initial shock and panic, with the aid of the cook and chambermaid a potential conflagration was averted. She longed for Gustav to arrive, which he did on the 15th of June. Yet even when they were reunited, Alma's feeling of isolation remained, for her husband's mind was once again fully concentrated on music and not on her. The completion of the *Seventh Symphony*, combined with the forthcoming 150th anniversary of Mozart's birth (the 27th of January, 1756), was uppermost in his mind. Alfred Roller paid them a visit to discuss the all-important Mozart celebrations due to take place at the Hofoper during the 1905-1906 season. Distracted by this Mahler found it hard to settle down to compose. So at the end of June he set off for the Dolomites to seek inspiration.

Suffering from a severe migraine, which had developed during the train journey, he arrived at Schluderbach close to the small town of Toblach. The pain of his migraine precluded any thoughts of working. He tried going for runs to shake it off, but to no avail, and when noisy Corpus Christi celebrations by local peasants, accompanied by soldiers from a nearby garrison, completely wrecked the tranquillity, he decided to move on. His next destination was another favourite of his, the nearby Lake Misurina, but on this occasion the magic of the Dolomites failed him. In a state of depression, and having achieved absolutely nothing, he began his return journey to Maiernigg.

Mahler's main problem was that the style of music of the two inner

Nachtmusik movements he had composed the previous summer was totally different from anything he had hitherto written. Staring at a blank sheet of manuscript paper, he had racked his brains in vain as to how he could begin the symphony. As it happened he did not have to wait long. Having alighted from the main line train at Klagenfurt, he changed onto the branch line to Krumpendorf. There he had expected to be met by Alma, but with no sign of her he crossed the Wörthersee in a rowing boat, and the rhythm of the oars awakened the inspiration that he had been seeking for the beginning of the opening movement. His imagination thus triggered the music began to flow with remarkable ease, and within four weeks the draft score of the *Seventh Symphony* was complete.

Seventh Symphony, in E minor
(In five movements)

The *Seventh* is the third and final work of Mahler's middle and purely orchestral period. As always there are links with previous works, notably the opening of the first movement and the finale, both having similarities to the equivalent parts of the *Fifth Symphony*. There are also echoes from the *Third* and *Sixth Symphonies*. Along with the *Sixth*, the *Seventh* is the least performed and understood of his symphonies. It is precisely because it has been performed less than the other symphonies that it has gained this reputation. It is in fact a very accessible work, the music free from the shackles of his angst-ridden inner self. With its swings from romanticism to Stravinskyesque 'modernism', its amorous moments alongside the jovial, the mysterious living beside the blissful and at times funereal, it embraces all of life's emotions. He used a palette of composition that would later re-emerge in the symphonies of Shostakovich. However, more than any of his other symphonies, Mahler was unsure of the work. He was to make extensive and repeated revisions, but he knew that the *Seventh* was in parts groundbreaking, even experimental, particularly the two *Nachtmusik* movements, which he had composed during the summer of 1904. Some consider it to be his weakest symphony, but it was an important learning experience for him and would lead him on to compose some of his finest music. According to Mengelberg it is thought that the initial source of inspiration had come to him after he had seen Rembrandt's huge painting 'The Night Watch' in Amsterdam.

First movement: Langsam (Adagio) – Allegro resoluto, ma non troppo

Despite Mahler's dislike of programmes for his symphonies, Mengelberg wrote one himself for the *Seventh*. In it he describes the first movement as being like a starless night, dark and foreboding. The images Mengelberg conjured up, together with the two *Nachtmusik* movements, have led to the symphony sometimes being called 'The Song of the Night' (<u>not</u> Mahler's words!).

The movement begins adagio, with a slow and deliberate rhythm – the oars of the rowing boat, we may presume. A horn call sounds, played by a tenor horn. 'Here nature roars!' stated Mahler. From out of the initial funereal atmosphere, the tenor horn breathes life. The tempo quickens. A brisk march follows, punctuated by imitations of the tenor horn theme played by other brass instruments. Dark the movement may be in parts, but there are moments of sheer ecstasy that penetrate the darkness like moonbeams – moments of light and love giving brief glimpses of hope in this dark night of the soul. These moments of bliss overcome the gloom, and the movement ends jubilantly.

Second movement: Nachtmusik – Allegro moderato

This, the first of the two *Nachtmusik* movements, Mahler envisaged as a night patrol. It opens with horn calls which echo out of the darkness. Sounds of nature are present: nocturnal birdcalls, babbling mountain streams and distant cowbells. Intermittently a waltz emerges out of the gloom representing nature's continuous merry-go-round.

Although the *Wunderhorn* symphonies ended with the *Fourth*, this movement is clearly a successor to such songs as *Revelge* and *Der Tamboursg'sell*. Here too there is a military feel with a slow march as the night patrol picks its way through the darkness, accompanied once more by the sounds of nature and the distant echoes of the horns.

Third movement: Scherzo – Schattenhaft (Shadowy)

Separating the two *Nachtmusik* movements is this strange *Scherzo*. This weird, even grotesque music is a *dance macabre* set in a world of spectres, a nightmare world with swings from the wild to the bleak and nasty shocks around every corner. In order to achieve the effects he sought in one section of the score, he instructed the celli and basses to play fffff so violently that the strings should actually impact against the sound boxes. He was also dissatisfied with the volume produced by a normal bass drum, so had an enormous one specially made. The effect, however, was not what he had hoped for, the drum only managing to produce a dull thud, so the traditional bass drum won the day!

Some have suggested that this movement was Mahler foreseeing the horrors of the Great War, the Holocaust or even man's self-destruction. More likely it was just Mahler at his most experimental creating a musical nightmare. To my mind there is more than a touch of sinister humour here, rather like 'A short ride in a ghost train' (apologies to John Adams!) with cobwebs, spooks and screams at every turn.

Fourth Movement: Nachtmusik – Andante amoroso

Following the nightmarish *Scherzo*, comes this wonderfully delicate love music, in which Mahler uses a guitar and a mandolin, supported by a harp and solo violin – instruments immediately associated with love ballads – in this most gracious of serenades. Whereas the first *Nachtmusik* dealt with a night patrol picking its way through the darkness of the wide outdoors, the second *Nachtmusik* is intimate and homely. With astonishing clarity Mahler weaves an emotional web of such a delicate nature.

Introduced passionately by a solo violin, a magical atmosphere is at once created, accentuated by the plucking of the guitar and the mandolin. Echoes of the night in the form of a slow march rhythm try to encroach, but these are soon dispelled. A solo cello introduces a sublime love theme, which is taken up first by the brass, then by the strings, building to a passionate climax. Harp and strings quietly lead the way towards the delicate music heard at the opening of the movement with the guitar and mandolin prominent once more. The music finally fades away in an atmosphere of perfect peace.

This second *Nachtmusik* was one of Mahler's most inspired and forward-looking creations, and was greatly admired by his young contemporaries Schoenberg and Webern.

Fifth movement: Rondo-Finale – Allegro ordinario

The hushed conclusion of the previous movement is suddenly shattered by a bravura timpani solo. Night is over, and the brass blaze forth announcing the rising of the sun and the dawning of a new day. There are suggestions of Wagner as Mahler nods towards *Die Meistersinger*, although not actually quoting Wagner's music. There are also allusions to Lehar's *Die Lustige Witwe* and Mozart's *Entführung*. Peasant dances and the march heard in the first movement, now in C minor rather than in its previous key of E minor, reappear. The cowbells are heard once more, now joined by tubular bells, and this wild and joyous music surges onwards towards its victorious conclusion. Leonard Bernstein considered that this last movement was Mahler finally ending the great European musical tradition of the nineteenth century.

The important difference between the *Seventh Symphony* and its predecessors is that it is music for music's sake. Mahler provided no programme, hidden or otherwise, other than by naming two movements 'Nachtmusik'. This symphony is not autobiographical in any way and does not deliberately mirror his own emotional conflicts, and this very fact has led some people to consider it to be inferior to his other symphonies. However entertaining it may be, by his standards it does lack the depth of its predecessors, but he needed a break from soul baring after the turmoil of the *Sixth*. Free from personal shackles, the *Seventh* gave him the opportunity to experiment on its victorious journey from darkness to light, from tragedy to bliss, from night to day – indeed a musical detoxification!

Mahler's summer in Carinthia ended early mainly due to the preparations for the Mozart 150th anniversary celebrations and the postponement of the planned new production of *Die Walküre*, brought about by funds not being made available. Before leaving Maiernigg on the 22nd of August, while visiting Justi and Arnold Rosé who were on holiday in Aussee, he wrote to Guido Adler telling him that he had completed the *Seventh Symphony*. He also broke the news to Strauss, at the same time asking him to send him a copy of the *Salomé* libretto. At this point Mahler was still optimistic about the opera being performed in Vienna. He even told Strauss his preferred cast, which included Eric Schmedes, Anna von Mildenburg and Friedrich Weidermann as well as an up-and-coming twenty-five year old soprano Elsa Bland whose looks and voice would fit the central role perfectly. Two well known names that Mahler had rejected straight away were Selma Kurz, whose lack of acting ability ruled her out, and Leo Slezak whom he regarded as being lazy and who rarely showed signs of genuine dedication. But, enthusiastic as he was about the project, he warned Strauss that the censor had yet to approve the work and that there were ominous rumours coming from that particular direction.

With Alma and the children staying on in Maiernigg, Mahler decided to spend a few days in the Semmering to the south of Vienna. During the course of the summer he had been suffering from a recurrence of digestive problems, and a local doctor had advised him to reduce his workload. Even though it meant commuting to the Hofoper, he felt that a few more days of fresh air and exercise, not to mention being unavailable around the clock, would be beneficial to his health.

In his letters to Alma he described the appalling weather, laced with intermittent thunderstorms, which as always appealed to his sense of drama. Nevertheless he kept up a routine of long walks and stated that the hotel food was excellent, but he told her that he missed her terribly.

The first opera he was due to conduct in the 1905-1906 season was *Fidelio* on the 24th of August, but he asked Bruno Walter to deputise for him so that he could prolong his stay in the Semmering until Alma's return to Vienna on the 30th. Reunited with Alma and the children, and having reopened their Auenbruggergasse apartment, they left Vienna once more to stay with industrialist and patron of the arts Fritz Redlich and his wife in their small château in Göding to the north east of the Austrian capital. They had been the guests of the Redlichs in May 1903, and were delighted to be able to stay with them again. However, Mahler was forced to return to attend to pressing business at the Hofoper, leaving behind Alma and his daughters so that they could spend a few more relaxing days away from city life.

An important meeting took place at the Hofoper with the thirty-four year old conductor Oskar Fried who had shown considerable interest in Mahler's music and who had been engaged in a regular correspondence with the composer for several months. Fiery, even arrogant, he was nevertheless totally dedicated to the cause of Mahler's works. Fried paid him a visit to discuss his *Second Symphony*, which he was planning to conduct in Berlin on the 8th of November. Fried, a fellow Jew by birth and born in Berlin, was deeply impressed by Mahler, despite the differences in their characters. It was therefore not surprising that they struck up a bond of mutual respect. He invited Fried to dine with him at the Auenbruggergasse apartment so that they could discuss the *Second*, rather than at the Hofoper where there would have been the inevitable interruptions. Mahler found him to be very sympathetic and receptive to his advice. Berlin, particularly the press, had not been very supportive of Mahler in the past, so he was especially eager that Oskar Fried's performance of the *Second* should be a success. In a letter to Alma, Gustav stated the importance of the event saying that he would take her with him to Berlin for the concert. (In 1924 Fried was to make the first ever recording of a Mahler symphony when he recorded the *Second* with the Berlin State Opera Orchestra).

As always when Mahler was on his own in Vienna he paid regular visits to Alma's mother, Anna Moll. The friendship and mutual respect between the two continued to grow from strength to strength. When time permitted he also enjoyed Fritz Löhr's company, going on long walks with him, thereby managing to escape for a short while from the demands of the Hofoper.

Mahler's fears and warnings to Strauss over the future of *Salomé* had been well founded. Matters came to a head towards the end of September. On the 22nd he wrote to Strauss telling him that the Court Opera censor was opposed to the libretto of *Salomé* on moral and religious grounds, and consequently permission would not be granted for the opera to be performed there. On the 10th of October Strauss wrote to him giving him the news that the première would take place in Dresden at the end of November (it actually took place on the 9th of December). In his letter of the 11th of October Mahler assured Strauss that he would do all in his power to have the censor's decision reversed, and that he hoped that it might be possible to stage the work in Vienna in the New Year.

Eleven days later he wrote to Strauss again giving him the encouraging news that the censor had had second thoughts, saying that permission might be granted so long as there were some minor changes to the libretto, including changing the name Jochanaan – Mahler suggested Bal Hanaan. Strauss was naturally delighted. He had no objection to this change of name, since, as he put it, the story was well known to every schoolboy! This positive news was however dashed when the censor had further thoughts, demanding more drastic and quite unacceptable changes, mainly to do with the sexual aspects – 'sexual pathology' as the official put it – in a libretto in which there were frequent implicit and explicit references to Christ.

Apparently the press had found out what was going on and had brought pressure to bear. It would be considered to be in thoroughly bad taste for such a work to be performed at the Court Opera, which had been founded and was funded by the Emperor himself. Mahler had the bit between his teeth, and he was determined not to lose this particular battle. He told Strauss that he would keep striving to obtain permission for *Salomé* to be performed at the Hofoper, but both men must have realised that for the foreseeable future their dream would not be realised.

Strauss entrusted the Dresden première to Ernst von Schuch. Some problems arose during rehearsals. One of these came about when Marie Wittich, the soprano cast as *Salomé* and a lady of ample proportions, declared that as a decent woman she would have nothing to do with certain stage movements demanded of her! This particular problem was overcome when a dancer was employed to deputise for her during The Dance of the Seven Veils, but this resulted in the première being put back to the 9th of December. At the end of the dress rehearsal, the invited audience sat in stunned silence, until Strauss, sitting immediately behind Schuch, turned and faced them and declared, 'Well, I enjoyed that!' This triggered off wild applause.

Even though the performance in Dresden had been a success, controversy continued to reign. At first *Salomé* was banned by a number of opera houses on both sides of the Atlantic, and Strauss joined Mahler as canon fodder for the cartoonists. Cosima Wagner stated that the opera was 'utter madness', and even Strauss's father declared that the music was like having cockchafers up his trousers!

Despite the earlier plan, Alma did not accompany her husband to Berlin on the 7th of November but remained at home with Putzi and Gucki. The final rehearsal of the *Second Symphony* took place on the day of Mahler's arrival, and he was unhappy with Fried's conducting. With his youthful gusto, Fried's tempi were too quick for his liking, but Fried welcomed the composer's advice. In addition the off-stage brass sounded far too prominent, and Mahler made this quite clear to the young man whose task it was to conduct this group of players – a young man of twenty who, like Fried, would become a dedicated champion of his music. His name was Otto Klemperer.

Klemperer had first seen Mahler in Hamburg as a boy. On his way home from school one day, he was fascinated by the strange jerky gate of the man he knew was the Kappelmeister from the Municipal Theatre, and followed him for several minutes.

After the rehearsal Klemperer had the audacity to ask Mahler if the off-stage brass had been to his liking, to which he replied that they had been awful and far too loud. Klemperer dared to point out that *fortissimo* was indicated in the score. Mahler agreed, but told him that it should sound as if from a distance!

Fried, having taken on board Mahler's criticisms, was then told that the allotted rehearsal time had run out so that he would not be able to go over certain passages again. He lost his temper, picked up a chair and launched it into the stalls, narrowly missing members of the invited audience. He then turned to the orchestra admitting his mistakes and told them that he would be taking quite different tempi at the performance, and he begged them to follow him very closely.

The evening of the 8th could have turned out to be an unmitigated disaster, but it was a triumph, and what is more Mahler told Klemperer that the off-stage brass had been very good. Mahler, who had tried his best to remain incognito sitting at the back of a box, was spotted, and the ecstatic audience insisted on his appearance on the stage. He had Berlin at his feet, and the gentlemen of the press had had the wind taken out of their sails. Had he been happy with Fried's conducting? Apparently not entirely, but the overwhelming success of the evening in a city which had hitherto been largely antagonistic towards him was what really mattered.

The following morning Mahler travelled to Leipzig to make four recordings of his music on piano rolls in the studio of M. Welte und Söhne. His mind must still have been in Berlin, and we have little idea as to his feelings towards the idea of recordings. No acoustic recordings of his conducting have been found, so maybe he had little time for such novel ideas. Certainly his playing on the piano rolls is not particularly polished, but they are nevertheless fascinating to listen to, giving us some idea of his approach to his own music. The works he recorded were two lieder, '*Ging' heut' morgens übers feld*' and '*Ich ging mit lust*', the fourth movement of the *Fourth Symphony* and the first movement of the *Fifth Symphony*.

Mahler was back in Vienna on the 10th with the Mozart celebrations about to begin. The two major events for 1905 were a refurbished production of *Cosi fan Tutte* in November, and a brand new one of *Don*

Giovanni in December. Leading the cast for *Cosi fan Tutte* were Leo Slezak and Marie Gutheil-Schoder. Gutheil-Schoder's voice was not what it had been, and the press picked up on this, but the production was praised as was Mahler's conducting. As far as the critics were concerned the main drawback was the work itself, for *Cosi* was generally regarded as being one of Mozart's less successful operas.

Further performances of Mahler's symphonies continued to take place far and wide, including the *Fourth* in London on the 25th of October under the baton of Sir Henry Wood, with his wife Lady Jessie as the soloist in the final movement. The reaction of *The London Times* was, 'the composer has little to offer us but a series of noises in the manner of Richard Strauss . . .' The correspondent of *The Musical Standard* was even less complimentary, referring to 'yards of whimsical fooling', the *Adagio* as 'unoriginal', and probably the most cutting remark of all, 'Seriously, we don't mind simple-minded people having symphonies written for them, but it is rather hard to expect rational music lovers to listen to them.'

Mahler was unable to attend a performance of his *Third Symphony* in Strasbourg, which received very mixed reviews, as it clashed with his *Second* in Berlin. He conducted the *Fifth* in Trieste on the 1st of December, where he was given a great reception and enthusiastic applause at the end of the concert, but it was more for Mahler himself than for his music.

Apart from the *Adagietto,* the *Fifth* continued to give rise to controversy, as it did when he conducted it again only six days later at the Musikverein in Vienna. There was a positive response from most of the audience, which of course included many of his friends and fellow musicians, although, as had become the norm there were a number of people present who were bent on disrupting the proceedings. The press predictably tore into the symphony. Most vitriolic of all was his arch critic Robert Hirschfeld. For him the *Fifth Symphony* typified a beautiless age. He accused Mahler of self-plagiarism (he often deliberately made reference to his earlier works!) as well as stealing ideas from other composers. He regretted that the public failed to appreciate what was healthy in art. This was quite probably a swipe at the Secessionist artists as well. Other articles also criticised the audience for showing such bad taste by applauding music of this nature. Theodor Helm doubted whether the *Fifth Symphony* would have been successful if it had been written by anyone other than by Mahler. The only critics of note who supported him and his *Fifth Symphony* were Julius Korngold and Max Kalbeck. Korngold made the important point that Mahler's symphonies should not be thought of as coming from the traditional classical mould. The music was intensely personal coming from the heart, and this gave his symphonies validity. For Kalbeck the *Fifth* was a considerable advance on its predecessors with its rich and beautiful scoring, the gentleness of the *Adagietto* and the triumphant last movement. For him this was the music of a master. Despite the largely positive articles by Korngold and Kalbeck, the Vienna press in the main remained hostile to his symphonies, and memories of the critical acclaim of his lieder concert the previous January must have seemed an age ago.

The final port of call in 1905 for Mahler and his *Fifth Symphony* was Breslau in Silesia. The concert took place on the 20th of December to great applause by audience and press alike, thus taking some of the sting out of its reception by the majority of the critics following its Vienna première.

Meanwhile, with Mahler dashing hither and yon conducting his symphonies, the major project at the Hofoper had been preparations for the new production of *Don Giovanni*. A new German translation had been commissioned from Max Kalbeck, although Mahler insisted that the title, 'Don Giovanni' should not be replaced by, 'Don Juan'. The original title had to be preserved. Anyway it would not have made musical sense to change it from the four syllables, 'Don Giovanni' to the shorter and far less attractive sounding, 'Don Juan', for example in the Commendatore's Curse. Mahler was determined to be as faithful to the original manuscript as possible, restoring cuts wherever feasible.

With its late Renaissance setting the cost of the production would be considerable. An estimate of 50,000 kronen was submitted. Alfred Roller planned to base his sets on a Renaissance concept of using omnipresent structures on the stage. These could be moved and adapted during the course of the opera. The idea of having two towers on the stage throughout at first worried Mahler, but after lengthy discussions with Roller and Koloman Moser, the Secessionist artist, neighbour and friend of Carl and Anna Moll, he finally agreed. One of the main advantages would be that there could be very rapid scene changes lasting no more than thirty seconds, which meant that there need not be any interruption in the action. These twin towers were basically grey. They could be used as walls, but had openings that could become windows or balconies. With Roller's use of creative lighting and drapes they could be transformed for any particular scene, and with their mobility the sense of space could be altered from a deep to a broad or an intimate nature. Instead of painted backdrops velvet drapes were used, black or coloured depending on the scene, and again the use of lighting played an important part.

Mahler, as always, was concerned with every aspect of opera production, not just the music. For him a successful production had to be a harmonious fusion of all departments, thus following Wagner's concept of a unified work of art.

Problems arose with the cast. Leopold Demuth, a fine and popular singer who had previously performed the role of Don Giovanni, understandably felt that he deserved the leading part in this new production. Mahler thought otherwise favouring the younger Friedrich Weidemann. Demuth was furious and threatened to resign from the Hofoper. Mahler, never one to give in on such matters, would not budge. Demuth, whose contract was due to run until 1907, asked Herr Direktor to accept his letter of resignation. Mahler, concerned about the public uproar that might arise, did not reply and Demuth remained. The part of Donna Anna went to Anna von Mildenburg and Elvira to Marie Gutheil-Schoder.

With controversy on and off the stage, it was no wonder that the press went to town over the production, although most of the critics praised Mahler's conducting. For example Korngold was in favour, delighting in the simplicity and the artistic use of lighting, whereas Hans Liebstöckl exclaimed that the production insulted the eyes. Max Graf bemoaned the fact that the orchestra was only allowed to whisper, that Mozart was being filtered through Mahler, and Berthold Viertel declared that Mahler was treating his singers merely as instruments. Some praise came from Hirschfeld who described him as a superb conductor and indeed the best contemporary Mozart conductor, yet he accused him of turning the opera into a music drama, thus losing the subtler aspects of the work including its humour. Hirschfeld slammed the cast as well as Roller's towers, which even Kalbeck had doubts about. On the other hand Berta Zuckerkandl supported Roller's ideas in an article in the *Allgemeiner Zeitung*. Satirists and cartoonists had a field day as the battle between the pros and cons raged.

It is thought that neither Roller nor Mahler was entirely happy with the effectiveness of the towers, but as Mahler is supposed to have told Ludwig Karpath they were just an experiment, and that new ideas had to be tried out to prevent stagnation. Yet a few years later, people would look back at the Mahler-Roller *Don Giovanni* of 1905 as a brilliant landmark in the history of opera production. Many of Roller's ideas for the sets remained in use for forty years until the Vienna State Opera House was severely damaged during an air raid in 1945.

This was just the beginning of the Mozart anniversary celebrations. Indeed the productions of *Cosi* and *Don Giovanni* took place prematurely, for the actual anniversary was in 1906. So a wildly hectic final three months of 1905 came to an end. Yet once again critical murmurings were heard concerning Mahler's frequent absences from Vienna to conduct his own works. It was partly for this reason, together with the considerable extra work connected with the Mozart celebrations, that prompted him to cut back on his travels, even though it meant that he would be unable to conduct some performances of his compositions. The only trips he had planned were to conduct performances of his *Fifth* in Antwerp and

Amsterdam in March, and the première of his *Sixth Symphony* in Essen in May.

As described by Alma in her memoirs, Gustav kept up a strict domestic routine. Typical was the early morning when he would rise at seven o'clock on the dot. Having shaved, the maid would bring him his breakfast and newspapers, although he barely looked at them for these would be read after lunch. According to Alma he would sit on the sofa discarding the newspaper sheets one by one until they were heaped up around him almost knee-deep. After quickly consuming his breakfast he went to his desk, which no one else was permitted to touch, to work on his scores. During the winter of 1905-1906 he concentrated on fine-tuning his *Seventh Symphony*. At nine o'clock sharp he would go into Alma's room, then see his daughters briefly before dashing off to the Opera.

1906, the Mozart Year, saw new productions of three of his operas: *Die Entführung aus dem Serail* in January, in which Roller's towers were again used, this time to better effect according to Alma, *Le Nozze di Figaro* at the end of March and *Die Zauberflöte* at the beginning of June. *Die Entführung aus dem Serail* was in fact the last production to utilize the original towers for safety reasons. It was reported that during one of the rehearsals, when Leo Slezak in the role of Belmonte climbed up a ladder in order to reach Konstanz's window, to everyone's horror the tower began to move causing Slezak to frantically windmill his arms! Although the cast, especially Leo Slezak and Selma Kurtz, were praised, the production itself was much criticised. As the least important of the new Mozart cycle, for budgetary reasons it had been staged as economically as possible, and as far as many of the critics were concerned this was clearly evident.

In his absence Mahler's works continued to be performed. His music had become an established part of the repertoire of many orchestras. The *Kindertotenlieder* sung by Friedrich Weidermann under Nikisch and Steinbach in Hamburg and Cologne respectively, continued to meet with widespread approval. Musicologist Paul Stefan wrote of their beauty and how they had touched everyone, and Anton Webern described them as marvellous. In January and February performances of his *Fifth Symphony* were given in Boston and New York where it was listened to with due respect, disliked in parts, yet approved of in others. Not surprisingly it was not fully understood after a single hearing, but neither was it dismissed. Most of the American critics were complimentary, and such sentiments as 'he captivates and conquers his audience', 'deeply felt and tremendously sincere' and 'a master-hand at instrumentation' must have given Mahler great satisfaction. *The Boston Evening Transcript* even referred to him, as 'a twentieth century Berlioz'. An understandable comment, if not entirely accurate.

Two further performances in Boston just three weeks later brought with them a greater understanding of the music and with it even greater applause. Of course there were still the unconvinced who found his chosen musical path incomprehensible, wayward in form and decidedly unattractive, but these were a minority. Mahler had become a name to be reckoned with in the United States.

In January he wrote to Willem Mengelberg (the date of the letter is unknown) regarding the planned performance of his *Fifth* in Amsterdam. He enclosed a much-revised copy of the score and asked Mengelberg to arrange for him to have three rehearsals. He also asked Mengelberg to hold preliminary rehearsals before he arrived, telling him that the *Fifth* was an extremely difficult work to play well, and well it had to be played to avoid him being ridiculed.

En route to Amsterdam Mahler was to conduct the same symphony in Antwerp. He left Vienna by train on the evening of the 2nd of March, arriving in the Belgian city the following morning. While unpacking his suitcase in his room in the luxurious Grand Hotel, he discovered that Alma had slipped in a photograph of herself and their daughters. He was delighted and placed it on his bedside table. He wrote to Alma thanking her, telling her that the hotel was excellent, but that the orchestra was dreadful and he feared that the performance might end up a shambles. He told her that he felt like packing his bags! Paul Clemenceau and Georges Picquart travelled from Paris to join him and give him some much needed moral support. They were devastated to discover that Alma had not travelled to Antwerp, and, as Mahler put it in a letter to his wife, they had sighed repeatedly for her throughout the course of their breakfast!

The concert on the 5th of March also included the overture to Carl Maria von Weber's opera *Der Freischütz* and Liszt's arrangement for piano and orchestra of Franz Schubert's *Wanderer Fantasy* with Eugen d'Albert as soloist. As things turned out the evening was a great success. Both Mahler and his *Fifth Symphony* were given rapturous applause, and the press responded very positively. With gratitude and with great relief he left Antwerp for Amsterdam on the 6th of March.

Mengelberg was at the station to greet him on his arrival. Together they went to the Concertgebouw for Mahler's first rehearsal with the orchestra. It was abundantly clear that the musicians had been extremely well prepared by Mengelberg during the preliminary rehearsals. Mahler was in good form, delighted to be back amongst friends in the city, which more than any other had taken him to its heart. Two concerts had been arranged. On the 8th of March he would conduct his *Fifth Symphony* as well as the *Kindertotenlieder* and *Ich bin der Welt abhanden gekommen*. Friedrich Weidemann from the Hofoper had been booked to sing the lieder, but shortly before the concert he fell ill and had to be replaced by the baritone Gerard Zalsman. At the concert on the 10th of March *Das klagende Lied* would receive its Dutch première.

The dedication and superb playing of the orchestra, the excellence of the chorus and the friendship shown by all concerned made the rehearsals a pleasure for Mahler rather than the hard and frequently negative atmosphere to which he had become accustomed at so many venues. This was largely due to Mengelberg whose enthusiasm for his music was infectious to say the least. Away from the concert hall, he enjoyed the hospitality of the Mengelbergs and was delighted to meet up once again with Alphons Diepenbrock and his wife Elizabeth.

Despite the typically positive mood that he adopted whenever he visited Amsterdam, concern lingered at the back of his mind over unrest that had been developing at the Hofoper. Ill feeling had been growing between Alfred Roller and the chorus during rehearsals for a new production of *Lohengrin*. Apparently the costumes he had designed were decidedly uncomfortable and very heavy, and several larger members of the chorus refused to wear them. Roller's reaction of dismissing those concerned had resulted in a threat of strike action.

In a letter to Alma, Mahler wrote that the *Fifth Symphony* had been well received by both the audience and the press. Predictably the performance had of course been excellent, but in fact the symphony had not met with the level of enthusiasm that he had expected. The applause had been polite, but many, including Diepenbrock, had failed to appreciate the work. Most of the critics liked the clarity of the orchestration and the more formal construction that he had used compared to the earlier symphonies, thus providing a greater unity. To make matters worse, following the symphony, the replacement singer gave a rather uninspired rendition of the lieder resulting in some of the audience leaving the hall before the end of the concert. Failure to fully appreciate the *Fifth Symphony* was one thing, but to have members of the audience departing during the course of *Die Kindertotenlieder* and *Ich bin der Welt abhanden gekommen* was quite another, for even in Vienna these latter works had met with almost universal praise. One can only presume that the audience had become 'punch drunk' after listening to the symphony, coupled with the lack-lustre performance of the lieder by Zalsman, who had probably not had sufficient time to prepare for the concert. This was a great disappointment for Mahler, especially in Amsterdam. Nevertheless plans had been made for Mengelberg to take the *Fifth Symphony* on tour to Rotterdam on the 12th of March, the 14th in The Hague, the 19th in Arnhem and the 20th in Haarlem, before returning to Amsterdam for two further performances on the 21st and 22nd of March. Upon a second hearing Diepenbrock was completely won over by the symphony, declaring Mahler to be the only true poet of that time, but despite Diepenbrock's conversion mixed feelings remained. On the 1st of April Mengelberg conducted a further performance of *Die Kindertotenlieder*, again with Zalsman as the soloist, as well as the *Adagietto* from the *Fifth Symphony*.

If Mahler's first concert had been a disappointment, the second – the Dutch première of *Das klagende Lied* on the 10th of March – was an undoubted success with the concertgoers. Bearing in mind that it was an early work, the mature Mahler could nevertheless be clearly recognised in the score and the work was given the type of applause he had hoped for the previous evening. So ended his 1906 visit to Amsterdam, and all in all it had been something of a disappointment.

Provisional plans had been made for the United Theatres of Breslau to take *Salomé* on tour. One of the cities being given serious consideration was Vienna. Mahler wrote to Strauss giving the project his unqualified support, telling him that Director Theodor Löwe had only to ask if extra musicians were required, and that Alfred Roller's expertise would be available regarding the sets and costumes. Strauss, as ever grateful for Mahler's support, begged him not to let his enthusiasm for the proposed Vienna performances endanger his position at the Court Opera. As much as he yearned for Vienna to see *Salomé*, Strauss stated emphatically that it was more important for Mahler, with his genius and vision, to remain at the helm of the Hofoper. As things turned out the Breslau company's production of *Salomé* was not seen in Vienna until May and June of 1907.

Vienna has always had a strange magnetic force, dragging musicians to her bosom and in some cases devouring them. Mahler of course had a love-hate relationship with the city and its institutions. Mozart was another case in point. Accepted in his hometown of Salzburg, lauded in Prague, it was nevertheless Vienna, 'Clavierland' as he described it to his father, that became an inescapable draw. Ambition and the size and vibrancy of what was the cultural capital of Europe – the temptation was too great. And where did Mozart end up? In an anonymous grave. It was only after his death that the city realised its loss and tried to make amends by erecting a statue in his honour behind the Opera on Mozartplatz, later to be moved to a garden beside the Imperial Court. Mahler's treatment by the Viennese proved to be similar in many respects.

When he returned from Amsterdam, it was straight back to work on the Mozart celebratory season – the city's homage to 'her very own' musical prodigy – and a new production of *The Marriage of Figaro*. There was a newly translated libretto in German by Max Kalbeck with what had become the customary spoken recitatives by Lorenzo da Ponte ('farcical prose' as Mahler described them) replaced by the original sung versions with words by Beaumarchais. As Alma wrote in her memoirs, Mahler knew the importance of this production of *Figaro*, carefully scrutinizing every detail. She considered it to be one of his most memorable achievements alongside the renowned *Tristan, Fidelio* and the recent *Don Giovanni*.

The first performance took place on the 30th of March, and Alma's feelings were shared by the audience as well as by the press. The cast, that included Richard Mayr, Berta Foerster-Lauterer and Friedrich Weidermann, was given much praise, and as for Marie Gutheil-Schoder's performance as Susanna, the critics could not find enough superlatives. They were also very positive with their views on Roller's sets and the production as a whole. As for Mahler's interpretation of the score, even his staunchest opponents found it hard to find fault. Words such as ecstasy, tenderness, serenity, brilliant, noble and radiant peppered the reviews. In retrospect many considered this production of *The Marriage of Figaro* to be the high point of his years at the Hofoper.

June the 1st saw the final opera to be staged in celebration of the 150th anniversary of Mozart's birth – *The Magic Flute,* an opera very close to Mahler's heart. With so much money spent on *Don Giovanni* and *The Marriage of Figaro,* the budget for *The Magic Flute* was tight, thus precluding any idea of an entirely new production. Instead Mahler and Roller were forced to adapt an existing one. But adapt Roller did in style, and what could well have turned out to be an anti-climax to the Mozart cycle instead became yet another success. As always among the Viennese critics there were those few who presumably felt that they were not doing their job properly without picking holes in anything Mahler and Roller produced, but they were a small minority with whom few agreed. Guido Adler wrote that each of the Mozart operas staged in 1906 had been rejuvenated, and that this festival marked the beginning of a renaissance of Mozart in Vienna.

Apart from the on-going Mozart Festival, May also saw another very important event for Mahler, the première of his *Sixth Symphony* in Essen. But before that came the first Austrian performance of *Salomé* which was to take place in Graz on the 16th of May. Already something of a sensation in Dresden, Prague and Breslau, this was to be the first time that Strauss himself would conduct.

Upon arrival at the Elephant Hotel in Graz, Gustav and Alma were met by Richard Strauss who had planned an excursion to a local beauty spot that afternoon, the Golling waterfalls. As Alma recalled they took refreshments at an inn within the vicinity of the falls. Having walked and wondered at the magnificence of nature, they returned to the inn for a bite to eat. Time was pressing, and Mahler began to show concern that they might be late for the performance, but Strauss was enjoying himself, declaring that they would not be able to begin without him. Mahler became fidgety and, suddenly springing to his feet, told Strauss that if he were not prepared to leave then he, Mahler, would conduct the performance himself. This persuaded Strauss to make a move, but when Mahler urged the chauffeur to put his foot on the accelerator, Strauss told him not to drive so fast. It was an amusing contrast with Strauss, the composer, conductor and the man of the moment, remaining very laid back, and Mahler behaving like a cat on hot bricks! The likelihood was that he was hoping against hope that this performance of *Salomé* would be a triumph for Strauss, for the sake of the masterpiece itself, but above all as a riposte to the biased attitude towards the work by the Vienna authorities.

Schoenberg, Berg and Zemlinsky had also travelled from Vienna for the occasion. There had been rumours of trouble from the local Christian Socialists, but this did not materialize, and the evening was a major success for all concerned. Graz's gain was Vienna's loss, and Mahler felt gratified that he had been proved right.

The following morning over breakfast Strauss castigated Mahler over the way he took everything so seriously. He told him that he should relax a little for it was not worth getting upset by matters at the Hofoper, which he described as a cow shed. Driving himself into the ground for that 'pig-sty', which would not even consider staging *Salomé*, was just not worth it. Alma agreed with Strauss, believing that every note of Gustav's compositions was worth more than anything he did at the Hofoper – fine thoughts from his companions, but he was dedicated to his work at the Opera; he had to be, after all it was his livelihood. Part of the problem was that he had become virtually a dictator, insisting on having full control over stage, music and administrative matters with the inevitable result that he made many enemies. He felt that without overall control, problems would have been even greater.

As director of the Court Opera he had adopted a policy similar to that of Wagner: the principle of *Gesamkunstwerk*, a composite work embracing all the artistic ingredients in a harmonious fusion. In the same way he believed that all departments of the Hofoper had to work together under his banner. He despised routine, and in his quest for freshness in every new production he welcomed constructive ideas from those around him. If he had written just one instruction for those with whom he worked, it might well have been 'Be inspired or go'. His concern for each individual knew no bounds, and at rehearsals he would spend almost as much time on the stage as he would on the podium.

He attached a great deal of importance to flexibility, and if he or anyone else for that matter came up with a better idea, he was always prepared to make changes. He himself frequently changed his mind on matters of staging, even down to the smallest detail. Everything that happened on the stage had to work hand in hand with the music. He detested what had become the traditional grand gestures used at every possible opportunity – these should be reserved for the great climaxes only. He favoured a more low-key, naturalistic style of acting, allowing the music itself to carry the emotional weight. He did not suffer fools gladly, as many found to their cost. It was essential that he had overall control, yet even those who disliked or feared him could not help but admire his dedication and search for perfection, something that they themselves did not aspire to. It was a lesson that his successor, Felix Weingartner, was slow to learn.

The podium fireworks for which he had become well known during the early part of his career had by this time largely disappeared, for he had mellowed with the passing of the years. He reserved excessive gestures for rehearsals, but during performances his conducting was no more energetic than it needed to be, for the last thing he wanted was to distract the audience's attention from the stage and indeed the music. He did not want to be the centre of attention, yet inevitably he frequently was. With the conductor of a given performance often not announced beforehand, when the small figure of Mahler hurried to the podium the audience anticipated a special performance. The grimaces, smiles, his piercing eyes and the flashing of his glasses, the passion was clearly visible, but only to the musicians and cast.

Also with the years and with the greater confidence that they brought, Mahler's sense of humour had developed, and he would laugh along with the rest of those present at unforeseen amusing incidents or the occasional leg-pull, so long as these did not disrupt the rehearsals unduly. He realised that a good laugh could relieve tension and have a positive effect. One of the biggest jokers (in both senses!) was of course Leo Slezak, famed for an aside he was supposed to have made during a performance of *Lohengrin*. Legend has it that just before his first and very dramatic entrance, when he was about to step on board the boat drawn by a swan, a stagehand had made a mistake and the boat left without him. Whereupon Slezak turned to those near him and asked, 'What time is the next swan?' He was well known for teasing other members of the cast, and sometimes his pranks would go on too long. On one such occasion Mahler, beginning to feel somewhat exasperated by the disruptions, told him to take rehearsals more seriously. The following day Slezak turned up long-faced and in full mourning regalia, and Mahler and the assembled company could do nothing but burst out laughing!

Such moments were indeed a relief from the tensions, arguments and sometimes excessive demands of Herr Direktor, who would frequently insist on a problematic passage being played over and over again, sometimes twenty or thirty times, until he was entirely satisfied. Inevitably there were some who did not share Mahler's constant quest for perfection, but those who did had the great satisfaction of knowing that they had been involved in the creation of something special. In retrospect few would deny his greatness as a director. Among these was Leo Slezak who thanked his lucky stars that he had had the privilege of working with Mahler, and wrote of his deepest gratitude to him.

Mahler's workload was quite clearly horrendous. One day he was quoted as declaring that by taking care of themselves some people would destroy the Opera, but he took care of the Opera and in so doing was in the process of destroying himself. It was no wonder that he held sacrosanct his daily brisk walks around the Ringstrasse, in the grounds of the Belvedere Palace or in the Prater to relieve the tension. He would also have relaxing breaks in the coffee houses where he would wryly read the newspapers, usually oblivious to the gazes and mutterings of the passers-by.

His interest in literature and philosophy, a love of books inherited from his father, continued to play an important part in his life. Goethe and Dostoyevsky alongside the thoughts of such philosophers as Kant, Schopenhauer and Nietzsche, were part of his daily intellectual diet. Politics and science continued to fascinate him, especially the wonders of nature and man's part in the scheme of things, and above all else the constant quest for an answer to the purpose of life and what lay beyond. His struggle to understand the true meaning of God, away from the doctrinal shackles of organised religion, which he continued to have little time for, had never and would never abate.

Returning from Graz on the 17th of May, he barely had time to dash to his office and repack before setting off once more on the 19th. His destination this time was Essen for the première of his *Sixth Symphony*. It was to be performed at the 1906 *Allgemeiner Deutscher Musikverein* Festival, once again organised by Richard Strauss. Industrial Essen, dominated by coalmines and the famous steel and armament firm of Krupp, was a world apart from the cultural Mecca that Vienna had become. Nevertheless its orchestra had a good reputation. Having devoted some hours two months previously playing through the score with the Vienna Philharmonic, for which he thanked his orchestra for their cooperation, he was confident that all was as ready as could be for this very important occasion, although he continued to work on the orchestra parts throughout the rehearsal period.

As usual the festival's main aim was to present new works by contemporary composers. Among those represented in 1906 were Frederick Delius (*Sea Drift*), Hans Pfitzner (*Trio in F major, op.8*) and Bruno Walter (*Quintet for piano and strings in F sharp minor*). With many new works to be performed during the festival, rehearsal time was at a premium. Even so Mahler required seven rehearsals, pointing out the sheer magnitude of his work, the complexity of the score requiring as much rehearsal time as possible. As it was unquestionably the main event of the festival, his request was granted.

Alma had remained behind in Vienna with the children but would travel to Essen with her mother for the concert. In his letter of the 21st of May Gustav told his wife that the first rehearsal had gone well, and the following day he wrote telling her that he had rehearsed the orchestra for five hours and had also spent seven hours working on the orchestra parts. The musicians were finding a number of passages difficult to cope with. This applied particularly to the large percussion section.

Mahler met a young Russian pianist and conductor by the name of Ossip Gabrilowitsch who had attended the rehearsals. He found his company very convivial and invited him to sit at his table at the hotel. Gabrilowitsch's enthusiasm was infectious and Mahler told him of the support he had among the young musicians of St. Petersburg. Also present at the rehearsals was Oskar Fried, whom Alma described as following Mahler like his shadow.

He was still not happy with the orchestra parts and continued to burn the midnight oil trying to iron out problems. To make matters worse Strauss, who had shown little interest in the *Sixth Symphony,* made a cutting remark saying that it was over-orchestrated. He was deeply hurt by this comment from the director of the festival and a man whom he had considered to be a friend.

Having arrived on the 25th, Alma and Anna Moll were present at the final rehearsal. After the last movement with its three huge hammer blows of fate, Mahler fled to his dressing room where he proceeded to pace up and down, emotionally overcome by the experience and with tears streaming down his face. While Alma, the young conductors Oskar Fried and Julius Buths and Ossip Gabrilowitsch stood dumbfounded watching him, Strauss burst in. Totally insensitive to the situation, he told Mahler he would have to conduct some suitably funereal music before his symphony on the morrow because the mayor had died. He then made an aside asking him what was bothering him and marched out without waiting for a reply!

According to Alma, he did not conduct well at the concert on the 27th. The frantic alterations as well as the nature of the music had left him totally exhausted. Many in the audience, who had presumed that they were at last coming to terms with Mahler's music world, were completely taken aback by the ferocity and anguish of the score, particularly the first and last movements. Nevertheless he was given a great acclamation by audience and musicians alike and was presented with the traditional laurel wreath.

Having left the stage for the final time he was in a state of near collapse. Alma and Willem Mengelberg, who had met for the first time that day, managed to revive him before taking him to the post concert meal.

Just as most of the audience had been disconcerted by the sheer ferocity in certain passages of the outer movements, so too the press failed to grasp the inner depths of the work. The general opinion was to agree with Strauss that the symphony was indeed over-orchestrated and its thematic material trite. Some considered it to be the weakest of Mahler's symphonies to date, with the exception of the *First* – rather ironic when considering the lambasting that the *Fourth* and *Fifth* had received after their first performances! Yet there were a few who praised his skill and sincerity. An anonymous article in the *Frankfurter Zeitung* stated that the *Sixth Symphony* represented an example of contemporary composition at its highest level and would be a legacy for generations to come. Following the première Alban Berg wrote to Anton Webern declaring that it was the <u>only</u> *Sixth*, despite Beethoven's *Pastoral!*

Mahler returned to Vienna to face several disgruntled singers who wished to negotiate new contracts entitling them to make guest appearances outside the city. He had always opposed this practice, believing that if singers had the privilege of being employed by the Hofoper they should show complete dedication to both him and the Vienna Opera. Two singers in point were Wilhelm Hesch and Leo Slezak, the latter having consistently objected to the restriction imposed upon him by Herr Direktor.

Mahler conducted two performances of *The Magic Flute,* but declined to conduct the performance of *Tannhäuser* in which Hermann Winkelmann bade farewell to Vienna after twenty-three years of sterling service as one of the leading singers. This he left to Bruno Walter, and although present in his box for the first two acts, he did not appear on the stage to thank the popular Winkelmann for his many years at the Hofoper. This was a bad diplomatic mistake on his part and invited adverse criticism.

One critic, and a much-revered one at that, had become both a supporter and friend of Mahler's. Julius Korngold, successor to the renowned and much feared Eduard Hanslick as chief music critic of the *Neue Freie Presse*, and whom many regarded as the most influential and level headed voice in the Vienna press, had a prodigiously gifted son Erich Wolfgang. He was nine years old and had recently completed a cantata, *Gold,* for solo singers, chorus and piano. Julius Korngold recalled how on a sunny day in June 1906 he had taken little Erich to Mahler's apartment on the Auenbruggergasse. With his head almost hidden from view under a large sailor's hat, he proceeded to play *Gold* by heart. Mahler, leaning against the piano, followed the score. After a few minutes he began pacing up and down the room with his irregular step, a sure sign that he was becoming excited. Deeply impressed by the inventiveness and power of the music he was hearing, he proclaimed, 'A genius! A genius!' He immediately advised Julius to send his son to study with Zemlinsky, advising him against the Conservatory, which would only inflict endless exercises on the child. Mahler had indeed recognised a genius. Erich's compositions, in particular his opera *Die Tote Stadt*, would become widely performed throughout Europe to great acclaim. He was one of a number of musicians forced to flee his homeland at the onset of the Second World War. He settled in Hollywood where he began a new career as a composer of music for films – 'operas without words' as he called his scores. He continued to compose concert works, including a violin concerto dedicated to Heifetz.

The final performance of the 1906 Mozart festival was to be *The Marriage of Figaro* in Salzburg on the 18th of August. Because this would interrupt Mahler's summer break in Carinthia, he managed to get permission to leave Vienna a few days before the end of the season. He was therefore able to travel to Maiernigg with Alma and the children on the 13th of June. His main target for the summer of 1906 was to complete a revision of the orchestration of his *Seventh Symphony*.

Remembering the frustration he had suffered the previous summer when inspiration had failed him for over two weeks, and being utterly exhausted after such a hectic season in Vienna, coupled with the amount of travel in conducting his own works, Mahler wanted to relax and rest. With his forty-sixth birthday less than a month away the years were beginning to catch up with him. All he wanted was a peaceful spell before having to travel to Salzburg. Revising the orchestration of the *Seventh* would not be too taxing.

On the first morning of the holiday, as he strolled up to his *Häuschen* clutching the manuscript and breathing in the fresh forest air, the turmoil of Vienna must have seemed a world away. But peaceful revision was soon cast aside. According to Mahler it was on that very first morning that the *spiritus creator* seized him and threw him headlong into an amazing burst of composition. The half forgotten words of the Latin hymn *Veni Creator Spiritus* filled his mind. Tired he may have been, but his outlook for the future must have been very positive. He was at the very pinnacle of his fame in Vienna and beyond. His family life was also at a high point. This is reflected in the score, for never before or afterwards would he compose a work that was so uplifting. Alma in her memoirs wrote that he had had his usual fortnight of compositional frustration. This is clearly wrong as on the 21st of June, a week after the first morning in his *Häuschen*, he wrote to Fritz Löhr asking him to send post haste the full text of the hymn for certain aspects of translation and scansion were concerning him. To his relief the music he had composed more or less fitted the full text with only minor adjustments needed. The excitement of writing the first fully choral symphony (Vaughan Williams' *Sea Symphony* following three years later) brought from within him hidden reserves of energy. He was determined to complete the short score of his monumental *Eighth Symphony* before his commitments in Salzburg. This he managed to achieve in the space of a little over eight weeks.

Eighth Symphony, in E flat
(for eight soloists, double chorus, children's chorus, organ and orchestra, with additional off-stage brass)

Mahler had had thoughts of composing a religious work, possibly a mass, but with his views on established religious doctrines he felt unable to set parts of the liturgy to music, in particular the *Credo*. His desire to compose a wholly choral symphony reflected his belief that an enlightened human spirit, filled with the love and compassion of the universal God, would overcome all the traumas and evils of earthly existence and consequently achieve eternal bliss. Scored for massive choral and instrumental forces as well as eight solo singers, it is often referred to as 'The Symphony of a Thousand', an advertising slogan thought up by Emil Gutman, the concert manager of its Munich première – a slogan Mahler did not sanction. But despite the huge forces involved Mahler rarely uses them en masse. The unheard of number of musicians gave him the widest possible choice of colours from his outsize musical palette, but there are many passages where the symphony takes on an almost chamber like quality. It was the largest symphony at that time, only to be superseded by Havergal Brian's *First Symphony, 'The Gothic'*, composed between 1919 and 1927.

Mahler's *Eighth Symphony* is divided into two parts: the first using the Latin hymn '*Veni Creator Spiritus*', and the second part the closing scene from Goethe's *Faust*. Mahler had not initially planned to use *Faust*. His original idea had been for a four-movement symphony. Following the *Veni Creator Spiritus*, there would be an adagio, '*Caritas*', which he had first intended to use as the slow movement for his *Fourth Symphony*, but had set aside with the arrival of the *Ruhevoll adagio*. Next would come a *scherzo*, 'Christmas games with the Christ-Child', incorporating two *Wunderhorn* songs. The symphony would end with a hymn, 'Creation through Eros'. At exactly what point Mahler abandoned this scheme in favour of using the final scene from *Faust* is uncertain, but his second thoughts were probably influenced by the fact that the *Caritas* and *scherzo* movements were clearly retrospective, and he wanted to explore new territory. One can presume that the initial plan was soon abandoned because of the remarkably short space of time in which the sketches for the complete symphony were completed. On the face of it, it seems to be a strange combination, the first part religious, a Whitsuntide mediaeval hymn, thought to have been written by Hrabanus Maurus, Archbishop of Mainz, and in Latin, the second secular and in German. But together they mirror Mahler's belief in God the creator and man's search for the eternal. However, there was another reason why he decided to use Goethe's *Faust*. Alma's memories of her father telling her stories from *Faust* were etched onto her mind, and how he had given her a copy of *Faust*, only for it to be snatched away by her mother as inappropriate reading matter. Gustav was fully aware of Alma's love of the work and he too was particularly fond of it. His use of this text in this grandest of symphonies was a token of his love for his wife to whom the work was later dedicated.

It was composed during his happiest summer and formed a part of a trinity of positives: his success at the Hofoper, a happy family life and the *Eighth*. Together they formed a trio before the storm clouds began to gather and 'the three hammer blows of fate' that he would suffer. The *Eighth* is a celebration and in a way an apotheosis of three eras of music combined in one glorious work: the Baroque in Part One, and the Romantic and Music Drama in Part Two. It marked the end of romanticism in Mahler's music. From this point on his compositions focussed on the future, the influence of his final works being felt right up to the present day.

There are no sounds of nature, nor the nostalgia so often depicted in the past by military band music and ländler in his earlier, more introspective works. There are no hints of personal gloom or fears. The *Eighth* is a work composed <u>for</u> the people, in much the same way as Beethoven's *Ninth*. Extrovert in nature, it beckons the world to unite and embrace all that is good in mankind. The combination of wisdom and the power of love, as seen by Goethe and Mahler, which is capable of overcoming all evil and misery, is as apt a message today as it was in their respective times – a pathway to salvation, which mankind continues to reject at its peril.

PART ONE – *Veni Creator Spiritus*
(Allegro impetuoso)

For sheer perfection of musical form Mahler considered Bach to be supreme, and he spent more and more time as the years went by studying his scores. This huge yet compact first movement, with its polyphony and spectacular double fugue, is his homage to the master.

His previous three symphonies had all opened with a march. With the *Fifth* and *Seventh* he had used funeral marches. In the case of the *Sixth* he composed a march with violence not far below the surface forecasting the grim conflict to come, before the music found temporary solace in the 'Alma' theme. With the *Eighth* he yet again opens with a march, but this time one bursting with energy, rousing, positive. The symphony bursts into life with an E flat major chord for organ, woodwind and lower strings before the combined adult choruses exultantly entreat the Creator Spirit to come. We are off on a musical roller coaster that would have utterly astonished that master of dramatic magnitude, Hector Berlioz! After this fortissimo opening the music subsides to pianissimo and four soloists beseech the Creator Spirit with the words *Imple superna gratia* – fill (our souls) with heavenly grace. A soprano sings *Et spiritalis unctio* – and the soul's anointing. This quiet interlude soon ends when the choirs ecstatically repeat *superna gratia*. A development of the *Veni* theme is played by the horns and trombones followed by a prayer for strength *(Infirma nostri corporis)*. This in turn leads to the magnificent *Ascende lumen sensibus* – inspire our minds with thy light – sung to a new theme that will reappear in Part Two of the symphony. With a double fugue the music surges towards its mighty apotheosis with adult and children's choruses and all eight soloists singing the words of the *Gloria,* accompanied by the full might of the orchestra, organ and additional off stage brass.

PART TWO – The closing scene from Goethe's *Faust*

The contrasts between Parts One and Two are considerable: Latin – German/ ecclesiastical – secular/ white-hot drama – lyrical/ hymn – symphonic oratorio. Yet musically there are links between the two parts. Whereas the first is basically a single movement, a sonata form *allegro,* the second part's construction is not so obviously clear. It could be argued that it is made up of three movements – *adagio, scherzo* and *finale* – fused into one. Part One is chorus-dominated, whereas in Part Two the orchestra plays a much more significant role with Mahler's magical use of subtle orchestral colours evident on many occasions. Only at the end is the full weight of the massed forces heard. Many passages are almost chamber-like in their delicacy with parts for such instruments as mandolin, celesta and harmonium.

Part Two, having moved from E flat major in Part One to E flat minor, opens with a lengthy orchestral prelude, which sets the scene for the story that is about to unfold. Creating a mysterious atmosphere the music describes Goethe's opening scene of mountain gorges, forests, cliffs and a prevailing sense of solitude with holy hermits huddled in rocky clefts. The opening barely audible chorus describes the scene already portrayed by the orchestra: the rocks, the swaying trees, the foaming water and the friendly lions that honour that sacred place. The dream-like quality of this prelude is brought abruptly to an end when Pater Ecstaticus (baritone) sings passionately of the joy and pain of love. The line *Pfeile, durchdringet mich* (Arrows penetrate me) refers of course to Eros, the Greek god of love, and the '*Accende*' motif from Part One, already heard being tossed around on the breeze, is now stated prominently by the brass. Pater Profundis (bass) takes over from Pater Ecstaticus. His descriptions of nature are far from peaceful for he uses them to illustrate burning desire and a full, overwhelming passion of love. He beseeches God to soothe his mind and enlighten his heart.

The mood changes with a chorus of angels and boys' voices as Faust's soul is borne upwards. This section is what remains of Mahler's originally planned *scherzo*, the *Wunderhorn* 'Christmas Games'. With its lightness of touch, this music harks back to the last movement of the *Fourth Symphony* and its child's vision of Heaven. Dr Marianus (tenor) sings in awe of the Queen of Heaven with her coronet of stars. As the Queen of Heaven, Mater Gloriosa (soprano) appears high above the orchestra and the choirs. The great love theme is heard, and the choirs continue their intercession for sinners. A group of penitent and now redeemed women sing in praise of her. These are Magna Peccatrix (soprano – Mary Magdalene), Mulier Samiratana (contralto – the woman of Samaria) and Maria Aegyptiaca (contralto – a converted prostitute from Alexandria who spent the last four decades of her life on her own in the desert to atone for her sins). They are joined by Una Poenitentium (soprano – the soul of Gretchen of the first part of Goethe's original). In this first part of Goethe's play, when Faust first sets eyes on her, he is consumed by desire, a desire that at first is held at bay by her innocence and integrity. Instead of satisfying his lust he tries to divert his mind by contemplating nature, but to no avail. He persuades her to give her mother a sleeping draft, which proves to be fatal, and he proceeds to seduce her. A distraught Gretchen becomes pregnant. Faust kills her brother, and Gretchen is thrown into prison accused of killing her child and is condemned to death. Faust seeks the healing power of nature to overcome Gretchen's demise.

Returning to Part Two of Mahler's *Eighth*, Gretchen, having herself sought forgiveness for her sins from the Queen of Heaven, is joined by the other penitent women and together they pray for the soul of Faust. Their prayers are answered as Faust is transfigured. Mater Gloriosa tells the redeemed Gretchen to raise herself to higher spheres, for when Faust sees her, he will surely follow. With the *Ascende* theme heard once more in the brass, the symphony reaches its magnificent climax with the *Chorus Mysticus* – '*Alles Vergängliche*' (All things are transitory) . . . '*des ewig-Weibliche zieht uns hinan*' (the Eternal Feminine draws us heavenward). The love theme and the *Veni Creator* motif, in a blaze of glory, reach for paradise in what must surely be one of, if not the most emotional finale in the history of music as the massed forces, accompanied by the full might of the organ and additional brass from above, lift our spirits along with those of Faust and Gretchen towards the gates of Heaven.

Of course Mahler had changed Goethe's ending. In the original Faust sells his soul to Mephistopheles, is damned and cast into Hell. In Mahler's version he seeks forgiveness, which he receives through the intercession of the penitent women, and is drawn heavenwards by 'the Eternal Feminine'. Obviously this provides a far more positive and uplifting ending, but one cannot help but wonder whether Mahler had cast himself as Faust and Alma as Getchen!

The sheer scale of the work, with its overwhelming emotional ending, was a virtual guarantee of popular acclaim, but even today it remains in the true Mahler tradition controversial. For example Neville Cardus stated that should Mahler's works be threatened with conflagration, and if he were only able to save but two of them, the *Eighth Symphony* along with the later *Das Lied von der Erde* would be his choice. On the other hand the American critic R. D. Darrell, writing in 1952, referred to it as 'masochistic aural flagellation', which added up to 'a sublimely ridiculous minus-zero'!

Incidentally, inspiration for the great hymn of redemption *Chorus Mysticus* came to Mahler while he was enthroned – not the first time that the muse had visited him under such circumstances! He wrote the preliminary sketch of the magnificent theme on a sheet of lavatory paper, which Alban Berg later acquired and had framed.

Before leaving Maiernigg for the Salzburg Festival he wrote to Willem Mengelberg giving him the news that he had completed his *Eighth*. He told him that it was his grandest creation to date, but found it impossible to describe. He suggested that Mengelberg should try to imagine the whole universe ringing and resounding, with the human voices becoming planets and suns rotating.

He arrived in Salzburg on the 15th of August, and in his letter to Alma the following day he wrote of the hideous crowds and the numerous and inevitable social events that had been planned. He told her that he missed her and the quiet life of his summer retreat. He spent as much of his spare time as possible away from the madding crowd in the company of Alfred Roller. Strauss was there too, already working on his next opera *Elektra,* as was Julius Korngold who later wrote that he had seen Mahler walking about Salzburg with a much-thumbed copy of Goethe's *Faust* sticking out of his pocket! He was clearly and understandably excited by his latest creation, as is evident in his letter of the 16th to Alma in which he deliberately mixed up the names of people and places. On one occasion Korngold, who was having a quiet conversation with Roller in a café, was spotted by Mahler from the street outside. He described him as being like a wilful cherub as he jumped in through the open window!

As well as performing in *The Marriage of Figaro* under Mahler and two orchestral concerts, the Vienna Philharmonic/Opera orchestra had been engaged to play in a production of *Don Giovanni*. This was produced by the artistic director of the festival Lilli Lehmann and was the opening event on the 14th with a second performance on the 16th. Mahler and Strauss attended the second performance, but they found the production and the conducting of Reynaldo Hahn so awful that they left after the second scene and returned to their hotel for a quiet meal. Their lack of tact was noted, but their feelings were mirrored in the press. The production of *Don Giovanni* might have been a shade better had Mahler not insisted on four days of rehearsal for *Figaro*, already performed several times in Vienna prior to the festival, leaving just two rehearsal slots for Lilli Lehmann. Mahler's excuse was that *Figaro* had to be adapted to the much smaller stage of the Salzburg theatre.

The adapted Hofoper production of *The Marriage of Figaro* was received with enormous enthusiasm by the audiences and the press. Korngold wrote of its enchanting grace, and that nobody who was there would ever forget the occasion. Everyone agreed that it had been the highlight of the festival. Josef Reitler declared it to be the ideal Mozart performance, calling it a marvel and stating how lucky Vienna was to have Mahler, the greatest director, producer and conductor of the day. As a sixteen-year-old, Reitler had been present at the première of Mahler's *First Symphony* witnessing the furore that the music had sparked off, and he had then and there decided to dedicate his life to the furtherance of his music. Angelo Neumann, writing in the *Wiener Fremden-Blatt* five years later, declared that in all his fifty years of opera going these performances of *Figaro* came closest to perfection.

Whilst in Salzburg, Mahler had an interesting conversation with the music critic Bernard Scharlitt during which he put forward his views on the future of opera. He told Scharlitt that the tradition of repertory opera was totally unsuitable for modern opera thought. With higher artistic aims, both musically and in the field of production, it was unreasonable to expect a contemporary opera company to stage several hundred performances during a season on a repertory basis and still expect standards of artistic excellence. Opera companies had to change with the times, and he hinted that he wanted to leave Vienna at a time when his achievements would be remembered if not immediately then in retrospect. He recognised that he was no longer 'new', and anyway he wanted to devote more time to composing. Did he foresee the troubles that lay in store for him, or was he beginning to feel the effects of burn out?

On his return to Maiernigg Mahler wasted no time in getting back to work on the orchestration of his *Eighth Symphony*. Only two weeks of his summer holiday remained, and he was determined to make the most of the little time that he had left before having to return to Vienna. He resumed his usual strict summer routine – rising at five-thirty, a swim, seven hours work before lunch, followed by his afternoon walk and more swimming. As ever fitness of body and mind were all-important to him. He continued to take great care over his diet, which was frugal to say the least, even when entertaining visitors. Among those who came to stay that summer were Alfred Roller and, following Mahler's return from Salzburg, Alexander Zemlinsky, the music critic Ernst Decsey and Julius Korngold. Korngold, so used to the stressed Mahler of Vienna, was pleasantly surprised to find him relaxed, friendly and in good humour, as well as being a good husband and father. During his very short visit Julius Korngold felt that for the first time he had begun to understand the real Mahler, the pain and exaltation that his compositions bestowed upon him, and not just the demons that haunted him in his Vienna existence. More relaxed he may have been, but his thoughts were never very far from the Hofoper, and those great imponderables – God and the meaning of man's existence – were constantly gnawing at his mind.

When Mahler boarded the train at Klagenfurt on the 3rd of September, his summer vacation over and the prospect of yet another year at the Hofoper looming, he could look back over the previous six months with justifiable pride. His achievements at the Vienna Court Opera and in the field of his own music had reached the highest point in his career to date. Little did he know what horrors fate had in store for him during the year to come.

Chapter 13

Vienna . . . Part Seven

The Three Hammer Blows of Fate

WITH ALMA AND the children remaining in Maiernigg together with Anna Moll, Mahler accepted an invitation to stay with Hugo and Ida Conrat in Dornach, a desirable suburb of Vienna. A very cultured and respected couple, their circle of friends had included Brahms and they held regular salons at their apartment in central Vienna. In her memoirs Alma described Ida as having been like a second mother to her when she was a child. Their younger daughter Erica had become one of Alma's friends and had stayed with the Mahlers in Maiernigg during the summer of 1904. Mahler thoroughly enjoyed the company and hospitality of his hosts. Staying with the Conrats enabled him to escape from the clutches of the Hofoper after his day's work. A solicitor by the name of Dr. Richard Horn visited Hugo and Ida while he was there, and described him as being a deep thinker who was content so long as he was able to consume Goethe and apples regularly! Ida's cuisine was a delight, and Gustav told Alma in his letters how smoothly his digestive system was working: no wind, and managing successfully 'to sacrifice to the gods'!

Replacements had to be found for those singers and musicians who had resigned or retired since the end of the previous season, as well as those whose departure was imminent. One appointment that Mahler made was Alexander von Zemlinsky as assistant conductor, which was fully justified on musical grounds. This move strengthened the bond between the two men. Arnold Schoenberg was overjoyed, as indeed was Alma! There was the usual backlog of administrative work to be dealt with, and the very day after his return to Vienna he was on the rostrum conducting a performance of *Tristan und Isolde*. But Mahler was not happy to be back at work. Ending a letter to Willem Mengelberg dated the 12th of September, he stated that he would not be able to take much more of the turmoil at the Hofoper, thus hinting that he was contemplating his future.

To mark the Emperor's name day on the 4th of October Mahler had decided to stage the Vienna première of *Le Juif Polonais* by the French composer Camille Erlanger. Although Mahler had attended a performance in Paris in 1900, it was a strange choice for such an occasion. Alma made a sarcastic comment in her memoirs that he had chosen it because of the use of sleigh bells, which gave it something in common with his *Fourth Symphony*. Perhaps he did have a point to make, with its story of an innkeeper who had killed a Polish Jew fifteen years before and how his deed comes back to haunt him in a nightmare during which he dies of a heart attack! But his enthusiasm for the opera was clearly not that great for, despite the importance of the occasion, he left the conducting to Bruno Walter. The press were unanimous in their condemnation of the work and of Mahler for having chosen it.

On top of this, only two days later, a gala concert was held with the star attraction being an appearance by the renowned Italian tenor Enrico Caruso. At this time Caruso was living in the United States and his agent was Heinrich Conried, the general manager of New York's Metropolitan Opera. Many considered Caruso to be the world's greatest tenor and there was the inevitable scramble for tickets, even at the inflated prices that were being charged. The evening was a fantastic success, but accusations were made that Jewish ticket touts had bought up a huge number of seats reselling them at extortionate prices, that there was a substantial Jewish presence in the audience and that 'good' Viennese people had been unable to attend. As a result anti-Semitism once again reared its ugly head and the knives were being sharpened.

Following this concert and its unfortunate aftermath, Mahler managed to escape to Berlin to attend a performance of his *Sixth Symphony* under the baton of Oskar Fried. He had made a number of revisions prior to this concert and he was well pleased with the results as well as with Fried's conducting. The performance may have been good but some in the audience were baffled, even hostile, with a good number walking out. It also aroused vehement condemnation by almost all the Berlin press. At the end of the same month Fried introduced the citizens of St. Petersburg to Mahler's music. The *Second* seemed to be a good choice, but the majority of the Russian audience, as well as the local critics, were not impressed.

Having returned to Vienna he looked forward to a visit from a group of Parisian friends of his and Alma's, among them General Georges Picquart and Paul and Sophie Clemenceau. To honour their visit he had organised the Hofoper schedules so that performances of *Fidelio*, *Le Nozze di Figaro*, *Die Entführung*, *Die Zauberflöte* and *Tristan und Isolde* might take place during their week's stay, he himself conducting. It had been one of Georges Picquart's greatest desires to be able to attend a performance of *Tristan* conducted by Mahler. The 19th of October was the day that this dream would be fulfilled. With Schmedes as Tristan and Mildenburg as Isolde,

Picquart was so excited that he left for the Hofoper almost an hour ahead of the rest of the party. Alas his dream was shattered, for a telegram arrived from President Georges Clemenceau, Paul's brother, telling him to return to Paris immediately to take over the post of Minister for War. He had no alternative but to leave Vienna by the first available train, thus missing the performance.

Two days after *Tristan* Mahler was once again on his travels, this time to Breslau where he was to conduct his *Third Symphony* as well as four of his orchestral songs, with Friedrich Weidemann as soloist. One can imagine the mutterings in Vienna of 'There he goes again!' As usual while he was away he wrote to Alma daily, and on the 23rd complained that she had not bothered to write to him – Alma was never a good correspondent. Apart from a few boos following the long first movement, the audience was enthusiastic; the press response predictably mixed.

Mahler's cherished plan to stage *Salomé* at the Hofoper was yet again dashed that autumn, for permission continued to be withheld on religious and moral grounds. Instead he arranged for performances of Rossini's *Barber of Seville* and Hermann Goetz's *The Taming of the Shrew*.

As always, and perhaps even more so in 1906, family life in Vienna was constantly disrupted due to Mahler's colossal workload and his frequent travels to further the cause of his own music. Alma had her children to look after, she had her mother on whom she increasingly leaned for support and she had an English nursemaid of a somewhat fussy disposition, but not surprisingly she felt frustrated at being virtually marooned from the social life for which she craved. When Gustav was at home he liked nothing better than to be with his elder daughter. Putzi would spend many private hours with him, and Alma remembered how special these times were for father and daughter. Frequently Putzi would enter the studio clean and tidy, only to emerge a while later covered with jam and with a beaming smile. The bond between them was so strong, and Alma wrote that Putzi was 'his child entirely'.

But these happy times could only take place when he was there, and on the 5th of November he left Vienna for Munich to conduct his *Sixth Symphony* as part of a charity concert to be given by the Kaim Orchestra. While there he went to a performance of Oscar Wilde's *The Importance of Being Ernest* which he thoroughly enjoyed. The Swiss writer William Ritter, who had become an ardent supporter of Mahler and his music, had also travelled to Munich and at last managed to meet the composer. He attended the rehearsals as well as the concert, describing Mahler's *Sixth* as an Alpine symphony of heroic proportions. In his detailed diary of those few days he described him as being far more on edge, more drained in appearance than when he had first seen him five years previously. His legs constantly twitched, yet he showed great patience with the musicians before him.

Preliminary rehearsals had been in the hands of Bernard Stavenhagen, a conductor for whom Mahler did not have a particularly high regard but nevertheless liked as a person. He found the musicians to be positive and hardworking. After the performance the audience insisted that he return to the stage no less than ten times. Having taken his final bow Mahler left the concert hall, leaving Stavenhagen to conduct the final work, Liszt's *First Piano Concerto*, for he had to return to Vienna by the night train. The acclamation must have pleased him, but the press castigated his *Sixth*. Writing to Alma the next day, he said that he had faced 'death by firing squad', quoting one of the reviews. Stavenhagen conducted a repeat performance a week later, thus adding fuel to the fire!

After the concert Ritter wrote to Mahler calling him 'master and friend' and renewed his dedication to him and his music, saying that he intended to write a book in French on the subject. The idol worship that Ritter continued to show him was somewhat surprising coming from the lips of one who was a self-confessed anti-Semite, but Mahler was grateful for his support, knowing that the French had yet to come to terms with his music.

Having returned to Vienna on the 9th of November he made an increasingly rare appearance on the rostrum at the Hofoper that same evening conducting Hermann Goetz's opera *The Taming of the Shrew*. The following day he travelled to Brno where he had been invited to conduct his *First Symphony* on the 11th. This time Alma accompanied him, together with Arnold Rosé and six other members of the Vienna Philharmonic – key players who would help to ensure a good performance. And a great success it was too with Mahler receiving a prolonged ovation, and even the press making complimentary remarks.

Just over a fortnight later he travelled south to the city of Graz having been invited to conduct his *Third Symphony* in support of the Stadttheater's pension fund. The success of the concert during the Graz Festival of June 1905, when thirteen of his lieder had been performed, had prompted the invitation. Again he took with him several reliable musicians from the Vienna Philharmonic. He found the Grand Hotel to be very comfortable, and he was greatly relieved that the vital preliminary rehearsals had been carried out efficiently by the Graz conductor, Friedrich Weigemann. The Graz composer Josef Marx related an amusing incident. Mahler, entering the rehearsal hall smoking a cigarette, was accosted by an attendant who squared up to him saying, '*Rauchen ist verboten!*', to which Mahler replied, '*Ich bin Mahler*'. *Maler* being the German for painter, the attendant told him bluntly that even for painters smoking was prohibited. So he had been called a disaster in Paris (*Malheur*) and a painter in Graz!

This performance of the *Third* was a phenomenal success and must have brought back memories of his Krefeld triumph in 1902. Although the audience was not entirely won over by the first movement, their enthusiasm increased and at the end of the final movement they were in complete rapture. So successful was it in fact that he was invited to conduct a further performance on the 23rd of December. However, Prince Alfred Montenuovo, Lord Chamberlain and administrator of the Hofoper, accused him of neglecting his duties as Director. Mahler's reply that by gaining prestige conducting his own works in other countries he would enhance the standing of the Vienna Opera was not entirely convincing. Although undoubtedly still concerned with maintaining high standards at the Hofoper, yet tired of the constant hassles there, he had given the furtherance of his own music precedence. For once his critics had a valid point, and secretly he would have had to agree with them.

At the beginning of 1907, the year that would turn out to be Mahler's *annus horribilis*, he had decided to conduct the Viennese première of his *Sixth Symphony*. The date of the concert was the 4th of January, but with a lack of interest being shown by the Vienna Philharmonic he reluctantly agreed to use the lesser talents of the Koncertverein Orchestra. The musicians were not used to his methods and his search for perfection, and he was reported as telling them that it was only through criticism, not compliments, that he had managed to achieve anything in the past. Fear spread throughout the orchestra, but he won them over. The symphony was greeted by a battle royal between his supporters and his foes. For the first time he had managed to virtually unite the press against him, even Korngold finding it hard to write anything positive. The general opinion was that his symphony was more catastrophic than 'Tragic'. Mahler was deeply hurt, but he should not have been surprised for he must have been fully aware of the increasing criticism being levelled at him as Director of the Hofoper. He wrote to Mengelberg saying that he felt unable to bring himself to conduct the planned performance in Amsterdam, scheduled for later that month. In fact he would never again conduct his *Sixth Symphony*.

The New Year also saw a concerted campaign against Mahler regarding his frequent absences from Vienna. He was accused of neglecting important works by revered composers and for showing favouritism to a few singers, some of whom were well past their prime, Anna von Mildenburg being one. Other very talented artists were being sidelined or used as understudies. There was a degree of truth in these criticisms, and those who remained close to him (not just singers, Bruno Walter being a case in point) began to be tarred with the same brush. Despite this mounting pressure, compounded by several members of the Hofoper company being absent on sick leave, Mahler continued on his merry-go-round of travels. Next on the list was Berlin for a performance of his *Third Symphony* on the 14th of January.

Upon arrival Gustav wrote to Alma admitting that the incessant travelling was wearing him down, but that there was no choice for the furtherance of his own music was of the utmost importance to him. He enjoyed the company of Arnold Berliner, and together they went to a performance of *Salomé*, Strauss having left two tickets at the hotel reception. There had been no problems of censorship in Berlin where Strauss was held in such high regard, both as a composer and the city's foremost conductor. In fact the German city was only too delighted to be regarded as more progressive than its archrival Vienna! Mahler's opinion of Strauss's opera remained as high as ever, describing it as brilliant and without doubt one of the most important works of that era. With *Salomé* Mahler's feeling towards Strauss as a composer had changed. No longer did he believe that his sole aim was simply to gain popular acclaim and financial rewards. He had now come to regard him as potentially a forward-looking musician like himself and consequently his respect for him had increased a hundred-fold. Two days later Mahler and Berliner attended a further performance of *Salomé,* afterwards joining Strauss and his wife Pauline for dinner.

Rehearsals for the *Third Symphony* had been going well, although Mahler found the musicians of the Berlin orchestra to be inferior to those of the Vienna Philharmonic. Nevertheless he described them as being very experienced and attentive. Open to the public, the dress rehearsal took place at midday on the 13th. Great applause rang out as he made his way to the front of the orchestra and at the end of each movement he received more applause. Unable to attend the performance the following evening due to his conducting commitments, Strauss made a point of being present at the final rehearsal. He wrote to Mahler afterwards saying how impressed he was with his 'magnificent work', and that he was pleased that at last audiences were beginning to understand and love his music. Lavish praise indeed from Strauss, but probably exaggerated. Perhaps it was more of a reciprocal gesture for Mahler's continued support and very genuine belief in *Salomé* as a work of genius. Strauss had never, nor would ever, consider Mahler to be a composer of stature. To him the importance of Mahler remained as an ally who could promote his works as well as being a quite exceptional conductor. For his part, Mahler still found it difficult to understand Strauss's character and his attitude to composing. In a letter to Alma he described him as being like a Vulcan living and working beneath a slagheap. Yet he could not help but respect the phenomenon that was Strauss. As for his wife Pauline, Mahler's feelings towards her had most certainly not altered. Her rudeness and cutting remarks aimed at her husband in company were a constant embarrassment. One of a number of utterances that Gustav related to Alma took place over lunch when Pauline suddenly exclaimed that if only they had a few million then her husband could stop 'manufacturing' music!

The audience who had come to hear the *Third* on the 14th were as generous in their applause as those who had been present at the final rehearsal. Mahler was delighted with the performance, describing it as 'magnificent', but most of the critics took a different view of the concert. Waiting for his train for Frankfurt, the next city on his itinerary, he read a report in the *Bösencourier* which stated that he was talentless and useless at orchestration, that the music lacked ideas and was at times nothing less than vulgar. Not all writers were quite so damning, but the general opinion was negative. The newspapers also carried stories that the Hofoper had run into serious financial difficulties and that Mahler had, or was about to, resign from his post as Director! According to Ludwig Karpath a witch-hunt was under way. However he stated that the rumours were entirely without foundation for as long as Prince Montenuovo remained in overall charge Mahler's position was secure. Nevertheless Mahler said that he felt like a stag being pursued by a pack of hounds in full cry. In another reference to the canine, he wrote that the 'dogs' were mistaking him for a lamp-post!

Having arrived in Frankfurt, he set about rehearsing his *Fourth Symphony* for a concert to be held on the 18th of January. Previously conducted there by Weingartner, he regarded this as a chance to redress the hostile reception it had received in 1901. The concert, which also included Schumann's *First Symphony*, was a qualified success. Most of the audience applauded him both as conductor and composer, although a minority made their feelings heard with a chorus of boos and whistles. The press, although not as vitriolic as their Berlin counterparts, were little more than polite.

He wrote to Willem Mengelberg saying that regrettably it would be unlikely that he would be able to travel to Amsterdam that year. Doubtless Mahler's heavy schedule as well as the increasing pressures in Vienna were to blame, for staying with the Mengelbergs and conducting his music in Amsterdam had in the past given him so much pleasure. He suggested that Mengelberg should go ahead with the planned performance of the *Sixth* without him.

The final port of call on this tour was Linz where he was booked to conduct his *First Symphony* as part of a concert that also included three of his lieder. One of the plus points of this particular tour had been the willingness and total cooperation of the musicians, no more so than in Linz where his *First Symphony* was generally well received. The time had come for him to return to Vienna to face the music, so to speak.

The press articles that he had read whilst waiting for his train to Frankfurt were only the tip of the iceberg. A vicious anti-Mahler campaign, stirred up by some of his arch critics such as Richard Wallaschek of *Die Zeit* and Hans Liebstöckl writing in *Illustrirtes Extrablatt*, had not only taken hold but was deepening in its intensity by the day. Even the government backed newspaper *Fremdenblatt*, hitherto on the whole supportive of Mahler's work at the Hofoper, began to criticise him. Conveniently forgotten by many of his foes were the vast improvements brought about during his tenure as Director: the improved discipline, the higher musical standards of both musicians and singers, the at times awe-inspiring albeit controversial productions, especially with his continuing partnership with Alfred Roller, and above all the consistent brilliance of his conducting. True, Mahler was tired out from the burdens of running the Hofoper; true, he himself wondered how much longer he would be able to cope with his responsibilities and the continual criticism; true, he wanted to devote more time to composition and the furtherance of his own music. But despite all these points it was not in his nature, nor in his interests to shirk his responsibilities at the Vienna Court Opera. However, most of the newspapers and journals were gunning for him and they would not rest until he had tendered his resignation.

His ever-increasing absences not surprisingly came top of the list, leaving the conducting to his not so capable assistants such as Franz Schalk and Bruno Walter, but he was attacked on several other fronts as well. The repertoire had become unimaginative with many popular operas being neglected in favour of second rate Vienna premières. The utter extravagance of some new productions had led to financial problems, and frequently the quality of performance had not justified the outlay. He was blamed for the loss of popular singers due to his favouritism of others and his harsh treatment of those who would not obey his every word. He was accused of being neurotic and a bully, and for milking the Hofoper for his own ends, the whole organization becoming totally demoralized. Yet even Liebstöckl had to admit that during the first two years of Mahler's reign he had managed to raise standards at the Hofoper. Underlying much of this vicious campaign was the steadfast determination by many to oust the 'Jew' Mahler from the premier post in the world of opera. There were a few critics who sprang to his defence, most notably Julius Korngold and to a lesser extent Ludwig Karpath, but their Canute-like efforts to stem the tide of abuse were to little avail. Even Korngold criticised Mahler's promotion of young talent at the expense of excellence. He stated that there were too many 'little people' being employed by the Court Opera, and that half a tenor and half a bass did not add up to a whole opera singer.

Despite this barrage of criticism and abuse that greeted Mahler's return to Vienna, work at the Hofoper had to go on. Having received an assurance of support from Prince Montenuovo the immediate task at hand was the new Mahler-Roller production of *Die Walküre*. One of his long held ambitions had been to stage a new and memorable production of Wagner's music drama. This would be his reply to those who wished him gone. Preparations had of course been going on during his absence. Realism not symbolism formed the basis of this important production with dramatic sets and lighting effects as usual replacing the old painted backdrops. Two revolving stages were used so that set changes would not interrupt the flow. Attention to detail was paramount, Roller taking note of Wagner's own ideas, although he overlaid these with his own particular brand of magic that included lightning effects, starry skies, spot-lit details and fire, along with re-thought costumes. A widely held criticism was that certain scenes, such as in Hunding's hut in the first act, were far too dark – not for the first time that Roller had been criticised on this front. Creation of a sense of intimacy complete with dark facial shadows was thought to be more appropriate in paintings than on a stage, for the audience, especially those not sitting at the front, found it difficult to see clearly what was going on. Anna von Mildenburg complained to Mahler who agreed and suggested that she should approach Roller herself!

If doubts were held by some regarding Roller's contribution to this new production of *Die Walküre*, musically it was a resounding success. The experienced cast had acquitted themselves magnificently with Mildenburg, Weidermann, Schmedes and Foerster-Lauterer earning extravagant praise. And what of Herr Direktor Mahler, the target of so much abuse? Even the majority of his arch critics found it hard not to be enthusiastic, especially in the face of the overwhelming acclamations of the audience. The standing ovations were clearly tempered by sympathy for Mahler and the problems he was facing. For the time being at least he had held the hounds at bay. He had replied to his critics in no uncertain terms as Richard Wallaschek had to admit. Even Hirschfeld used words such as 'inspired . . . rapture . . . passionate . . . the last act imbued with a strength and purity not heard until now' – these comments from one of his severest critics. Otto Klemperer was lost for words – to him it was perfection.

On the 5th of February he attended the first performance of Schoenberg's *String Quartet, Op. 7* in the Bösendorfer Hall, played by the Rosé Quartet, founded by Arnold Rosé and his brother Eduard. Mahler was always prepared to support up and coming composers, not least Schoenberg. Alma recalled how the performance began quietly until an unnamed critic suddenly shouted 'Stop!' This triggered off an anti-Schoenberg demonstration with one individual apparently confronting the composer and hissing at him. Mahler leapt to Schoenberg's defence. The abuser was all set to physically attack Mahler when Carl Moll burst through the audience and managed to separate them. Moll, a man of far larger stature than the demonstrator, proceeded to march him out of the hall, whereupon he made a parting comment that he also hissed at Mahler's concerts.

Three days later Schoenberg's *Chamber Symphony, Op. 9* was performed in the Musikvereinsaal. When noisy scraping of chairs started to accompany the music as members of the audience began to leave midway through, Mahler again took action, standing and insisting on silence, and at the end he very publicly applauded. Afterwards Guido Adler told Alma that such actions by her husband might well cost him his job. He told her that she should try to dissuade him from making any further exhibitions of such a nature. Adler added that he went home and wept at the path that music was following.

Mahler freely admitted that he did not understand Schoenberg's music, saying that he was old and perhaps the young man was right; only time would tell. But disrespect for a genuine artist he would not tolerate, a sympathy born out of his own experiences and the frequently rough and unfair treatment he himself had so often suffered when his own ground-breaking music had been performed. Mahler's very public support for Schoenberg did indeed weaken his position still further, for Schoenberg and his music, widely regarded as a sick joke, were being ridiculed and attacked even more than Mahler and his symphonies. Nevertheless he had been greatly impressed by the quartet and wrote to Richard Strauss recommending the work for the forthcoming Dresden Festival. He told Strauss that the Rosé Quartet, led by his brother-in-law Arnold Rosé, would be prepared to perform it without fee so long as their expenses were met. He ended his letter by thanking Strauss for sending him the score of *Salomé*, which never left his desk.

Following the success of *Die Walküre* Mahler's foes prepared themselves for their next onslaught, but what they had not anticipated was a production that many considered to be his finest achievement at the Hofoper: Gluck's lyric tragedy *Iphigénie en Aulide* in the version revised by Richard Wagner in 1847 and sung in German. For Mahler this was a labour of love, and not just because it was one of Wagner's favourite operas. He knew that his days at the Hofoper were numbered and, as he told Berta Zuckerkandl, he had put his all into this production, which might well turn out to be his farewell.

The Roller-Mahler wizardry had cast its spell. Performed behind a thin gauze curtain, a dreamlike atmosphere was created, a continuous flow of classical 'paintings' of ancient Greece. Many of Roller's ideas were based on designs used on Greek pottery. Following meticulous research Roller's sets and costumes worked to perfection and his lighting effects were quite magical. On the 18th of March, the day of the first performance, Emil Zuckerkandl saw Mahler staring at a poster on an advertising pillar on the Ringstrasse. Upon asking him why he was so absorbed, Mahler replied that he could not take his eyes off the *Iphigénie* poster, that every time he saw one he could not help but stop and stare. He found it hard to believe that this long-cherished dream was at last about to come true that very evening. Emil was very moved by Mahler's demeanour, and on returning home told Berta that there had been almost an aura of holiness about him – a far cry from the popular cartoonist's image of a foot stamping, shouting little dictator.

With a superlative and inspired cast led by Mildenburg, Gutheil-Schoder and Schmedes, matched magnificently by the orchestra in top form, this production marked one of the highest achievements in the history of the Vienna Opera. Lilli Lehmann wrote in 1913 that it was Mahler's greatest. In her view it had more clarity and spiritual harmony than any other classical work of art that she could think of. With the anti-Mahler press campaign virtually silenced by *Die Walküre*, *Iphigénie* left the critics with little alternative other than to launch into superlatives. However, despite this enthusiasm, anti-Mahler mutterings continued. Like a cancer the movement to rid Vienna of his services had taken hold and was spreading relentlessly. With no further progress on the *Salomé* front and a tightening of the Imperial purse strings, which meant a shelving of any idea of completing the new *Ring*, Mahler knew that it was only a matter of time before he would be forced to resign on artistic grounds if nothing else.

Despite the brilliance of *Iphigénie*, and the widespread praise that it had justifiably earned, unrest was continuing to spread at the Hofoper with many singers and musicians looking forward to the day when they would have a new director. Opera audiences too were becoming tired of the now regular anti-Mahler demonstrations that frequently disrupted performances, and many seats remained unsold, even for the remarkable *Iphigénie en Aulide*. More serious still was a rift that had developed between Mahler and Prince Montenuovo.

As usual the Opera was to close over Easter. Mahler had been invited to conduct two concerts in Rome, returning to Vienna on Easter Tuesday. He had entered the dates in the Hofoper diary. However the Easter break of 1907 was shorter than usual with the Opera opening its doors on the very day that he was due to return to Vienna. Unfortunately he had failed to seek permission to be absent and, in a climate of considerable unrest and instability, Montenuovo was understandably furious when he was told. Mahler was duly summoned, rowed with his most important ally and offered to resign. He was somewhat taken aback when Montenuovo accepted that when the time was right he could go, and set about discussing such matters as severance pay! Petty this may have seemed, but Montenuovo himself was becoming increasingly worried that his support for Mahler might be weakening the foundations of his own authority.

Shortly before this Montenuovo's support for him had been brought into question over another matter. It was no secret that Mahler had little time for ballet, but as Director of the Hofoper he was obliged to supervise the staging of this particular genre. Roller, to whom he habitually gave his full backing, requested that he be given the opportunity not only to be the designer of sets and costumes but also to be responsible for the choreography. Mahler had agreed to this proposal and consequently charged Roller with a new production of Auber's *La Muette de Portici*. The resident ballet-master Josef Hassreiter, who had been in his post for twenty years, was understandably furious and insisted on seeing Prince Montenuovo immediately! The latter was sympathetic with his ballet master. When Mahler continued to back Roller, Montenuovo showed his displeasure in no uncertain terms saying bluntly that he had deliberately supported an irregularity. Alma later stated that it was this confrontation that finally persuaded Montenuovo that he would have to be replaced. Mahler knew full well that his position was becoming increasingly untenable for many were watching his every move, taking every opportunity to publicly criticise him and frequently doing so by distorting the truth. However, following the double successes of *Die Walküre* and *Iphigénie,* he had once again proved his worth. There was no young pretender waiting in the wings whose ability and dedication could in any way be compared to his. With his letter of resignation already lying in one of the drawers of his desk, his imperial masters were, for the time being at least, loath to let him go.

Without waiting for the plaudits resulting from *Iphigénie,* Gustav and Alma boarded a train for Rome for the two concerts he would be conducting on the 25th of March and the 1st of April. The journey turned out to be rather eventful. Alma wrote how the train suddenly jolted to a halt at Semmering with passengers leaping from their bunks – not Mahler, who took the opportunity to get some sleep. It was three hours before the train was able to proceed, but the engine broke down on two more occasions, resulting in the Mahlers missing their connection, and even worse their luggage went astray in which were the orchestral scores for the two concerts!

With only the clothes they were wearing and the score of Mahler's own *Seventh Symphony,* top priority on reaching their destination was a shopping expedition and for Gustav to hire a dress suit for his appearances on the Roman rostrum. Accustomed to fine materials he found the shirts in particular very uncomfortable. Being small of stature the only dress suit available for hire had been designed for a much taller man and made Gustav look decidedly Chaplinesque! There was no alternative, but he refused to let Alma make any alterations other than a few tucks in the sleeves and minor adjustments to the trousers aided by a large gold safety pin situated in a strategic position at the front.

Alma recalled how her husband enjoyed the historical aspects of Rome, especially the Forum and the Via Appia, but that he was constantly on edge, irritable and abrupt both when they were on their own and in company. Doubtless the problems in Vienna and what the future might have in store for him weighed heavily on his mind. The orchestra he found to be not of the highest calibre, which hardly helped his tense mental state. The musicians were tired after a busy schedule and less committed than those that Mahler was used to dealing with. They were in dire need of inspiration and Mahler's renowned brand of discipline.

He had intended to include some of his own music in the concerts, but with the scores gone astray together with his doubts about the ability and attitude of the orchestra he decided otherwise. He played safe putting together two classical programmes, the main works being Beethoven's *Third* and *Seventh Symphonies*. Many of the musicians found his demands to be an unpleasant shock, but it was generally agreed by audiences and press alike that the standard of playing and Mahler's very personal interpretations of the works performed came as something of a revelation.

Mahler broke his return journey from Rome for a concert in Trieste on the 4th of April. Performed were Beethoven's *Fifth* and his own *First Symphony*, and both were enthusiastically received. His all too brief escape from Vienna thus came to an end and he braced himself for the barrage of criticism that he knew would greet him.

Alma felt unwell on their return from Italy, and to make matters worse they discovered that their English nurse, Lizzie Turner, had scalded three of Gucki's fingers. Alma wrote however that their younger daughter was not just suffering from burnt fingers, she had also developed a fever – scarlet fever was diagnosed. Putzi was immediately taken to the Molls to avoid contagion. When Gucki had recovered sufficiently Alma went to a nursing home for an operation. As usual Anna Moll stepped in to look after the children. Mahler too had been under the weather. In addition to his susceptibility to migraines, for some weeks he had been suffering from an increasing number of sore throats. Understandably these he linked to the mounting tension in his work life. With the summer holiday only a few days hence, he believed that plenty of fresh air and exercise would soon restore his normal fitness.

Before Mahler had left Vienna for his Italian tour, with the help of his lawyer friend Emil Freund, he had managed to negotiate an increase in his pension, payable after ten years of service, from 11,000 to 14,000 kronen. In addition there would be a one-off sum of 20,000 kronen as an expenses payment when the time came for him to leave Vienna. These details became known to the *Deutsche Zeitung,* which considered such unheard of increases to be scandalous for one who had mismanaged the Vienna Opera, which, according to the article, was going to rack and ruin while Mahler was on yet another conducting tour abroad simply for his own ends. This article signalled a new and more vicious than ever campaign against him. Rebellion was in the air, compounded by popular tenor Fritz Schrödter's refusal to accept a new contract with a remuneration of only two-thirds of his previous one. Schrödter complained to Prince Montenuovo who summoned Mahler. Another unfortunate confrontation resulted during which Mahler produced his resignation in waiting, which the prince immediately accepted, much to his surprise. When tempers had cooled both men agreed that it was in their own best interests that their confrontation should not be made public. Anyway, any termination of his appointment had to be agreed to by the Emperor himself, and then only after a suitable replacement had been found. More problems arose with Lucy Weidt resigning after what she considered to be a broken promise by Mahler for her to sing the part of Desdemona in *Otello.* Then Schmedes refused to step in for the sick Slezak, the former having arranged to appear in Frankfurt. The press began to attack Montenuovo for constantly backing Mahler, yet the resignation issue was still on hold and plans were being laid for the 1907-1908 season. Mahler and Montenuovo managed to hold the hounds at bay for a while at any rate by arranging an increase in pay for the musicians, chorus and dancers of the Hofoper.

Alarmed by the rumours of Mahler's departure, many influential names in the world of the arts signed a statement declaring how devastated they were at the possibility of Vienna losing his services as a result of the disgraceful campaign that was being waged against him. A long list of signatories included Gustav Klimt, Kolo Moser, Arnold Schoenberg, Ludwig Bösendorfer, Julius Epstein, Hugo von Hofmannsthal and Max Burckhard, later joined by others including Sigmund Freud and Lilli Lehmann. Although touched by their very public support, Mahler nevertheless made it clear in an interview he gave for the *Neues Wiener Tagblatt* that it was not true that he was being forced to leave as a result of the press campaign against him. Rather he was planning to leave in order to have greater freedom and more time for composing. He also hit out at the accusations levelled against him that he had been personally responsible for running the Hofoper into a state of serious and increasing deficit. He pointed out that budgets were drawn up a year in advance, and that short-term fluctuations would always occur, such as the recent fall in receipts due to unusually hot weather. Indeed he predicted that 1907 would end on a profitable note. Yet in a letter to his friend Arnold Berliner, he admitted that he would be leaving the Hofoper because he could no longer tolerate the rabble. Likewise he told Bruno Walter that his mind was made up. After working for ten years at the Hofoper he felt that he had completed a cycle. It was time to go, as confirmed by Roller in a letter to his wife in which he wrote, 'if only it be known how relieved he was to depart'.

Despite the escalating turmoil, Mahler remained dedicated to his work, refusing, outwardly at least, to be affected by the barrage of attacks. The journalist Josef Reitler confirmed this. Having just arrived in Vienna from Paris to take up a post with the *Neue Freie Presse*, Mahler invited him to meet him at the Opera and to attend a performance of *Fidelio*, saying that the auditorium would probably be half empty. Arriving at five o'clock, he found Mahler already changed and studying the score, which of course he had conducted many times and knew by heart, but every time he studied it he had new insights and with them renewed inspiration. Conducting such a masterpiece was a sacred duty and privilege, and no amount of external pressure would distract him.

The apparent water off a duck's back attitude that he had adopted was undoubtedly helped by the knowledge that he would be leaving soon anyway, yet he remained determined that his departure would be of his own accord, on his own terms and that under no circumstances would he be forced out by his enemies. But the pressure continued to mount, despite the efforts of his supporters and the occasional pro Mahler article.

Three possible replacements had been discussed: Nikisch, who declined the offer, Ernst von Schuch of Dresden and Felix Mottl of Munich (Mahler's preferred candidate). According to Alma nobody liked the idea of being Mahler's successor, nor to take on such enormous responsibilities for so little money. By this time news of Mahler's likely exit from Vienna had spread throughout the music world. A number of opera houses had begun to show interest, none more so than the Metropolitan Opera of New York and its chief administrator Heinrich Conried who just happened to be in Berlin. On the 4th of June Mahler caught a train for the German capital to discuss Conried's proposals. He soon discovered just how poorly paid he had been in Vienna by comparison. With offers on the table of four year contracts of either six months a year totalling half a million kronen or six to eight week guest contracts totalling two hundred thousand kronen, Mahler was understandably very tempted. But he wanted to spend most of each year in Europe, to devote far more time to composing and enjoying family life. Finally they agreed on a three-month contract, initially for one year, running from the 15th of January to the 15th of April at a salary of seventy-five thousand kronen ($15,000) plus expenses. The main works to be performed were to be by Wagner and Mozart, as well as his own *Second Symphony*! A week later, leaked news of Mahler's engagement at the Metropolitan Opera appeared in the New York press. With final details still to be worked out, the die had now been cast and the relief for Mahler must have been considerable.

A final petition, a statement of support penned by Anna von Mildenburg and Marie Gutheil-Schoder, was circulated amongst the staff at the Hofoper, but it was largely ignored.

Meanwhile problems began to arise regarding the appointment of a successor. When news broke in Munich of Felix Mottl's possible move to Vienna there was uproar. A combination of embarrassing revelations of Frau Mottl's financial improprieties and of generous offers, awards, rewards and an extended contract for her husband resulted in Felix Mottl stating publicly that he was not a candidate. Doubts also began to arise over Schuch's availability, let alone the fact that he was in his sixty-first year. Prince Montenuovo began to panic and begged Mahler to reconsider and stay, but to no avail. His mind was made up, and no amount of bribery, financial or otherwise, would get him to change his mind. Yet the key problem still existed: he would not be able to go until a successor had been found. An article in the *Neue Freie Presse* by Max Burckhard, which appeared on the 16th of June, criticised the authorities, asking what on earth were they doing letting Mahler go after the many great artistic achievements at the Court Opera during his tenure. Three days earlier a poll of Vienna's music establishment indicated that most wanted him to stay. New candidates were sought including Karl Muck and Franz Schalk, already associated with the Hofoper. Richard Strauss's name was mentioned, but that was wishful thinking, especially after the Hofoper's repeated rejection of *Salomé*. Another name put forward was Felix Weingartner, at that time working in Berlin. The foreign press joined in the criticism of Vienna, the *Prague Tagblatt* insinuating that the authorities did not know what they were doing allowing such a genius as Mahler to leave.

Having signed the contract for the 'Met' on the 21st of June, the time had come for Mahler to extricate himself from the Vienna maelstrom. He set off by train for Hochschneeberg to the south west of Vienna and en route to Maiernigg. Coincidentally two of his travelling companions were Anna von Mildenburg and Hermann Bahr. Despite the foggy weather and still suffering from migraines, which he did his best to walk off, he relished the peace and quiet and a much needed chance to unwind. He wrote to Alma saying how wonderful the place was and that he had reserved a room for her for September. But this peace and quiet turned out to be the calm before a particularly tragic storm.

On the 1st of July Gustav, Alma and the little girls were reunited at their holiday home in Maiernigg on the southern shore of the Wörthersee. Home at last in the countryside that was closest to his heart, the setting of so much happiness, and his *Häuschen* in the forest where the muse had spoken to him so clearly in the past.

Hardly had they settled in when, on the third day of their holiday, Putzi fell ill. An unintentional but dreadful mistake had been made – Gucki had rejoined her sister too soon. Still contagious from scarlet fever she had passed on the illness she no longer appeared to be suffering from to her sister. A local doctor by the name of Blumenthal examined her. She was developing diptheria as well as scarlet fever. Initially, although obviously concerned, Gustav and Alma were positive about Putzi's recovery. Surely with the peace and quiet of Maiernigg and with plenty of fresh air she would recover. On the same day as Dr. Blumenthal's diagnosis Mahler wrote to Arnold Berliner telling him that his contract with Conried had been drawn up. It would be for four years at the previously agreed sum of a total of 300,000 kronen ($60,000) plus expenses. He asked Berliner if he would be able to visit them during August.

Their optimism was short lived, for the little girl's condition deteriorated rapidly. The sense of doom was echoed by the weather with gloomy skies and thunderstorms. Under normal circumstances Mahler loved the 'Wagnerian' drama of such weather, not then. With Putzi struggling to breathe her father spent most of his time shut away in his study where he was unable to hear the agony that his beloved daughter was going through. The night came when Putzi's breathing became so critical that she was in danger of suffocation, and consequently Dr. Blumenthal made preparations to carry out a tracheotomy. Gustav's servant Anton was posted outside his room to prevent him from witnessing what was about to take place, and Alma was told by the doctor not to be present either. She fled the house and ran along the shore of the Wörthersee crying her eyes out. At five o'clock in the morning the English nurse, Miss Turner, found Alma and told her that the operation was over. Alma described how her beautiful daughter lay wide-eyed and gasping for breath. Gustav, totally inconsolable and unable to stand the sound of Putzi's final struggle for life, left the house.

The following day, on the morning of the 12th of July, four-year-old Maria Anna died. The daughter whom he had doted over so much and with whom he had spent so many happy secret hours was gone, and Alma's superstitious fears over his composing *Die Kindertotenlieder* had become a reality. With her Gustav had enjoyed a childhood happiness he had been deprived of during his own tender years; guilt and bitter early memories enhanced his grief. Anna Moll made haste to Maiernigg, and together they shared a room for they felt like 'birds in a storm', fearful of what the future had in store for them.

Two days later, Gustav told Alma and her mother to go for a walk along the shore of the Wörthersee while he remained at the house. Anna Moll then fainted from exhaustion at the water's edge. Distraught, and she too in a state of near collapse, Alma looked up when she heard footsteps approaching. It was Gustav, his face drawn and ashen, and behind him she saw the little coffin being lifted into the hearse.

Totally drained by the traumas of the past week, Alma began to suffer from palpitations. Dr. Blumenthal was immediately summoned to examine both women. He found Anna to be tired but healthy and he told Alma that it was essential for her to have a long and complete rest. Relieved that neither Alma nor Anna had a serious heart problem, Gustav, in an effort to distract them, suggested that perhaps Dr. Blumenthal could check him as well. Gustav lay down on a sofa, but while examining him and listening to his heart, the doctor's expression turned very serious, and he commented 'You've no right to be proud of having a heart like yours!' For Mahler the fitness fanatic this came as a bombshell.

An appointment was made straight away for him to see a Viennese specialist, Professor Kovacs. He travelled to Vienna on the 17th of July leaving Alma and Anna Moll, with the help of the servants, to pack and to be ready to go to whatever destination they decided upon following his meeting with Kovacs.

Dr. Kovacs confirmed that Mahler had a heart problem, but his prognosis that it was life-threatening is thought to have been far from correct. Certainly he had a valvular irregularity as described by Alma and indeed later by Mahler himself in the first movement of his *Ninth Symphony*. This was partly inherited, but had been exacerbated by his frequent bouts of streptococcal infection that had resulted in lesions. Before being examined by Dr. Blumenthal he had felt physically fit, and writing to Alma the day before his appointment with Kovacs he reminded her to pack his cycling clothes. Therefore, with no obvious physical impairment, it is clear that Kovacs had clearly exaggerated Mahler's condition. Although there is no concrete evidence it is possible that Alma, who had herself been treated by Kovacs in the past, had asked him to persuade Mahler to slow down on his physical exertions – apart from his heart, less physical activity would mean more attention to her! Whether this is true or not, Kovacs told Mahler bluntly that he should avoid any form of physical exertion such as long walks, swimming, rowing and cycling. Despite the important part that such forms of exercise had played in his life, both for fitness and as a catalyst for inspiration, Mahler had been frightened by Kovacs' erroneous advice, and he now feared that such activities might indeed kill him. Consequently with immediate effect he changed his routine. With watch and pedometer as his companions, and taking his pulse at regular intervals, he had to learn to walk slowly – a new experience for him! His walks were to be limited initially to five minutes, to be increased gradually in five-minute stages.

The Mahlers spent the remaining days of their summer holiday at a hotel in the small hamlet of Schluderbach between Toblach and Lake Misurina, one of Mahler's favourite areas with its spectacular Dolomite scenery. With the recent tragedy still haunting them, they felt unable to return to Maiernigg. Grieving in silence, as was his nature, and very much on edge, he insinuated that Alma's mother was largely responsible for Putzi's illness and subsequent death by sending Gucki home too soon after her bout of scarlet fever. This inevitably created added strain to an already very fraught situation. However, with the inspiring scenery laced with his own sorrow, the seeds of his next composition were sown. As Alma noted, Putzi's death and Gustav's grief had changed his perspective of the importance of things and this is clearly reflected in his music from this point onwards.

Theobald Pollak, a retired civil servant and close friend of Alma's late father Emil Schindler, had sent Mahler an advance copy of a collection of poems entitled 'Die Chinesische Flöte' (The Chinese Flute). Pollak considered that these poems translated by Hans Bethge, based on the Chinese originals by poets including Li-Tai-Po in a French translation, might give Mahler some much needed inspiration during those dark days. Pollak was right. During the early years of the 20th century an interest in Chinoiserie had become fashionable, and for some time Mahler himself had shown a growing regard for eastern philosophy. He was greatly moved by the poems and made the first tentative sketches of a new work during their stay at Schluderbach and at Fischleinboden where they spent the final days of their holiday before returning to Vienna via Maiernigg.

Amidst all the gloom came a ray of light. In a letter dated the 10th of August, Prince Montenuovo informed Mahler that Felix Weingartner had been appointed as his successor with effect from that autumn. At last he would be free from the shackles of the Hofoper and could make definite plans for his future at the New York Metropolitan Opera. Montenuovo also confirmed that his financial demands had been met in full: 20,000 kronen to cover the costs of the move, a 14,000 kronen pension and a 2,000 kronen a year widow's pension for Alma.

With this good news the Mahlers returned to Maiernigg to pack their belongings before putting the villa on the market. After the tragedy in July there was little choice for they knew that they could no longer stay there. The replacement would be their main home with Mahler's New York contract committing him for just three months each year. And yet they felt a certain sorrow at the thought of leaving Maiernigg, the scene of so much inspiration and happy times.

Emil Freund had joined them at Maiernigg to discuss various legal matters in connection with the sale of the villa and, of course, Mahler's future. Leaving Alma and the servant Anton to finish packing, the two men returned to Vienna. Mahler stayed with the Molls, and in his letter to Alma dated the 25th of August, he informed her that there was a threat of a smallpox epidemic in Vienna, and advised her to get Dr. Blumenthal to vaccinate her, Gucki and nurse Lizzie Turner as soon as possible. He also mentioned that Julius Korngold had sent a reporter to interview him for the following day's edition of the *Neue Freie Presse*. In this article Mahler stressed that he would continue to dedicate himself to the Hofoper until Weingartner was able to take up the reins, and that he planned to sail for America the following January. A somewhat fictional piece appeared the same day in the *Wiener Mittagszeitung* stating that he had apparently sold his Maiernigg home, bought a villa in Mödling (just south of Vienna) and had written a symphony about Faust's death! He sent both articles to Alma saying how much the latter had amused him!

A third and very accurate article appeared as a result of an interview with Josef Reitler, also for the *Neue Freie Presse*. This was one that Mahler was pleased to give, for he knew that through Josef Reitler, a loyal supporter of his music, he would be able to speak his mind on certain points without the fear of his views being distorted. In it he pointed out that most people were simply unaware of the problems arising from running an organisation like the Hofoper in the manner that was expected. With such a variety of works and different styles, nightly performances and an inevitable lack of rehearsals, it was no wonder that the highest standards could not always be maintained. He told Reitler that when he had first taken on the directorship of the Hofoper ten years before he had felt that it was possible to achieve consistently high artistic standards, but that he had come to realise that with the system as it was this goal was simply not possible. The organisation was at fault, and the fact that commercial considerations had become more important than artistic ones had meant that he was unable to reconcile the demands made upon him with his artistic principles. He ended by once again stressing that the decision to resign was entirely his.

He also received a letter from Weingartner in which he said how much he hoped that their past friendship, despite lying dormant for some years, might be renewed and that he looked forward to their next meeting in Vienna. Mahler did not have the greatest respect for Weingartner, especially after his withdrawal of the *Fourth Symphony* from already scheduled concerts in Munich and Berlin due to hostility at previous performances.

He presumed that this 'making up' on the part of Weingartner was shallow, his intention being to placate him in order to seek his help and influence when settling into the very hot seat at the Hofoper! In a letter to Alma, Mahler referred to Weingartner's message as 'a love letter'.

Having told Alma to make sure that both she and Gucki were vaccinated against smallpox, he did likewise and at the same time asked the doctor whom he saw to give another opinion about his heart condition. The doctor's words came as a relief. He did have a minor valvular defect, but it was fully compensated and therefore should not cause any problem. In his opinion he could lead a perfectly normal life, but recommended that Mahler should not over-exert himself. A dark cloud had been lifted – hiking was once more on the agenda.

With unbearably hot weather in Vienna and suffering from a fever and a very sore arm as a result of his vaccination, Mahler was feeling thoroughly run down, but he nevertheless returned to his walking routine, albeit taking good care. Bruno Walter paid him a visit and asked him for his opinion on a symphony he had composed, but Mahler was unimpressed, which inevitably upset Walter. Before Alma's return to Vienna, Mahler sat for a series of photographs taken at the Opera. He had always disliked being photographed, but he agreed to these being taken as they were for the archives and because the session was under the supervision of Alfred Roller.

The family was reunited in their Auenbruggergasse apartment in the first week of September (the exact date is not known). As with their return to Maiernigg, memories of Putzi came flooding back, but they knew that they would not be living in their Vienna home for much longer. Mahler was still suffering from the after-effects of his smallpox vaccination. His right arm remained very sore, which resulted in him being unable to conduct the opening performance of the season, *Die Zauberflöte*. In addition he had had a recurrence of his digestive problems. His choice of this particular opera to open the 1907-1908 season was understandable. He loved Mozart, and so did the Viennese. He wanted his last weeks at the Hofoper to be as free from controversy as possible. By conducting *Die Zauberflöte* on the opening night, his first appearance on the podium after the news had broken that he had resigned from his post at the Hofoper, he had hoped to bury old hatchets and win over the hearts of staff and patrons alike. Alas his plan failed. With his conducting arm more painful than ever, Zemlinsky had to deputise for him. However, with Mahler's desire not to ruffle feathers and many of his old adversaries feeling that they had won their battle to be rid of him, a greater calm settled over the Vienna Court Opera. That is apart from the usual squabbling and jealousies amongst some of the star singers, and the continuing vitriol of the anti-Semitic extremist members of the press.

A week after the performance of *Die Zauberflöte* he resumed his conducting with a performance of *Tristan und Isolde*. This was followed by *Don Giovanni, Die Walküre, Figaro* and his recent great success Gluck's *Iphigénie en Aulide*, which all took place during the succeeding fortnight. He had made it clear that it was business as usual until the day came when he left the Hofoper.

On the 20th of September he made a flying visit to Munich to meet Conried in order to finalise plans for his first season at the Metropolitan Opera. He told Conried that it was essential that he should have more time to settle in and to rehearse before his season in New York began. It was therefore agreed that Mahler would sail from Cherbourg on the 12th of December, a month earlier than had originally been planned. This resulted in him having to cancel a number of engagements in Holland, Germany and Russia. He sought compensation from Conried even though the cancellations were his own decision. Not surprisingly Conried showed little sympathy, but eventually agreed to pay Mahler 25,000 kronen ($5,000) – half the amount he had asked for – in exchange for conducting twice a week during the extra month. In addition Conried made the ridiculous stipulation that Mahler should become teetotal during his contract – Mahler, who had always been so health-conscious and abstemious! He must have begun to have doubts about Conried's character, but this strange demand could well be attributed to Conried's increasingly poor health, which would result only a few months later in his resignation.

Hasty arrangements were made for the two concerts that Mahler had been due to conduct in St. Petersburg to be brought forward to the 26th of October and the 9th of November. Between these dates he was invited to conduct in Helsingfors (Helsinki) on the 1st of November. More immediately he had an engagement in Wiesbaden, one, as he told Alma, that he could well have done without. With hotels that left much to be desired (he left the first without unpacking) and the persistent noise of the crowded fashionable spa town, he could not wait to escape. But the concert itself was a great success. The programme was virtually guaranteed to be popular, the main works being Beethoven's *Fifth Symphony* and the *Prelude and Liebestod* from *Tristan und Isolde*. The glittering audience duly rose to its feet, the press loved it and, as he told Alma, it would pay for a fur coat for the forthcoming Russian trip! Before that Mahler dashed back to Vienna for a very important event scheduled for the 15th of October – his farewell performance at the Hofoper. For this special occasion, which also happened to mark his tenth anniversary as Director, he had chosen an opera very dear to his heart – *Fidelio*. He loathed any idea of public demonstrations either for or against him so he insisted that this final performance should be like any other, even refusing a prior announcement that he himself would be conducting. According to Alma the last performances that Mahler conducted at the Hofoper suffered from poor attendances and were shunned by many of the regular patrons.

Four days later he was on his way to St. Petersburg, without Alma for she was feeling unwell. It was a long but uneventful journey during which he spent much of his time making revisions to the score of his *Fifth Symphony* in preparation for its performance on the 9th of November. He arrived on the 21st to be met by his cousin Gustav Frank who took him to the Hotel d'Angleterre. Memories of his previous visit five years before came flooding back. It was the same hotel where he and Alma had stayed during his working honeymoon, but he wrote that it looked shabby and the food was disappointing despite the increased prices. His room, next door to the one he and Alma had shared, overlooked a noisy courtyard. Nevertheless he found the people to be as hospitable as ever, many of whom remembered their previous visit and asked after Alma. His cousin Frank was his usual agreeable self, and he told Alma that the Russian pianist Ossip Gabrilowitsch had given him a large box of apples, which he had already begun to enjoy.

Mahler's first concert on the 21st of October was a resounding success. With musicians who were totally committed to his interpretation of the score of Beethoven's *Fifth Symphony,* the main work on the programme, he received widespread praise. Buoyed on by this success, Mahler left St. Petersburg to conduct the second concert of his tour in Helsingfors. His only concern was that despite his usual daily letters to Alma, he had not heard from her, and was understandably worried about her health.

On the evening of his arrival, the 29th of October, Mahler attended a concert given by the Philharmonic Society under their esteemed conductor Robert Kajanus. Two of the works performed were *Spring Song* and *Valse triste* by a certain Finish nationalist composer by the name of Jean Sibelius whose popularity was growing both in Finland and abroad. Mahler was not particularly impressed by his music, referring to *Spring Song* as 'kitsch spiced with a Nordic sauce!' But despite his feelings towards these two works, he found Sibelius to be friendly and intellectually stimulating. The two men enjoyed each other's company on several walks and a deep mutual respect developed between them, despite their differing views on music. The main point of disagreement centred on what form a symphony should take. Sibelius, having just completed his *Third Symphony,* believed in traditional structure with its strict form and logical development. Mahler on the other hand proclaimed his view that a symphony 'must be like the world – all embracing'. They begged to differ.

The concert on the 1st of November turned out to be another outstanding success. The programme consisted of Beethoven's *Coriolan*

Overture and *Fifth Symphony,* the prelude to *Die Meistersinger* and the *Prelude and Liebestod* from *Tristan und Isolde.* The audience, many of whom had travelled considerable distances to attend, gave Mahler one of the greatest ovations of his career and the local press praised his fresh approach to the works performed. The general opinion was that they had been privileged to hear these well known works conducted by one of the greatest conductors of that era.

Another eminent member of the Finnish artistic world whom he met was Akseli Gallen, a painter he described as being like a Viking and that he could quite imagine women falling at his feet. The morning after the concert Gallen and Eliel Saarinen, an architect of considerable repute, took Mahler on a boat trip through the Skerries to the home that Saarinen shared with fellow architect Herman Geselius. Designed and decorated by Saarinen and Gallen, Mahler was very impressed by the building describing it as being like a Finnish Hohe Warte house, the street in Vienna where the Molls lived. With daylight fading and sitting in front of a large log fire Gallen put up his easel and painted Mahler's portrait. Under normal circumstances he was none too keen on sitting for portraits, whether photographic or artistic. However on this occasion, in the warm and relaxed atmosphere, he sat willingly. At least he did so for half an hour until he became restless and went for a walk while Gallen put the final touches to the portrait. It is one of only a very few paintings that exist of Mahler, and in many ways captures his character the best. Mahler himself was very impressed, describing it to Alma as being rather like a Rembrandt.

With his short but enjoyable stay in Helsingfors over, Mahler returned to St. Petersburg to prepare for the third and last concert of this tour to be held on the 9th of November. He had demanded a change of rooms at the Hotel d'Angleterre, the new one being on the top floor overlooking a fine square and St. Isaac's Cathedral. Upset that Alma had not taken the trouble to write to him in reply to his usual daily letters, he was much relieved when he received a cable from her saying that all was well. Rehearsals for the lengthy concert began. Mahler was to conduct his own *Fifth Symphony,* Beethoven's *Coriolan Overture* and the *Prelude and Liebestod* from *Tristan und Isolde.* The Russian conductor Mikhail Vladimirov would conduct Rachmaninov's *2nd Piano Concerto* as well as two movements from Mozart's *22nd Piano Concerto* with French pianist Raoul Pugno as soloist.

With the warm reception he had received after the first concert in St. Petersburg still fresh in his mind, the very positive attitude of the musicians was underlined when a delegation visited him at his hotel asking him if he would be able to conduct two concerts in February. Flattered as he was by their request, he had to decline the invitation, as he would no longer be in Europe. Unfortunately the generally positive attitude in St. Petersburg was in the process of being marred by seeds of antagonism that were being sown by Rimsky-Korsakov. He detested Mahler's music, considering it to be even worse than the scores of Richard Strauss! Following the performance of Mahler's *Fifth* Symphony, most critics, while admitting that there were moments of beauty, concluded that the music was bombastic, long-winded and chaotic. One even suggested that it would have been better suited to Paris than St. Petersburg – a particularly cutting remark as Parisians had never really warmed to his music! An exception was Isaiah Knorozovsky whose long and well-balanced review in *Teatr i Iskusstvo* praised Mahler the composer, saying that he had a great talent and that his orchestration was masterful. If most of the critics were very negative about his *Fifth Symphony*, Mahler the conductor was once again given lavish praise. Sitting in the audience had been a young Russian composer of twenty-five who would soon shake the music world with his ballet *The Rite of Spring* – Igor Stravinsky. Unfortunately his opinion of this performance of Mahler's *Fifth* is unknown, but as a pupil of Rimsky-Korsakov one might presume that he would not have been impressed. Indeed years later Stravinsky poured scorn on Mahler's music. Nevertheless he had been impressed with his conducting.

Returning to Vienna on the 12th of November Mahler spent a few days helping Weingartner settle into the 'hot seat' at the Opera. About to vacate his office, it was drawn to his attention that he had forgotten numerous decorations that had been bestowed upon him by Emperor Franz Joseph as well as those he had received from countries he had visited. Typical of his attitude to such matters, he shrugged his shoulders and muttered that his successor could have them! With his obligations to the Hofoper at an end, there was one more occasion that interested him. His *Second Symphony* was due to be performed in the Musikvereinsaal on the 24th of November with Franz Schalk conducting. Despite the prevailing antagonism towards him from some quarters he felt that he would like to conduct this particular concert himself. Apart from the fact that it was his music, he wanted to make it quite clear to Vienna that he was not about to leave with his tail between his legs. Schalk agreed to hand over the baton, although somewhat reluctantly.

Mahler had judged the up to the minute mood of Vienna's music circle to perfection. The final rehearsal and the performance itself in the Musikvereinsaal took place in front of packed audiences. If *Fidelio* had been his farewell at the Hofoper, this occasion, on the afternoon of the 24th of November, was to mark his departure as a composer. Some undoubtedly attended simply to cheer him on his way, but many others were overwhelmed by the occasion. Among these was Alban Berg who declared to his fiancé that while listening to Mahler's *Second* he had been unfaithful to her! The applause at the end by Mahler's friends and supporters, as well as the musicians and chorus, meant that he was forced reluctantly to return time and again to acknowledge the seemingly endless cheers. This he did with a straight face – he had made his point.

Korngold reported that the audience reaction had been heartfelt, almost unique, for they recognised just what Vienna was about to lose. Indeed the critic Albert Kauders wrote that Vienna was only just waking up to their impending loss – a valuable possession. People were beginning to realise that his often fiery personality was of little significance when set beside the noble values that he steadfastly stood for. But not all correspondents were so positive of his achievements during his tenure as Director of the Vienna Court Opera. Some actually hated the idea of him being applauded by the public, Max Graf and Richard von Perger among them. But perhaps Korngold summed up the public feeling when he wrote that he was lost to Vienna, and hoped that the words of the *'Aufersteh'n'* at the end of his *Second Symphony* would indeed come to pass: 'Arise again my soul after just a short rest!'

Hermann Bahr, a friend of Mahler's of course, wrote that his ten years at the Hofoper had been the greatest in its history from the point of view of artistic integrity. On the other hand Max Graf's opinion was that he believed that his years at the Vienna Court Opera had been destructive. He had not entered into Viennese society, remaining aloof and against tradition. With the passage of time, and no longer concerned with hitting the headlines, Graf changed his mind about him saying that his time at the Hofoper had been a golden age!

As a final gesture Mahler wrote a letter addressed to the employees bidding them farewell, which he pinned to a notice board. In it he wrote of their time together, how they had become dear to him and how they had striven together towards a goal that remained incomplete, yet many matters remained unfinished, as is Man's fate. He admitted that despite his best efforts success had not always been achieved. Not sparing himself, he felt that he had been able to ask others to pull their weight too. He acknowledged that there had been times when stress had led to hurt feelings, but that these had disappeared when their combined efforts had been rewarded with success. Together they had made progress, and he thanked them for their support especially in times of difficulty. He wished them all well for the future, and for the Hofoper too. Despite the obvious sincerity of his letter, and the indisputable success of his final concert, it was found torn up and thrown onto the floor. Having just written the above message to 'All members of the Court Opera Company', he wrote a note to Anna von Mildenburg who was in the Semmering. He told her that he had been hoping to catch sight of her before she left for her holiday to say good-bye. He wished her every success for the future, and hoped that they would meet again in more peaceful times. He would remain a good friend whom she could depend on, ending his letter affectionately with the words 'your old friend'.

It is easy to think that Mahler had constantly had his back to the wall in Vienna, but this was not always so. Typically some Viennese newspapers and journals were forever on the look out for sensational stories, true or false. Mahler, his celebrity status second to none outside royalty, was always bound to hit the headlines whether for good or ill, justly or unjustly. But those who persistently strove to bring him down, mainly the dedicated anti-Semites, were in a minority. He had many friends and supporters, and he had regarded it as a privilege to be at the centre of what was undoubtedly the cultural capital of the world at that time. Ironically among his admirers had been one Adolf Hitler. Still in his teens he was able to forgive Mahler his Jewish background for he was without question the supreme conductor of Wagner's operas of that era. A love-hate relationship it may have seemed at times, but Mahler's years as Director of the Vienna Court Opera had provided the inspirational impetus he had needed to create many of his greatest works.

Suddenly the enormity of the new direction that his life was about to take hit him. He paid visits to many of his Viennese friends, including Emil and Berta Zuckerkandl bidding fond farewells and seeking reassurance that he had made the right decision to leave. Richard Strauss, in Vienna to conduct a concert on the 1st of December, typically advised Mahler just to think of the money he would receive! But the relief he felt at not having to return to the Hofoper was immense, as was the fact that he could at last turn his back on those music critics who had plagued him for so long. Two correspondents whom he took the trouble to contact were Julius Korngold and Ludwig Karpath, both of whom had been consistently fair to him.

With an uncertain future ahead of him, both in a professional capacity and as far as his health was concerned, Alma and Gucki were now uppermost in his mind. He had begun to realise just how much Alma had sacrificed for him during the past ten years. She had given up ten years of her youth, subordinating herself to him and his work unquestioningly.

Gustav and Alma had taken the decision not to take their three and a half year old Gucki to New York. During their four months in America she was to live with Anna and Carl Moll. On the face of it this decision is difficult to understand. Having recently lost their elder daughter, surely they would not have wanted to be separated from Gucki, nor Gucki from her parents. Perhaps stability came into their minds for this first visit to America was very much a journey into the unknown with probably little time available for looking after their daughter in a new and strange environment.

Meanwhile a twenty-eight year old Thomas Beecham had been preparing to conduct Mahler's *Fourth Symphony* at the Queen's Hall in London. The young English conductor was enjoying making a name for himself by conducting contemporary works. The *Fourth* had been performed two years previously under Henry Wood without gaining many plaudits. This second performance, held on the 3rd of December, resulted in a torrent of adverse criticism in the press. From this moment on Beecham cried shy of Mahler's works, considering them to be imbued with emotional over-indulgence. London was still not ready for his music. What Beecham himself thought of the symphony is not known. A pity as he might have produced one of his famous quips such as his well known comment regarding Bruckner's *Seventh Symphony*, that in the first movement alone he had taken note of six pregnancies and at least four miscarriages!

The day of their departure came. Early on the morning of the 9th of December Gustav, Alma and Gucki arrived at the West Bahnhof to board their train for Paris. Waiting for them was a large crowd of friends and past colleagues. Among them were Arnold and Justine Rosé, Roller, Klimt, Schoenberg, Berg and Webern, a co-signatory of a flysheet that had been circulated amongst 'the admirers of Gustav Mahler' inviting them to be present at the station. Also there were members of the Philharmonic and several singers from the Opera including Eric Schmedes and Marie Gutheil-Schoder. There were flowers, there were tears, not least from Gustav and Alma whose compartment had been bedecked with blooms. There were the inevitable tearful goodbyes to their friends and especially to Gucki.

As the train pulled out of the station, Klimt was overheard saying, 'Vorbei' – It is over. Soon too were the principles and standards that Mahler had striven for at the Hofoper. His reforms and inspiration had dragged the Vienna Court Opera from the depths of indifference and stagnation where it had been wallowing for years. It had become the envy of the operatic world, its standards and artistic excellence unparalleled. Mahler and Roller between them had injected a freshness of new ideas for a new century. Now he was gone, and although the Secession remained along with the beginnings of the Second Viennese School of composers, whom he had encouraged with all his heart, the Hofoper would soon revert to its previous attitude of indifference. Weingartner found the thankless task of stepping into Mahler's shoes impossible. Faced with a barrage of criticism, his work constantly being compared with the high standards of his predecessor, he gave up the battle and left in 1911. Roller, co-founder of the Secession and elected their president in 1902, left the Hofoper in 1909 to become the director of the Kunstgewerbeschule. Bruno Walter departed in 1912 to take up a post at the Munich Opera.

As the Orient Express headed for Paris, a sense of relief came over

Gustav and Alma. Freed from the shackles of Vienna they could look forward to a new life, more time to spend together and no financial worries. During the journey he mentioned to Alma that one of the reforms he had intended but had not had the opportunity to bring about was to put an end to repertory opera. He believed that such programming went counter to improving or even just maintaining artistic standards.

Among those who met them on their arrival at the Gare de l'Est in Paris was Ossip Gabrilowitsch, the twenty-nine year old Russian pianist who had given Mahler the box of apples during his recent visit to St. Petersburg. Together they went to the Hotel Bellevue. Gabrilowitsch, whose enthusiasm for Mahler and his music knew no bounds, nearly caused a major upset. Left alone with Alma for a short while that evening and sitting with her in the dark, he suddenly declared that he was falling in love with her. He told her that his mind was in turmoil, for the last thing he wanted to do was to hurt her husband. Just as he was about to take her hand, Mahler entered the room and switched on the light. He suspected nothing and a crisis was averted, but Alma was nevertheless flattered that the young pianist had made her the object of his desire!

On the 12th of December they left Paris for Cherbourg. Night had drawn in when they boarded a tender, which ploughed its way through a choppy sea towards the liner *Kaiserin Augusta Viktoria*. Bathed in lights, the ship was a welcoming sight. With the strains of the *Marseillaise* ringing in their ears, they were conducted to their state-cabins. A telegram lay in wait; it was from the playwright, friend and admirer Gerhardt Hauptmann. He hoped that the crossing would be smooth, and that Gustav would return happily, for Europe needed men like him as much as their daily bread.

Mahler had been dreading the voyage, convinced that he would be seasick. They had just settled down to an excellent meal in the dining saloon when Alma told him that the ship had started to move. He was not best pleased. When conditions were rough and Mahler feeling likewise, Alma described how her husband lay rigidly in a horizontal position 'like a cardinal on a tomb' until his nausea abated. New York awaited them with bated breath.

Chapter 14

New York . . . Part One

Das Lied von der Erde

AILING TO THE United States of America was as much to do with
escaping from the horrors of the recent past as with the excitement
of the new challenges that lay ahead. As the *Kaiserin Augusta
Viktoria* neared journey's end, the New York skyline almost took their
breath away. Fascinated by the sights, the sounds and the general hustle
and bustle of this foreign city, they were driven to the Hotel Majestic in
Central Park West where a suite complete with two pianos had been
reserved for them on the eleventh floor.

An invitation arrived for them to take luncheon with Conried in his
apartment. German born and trained in Vienna, he was a shrewd
businessman, yet often tactless and unfair and consequently not noted for
his popularity. He did not command great respect from either musicians or
singers, especially as he lacked a deep knowledge and experience in the
field of 'serious' music. As a theatre manager however he was an expert
manipulator, which explained his survival at the Met for five years! Alma
described him as suffering from the wasting disease tabes and as a
megalomaniac with a total lack of taste. This was typified by his smoking-
room, which was dominated by a couch complete with canopy and
surrounded by twisted pillars, gawdy lights and a suit of armour emanating
an internal red glow. It was in these vulgar environs that Conried held
court to members of the opera world and would-be investors. Doubtless his
intention had been to impress Gustav and Alma, but as soon as they
managed to escape from the building they doubled up laughing!

Alma admitted that for the time being they managed to forget their
troubles, but with the approach of Christmas, separated from Gucki and
far from home, they began to feel very lonely. In Alma's words Christmas
Eve was 'our saddest evening.' Mahler must have remembered another sad
Christmas Eve many years before when he was in Leipzig, alone, staring
out of the window and weeping for his sick parents. At least now he had
his Almschi with him. At the last moment Austrian-born journalist Maurice

Baumfeld insisted that they go to a family dinner party, but when a group of thespians arrived, one of whom was an unkempt actress called Putzi, they made a hurried exit.

Alma's loneliness and frequent bouts of boredom continued, but Gustav's life, Christmas apart, had become a whirlwind of activity. His debut at the Metropolitan Opera was to take place on New Year's Day with a performance of *Tristan und Isolde*. It was very important to begin with a success, to win over the critics and patrons especially as his reputation as an inspired conductor and perfectionist had preceded his arrival. An editorial in *Musical America*, as early as the previous June, had referred to him as an imposing personality with high ideals who was intolerant of failure and who had no time for the 'star' system. He meant to live up to his reputation.

Some suspected that he would find the prevailing lackadaisical attitudes at the Met to be totally unacceptable and that he might even have second thoughts about fulfilling his contract. Problems there may have been, but to the surprise of many he simply rolled up his sleeves and got on with the job in hand. As reported in *The New York Times*, Mahler exercised his authority from the word go. Having been introduced to the musicians by Conried, he began conducting the prelude to *Tristan und Isolde*, but hardly had the orchestra begun to play when he put down his baton. Extraneous sounds of another rehearsal could be heard, a situation that other conductors had complained about on several occasions but without much success. Mahler insisted that it be stopped at once – it was!

Whereas in Vienna Mahler had felt a total responsibility for every aspect of a production, he was now able to concentrate entirely on the music, even if he did have to turn a very blind eye to some of the sets, costumes and production ideas the like of which he and Roller had striven so hard to dislodge at the Hofoper.

The evening of his debut got off to a bad start when he arrived late at the opera house. An incident occurred in the hotel lift when he had accidentally trodden on Alma's train, which duly parted company with her dress. While repairs were being carried out an urgent call came from the Opera wondering what had happened to maestro Mahler. Was this mishap a bad omen for the evening? Not a bit of it. Mahler dashed into the orchestra pit, and as he launched into the prelude, the previously impatient audience was immediately won over by his conducting.

With the Swedish soprano Olive Fremstad making her debut as Isolde and German tenor Heinrich Knote as Tristan, Alma stated that musically this was the finest performance of her favourite opera that she had ever heard. Most of the critics, who had a reputation for giving foreign conductors a hard time, wrote glowing reviews. The reporter of *The New*

York Times spoke of Mahler's brisk tempi in certain passages, 'elastic, but full of subtle variations . . . though all with the pulse of dramatic passion . . .' Also mentioned was the way he never let the orchestra overwhelm the singers whose every word could be heard by the audience with unusual clarity. Reginald De Kovan in *The World* stated that 'Mahler caught his audience at once, and I predict for him the popularity and influence which his great talent should demand'. *The New York Sun* declared the performance to be 'notably good . . . the guiding hand of Mahler was discernable in every musical detail of the interpretation'. As so often there just had to be a critical voice. Lawrence Gilman in *Harper's Weekly* used words such as 'portentousness' and 'analytical', that he had failed to lay bare the heart of 'this music'. However Mahler was delighted by the response of the packed house, and as reported in *The Sun*, 'the applause was general and prolonged. Many stood up and cheered. Mr. Mahler looked happy'. And so did Conried! There were four further performances of *Tristan* during the month that followed.

Later the same month the Metropolitan Opera Company gave a performance of *Tristan* in Philadelphia. Alma recalled how, sitting in the front row, she suddenly became aware of an expression of deep suffering in Mahler's face. She was so shocked by this and the fear that she might lose her husband that she had to be helped backstage where she fainted. Mahler, who had always made a point of glancing at his wife during performances, suddenly noticed that her seat was empty. As soon as the curtain fell on the first act he dashed to her side, but by then she was already sitting up.

Speculation had arisen, even before Mahler's arrival in New York, as to whether he might replace Conried who had already decided that this would be his last season as Director of the Metropolitan Opera. This was of course pure conjecture, for Mahler had no intention of doing so. His present contract of three months a year, relatively stress free, giving him time to compose and yet with an exceptionally good salary so that his family would be well provided for in the future, was exactly what he wanted. In a letter to Alfred Roller, dated the 20th of January, he wrote that Conried had actually been given notice and that there was a plan to offer the post to Giulio Gatti-Casazza, the director of Milan's La Scala Opera. There was also talk of a plan to procure the services of Arturo Toscanini to conduct the Italian operas so that Mahler could concentrate on the German repertoire. He described the audiences, as well as the multi-millionaire board, as lacking sophistication yet eager to learn and hungry for novelty. He told Roller that he had complained to the board about the lack of artistic taste and vision in the productions, and that he knew of only one man suitable to bring about the necessary reforms – Alfred Roller. Thus he hoped that he might be able to pave the way for their creative partnership to be renewed. He warned

Roller that, should he be approached by the Metropolitan Opera, he must insist on having total control over all stage matters.

Mahler also wrote to Willem Mengelberg forewarning him that he would probably be receiving an offer to take over the directorship of the Boston Symphony Orchestra. He advised him to accept without hesitation for the orchestra was America's finest, second only to the Vienna Philharmonic, and that the post would come with a sizeable salary of $20,000. He told Mengelberg that he would very likely spend the next few years in America, adding that he was entranced by the country. Whatever his plans for future seasons in New York, the idea of having his staunch supporter from Amsterdam close by must have been a very appealing proposition. However, Mengelberg was not tempted by the offer. He remained with the Concertgebouw Orchestra with whom his standing continued to grow from strength to strength.

Meanwhile Alma, utterly depressed, had taken to her bed. A doctor diagnosed a weakness of the heart and nervous exhaustion. Her illness was almost certainly psychosomatic. Throughout her life there were occasions when under stress she would succumb to mysterious illnesses. In fact she had a very strong constitution and lived until 1964 when at the good age of eighty-four she died from pneumonia. Alma wrote that Gustav spent half of each day in bed to conserve his energy!

The second opera that Mahler conducted was *Don Giovanni* on the 23rd of January. The several weeks of rehearsal that he had become used to at the Hofoper was out of the question at the Met. However, having had only nine days for *Tristan*, he had managed to arrange fifteen for *Don Giovanni*. Despite the predictably poor production, musically the performance was another success. With a very strong cast that included the delectable and very popular Emma Eames as well as Marcella Sembrich and Antonio Scotti, Mahler himself played the continuo for the recitatives. He used the full complement of the string section of the orchestra, which he felt was needed in a building of that size. He had reduced the usual four acts to the original two and had used tempi more akin to those used in Mozart's day – not what New York audiences had become accustomed to. Taken aback as some were, the general opinion was that musically the results were outstanding. Adjectives such as ravishing and exquisite appeared in the reviews. *The New York Sun* declared that Mahler had correctly treated *Don Giovanni* as a music drama and not merely as the frequently heard collection of set pieces for the singers. In a letter to the Viennese businessman Paul Hammerschlag, Mahler, whilst obviously missing the quality of his Vienna production of *Don Giovanni*, nevertheless stated that the singing was 'almost unsurpassable' (the one member of the cast who had been singled out for adverse criticism being Feodor

Chaliapin). In his letter Mahler enthused about the climate, the people and the fact that in New York there were no commercial factors to interfere with the musical standards he sought.

Concern was voiced in the New York press over the forthcoming arrival of 'Mr. Toscanelli' (*sic*. – editorial in *The New York Times*) and how well the division of authority between the two conductors would work. The *New York Herald*, describing Mahler as the tsar of the Vienna Imperial Opera, said that he 'had proved himself to be a wit and diplomatist'. The article added that musicians and singers were more than willing to do what he asked of them, which was a notable achievement, ' for everyone knows that singers and snakes cannot be charmed too easily'. As an example it cited an occasion during a rehearsal of the Valkyries in *Die Walküre*, the opera he conducted following *Don Giovanni*. He had complimented the female singers before him saying that never before, not even in Vienna, had he heard such voices brought together to sing the Valkyrie chorus. The ladies were naturally overjoyed by this compliment. Mahler then continued,

'And now ladies, finding that you are possessed of such wonderful voices, I must ask you to use them!' Apparently the effect on their singing was remarkable. The critics were once again delighted by his inspired conducting. *The New York Times* enthused, 'how lovingly can he linger over certain passages with a special emotion and fill them with rich expressiveness.'

On the 11th of February Conried's anticipated resignation was accepted and Gatti-Casazza was officially appointed as his successor. Reforms were in the air. One of these was to produce operas in English, thereby making the Metropolitan Opera more of a national institution as well as helping to develop home grown talent. With the Conried era all but over, the time had come for Mahler to encourage Roller to join him in New York. On the 15th of February he wrote to him saying that he would be receiving a telegram inviting him to visit New York to discuss the possibility of being appointed Chief Stage Manager. He told Roller that he himself did not plan a lengthy commitment to the Metropolitan Opera, although he did intend to return the following season, so long as he was still in good health.

Despite the more reassuring second prognosis he had received before leaving Vienna, Mahler was nevertheless worried. Whether psychological or not, he felt constantly tired, spending more and more time in bed and resting, conserving his energy for rehearsals and performances. He was ageing rapidly. Nevertheless he was enjoying his work and looking forward to a peaceful summer in the Tyrol with Alma, Gucki and his manuscript paper.

On the 16th of February he wrote to Carl Moll. The letter had a generally cheerful tone. Whilst warming to the gratitude he was receiving in New York, he regretted the apparent inability of many to discern the difference between good and bad taste – this he put down to an excess of enthusiasm. He ended the letter on a positive note, saying that Alma's depression seemed to be lifting and that she was quite lively.

On the same day an event took place that had a profound effect on both Gustav and Alma. While they were sitting relaxing in their suite on the eleventh floor of the Hotel Majestic, they heard the sounds of a procession coming from the street below. It was the funeral cortège of New York Fire Department's deputy chief, Charles W. Kruger who had died tragically but heroically in the line of duty. It came to a halt outside their hotel where an address was made, the words of which Gustav and Alma were unable to make out. Following a pause they heard the dull thud of a muffled drum, then silence. They were both very moved, and Alma wrote that tears were streaming down her husband's face. Memories of Putzi's death and the sight of the hearse taking away her little body from their Maiernigg home came flooding back – the sound of the drum so reminiscent of the fateful hammer blows of his *Sixth Symphony*. Mahler would later use the sound of the muffled drum stroke in his unfinished *Tenth Symphony*.

Without the intolerable burdens of responsibility that he had been forced to shoulder in Vienna, together with the tragic loss of Putzi and worry over his own health, his attitude to his work had changed. Mahler, the stern, sometimes ruthless dictator had taken a back seat and he bowed to many of the wishes of his new employers even if at times they went against the grain. One example of this concerned cuts in Wagner's operas. In Vienna he had crusaded to have all cuts reinstated; in New York he not only accepted the traditional cuts but agreed to others as well. This may not have been to his liking, but he was not going to be stressed by such decisions. The constant battles at the Hofoper might be in the past, but memories still gave him nightmares.

On the 19th of February *Siegfried* was performed and once again most critics praised his conducting unreservedly, although the *New York Times* disagreed, regarding his interpretation as being 'more scholarly than passionate'!

The same evening saw the American première of Debussy's opera *Pelléas et Mélisande*, which took place at the Manhattan Opera House. Gustav and Alma were present the following evening for the second performance. It was well received and regarded as an important event in New York's opera history. Alma was very impressed by Debussy's opera; Gustav commented that it was harmless!

Mahler's high hopes of securing a contract for Alfred Roller at the Met were suddenly called into question. In a letter to Roller dated the 27th of February he warned him that the initial enthusiasm over securing his services had suddenly cooled. He wondered if Roller had unintentionally said something that had annoyed Rawlins Cottenet, a member of the Metropolitan board who had recently met him in Vienna. In his reply, Roller suggested that the upset might have been the result of his poor English. He had told Cottenet that he would insist on a completely free hand as far as stage direction was concerned, and that he expected to be very well paid for his services. Cottenet countered this by telling him that he would be expected to work for the whole season, on German opera with Mahler and Italian opera with Toscanini. Roller had agreed in principle, but suspected that the recently appointed general director, Gatti-Casazza, might be at the heart of this disagreement, combined with the unfair criticism which was being levelled against him in Vienna for being over extravagant. Whatever the cause, Mahler feared that his cherished dream was in danger of slipping away. His ideal of a Mahler-Mengelberg-Roller triumvirate to influence the course of music history in America now appeared to be something of a forlorn hope.

An interesting article appeared in the *New York Herald* on the 8th of March on Mahler's attitude to using a score during performances. The subject had arisen because rumours were rife that in Europe he rarely referred to scores while conducting. When asked about this Mahler admitted that as a young conductor he had not only refused to have an open score in front of him, but had actually made a point of having it removed in full view of the audience! He told the interviewer that such youthful demonstrations were no longer part of his make-up; he had become more restrained in his conducting and did not wish to upset those before him. Another point that Alma made in an interview many years later was that by not using a score Mahler had felt that it would be easy to forget details of interpretation. His changed attitude to using a score reflected his changed attitude to conducting as a whole. No longer was he the young highly energetic firebrand of the podium out to impress the public on a series of ego trips. Over the years he had mellowed. Still as insistent as ever on the dedication of musicians and singers, he had come to realise that he was the privileged servant of the masterpieces and their creators.

The last and greatest success of his first season at the Met was *Fidelio*. For the first time he was able to influence every aspect of a production. Based on the tremendously successful Vienna one, the original plan had been to transport the Roller sets to New York. Logistics and costs had prevented this, but near replicas were created. Musically too it was the Hofoper version, with Mahler's minor alterations to the score and the switching of the *Leonore Overture No. 3* from its traditional place after the first act to cover the scene change before the second act. Inevitably questions were asked and some eyebrows raised, but praise was generally lavish. The *New York Times* used words such as 'remarkable . . . thrilling

... subtle ...' and that Mahler was 'a great conductor'. The *Musical Courier* went as far as to state that there was no point in going to New York concerts after such 'a magnificent performance'.

Alma wrote to Guido Adler telling him that *Fidelio* had been nothing short of a triumph, and in a letter to Anna Moll Gustav described the evening as a total success. He also told her that there was a possibility that a new orchestra might be formed to be at his disposal to perform works of his own choice, including his own music. He hoped that the people of New York, being unbiased, would enable him to discover fertile soil for his works, and that as a result New York would become for him a spiritual home. This would be a dream come true, for he had longed to have this facility ever since he had relinquished responsibility for the subscription concerts with the Vienna Philharmonic in 1901.

Behind this ambitious plan was a committee mostly made up of ladies led by one Mrs George R. Sheldon, the wife of a wealthy and powerful Republican. Forty-five year old Mary Sheldon was the daughter of a banker, George Seney, who had become noted as a patron of the arts as well as other good causes. In 1881 she had married George R. Sheldon, also in banking. When her father died in 1893, she decided to continue in his footsteps by supporting charitable causes, one of which was an ambition of hers to create 'the greatest orchestra America has ever heard'. The committee was convinced that Mahler was the man to achieve this noble aim. Alongside Mary Sheldon was another influential and wealthy lady of a similar political persuasion, Minnie Untermeyer. Several members of this committee had been promoters of the New York Symphony Society, but they had become dissatisfied due to declining standards under conductor Walter Damrosch, as well as the equally unsatisfactory New York Philharmonic.

The initial plan was for Mahler to conduct four Festival Concerts at Carnegie Hall during the following season. $17,000 would be made available to cover his expenses and he would be personally involved in the selection of musicians. These four concerts would be but a start in the formation of a permanent orchestra that the great city of New York could be proud of. With financial backing coming from a number of America's wealthiest citizens, including John D. Rockefeller and Joseph Pulitzer, the aim was for a re-built New York Philharmonic to rival the Boston Symphony as America's finest orchestra.

Alma's spirits had continued to improve. She had met and befriended Marie Uchatius, a Viennese artist, and with Mahler's continued rise in popularity social events were hardly in short supply. One of these made the meeting with Conried in his somewhat surreal apartment seem to have been quite tame. Dr. Leon Corning, who had rescued Alma when she had fainted during the performance of *Tristan* in Philadelphia, was a prominent and very wealthy neurologist. He had invited the Mahlers to dinner and had sent his chauffeur driven car to pick them up. Another passenger, a man also invited to the party, was a deaf-mute. Having been ushered into an upstairs room, which Alma described as being like that of 'a medieval alchemist' filled with all manner of weird contraptions, they met Corning's wife who was dressed in black and looked like a death mask. They were then led into the music room in which there were no less than four grand pianos. Corning proceeded to pick up a flute and began pacing up and down the room playing the instrument. Joined by Corning's brother and sister-in-law, they sat down to a meal of tiny portions of food of a doubtful origin, accompanied by a half bottle of champagne shared between all present. With the only light coming from a few small candles and a string of rather ineffective fairy lights, the hollow-cheeked wife, who was prevented from speaking, and the deaf-mute, the atmosphere was one of a haunted house. Yet Gustav and Alma realised that Corning, a miser by reputation who seldom invited guests, had done his best to entertain them in a fitting manner, and they were touched by the novel idea of having little bronze gifts instead of the traditional place cards: a miniature music stand for Gustav and a piano for Alma. As so often one has to take Alma's descriptions with a pinch of salt. Her tendency to exaggerate the eccentricities of acquaintances whom she did not particularly like or who lacked physical appeal is well known.

Another man from the world of medicine whom they met was Dr. Joseph Fraenkel. A man of considerable wit, an immediate bond of friendship was struck up between them. He would play a very significant role in their lives in the not too distant future.

With *The New York Times* declaring that Mahler was responsible for bringing a new spirit and beauty to performances at the Met, their first season in America drew to a close on a very positive note, even though Mahler continued to worry ceaselessly about his health. They now looked forward to a return to Vienna. Whatever the pleasures of New York, they missed family and friends, especially little Gucki. On the 23rd of April they boarded the *Kaiserin Augusta Viktoria* and bid farewell to America for the time being.

After an uneventful voyage they disembarked at Cuxhaven on the 2nd of May, where a customs officer presumed that Gustav, looking totally exhausted, was Alma's father! Vienna and a return to composing in the Tyrol seemed a little closer, but before that two important engagements had to be fulfilled, the first being in Wiesbaden. They travelled via Hamburg, Alma staying on for two days for social reasons before rejoining her husband.

Arnold Berliner and Ossip Gabrilowitsch had also travelled to Wiesbaden for the concert, which was to include Mahler's *First Symphony*, Mendelssohn's *Hebrides Overture* and the third *Leonore Overture* from Beethoven's *Fidelio*. The event turned out to be virtually a waste of time and effort. Due to an unreasonable increase in ticket prices the public had to all intents and purposes boycotted the concert. Alma wrote that she, Berliner and Gabrilowitsch were almost the only members of the audience! Mahler, tired and understandably upset by the poor attendance, showed his displeasure during the post concert meal. Apparently he was in the habit of removing the labels from wine and beer bottles when dining out, and as a joke Berliner asked the waiter to carry out this task before bringing them to their table. Mahler, realising who was at the bottom of this, was not amused and remained decidedly irritable for the rest of the evening.

The 10th of May saw their return to Vienna where they were at last reunited with Gucki. They stayed for a few nights with Alma's mother and stepfather while their Auenbruggergasse apartment was made ready for their return. The talk of the city, and indeed of the whole of the Austrian Empire, centred around the celebrations to mark the diamond jubilee of Emperor Franz Joseph in June. A series of ten concerts had been planned in Prague and Mahler had been invited to conduct the Czech Philharmonic in the first of these. Therefore after less than a fortnight, but feeling refreshed and almost back to his normal self, he set off on the 21st for the capital city of the land of his birth.

Following his departure, Alma and Anna Moll travelled south to the Tyrol, their mission to find a suitable place for the summer where Gustav could compose in peace. Arriving in Toblach, their search led them to an ideal house close to the hamlet of Alt-Schluderbach and just south of Toblach. It was owned by the Trenker family who lived on the ground floor, the Mahler's would rent the first floor. It was an eleven-room farmhouse with two verandas and two bathrooms. There were delightful and very peaceful views over the Pustertal Valley to the north with Toblach and its church in the distance, nestling beneath wooded hills. By contrast, to the south rose the jagged and dramatic peaks of the Dolomites, an area to which Mahler had escaped on several occasions in order to seek inspiration.

Meanwhile his concert in Prague on the 23rd of May, the main work being Beethoven's *Seventh Symphony,* was a major success. He had been welcomed home as the nation's favourite and most celebrated musician. The press had anticipated the event in style, using phrases such as 'a festive day' and referring to him as 'one of the greatest living musicians'. He found the Czech Philharmonic to be splendid and he was lauded wherever he went. Among those present was Otto Klemperer who had recently completed a piano arrangement of Mahler's *Second Symphony*, which the latter thoroughly approved of. The final accolade of his visit came when he was asked if he would be prepared to conduct the first ever performance of his own *Seventh Symphony* at the final concert in the series in September. Needless to say he gladly accepted the offer, and returned to Vienna feeling rejuvenated and more positive about the future, and a noticeable spring had returned in his irregular step!

Before setting off for Toblach he contacted Alfred Roller, forewarning him that it was quite possible he might receive a letter from Andreas Dippel, a theatre director at the Metropolitan Opera. If Dippel was as good as his word, Roller would be offered *Tristan* and *Figaro*. The prospect of the Mahler-Roller partnership being renewed in New York was still a possibility, if only for occasional selected productions. This, however, was thrown into doubt when on the 9th of July Andreas Dippel wrote a long letter to Mahler concerning arrangements for the 1908-1909 season. In it he mentioned Roller's excessive financial demands, which he deeply regretted as he had hoped to be able to use his talents in New York. Mahler must have wondered if he had done the right thing in advising him to seek high remuneration. Dippel also told Mahler of the possibility of Toscanini, who would be joining the Met for the forthcoming season, conducting a few performances of *Tristan und Isolde* before he returned to work at the Opera. In his reply Mahler made it abundantly clear that under no circumstances would he agree to Toscanini conducting *Tristan*. He told Dippel that he had taken great pains with the production during the previous season and musically he regarded it as his 'spiritual property'. He threatened that if Toscanini were to conduct it before he himself took up the baton at the Met, the whole character would change and consequently he would not be prepared to take over further performances. Nevertheless, he pointed out that he did in fact have great respect for the Italian conductor.

On their arrival at Villa Trenker the first task was for Gustav to lead a tour of inspection. Alma, Anna Moll and Gucki followed him until he had decided which two rooms would serve his purposes best, the three criteria being light, good views and least possible disturbance. Top priority was to hire a local carpenter to build a composing hut nearby. A spot was chosen which had a good view across the valley yet was surrounded by trees on the other three sides. When completed Mahler had an upright piano installed, in addition to the two grand pianos in the house. Close by was another, much smaller hut. On one occasion a visitor asked Alma what it was used for. Much amused, she replied that it was a lavatory. The visitor, slightly taken aback, remarked that there was no privacy for the window at the front had no curtains. To which Alma explained that her husband needed to be inspired by the mountains and trees for his digestive system to function properly!

Everything was ready for a return to his old composing routine, but his more positive attitude to life that had been building only a short time before began to diminish. In the peace and quiet of the Tyrol and deprived of intense musical activity, once again he began to dwell on his health, his heart and the over-cautious advice he had received from doctors. Despite the presence of his family and visiting friends, among them Julius Korngold, Oskar Fried, Alfred Roller and of course the Molls, a new loneliness had overcome him. Writing to Bruno Walter he spoke of his fear of solitude and the difficulty he found working for hours on end at his desk without the complementary vigorous exercise he had been used to in the past. He even stated that he wished that the summer holiday would end. Always with a pedometer and constantly aware of his pulse rate, his anxiety fuelled palpitations even on the shortest of walks. For him the combination of composing and physical exertion had become a type of yin and yang. Deprived of one, his mental balance was upset. Once again he adopted a negative attitude and longed to be able to lose himself in his merry-go-round of conducting commitments. And yet, unable to climb mountains, he channelled even more energy than usual into his work, into which he launched with a frenzy, spending hours in his newly built *Häuschen*. Convinced that Father Time was lurking in the shadows, creativity became an obsession.

Das Lied von der Erde, preliminary sketches of which he had begun the previous summer in the wake of Putzi's death, was rapidly taking shape. Mahler had originally considered calling the new work 'Symphony for tenor, alto and orchestra', but he had second thoughts about this title, probably because of the 'Ninth Symphony' connotation. He renamed it 'The Jade Flute'. The next title he gave it was 'Song of Earth's Misery' before finally settling on *The Song of the Earth*.

With the Prague concert on the 19th of September, his aim was to complete the work by the end of August. This he did with the final notes of the short score penned on the 1st of September. Despite everything, Alma's description of that summer as the saddest they had ever known might seem to be an exaggeration. Surely the previous one would have qualified for that. Even if at times the atmosphere was tainted by feelings of grief and foreboding, Mahler described their new summer retreat as 'wonderful', and the music he composed during their stay was truly inspired. Also, in a letter to the Molls, he had written that he hoped that the summer break would be both peaceful and enjoyable. In an undated letter to Bruno Walter at the beginning of September, he wrote that he had been given 'a time that was good'. Perhaps Alma's remark referred more to herself than to them both.

Das Lied von der Erde
The Song of the Earth
(for alto (or baritone), tenor and large orchestra)

Mahler knew that he had created something very special. When later Bruno Walter, having studied the manuscript, handed it back to him, he was virtually speechless with admiration. With a touch of jest Mahler asked him if he thought it was bearable, or whether it would make people do away with themselves. Amused by the expression on Walter's face, he then asked him if he had any idea how it should be conducted, because he hadn't!

So began the final period of Mahler's works. Following the *First*, there had been the three *Wunderhorn* symphonies, then the middle trio of purely orchestral works, followed by the monumental *Eighth*, which inevitably stands alone. The last three works are Mahler at his most self-reflecting. Before leaving Toblach he wrote to Walter saying that he thought that *Das Lied von der Erde* was without doubt the most personal work he had created so far.

As previously mentioned, Mahler had intended *Das Lied von der Erde* to be his ninth symphony, but he had not numbered it as such due to his 'nine symphonies' superstition, with Beethoven, Schubert, Bruckner and Dvořák all having departed this life after their ninth numbered symphonies. In it Mahler the undisputed master of the lied meets Mahler the composer of great symphonic works. *Das Lied* is not just a song cycle, although initially he had intended it to be so. It is a symphony of songs or a song symphony. In the past Mahler had used material from his lieder in his symphonies, either sung or instrumentally. With *Das Lied* he reversed the procedure applying symphonic principles to a collection of songs. This was an entirely new and ambitious form, which has rarely been attempted successfully since, notable exceptions being Zemlinsky's *Lyrische Symphonie* and Shostakovich's *14th Symphony*. From the anthology of eighty-three poems by thirty-eight poets, the seven that Mahler chose and adapted from this collection of ancient Chinese verse translated by Hans Bethge are:

1 *Das Trinklied vom Jammer der Erde*
   (The Drinking Song of the Earth's Misery)
2 *Der Einsame im Herbst*
   (The Lonely Man in Autumn)
3 *Von der Jugend*
   (Of Youth)
4 *Von der Schönheit*
   (Of Beauty)

   5 *Der Trunkene im Frühling*
      (The Drunkard in Spring)
   6 *Der Abschied*
      (The Farewell)

Der Abschied is in fact a combination of two poems, *In Erwartung des Freundes* (In Expectation of the Friends) and *Der Abschied des Freundes* (The Farewell of the Friends), with Mahler himself adding the final lines. His tinkering with the poems to meet his own requirements was perfectly reasonable for Bethge's translations were very loose and had been based on translations by others including Judith Gautier (thought to have been Wagner's last mistress!). It is possible that she might even have written *Der Einsame im Herbst* and *Von der Jugend* herself!

   As we have seen, Mahler's life-long search for the truth and the whole meaning of life had led him to explore and reject most of the prescribed doctrines of the main religions, but Eastern philosophy, and in particularly Buddhism, fascinated him. With its rejection of a God or heavenly kingdom, it seeks to be one with creation in a celebration of life, an acceptance of suffering and sorrow as inescapable elements of existence and a belief that these may be overcome. This side of Buddhism appealed to Mahler at this stage in his life. There is a suggestion of this influence in *Die Kindertotenlieder*, but it is clearly mirrored in *Das Lied von der Erde*. This despite the fact that the translations of the Chinese verse by Judith Gautier and Henry-Saint-Denys into French, with Gautier's extensive alterations resulting in her versions showing scant resemblance to the original poems. These of course had not only changed at the hands of Gautier, but also through the translation into German by Bethge before being adapted, amended and added to by Mahler himself in what could almost be described as a game of Chinese whispers!

   Despite the very large orchestra required, the scoring frequently has a chamber-like quality. It utilizes instruments of delicacy such as the mandolin and celesta to superb effect and a repeated use of the pentatonic scale creates an exotic, quasi-oriental quality. Mahler, although basically a composer of diatonic, western music, made extensive use of chromaticism in order to achieve the musical effects he sought. With *Das Lied von der Erde*, its Chinese verse and eastern philosophy, he added the use of the pentatonic scale most significantly in the third and fourth movements, skilfully blending it with his own highly individual style, itself in addition influenced by the Hebraic music of his Jewish background.

   It is no surprise that Schoenberg later re-scored *Das Lied* for chamber orchestra to very good effect. The songs of the *Kindertotenlieder* cycle (*Das Lied*'s predecessor) certainly show a relationship with each other, but *Das*

Lied goes further with orchestral passages, as well as the words, forming a symphonic and emotional cohesion on an entirely different level. As a symphony of songs it was not surprising that Mahler also wrote a version for piano accompaniment for performance in more intimate surroundings, just as he had done with *Die Kindertotenlieder*. With today's shortage of contraltos, the alto movements, numbers 2, 4 and 6, are usually sung by a mezzo-soprano.

Das Trinklied vom Jammer der Erde
(Drinking Song of Earth's Sorrows)
(tenor)
A minor

The work opens with a blazing fanfare from the horns followed by wild laughter from the woodwinds and strings. With heldentenor strength, the soloist declares that wine is already in the golden goblet to drown away earth's sorrows . . . but first, a song. Apart from the idea of drowning one's sorrows, this first movement is a clear reflection of Mahler's own state of mind, although of course he himself drank in strict moderation. The tenor sings three stanzas all ending with the words 'Dark is life; dark is death!' each time sung a semitone higher. The brevity of man's existence on this earth permeates the song. At the beginning of the third stanza there is a sense of clinging onto the beauty of nature: 'The firmament is eternally blue', to which Mahler himself added, 'and the Earth will long endure and blossom again in spring'. These words pre-echo the very end of the work. For Mahler the new life of spring equated with spiritual renewal, but will the singer ever see it? There follows the almost surreal, nightmarish scene with a terrified ape howling in a moonlit graveyard. There is no *Komm, süsser Tod* here, rather it is more akin to Dylan Thomas's 'Rage, rage at the dying of the light!' It is time to drink the wine right down to the dregs, for 'Dark is life; dark is death!'

Der Einsame im Herbst
(The Lonely Man in Autumn)
(alto)
D minor

Following the often brash outbursts from the despairing individual about to drown his sorrows in *Das Trinklied*, the second movement is in total contrast. Opening with muted undulating violins and a solitary oboe, the music has a chamber quality. Both words and music convey a scene of loneliness. The joys and beauty of spring and summer have gone. There is no more blossom, the flowers have lost their fragrance, the golden leaves will soon fall to earth. Frost and mist pervade the scene, and there is an overwhelming feeling of weariness, even depression. Mahler wrote in the score 'dragging and weary'. The words 'My little lamp has spluttered out' refers as much to the light within as to the light from the lamp itself. There is something of 'the dark night of the soul' (St. Teresa of Avila) about this poem. There is a longing for rest, peace and solace. From the physical despair of *Das Trinklied* we now have despair of the soul: 'Sun of love, will you never again shine to tenderly dry up my bitter tears?' With these words the music briefly surges upwards, before the oboe returns with its doleful lament.

Von der Jugend
(Of Youth)
(tenor)
B flat major

In artistic terms, whereas *Der Einsame im Herbst* may remind us of Chinese watercolours, *Von der Jugend* is more like the Willow pattern on china. It is about the triviality and transience of youth. This brief song describes a pavilion of green and white porcelain which stands in the middle of a pool. A jade coloured arched bridge leads up to the house. The water is like a mirror, and inside the pavilion a group of young friends sit happily chatting, drinking, with some writing poetry. One can presume that it is spring or early summer, and after the gloom of the previous two songs this comes both as a contrast and much needed relief. There is even a touch of humour when the singer, referring to the pool's mirror image, declares that everything is standing on it head, a line which suggests that perhaps the scene itself is but a mirage.

Von der Schönheit
(Of Beauty)
(alto)
G major

Continuing with the theme of youth and beauty, *Von der Schönheit* is far more intimate, at times even sensuous, than its rather detached predecessor.

The song opens with a description of an idyllic scene. A group of young girls gather flowers beside a river, laughing and teasing each other. The sun's rays weave around their forms that are reflected in the water and the breeze gently lifts their sleeves. The mood changes with the arrival of a group of young men on horseback. After the delicate opening of the song, the music suddenly becomes macho, even wild with excitement. With trumpets and timpani to the fore, a vigorous march rhythm takes over, at one point strangely reminiscent of the 1812 Overture. Was this Mahler having a dig at Tchaikovsky – not one of his favourite composers? The horses gallop by, while one young man rides his steed across a carpet of flowers and fallen blossom. The horse tramples the blooms, whinnies and tosses its mane in a frenzy with steam blowing from its nostrils. And then as quickly as they had come they are gone, and the fairest of the maidens gazes longingly into the distance. Is it all a mirage, like the reflections in the water? The music fades away as if the whole scene had been but a dream.

Der Trunkene im Frühling
(The Drunken Man in Spring)
(tenor)
A major

Although *Das Lied von der Erde* has six movements, it is, to all intents and purposes, divided into two parts. The first five form the first part, followed by the sixth and last (*Der Abschied*) which is almost as long as the first five put together. *Der Trunkene im Frühling* is the second 'drinking song', and neatly rounds off part one. So far we have had a song about a man drowning his sorrows, loneliness, a dream of forgotten youth and a dream of love and desire unfulfilled. Now it is time to return to the bottle and seek alcoholic oblivion, despite the fact that it is spring when 'a young man's fancy lightly turns to thoughts of love'. This is no reflection on Mahler himself, of course!

The bucolic, jig-like opening as the drunkard staggers about trying to blot out life's misery, gives way to a delightful middle section. He is awakened by a bird that sings of the arrival of spring during the night while he had been asleep. With exquisite delicacy from solo violin and piccolo, the drunkard is at first won over by the singing of his feathered friend, but as far as spring is concerned he is not interested. With a return to the drinking music of the opening section he states that he will fill his glass once more and drink till he falls asleep, for what has spring got to do with him?

Der Abschied
(The Farewell)
(alto)
C major and minor

It is so easy to overlook the qualities of the first five songs – the first part of the work – and dwell on the quite stunning sixth, which is considered by many to be the finest and most personal symphonic movement that Mahler ever wrote.

The escapist mood of the previous song is dispelled at a stroke – on the tam-tam. The two instruments whose roles come to the fore in this final movement are the tam-tam and the celesta. The tam-tam, with its harsh and often menacing timbre, represents death and foreboding, the celesta eternity and bliss. *Der Abschied* is about the final journey, the farewell and the transfiguration.

For the opening section he wrote in the score *Schwer* (heavy), an atmosphere duly created by the tam-tam, contrabassoon, horns and double basses. Above the dark and sombre atmosphere, an oboe plays a shepherd-like melody, similar in mood to the opening of Act Three of *Tristan und Isolde*. This is the beginning of Mahler's journey from darkness to light. The oboe's melody is sad and it yearns for a release from the darkness.

His instruction for the soloist at the beginning of the song is *In erzählendem Ton, ohne Ausdruck* (in narrating tone, without expression). This is important as the opening and very evocative descriptions of sunset and the onset of night cry out for a good deal of expression! However, by beginning the song with a sense of detachment, the gradual emotional build-up during the course of the movement is that much more effective. With the entry of the singer, a solo flute replaces the oboe and there is a noticeable lightening of the orchestral sound as harps, clarinets and upper strings join in to depict the peace of the scene. Yet the lament is still present. There is a sense of loneliness, which is temporarily dispelled by birdsong of the dusk chorus.

Descriptions of the close of day completed, the human element enters with the words 'I stand here waiting for a friend'. It is at this point that the singer's emotion takes flight. This longed-for meeting will be a farewell. 'But where are you? You have left me alone so long!' Here Mahler inserted a line of his own to superb effect: 'O beauty! O world for ever intoxicated with love of life!' The friend arrives and dismounts, but there is only sadness at this their last meeting. 'I shall wander in the mountains to find peace for my lonely heart', just as Mahler had done following Putzi's death. With aching intensity the music prepares for the ultimate release from life's torments. We now come to the final and most well known passage: the coda in C major with Mahler's own words expanding the ecstatic symbol of springtime and renewal that he used towards the end of the first song, opening the gates to eternity.

> 'Everywhere, the dear earth blossoms
> forth in Spring and grows green once more.
> Everywhere, eternally,
> distant horizons shine blue:
> forever . . . forever . . . forever . . .

Accompanied by harp, celesta, mandolin and sustained chords from the strings, the music and soloist fade away into eternity. It is the soul's release from earthly woes, and for the listener, just for a moment, time seems to stand still.

Despite its preoccupation with departure from this life and the drunken despair of the first and fifth movements, *Das Lied von der Erde*, and *Der Abschied* in particular, is not a work weighed down by gloom and doom. It is a celebration of the wonder and beauty of creation, of constant rebirth and renewal. It reflects both Mahler's own approaching final farewell and the end of late Romanticism. It embraces ecstasy alongside feelings of dark foreboding.

In a letter to his friend Henry Boys, Benjamin Britten wrote how he could go on playing *Der Abschied* indefinitely. He stated how cruel it was that music should be so beautiful. For him it had been worth living just to 'bask in its heavenly light'. The great conductor Jascha Horenstein made a similar comment, saying that one of his deepest regrets in dying would be that never again would he be able to hear *Das Lied*. Klemperer regarded it as Mahler's very moving farewell to life and that it expressed the lonely side of his nature. But again it must be stressed it is not a morbid work, but ultimately one of celebration. As far as being his farewell to life, surely *Der Abschied* is as much or even more to do with Putzi's death the previous year than with his own mortality, or perhaps it was a longing on his part to join her in the hereafter, who knows. As baritone Thomas Hampson pointed out in a BBC television interview for a documentary on Mahler, you could probably find a germ of every piece of music he ever wrote in *Das Lied*. In his opinion it was 'a huge testimony'. In Michael Kennedy's words, 'its final effect is to uplift the heart . . . it is the best of Mahler'.

His summer holiday over, Mahler returned to Vienna on the 5th of September en route to Prague for the première of his *Seventh Symphony*. As usual, Alma, Gucki and Anna Moll remained behind to enjoy a few more days in the Tyrol. He wrote to Alma from Vienna saying that he had had a comfortable journey, sleeping most of the way. He had met Alfred Roller and Bruno Walter at the Café Schwarzenberg, and both had remarked how well he looked. Roller had said that he was utterly fed up with the constant aggravation and political manoeuvring at the Hofoper, and was longing to find pastures new. Mahler reported to Alma that his appetite and digestion were excellent! That afternoon he caught a train to Prague with a little less than a fortnight before the red-letter day – the 19th of September.

This eagerly awaited event in the Prague music calendar had not only attracted a great deal of attention in the press, but had resulted in many musicians and friends of his travelling to the Czech capital. Among these were Arnold Berliner, Ossip Gabrilowitsch, Otto Klemperer, Bruno Walter and the German artist Emil Orlik, whose engraving of Mahler is very well known.

Mahler had arranged to stay at the Hotel Blauer Stern where he had stayed on a previous visit. Unfortunately the occupant of the adjoining room snored resoundingly, regularly waking him up with a start. Luckily the man left after the first few nights, whereupon Mahler reserved the room for himself in order to prevent the possibility of any further nocturnal disturbance from that direction!

His first task was to correct and revise the orchestral parts following section rehearsals before launching into the main, full rehearsals. Several young musicians, including Otto Klemperer and Bruno Walter, volunteered to help him with this urgent and onerous undertaking, but according to Klemperer he declined their offer. In the evenings he would find time to relax and enjoy their company in his hotel. Klemperer was at the time a junior conductor and chorus master at the German Theatre on Mahler's personal recommendation, the same theatre where he himself had been conductor in 1885.

Alma arrived on the 15th, four days before the concert. She accompanied her husband to the large exhibition concert hall for a full rehearsal. When they arrived they found the auditorium, which was also used for banquets, to be a hive of activity with waiters scuttling about laying tables! Mahler was not amused but was unable to do anything about it. William Ritter, the Swiss journalist and long time supporter of his, was present and described the occasion. A chair was found for Alma and placed about thirty feet from the podium. For a few moments all eyes were turned on her, then Mahler raised his baton and the rehearsal began. Ritter wrote that after the final chord of the Finale had died away, 'a stunned silence' filled the hall. Following a few words with the orchestra, Mahler closed his conductor's score and went to sit next to his wife. Once more all eyes were on her, anticipating her reaction. Embarrassed she smiled politely, but according to Ritter it was apparent that she neither understood nor particularly liked the work.

Alma's first impressions of the *Seventh Symphony* were shared by many of those who attended the première. True, Mahler was called back to the podium many times during a fifteen-minute ovation, but this generous applause was more for him than for the music. He was after all their famous fellow countryman, most of whose previous works, as well as his conducting, had enraptured the citizens of Prague in the past. This symphony had taken many by surprise for it had not been what they had anticipated. It was after all a new direction for Mahler and for music. Nevertheless the majority were grateful and felt honoured that he had chosen Prague for its première.

A month later he was in Munich preparing for the second performance.

He was joined there by Anna Moll, but Alma remained in Vienna to finalise the arrangements for their second voyage to New York. Supervised by Emil Freund, there was also the impending sale of their Maiernigg villa to attend to with contracts due to be exchanged at the beginning of November.

Mahler was in good spirits. He greatly approved of Munich and its climate, and having discovered how low the cost of living was he even suggested to Alma that buying a villa there might be well worth considering. With a very comfortable hotel and a dedicated orchestra he appeared to be on top form, but William Ritter, who had travelled to Munich for this second performance of the *Seventh,* thought that in Prague he had detected signs that Alma's feelings towards her husband had begun to cool. There was further evidence of this in Munich when Ritter overheard Mahler muttering to himself about someone else being 'the ruler of that heart'. Was it Ossip Gabrilowitsch? Perhaps this was one reason for his request to Anna Moll to be with him in Munich. The concert itself ended with generous applause, but as in Prague many in the audience did not quite know what to make of the *Seventh Symphony.* As for the German press, they slated the work, which would not have come as any surprise to Mahler!

One last engagement remained before departing for America. He had agreed to conduct a concert in Hamburg, which was very convenient as it was close to the port of Cuxhaven where they would be boarding ship. The programme was to include Beethoven's *Seventh Symphony* and *Coriolan Overture,* the prelude to *Die Meistersinger* and Tchaikovsky's *Romeo and Juliet Overture.*

However, before he left Vienna a rather unpleasant disagreement was said to have taken place between Gustav and Justine, as recalled by Alma in her memoirs. When Justine had married Arnold Rosé she had taken with her an assortment of books and papers that were hers. Apparently, unknown to Mahler, she had also removed his libretto for the fairy-tale opera *Rübezahl,* written in direct competition with Hugo Wolf many years before and which had caused a rift between the two composers. Arnold Rosé just happened to mention that his wife had shown him this youthful libretto. Mahler then accused his sister of taking it. Justi at first denied this, then said that she had burnt it! It transpired that she had lent the manuscript to Alfred Roller who was hoping to stage a ballet based on the same subject at the Hofoper. According to Alma, Mahler was livid and declared that he would not speak to his sister until she returned it. Fortunately Justi had not burnt it, for it was found amongst Alma's possessions after her death. To confuse matters further, a parcel from Justi arrived in Hamburg containing an even earlier libretto of Mahler's, *Die Argonauten,* which he had written in 1879-1880. It is quite possible that

Justi had taken these early works for safe keeping, lest Mahler should destroy them as he did with letters he had received and any other papers that he considered no longer relevant. Unlike her brother Justi had always made a point of preserving all his correspondence and papers for posterity.

One can't help but feel this story has been exaggerated, for Mahler and his sister had always been very close. He had always needed a 'mother figure' to lean on in times of stress. Both Justi and Natalie Bauer-Lechner had fulfilled this role in the past, a mantle taken over by Anna Moll. It is more than likely that Alma had become jealous of the reliance that her husband put on her mother, 'Little mamma' as he called her, just as she had been when Justi and Natalie had played that role. It is for this reason that Alma probably exaggerated the incident in her memoirs, for the bond between Gustav and Justi was surely too strong for him to threaten never to speak to her again! This is confirmed in a letter he wrote to Justi from Hamburg on the 9th of November, in which he said that it would never cross his mind to be angry with her. Therefore it appears that a 'ticking off' was exaggerated out of all proportions! Nevertheless, he may have been concerned that the libretto would fall into the wrong hands, and in some ways he might well have felt happier if it had been burnt!

Already standards at the Hofoper were in decline. In an article by Richard Specht, the author wrote that, in just half a year, all that Mahler had achieved had been lost or even deliberately wiped out by Weingartner. Such reports must have been painful, but the Hofoper was in the past, and on the 6th of November Mahler travelled to Hamburg, again accompanied by Anna Moll. In his letter to Alma on the 7th he said that the Hotel Esplanade was delightful, the people friendly and asking after her, and that 'the package' from Justi had arrived!

Alma, little four-year-old Anna and the rather stern new twenty-two year old English nurse Maud Turner joined Gustav and Anna Moll in Hamburg. With a good orchestra and with no work of his own in the programme, the rehearsals went smoothly and did not tax him as much as his two previous concerts. With the applause still ringing in his ears, the time had come to set sail for America. This time Gucki and her nurse would also be making the crossing.

The *SS Amerika* was about to set sail from Cuxhaven. Having boarded the tender, Gucki, seeing the huge liner towards which they were heading, suddenly gave a shout of delight and started jumping up and down. Miss Turner reprimanded her, telling her not to get so worked up, upon which Mahler picked up his daughter, sat her on the taffrail and told her 'Now go on, get excited!' He too was excited, and delighted that Gucki would be with them in New York this time.

Chapter 15

New York . . . Part Two

Ninth Symphony

THE *S.S. AMERIKA* berthed in New York on the 21st of November 1908. For his second season Mahler had booked a suite on the eleventh floor of the prestigious Hotel Savoy on Fifth Avenue, a hotel much favoured by stars of the Metropolitan Opera such as Caruso and Sembrich.

Mahler's firm stand over the Toscanini-*Tristan* dispute had paid dividends, Toscanini making his New York debut only five days before Mahler's return with a performance of Verdi's *Aida*. This came as a great relief to Mahler who had not wished to set off on the wrong foot with the new manager, Gatti-Casazza.

During the summer the proposed plans of Mrs Sheldon and the 'ladies' committee' to create an orchestra for Mahler (a reorganised New York Philharmonic) had fuelled controversy in the press. The conductor Walter Damrosch, writing in *The Tribune*, referred to them as 'two or three restless women with no occupation and more money than they seem to know what to do with'. The truth of the matter was that Damrosch felt that Mahler could well become a serious rival on the concert platform. This article was contested by *The Musical Courier,* which considered that the restlessness was more to do with New York music lovers who longed for 'a worthy orchestra' with a conductor of Mahler's calibre. Fortunately by the time of Mahler's return the dust had largely settled on this matter.

As had been planned at the end of his first season in New York, his initial engagements were not at the Opera, but to conduct the New York Symphony Orchestra in three concerts. The first of these was held on the 29th of November in Carnegie Hall. The programme consisted of Schumann's *First Symphony* and the *Coriolanus, Battered Bride* and *Meistersinger* overtures by Beethoven, Smetana and Wagner respectively. The correspondent of the *New York Times* praised the performance as well as Mahler's restrained yet authoritative conducting, even if his left hand was in his pocket at times! But this was not a universally held view.

Criticism was levelled at him over some of his tempi. It was also reported that he had considered the concert to be something of a farce, as many of the musicians had either failed to turn up for rehearsals or had been unwilling to remain as long as he had asked them to. And who was their regular conductor? Walter Damrosch! Mahler complained, and irritating as this might have been for him, it did underline the importance of having a truly professional orchestra in New York. The plans of the 'ladies' committee' gained wider support as a result.

The regrettable attitude of certain members of the New York Symphony Orchestra must have been of particular concern to Mahler regarding the second concert of the series, which was to take place on the 8th of December. There would be only one work, his own *Second Symphony*. It would be its American première. Once again the rehearsals proved to be frustrating as is evident in a letter he wrote to William Ritter in which he complained of inadequate forces and that America really did not know 'what to do with me', or even art in general for that matter.

Joining the New York Symphony Orchestra for this important event were the two hundred-strong Oratorio Society chorus, Laura Combs (soprano) and Gertrude Stein-Bailey (alto). Even if Mahler himself considered the performance to be below par, the audience was very moved and gave him a lengthy ovation, as did the participants. The press too were generally in favour, although some critics could not resist attacking his music with remarks such as 'portentously insignificant', that he was 'an unrepentant denigrator of programme music', that he had 'no true vocation as a music maker'. The correspondent in *Harper's Weekly* even went so far as to say that his music was unoriginal and unimaginative.

On the 11th of December Toscanini made his Wagner debut at the Met with *Götterdämmerung*, a performance generally considered to be good without being in any way revelatory. On the same day a long letter appeared in the *New York Times*, in which Mary Sheldon stated certain facts regarding the reorganization of the Philharmonic Society. She pointed out that the Society had been in existence for over sixty years and was the oldest orchestral organization in America. Its members realised that reorganization was essential for its continued existence and were totally supportive of the proposed reforms. These included having a conductor with complete control to be appointed by a board of trustees. Mrs Sheldon stated that there was no question of 'eliminating' anyone (she presumably had Walter Damrosch in mind), but merely to put the Philharmonic Society on a firmer footing.

Mahler's third and last concert of the series with the New York Symphony Orchestra took place on the afternoon of the 13th of December. The publicised programme consisted of two overtures, Wagner's *Faust* and

Weber's *Oberon*, to be followed by Beethoven's *Seventh Symphony*. It was a programme designed to be non-controversial and popular. However, without due notice to the public and to the annoyance of some of the patrons, Mahler decided to substitute Beethoven's *Seventh* with the same composer's *Fifth Symphony*. The *New York Herald Tribune* reported that the best part of the afternoon had been the tremendous applause that Mahler had received before, during and after the concert. As for the performances, the reporter considered them to be far from satisfactory, with 'crudeness and impurity of intonation'. Both he and the correspondent of the *New York World* put part of the blame on Mahler himself, saying that he appeared to be in a highly nervous state and that there was a lack of emotion. This is quite possible, for having to work with musicians who had an unprofessional attitude must have gone against the grain. Quite clearly all he wanted was to get this last concert out of the way and to sever his links with the New York Symphony Orchestra.

Away from work, Gustav and Alma continued to enjoy their leisure time. At a ladies' lunch, held in very luxurious surroundings, Alma met a woman who had become something of a celebrity – Natalie Curtis. Unlike the rest of the ladies present, whose elegance matched the surroundings, Natalie Curtis's eccentric attire left a lot to be desired, yet on her arrival she had automatically become the centre of attention. She was something of a legend, living for years among the American Indians studying and writing about their life style, legends and music. Alma found her fascinating, and a friendship was soon struck up. Another social event that she mentioned in her memoirs was a visit they made to the home of Karl Bitter, the Austrian sculptor who had emigrated in 1889. His house was perched high up on the cliffs overlooking the Hudson River. The occasion was a great success. Having received them dressed in a chef's outfit, he proceeded to grill fish Indian style on an ebony slab, a method of cooking that Gustav thought delightful. Before they left, Bitter invited his guests to a party on New Year's Eve. They also spent several very enjoyable evenings with Enrico Caruso, the great Italian tenor, who was also staying at the Hotel Savoy. It was during one or more of these evenings that Caruso drew the well-known caricatures of Mahler, refusing to let him see them in case they caused offence! In fact not only was he not offended when he later saw them, but when one appeared in a newspaper the following April, he sent a copy stuck to a postcard to his old teacher Heinrich Fischer in Iglau.

Mahler's seasonal debut at the Met on the 23rd of December was very fittingly *Tristan und Isolde*. Having turned a blind eye during his first season to a number of traditional cuts, he now felt it was time for some restoration. With Eric Schmedes as Tristan and Olive Fremstad as Isolde the performance was a major success. The reviews in the Christmas Eve papers were full of praise for Mahler, the *New York Times* stating that it was 'a remarkable performance'. The key to its success was the way Mahler held back the orchestra so that the words could clearly be heard. Yet this had been criticised by some the previous season, for by so doing it was felt that a good deal of the orchestral drama had been lost, especially at climaxes. The correspondent of the *New York Times* considered this to be a false argument, stating that greater drama was achieved by giving the singers prominence.

Gustav and Alma spent Christmas Eve with their friend the Austrian physician Joseph Fraenkel, and on Christmas Day they were the guests of the Polish soprano Marcella Sembrich. With several of those present inevitably being connected with the Met, including Caruso, Gustav was treated as the unofficial guest of honour. Pleasant as the party was, the undoubted highlight for him was when the Christmas tree caught fire!

Two interesting articles appeared in the *New York World* and the *New York Sun* on the 27th. In the former, a rumour was reported that a new opera house might be built in the city with greatly superior acoustics to the Met and would consequently become a serious competitor. The man thought to have been behind this plan was wealthy businessman Oscar Hammerstein, grandfather of the writer, producer and director of musicals of the same name. As a rival of the departed Conried, and director of the four-year-old Manhattan Opera House, he had acquired the rights to several operas during the 1906-1907 season, among them Massenet's *Thaïs* and Debussy's *Pelléas et Mélisande*. He had also attracted a number of stars including the Australian, Nellie Melba, probably the greatest prima donna of that time. The rumours were therefore quite believable. Hammerstein denied being involved in any such plan, but it was thought that discussions on the matter had taken place. In the same article the music-loving New Yorkers were described as 'this opera-mad community'. In complete contrast to the latter remark, the article in *The Sun* reported how many patrons who attended Wagner operas would arrive anything up to an hour late, would consider the long interval to be the main point of attending so that they could parade about displaying their finery and jewellery, and that shortly after eleven o'clock they would depart. The correspondent concluded by saying that few of the subscribers had any idea how *Tannhäuser* ended!

The New Year's Eve party at Bitter's studio turned out to be a disappointment to say the least. Alma, pregnant once more, felt unwell so Gustav had to go alone. The bad weather deteriorated, a blizzard setting in. With a biting wind and the snow becoming heavier by the minute, Gustav decided to leave Bitter's studio shortly after midnight. Beginning his return journey in a bus full of drunks, he alighted at the first opportunity and caught a hansom cab, which was blown over, fortunately not far from his hotel. As he crawled out from underneath the overturned vehicle, unhurt but nevertheless shaken, his pince-nez was blown off into a snowdrift. After retrieving it with some difficulty, not helped by well-intentioned assistance from the rather inebriated driver, he battled his way against the elements, arriving back at the hotel at around two o'clock feeling frozen and utterly exhausted.

The first major event of 1909 at the Metropolitan Opera was a new production of *Le Nozze di Figaro*. Following almost two weeks of rehearsals, an almost unheard of amount by New York standards, the first performance took place on the 13th of January. With new sets and costumes, the cast included Marcella Sembrich, Emma Eames, Geraldine Farrar and Antonio Scotti. With Mahler conducting from a piano with paper-covered strings so that it sounded rather like a harpsichord, the performance resulted in great praise from the press, with comments such as it 'sparkled and flashed like champagne', 'delightful and brilliant', that Mahler's interpretation was 'masterly', and that with Mahler in charge 'it could hardly have been otherwise than good'. Emma Eames later wrote that of all the conductors she had performed with, Mahler was the greatest, a true genius, modest and considerate. He was a collaborator, not a dictator.

On the 4th of February Emma Eames was in the cast of Catalani's *La Wally,* in which Marcella Sembrich sang the title role – her farewell opera performance at the Met. Two days later she was honoured at a special gala to mark her twenty-five years at the Metropolitan Opera. Her appearance on the stage with Giulio Gatti-Casazza was accompanied by the march from *Le Nozze di Figaro* with Mahler conducting. The gala was followed by a banquet in the ballroom of the Hotel Savoy with many friends from the world of music present, including the Mahlers. She, like Emma Eames, had a very high opinion of him, and she later wrote that he was 'wonderful' and that it had been 'a great delight' to sing for him.

The 19th of February saw another triumph for Mahler. The music of his fellow countryman Smetana had always been very close to his heart, and on this particular evening he conducted the first American performance of *The Bartered Bride*. With fellow Bohemian Emmy Destinn as Marie and dancers who had been brought in specially from the Prague National Theatre, it was in the words of the *New York Daily Tribune*, 'an evening of unalloyed delight'.

With such high appreciation of his work at the Met and the prospect of conducting the Philharmonic Orchestra, Mahler was enjoying life in New York. This is clearly reflected in his letters to Alfred Roller and Bruno Walter. He told Roller that he had only good news to send. He mentioned the recently highly acclaimed *Figaro* and *Bartered Bride,* that he was in good health, but that he would nevertheless be leaving the Met at the end of the season in order to concentrate on concerts with the Philharmonic. To Walter he wrote that, despite everything that he had been through during the previous eighteen months, his thirst for life had never been greater. He said that it was through music that he managed to find answers to his questions, providing him with a certainty that meant they were no longer questions at all. One can presume he was referring to the meaning of life and the hereafter, so he had obviously adopted a far more positive outlook than he had had only a few months before.

An added pleasure during the month of February was the arrival of Anna Moll who had come to spend the last few weeks of the season with her daughter, granddaughter and son-in-law. Unfortunately during her visit she fell ill. At first they were all afraid that it was a recurrence of the suspected heart problem that had manifested itself after the death of Putzi. Dr. Fraenkel was summoned, but he reassured her that her heart symptoms were only secondary and that she was suffering from a kidney complaint. She was advised to contact a specialist on her return to Vienna, and if she stuck to a strict diet she should make a full recovery. Added to this upset was the fact that Alma had a miscarriage. Mahler mentioned this at the end of his letter to Carl Moll dated the 10th of March. He reported that she was well and that she had been 'relieved of her burden', and that this time it was with regret. His use of the word burden suggests that Alma's feelings towards pregnancy were not entirely positive, although her regret on this occasion was probably genuine, wanting another child after the death of Putzi, so this loss must have had added poignancy. From his remark 'this time' we can assume that she must have already had a miscarriage.

One evening, much to Alma's surprise and delight, Ossip Gabrilowitsch paid them a visit at their hotel. After dinner, Mahler, saying that he wished to retire, left them in the salon. Gabrilowitsch went to the piano and played for Alma the *Intermezzo in A minor* by Brahms, one of her favourite pieces. An air of intimacy thus set in and it was not long before they were declaring their passionate feelings towards each other. Gabrilowitsch played the Brahms *Intermezzo* again and then departed. Although nothing physical had occurred between them, Mahler had overheard their conversation. He felt deeply wounded, despite Alma's assurances that they had done nothing untoward, for he remembered only too well the previous occasion when such an encounter had occurred in a Paris hotel. Gustav was upset and Alma very embarrassed, but this would be her last intimate encounter with Ossip Gabrilowitsch who was to marry Clara Clemens, the singer and daughter of Mark Twain, the following year.

For Mahler the season at the Metropolitan Opera ended as it had begun with performances of *Tristan und Isolde* and *Le Nozze di Figaro*. *Tristan* was staged on the 12th of March and, judging by the report in the *New York Sun*, he had obviously taken note of the criticism levelled at him from some quarters after the performance on the 1st of January that, great as it had been, it had lacked the dramatic punch that many had expected. This time *The Sun* correspondent wrote of 'white heat', 'a torrent of vital sound' and 'power and passion'. His final appearance of the season at the Met was to conduct a further performance of the much-acclaimed production of *Le Nozze di Figaro*. Thus he ended his season and his contract with the Opera with two outstanding performances of works by his two favourite opera composers. The inevitable had happened with the Italian duo of Gatti-Cassaza and Toscanini gaining control of future plans for the Met. But Mahler's mind was made up anyway, for he wanted to focus on his new three year contract with the Philharmonic Society which would take effect in November, one that would give him total control over the orchestra and the works they were to perform.

Before leaving for Europe he had been invited to conduct the Philharmonic in two concerts, the first to take place on the 31st of March. The musicians were on their mettle knowing full well that Mahler would soon have the power to hire and fire. For the time being he could not put his plans into action. With the status quo, the Philharmonic had a minority of just thirty-six musicians, the majority having to be hired concert by concert. It was no wonder that the musical standard of the orchestra took a lot to be desired. Nothing could be done about this unsatisfactory situation for the two end-of-season concerts, especially as the Musicians Union was standing in the way of any immediate reforms. Nevertheless, with his future in New York being linked with the Philharmonic Society, Mahler did his utmost to shake up those he had at his disposal. He played safe with the programmes. The first concert on the 31st of March in Carnegie Hall consisted of Schumann's *Manfred Overture,* Wagner's *Siegfried Idyll* and *Tannhäuser Overture* to be followed by Beethoven's *Seventh Symphony*. Although the audience was not large they were appreciative of the efforts made by Mahler and the orchestra. Both *The New York Times* and the *New York Sun* were generous in their praise of the Philharmonic's new conductor. The correspondent of *The Times* wrote that Mahler's authority was very evident, resulting in precision and a vitality that had long been absent; *The Sun* stated that the concert 'achieved much' and 'promised more'. The *New York Tribune* described Mahler as a 'quiet, undemonstrative, masterful man' who had complete control over the musicians.

The second of the two concerts took place on the 6th of April and consisted of Beethoven's *Egmont Overture* and *Ninth Symphony.* Mahler decided on this programme so that he could end his second season in New York on a grand and popular note. As with the first concert it was well received by both the audience and the press. The only questions raised were regarding his minor revisions. Most of these were to do with adapting the score for a modern orchestra and venue, such as the doubling of some instruments and refining certain voices of the brass for the more powerful instruments being used. Such revisions were generally regarded as acceptable, but questions were asked over the greater prominence he gave to the timpani which, according to the *New York Tribune*, 'assaulted' the ear of the audience. In the *New York Sun's* review the kettledrums were not just beaten, 'they were castigated. They volleyed and thundered . . .' often swamping the melodic instruments. *The New York World*, however, described the performance as 'magnificent'. The day after the concert good news reached Mahler that permission had been granted for him to seek and engage a concertmaster (leader) for the Philharmonic as well as a first flute player.

On the 10th of April, Gustav, Alma, Anna Moll, Gucki and her nurse left New York for Cherbourg. After an uneventful crossing they travelled to Paris for a brief holiday, shopping and the inevitable round of social events that Mahler could well have done without, but which Alma thrived on. One such occasion, as recalled by Alma, had been arranged by their friend Georges Picquart. He was now Minister for War, and he had invited them to lunch at the Ministry. When they arrived, to their great surprise, they were greeted by a guard of honour in full uniform and with presented arms. Picquart, standing at the top of the steps, told them that to him they were like royalty! The lunch itself turned out to be enjoyable for among the other guests were their friends Paul and Sophie Clemenceau.

The most important event historically speaking, however, had been secretly arranged by Alma's stepfather Carl Moll with the help of Paul Clemenceau. The seventy-year-old sculptor Auguste Rodin had been approached with the idea of producing a bust of Mahler. Keeping the matter secret had been essential, for if Mahler had had any indication that such a plan was afoot, he would almost certainly have declined. He had always disliked being painted, drawn or photographed. On this occasion, however, with arrangements already in place, he felt that he had to agree, even though the thought of having to sit still for hours on end must have gone right against the grain. It was probably because it was Rodin, the most revered sculptor of his time who had generously agreed to reduce his fee to make the commission possible, that Mahler was prepared to resign himself to the project. Paul Clemenceau later recalled that the two geniuses actually got on extremely well, sharing a deep mutual respect, and that Mahler had been a very cooperative model.

The bronze bust of Mahler is of course an outstanding work of art and the original clay moulding can be seen in the Rodin Museum in Paris. Rodin was fascinated by Mahler's features, seeing in them a combination of Frederick the Great, Benjamin Franklin and Mozart! He later carved a marble bust based on his memories of Mahler, which when displayed in the Rodin Museum in Paris was labelled by a curator 'Mozart'.

An invitation arrived from the Chief of Police for Gustav and Alma to join him as his guests for a gala performance at the Opéra of *Tristan und Isolde*. Picquart and the Clemenceaus had also been invited, so the invitation was gratefully accepted. The evening began well enough until, that is, the second act, when Tristan, sung by the Belgian tenor Ernst van Dyck, whom Mahler remembered from his Vienna days, began to ignore his Isolde (Louise Grandjean) and repeatedly went to the front of stage doing his utmost to milk the audience. For a short while Mahler fumed in silence, then stood up, and without saying anything, marched out of the box. The Chief of Police, Picquart and the Clemenceaus were astonished. Alma was deeply embarrassed.

After an on the whole successful visit to Paris they returned to Vienna where Mahler had business to attend to. Top priority was to find a concertmaster for the Philharmonic. As the key musician in the orchestra, the candidate had to be right. Ideally, he would have preferred a German-speaking musician for practical reasons, but no one suitable was available. In the end he settled for American-born Theodore Spiering.

A violinist and conductor, Spiering's previous posts had been in Chicago and Berlin. Founder of the Spiering Quartet and Director of the Chicago Music School until 1905, he had then embarked on regular concert tours in Europe. He had applied for the position of concertmaster of the New York Philharmonic on the advice of fellow violinist Fritz Kreisler. By chance Spiering had happened to meet Mahler in the street, and as they walked together, Mahler had told him of his plans for the orchestra. The official interview took place that same afternoon in the Auenbruggergasse apartment with Arnold Rosé present. Mahler's search for a flautist, however, came to nothing.

Mahler wrote to Willem Mengelberg concerning his autumn visit to Amsterdam when he would conduct performances of his *Seventh Symphony*. He told him that the score was to be published by Bote and Bock and that it should be ready in good time for the preliminary rehearsals in September.

Before leaving Vienna he bought a burial plot in the cemetery in Grinzing, a northern suburb of Vienna, and made arrangements for Putzi's body to be disinterred and laid to rest there where he himself wanted to be buried. The transfer of Putzi's remains would take place in July, after he had left Vienna for his summer break in Toblach.

Following a hectic and very successful season in New York and the visit to Paris, the rush of adrenalin had ceased, and Mahler once more began to dwell on his health and what the future might hold for him. Alma too was under strain. She felt exhausted, suffering depression from the miscarriage and feeling increasing sexual frustration; not yet thirty, she was still young and attractive, her husband ailing and aging beyond his years. Mahler would go to Toblach and bury himself in composition. This was his vocation, his main purpose in life, and his music continued to take precedence over all else, including Alma. He had warned her of this before they were married, but that was when she was in the full flush of youth with stars in her eyes! Now she had begun to feel trapped and unable to live life to the full. William Ritter's observations of the previous autumn that there appeared to be a cooling of Alma's feelings towards her husband were proving to be correct. With her mind in turmoil she was persuaded to go for a rest cure in Levico, a spa in Italy some one hundred and twenty kilometres southwest of Toblach.

The Mahlers left Vienna on the 8th of June. They travelled together to Toblach, before Alma, Gucki and Miss Turner set off for Levico leaving Gustav alone to concentrate on composing. If her memoirs are anything to go by, Alma was certainly in a bad way. She described how every evening she would sit on her balcony in tears, with the sounds of laughter and merrymaking from the crowds below grating on her ears. She desperately wanted love of a physical nature and of an intensity that she felt Gustav just could not provide. She yearned for the excitement that she had once enjoyed and that now she felt she had lost. Yet at the same time she wanted to support her husband, the great composer, the conductor of fame. And then there was Gucki to consider . . .

With Alma away in Levico, Mahler had to attend to business matters regarding the forthcoming season in New York, as well as arrangements for the performance of his own works in Europe and the publication of the *Eighth Symphony* by Universal Edition. He also made a point of contacting many of his old friends such as Fritz Löhr, Emil Freund, Arnold Berliner and Siegfried Lipiner. He wanted to heal old wounds inflicted on several of them by Alma shortly after their marriage when she had made it clear that she did not want them to be part of their lives. In a letter to her, Gustav pointed out that it was time for reconciliation. Among these friends who had ceased to be part of his life Lipiner had been the cause of deepest regret. Lipiner was so delighted by the prospect of renewing their friendship that he wrote a poem, *Der Musiker spricht*, which he gave Mahler in celebration of his fiftieth birthday the following year. Finding it hard living alone, Mahler sent a number of invitations to friends to come and stay at Villa Trenker.

Writing to Anna Moll, whom he addressed as 'dearest Mama', he stated that Alma's letters were full of lamentation, thus presuming that the cure she was undergoing was a stressful affair. He wondered whether it was right for her to be alone, even though she had Gucki with her. He asked Anna to buy a number of items for him: honey, pen-ink, two key-chains and a peppermint mouthwash. In a letter to Carl Moll he wrote how marvellous it was in Toblach and that he should visit sometime. He told him that he was well, that he was able to cope with the solitude of his present situation, which he believed was good for the mind. He referred to it as a kind of '*purgatorio*'. But *purgatorio* implies suffering, and Mahler always suffered during long periods of solitude. He could not wait for Alma and Gucki to return.

During Alma's absence he had to deal with certain domestic matters, which were normally her domain, including keeping an eye on the servants. One of these, Kathi, the cook, complained that Mahler had been very abrupt with her. Alma supported her and reprimanded Gustav over his attitude towards Kathi. He was extremely upset that his wife had had the audacity to take the side of a servant. In a very long letter he denied any inappropriate behaviour and more or less accused Alma of being disloyal to him.

Meanwhile he had returned to composition. He had begun work on a new symphony, the *Ninth Symphony*, although he was reluctant to call it by name! He felt that he had tricked fate by considering *Das Lied von der Erde* as his Ninth, but his superstition still held firm. In his letters to Alma he mentioned that he had been spending time in his *Häuschen*, but he gave no details of the work he was doing.

His concentration on composing was however severely disrupted by the arrival of Richard Arnold, the vice-president of the New York Philharmonic, and his wife. Emil Freund, his lawyer friend, then arrived for 'health reasons', followed by the conductors Oskar Fried and Gustav Brecher. Welcome as these visitors were, their presence distracted Mahler from work on the new symphony, and he made it clear to Alma that no visitors would be staying at the Villa Trenker when she and Gucki returned from Levico. And with their return Mahler knew that he would once again find inspiration.

Alma was due back on the 13th of July. Gustav went to meet her at the station in Niedendorf, calling in at a barber's in Toblach on the way. He wanted to look his best, but his absentmindedness got the better of him. His intention to have a trim turned out to be a severe short back and sides, and Alma described him as looking ugly, like a convict!

Relieved that Alma had returned from what had obviously been a pointless stay in Levico, Mahler, freed from all domestic concerns, was able to concentrate on his new symphony. He had arranged to take Alma to Salzburg for a few days in mid-August, so he had a month to fulfil his aim of completing the short score. But as for Alma's mental state, no amount of rest could cure that. She had returned as depressed as when she had gone to Levico, for the problem lay with the state of their marital relationship. Yet Mahler's love for her remained as strong as ever; he just seemed to be unable to understand what she was going through.

Before they left for Salzburg, Mahler wrote to Bruno Walter telling him that he had been working very hard on the new symphony and that it was 'a very satisfactory addition to my little family'. He told him that he had been writing at such a speed that the manuscript would probably be illegible to anyone else, and that he hoped that he would be able to make a fair copy during the winter to come.

Upon their return more guests arrived. Anna Moll, concerned about her daughter, came to help her back onto an even keel. Mahler was of course delighted that she had come, as he was with a visit from Alfred Roller. On the 3rd of September Richard Strauss and his wife made the journey to Toblach. Mahler met them in front of the Südbahn Hotel where they had booked to stay. According to Alma's memoirs, Pauline Strauss had not changed, for as soon as she saw him she shouted across the square, 'Hello, Mahler! How's America? Lousy? I hope you made a pile anyway!' It was hardly surprising that after such a public display of bad manners, he felt deeply embarrassed. Following this unfortunate reunion, Richard Strauss invited the Mahlers, as well as Alfred Roller and Anna Moll, to dinner at their hotel. When Strauss suggested that Mahler should sit next to her, Pauline retorted 'only if he doesn't fidget!' whereupon he went to the other end of the table.

With Alma's return, despite her ongoing problems, and the music flowing, Mahler's spirits had been lifted during the last weeks of their summer break, and before he travelled to Vienna on the 6th of September, not only had he completed the short score of the new symphony, but he had also begun the orchestration of the last movement. His rush to complete the work is clearly evident on the manuscript paper with frequent and often ferocious crossings out and obliterations. He managed to finish the short score of the *Ninth* in just ten weeks, although he continued to work on the orchestration and the fair copy until the following spring. But even this 'fair' copy was completed in a rush with a great deal more alterations when compared to his earlier fair copies of scores. His first mention of the dreaded 'nine' was in an undated letter to Oskar Fried later in the month, when he wrote *'Die 9 ist fertig'* (The 9th is finished).

Ninth Symphony, in D minor
(in four movements)

Das Lied von der Erde and the *Ninth Symphony* are not only linked by the 'number nine' factor, but also by a sense of passing. *Das Lied* ends with *'Der Abschied'* (The Farewell), and the *Ninth* continues in this vein.

'The most heavenly piece that Mahler ever wrote': these are the words of Alban Berg on the first movement of Mahler's *Ninth Symphony* in a letter to Schoenberg in June 1912, shortly before the posthumous première of the symphony by its dedicatee Bruno Walter. Having studied the score in a four-hand piano arrangement, Berg described the work as 'music no longer of this world . . . a mysterious miracle of nature'. Bruno Walter wrote of the enormous responsibility placed upon his shoulders to introduce his friend's masterpiece to the world; he would dedicate his future to the furtherance of Mahler's music.

The *Ninth* is a totally different world from its predecessors. Gone are the heroic struggles, the glorious approaches to the gates of Heaven at the end of the *Second* and *Eighth Symphonies*, the devastating *Sixth* with its hammer blows, the journey from dusk to the dawning of a new day in the *Seventh*. The *Ninth* begins and ends with a slow movement. The first is filled with a combination of nostalgia and the fear of mortality, the last with a sense of resignation, a message of 'Rest in Peace', with the music never reaching a proper conclusion, but just peacefully dying away. Sandwiched between these two great movements are the two much shorter ones, the *Ländler* and a *Rondo-burleske*. It is a most unusual layout for a symphony, but the sheer magnificence of the outer movements holds the work together.

First movement: Andante comodo

In the opinion of many, including Georg Solti, the *Ninth Symphony* is regarded as Mahler's greatest symphony, and the first movement the finest symphonic movement he ever composed. It is both highly personal and at the same time forward looking, and its influence on the composers of the Second Viennese School, notably Berg, Webern and Schoenberg, was colossal. The symphony is often described as being death obsessed, but this is an over-simplification. The first movement of his least 'personal' symphony, the *Seventh*, opens with the rhythm of the oars of a rowing boat on the Wörthersee, whereas here, in the opinion of Leonard Bernstein, the rhythm of the opening bars is a depiction of Mahler's irregular heartbeat; quite probably so. Mahler was clearly aware of his approaching end, but he was still looking to the future, planning concerts in New York and elsewhere, not just for the approaching season, but for the year after as well. He had even considered, although turned down, a request to conduct a Wagner festival in Buenos Aires. There was plenty of life in him yet.

One of the reasons for the 'death obsession' so often linked with the *Ninth* stems from the inscriptions that he wrote on the draft score. One of these appears on the penultimate page of the first movement: '*Leb Wol! Leb Wol!*' (Farewell! Farewell!). But this is not Mahler giving up on life, rather a farewell to the music of the past, the end of Romanticism and the music that he loved. In short it was a farewell to tonality.

With a running time of around twenty-eight minutes, this movement is one of his longest and most forward-looking with its roots firmly in the soil of the first movement of the *Seventh*. It is a mighty struggle between life and death, tonality and atonality, and a raging against vanishing beauty. '*O Jugendzeit! Entschwundene! O Liebe! Verwehte!*' (Oh youth! Disappeared! Oh Love! Scattered!). This inscription in the middle of the movement clearly shows the emotional turmoil that he was going through.

Following the introductory 'heart' motif, played by the celli and horns there is an unsettling tolling of a harp, which brings to mind the opening line of Thomas Gray's *Elegy*: 'The Curfew tolls the knell of parting day.' The first principal melody appears, a melody that will reappear in different guises. This 'farewell' motif, given to the second violins, is also a direct link with the very end of *Das Lied von der Erde* with its oft-repeated '*Ewig*' (forever), which is sung to a similar falling two notes. This sighing theme is in part in homage to Beethoven, for it recalls his *Piano Sonata, Op. 81a*. '*Les Adieux*' (Farewell), but each time the melody tries to take wing, a sense of dark foreboding intervenes. The title '*Les Adieux*', although known as Beethoven's 'Farewell' sonata, is in fact in the plural, hence Mahler's '*Leb wol! Leb wol!*' It also just happens to be the piece he played at his audition for the Vienna Conservatory in 1875. Maybe this is nostalgia getting the better of him as he rages against the passage of time. Out of this passionate conflict, the horns blare out the opening theme before the music subsides into a '*schattenhaft*' (shadowy) passage. But this is merely a brief respite before the next onslaught in which the trombones, their bells raised for maximum effect, play the opening heart beat motif violently, while the timpani pound out the bell motif which had been played by the harp at the beginning of the movement. Then, almost inevitably, the music breaks into a funeral-march rhythm, but an undignified one with the timpani pounding on relentlessly. Quite suddenly there is a change of mood. The orchestra is reduced to chamber proportions, Mahler instructing the musicians to play in a mysterious manner, hesitantly and floating, as the movement moves towards its conclusion with the 'farewell' motif fading away as if vanishing into the ether.

Second movement: Im Tempo eines gemächlichen Ländlers
(In the tempo of a leisurely ländler)

The epic first movement is followed by two much shorter, yet brilliantly executed ones. The first of these is a *scherzo*. Whereas a ländler is normally a dance associated with merrymaking, here it is satirical, cold and at times even disturbing. At one point Mengelberg wrote in his copy of the score: 'grimly with fury', and Adorno referred to the movement as a *totentanz*. It is Mahler 'cocking a snook' at both the artistic emptiness of the peasant and his rustic ländler and at the shallowness and hypocrisy of high society.

Mahler's opening instructions are *'Etwas täppisch und sehr derb'* (somewhat clumsy and very coarse). This is followed by *'schwerfällig'* (ungainly). It is a ländler danced in seven league boots! There are lighter moments, even humorous at times, but these are short lived. The opening ländler 'waltz' is suddenly interrupted by a swirling one of the Viennese, Johann Strauss variety, but deliberately bloated; it has a scowl on its face rather than the usual smile. The two dances almost trip over each other in a bizarre, bacchanalian fashion with suggestions of the 'farewell' motif trying to make its presence felt. To add to the confusion a second slower waltz theme enters the fray, but it is not long before the hyper-active, overblown orchestration begins to calm down to an almost chamber level and a return to the opening material before the movement ends inconclusively.

Third movement: Rondo-Burleske
(*Rondeau-Burlesque* as Mahler wrote on the original manuscript)
Allegro assai: sehr trotzig (very defiant)

The final movements of the *Fifth* and *Seventh Symphonies* bear the title *Rondo*. In both cases these lively movements journey towards a bright, very positive and even ecstatic conclusion. With the third movement of the *Ninth* however, the word *Rondo* is qualified by *Burleske* and is of an entirely different nature. It is wild and bitter music and is Mahler's riposte to the cynicism of his critics. He dedicated the movement to his 'brothers in Apollo', a sneer aimed at those who had accused him of lacking the ability to write true counterpoint, which criticism stemmed in part from the fact that he had been excused from attending counterpoint lessons whilst at the Vienna Conservatory. It is also the most forward-looking movement he ever composed. At times it verges on the chaotic, intended of course, with dissonant and disjointed counterpoint. If he had levelled sarcasm at the ländler and waltz in the second movement, here he portrays the 'dance of life' as being little short of poisonous – a sick joke! A march, a burlesque of the march in the first movement of the *Third Symphony*, tries to make itself felt, but is soon submerged in the general pandemonium. As the storm temporarily abates, a lyrical and passionate theme emerges, played first by the trumpets and then handed over to the violins. It is not long however before cynicism strikes and the theme becomes a self-parody. The movement ends in a frenzy with a coda marked *'presto'*, the music becoming faster and faster, boiling over with fury.

Fourth movement: Adagio: Sehr Langsam.

Is the final movement Mahler's farewell to this world? Is it a farewell to Romanticism and tonality? Is it a requiem for his lost daughter as Michael Kennedy suggests? Is it a plea to Alma to stay with him and return his love during whatever time he had left? Perhaps it is a combination of all of these, but of one thing there is no doubt; the *Adagio* is a miracle of music at the end of which, in the words of Thomas Hampson, you become 'unbalanced . . . transported to some other place within your own consciousness . . . to reflect on what it is to be a human being and alive'. The final, slow movement of the *Third Symphony* originally bore the title 'What love tells me' (titles were later dropped by Mahler), and it is a passionate yearning for love, both physical and spiritual. It is forward looking, whereas the *Adagio* of the *Ninth* is nostalgic; it is Mahler's desperate desire to cling onto love despite physical loss and the passage of time. It is also Mahler at his most compassionate reflecting his concern for the future, not just his own, but of mankind.

With a passionate statement from the strings, the frenzied cynicism of the previous movement is immediately banished and the music adopts a hymn-like quality. There is a striking resemblance to the music of *'Abide with Me'*, and variations of this theme weave in and out throughout the movement.

'Abide with Me' was composed by William Henry Monk to words by the Reverend Henry Francis Lyte. Monk's original title was 'Eventide', and it was first published in Hymns Ancient and Modern in 1861. It is quite possible that Mahler had heard this popular hymn either during one of his voyages across the Atlantic, or in New York itself. Or had it not been just the muffled drum that had moved him to tears during the fireman's funeral procession? Had he heard the hymn on that occasion? Pure conjecture of course, but the resemblance is very clear, and certainly the words of the hymn 'Abide with me, fast falls the eventide' fit perfectly with his mental state at that time. Was this his plea to Alma not to desert him in his hour of need?

The movement is <u>not</u> one long twenty-five minute lament imbued with despair. Mahler's instructions alternate between *ohne Empfindung* (without emotion) and *Adagissimo, mit inniger Empfindung* (extremely slow, with deepest emotion). Only once is the music overwhelmed by heartbreak, the passionate *fff* climax before the almost hypnotic coda. At this point comes the very significant quote from *Die Kindertotenlieder*. It had been hinted at on several occasions earlier in the movement, but now it takes wing. It is from the penultimate song, when despair is countered by a vision of the lost children up on the hills in the sunshine. Surely this is in remembrance of Putzi, as well as those of his brothers and sisters who had died tragically at such an early age. This quotation, with its positive rising notes, is Mahler himself reaching out to them, longing to be reunited. From *pp* to *ppp* and finally to *pppp*, marked *ersterbend* (dying away), the music fades into eternity with a sigh, described so aptly by Bruno Walter as being 'like the melting of a cloud into the ethereal blue'. Peace and stillness reign, and it is quite normal for audience and musicians alike to be left stunned, almost paralysed, before anyone dares to applaud.

There are few, if any, pieces of music that have such an emotional impact. As Leonard Bernstein put it in his book *Findings*, 'No person of sensibility can come away from the *Ninth Symphony* without being exhausted and purified'. Leonard Bernstein, who considered his main mission in life was to further the cause of Mahler's music, once stated that he felt himself to be 'in direct contact with Mahler's message'. He pointed out that Mahler himself had conducted the first eight symphonies, showing the world how they should be performed, but had not lived to conduct his *Ninth*. He declared, 'This one he wrote for me'! Of course Mahler had dedicated it to Bruno Walter who conducted its première in 1912. Perhaps it might be fitting to leave the final comment on this great work to Mahler's granddaughter Marina, made in a BBC film on the composer: 'His music takes one beyond what one is able to bear, because it's a relief and because it's a freedom'.

Although this profound and visionary score alternates between hope and despair, existence and death, it must again be stressed that it was not Mahler giving up on life. Apart from his intensive conducting plans in New York and his understandable enthusiasm of having an orchestra at his beck and call, he was already contemplating buying a new home in the Semmering area to the southwest of Vienna, where he planned to retire and devote his remaining time to composing.

On the 6th of September he left Toblach for Vienna. After spending two days with the Molls, he returned to the Auenbruggergasse apartment where he planned to put the finishing touches to *Das Lied von der Erde,* a task which he had been obliged to shelve during the summer due to work on the *Ninth Symphony.* Unfortunately builders were hard at work in the apartment below, forcing him to seek peace elsewhere. He therefore decided to spend a few days with his industrialist friend Fritz Redlich and his wife Emmy in their small *Schloss* in Göding (now Hodonín) on the borders of Moravia and Austria. While he was completing the full score of *Das Lied,* Alma and Gucki returned to Vienna. Alma had been having recurring throat problems during the summer, and it had been recommended that she should have a tonsillectomy. This was duly carried out at a sanatorium in Vienna, her daughter having the same operation as well. In a letter to Alma, Mahler congratulated her on her bravery, having twenty-four incisions without any anaesthetic!

He returned to Vienna on the 22nd of September, staying at the Molls' where Alma and Gucki were recuperating. With the onset of autumn the new season in New York loomed large – forty-four concerts had been booked for him during the five-month period. But first he had to travel to The Hague and Amsterdam to conduct performances of his *Seventh Symphony,* the only European concerts that he had agreed to conduct that year. This of course was something he had been looking forward to, returning to Holland and his many friends there, especially the Mengelbergs. Meanwhile Alma, helped by her parents, would clear the apartment, putting most of their belongings into store, for their Auenbruggergasse home that had served them so well over the years, was no longer needed. Alma had clearly not recovered from her operation as is evident in a letter from Gustav, written on the 28th of September on his way to Amsterdam, in which he wrote that he had been upset to leave, especially as she was looking so poorly.

He was met at the station by Mengelberg, whom he described as being his usual hospitable self. He had put the Concertgebouw Orchestra through an intense rehearsal schedule during the week before Mahler's arrival, and when the latter took charge at his own first rehearsal he was very impressed by the groundwork carried out by his friend. He told Alma that the orchestra sounded wonderful and, with Alphons Diepenbrock present at his first rehearsal, he declared the occasion to be pure pleasure, not work.

Several musicians approached him with the suggestion that he might conduct them in music by Beethoven and Wagner in addition to his own, and that the orchestra would be prepared to have extra rehearsals. Mahler not only agreed with the proposal but showed delight at the prospect. After further discussion it was decided that he would conduct the overture to *Die Meistersinger* at the third and final concert on the 7th of October, and that Mengelberg would conduct Beethoven's *First Symphony* after the interval at the first two concerts on the 2nd in The Hague and the 3rd in Amsterdam.

The *Seventh Symphony* was warmly received at all three concerts. Mahler was overjoyed – this was just the boost that he needed before setting off for America. Following the symphony's acclaim, Mengelberg himself conducted the work no less than five times during the 1909-1910 season. But Mahler decided that the Seventh, with its forward-looking score and associated difficulties for musicians, would not be a wise choice for New York, for the time being at least. An added bonus came after he had played parts of his *Eighth Symphony* to Diepenbrock and Mengelberg. The latter was so impressed that he urged Mahler to choose Amsterdam for its première. Needless to say, Mahler was very enthusiastic about the proposal, knowing that under Mengelberg all preliminary arrangements and rehearsals would be carried out with the utmost efficiency.

On Friday the 8th of October, Mahler left Amsterdam for Paris, arriving on the same day as Alma, Gucki and her nurse. Thence they took the train to Cherbourg where they boarded the *Kaiser Wilhelm II* and set sail for New York.

Chapter 16

New York . . . Part Three

Tenth Symphony

THEIR FIFTH CROSSING of the Atlantic proved to be a particularly unpleasant one. With unusually rough seas Mahler spent much of the time horizontal in his cabin. Among the other passengers was the violinist Fritz Kreisler, who provided him with a welcome distraction from the adverse elements by showing a particular interest in discussing his scores. Kreisler was overwhelmed by the skill of Mahler's orchestration and his utter sincerity. When interviewed three weeks later, he declared that it would not be long before the world recognised Mahler with unreserved enthusiasm.

The *Kaiser Willem II* docked in New York harbour on the evening of the 19th of October 1909, arriving several hours late due to the stormy seas. Alma later wrote how the magnificent New York skyline had once again moved them to tears, possibly partly due to their relief at being able to put their feet on dry land. Following what she considered to have been an unpleasant search by customs officers, they were driven to the Hotel Savoy on Fifth Avenue, the same hotel where they had stayed the previous year.

The enticing prospect of having total control over the reformed Philharmonic orchestra, as well as the programming for the season, proved to be at least in part wishful thinking. To start with Mahler was obliged to bow to the wishes of the Guarantors' Committee by including several works by Tchaikovsky, including the *First Piano Concerto* and the *Sixth Symphony*. Mahler had never been over-fond of Tchaikovsky's non-operatic music, especially the symphonies, but he acknowledged its growing popularity ever since the Russian composer's visit to New York in 1891.

As regards the orchestra itself, the complement of 102 players had been pared down to 92, 55 of whom had been involved during the previous season. No expense had been or was being spared in the quest for the best musicians, one of whom was the principal horn player Reiter who had been enticed away from the Metropolitan Opera! The string section was least affected, while other musicians were forced to accept demotion or leave.

Only half of the brass and woodwind players remained, and the whole of the percussion and timpani section had been replaced. During the summer Mahler had purchased a new set of timpani from a Viennese supplier, paid for by Mrs George R. Sheldon. Such was his search for excellence, and with it came a workload that greatly surpassed that of his first two seasons in New York. During the 1909-1910 season no less than 97 works by 33 composers would be performed, not just in New York but in other American cities as well.

In an interview with a *New York Daily Tribune* reporter on the 20th of October, Mahler declared his hope to be able to arrange special concerts during the course of the season at prices affordable to all. He firmly believed that music should be available to everyone, not just to the wealthy. He told the reporter that he intended to include well established music as well as new works of merit, but that in his programming he would nevertheless take into account what the critics and public wanted. In another interview, this time with a correspondent of *Musical America*, he spoke of his ambition to put the Philharmonic on a par with the best orchestras of Europe such as those of Vienna and Berlin. He also emphasized that his aim was to educate the public. The correspondent wrote that Mahler conveyed 'the impression of a philosopher and an idealist of lofty aspirations', and that it was clear that he had a 'determination to fight down obstacles in the way of all that is purest in art'. He also stated that he, Mahler, was a man of 'personal charm and magnetism'. Thus Mahler the diplomat smoothed the way ahead for the reformed New York Philharmonic's 68th season, the first in his charge.

With a combination of determination and infectious enthusiasm, as reported by his newly appointed concert master Theodore Spiering, Mahler embarked on a series of nine rehearsals with his orchestra in preparation for their first concert to be held in Carnegie Hall on the 4th of November. The programme consisted of Beethoven's overture *The Consecration of the House* and *Third Symphony,* the symphonic poem *Mazeppa* by Liszt and *Till Eulenspiegel* by Richard Strauss. Anticipation of this concert had been white hot, but as things turned out the general opinion was one of slight disappointment combined with a hope of great things to come. This feeling was summed up by the review in *The World*, which stated that 'Rome was not built in a day'. After only nine rehearsals, how could anyone expect the emergence of a top rank orchestra, even at the hands of Mahler? Yet it was generally agreed by the critics that great strides had been made and that the future for the orchestra as a first rate ensemble was without question, and Mahler himself was given thanks and praise for his efforts. The only questions asked, not unexpectedly, were over his approach to the *Eroica*. His very personal interpretation, and at times unusual tempi, had not come as a surprise to those who had attended the performance of Beethoven's *Ninth* the previous April. This opening concert set the tone for the months to come with Mahler conducting more works by Beethoven than by any other composer and with the music of Richard Strauss, the main representative of the new music (*Till Eulenspiegel* was performed ten times during the course of the season!).

The second concert, which took place six days later, was of particular note for the first performance of a *Bach Suite* compiled and arranged by Mahler himself. With his admiration and love of Bach's music and the inspiration it afforded him with his own composition, he determined to introduce Bach to a wider audience. For this arrangement he chose the *Overture, Rondeau* and *Badinerie* from Bach's *Suite No. 2*, coupled with the *Air* and *Gavottes 1 and 2* from the *Suite No. 3*. Mahler himself composed the continuo part, which he played on a specially prepared Steinway piano made to sound like a harpsichord. It must have come as something of a surprise to many in the audience to see the conductor, renowned for performances of large-scale dramatic works, sit down at the prepared piano and proceed to play the continuo part. Although giving the impression of free improvisation it had of course been written down. He gave the part greater importance than the traditional Baroque continuo, promoting it to first chair orchestral status and using it to add additional colour to the score. (He also wrote a version for organ continuo). The half-expected cries of 'sacrilege' did not materialise. A few purists were inevitably offended, but the general reaction was 'very interesting'.

Mahler's *Bach Suite* became very popular and was performed on numerous occasions with Mahler altering the continuo part at every performance to give the impression of freshness of improvisation. On each occasion he would ask Alma for her opinion. He clearly enjoyed performing the work, as is evident in a letter dated the 19th of November to his Austrian banker friend, Paul Hammerschlag, in which he wrote that he had been having 'great fun recently with a Bach concerto'.

On the 3rd of November 1909, Mahler's *Seventh Symphony* had been given its première in Vienna. Unlike the performances in Prague and Amsterdam, it met with a predictable barrage of Viennese hostility. The conducting of Ferdinand Löwe had not helped. In a letter to Guido Adler, Mahler wrote that however well intentioned he might have been, Löwe clearly had not fully understood the work and was a 'four-square' interpreter. On the other hand, Schoenberg told Mahler that Löwe had made every effort to follow the score's directions to the letter, although without achieving much more. Even so, it is clear from his letter that the young composer greatly admired the *Seventh*, its experimental and forward-looking aspects in tune with what he himself was endeavouring to achieve.

The New York season continued apace with the next in Mahler's Beethoven series when on the 20th of November the *Second Symphony* and four overtures were performed. His doubling of the woodwind met with general approval as did his conducting, and it was noted that the Philharmonic was improving with every concert.

The 22nd saw the first of Mahler's Sunday concerts, the 'popular' events at affordable prices. Some questioned the wisdom of these, both on religious and financial grounds. The first major success however was on the 25th with a performance of the *Third Symphony* by Brahms. The review in the *New York Daily Tribune* the following morning stated that 'nothing finer than the finale . . . had been heard in our concert rooms for years'. Not even Toscanini's first performance of his treasured *Tristan und Isolde* at the Met managed to distract Mahler's enthusiasm and determination.

Then controversy came. Once again it was his interpretation of the classics that came under fire. This time it was Beethoven. The concert concerned took place on the 8th of December; the work in question was Beethoven's *Fifth Symphony*. An article in *Musical America* referred to it as 'Mahler's Fifth Symphony', that he had taken liberties of tempo and in so doing had distorted Beethoven's intentions and spirit. The same work was repeated four days later on the 9th at the second of the Sunday concerts, and the review in the *New York Daily Tribune* criticised Mahler for allowing the 'fearful beating of the kettledrums and the violence of some other noise-making instruments'. Yet despite these acerbic comments from some directions, he remained the talk and toast of the town for his sterling work. However, the signs were clear; his honeymoon period, at least as far as the critics were concerned, was beginning to show signs of nearing its end. Would New York become another Vienna? – probably not. For one thing, anti-Semitism was on no one's agenda, but Mahler knew that battles could well be just over the horizon. Yet the aforementioned article by composer and teacher Arthur Farwell in *Musical America* on the 18th of December was countered in the same edition by an accurate and very positive character study. It referred to Mahler as 'a stern disciplinarian at rehearsals', yet charming in private, never seeking praise for either his conducting achievements or his own compositions and that he was 'the personification of courtesy' at home.

Alma reported that an event of considerable embarrassment took place on the 17th of December. The Guarantors' Committee, with the best of intentions, had arranged for Mahler to conduct his own *First Symphony*. He had agreed and the rehearsals had gone as smoothly as he could have expected. Come the evening of the performance, according to Alma, he was in for a shock. The good ladies had secretly made arrangements to pay homage to him by spotlighting the podium and festooning it with wreaths.

To make matters worse they had apparently rearranged the seating of the musicians with the brass players at the front surrounding him and the strings forming a semi-circle behind them. The result needless to say would have been a total imbalance of sound. However, none of the reviews mentioned this, so perhaps this was another case of Alma's imagination running riot! Nor did Mahler mention it in his letter of the 19th to Bruno Walter in which he gave the impression that he had been quite pleased with the performance, even though many of the critics had been far from complimentary. The general opinion was that this was an early work, and as he had since established himself as a composer 'his symphony cannot therefore be summarily dismissed as we are inclined to think that it ought to be . . .' (*New York Daily Tribune*). Some repeated the common complaint in Europe that he had forbidden the use of a programme for what was clearly programme music. The *Musical Courier* was more positive, praising the 'picturesque detail in melody, harmony and orchestration' and 'excellent orchestral writing', and as it was Mahler's *First Symphony*, 'it is a truly remarkable achievement' which foreshadowed the works to come. The review in *Musical America* commented that it was a symphony of 'youthful ardour and exuberance . . .'. Henry Krehbiel, in the *New York World*, wrote that there was no reason why Mahler should be 'a prophet of the ugly' as in parts of the last movement. He added that this was evident by the way he interrupted 'a painfully cacophonous din' with a melody that was 'exquisitely lovely and profoundly moving'. When Krehbiel – New York's equivalent of the feared Hanslick in Vienna – hinted that he himself might in future provide programme notes for Mahler's symphonies, the latter stepped in and forbade him from doing so.

The following month Mahler wrote to Schoenberg saying that his *First Symphony* had been a failure in New York, and that he was longing to return home.

It is worth returning to the letter that he wrote to Bruno Walter on the 19th of December. He was clearly becoming disillusioned both with his orchestra and with the American music scene in general. He complained about overwork, union interference, musicians who lacked talent and were phlegmatic, and that he felt he was fighting a losing battle. Nevertheless he singled out the audiences as being lovable and attentive. The problem was of course a combination of the press, traditionalism and petty politics, all of which he had hoped he had left behind in Vienna. He congratulated Walter on the success of a performance of the *Third Symphony*, which he had conducted in Vienna on the 25th of November, saying that the news had given him great joy and that judging by the reviews it must have been superb.

Overworked he may have been, but he still found time to attend numerous social events with Alma. Often in the past he had done his utmost to avoid such occasions, but in New York, away from his friends, they were a welcome distraction from his music responsibilities. These came in a variety of guises. Some were professional, such as a dinner party with the music publisher Ernest Schirmer and his wife, while others were purely for pleasure like the day they spent with Laura Roosevelt's family at their seaside home in Oyster Bay, a hamlet on the north shore of Long Island. Their hostess took them to see her brother-in-law and ex-president Theodore Roosevelt's house, Sagamore Hill. He was not resident at the time, for having left office earlier in the year he had gone on an extended safari in Africa.

On another memorable occasion they attended a séance at the house of one Eusapia Palladino. Otto Kahn, one of the chief financial backers of the Met, his wife and Gustav and Alma's doctor friend Joseph Fraenkel accompanied them. Alma's description of a flying mandolin, the table hitting the ceiling and phosphorescent bodies would seem to be either another touch of her excessive imagination or the result of the influence of some substance or other! Palladino, who had been brought up in the back streets of Naples and who had married a conjuror, had become notorious in various European countries for instigating strange happenings during her séances. Although initially she had managed to baffle the experts, she was eventually exposed as nothing more than an expert trickster.

Another memorable social occasion was their visit to the home of Louis Tiffany, the American artist, designer, philanthropist and something of a recluse. The invitation had come after he had attended one of Mahler's rehearsals incognito. His home was palatial and suitably exotic, and as the Mahlers went up the imposing staircase they heard the strains of the prelude to *Parsifal* being played on the organ by a grandson of Shelley! Tiffany greeted his guests and then, according to Alma, disappeared almost immediately because he was addicted to hashish! Gustav and Alma found themselves in the midst of a large gathering, with footmen distributing champagne and women adorned in attire entirely in keeping with the surroundings. In her memoirs Alma described the scene as being like *One Thousand and One Nights*, New York style!

The concert schedule was gathering pace. On the 29th of December the violinist Maud Powell was the soloist in a very fine performance of Mendelssohn's *Violin Concerto*, Schubert's *'Unfinished' Symphony* being the accompanying work. Maud Powell later wrote that she worshipped the memory of Mahler both as a man and as a musician. To her he was an inspirational genius, a sensitive man whose character had often been misunderstood and maligned. She was again the soloist the following day playing Beethoven's *Violin Concerto*.

On New Year's Day Mahler wrote to his friend, the musicologist Guido Adler. He was quite clearly upset by certain false rumours and misunderstandings that had surfaced in Vienna. These were on two fronts, his overwork and Alma. The former may have stemmed from the well-publicised ambitious programme for the New York season, as well as from Mahler's own correspondence. Among these letters was one to Adler himself written in November in which Mahler told him that he had to conserve his energy by going to bed in the afternoons, mentioning also how much he looked forward to settling down to composing so long as he managed to survive the next two years. As for the gossip concerning Alma, he accused Adler of making unjust comments. These were the result of rumours concerning Alma's flirtations with Gabrilowitsch, which had given rise to understandable criticism being voiced by Mahler's friends in Vienna. Mahler made it quite clear that Alma had his welfare at heart, that she was faithful and a good organiser, both of domestic and financial affairs. He ended by stating that any such unjust comments aimed at his wife were aimed at him as well! Considering that Guido Adler had been one of Mahler's staunchest supporters as well as a close friend who had grown up in his home town of Iglau, his remarks in this letter were sharp to say the least.

How this unfortunate matter arose is unclear, but Alma's mental state the previous summer, the cooling of her physical relationship with her husband and her flirting with Ossip Gabrilowitsch may have sparked off coffee house talk in Vienna. As regards the overwork, with such a hectic schedule well publicised, with his health not what it used to be and the fact that he had told others such as Schoenberg and Walter that he was suffering from overwork, meant that his denial to Adler was simply not true. Just five days later he wrote to Roller saying that there were too few hours in a day, that Alma's initial enthusiasm for America was growing thin and that he himself longed to return to Austria and not go away again!

Earlier in his letter to Adler, and on a more positive note, he had said that he was convinced that many of the shortcomings in the orchestration of his music in the past had been due to spending most of his time in the very different acoustic of the opera house rather than the concert hall. Always striving to improve his techniques, he felt that he was learning a good deal about orchestration and acoustics since he had become a concert conductor.

Mahler's heavy workload, and his need to go to bed in the afternoons, meant that there was little room for family life, but Alma wrote of an amusing incident concerning little Gucki. She would sometimes stand beside her father while he was working. On one occasion when he was revising a score she watched wide-eyed as he began to scratch out note after note. Alarmed, and with her imagination taking wing, she blurted out that she wouldn't like to be a note. When her father asked her why, she replied that he might scratch her out and blow her away!

Two concerts of note, especially so because of the pianists who performed, took place on the 6th and 16th of January 1910. The first consisted of the *Symphonie Fantastique* by Berlioz and Beethoven's *5th Piano Concerto* with Ferruccio Busoni as the soloist. The *New York Daily Tribune* described the performance of the symphony as 'graphic, vivid and powerful'. The *New York Post* stated that no conductor, not even the Berlioz specialist Felix Weingartner, had managed to rouse an audience 'to such a state of frenzied excitement'. The correspondent regarded Mahler as a miracle worker, and that it was little surprise that 'the Mahlerites are growing so fast in numbers'. He even compared his conducting of the Berlioz to Paderewski playing Liszt! The concert on the 16th saw Sergei Rachmaninov playing his own *Third Piano Concerto*.

Between these two celebrity events came the next in Mahler's controversial Beethoven series, with the *Fifth* and *Sixth Symphonies* being played. He had already been criticised for his interpretation of the *Fifth* two months before, so attention this time was focused on his treatment of the *Sixth*. With some negative reviews virtually pre-planned, the journalists concerned were disappointed. The only point of interest they managed to raise was that he had added an additional set of timpani to heighten the thunder effect.

The truth of the matter was that his fresh interpretations of the classics were becoming accepted, even lauded, as was the performance of Beethoven's *Fifth* at the Academy of Music in Philadelphia on the 17th of January. The review of this concert in *The Philadelphia Inquirer* pointed out that performances of the classics did not have to be dull and impersonal, and praised Mahler for giving 'one of the most highly coloured and strongly accentuated renderings'. The author considered Mahler's reading to be sincere, dignified and altogether very fine. His ambition of educating the American concertgoer was beginning to bear fruit.

Yet it seems that he had to keep the pressure up on his musicians at rehearsals, not just with their playing but their attitude as well. Theodore Spiering, the recently appointed concertmaster, remarked that at one rehearsal Mahler had told the orchestra that when he conducted he did so with his heart and soul, and that his aim was to bring to life the intentions and spirit of the composer without any suggestion of personal glory or gain. He then stated that any member who felt otherwise he would regard as being an enemy!

The 26th of January marked an important occasion for him with a performance of *Die Kindertotenlieder*. The song cycle was well received, and the reviews the following day spoke of sincerity, skilful orchestration and beauty. Even Henry Krehbiel, Mahler's chief adversary among the gentlemen of the press, wrote that they were individual, poignantly sincere and clearly had 'autobiographical significance'. Mahler had as usual declined to include in the programme any mention of their background, so Krehbiel was once again deprived of any information that would place the songs in a personal context.

Four days later a very embarrassing confrontation took place at the final rehearsal of Schumann's *Piano Concerto*. The pianist was Josef Weiss from Leipzig. Alma described him as having a square, bald head with a little tuft in the middle and having slit eyes which, in her opinion, meant that he was either insane or a genius! Mahler, who had known him for some time and recognised him as being exceptionally gifted, had heard that he was going through hard times. He therefore arranged for him to travel to New York especially for this concert and to receive a very high fee.

The earlier rehearsals had gone smoothly, but at the dress rehearsal Weiss was nervous and below par. Mahler made some positive suggestions as to how the music should be played, but Weiss was on edge and made an unfortunate aside about Mahler's breath! He pretended not to hear this remark, but suggested that he should play more and speak less. At which point Weiss leapt to his feet, slammed down the piano lid and stormed out! He was replaced by Paolo Gallico.

The 1st of February saw the American première of Richard Strauss's opera *Elektra*. Mahler already had a poor opinion of the work, considering it to be no match for its predecessor, the masterpiece *Salomé*, but he felt a certain duty to attend the performance at the Manhattan Opera House. Alma recalled that her husband had wanted to leave half way through. She had persuaded him not to do so, but afterwards they both agreed that it had been one of the most boring evenings that they could remember. Some in the audience merely applauded politely, while others appeared to actually like the opera. Members of New York's Greek community, however, were appalled and demonstrations took place led by Raymond Duncan, brother of the famed dancer Isadora Duncan. To him the beauty of the *Elektra* of Sophocles had been desecrated, and he urged that steps should be taken to educate the American people in genuine Greek art.

Meanwhile plans were well under way for the première of Mahler's *Eighth Symphony* to be held in Munich later in the year. He wrote to Emil Hertzka of the publishers Universal Edition enclosing a revised piano score, asking him to transfer the revisions to the full score. He also requested that copies of the vocal score be sent to Richard Strauss, Willem Mengelberg, Bruno Walter, Oskar Fried and Julius Korngold among others. With Mahler still in New York, the rehearsal arrangements were in the hands of the German impresario Emil Gutman who was based in Munich. On the

27th of February Mahler wrote to him voicing his concern over the preparations. A combination of two delays, the publication of the score and the start of rehearsals by the Riedel-Verein choral society of Leipzig (one of several choirs from different cities involved), worried Mahler to such an extent that he urged Gutman to consider cancelling the première. He pointed out that it would be bad for both of them if the occasion turned out to be a disaster or if it had to be cancelled at the last moment. He suggested replacing the *Eighth* with another of his symphonies.

Towards the end of February, Mahler and the Philharmonic left New York for a short four-day tour, performing in New Haven (Connecticut), Springfield (Massachusetts), Providence (Rhode Island) and finally Boston, the city whose orchestra had hitherto been generally regarded as America's finest. With such a tight itinerary Alma remained behind with Gucki.

The main work in New Haven was Grieg's *Piano Concerto*, played by Olga Samaroff. She had become a friend of the Mahlers, and she later described Alma as one of the most beautiful women she had ever seen. After a well-received performance, Olga Samaroff dined with Mahler. Being the town of Yale University, he had hoped to experience some student *joie de vivre*, but he was disappointed. The cafés and restaurants were quiet and rather lifeless, their meal subdued. American students were clearly very different from their Viennese counterparts.

In Springfield he conducted the *Symphonie Fantastique*, and once again his reading was praised without reservation. He wrote to Alma telling her how he hated Springfield, that his stomach was troubling him, it was bitterly cold and that there was a constant roar of traffic. From Springfield they moved on to Providence, where the attendance turned out to be disappointing mainly due to a recital being given by Fritz Kreisler the same evening at a nearby venue.

The tour ended with the concert in Boston's Symphony Hall. The *Symphonie Fantastique* was again the main work along with Beethoven's *Leonore Overture No. 3* and Richard Strauss's symphonic poem *Till Eulenspiegel*. Whereas the orchestra had been considered to be 'well-trained', 'superb' and 'magnificent' after the first three concerts, the *Boston Sunday Globe* was more restrained in its praise, mentioning 'limitation of the orchestra's technique' and that it was 'unequal to the execution of Strauss's score'. Nevertheless the review was very complimentary towards Mahler and his interpretation of the scores. As the home of America's 'top' orchestra, perhaps the correspondent felt that he had to be restrained in his review. The organist and composer Arthur Foote, who had attended the concert, wrote that from that performance alone it was clear that Mahler was 'one of the greatest conductors of all time'.

With the tour over, his next assignment was to make a return to the

Metropolitan Opera to conduct the first American performance of *Pique Dame* by Tchaikovsky, which he had already conducted in Vienna. The cast included Leo Slezak and Emmy Destinn. Slezak later wrote that rehearsals had often been marred by absenteeism, and that frequently he and Mahler were alone. He remembered him as being tired and ailing, the fiery spirit of old gone. Tired he may have been, which is more than likely following his very hectic schedule over the months gone by, but determination of the spirit remained, even if the flesh was weaker. Rumours were rife of a strained atmosphere at rehearsals with Mahler's usual quest for perfection over-riding everything. Emmy Destinn was said to be in fear of him, while another singer apparently cracked under the strain. The fiery spirit of old gone? – Unlikely. Wherever the truth lay, the première was a success and his conducting praised unanimously. Three further performances took place before the month ended.

The following Thursday Mahler was back in front of the Philharmonic. The main work was Brahms's *Violin Concerto,* played by Fritz Kreisler. Also included in the programme was Busoni's *Turandot Suite*, completed in 1906. Busoni afterwards remarked on the love and dedication that Mahler had shown during the rehearsals and that the performance itself was perfect. At the end, Alma went to Busoni's box and managed to persuade a very shy composer to join her husband on the platform to receive a well deserved round of applause.

With the season drawing to a close Mahler wrote a letter to Anna Moll in which he stated that he had coped with the New York season well yet without sparing himself, adding that he was the fittest of the three of them, but that he was impatient to return home. Even while he was in America he remained loyal to his friends in Europe. A typical example of this occurred when Otto Klemperer crossed swords with Angelo Neumann, director of the Prague Opera, and was obliged to resign as a result. In his memoirs Klemperer wrote how he had applied for a similar post in Hamburg and had sent a telegram to Mahler asking him if he would consider recommending him for the job. This Mahler did immediately, telling the director of the Hamburg Opera to 'Grab Klemperer'. He was signed forthwith.

The penultimate concert of the Philharmonic's season was notable for a very fine performance of Bruckner's *Fourth Symphony.* Mahler's respect for the man and his music had never faltered since his student days at the Vienna Conservatory, and it gave him the greatest pleasure to be able to conduct his *Fourth.* Alas the attendance at Carnegie Hall on the 30th of March was very poor, but the *New York Times* eulogized over Mahler's conducting with words such as 'superb' and 'masterly', that the performance was brilliant and that the orchestra was gaining 'the right to be called a virtuoso organization'.

The final concert of the season took place on the 1st of April with an all Beethoven programme – the *Choral Fantasia* and the *Ninth Symphony*. While the performance of the *Choral Fantasia* met with widespread approval, Mahler yet again drew criticism over his minor revisions in the orchestration of the *Ninth* and his 'accentuation of details and his originality in the regulation of tempi' (*New York Sun*). As for his use of a second set of timpani, the *New York Times* found it at times to be 'nerve-racking'!

Thus Mahler's third season in New York ended. Before leaving he agreed to give two interviews. One appeared in the *New York Herald Tribune*, Mahler stressing that today's radical is tomorrow's conservative. He pointed out that what really mattered, and should be respected, was 'genuine self-expression' and sincerity, even if traditional rules were broken. Yet sadly this was frequently not the case with conservatives condemning new ideas. He told the correspondent how he held Strauss and Debussy in high esteem for their originality, but that only time would be the judge as to whether their works were decadent or not. He ended by stressing that nothing was immortal, including dogmatic standards, 'and the critic should be enough of a philosopher to realise this'. In the second interview, he told the correspondent of the *New York Times* that he was pleased with the results of his work so far and that the orchestra had improved with every concert. He had found the New York public to be serious and attentive. He told the reporter that as yet he had made no plans for the following season, other than that the repertoire would consist of both classical and modern works, and would include 'good music of all nations'. In the same interview he also mentioned that he had cancelled a proposed music festival organised in his honour in Mannheim that May. This festival would have included a performance of *Die Meistersinger* and symphonies by Beethoven as well as some of his own. However, he said that he felt tired and needed a rest. Unfortunately his words were twisted by a Munich newspaper, quoting Mahler as having said that he was 'tired of America'!

He probably was tired, but uppermost in his mind were the organisational problems concerning the preparations for the première of his *Eighth Symphony*. These were not being helped by the fact that they were in the hands of Emil Gutman whose efficiency he held in serious doubt. This was made clear in a letter he wrote to Gutman in which he stated that if, on his return to Europe, he found that musically matters were not up to scratch, he would cancel the performance. On the other hand if he felt that satisfactory progress was being made, he would go ahead but without what he referred to as Gutman's 'Barnum and Bailey' methods! (Barnum and Bailey were entrepreneurs renowned for their brash marketing and famous for their circus extravaganzas, most notably 'The Greatest Show on

Earth'!). He wrote to Bruno Walter expressing the same sentiments, saying that he relied on his help to sort out a possibly disastrous situation. He asked him to contact him at the Hotel Majestic in Paris where he would be staying until the 17th of April. He also told Walter that he had completed the fair copy of the score of his *Ninth Symphony*. Remaining Mahler's top priorities for the immediate future were, needless to say, a much-needed holiday and a return to composing.

With disappointing attendances at many of the concerts, the season had shown a deficit. Nevertheless Mahler was given permission to replace no less than twenty-six members of the orchestra before the autumn. With the quality of the orchestra thus improved, and with the appointment of a full-time manager, Mahler's workload would be eased and attendances at the concerts would hopefully improve.

The Mahlers left New York on the 5th of April 1910, arriving in Paris a week later for the first performance in France of his *Second Symphony*, to take place on the afternoon of the 17th at the Théâtre du Châtelet. Anna and Carl Moll had travelled to Paris for this important occasion, and while Gustav launched into the rehearsals, Alma and Gucki spent much of their time with them.

The orchestra booked for the concert was the Orchestre Colonne. The founder and conductor of the orchestra, Edouard Colonne, had died on the 28th of March. Not surprisingly, the concert, scheduled to take place only three weeks later, had been in danger of cancellation until assistant conductor and composer Gabriel Pierné agreed to take on the onerous responsibility for the rehearsals prior to Mahler's arrival.

Pierné held a dinner party at his home with Alma and Gustav the guests of honour. Among the other guests were Paul Dukas, Gabriel Fauré, Claude Debussy and Paul and Sophie Clemenceau. A combination of communication problems and with his mind firmly fixed on the concert did not make the evening a great success for Mahler and, according to Alma, Dukas, who was sitting next to her, spent much of the time relating unpleasant stories concerning Debussy's past!

The music of Mahler and French tastes did not mix particularly well. This is not really surprising when one considers the differences between the French and Austro-German cultures at that time. One need only look at the very different paths that contemporary music was taking, with the French impressionists on the one hand and on the other the music of Mahler and the emerging Second Viennese School. (A few French composers were genuinely interested in his music, the eighteen-year-old Darius Milhaud being one). Music apart, there was also an ambivalent attitude towards Germanic culture in general stemming from the Franco-Prussian war, only forty years before, and the siege of Paris of 1870-71 which remained in the memory of many. Nevertheless, the Paris première of Mahler's *Second Symphony* was by and large a success. The audience applauded generously and most of the critics, although voicing some reservations, were on the whole courteous to him and wrote in favour of the work.

According to Alma her husband had been deeply upset by the sudden departure of Debussy, Pierné and Dukas during the second movement. They had apparently found the music to be 'too foreign . . . too slav . . . too Schubertian'. Henry-Louis de la Grange has cast serious doubts as to whether this actually happened, certainly as far as Pierné and Dukas were concerned. The *Second* was the most consistently popular of Mahler's symphonies and the audience had applauded after the first movement. Even if the first movement had not appealed to the tastes of the three French composers, the second movement, the delightful and delicate *Andante*, could hardly have given offence. It is almost unthinkable that Pierné, who had after all taken over the rehearsals before Mahler's arrival in Paris, would have shown such bad manners and lack of etiquette by walking out. Dukas, who had spent most of the evening at Perné's dinner party talking to Alma, and whose opera *Ariane et Barbe-Bleue* Gustav and Alma had attended at the Opéra-Comique the previous evening, was also most unlikely to have done so. Which leaves Debussy who was well known for demonstrating his feelings about anything he disliked, especially anything Germanic. Although Mahler was not over-enthusiastic about Debussy's music, after all he had described the opera *Pelléas et Mélisande* as 'harmless', he had conducted a number of his works in New York. Debussy, however, was known to be a strange person with a definite dark side to his character, epitomised by the way he had treated his wife who had tried to poison herself, recovered and who then divorced him. Etiquette and good manners were not part of Debussy's make-up. It is therefore possible that he did walk out, although there is no mention of him having done so in the press, nor in any of Mahler's letters. Alma's account therefore, at least in part, might be considered as being a further example of her penchant for artistic licence.

Having said farewell to their Parisian friends, and with little Anna and her nurse returning to Vienna with the Molls, Alma and Gustav departed for Rome for three concerts with the Academy of St. Cecilia. These Mahler could well have done without, especially as the orchestra was bereft of most of its best musicians who had left Italy for a South American tour. Tired and longing for a rest and a return to composing, it was little wonder that Mahler set about haranguing the make-shift orchestra whose performances at the first two concerts were so embarrassing that he cancelled the third.

He returned to Vienna on the 3rd of May to stay with the Molls, but he could not settle down and enjoy his holiday yet, for work had to be done in preparation for the première of his *Eighth Symphony*. Emil Gutmann paid him a visit to update him on the arrangements. Gutmann had booked as the two main choirs the Vienna Singverein and Leipzig's Riedel-Verein, and plans had been made for Mahler to rehearse these choirs during the following month. Mahler entered into a contract with Universal Edition for the publication of his *Ninth Symphony* and *Das Lied von der Erde*. The peace and quiet he craved seemed to be as far away as ever. To make matters worse, he and Alma were devastated by bad news. Their friend of so many years, Emil Zuckerkandl, died of cancer. Mahler's friend Siegfried Lipiner was also diagnosed with the disease, and news reached Alma that Max Burckhard, family friend and former director of the Burgtheater who had been the first to encourage her to compose, was also seriously ill.

They were both under enormous stress, and Alma, also suffering a recurrence of sexual and creative frustration, was almost at breaking point. Once again it was agreed that she should take a rest cure. This summer it would be at Tobelbad, a spa near Graz where she would relax and take the waters. As with the previous summer, Gucki, now turned six, and nurse Turner would accompany her, to be joined later by her mother. Alma's mental problems could possibly have been inherited, at least to a certain extent, for her father, the artist Emil Jacob Schindler, was known to have had bouts of depression. Schindler also had shown little or no love towards Alma when she was a baby.

Having managed to attend some rehearsals of parts of his *Eighth* by the Vienna Singverein under Franz Schalk, which thoroughly displeased him, Mahler took Alma, Gucki and Miss Turner to Tobelbad. He returned to Vienna the following day, once again staying with the Molls. He went to another choral rehearsal, this time with the men of the Singverein again under Schalk, hoping that it might prove to be more encouraging than the previous one he had attended. It was not. In fact it was even worse. At the appointed time only fourteen were present. Gradually more began to drift in, but he soon found out that Schalk had no idea about the correct tempi. Mahler took charge of the proceedings, but it was not long before he discovered that the singers had not learnt their parts properly. The women of the Singverein most certainly had done their homework; it was clear that the men definitely had not. Surrounded by such incompetence he once again began to doubt the wisdom of letting the concert take place.

Writing to Alma, he told her that his lawyer friend Emil Freund had been to visit him, a pleasure he considered to be greater than a torte from Vienna's famous Sacher coffee house! In one of her letters Alma had asked Gustav if he still loved her. His reply was not to be so silly! He urged her to take whatever course of treatment she thought was best for a full and swift recovery so that they could resume their family life in the beautiful surroundings of Toblach as soon as possible. He stressed his love for her, saying that he only lived for her and Gucki and that nothing, not anyone could ever come between them. Still he was unaware of Alma's real problems. These did not stem simply from sexual frustration, nor from the knowledge that she came very much a second to Mahler's work, but from an increasing longing for a return to composing music of her own.

Little did he know. Alma had found a cure, but it was not the result of any medicine or from taking the waters. Existing mainly on a diet of lettuce and buttermilk and taking the recommended regular bathes in the hot springs, she was also advised by the doctor to seek someone suitable to accompany her on her walks. Perhaps she might find a partner by attending some of the dancing sessions. At one of these she met a young, handsome and very gifted architect by the name of Walter Gropius, and almost immediately they became infatuated with each other. 27-year-old Gropius was on holiday in Tobelbad, presumably taking the waters as well. He later became famous as a co-founder of the innovative school of architecture and design known as the Bauhaus.

A guilty conscience began to plague Alma. She still felt an irresistible desire to support her husband in his work, especially now that he was not in the best of health, and he was, after all, Gucki's father. One set of problems had been replaced by another, and Gustav, totally unaware of what was going on, began to get worried when her letters ceased to arrive.

On the 10th of June, before leaving Vienna for Leipzig where he was to hold rehearsals with the Riedel-Verein choir, Gustav wrote to Alma telling her of his concern at not having heard from her for a while, almost begging her to write to let him know how she and Gucki were. The rehearsals in Leipzig went very well and the tenor he had chosen, Felix Senius, turned out to be quite exceptional. Six days later he was in Munich to hold orchestral rehearsals. He found the orchestra to be excellent and well disciplined, and his opinion of Gutmann and his organisational ability increased greatly. As well as being very pleased with the rehearsals he was delighted to meet up with Rudolf Krzyżanowski, his friend from student days, and in the evenings they dined together at a local inn, doubtless reminiscing. Having told Alma all the news, the second half of his letter launched into a decidedly heavy discourse on the philosophy of love, using Plato, Socrates and Goethe as examples, and laced with *Zeitgeist* (the spirit of the times) – not at all what Alma needed!

The orchestral rehearsals were going well and Mahler had his first session with the children's choir, which was mostly made up of girls whom he described as 'chattering like sparrows'. His *Eighth Symphony* was becoming the talk of the music world and a number of fellow musicians, including

Oskar Fried and Otto Klemperer, came to pay their respects. With the adrenalin flowing he was able to cope with his exhaustion, even managing to attend a performance of Richard Strauss's *Don Quixote,* at the end of which he apparently applauded wildly. The only physical problem that he suffered from was a pulled muscle in his arm acquired while he was conducting.

In a letter dated the 21st of June, he told Theodore Spiering, leader of the Philharmonic orchestra, that the rehearsals for the *Eighth* were going well, although he had certain reservations about the leader of the orchestra saying that he did not really lead. In the same letter he expressed his concern over the fact that the newly appointed manager of the Philharmonic had plans for sixty-five concerts during the forthcoming season instead of a maximum of forty-five as stipulated in his contract. He had complained about the increase, but as yet had had no reply.

His mounting concern over Alma's condition was not helped by the infrequency of her letters, and in those that he did receive he began to notice a worrying change in both content and her style. He began to sense that all was not as it should be, so he wrote to Anna Moll asking her if she knew what the problem was.

Despite the importance of the rehearsals, he was desperate to rejoin Alma and Gucki. His original intention had been to spend a few days resting at the Villa Trenker in Alt-Schluderbach, near Toblach, before travelling to Tobelbad, but under the circumstances he decided to go straight to the spa via Vienna. Before continuing his journey he asked Carl Moll to arrange to have a diadem made as a surprise birthday present for Alma. On his arrival at Tobelbad on the 30th of June, he found to his great relief that she appeared to be in much better health than he had feared, and he wrote to Anna Moll saying that the treatment was clearly doing her good! His mind at ease, he left the spa after two days, having promised Alma that he would devote all his time to her when she rejoined him at the Villa Trenker and that he would not pick up a single sheet of manuscript paper – wishful thinking!

When Anna Moll arrived at Tobelbad on the 4th of July, the eve of the third anniversary of Putzi's tragic death, she found out about her daughter's passionate affair with Gropius and to Alma's surprise and relief she showed sympathy rather than anger. As fond as she was of Gustav, as far as Anna was concerned, Alma's mental state took priority and it appears that she considered that under the circumstances her daughter's extra-marital affair was the best treatment for her problems.

Alma's blossoming affair with the brilliant young architect did not lessen her sense of duty towards her husband as a world famous conductor and composer, and to continue to be his companion and muse. Her admiration for him as one of the most influential musicians of that time remained intact. Intellectually they had much in common both in their love of music and also literature. She could have been in no doubt as to his love for her, even if he did not satisfy her physically and spent less and less time in her presence. She was torn in two directions; the intellectual side of her wanted Gustav, the physical Walter Gropius, and this divide inevitably brought about its own stress.

In his letters to Alma, Gustav complained of the noise emanating from the Trenker family who were living on the ground floor, especially the children and a baby who spent most of the time bawling with its mother shouting in reply! He feared that they might even follow him to the privacy of his *Häuschen*. But despite the noise from the children, Mahler got on well with the Trenkers. They later remembered his visits with fondness. Never would he consider himself to be above their station, and frequently told them stories about the struggles of his own childhood. He mentioned that the two new servants had settled in well, and that it was a great relief to be rid of their former cook Kathi. He told Alma not to return until she felt that she had fully recovered and to stay at the spa as long as she could.

Mahler did take refuge in his *Häuschen*, and despite his promise to Alma, took out the manuscript paper and began to compose his *Tenth Symphony*. Alfred Roller wrote of an incident that took place while Mahler was at work. A jackdaw, chased by a hawk, seeing Mahler's hut as a safe haven, crashed through the window pursued by the hawk. The little room was filled with flying glass, screeching and feathers. At first Mahler continued to work, so lost was he in his music. When he returned to reality and saw the terrified jackdaw hiding in the corner, he marched briskly to complain to Herr Trenker, who laughed at the expression on Mahler's face, and they both ended up seeing the funny side of the incident.

The 7th of July marked his fiftieth birthday, but his mind was concentrated on music rather than any celebrations. The inevitable telegrams, letters and greetings cards arrived, much to his annoyance for this meant that he had to waste valuable time writing replies. He received greetings from Anna Moll, but nothing from Alma. The letter that pleased him most came from Siegfried Lipiner, and he took the trouble to reply at length. As well as telling him about his own news, he wished his old friend well, saying that he hoped that he had recovered from the side effects of the radium treatment that he had undergone and that he hoped he would be able to make the journey to Munich in September for the première of the *Eighth Symphony*.

Another distraction was the on-going dispute with his employers in New York over the additional concerts planned for the 1910-1911 season. Realising that a refusal to conduct them would cause even more trouble, he demanded an extra $25,000. He was offered £20,000. Eventually a compromise was reached for $23,000. Even though he could well have done without this extra work, he was prepared to agree to conduct the extra concerts for financial reasons. After all, the whole New York venture was undertaken in order to provide him with a comfortable retirement during whatever time his heart and fate would give him, and to guarantee financial security for Alma and Gucki after his death. Meanwhile another gap had appeared between Alma's letters and again he complained, calling her 'a child-wife'! He voiced his concern in a letter to Anna Moll, adding how lucky they were to have her around during these difficult times!

During Alma's absence he worked hard on his *Tenth Symphony*. After apparently outwitting fate by already having composed ten (nine and *Das Lied von der Erde*), he felt more relaxed about writing a new symphony. Soon Alma, his muse, would be home with Gucki, and he looked forward to spending a few weeks of intense creativity before having to leave Toblach to conduct the première of the *Eighth*.

Just over a week after his birthday, he met Alma and Gucki at the station in Toblach. What he did not know was that his wife, having left Tobelbad, had gone to Vienna for a secret assignation with Gropius. This meeting had been arranged with the help of Anna, to whom Gropius wrote a few days later thanking her, saying that his heart was 'filled with love'. The emerging *ménage à trois*, encouraged by Anna, mirrored a similar situation in her own life when she was having an affair with Carl Moll while at the same time being supportive of her artist husband, Emil Schindler.

Still Mahler had no idea of what was going on behind his back and he presumed that their summer routine would be resumed as in the past. In a way this is what Alma would have liked as well, at least for the time being. With Mahler's deteriorating health, the ideal situation would have been to continue her family life as normal with just the occasional foray in the direction of Walter Gropius. Both she and Gropius had agreed to keep him in the dark about their affair and that Gropius should send his letters *postlagernd* (to be collected by the recipient). Gropius not only broke this promise, but sent a letter to the Villa Trenker addressed to 'Herr Direktor Mahler'. In it he expressed his undying love for Alma, saying that he could not live without her! Gustav read the letter sitting at his piano and was understandably devastated; Alma embarrassed beyond words. She wrote to Gropius admonishing him for such insensitive and hurtful behaviour, insisting once more that he send any future letters *postlagernd* as they had originally agreed. Gropius then declared his intention to travel to Toblach so that he could meet Mahler. Alma told him he should not do so under any circumstances.

The tension arising from this incident triggered off the beginning of a change in their marital relationship, almost an exchange of roles. Gustav, the former 'feudal lord' who had ruled Alma's every move, began to become submissive, and Alma, her well being and confidence renewed by the combination of Tobelbad, Gropius and her mother's support, began to become the more dominant partner. Gustav asked Alma if the letter was a prelude to a proposal of marriage. She replied that she would never leave him but that she had become desperate for the physical love for which she had yearned for so long. Gustav was not only relieved but, partly through a feeling of guilt, his love for her actually deepened. Alma wrote how he insisted that the adjoining door between their rooms had to be left open so that he could hear her breathing and that frequently she would wake up to see him standing beside her bed. It was a potent mixture of undying love and despair at the thought of losing her. He found it almost impossible to sleep and would frequently leave love letters on her bedside table. On one occasion he collapsed on the landing with Alma and the servants having to carry him back to his bed. To make matters worse they both went down with a throat infection.

Not surprisingly Mahler was flung into a state of deep depression bordering on a nervous breakdown. On some occasions when Alma went to his *Häuschen* to fetch him for his midday meal, she would find him lying on the floor in tears. They agreed that Anna Moll should be asked to make haste to come to Toblach to calm the waters, for, as his mother figure, Gustav had total confidence in her.

The drama drew to a climax. While Alma was out in a pony and trap she spotted Gropius hiding under a bridge. On her return, she told Gustav who said that he himself would go and find him and bring him back to the house. Mahler set off on foot. By the time he found him darkness had fallen. He told Gropius unceremoniously to follow as he strode on ahead, lantern in hand. They walked for around half an hour in total silence. When at last they arrived at the house, a grim faced Mahler left Gropius with his wife telling them to get the matter sorted out, before retiring to his room. Shortly afterwards Alma found her husband pacing up and down reading the Bible. His one comment was that whatever she decided to do would be right. Alma had to make the choice there and then, but for her there really was no choice. She had to stay with Gustav, for without her support she feared he would die. Yet she could not totally abandon Gropius. For the time being at least he would have to remain in the background. Mahler knew that his marriage was safe, but also that Walter Gropius would remain in Alma's affections. Indeed, in one of her letters to him she declared how she longed to lie in his arms and to have his child. He even had the temerity to write to Mahler before boarding the train at Toblach station. While apologising for his bad behaviour, he thanked

Mahler for his dignity, and, figuratively speaking, offered his hand in reconciliation.

A short while later Alma wrote to Gropius saying how Mahler had changed, how in spite of everything his expressions of love had become almost overwhelming and that he had become 'like a sick, wonderful child'.

An incident occurred which clearly shows Mahler's mixed feelings of guilt at the way he had treated Alma in the past, his fear of losing her and his new-found expressions of love towards her. Alma and Gucki had been out for a walk and as they were returning they heard him playing the piano. This, of course, was not unusual but the music was. He was playing Alma's songs. They stopped and listened. Alma froze with shock and surprise at hearing her 'forbidden' music of so long ago. It ceased and then Gustav came rushing out to meet them. There was a beaming smile across his face, yet at the same time he was reprimanding himself for having prevented her from composing all these years. He declared that the songs were excellent, that they must work on them and get them published. He told her that she must start composing again immediately. Likewise Mahler put in a final burst on his new symphony, for soon their summer holiday would be over.

Tenth Symphony, in F sharp
(In five movements)

With each new symphony that he wrote, Mahler moved forward to explore new musical territory. The personal and the autobiographical elements remained, but his symphonies were never simply a wallow in nostalgia. The *Tenth*, even in its unfinished state, saw another leap forward in that, for the first time, the past took a back seat. It was moulded both in the present and the future; the traumatic emotional and physical crises that he was going through and a foretaste of the path that music would dare to follow in the years to come. Yes, he drew on ideas from the past, from his own works, even Bach and Gregorian chant, not to mention the muffled drum strokes of the fireman's funeral, but in the context of a new and, for its time, daring vision. This symphony prophesied the works of such composers as Berg, Stravinsky, Britten and Shostakovich.

Mahler was unable to finish this revolutionary work. Indeed it is astonishing that he managed to compose as much as he did, given the inevitable distractions arising from the preparations for the première of the *Eighth Symphony*, Alma's problems, including her affair with Gropius, putting the final touches to his *Ninth Symphony* and planning for the next season in New York!

Of the five movements, he completed only the first, the first thirty bars of the third movement and parts of the second in draft orchestral score. The rest of the symphony exists only in a combination of a four stave short score and sketches. Because of the particularly personal nature of the manuscript, which includes very emotional exclamations and messages to Alma mirroring their marital crisis, it is little wonder that she kept the score under lock and key for a number of years.

It was not until 1924, thirteen years after her husband's death, that she could be persuaded to have a facsimile of a large part of the manuscript published, and immediately it became clear what an astonishing work the *Tenth* might have become. Alma permitted the young composer Ernst Křenek, Anna ('Gucki') Mahler's husband, to create a performing version of the first and third movements, helped by Alban Berg. Some unauthorised changes were made by Franz Schalk before he conducted the first performance in Vienna that autumn and further changes by Alexander von Zemlinsky before the second performance in Prague. Alma sent a copy of the score to Mengelberg who made additional revisions, favouring a larger orchestra. His version was first given at the Concertgebouw on the 27th of November 1924. But there were many in the world of music who objected to any part of the *Tenth* being played, for they believed that as an unfinished work Mahler's vision could not and should not be presumed. To do so, in their opinion, was almost musical sacrilege, showing disrespect to the late composer. It was not until 1951 that these two movements were finally published.

The next stage in the *Tenth's* history took place in 1960, the centenary of Mahler's birth. The B.B.C., having made plans for a Mahler cycle, approached the musicologist Deryck Cooke suggesting that he might write an accompanying booklet. He agreed to carry out this task. In so doing, his curiosity and imagination regarding Mahler's unfinished symphony led him to suggest the idea of producing a programme about the work, complete with musical illustrations. However, one major problem existed – Alma. After fruitless overtures to Schoenberg, Shostakovich and Britten to create a performing version of the entire symphony, she had since banned any idea of anything other than the first and third movements being played. It was then pointed out to her that it would not be long before the score came out of copyright, and that it would therefore be wise to let a performing version be created in the safe hands of Deryck Cooke. Finally she agreed to a partial version to be used solely as illustrations for the programme about the symphony. Cooke was aided by the composer and conductor Berthold Goldschmidt, the latter conducting the first, although incomplete performance, on the 19th of December 1960 – incomplete because several pages of Mahler's manuscript of the two *Scherzi* could not be found. Alma, who had not heard the broadcast, felt that she had been misled. What she had presumed would have been just musical examples had turned out to be, to all intents and purposes, a complete performance! She reimposed her ban.

Having progressed so far, and having become more and more fascinated with the task he was undertaking, Cooke had no intention of calling a halt at this stage. Alma was persuaded to listen to the recording of Goldschmidt's performance, and was so moved that she immediately lifted the ban. The final pieces of the jigsaw fell into place when her daughter Anna and Henry-Louis de la Grange discovered the missing pages from the *Scherzi* in rooms that Alma owned above her New York apartment and sent them to Cooke. The première of Deryck Cooke's complete performing version took place at a promenade concert in the Royal Albert Hall on the 13th of August 1964, played by the London Symphony Orchestra and conducted by Berthold Goldschmidt.

Following the prom performance and another in America under Eugene Ormandy, who also made the first recording of the work, Cooke, in the true Mahler tradition, felt the need for revisions. In this he was helped by Colin and David Matthews, the revised version being first performed in 1972 under Wyn Morris. The Matthews brothers then carried out further revisions, these being published in 1989.

There have been a number of other versions, most notably by Rudolf Barshai, Clinton Carpenter, Joe Wheeler and Remo Mazzetti, jr., all of which have been recorded, but the Cooke-Mathews brothers version is generally regarded as being the finest and least speculative. One final point, it was made very clear that the Cooke-Matthews *Tenth* was 'a performing version', not a completion as were the other versions, hence the leanness in the orchestral texture.

First movement: Adagio

The symphony opens with unaccompanied violas playing a wistful, searching, yet bleak melody that soars upwards, almost coming to a standstill before the main adagio theme enters. Played by the violins it is intense and warm. They are joined by the horns and a return of the viola theme in counterpoint. Here Mahler employs one of his trademarks, the switching between major and minor. The tension builds, leading towards a shattering climax of unheard-of dissonance that culminates in a nine-note chord with screaming strings and a sustained trumpet that pierces the tumult like a knife through the heart. Once again this massive chord erupts before this terrifying climax subsides and the gentle coda emerges, and the movement draws to a relatively peaceful conclusion that is both touching and has a feeling of resignation.

Second movement – Scherzo 1

Mahler originally designated this movement as *'Scherzo-Finale'*, which leads one to suspect that his initial plan had been for the symphony to be in two parts with this movement ending the first of these. In total contrast to the tension and drama of the first movement this scherzo opens with vigorous rapid changes in time signature, irregular rhythms and shrill harmonies. Following the brash, almost sarcastic opening, the music becomes gentler as a ländler takes over – a transformation of the main string theme of the first movement – which is occasionally interrupted by the earlier brash ideas. Following a radiant passage, the movement surges forward in a series of climaxes, finally ending exuberantly.

Third movement – Purgatorio (oder Inferno)
(Mahler deleted the *oder Inferno*)

This is the shortest of the symphony's five movements at around four minutes. It opens 'part two' of the symphony, and the title 'Purgatory or Hell', as well as the music itself, clearly reflects Mahler's unsettled state of mind. An *ostinato* from the *Wunderhorn* song, *Das irdische Leben* is used. A brief passionate outburst is followed by a sinking, almost suicidal sounding motif. On his manuscript Mahler scribbled the first three of a number of exclamations: 'Have mercy!', 'Oh God, Oh God, why hast Thou forsaken me?' and then 'Thy will be done'. Perhaps this was the only way he was able to communicate his feelings to Alma. Some have suggested that these despairing words might have been written after he had composed the music, but there is no doubt that they clearly reflect his anguish and pain at the thought of losing his Almschi to the younger and more virile Walter Gropius.

Fourth movement – Scherzo 2

This second scherzo is often described as being 'demonic', partly because of the longest of Mahler's inscriptions:

> 'The Devil dances with me,
> Madness seize me, the accursed!
> Destroy me, that I may forget my existence,
> that I may cease to be,
> that I for . . .'

Mahler was unable to continue. The movement is a *danse macabre*, a satirical almost satanic waltz. It contains fleeting fragments of the *Purgatorio* as well as *Das Lied von der Erde* (a quotation from the first song, 'The Drinking Song of Earth's Misery' with the words 'Joy and song fade and die'). The dance-like coda is scored mainly for percussion, almost Stravinsky in style. It ends with a muffled drum stroke, under which Mahler addressed Alma with the words, 'You alone know what it means', referring to the muffled drum stroke that had so moved them during the fireman's funeral procession in New York. It could also have been symbolic of the 'funeral' of their marriage and his fear of having to live without her, for he added 'Farewell, my lyre! Farewell . . . Farewell . . . Farewell'.

Fifth movement – Finale

The Finale begins where the previous movement ended, with a muffled drum stroke, which interrupts a foreboding rising scale from the tuba. This is followed by a further five strokes which continue to interrupt the tuba and a motif from the horns. Out of this doom-laden atmosphere emerges a plaintive flute solo. At first hesitant, but gaining confidence, it plays a slow and exquisitely beautiful transformation of the disquieting waltz theme from the previous movement. This in turn leads to a soaring string passage of great yearning bordering on rapture, only to be extinguished *'coitus interruptus'* by the return of the drum stroke and the previous sombre atmosphere.

The resumed aura of gloom begins to turn to bitterness with a wild development of material from the *Purgatorio*, which becomes almost a parody of the *Burlesque* of the *Ninth Symphony*. This savage development builds towards the climax of the movement with a return of the cataclysmically dissonant nine-note chord of the opening *Adagio*, complete with the shrill stabbing of the solo trumpet. On this occasion a horn competes with the cacophony with a theme from the opening movement, and then, emerging from this agony, returns the soaring melody, previously cut short so cruelly by the muffled drum stroke. This blissful stream of melody, beautiful and serene though it is, has an undercurrent of sadness. It is a longing for what might have been, regrets over his treatment of Alma, a desperate reaching out, trying to hold on to her love, to all that is beautiful in life, and with it all there is the continuing agony of the loss of his beloved daughter – all this is in the closing bars. These final bars, the last he would write, are the most ardent, tender and at the same time bittersweet that he ever wrote. They are his final musical declaration of love for Alma. After a final passionate two note surge, as if exclaiming 'Almschi', this astonishing symphony ends, not in glory, but moving from major to minor with a sigh. And the world of music sighs with him, asking a question that can never be answered: what would the transcendent *Tenth* have been like if he himself had completed it? And following the *Tenth*, what new paths would he have taken? Of course we shall never know, but we must be grateful to those whose dedication have made this landmark symphony accessible to all, and objections to the tampering of Mahler's unfinished score are tantamount to wanting a unique and great treasure to be buried and hidden from the world – 'Lost to the world'.

At the end of the manuscript, Mahler wrote the following words:

> *'Für dich leben! Für dich sterben!*
> *... Almschi'*
> (To live for you! To Die for you!)

Some have stated that this final movement is Mahler relinquishing his will to live, in much the same way as *Der Abschied* and the last movement of the *Ninth* have attracted similar opinions. I beg to differ. If death has a part here, then surely it should be regarded as his 'Death and Transfiguration'. Whereas some of his earlier symphonies end with the declaration that his 'hero' shall live forever, here it is almost as if he is quietly affirming 'I will live for ever', or like St. Joan in Honegger's 1935 oratorio *Jeanne d'Arc au Bucher,* when she exclaims from the stake that the chains are broken. Mahler had been through hell, or perhaps Purgatory! Now he could see the light ahead. He would embrace his destiny, whatever form it might take.

This is what he was saying in his music, but the fact was that his mind was in a state of turmoil. This is evident from the love notes and poems that he had left for Alma to find, several written on manuscript paper, with lines that are 'over the top' with alternating images and messages of sensual desire and despair. Another indication of his mental instability arose during a visit from Oskar Fried. Mahler had asked his wife to play her songs for their guest. Apparently Fried's reaction was a polite 'very nice', which upset Alma who considered the songs to be worth a far greater compliment. Mahler's temper snapped, and it was with great difficulty that Anna Moll managed to prevent him from verbally, if not physically, assaulting Fried – Fried, who had always been one of his staunchest allies. Fortunately he fully understood the strain his host was under, and took the sensible course of departing the following morning.

Alma and her mother decided that the best course of action would be to contact Dr. Richard von Nepallek, a distant cousin. He in turn recommended that Mahler should see one of the leading psychoanalysts of the day, Sigmund Freud, who had actually lived quite close to their Auenbruggergasse apartment in Vienna. Mahler had hitherto had little time for psychoanalysts, even though Bruno Walter had found Freud's advice very helpful when he had been suffering from a weakness in his conducting arm four years earlier. At first Mahler dismissed the idea, but with persuasion coming from both Alma and Anna Moll and the realisation that he had to unburden himself to someone, reluctantly he agreed. The first two appointments he cancelled, but he was finally persuaded to accept a third. This would mean travelling to Leiden in Holland close to where Freud was on holiday.

This lengthy rail journey from Toblach meant a change onto the main line at Franzenfeste, the express going via Innsbruck and Munich to Cologne. There, Mahler had enough time for a brief walk before boarding the train to Amsterdam, and thence to Leiden. Even with today's high-speed services this journey would be somewhat tedious, but in 1910 it must have seemed interminable! At various points during the journey he sent telegrams to Alma, and from Amsterdam another soul-searching poem.

The consultation with Freud took place shortly after his arrival in Leiden late in the afternoon of the 26th of August, not on a consultant's couch, but during a long walk through the streets of the old town and along the tree-lined canals. Exactly what course their conversation took regrettably we shall never know, but a meeting between the fifty-four year old father of psychoanalysis and the most revered musician of the day has led to numerous suggestions as to the ground covered during their four hour meeting. The two men had much in common. Both were in their early fifties, both of Jewish parentage, both steeped in the works of such writers as Nietzsche and Dostoyevsky, and both had suffered from psychological problems.

Many years later, with Mahler long departed, Freud was persuaded to talk about this meeting. He referred to Mahler as a genius and that his main problem was sexual. He had considered him to be potent, but that he had withdrawn his libido from Alma. It would seem more likely that Alma had rejected him sexually, mainly because of the constant battle between her and his music, the latter always winning his attention. Apparently Freud had told Mahler that he was suffering from *Mutterbindung* (mother fixation, or 'Holy Mary' complex), a mother-son tie that he had never been able to break. This had developed during his unhappy childhood, resulting in his constant search for his mother in the women he met. This is evident in his obsessive feelings towards both Alma as well as Anna Moll, 'little mama' as he called her. Freud told him that he had a separation anxiety, equating a loss of Alma with the loss of his mother.

At one point during their walk, Freud commented that Mahler should have married a woman with the same name as his mother, Marie. This buoyed up Mahler, and he replied that Alma's second name was Maria and that he sometimes called her Marie, although he never addressed her this way in any of his letters. He was worried about their age difference, but Freud pointed out that Alma had need of an older man. This was correct judging by her earlier affairs although not those that followed his death.

Alma had had a particularly strong love for her artist father, which had resulted in a need for a 'father-figure'. The fact that *Maler* (without the 'h') is German for 'painter' might have added to the attraction! One question remains unanswered: did Mahler mention Walter Gropius? Freud's advice was to calm down and relax, for then both he and Alma would feel much better.

The problems remained, but as is clear from his telegram to Alma before his return trek to Toblach the following day, he had certainly benefited from his session with Freud. He said that he was feeling cheerful, that the discussion had been interesting and that he had decided to catch a later train so that he could have a stroll around Leiden.

His return to Toblach, however, would be brief for he had to travel to Munich for the final rehearsals of his magnum opus, the mighty *Eighth Symphony*, which was to be performed for the first time on the 12th of September. Alma was delighted that her husband was in a more composed frame of mind and excited about the forthcoming première. As a result she too felt more relaxed, and together they celebrated her 31st birthday on the 31st of August. Mahler later told Carl Moll that the diadem he had commissioned had been received with great delight. Nevertheless, even though she made a point of accompanying her husband to Toblach station on the 3rd of September, her feelings towards Gropius were as strong as ever. Anna Moll continued to be a willing accomplice, passing on her letters and arranging trysts, one of which would be in Munich only a few days later.

As usual, Mahler sent messages to Alma during the journey, and a curious mixture they were. In a telegram sent from Innsbruck he stated that he had been shaken by recent events, but that he accepted his fate. In a poem, whilst referring to her as 'my love', he predicted new tribulations and shocks to follow, and that in the future he would go to the station on his own! Yet this poem was followed by a love letter, as of old, addressing her as his beloved and using his pet name for her – Almschili. Not surprisingly, Alma was taken aback, if not upset, by the telegram and the poem, and Mahler immediately sent her another telegram, followed by a letter, telling her that he had only been joking! He also reported that he had gone down with a fever and severe septic throat. This was quite likely the streptococcal infection that was widespread at the time.

A very alarmed Emil Gutmann (the Austrian impresario in whose hands were the arrangements for the concert) dashed to the Grand Hotel Continental to mop the maestro's brow! Now physically as well as mentally upset, Mahler once more filled his letters to Alma with purple prose and words of obsessive love. He even declared to her that fidelity would win in the end. He sat swathed in blankets, sweating out the infection, determined that in no way should it interfere with the rehearsals. He also resorted to taking a Turkish bath.

Alma and her mother arrived at the Hotel Continental on the 9th of September, just three days before the concert, and Gropius at the Hotel Regina. When Alma and her mother entered the hotel suite, they found to their delight that Gustav had arranged for their rooms to be filled with roses. There was another surprise too, for Anna found on the table in her room the piano score of the *Eighth Symphony* with a dedication to her. The full score, of course, he had dedicated to Alma.

Mahler managed to dig deep into his reserves of strength. With the invaluable help of Alfred Roller as stage manager, the rehearsals progressed smoothly. Many present, though, remarked on how frail Mahler looked. Yet the sight of the clearly sick man in front of them increased their determination to perform to the peak of their ability. He was particularly enamoured by the enthusiasm shown by the 350 strong children's chorus with whom he had a strong rapport, and it was reported that he had been moved to tears as their angelic voices soared above the huge orchestra.

It goes without saying that this much-anticipated concert (to be repeated the following day) was to be Europe's cultural event of the year. Friends and the famous flocked to Munich. It would be one of the last such occasions before Europe became engulfed in the horrors of the First World War, just four years away. The world of music was represented by such names as Richard Strauss, Siegfried Wagner, Anton Webern, Bruno Walter, Willem Mengelberg, Leopold Stokowski, Erik Schmedes, Alphonse Diepenbrock, Alfred Casella, Lilli Lehmann, Selma Kurz, Guido Adler, Rudolf Krzyżanowski and Anna von Mildenburg. Many from the world of literature arrived, such as Gerhart Hauptmann, Thomas Mann and Stefan Zweig. There were Mahler's friends and family: the Clemenceaus, Arnold Berliner, his sisters Justine and Emma with their husbands Arnold and Eduard Rosé. Anna and Carl Moll were already in Munich of course, as was Walter Gropius, Alma taking every opportunity to visit him while her husband was at rehearsals.

Present at one these were Julius Korngold and his thirteen-year-old son Erich, whom Mahler had earlier proclaimed to be a genius, and who subsequently, whenever asked what he wanted to be when he was grown up, replied 'Direktor Mahler'. Otto Klemperer also attended some of the rehearsals, although he was unable to attend the performance due to his conducting commitments.

Emil Gutmann's advertising slogan 'The Symphony of a Thousand' proved to be correct, for the orchestra numbered 171, the massed choirs 858 with 8 soloists in addition. The specially extended stage in the huge Exhibition Hall was set for Mahler's greatest triumph. As soon as the audience saw him appear, looking pale and drawn, they rose to their feet. Royalty, celebrities, everyone stood in silence until, somewhat taken aback, he acknowledge their reception. The silence was soon broken when he greeted the children who responded as one. This was followed by cheering until he raised his baton and unleashed such a volume of sound as no one had ever before experienced.

The première was a magnificent success, and the audience moved beyond words. As the final, mighty chord faded, and following a few seconds of stunned silence, an ovation almost as overwhelming as the music broke out, lasting for nearly thirty minutes. It was not just the audience who were applauding, the thousand performers did so too with abandon. Bruno Walter remembered how Mahler, even though he was completely exhausted, climbed the steps to where the cheering children were and shook hands with as many as he could. This was Mahler's greatest hour and the last time he would conduct in Europe. It was almost as if he had been deified.

Thomas Mann wrote to him the following day thanking him for the wonderful experience, saying that he sincerely believed that he, Mahler, expressed the art of that time 'in its profoundest and most sacred form'. He enclosed a copy of his latest novel *Royal Highness* as a very small 'thank you'. Inspired by the occasion, Mann later wrote his novel *Death in Venice* about a writer in cholera-stricken Venice, with the central character, Gustave von Aschenbach, clearly based (in some respects!) on Mahler.

Despite the great emotional impact of what Mahler considered to be his greatest work, the *Eighth* has remained his most controversial symphony. Audiences love it; critics and some fellow composers continue to have doubts. Hans Pfitzner, considering the first part, '*Veni Creator Spiritus*' (Come Holy Spirit) once asked, 'But what if he doesn't come?' More recently, the composer Robert Simpson, normally a staunch advocate of Mahler's music, described the second part as 'An ocean of shameless kitsch'. Nevertheless, and this cannot be denied, the *Eighth Symphony* has always, and will always, be an unforgettable emotional experience for audiences, and one can just imagine the effect that it had on those present at its first performance.

On returning to Vienna, Mahler saw a doctor about his recurring throat problems. He did not want to have his tonsils removed, so it was decided that they should be cauterised. As usual they stayed with the Molls, with 'little mama' helping him on the road to recovery. During his brief stay at the Villa Moll, his old friend, the archeologist Fritz Löhr, paid him a visit. Together they walked to the cemetery in Grinzing where they stood before Putzi's grave, the grave where Mahler himself wished to be buried.

More than ever Alma was torn between the fame of her husband and the sexual attraction of Gropius. She wrote telling him that she would be travelling to Paris on the 14th of October, two days before her husband, and that her compartment would be number 13 in the 2nd sleeping car. She suggested that he should travel under a false name, Walter Grote of Berlin.

While Alma and Walter Gropius travelled to Paris, Mahler took a different route, visiting Oscar Fried in Nikolassee. Clearly the purpose of this visit was to renew their friendship after the unfortunate row over Alma's songs. The two men embraced fondly. Apparently no discussion took place as to future plans, Mahler spending most of the time playing with Fried's children in their garden. This was to be their last meeting.

On the 26th of September, Mahler had written to Mengelberg saying that he would be sailing on the *Kaiser Wilhelm II* from Bremen on the 18th of October. Alma also mentioned this in her memoirs, but said that she rejoined her husband on board at Cherbourg. However, Mahler's visit to Oscar Fried meant that he would have had a very tight schedule and, as Alma had told Gropius, she would be travelling to Paris two days before her husband. So it is probable that he was reunited with Alma and Gucki in Paris and that they travelled to Cherbourg together.

On the 19th of October, the *Kaiser Wilhelm II* set sail for New York; Mahler's final season was about to begin. Despite his dislike of sea travel, he at least managed to get some rest. His only commitment during the voyage was to fulfil a promise to be the accompanist for the tenor John McCormack at a charity recital in aid of the widows and orphans of sailors.

Chapter 17

New York . . . Part Four

The Final Farewell

T HE *KAISER WILHELM II* sailed into New York harbour on the 25th of October. Once again a suite had been booked at the Hotel Savoy. The Alma-Gropius affair continued unabated by post, yet Alma remained adamant that she would not leave her husband, for in so doing she would almost certainly have hastened Mahler's death, thus tarnishing her name internationally. Anyway, it was more than likely that she was enjoying being the dominant partner!

Mahler, hardly rested after the potent mixture of trauma, elation and ill health that had constituted his summer break, was about to face an even greater workload than he had during his previous visits to America. The 1909-1910 season having resulted in a deficit of around $100,000, the Guarantors' Committee had sought the services of Loudon Charlton, head of an artists' agency (thus with inevitable divided loyalties) to take charge of financial affairs for the coming season.

Feelings were not exactly harmonious between Mahler and the orchestra's management committee. His demand for an extra $5,000 for the additional concerts entrusted to him had still not been formally agreed to. In fact this did not come about until the New Year when Mahler made the good will gesture of reducing the sum to $3,000.

Sick as he was with his throat problem still plaguing him and exhausted before the season had even begun, he nevertheless remained as determined as ever to tackle the challenges that lay ahead.

The main reason for the increase in concerts for the 1910-1911 season was to reduce the deficit of the previous one. Ticket prices were lowered in an attempt to attract larger audiences, but a matter of considerable concern for the Guarantors' Committee was the demand made by the musicians union for higher wages. This would not affect the Philharmonic until the 1911-1912 season, but Loudon Charlton had to take this into account. It was with this in mind that he proposed increasing the number of concerts for 1911-1912 from the already increased schedule of 63 to 100. Whether or not Mahler had any thoughts of renewing his contract, such an increase would not have appealed to him for three reasons. Firstly he was neither willing nor able to undertake such a task single-handed. Secondly, the idea of sharing the conducting of 'his orchestra' would certainly not have met with his approval, and thirdly such a workload for the orchestra, let alone the conductor, would more than likely result in a fall of standards, which of course he had been striving so hard to improve. During the summer no less than twenty-three members of the orchestra had been replaced. Mahler, who in Vienna had been very much his own master, was now beginning to feel like a dispensable tool.

Alma wrote in her memoirs how he had begun to pay extra attention to his appearance, wearing smart suits and waistcoats and with his shoes always polished to a mirror finish. Reportedly he had taken to declaring, 'Spitting on the floor doesn't help you to be Beethoven!' True, but this sudden desire to improve his appearance was more than likely to have been part of his every effort to please Alma!

The press were becoming more critical, his novelty value beginning to wear thin. This was evident in the reviews of the first two concerts of the season, which took place on the 1st and 4th of November at Carnegie Hall. Mahler was given a generous 'welcome back' by the audience and the playing of the orchestra met with general approval. But the press criticised him for his 'grandiose' interpretation of Schubert's 'Great' C major Symphony, and for his 'far-reaching modifications of tempo', even though there were 'passages of exquisite poetical insight' (New York Times). Despite the enthusiastic applause, the New York Sun remarked that Mahler was trying to make Schubert sound like Strauss, and the New York Daily Tribune objected to the overwhelming brass and 'the fairly ear-splitting kettle drums'. The same critic complained that the audience, at the end of a lengthy two-hour concert, had been subjected to Strauss's Also sprach Zarathustra and sent home with the 'cacophonous' ending 'outraging the aesthetic sense . . .' The only work that failed to get a mention, as popular as ever, was Mahler's Bach Suite with the composer once again conducting from the prepared piano.

At a concert on the 15th of November he introduced his American audience to a new work by Claude Debussy, Rondes de Printemps. It was received with polite applause. The critics, however, voiced their displeasure with expressions such as 'acrid harmonies' and that the music 'sounds as if the composer had plentifully and indiscriminately sprinkled his score-paper with a haphazard collection of notes' (The New York World).

Rumours began to abound concerning Mahler's future in New York. Mrs Sheldon, in an interview with a correspondent of The Musical Courier, came to his defence saying that if he should not return the following season, the people of New York would find out just what the city had lost, for 'He is a wonderful organizer and a great conductor'. The rumours were not ill founded, and not just due to his poor health or to the gossip about a possible return to the Hofoper. Mahler rejected such speculation as nonsense in a letter to his lawyer friend Emil Freund dated the 21st of November. Felix Weingartner had failed to impress as his successor in Vienna and was to be replaced in March by Hans Gregor, former director of the Berlin Opera. Mahler told Emil Freund that it had never crossed his mind to work with Gregor who had the reputation of being an unpleasant man. It was on the same day (the 21st of November) that *The Musical Courier* made the speculative announcement that he would not be returning for the 1911-1912 season.

With the prospect of an even greater workload in the future, combined with the increasing adverse criticism that was being thrown at him by the New York press and the fact that he no longer felt that he was in total charge of the orchestra, it was not surprising that he considered that it might be the right time to retire. Yet he still liked the American public and the audiences remained very appreciative, but he had begun to crave for a more relaxed existence with Alma and Gucki and to devote whatever time he had left to them and to composing. His thoughts were helped by the fact that Carl Moll, aided by Emil Freund, had managed to buy a farm at Breitenstein am Semmering to the south-west of Vienna. With meadows, forests as well as arable land, and a plot ideal for the building of a new Villa Mahler, this would be their future idyllic home. At last Gustav and Alma would have a place of their own in an area that they both loved. Emil Freund signed the contract on the 3rd of November on Mahler's behalf, having asked Freund to ensure that the land should be registered in both his and Alma's names. But the season had hardly begun and a hectic schedule lay ahead that included concerts in a number of other American cities.

On the 22nd of November he conducted a performance of Schumann's *Second Symphony*. The audience liked it; the press once more questioned his right to make alterations to the score, albeit minor ones. Also in the programme were performances of two of Mahler's songs, 'Morning in the Fields' and 'A Tale of the Rhine' (*Ging' heut' morgen übers Feld* and *Rheinlegendchen*) sung by Alma Gluck to considerable acclaim.

He began the concert on the 29th with a well-received performance of Elgar's *Enigma Variations*. What happened next took everyone by surprise. Half of the orchestra left the stage before the work that followed, Mozart's *40th Symphony*. Instead of using the expected enlarged orchestra that Mahler favoured for performances in a large auditorium, he had actually reduced it to give a 'period' performance as in Mozart's time! The general opinion was, 'we prefer a more modern approach'! Mahler, presumably with his tongue in his cheek, had made his point.

The time had come for the Philharmonic's first away concerts of the season. The first of these was in Pittsburgh on the 5th of December. With almost every one of the 2,600 seats in the Memorial Hall sold, Mahler and the orchestra were given a rapturous reception. His *Bach Suite* was followed by Beethoven's *6th Symphony*, and while the *Pittsburgh Dispatch* accepted that Beethoven's score had been 'Mahlerized', it praised the performance unreservedly. The tour continued with concerts in Cleveland, Buffalo, Rochester, Syracuse and Utica, and in all these cities they enjoyed unfettered applause. 'Little Mahler, whose gigantic power makes the other conductors seem like pygmies' (*Cleveland Plain Dealer*); 'The Beethoven *'Pastorale' Symphony* was given a remarkable reading' (*The Buffalo Express*); 'Mr. Gustav Mahler and his splendid organization of men' (Rochester's *The Union and Adviser*); 'Mr. Mahler seemed to throw himself heart and soul into the spirit of the music' (*Utica Observer*) and the *Utica Daily Press* described his conducting as 'hypnotic'.

As was so often the case, adrenalin had come to his rescue. Theodore Spiering spoke of his 'indomitable will', and the way he managed to inspire the musicians even after travelling for several hours. Away from the New York sniping, Mahler and his orchestra were on a high, and he must have been wondering whether to accept perhaps just one more season.

Before the concert in Buffalo, Gustav and Alma visited the nearby Niagara Falls. It was a crisp, frosty winter's day and as they stood on the observation platform, they were awe-stricken by the sheer size and the deafening roar. That same evening, having just conducted an overwhelming performance of the *Pastoral Symphony*, he exclaimed 'A fortissimo at last!' Alma wrote how he told her that he now realised that 'articulate art is greater than inarticulate nature'.

Maurice Baumfeld, a Viennese-born journalist, remembered how Mahler relaxed after concerts in his suite at New York's Hotel Savoy. Very often a few friends and supporters would be invited back to the hotel. He wrote that Mahler was an expert mimic and frequently had everyone doubled-up with laughter. He would usually end up horizontal on a divan, and when tiredness began to overcome him he would retire to his bedroom, telling his guests that they could go ahead and enjoy themselves, but if they made too much noise he would throw his boots at the wall! Baumfeld also wrote of the tenderness he showed to Gucki, how he adored playing with her and acting out stories for her, and that his love for Alma was without question. She in turn described how Gustav's love for his daughter was growing almost daily, and how he took her for walks in Central Park and played snowballs with her.

Mahler made sure that his wife enjoyed an active social life. They had a box at the Metropolitan Opera and among their regular visitors was Dr. Joseph Fraenkel. Shortly before Christmas, his visits took on a professional role as well, for Mahler had begun to suffer from a recurrence of his septic throat problem. Fraenkel, like so many before and after him, had secretly fallen head-over-heels in love with Alma, although for the time being at least he made every effort to hide his feelings. Alma, though, remained besotted with Walter Gropius, and their secret love letters continued to cross the Atlantic.

Gustav had made a special effort to make Christmas 1910 a memorable one for Alma. She had suspected that he was up to something when one day he put his chequebook into his pocket, which was almost unheard of, and set off on his own. The results of his shopping expedition came to light on Christmas Day. She described how they had spent the day alone in a room festooned with pink roses in the middle of which was a table covered with presents for her, as well as two notes promising the purchase of a solitaire with a value over $1000 and a $40 shopping spree in Fifth Avenue. She was genuinely touched by these tokens of love, so unselfishly given and with her tastes entirely at heart.

Joseph Fraenkel celebrated the New Year with Gustav and Alma in their suite on the ninth floor of the Hotel Savoy. Alma described the city as being bathed in a 'milk-white haze', and that at five minutes to midnight sirens and church bells began to sound from every quarter of the city. The three of them stood together by the window holding hands, mesmerized by the occasion and shedding a few tears. It was a situation reminiscent of the fireman's funeral nearly two years before. What should have been a joyful occasion had become one of sadness and foreboding, but as Alma wrote, they did not know why – or perhaps they did.

With his health deteriorating and his strength diminishing all the while he must have begun to realise that time was short. Consequently he wrote to impresario Emil Gutmann asking him not to arrange any concerts during the summer to come so that he could rest and concentrate on composing.

Since resigning as Director of the Vienna Court Opera and transferring his attention to New York, Mahler had become more distant from his own circle of friends. Some of these, of course, Alma had shunned early in their marriage. With his new commitments, opportunities for socialising had become fewer. The situation was not helped by his state of health, or by rumours of Alma's infidelity. His focus had been more and more on Alma's parents; Anna, 'little mama', who gave him maternal comfort, and Carl to whom he frequently turned for advice. In many ways he had become his agent in Vienna, dealing with legal and business affairs on his behalf.

Despite adverse criticism of Debussy's music in the past, 'Iberia', from his *Images pour orchestre*, was included in a programme of French music on the 3rd of January. His music continued to be controversial, as voiced by the critic of the *New York World* who wrote that, with no 'harmonic design or real melodic thought', it might be clever, but was it music? Georges Enesco's *Suite for orchestra* did not impress the critic either, although Chabrier's *Ode à la musique* did, as well as Mahler's conducting and the playing of the Philharmonic.

Meanwhile rumours concerning Mahler's future in New York continued to abound, fuelled by Mrs Sheldon's riposte of 'no comment', and the fact that an approach had been made to violinist Franz Kneisel, offering him the post of conductor of the Philharmonic for the 1911-1912 season. The truth was that Mahler himself had not yet made up his mind. On the one hand the peace and quiet of a new house in the Semmering prompted him to say enough was enough, but on the other one more season would mean a considerable sum towards the cost of their new villa and added security for Alma and Gucki. But he must have had doubts as to whether he had sufficient strength to cope with another season, especially with the proposed 90 to 100 concerts. It is strange that he had even considered such a burden having thought twice over the increase of the current season from the previous 45 concerts to 63. Nevertheless he said that he might be prepared to do so for $30,000, double the salary of his first season in New York and no less than ten times his basic salary at the Vienna Court Opera! Perhaps he felt that by making such a demand he might be turned down. He was not, for he was a valuable asset. With growing popularity and standards of performance, the Philharmonic would go from strength to strength under his leadership. Without his presence on the rostrum ticket sales would almost certainly fall.

If the prospect of the following season's schedule was not bad enough, ill feeling began to brew up in the orchestra. The leader of the second violins, Theodor Johner, had manoeuvred his way into Mahler's confidence and had become his spy, informing him of any problems in the ranks. When the members of the orchestra discovered this, inevitably friction surfaced. Complaints were made to the Guarantors' Committee, together with a demand that Johner should be dismissed by Mahler, who, not surprisingly, refused outright. A bitter atmosphere began to develop, not just between Mahler and the orchestra but with some members of the committee as well, who took it upon themselves to attend rehearsals, take notes, criticise and even try to interfere with the programming of future concerts. On the 1st of February a Programme Committee was set up to supervise the selection of works to be performed. Mahler was understandably infuriated by these attacks on his autonomy.

Tired and under increasing stress, he had two imminent and important concerts to focus on. Opening with Hans Pfitzner's overture to *Das kätchen von Heilbronn* and ending with *Ein Heldenleben* by Richard Strauss, the central work to be performed would be his own *Fourth Symphony*. The concerts were to be held on the 17th and 20th of January. His *Fourth* had been performed before in New York in 1904, but he had since substantially revised the orchestration. He was very satisfied with the results of his labours. The audiences applauded; the critics carped.

The review in the *New York Sun* commented that 'idyllic moods are continually interrupted by the rude invasion of acrid modern harmonies'. It went on to mention the advice given to an Englishman who was trying to catch a rabbit to 'go behind a fence and make a noise like a turnip'! The opinion of the correspondent of the *New York Times* was that while the symphony was a powerful work and the performance brilliant, it was hard to take it seriously, and *Musical America* considered that it was clever but superficial. *The Musical Courier*, whilst praising Mahler's conducting as being second to none, described it as seeming 'puny and futile' alongside Strauss's *Ein Heldenleben*.

Yet the *Fourth Symphony* had been very well received by the audiences, and on each occasion Mahler had been called back many times to acknowledge their applause. Although understandably upset by adverse press comments, something he had become very used to, his fondness for the American public remained as strong as ever. This is made clear in a letter to his Swiss writer friend William Ritter, dated the 27th of January, in which he said that the love they showed him and their determination that he should stay made it almost impossible for him to leave.

Early in February (the letter is undated) Mahler wrote to Anna Moll saying how much they were looking forward to her arrival in New York, and that they hoped that she could arrange to travel back to Europe with them on the 20th of March. He told her that Gucki and Alma were both in excellent health, and that having abstained from alcohol, Alma was looking younger daily. He also mentioned that she had written some new songs, which were delightful.

On the 8th of February, Mahler wrote to Georg Göhler, the German composer, writer and conductor of the Riedel-Verein Chorus of Leipzig, whom he had met the previous year in connection with the première of his *Eighth Symphony*. Göhler had written an analysis of his *Fourth*, and Mahler told him that it was 'enchanting'. As a postscript he stated that he had completely re-orchestrated his *Fifth Symphony*, saying that he could not understand why he had made so many mistakes, like a beginner. He put it down to the fact that the new style of the *Fifth* had required a completely new technique, which he had not mastered at the time.

Mrs Sheldon continued to support Mahler, declaring in an interview for *Musical America* that he was the greatest conductor in both Europe and

America, and that she was hoping that he would remain at his post for at least one more year. In the same interview she attacked the press for their biased criticism of him and at the same time praised the public for their loyal support. But this interview masked the whole truth. She clearly wanted him to return for one more season, especially as there appeared to be no obvious successor waiting in the wings. However, the mounting disquiet among the musicians following the Johner affair and his refusal to dismiss him resulted in Mahler being summoned to Mary Sheldon's home.

On his arrival he was faced by several other members of the Committee who proceeded to level accusations at him concerning numerous instances of misconduct, all of which he utterly refuted. With his most loyal supporters on the committee, Minnie and Samuel Untermeyer away at the time, one is tempted to speculate if this 'emergency meeting' had been deliberately called in their absence! Consequently Mahler was dictated to, new lines were drawn up and his autonomy thrown out of the window! According to Alma, with this unpleasant exchange at an end and the results documented, Mrs Sheldon signalled for a curtain to be drawn aside to reveal a lawyer who had been making a detailed record of the meeting. Alma wrote that Mahler returned home trembling with rage. To make matters worse, and to underline the fact that he was no longer autonomous, plans were laid for the termination of Johner's contract, to take effect the following month.

Stress had mounted upon stress and, with his already weakened constitution providing little resistance to disease, his throat problem suddenly worsened. Although very unwell and suffering from a high fever he went against the advice of Dr. Fraenkel and insisted on conducting the concert on the 20th of February. Alma and Fraenkel drove him to Carnegie Hall for the 'Italian' concert, which would include Mendelssohn's *Fourth Symphony*, the 'Italian'. Among the other works on the programme was the world première of Ferruccio Busoni's *Berceuse Elegiaque* – '*Cradle Song at the Grave of My Mother*', which in retrospect would turn out to be so appropriate. Busoni, who was present sitting next to Toscanini in a box, stood to acknowledge the applause. By the interval Mahler felt exhausted and was suffering from a severe headache. Nevertheless he insisted on returning to the rostrum to conduct the rest of the concert. Alma reported that on their return to the Hotel Savoy, Fraenkel had told him that his temperature had gone down to normal, which led Mahler to joke that conducting was the cure!

This partial recovery was only temporary. Dr. Fraenkel's increasing concern led him to contact Dr. Emanuel Libman of Mount Sinai Hospital, one of the leading diagnosticians of the day. Fraenkel had begun to fear that Mahler was suffering from bacterial endocarditis. Libman agreed and arranged for a blood sample to be taken and sent to the hospital laboratory. The diagnosis was *streptococcus viridans*. Antibiotics had yet to be discovered so there was no medical cure.

On the afternoon of the 24th, the 'Italian' programme of the 20th was repeated, but Mahler's state of health prevented him from conducting. His place was taken by the leader of the orchestra, Theodore Spiering, Busoni himself conducting the '*Berceuse Elegiaque*'.

Mahler had conducted his final concert.

Spiering continued to deputize for him. With uncertainty over Mahler's future, the Committee set about contacting Felix Weingartner as a possible successor.

Busoni wrote of the poor taste shown by the people and the press of New York who did not wait long before declaring Spiering to be a great maestro who should be seriously considered as the Philharmonic's new permanent conductor. Even if his performance had been good, according to Busoni 'not a word of regret' was uttered concerning Mahler's absence and well-being.

Mahler, who was obviously aware of the seriousness of his condition, demanded that he be told the full facts. His immediate wish was to return to Vienna so that he could spend his last days there. Even though he liked the American public and had not suffered from anti-Semitism and the same level of intrigues as he had during his directorship of the Hofoper, he remained Viennese at heart. As early as 1908, in a letter to Countess Wydenbruck, he had written of his homesickness and a longing to return to Vienna, the city of his dreams, his Jerusalem, his Golgotha. The city described by Schoenberg as 'our hated and beloved Vienna'. Alma contacted her mother asking her to make haste to New York so that she could help them on their return to Europe.

The strain of nursing her husband had begun to tell on Alma, and Fraenkel, becoming increasingly concerned for her own health, arranged for Dr. Joseph Brettauer to visit her regularly. A friend and colleague of Fraenkel's, he was Austrian, he had trained in Vienna and was acquainted with the Zuckerkandls. His task was to give whatever comfort and support he could during their last weeks in New York.

Despite her genuine concern for Gustav, Alma's longing for Gropius remained as ardent as ever. Even at this time of crisis she began a letter to him with the words 'my love' and ending 'your bride'! She told him that she had become nurse, mother and housewife to Gustav, and exclaimed 'I want you, do you want me?'

A brief glimmer of light in the gathering gloom was a performance of one of Alma's songs, *Laue Sommernacht* (Mild Summer's Night) as part of a recital given by soprano Frances Alda Casazza, wife of Giulio Gatti-

Casazza, manager of the Metropolitan Opera. It goes without saying that Mahler was unable to attend the recital in the Mendelssohn Hall, so Fraenkel accompanied Alma. Upon her return she told Gustav, who had been in a state of extreme excitement, that it had been a success and was encored, to which he apparently said repeatedly, 'Thank God'. The feeling of guilt that he had felt over his suppression of her music for so long had eased. His remorse, the publication of her songs, his encouragement for her to write more and now the first public performance had taken place.

Among her compositions were around a hundred songs, a piano sonata and sketches for an opera. Most of her works are now lost without trace. However, seventeen songs survive, fourteen of which were published during her lifetime: *Fünf Gesänge* in 1910, *Fünf Lieder* in 1915 and *Vier Lieder* in 1924. A further three songs were found among her possessions after her death, composed while she was married to the author Franz Werfel. Two of these were published in 2000, the third remaining unpublished. Although rarely performed, a few recordings of her songs have been made in recent years.

Mahler's condition continued to weaken and Alma had to administer to his every need, including having to spoon-feed him. She slept in his room, frequently not undressing so that she could take immediate action should a crisis occur during the night. He could not bear strangers, even nurses, attending to his needs so the full burden fell on Alma's shoulders. Now that rumours of the severity of Mahler's illness had begun to spread, genuine sympathy began to be shown even by complete strangers. A constant stream of messages wishing him a speedy recovery and numerous gifts were delivered daily to the Hotel Savoy.

Blood tests were carried out, other specialists were consulted, but in the absence of antibiotics little could be done. Experiments might have been carried out on a lesser patient, such as a complete blood transfusion, but no one dared to take on the responsibility of any such course of action on Gustav Mahler. The general feeling was to leave any slight hope of a cure to nature herself.

Still nothing was made official regarding his future with the Philharmonic. In interviews with the press Loudon Charlton strongly denied that Mahler's absence was due to disagreements between conductor and management, and that they were 'working in perfect harmony'. However, the 18th of March editorial of *Musical America* contradicted Charlton's efforts at placation, and a week later the same journal clearly inferred that all was not well behind the scenes and that the removal of Johner had been the final straw. It went on to state that Mahler had been driven to the verge of a nervous breakdown and that he had succumbed to 'an attack of the grippe'. The truth about his real condition had not yet leaked out. The same edition stated that they had had it on 'the highest authority' that Mahler's tenure as Director of the Philharmonic was over and that he would not be returning to New York the following season. Not surprisingly speculation soon became rife as to who would be his successor, one name mentioned was Sir Henry Wood, founder of London's Promenade Concerts in 1895.

Mahler was too weak to travel back to Europe on the 30th of March, so they were forced to cancel their suite aboard the luxurious *George Washington*. The following day Anna Moll arrived to help her exhausted daughter. With Mahler's condition continuing to deteriorate and with preparations for their return to Europe (Alma wrote that she had forty items of luggage!), 'Little Mama' had insisted that he should allow a nurse to help look after him. Reluctantly he agreed, but on one condition: that she did not look directly at him!

Alma related an unfortunate incident that took place in their hotel suite. Anna Moll was in the middle of stewing some fruit on a spirit stove when it suddenly exploded, setting the curtains and carpet alight. After a fair amount of panic and dowsing with water, Anna, Alma and Miss Turner, Gucki's English nurse, managed to control the situation before the hotel staff arrived on the scene.

The 8th of April arrived, and Gustav, Alma, seven year old Gucki and Anna Moll, together with Miss Turner, prepared to leave New York. Alma described how her husband, pale and unsteady on his feet, had nevertheless refused to use the stretcher provided, preferring to take his time helped by Joseph Fraenkel. The liftboy fought to keep back the tears; the hotel lounge and lobby had been cleared to prevent any onlookers. Minnie Untermeyer, one of Mahler's closest allies on the Guarantors' Committee, had arranged for her chauffeur-driven limousine to take them to the harbour, Alma remaining behind to settle bills and thank the staff.

Their suite aboard the *SS Amerika* was filled with flowers and gifts from friends and well-wishers. Dr. Fraenkel insisted that Mahler should go straight to bed. Having warned Alma not to involve the ship's doctor unless absolutely necessary, he bade Mahler a sad goodbye knowing that they would never meet again. Fraenkel having departed, Alma and her mother once again took charge of the nursing.

With Mahler gone, Theodore Spiering gave up his post at the Philharmonic to return to Berlin and continue his career conducting European orchestras. He must have been upset by an article that appeared in *Musical America* that praised Mahler as a conductor, but went on to describe him as being tactless and self-centred.

His four seasons in America had only been a partial success. The eager anticipation of some sort of musical miracle that had preceded his arrival in the autumn of 1907 had not been entirely fulfilled. Such expectations, fuelled by Mahler's status as a legendary figure, had been unrealistic especially after the cruel 'hammer blows' he had suffered. Nevertheless he had improved standards both in the operatic and orchestral fields, and he had set America on a course of musical excellence that would rival the best in Europe. Many singers and musicians later wrote in awe of his achievements. One of these, the Italian baritone Antonio Scotti, said that during the course of his career he had held no conductor in greater esteem, and the violinist Maud Powell wrote, 'I worship the memory of Mahler, the man and the musician!' She went on to say that New York had never really understood him and that the criticism he had suffered was 'an ineffaceable blot on our musical history'.

During the voyage Mahler insisted on rising daily and dressing, if only for a short while, and on at least one occasion he went up on deck where the last known photograph of him was taken. Among the other passengers was his young friend and fellow composer Ferruccio Busoni, who did his best to amuse him by sending him what Alma described as 'crazy specimens of counterpoint'.

Following an uneventful crossing, during which Mahler's condition showed further deterioration, they travelled by train to Paris, Carl Moll joining them en route. They arrived in the city at five o'clock on the morning of the 18th. Utterly exhausted, they went straight to their rooms at the Elysée Palace Hotel. Their reason for going to the French capital was not just to break the journey, but, on Fraenkel's recommendation, to seek further medical advice. He had recommended that Alma should contact two specialists, one in Berlin and the other in Lyon.

Early the next morning, Alma thought she had seen a vision! There before her stood Gustav dressed and shaved, and suggesting that it would be good day for a drive in the Bois de Boulogne. She was so taken aback by this seemingly miraculous recovery that she agreed at once. Having got into the car Gustav, laughing and full of the joys of the spring, suggested planning a holiday in Egypt, and even talked about possible future opera plans, which would include a new production of Peter Cornelius's *Der Barbier von Bagdad*. But this recovery was a mirage for within an hour he was back in bed, deathly pale, weeping and telling Anna Moll of his desire to be buried next to Putzi in the Grinzing cemetery.

Alma had been unable to make contact with either of the specialists whom Fraenkel had recommended due to the Easter holiday. So, with Mahler's condition causing great concern, the eminent bacteriologist Professor André Chantemesse of the Pasteur Institute was summoned. He made immediate arrangements for him to be moved to a clinic in the elegant northwest suburb of Neuilly, just to the north of the Bois de Boulogne. Mahler's family accompanied him.

A correspondent of the *Neue Freie Presse* spoke to André Chantemesse after his first visit to Mahler at the sanatorium. The Professor stated that his patient was feeling better than he had the previous day and that his heart was functioning in a satisfactory manner. Having grown a culture from a sample of Mahler's blood he somewhat insensitively remarked that in all his years in medicine he had never come across streptococci 'in such a marvellous state of development'! He even invited Alma to look through the microscope. He immediately prescribed a serum treatment, but Mahler became so weak that he was unable even to hold a book – the only way he could read was to tear out pages one by one. His mind, however, remained alert, for the book he was struggling to read was the philosophical work, 'The Problem of Life' by Eduard von Hartmann.

His thoughts began to drift towards Schoenberg and the other young composers whom he had gone out of his way to encourage. He told Alma of his concern for them once he had gone, for who then would support them? Voicing this was to bear fruit. Both Alma and Carl Moll promised to further their cause and set up a bursary fund to help young composers. Trustees would include Richard Strauss, Ferruccio Busoni and Bruno Walter. Schoenberg himself became one of its first beneficiaries, despite comments made by Strauss to Alma that only a psychiatrist could help Schoenberg, and that he would be better employed shovelling snow than scribbling on manuscript paper!

With Mahler's condition in such a perilous state, another leading specialist was summoned. Professor Franz Chvostek, one of Vienna's foremost experts in bacteriology, made haste to Paris. His initial approach was psychological; his aim to boost Mahler's morale. Jovially bursting into his presence, he told him that he had been working too hard and that in future he should take a six-month break every year. At first Mahler half believed him, asking Chvostek if he was serious in thinking that he might work again. The professor replied that of course he was, yet he knew full well that Mahler's days were numbered. He was under no illusions, and made immediate plans for Mahler's return to Vienna. Chvostek's approach, however, had had the desired effect of putting him into a far more positive state of mind, for the time being at least, and consequently he would be better able to cope with the journey.

Carl Moll hurried to the station to book sleeping compartments on the Orient Express that would depart that very afternoon, for they were all only too aware that should Mahler suffer a relapse, then his wish to return might not be fulfilled. Moll and Chvostek would accompany Alma and her husband, while Anna Moll, Gucki and Miss Turner would travel the following day.

The train left Paris on the afternoon of the 11th of May. Alma had been upset by Chvostek's rather theatrical approach to Mahler at the clinic, but he now told her the truth that her husband might die at any time, and even if by some miracle he were to survive, he would be condemned to a wheel chair for the rest of his days. He told her that his aim had been simply to enable him to think more positively, his only option if he were to have any chance of returning home.

On the same day Richard Strauss, unaware of the true situation, wrote to Mahler saying how pleased he was that he was recovering from his long illness and in better spirits. He told him that he had the very good news that his *Third Symphony* was to be performed in Berlin the following winter, and that if he felt like conducting it, Strauss himself taking charge of the rehearsals, it would give everyone added pleasure.

Alma described the journey as being 'like that of a dying king'. Crowds of well-wishers, as well as journalists, had gathered at every German and Austrian station, all eager to get the latest news.

Just before six o'clock on the morning of the 12th the train arrived at the Vienna West Station. Unlike the many that they had passed en route, huge crowds had not gathered. This was not due to any lack of respect, but a sympathetic response to requests not to do so for fear of creating further and unnecessary stress to the patient. A few close friends and family were waiting on the platform, including Justine and Arnold Rosé, Bruno Walter and Albert Spiegler. On alighting from his carriage Carl Moll is reported to have stated that the journey had gone smoothly, but that Mahler was very weak. And then they saw him, frail and deathly pale, being carried on a stretcher to the waiting ambulance, which then left the station and headed for the Löwe sanatorium in Mariannengasse to the north west of the city centre.

A large room with a veranda had been reserved and both the room and the adjoining corridor had been decked with flowers, including a bouquet with a card signed 'From the Philharmonic'. When Mahler saw this he muttered repeatedly, '*My* Philharmonic!'

The following day, *Musical America* carried an article which had been partly based on an interview that their Paris correspondent had had with Alma a week or so previously. In it she was reported to have blamed Mahler's illness on the New York Philharmonic and its management. She was quoted as having said that whereas in Vienna he had been all-powerful, not even the Emperor interfering, in New York he had been like a puppet on a string being ordered about by the 'Ladies' Committee'. The article went on to state that the Philharmonic rejected the idea that his illness had, in any way, been caused by stressful relations, that these had always been 'agreeable' and that Mahler's illness was a result of 'his extreme nervousness'. The same edition went on to report that they had had it on good authority that Sir Henry Wood had declined the offer to become the new conductor, and that Joseph Stransky of Berlin had been appointed.

While the American press showed little feeling over Mahler's approaching death, their Viennese counterparts, including many who had done their utmost to end his tenure at the Hofoper, now began to wallow in sympathetic gestures. Every medical bulletin and scrap of news was seized upon.

With a combination of intermittent bouts of fever, the constant weakening of his strength and the drugs that were being administered, his mind began to drift. He muttered repeatedly 'My Almschi!' On one occasion when Justi visited him he failed to recognise her, asking who the lady was. Justi, understandably upset, had left in tears. But he recognised Gucki, telling her to be a good girl. He was given radium treatment for swellings that had appeared on his legs, the morphine doses becoming more regular and he was given oxygen to help his faltering breathing. Alma described how at one point his finger appeared to be conducting, and then, with a half smile, he uttered his last words: 'Mozartl . . . Mozartl' ('Little Mozart . . . Little Mozart').

With the onset of the death agony, Alma was escorted from the room. Dr. Chvostek and Carl Moll remained by his side. During the course of the evening the atmosphere had become increasingly oppressive. The distant rumble of thunder could be heard. Shortly after 11 o'clock, on the 18th of May, amidst flashes of lightning and the crashing and booming of thunder, Gustav Mahler lost his final battle.

After Mahler's features had settled, Carl Moll made the death mask. He then picked up Mahler's music notebook that had, as always, been at his side. He went into the room next door and gave it to the tearful Alma. She wanted to see her husband's body, but, as much as she protested, he prevented her from doing so, telling her that it would be for her own good that she should not. Mahler's request had been that his heart should be pierced and this was duly carried out. As news of his death spread, bells of the city's churches began to toll. Vienna was in mourning.

The following evening his body was taken to the little chapel at the Grinzing cemetery. On the 22nd of May the funeral took place. Prayers were said and hymns were led by singers from the Vienna Opera before the coffin was carried the short distance to the grave. Friends and enemies stood side by side, the world of music and the press amidst a multitude of anonymous faces. Mahler's wish for a simple burial, free from any pomp and speeches, was respected. Bruno Walter remembered how, just as the coffin was being lowered into the grave next to little Putzi, the clouds parted and the sun broke through, the birds sang and a rainbow arced across the sky. His grave was strewn with flowers, among them a wreath with a ribbon upon which was inscribed, 'From the children of the *Eighth Symphony*, Munich.' As he had requested, his gravestone, designed by Josef Hoffmann, bore just his name, for as he himself had said, 'Any who come looking for me will know who I was; the rest do not need to know'.

What was the real cause of Mahler's death? Alma blamed New York, while many blamed Alma and her infidelity. Neither accusation was true in itself, and certainly she had in all matters other than sexual remained devoted to her husband to the end. Then there was the streptococcal infection that he had been suffering from for which a cure had yet to be found. Probably all of these played their part. Throughout his career Mahler had been a workaholic, a music obsessive who was constantly frustrated by his inability to achieve perfection. He had expected those around him to show equal dedication, but the inevitability that few had shared his blinkered view of life had brought its own stress. His unhappy childhood, the loss of almost all of his siblings, Otto's suicide, Putzi's tragic death, the discovery of his own heart defect, the struggles to get his music appreciated, anti-Semitism and then, finally, Alma's infidelity – it was no wonder that he had been laid low and had become a ready recipient for the disease which was to prove fatal. Mahler died from heart failure, the normal cause of natural death whatever the circumstances leading to it, but in another sense he had died from a broken heart.

In the many obituaries that appeared on both sides of the Atlantic, even in death he remained a controversial figure. Henry Krehbiel wrote in the *New York Daily Tribune* a predictably unsympathetic piece accusing him of having tried to 'out-Strauss Strauss' in his music and that he had failed. He could not see how 'his music can long survive him'. He had been expensive and had meddled with the classics – he 'banged' on about his excessive use of kettledrums and brass! He went on to say that he had done considerable damage to the reputation of the New York Philharmonic, and that his relationship with both the orchestra and the subscribers had been an unhappy one.

Ossip Gabrilowitsch slated Krehbiel's piece in an open letter to the same newspaper in which he accused the critic of taking 'every occasion to attack and abuse him', and that the hatred he had displayed in the obituary was an insult. Gabrilowitsch went on to remind the readers of the great service that Mahler had given to music in Vienna and throughout Europe, quoting *Die Musik*, which had stated that the world had lost its greatest artist. He equated Krehbiel to Beckmesser in Wagner's *Die Meistersinger von Nürnberg* – a miserable faultfinder and hater of genius! He went on to remind 'Mr. Beckmesser-Krehbiel' that Richard Wagner had himself retouched the orchestration of Beethoven's symphonies.

The *New York Sun* did not wish to be drawn into the controversy over his time with the Philharmonic, preferring to remember Mahler's outstanding performances of Mozart's operas and Beethoven's *Fidelio* at the Metropolitan Opera. The *Musical Courier*, while pointing out that the world was divided between those who had loved him and those who had hated him, stated that without question he was a great man and that the world would be a poorer place without him. *Musical America* praised him as a conductor rather than as a composer with his intellectual approach, commanding nature and economy of gesture on the rostrum, and concluded that his death was a great loss to the world of music.

Most of the obituaries in Europe bent over backwards to praise him and mourn his passing, in keeping with the prevailing feeling in the music world. Even those critics who had been his adversaries and had done their level best to oust him from the Hofoper, somewhat hypocritically joined in. This was pointed out in the *Sonn und Montagzeitung*, which spoke of the deceit that was being shown, and how many of them had thought him to be ugly and bizarre. Yet now that he was dead his music was being regarded as noble and original. This particular obituary neatly summed up the Viennese attitude, saying that one had to be dead in order to live comfortably in Vienna!

Julius Korngold (*Neue Freie Presse*) considered Mahler to have been one of the last great idealists of that era; he had always sought to achieve the impossible. He was a virtuoso conductor who possessed a rare magic, and when those around him came under his spell, they remained loyal supporters of his art. Korngold compared his outward ugliness with his inner spiritual beauty, and declared that Vienna had become a poorer city with his passing.

Ernst Decsey (*Die Musik* – Berlin) wrote that with Mahler's death 'a window on the universe had been shattered', yet as a legend he would live on. In a similar vein, Maurice Baumfeld spoke of the infinite loss that art and humanity had suffered. Only with his death would people begin to realise just what they had failed to appreciate during his lifetime. Truer words could not have been written. Baumfeld went on to say that few really got to know him well as a man, but those who had knew him as a great human being as well as a great musician.

Similar sentiments were voiced by most of the artistes with whom he had worked. Leo Slezak felt real gratitude that he had had the privilege of working with Mahler, describing him as having been 'a martyr to the consuming flames of work'. Selma Kurtz commented that 'he compelled one to give of one's very best', and Lucie Weidt wrote that singers under his direction managed to achieve unheard of heights of expression. Theodor Reichmann described the fantastic inspiration that radiated from him, and Emma Eames stated that of all the great conductors she had performed with, none was greater than Mahler. Ernestine Schumann-Heink considered the various sides of his character: on the one hand he was kind and lovable, yet when he was conducting he became 'a despot', although he never bore malice. In her opinion his main weakness was that he never came to terms with the fact that perfection did not exist in the world. The English composer Ethel Smythe also felt that he had been the finest conductor she had known. She wrote, 'His passionate refusal to abate one jot or tittle of his artistic demands, the magnitude and purity of his vision, these are things that start a tradition and linger after sunset . . .'

Mahler was the bridge between late Romanticism and the music of the twentieth century. In his last three great works, *Das Lied von der Erde*, the *Ninth Symphony* and the *Tenth* he had explored a new world of music. His use of atonalism always contrasted with passages of sublimity, a contrast that makes these works so magnificent and moving. The effect he had had on the young composers of the Second Viennese School was immense, and Schoenberg, Berg and Webern adopted his increasing use of atonalism as the keystone for their own compositions. And yet historically his greatest influence lay elsewhere, following another route that led to such composers as Shostakovich, Benjamin Britten and even Elgar, whose *Cello Concerto* seems to reflect Mahler's *Ninth Symphony*. Another area greatly benefiting from his music was that of Hollywood film scores. Composers such as Korngold, Waxman and Steiner, who had fled from Nazi oppression in Europe, were undoubtedly inspired by Mahler's music. It spoke so eloquently of not only his time but theirs too, and it was no surprise that they had a great empathy with it.

Mahler's love for the music of Bach, Mozart and Beethoven and, of course, Wagner, not to mention the ahead-of-his-time Berlioz, was a constant inspiration to him. These were the scores that he grew up with, and their influence, blended with his own creative brilliance, led music into a new era. But his music was not created simply as entertainment or to be used at church services as that of many composers in times past. His was a new concept, deeply emotional and personal, even autobiographical and as such incredibly moving.

Although he never completed an opera of his own, his 'symphonic worlds' are almost operatic. Despite his rejection of programmes (as much to distance himself from the increasingly popular symphonic poems of such composers as Richard Strauss as to persuade his audiences to interpret his music in their own way), each of his symphonies is a drama. Inspirational passages coexist with banality, grandeur with tenderness, happiness with sorrow, beauty with ugliness. Theodor Adorno likens moments of ugliness to pieces of broken glass, which, when held up, refract the light into a rainbow of colours, or, in the words of singer Charlotte Hellekant, 'Ugliness is sometimes beautiful in its truth, in its reality'. Mahler's message is that if you look deeply enough you will see that beauty will flow from ugliness. It is the beauty of a troubled soul. It is Mahler.

Even though there are frequent cross-references between symphony and symphony, and symphony and song, it is remarkable how individual each work is. There is no suggestion of a single formula clothed in different garments, as is the case with so many composers, Bruckner being a prime example. Each is unique, a new voyage of discovery, a new world.

Freed from her obligations towards Gustav, Alma's life continued along the path of association with the famous. Walter Gropius, one of the foremost architects of his time, was of course next in line, alongside a steamy affair with artist Oskar Kokoschka. She married Walter Gropius on the 18th of August 1915. On the 5th of October the following year she gave birth to a little girl, Manon. At the end of 1917, Alma met and fell in love with Franz Werfel, a twenty-seven year old Jewish poet whose reputation as a writer was gathering momentum and who would later gain international fame as a playwright and author. She became pregnant and had a son by him, Martin, who was born prematurely and was not expected to survive. He died ten months later. Walter Gropius's patience with Alma waned and he left her, and their marriage ended in 1920. Nine years later she married Franz Werfel.

Another tragedy lay in wait for Alma. The beautiful, clever and universally loved Manon, whom Bruno Walter described as angelic, was struck down by poliomyelitis. After months of suffering she died aged just eighteen in 1935. Courageous, loving and witty to the end, her final words to her mother were a request that she might be allowed to die peacefully, and that her mother would get over her demise as indeed she managed to get over everything! Alban Berg was particularly upset by Manon's death, and he dedicated his *Violin Concerto* 'to the memory of an angel'.

At the outbreak of the Second World War, Alma and Franz fled Europe and settled in America, taking with them many of Mahler's manuscripts. Franz Werfel achieved Hollywood fame when his book 'The Song of Bernadette' was made into a very successful film. He died on the 26th of August 1945.

Alma's dependence on Benedictine grew in tandem with her failing hearing. Dressed in black, she spent much of her time playing the widow of the famous, enjoying the spotlight in the company of the likes of Leonard Bernstein and Georg Solti. On the 11th of December 1964 her eventful and long life drew to a close. She died of pneumonia at the age of 85, her daughter Anna by her side. Her body was taken back to Vienna where she was buried next to Manon, the grave almost back to back with that of Gustav and Maria.

Anna's love life followed a similar line to her mother's. Aged just sixteen she married a family friend, Rupert Koller. Four years later she married composer Ernst Křenek, only to leave him after ten months. She fled to London at the onset of the *Anschluss* and married publisher Paul Zsolnay. She gave birth to a daughter, Alma, in 1930, but this latest marriage also ended in divorce. She took up sculpture and was awarded the Grand Prix in Paris in 1937. In 1947 she married the conductor Anatole Fistoulari and had another daughter, Marina. Her next husband was Albrecht Joseph, a Hollywood film editor and writer. Aged seventy-five she left Joseph and moved to Spoleto in Italy. She died in London in 1988. As a sculptress she carved a number of stone busts of musicians including Schoenberg, Berg, Klemperer and Bruno Walter. She also carved one of her father, but destroyed it. Perhaps she felt that she could not compete with Rodin.

1911 saw the beginning of the fifty years that Mahler had predicted before his music would begin to be widely understood and appreciated. Leonard Bernstein was yet to be born, but the flame of Mahler's music was kept alight by a number of dedicated musicians including Willem Mengelberg, Bruno Walter, Otto Klemperer and Oskar Fried. Despite frequent bitter attacks, Fascism and the Nazi scourge, the flame continued to burn, awaiting the resurrection of his music in Europe during the post war years.

Whereas there continued to be a struggle for most of his works to gain acceptance in America, a notable exception was his *Eighth Symphony*, the American première taking place on the 2nd of March 1916 with Leopold Stokowski conducting the Philadelphia Orchestra. Regardless of the comments of some critics, it was such an overwhelming success with the audience that a further eight performances were hastily arranged in Philadelphia and one at the Metropolitan Opera. Stokowski had been present at the world première in Munich and had made it his mission to further the cause of the work that Mahler himself had considered to be his greatest.

Successful as the *Eighth* had been in America, the struggle was far from over. Typical was a piece by Deems Taylor in 1932, which suggested that should the *Ninth Symphony* be 'pruned so that Mahler's musical ideas and the amount of development they are worth' were left, the symphony would last around twenty minutes. He felt lukewarm about the other symphonies as well, and he commented that if such pruning should take place 'the great Mahler war will be over'. Adolfo Salazar wrote that Mahler's music was 'like a flood where float the wrecks of many a proud hope and where great gifts are lost in a vast disorder'. Romain Rolland spoke of 'opulent and brash bric-a-brac'.

Of all the conductors with whom Mahler had worked, none did more to further the cause of his music than Willem Mengelberg. In 1920 Mengelberg organised a *Mahler Feest* in Amsterdam to celebrate his quarter century as director of the Royal Concertgebouw Orchestra. Mahler had been the guest of Mengelberg and the Concertgebouw four times between 1903 and 1909, rehearsing and conducting his first five symphonies and the *Seventh*, as well as *Das klagende Lied* and *Die Kindertotenlieder*. All of Mahler's symphonies and orchestrated songs were to be performed, culminating in the massive *Eighth Symphony*. Guest of honour of course was Alma who should have been accompanied by Franz Werfel, but apparently his invitation did not arrive. To commemorate this important event, she presented Mengelberg with Mahler's original fair copy of his *Seventh Symphony* in gratitude for all that he had and was continuing to do for her late husband's music.

The 1920 Mahler Festival was an undoubted success; hardly surprising since the Netherlands, and Amsterdam in particular, had long been the 'home' of Mahler's works. The world of music could not do otherwise than to take note. This success spurred on Mengelberg to make even greater efforts to get his works accepted in other countries. It was no easy task, especially in the English-speaking world, for in many cities sections of the press and public lay in wait with daggers drawn. Like Stokowski, Mengelberg bit the bullet and went to America. It was through his dedication and sheer persistence that New York began to warm to Mahler's music, in spite of continued abuse in the press with such words as 'trash' and 'piffle' being bandied about.

An important event took place on the afternoon of 14th of November 1943. Bruno Walter became ill and was unable to conduct the New York Philharmonic Orchestra in a concert to be broadcast nationwide. At the very last moment, his twenty-five year old 'rookie' assistant, one Leonard Bernstein, had to step into his shoes. The works to be played were Schumann's *Manfred Overture*, the *Theme, Variations and Finale* by the Hungarian composer Miklós Rózsa, Richard Strauss's *Don Quixote* and the prelude to *Die Meistersinger*. Fortunately Walter had already prepared the orchestra well, making Bernstein's unexpected task that much easier, although the thought of a live broadcast must have brought about its own anxiety. Nevertheless the performance was an outstanding success and the charismatic young conductor became the focus of attention throughout America and beyond. Fifteen years later Bernstein himself was appointed music director of the New York Philharmonic, the very post that Mahler had held. He set about dedicating his life to the cause of Mahler's music. With Bernstein's film star image, the fast developing media and the long-playing record, Mahler's compositions began to achieve widespread popularity. One of Bernstein's initial projects was indeed to record the first complete cycle of Mahler's symphonies.

In 1912 Schoenberg had written, only months after his death, that young people worshipped Mahler like a God, and predicted that his time would come in at most five or ten years. But Mahler's own prediction of fifty years proved to be more accurate. Now his time has truly come, his music as apt a reflection of today's world as it was during his day, for it is the music of life. It remains both retrospective, yet at the same time takes a tremulous glance into the troubled waters of the future. In his symphonic worlds weakness plays its part alongside inspiration – a true reflection of man and creation. It is the music of experience, of the heart rather than an intellectual exercise along the well-trodden paths of the textbook. The English writer and critic Neville Cardus wrote, 'His pursuit of truth and beauty was fanatical, and in the end the world broke him'. Cardus saw him 'as a shell left on the shore of his century's romanticism, a shell in which we can hear the sound of a withdrawing sea'. What should be added today is his 'resurrection' at a time of a new, often frightening, incoming tide.

There was, and is, a danger of putting Mahler the man on a pedestal. He was not a saint, but he was a visionary. He was a man of extremes, at one moment plummeting into the depths of despair, and at the next reaching for the heights of Heaven. He was a man of courage, never afraid of fighting for what he considered to be right, whatever the cost. As the conductor Rafael Kubelik put it, he was a man with a mission 'to fight for the good of mankind'. What the world of music owes Gustav Mahler is beyond evaluation.

Biographical Notes

ADLER, GUIDO (1855-1941). Austrian musicologist. Brought up in Iglau and educated at the Vienna Conservatory, he became Director of the Institute for Music History at Vienna University. Having studied under Bruckner at the Conservatory, he had known Mahler since their student days and became a close friend and supporter of Mahler.

ADLER, VICTOR (1852-1918). Austrian journalist and founder of the Austrian Social Democratic Party whom Mahler first met while he was a student.

APPONYI, COUNT ALBERT (1846-1933). Hungarian politician of noble birth. He fervently supported Mahler's application for the directorship of the Vienna Court Opera.

BAHR, HERMANN (1863-1934). Austrian writer, playwright, critic and theatre director. He worked with Max Reinhardt in Berlin. He was an active member of the Austrian avant-garde. He married the soprano, Anna von Mildenburg in 1909.

BAUER-LECHNER, NATALIE (1858-1921). Viola player and violinist, who first met Mahler at the Vienna Conservatory. She became a close, faithful friend, remaining so until Mahler's marriage to Alma Schindler, and wrote her invaluable biographical sketches of Mahler covering the period of their friendship. She was a member of the Soldat-Röger Quartet.

BEHN, HERMANN (1859-1927). After studying law, Behn turned to music and became a pupil of Bruckner. Although composing a number of lieder and a piano sonata, he concentrated on transcribing and arranging works by other composers including Mahler's *Second Symphony*. Mahler first met him during his time in Hamburg.

BERLINER, ARNOLD (1862-1942). German physicist. He befriended Mahler during his first year in Hamburg. Despite a gap of a few years caused by Alma's rejection of many of Mahler's former close acquaintances, their friendship survived. As well as helping Mahler with his study of natural science, Berliner gave him a crash course in English before his first engagement in London.

BÜLOW, HANS VON (1830-1894). Eminent German pianist and conductor. He studied with Liszt whose daughter Cosima he married in 1857. He remained a staunch supporter and conductor of Wagner's music dramas even after Cosima left him to become Wagner's mistress and then wife. He was also a strong advocate of the works of Liszt and Brahms.

BURCKHARD, MAX (1854-1912). Author who became director of Vienna's Burgtheater. A friend of Carl and Anna Moll, he was one of Alma's early admirers.

BUSONI, FERRUCCIO (1866-1924). Pianist and composer. He became a close friend and supporter of Mahler and his music. Mahler conducted several of Busoni's works, and Busoni was the soloist in a number of concerto performances conducted by Mahler.

CONRIED, HEINRICH (1848-1909). General manager of the Metropolitan Opera in New York from 1903 until 1908. He was instrumental in persuading Mahler to accept the post of music director in 1907.

DAMROSCH, WALTER (1862-1950). American conductor of German parentage, who first met Mahler in Hamburg in 1895, and who, in 1904, conducted the first performance of a Mahler Symphony (the *Fourth*) in New York.

FOERSTER, JOSEF BOHUSLAV (1859-1951). Czech composer and music critic who became a friend of Mahler. He married the soprano Berta Lauterer who was engaged by Mahler at both the Hamburg and Vienna Court Operas.

FREUND, EMIL (1859-1928). Austrian lawyer and a close friend of Mahler. They first met in 1873. Freund helped Mahler with his financial affairs and contracts with publishers.

FRIED, OSKAR (1871-1941). German conductor who became a staunch supporter of Mahler and his music. He conducted the first recording of a Mahler symphony, the *Second*, in 1924.

HANSLICK, EDUARD (1825-1904). Austrian musicologist and prominent, although frequently outspoken, critic. Czech by birth, he was the chief music critic of the influential *Neue Freie Presse*.

KALBECK, MAX (1850-1921). Austrian conservative music critic of the *Neues Wiener Tagblat*. Kalbeck wrote the first biography of his friend Brahms. Although very anti-Bruckner, he was objective in his criticism of Mahler's music. He collaborated with Mahler writing new German translations of the libretti of Mozart's *Le Nozze di Figaro* and *Don Giovanni*.

KARPATH, LUDWIG (1866-1936). Austrian music critic. His initial ambition had been to become an opera singer, only to be rejected by Mahler during his tenure as director at the Royal Hungarian Opera in Budapest.

KORNGOLD. JULIUS (1860-1945). Moravian-born, he succeeded the redoubtable Eduard Hanslick as chief music critic of the *Neue Freie Presse*. He was always very fair in his writings on Mahler and his music, especially after Mahler had proclaimed his composer son, Erich Wolfgang, a genius!

KRZYŻANOWSKI, RUDOLF (1859-1911). Austrian conductor. He struck up a close friendship with Mahler while they were students at the Vienna Conservatory. He became Mahler's assistant at Hamburg.

LIPINER, SIEGFRIED (1856-1911). Austrian writer, poet and philosopher. He and Mahler became friends as students, remaining close until Mahler married Alma, who took a dislike to him. Mahler later made every effort to rebuild their friendship. Both Wagner and Nietzsche were impressed by his early poems.

LÖHR, FRIEDRICH (FRITZ) (1859-1924). Austrian archaeologist. He was appointed Secretary of the Austrian Archaeological Society in Vienna. He first met Mahler in 1876 and became a lifelong friend. Among Löhr's pupils at Vienna University were Otto and Emma Mahler.

MARSCHALK. MAX (1863-1940). German musicologist and composer. He was the brother-in-law of the dramatist Gerhardt Hauptman for many of whose plays he wrote the incidental music. Mahler had a high regard for him as a music critic.

MENGELBERG, WILLEM (1871-1951). Dutch conductor of Amsterdam's Concertgebouw Orchestra, a post he held for fifty years. Following his first meeting with Mahler in Krefeld at the very well received première of Mahler's *Third Symphony*, he became a close friend and staunch advocate of his music. Mahler regarded Amsterdam as his musical home, and Mengelberg as the most trustworthy interpreter of his scores.

NEUMANN, ANGELO (1838-1910). Austrian impresario and former opera singer. He directed the first *Ring* cycle staged outside Bayreuth, and became director of the German Theatre in Prague in 1885.

POLLINI, BERNHARD (1838-1897). German impresario and former opera singer. He became manager of the Hamburg Stadttheater. He engaged Mahler as his First Kapellmeister in 1891.

RICHTER, HANS (1843-1916). Hungarian-born conductor. Having been a copyist for Wagner, he conducted the first performance of *Der Ring des Nibelungen* in Bayreuth in 1876. He conducted at the Vienna Court Opera from 1880 until 1898 before moving to England where he became the principal conductor of the Hallé Orchestra.

RITTER, WILLIAM (1867-1955). French-Swiss writer, educated in Paris and who then settled in Munich. He was a painter, art critic and music lover. His first experience of a Mahler symphony was the *Fourth* in Munich in 1901. He, along with most of the audience, hated it, yet he was nonetheless affected by it. Despite his early negative opinion of Mahler's music, he later became a Mahler enthusiast and one of his most dedicated supporters.

ROLLER, ALFRED (1864-1935). Austrian artist and stage designer. His innovative ideas changed the course of opera production. Mahler first met him in 1902, and together they launched opera into a new era.

ROSÉ, ARNOLD (1863-1946). Violinist and founder of the renowned Rosé Quartet. He became the leader of the Vienna Court Opera/Philharmonic Orchestra at the age of eighteen. In 1902 he married Mahler's sister Justine.

SCHALK, FRANZ (1863-1931). Austrian conductor and former pupil of Bruckner. Mahler persuaded him to become his assistant conductor at the Vienna Court Opera in 1900, eighteen years later becoming its Director. Mahler was not over-impressed by his conducting.

SPIEGLER, ALBERT (1856-1940). Austrian doctor, dietitian and philanthropist. His wife Nanna had a deep understanding of music, and both she and her husband became close friends of Mahler. Albert Spiegler's sister married Siegfried Lipiner (see above).

ZICHY, COUNT GÉZA VON (1849-1924). One-armed Hungarian aristocrat, composer and pianist. A former pupil of Liszt, he became Intendant of the Budapest Opera.

ZUCKERKANDL, BERTA (1864-1945) and EMIL (1849-1910). In 1886,
Berta Szeps married Viennese anatomist Emil Zuckerkandl, and in the
same year her sister Sophie married industrialist Paul Clemenceau, brother
of the French statesman Georges Clemenceau. Mahler first met Paul and
Sophie Clemenceau at their Paris home, a regular meeting place for artists,
among them Rodin. Meetings at Berta and Emil's salon in Vienna were
renowned and it was there that the first thoughts on the Secession were
mooted. Emil and Berta were close friends of Carl and Anna Moll, Alma's
stepfather and mother.

Bibliography

Adorno, Theodor: Mahler – A Musical Physiognomy. (University of Chicago Press, 1992)

Bauer-Lechner, Natalie: Recollections of Gustav Mahler (Faber Music Ltd, 1980)

Beaumont, Anthony: Alma Mahler-Werfel Diaries 1898-1902 (Faber & Faber 1998)

Bernstein, Leonard: Findings: Mahler, His Time has Come (Macdonald & Co. 1982)

BBC Great Composers: Mahler (BBC TV)

Blaukopf, Kurt: Mahler (Allen Lane 1973)

Blaukopf, Kurt & Herta: Mahler: His Life, Work & World (Thames & Hudson 1991)

Blaukopf, Herta: Mahler, Unknown Letters (Gollanz 1986)

Blaukopf, Herta: Mahler/Richard Strauss Correspondence 1888-1911 (Faber & Faber 1984)

Boyden, Matthew: Richard Strauss (Weidenfeld & Nicolson 1999)

Burton, Humphrey: Leonard Bernstein (Faber & Faber 1994)

Cardus, Neville: Gustav Mahler, His Mind and His Music – The First Five Symphonies (Gollanz 1972)

Cardus, Neville: Ten Composers (Jonathan Cape 1948)

Carpenter, Humphrey: Benjamin Britten (Faber 1992)

Carr, Jonathan: The Real Mahler (Constable 1997)

Carroll, Brendan G.: The Last Prodigy (Amadeus Press 1997)

Cooke, Deryck: Gustav Mahler – An Introduction to His Music (Faber & Faber 1988)

Duchen, Jessica: Erich Wolfgang Korngold (Phaidon 1996)

Feder, Stuart: Gustav Mahler, A Life in Crisis (Yale University Press 1004)

Franklin, Peter: The Life of Mahler (Cambridge University Press 1997)

Gartenberg, Egon: Mahler, the Man and His Music (Cassell 1978)

Giroud, Françoise: Alma Mahler, or the art of being loved (Oxford University Press 1991)

Graf, Max: Composer and Critic (Chapman & Hall 1947)

Graf, Max: Modern Music (Philosophical Library, New York 1946)

de la Grange, Henry-Louis: Mahler Volume One (Gollanz 1974)

de la Grange, Henry-Louis: Vienna: The Years of Challenge (1897-1904) (Oxford University Press 1995)

de la Grange, Henry-Louis: Vienna: Triumph and Disillusion (1904-1907) (Oxford University Press 1999)

de la Grange, Henry-Louis: A New Life Cut Short (1907-1911) (Oxford University Press 2008)

de la Grange, Henry-Louis & Günther Weiss in collaboration with Knud Martner: Gustav Mahler, Letters to His Wife (Faber & Faber 2004)

Holbrooke, David: Gustav Mahler & the Courage to be (Vision Press 1975)

Holmes, Quentin: An Affinity with Gustav Mahler (Elius Books 1999)

James, Burnett: The Music of Gustav Mahler (Associated University Presses 1985)

Kaplan, Gilbert: The Mahler Album (Thames & Hudson 1995)

Keegan, Susanne: The Bride of the Wind, the Life of Alma Mahler (Secker & Warburg 1991)

Kennedy, Michael: Mahler (J.M. Dent 1990)

Kennedy, Michael: Richard Strauss (Oxford University Press 1995)

Klemperer, Otto: Klemperer on Music (Toccata Press 1986)

Lebrecht, Norman: Maestro Myth (Simon & Schuster 1991)

Lebrecht, Norman: Mahler Remembered (Faber & Faber 1987)

Mahler, Alma (ed. D. Mitchell): Memories & Letters (John Murray 1973)

Mahler-Werfel, Alma: And the Bridge is Love (Hutchinson 1959)

Martner, Knud: Selected Letters of Gustav Mahler (Faber & Faber 1979)

McClatchie, Stephen: The Mahler Family Letters (Oxford University Press 2006)

Mitchell, Donald: Gustav Mahler, The Early Years (Faber & Faber 1980)

Mitchell, Donald: Gustav Mahler, The Wunderhorn Years (University of California Press 1980)

Mitchell, Donald: Songs & Symphonies of Life and Death (Faber & Faber 1985)

Mitchell, Donald: Cradles of the New (Faber & Faber 1995)

The Mahler Companion (ed. by Donald Mitchell & Andrew Nicholson) (Oxford University Press 1999)

Gustav Mahler - The World Listens (ed. by Donald Mitchell) (Tema Uitgevers, Haarlem 1995)

Monson, Karen: Alma Mahler: Muse to Genius (Collins 1984)

Painter, Karen: Mahler and His World (Princetown University Press 2002)

Redlich, H.F.: Bruckner & Mahler (Dent 1955)

Reed, Philip: On Mahler and Britten (Boydell Press 1995)

Reilly, Edward R.: Gustav Mahler & Guido Adler – Records of a Friendship (Cambridge University Press 1982)

Roman, Zoltan: Gustav Mahler's American Years 1907-1911 – A Documentary History (Pendragon Press Stuyvesant NY 1989)

Seckerson, Edward: Mahler: His Life and Times (Midas Books 1982)

Seckerson, Edward: Michael Tilson Thomas – Viva Voce (Faber & Faber 1994)

Secrest, Meryl: Leonard Bernstein – A Life (Bloomsbury 1995)

Shmith, Michael: Mahler Musician of the Century (pub. RPO 1998)

Solti, Georg: Solti on Solti (Chatto & Windus 1997)

Walter, Bruno: Gustav Mahler (Hamish Hamilton 1958)

Wiesmann, Sigrid: Gustav Mahler in Vienna (Thames & Hudson 1977)

Index